THE SYMPOSIUM IN CONTEXT

Hesperia Supplements

The *Hesperia* Supplement series (ISSN 1064-1173) presents book-length studies in the fields of Greek archaeology, art, language, and history. Founded in 1937, the series was originally designed to accommodate extended essays too long for inclusion in the journal *Hesperia*. Since that date the Supplements have established a strong identity of their own, featuring single-author monographs, excavation reports, and edited collections on topics of interest to researchers in classics, archaeology, art history, and Hellenic studies.

Hesperia Supplements are electronically archived in JSTOR (www.jstor.org), where all but the most recent titles may be found. For order information and a complete list of titles, see the ASCSA website (www.ascsa.edu.gr).

Hesperia Supplement 46

THE SYMPOSIUM IN CONTEXT

Pottery from a Late Archaic House near the Athenian Agora

KATHLEEN M. LYNCH

The American School of Classical Studies at Athens
2011

Cover illustration: Type C cup showing komast with skyphos (P 32420),
500–480 B.C. Photo courtesy Agora Excavations

Library of Congress Cataloging-in-Publication Data

Lynch, Kathleen M.
The symposium in context : pottery from a late archaic house near the Athenian
    agora / Kathleen M. Lynch.
      p.   cm. — (Hesperia supplement ; 46)
    Includes bibliographical references and index.
    ISBN 978-0-87661-546-1 (alk. paper)
    1. Athens (Greece)—Antiquities—Catalogs. 2. Agora (Athens, Greece—
Antiquities—Catalogs. 3. Excavations (Archaeology)—Greece—Athens. 4. Pottery,
Greek—Greece—Athens—Catalogs. 5. Symposium (Classical Greek drinking
party) I. Title
DF287.A23L96 2011
938′.5—dc23   2011030246

For my spouse

CONTENTS

Appendix III
THE FOOT IN THE WELL WITH OSTEOLOGICAL
IDENTIFICATION   329
    by Lisa M. Little

ILLUSTRATIONS

COLOR ILLUSTRATIONS

(following page 90)

TABLES

ACKNOWLEDGMENTS

This project began as my dissertation, *Pottery from a Late Archaic Athenian House in Context,* University of Virginia (Lynch 1999), but has expanded and shifted focus over the intervening years. For permission to study well deposit J 2:4, which forms the core of this study, and its archaeological context I thank John McK. Camp II, director of the excavations of the Athenian Agora. I owe him enormous gratitude for his support and encouragement throughout this project. I thank excavation supervisors Christopher Pfaff and John Camp and the volunteer excavators of 1994 and 1995 for their daring and meticulous excavation of well J 2:4. The house of well J 2:4 was excavated in 1993 under the supervision of Julia Shear and then-director T. Leslie Shear Jr.

Predoctoral stages of this project were supported by the Homer and Dorothy Thompson Fellowship and the Samuel H. Kress Fellowship from the American School of Classical Studies at Athens. The Solow Foundation for Art and Archaeology and grants from the Semple Classics Fund provided postdoctoral support. I would not have been able to complete the project without this generous assistance, for which I am immensely grateful. The Loeb Classical Library Foundation and the Semple Classics Fund have also generously provided publication subventions.

The staff of the Agora excavations, including Jan Jordan, Sylvie Dumont, Richard Anderson, Anne Hooton, Craig Mauzy, Bruce Hartzler, and the many members of the conservation staff, have made research at the Stoa of Attalos a productive and nearly ideal experience, in addition to being my second family. Two colleagues from the Stoa of Attalos deserve special mention. Susan Rotroff accepted me as an assistant in the summer of 1997, introducing me, literally, to the basement of the Agora excavations. The experience of working alongside such a sensible scholar continues to influence my research, although she is not responsible for my insensibilities. Barbara Tsakirgis generously allowed me to study the house of well J 2:4, although it falls within her responsibility for publishing the Greek and Roman houses around the Classical Agora. I thank both Susan and Barbara for being mentors, role models, and friends, and the best thanks I can give them is that I try to emulate their support and encouragement of me when I work with my own graduate students.

When one loves a project as much as I have this one, it is hard to refrain from discussing mind-numbing details with everyone from experts to unfortunate cocktail-party companions. I am in debt to a great number of people who offered encouragement, interest, and suggestions along the way. In particular, my committee at the University of Virigina, Malcolm Bell III, Thomas Carpenter (Ohio University), John Dobbins, and Patty Wattenmaker, provided guidance from the start when my enthusiasm outweighed my sense. At the American School of Classical Studies, where I spent two years during the research and writing of my dissertation, I benefited from discussions with Beryl Barr-Sharrar, Judith Binder, Susanne Hofstra, Elizabeth Langridge-Noti, Mark Lawall, John Lee, Richard Neer, Jenifer Neils, John Oakley, John Papadopoulos, Molly Richardson, and Alan Shapiro, among many others. John Oakley also facilitated my contact with Elke Böhr, Bettina Kreuzer, and Matthias Steinhart. Lynn Snyder has studied the faunal material from well J 2:4, and the preliminary results of her work are included here. Andrea Berlin and Leena Pietilä-Castrén have offered consummate advice and friendship. At the University of Cincinnati, students Lynne Kvapil, Ols Lafe, Shannan Stewart, Katherine Swinford, and Jed Thorn have assisted me with the final stages of the project, and my colleagues here provided inspiration for my own research aspirations. As helpful as this group of friends and scholars has been, any errors contained within are, unfortunately, my own.

I have given many talks on the material from the deposit at the heart of this project, and I am grateful for the many questions from audience members that have caused me to see aspects of this project in a new light. The anonymous (and not so anonymous) *Hesperia* reviewers offered very helpful and insightful suggestions, and I especially thank "Reader 2" for bringing the Sardis houses to my attention. I thank them all for their interest in the project and their ideas for making it even more useful to a broader audience.

I dedicate this work to my spouse, Steve Matter, who has endured endless discussions about pots and all things Classical. I am very lucky to have him, both because he can always make me laugh and because he is a wonderful cook. The most important person in my life has been my grandmother, Elizabeth Stetler, without whom I would not be where I am now. She is a model of strength and unconditional love. Finally, I must also thank Tigerlilly for her warm support.

Cincinnati, Ohio
December 2006

Addendum

Sadly, Tigerlilly died in 2008, but she had a very good life as a Greek immigrant in America. She never lost her *kefi*.

I am grateful to a number of people who assisted in the final preparation of this book: Timothy Wardell and Carol Stein in the ASCSA publications office have offered excellent advice and guidance; Timothy shepherded the book to its end with great care and kindness; the freelance editor improved the manuscript tremendously and provided excellent suggestions for presentation of information; and University of Cincinnati graduate students Bice Peruzzi and Alison Fields helped with the final preparation of images and the bibliography. I continue to be grateful for the community of scholars and students at the University of Cincinnati who encourage my work and broaden my understanding of the Classical world. The librarians who maintain the outstanding collection at the University of Cincinnati Burnam Classics library have my greatest gratitude. They make research a great pleasure. My husband, Steve, continues to make sure a day does not go by without laughter or food. I can't imagine life without him.

I have chosen not to update the text and references substantially other than for clarity. However, I have added more recent references that support the points made in the original manuscript when possible. The subject of the symposium continues to be of interest to scholars, and in the past decade the field of vase painting studies has embraced the study of context, that is, the relationship of figured pots to their findspots, use, and users. I hope that this book will contribute to these and other conversations within the study of vase painting, pottery, and Greek culture.

Cincinnati, Ohio
September 2010

CHAPTER I

INTRODUCTION

In 1993, during excavation within the substantial foundations of the Roman podium temple north of the Agora square, excavators found the remains of a private house built in the Late Archaic period.[1] Late in the 1994 season, continued excavations in that area revealed the top of a well within the house. From the first bucketful of figured pottery it was clear that this would be an exciting find. The well, deposit J 2:4, was cleared to the bottom in the subsequent season (1995). All artifacts from the well deposit were kept, producing 48 tins of context pottery and 233 inventoried objects.[2] The material in the well fits the profile of Persian destruction deposits as described by T. Leslie Shear Jr., and thus becomes the twenty-second such closed deposit from the Athenian Agora and the first within the new excavation area north of Hadrian Street.[3] This is the first Agora well from the Late Archaic or Early Classical period for which all excavated material was saved, and thus presents an unusually complete view of an Athenian household assemblage. Although domestic plain-ware pottery abounds in every excavation, this is the first opportunity to study the relationship between typical household wares and figured wares. Most significantly, this deposit provides evidence for the use of figured wares for symposia in an Athenian domestic setting.[4]

The goal of this project is to contextualize the material from deposit J 2:4. Contextual studies of artifacts aim to situate the artifacts in their temporal, spatial, and/or cultural environment in order to understand better their association with other artifacts and cultural activities.[5] The method of reestablishing context varies according to the particular aspect of "context" to be considered, for there are numerous dimensions to an artifact's context. First, there is archaeological context: the physical environment

1. All dates in this study are B.C., unless otherwise noted.
2. Wet sieving and soil flotation were performed, but no significant data resulted.
3. Shear 1993.
4. Scholars have recognized a need for archaeological data for symposia in Greek households for some time; see Fisher 2000, pp. 360–361. Cahill (2002a, pp. 180–182, 186) had to compare his domestic Olynthian sympotic assemblages to the material published in Rotroff and Oakley 1992, a public not private sympotic assemblage, since this was the most comparable data available at the time.

5. Whitley (1994, pp. 52–53) discusses the application of context to pottery studies. See also Hodder 1991, pp. 121–155. On the relationship between original context and archaeological formation processes, see Schiffer 1987.

from which the artifact was excavated. The archaeological context includes stratigraphy, features, relationship to other artifacts (kept or not), soil type, and floral and faunal remains. Archaeological context, then, is a type of spatial and temporal context. It can provide relative information about the use and abandonment of the object, including its chronological context. Archaeological context, in turn, provides information about the artifact's use within the culture by associating it with specific activity strata and other artifacts contained within them. A group of artifacts found together, some of which functioned in complement, is an assemblage, and the types of objects within the archaeological assemblage also reflect the artifact use at the location.

Beyond the archaeological context, there are more artifact-specific contexts, such as chronological, typological, stylistic, and iconographic. Studies of an artifact's formal characteristics can place the object in a developmental framework. Development can, in turn, elucidate change and prompt questions regarding the process of and motivation for change. In addition, placing figured wares in their iconographic context permits inquiries that aim to understand the meaning of the images to the culture in general and to the creators and viewers of the images in particular. Although some images—for example, those that are taken as straight forward illustrations of an activity—can be studied without concern for their milieu, such study fails to explore fully the power of image design to impart cultural meaning. Only after the image has been placed in the context of iconographic trends and painter preferences will meaningful patterns appear. Additional contexts such as correlations between shape and image will illuminate further meaning.

Finally, context of use, perhaps the most vital of contexts, refers to the occasion, place, purpose, and user of the artifact in antiquity. In the case of pottery, a reconstruction of context of use focuses on who used the object, when, and for what purpose. This includes cultural uses such as the symposium, cooking, transportation, or storage. Examination of context of use emphasizes the interactive role of the objects in activities. We ask how the objects reflect their social use while simultaneously defining the nature of that social activity. For figured objects, a study of context of use allows us to associate the imagery with an activity: Is there a relation? If so, what is the nature of that relation?[6] To what extent does the intended use affect image choice? This last question is tied to the iconographic context discussed above: patterns of images can be associated with specific use contexts, thus allowing us to investigate the nature and meaning of the patterns.

The past decades have seen the study of Greek pottery embrace the concept of contextualization. Numerous conference proceedings have had "pottery and context" as their themes, with papers relating to various aspects of context from workshop to iconographic to geographic.[7] Monographs and exhibitions, also, have explored pottery in the context of its export and even its reception in modern times.[8] The goal is to move away from description and cataloguing into analysis and discussion.[9] This trend is welcomed by current scholars who want to know as much about "why" as "what," and in particular, want to rediscover the "who."[10] Excavation pottery is especially

6. See Gell 1998, but also Layton 2003 and Bowden 2004.

7. Oakley et al. 1997; Villaneuva-Puig et al. 1999; Scheffer 2001a; Schmaltz and Söldner 2003; Bentz and Reusser 2004; Marconi 2004; La Genière 2006; Nørskov et al. 2009; Oakley and Palagia 2009; Tsingarida 2009. Some papers in Brijder 1984 and Christiansen and Melander 1988 address context.

8. Nørskov 2002; Reusser 2002; Rouillard and Verbanck-Piérard 2003; Bentz and Reusser 2004.

9. Yet, description and cataloguing go hand in hand with analysis and cannot be abandoned. Without the typological and chronological frameworks established for the study of figured wares, observations of patterns associated with use and meaning would be impossible.

10. Rouillard and Verbanck-Piérard 2003, pp. 15–16.

well suited for engaging the issue of contexts because it usually comes from a documented archaeological context that can inform some aspect of its context of use or production.[11]

It is the goal of the current project to utilize the full "contextual" power of pottery and to consider the interrelationships between the various contexts discussed above. In particular, this study considers to what extent the context of use—in this case, activities within a house—affects the choice of shape and imagery of figured pottery. Frequently, art-historical studies of the stylistic context of figured pottery—particularly studies of painters and iconography—do not consider archaeological find context or context of use.[12] The key to the current project is the recognition that pottery is made for a purpose, no matter how broad, which permits us to ask how much the intended cultural purpose affects stylistic characteristics of the pottery. Specifically, how does the figured ware function within the context of activities in this house, and how does its iconography relate to these activities? The sum of these considerations of archaeological and stylistic contexts will be a broader understanding of the cultural meaning of the pottery in use in an Archaic Athenian house.

This study is organized according to the different contexts into which the material from well J 2:4 can be placed. The archaeological context is considered first, in discussions of the house of well J 2:4 (Chapter 2) and the contents of the well (Chapter 3). Second, I consider the sympotic context and how the pottery forms and their decoration relate to the practice of communal drinking in this house (Chapters 4 and 5). Third, I look at the everyday domestic context and the artifacts needed to run a household in Late Archaic Athens (Chapter 6). The final section (Chapter 7) gathers all of the information together to consider the larger social context. A Catalogue and three appendices follow.

In sum, the multifaceted approach to the material record proposed here permits an interdisciplinary study that harnesses archaeological data with art-historical and cultural studies. The objective is to show that meaning and use are inherently related, and that through archaeology we can restore a context of use for a class of objects frequently studied in isolation.

11. Ann Steiner (1998), in her review of *Agora* XXX, observes that "excavation pottery begs to have its character analyzed in terms of its context and use."

12. E.g., Neer 2002; Ferrari 2002.

CHAPTER 2

THE ARCHAEOLOGICAL CONTEXT OF WELL J 2:4

Well J 2:4 is located within the northern extension of the Athenian Agora excavations, north of the Piraeus–Kiphissia railroad tracks and across Hadrian Street (Figs. 1–4). Situated within the rubble foundations of a Roman podium temple,[1] the well and its house lie in a neighborhood formed by the intersection of the Panathenaic Way to the south and a north–south street to the east (Fig. 2). Between the house and the Panathenaic Way lies the Archaic altar of Aphrodite, presumably within a sacred precinct (Figs. 2–4).[2] This chapter will first examine the well and its stratigraphy, then the house it served, and conclude with a discussion of the chronology of the house and well and the identification of the well fill as Persian destruction cleanup debris.

WELL J 2:4

STRATIGRAPHY

As preserved, well J 2:4 is a 5.80 m shaft cut into soft bedrock (Fig. 5). The wellhead does not survive in situ, and the ground level at the time of use is not precisely known, although the excavator noticed a patch of light clay bordering the top of the shaft on the east side, which he suggested may represent contemporary ground level.[3] Nevertheless, the well was recognized at 51.03 m above sea level, which probably approximates original ground level.[4] The top of the cylindrical shaft is cut through fill on the northern side, but below and on all other sides it is cut into the soft, gray bedrock. The shaft had a fieldstone lining, with individual stones ca. 15–30 cm long, preserved to a height of 49.00 m above sea level on the north and 49.40 m above sea level on the south and east. This lining technique is not unknown for the Archaic period at Athens, but it is rare and indicates particular care in the construction of the well.[5] The interior diameter of the lined portion of the well was 1.05 m at 49.00 m above sea level and 0.92 m at 48.30 m above sea level. The northwestern side of the shaft had collapsed, displacing the fieldstones and permitting a section of the bedrock to fall away. With the collapse of the lining and the intrusion of later features, it is difficult to estimate the precise diameter of the well at

1. Shear 1997, pp. 485–507; excavated as section BZ.

2. For the altar of Aphrodite, see Shear 1984, pp. 24–33; for excavations in this general area, see Shear 1984, 1997; Camp 1996, 1999, 2007.

3. Pfaff 1994, p. 1.

4. This elevation agrees with the elevation of floor levels in the southeastern room, suggesting that the top of the well as excavated is close to its original surface level.

5. Camp 1977, p. 177 and n. 6. Of the 62 Archaic wells Camp studied, only four had stone linings. Well Q 21:3, mentioned below, was one of those four.

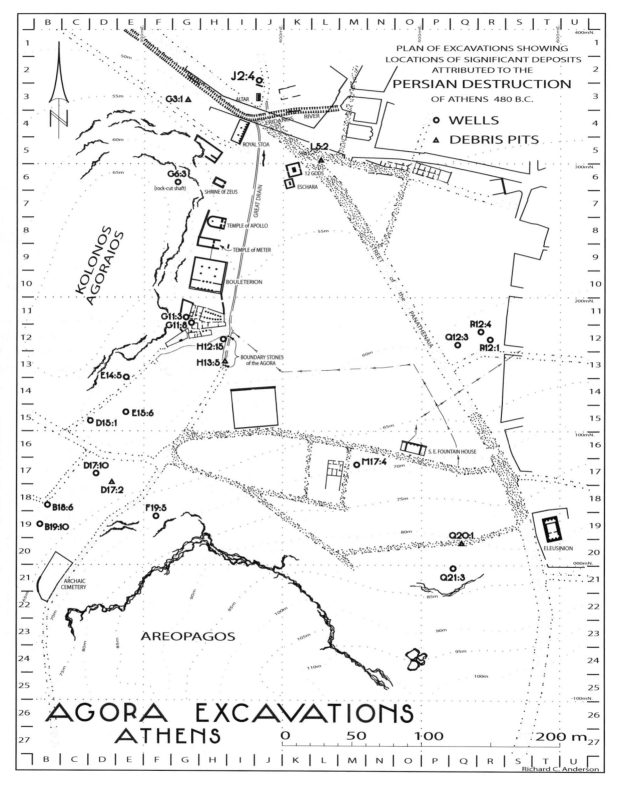

Figure 1. Plan of the Athenian Agora ca. 480, with Persian destruction deposits indicated. R. Anderson

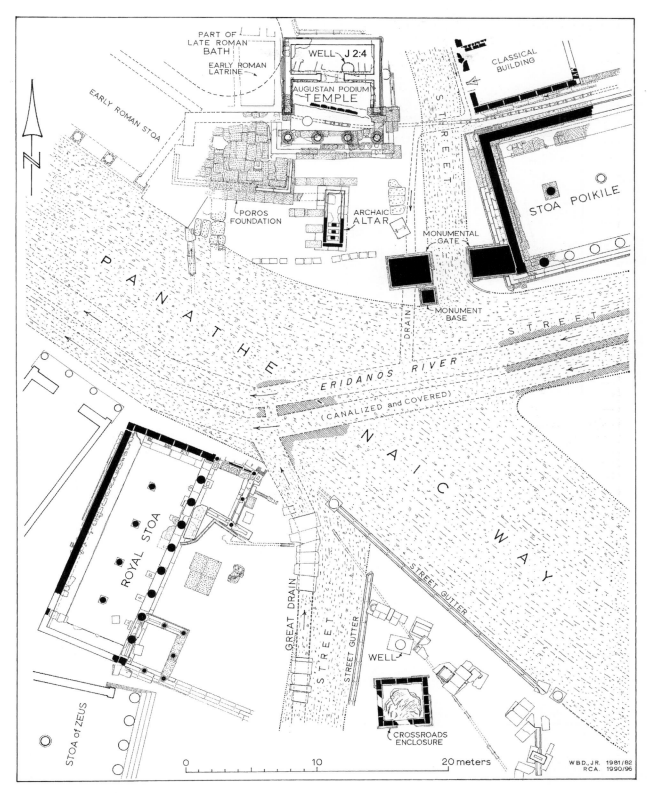

Figure 2. Northwest corner of the Agora, partially restored plan.
Shear 1997, fig. 1

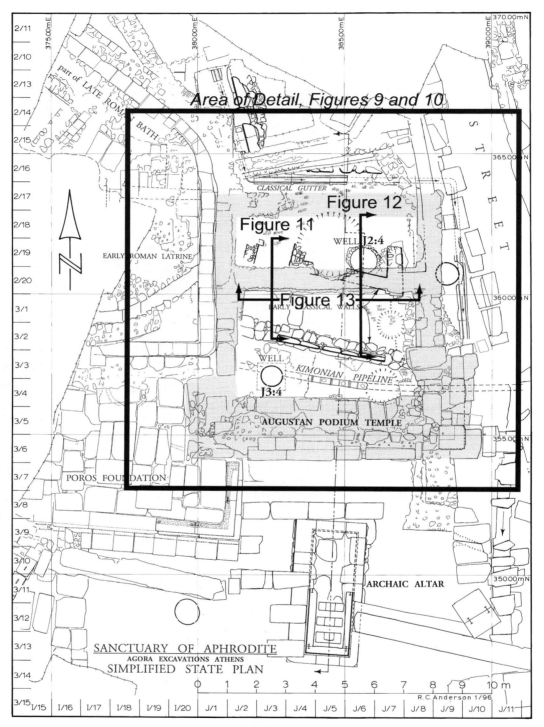

Figure 3. Detail, state plan of sanctuary of Aphrodite and Roman temple. Plan of Roman temple indicated in gray. Area within box enlarged in Figures 9 and 10. Lines indicate orientation of stratigraphic sections in Figures 11, 12, and 13. Author after Camp 1996, fig. 5

Figure 4. View of excavation of sanctuary of Aphrodite and Roman temple to the north. Agora Excavations

6. Camp 1999, p. 265. A second, similar grave, J 2:10, was found 1.5 m north of the well in 1996; see Camp 1999, pp. 263–265.

7. Skeleton AA 343; see Appendix III for full analysis.

8. See deposit P 8:5, a well filled with material of the 6th century with the exception of a Mycenaean feeder, *Agora* XIII, p. 264, no. 490, pl. 64 (P 12680), and a Mycenaean figurine (T 1653). The excavators speculate that well diggers disturbed a child's burial of the Mycenaean period; see Shear 1939, p. 212, fig. 11.

its mouth, but ca. 1.00 m is likely. The excavator did note that the sides of the uppermost portion of the shaft descended vertically for about one meter, then sloped outward for another meter so that the actual diameter of the shaft (without the fieldstone lining) at 49.00 m above sea level was 1.50 m. It is possible that the original builders of the shaft recognized the danger of the soft, unstable bedrock and then shored the well up with the reinforcement of the fieldstone lining.

A nearby Submycenaean grave sheds light on the chronology of the collapse of the fieldstone lining. Among the pottery from the period of use deposit in the well (Level 6, see below) the excavators encountered twelve bones of a human foot dispersed from 46.60 to 45.23 m above sea level. Two years later, in the 1997 season, excavators found a Submycenaean inhumation grave, J 2:11, west of the well, and abutting the northwest edge of the excavated well shaft.[6] The bottom of this grave was reached at a level of ca. 49.90 m above sea level, which is slightly higher than the collapsed level of fieldstone lining on this side of the well, approximately 49.00 m above sea level. It seems that the original builders of well J 2:4 missed the Submycenaean grave by centimeters, and the weakened bedrock between the two features soon gave way, dislodging the fieldstone lining. Grave J 2:11 was excavated with the assistance of a physical anthropologist, who recognized that the inhumed skeleton lacked a left foot.[7] After the initial collapse of the fieldstones and bedrock, the skeleton's foot dropped into the well and settled among the period of use fill in the well.[8] Since the foot bones were distributed in the well from 46.60 m to 45.23 m above sea level, the bones must

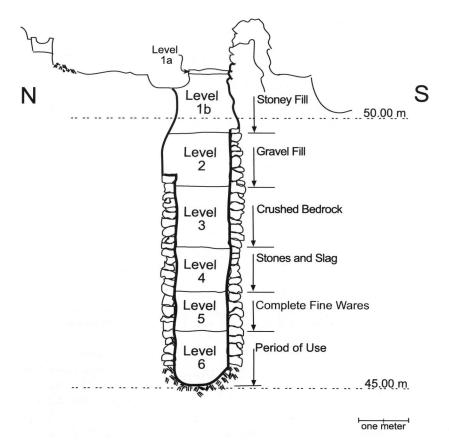

Figure 5. Simplified stratigraphic section of well J 2:4, looking east.
Author after Camp 1996, fig. 6

have fallen into the well slowly over the period of the well's use. The highest fragment of the foot was found within the lowest dumped fill deposited intentionally during the post–Persian destruction cleanup operation (Level 5, see below). The correspondence of the foot bone with the lowest level of cleanup debris suggests that the bones—and possibly bedrock—continued to fall into the well throughout the period of use down to the closing of the well with the destruction debris. Since the foot bones were present throughout the period of use, this indicates that the well continued to be used after the partial collapse of the fieldstone lining and bedrock wall.[9]

The fill of the well has a recognizable stratigraphy with six distinguishable levels, the bottommost being the period of use deposit (see Fig. 5 and Tables 1 and 2).[10] The pottery from the upper five levels represents fill deposited intentionally soon after the Persian destruction of Athens. Each "Level" (e.g., Level 1) represents a continuous portion of the deposit with generally similar characteristics. The levels are assigned and described in order to facilitate discussion and may not accord precisely with the original, natural stratigraphy of the well fill, since excavating a well below the modern water table makes recognition of subtle changes in soil and stratigraphy difficult. Each level represents a component of the cleanup event and can be likened to wheelbarrow loads of debris tossed into the well.[11]

Joins of fragments between the discernible stratigraphic levels of the well deposit confirm that the fill is one depositional event. Joins between pottery fragments from the upper portion and the lower portion of the fill are numerous, but figured-ware joins were the easiest to identify and

9. Not all bones of the foot are accounted for; see Appendix III. It is possible that an occasional toe was brought up with a bucket of water.

10. My "Levels" and section drawing deviate slightly from those presented in Camp 1996, p. 244. "Lots" refer to the pottery storage tin numbers corresponding to each level. Lots BZ T732 and T733 are mixed fragments from 46.00–45.20 m from the processing of the well mud after the initial removal of large pottery fragments. T735 contains bones from all levels, separated into individual plastic bags.

11. Cf. well E 15:6, with its alternating layers of potter's clay and sherds: Shear 1993, p. 403, fig. 7.

TABLE 1. STRATIGRAPHY OF WELL J 2:4

Level	Elevation	Description	Lot
1a	51.00–50.88 m*	Gray, clayish soil with little pottery	BZ 680, 681
1b	50.88–49.75 m	Densely packed 10–15 cm stones set in dark gray clay; large fragments of pottery	BZ 682, 683
2	49.75–48.60 m	Gravelly brown mud, fewer large stones; much fine pottery with many fragments of black figure, some red figure. Ca. 48.75 m gives way to gravelly fill with fist-sized stones containing little pottery	BZ 684–686, 704, 705, 734
3	48.60–47.60 m	Nearly sterile fill of crushed bedrock	BZ 707
4	47.60–46.65 m	Fist-sized stones, loosely packed stony fill with nodules of slag, fair amount of pottery, especially large coarse fragments. First intact pot at 46.63 m (**184**)	BZ 708–711
5	46.65–45.90 m	Loosely packed stones, high concentration of black-glazed, black-figured, and red-figured complete pots	BZ 712–723
6	45.90–45.20 m	Period of use: Mixed stones, silt, and large fragments of household water jugs; more fine-ware fragments with many joins with Level 5 for complete vessels	BZ 724–731

* The elevations within the well should be understood as "meters above sea level," but are shortened to "m" for the sake of space.

are used here to illustrate the point (Table 2). A large fragment of **79**, a black-figured lekanis lid with a double ivy pattern on the rim, came from Level 5, but two other nonjoining fragments from the same lid come from Level 2. The ivy-leaf pattern, the distinctive figural style, and the estimated diameter confirm that all are fragments from the same lid, even though they do not join. Joining fragments of a black-glazed lid (**162**) with rays at the base of the handle come from Levels 2 and 5. Fragments from a thin-walled black-figured skyphos (**77**) with the leg of a warrior running to the right with his right hand extended behind him holding a spear, the line of which overlaps the leg, come from Levels 2 and 5. Joining fragments from a black-figured kalpis (**6**) with a distinctive matte black-glazed surface, ivy frieze between the handles, and a shoulder panel preserving the rear legs of a feline and a hoofed quadruped come, again, from Levels 2 and 5. Joining fragments from a black-figured amphora of small-scale Panathenaic shape (**2**), unfortunately with only the neck preserved, come from Levels 2 and 4. Joining fragments from the body of an amphora (**1**), come from Levels 1b, 2, and 5. Joining fragments of a black-figured skyphos (**34**), perhaps with a bird between handle attachments, come from Levels 2 and 5. Both **39** and **41** are fragments of black-figured skyphoi consisting of joining fragments from Levels 2 and 5. Many of these joins occur between levels above and below one meter of generally sterile fill of crushed bedrock. Undoubtedly, the plain and coarse wares would show the same pattern of cross-level joins if attempts were made to find joins.

Fragments of a wellhead were found in both the upper and lower portions of the well. Although fragmentary and poorly preserved, the form is the drum-shaped variety, most closely resembling A 957 from a well on the north slope of the Acropolis.[12] Parts of the rim and base were found in Level 6, but other parts of the base were in Levels 5 and 1b. Some fragments of the base were tinged gray from exposure to fire. The distribution of wellhead fragments indicates that a portion of the wellhead was dismantled and

12. From deposit T 24:3: see Lang 1949, p. 126, no. 10, pl. 7, fig. 3; *Agora* XII, p. 194, n. 11. Downturned, projecting rim; three raised narrow molded bands; thickened base, offset from wall on exterior; streaky black glaze on molded bands and base. Dates to late 6th century. A 957 and others feature at least two large holes below the rim. No fragment of the wellhead from J 2:4 preserved this feature.

TABLE 2. CATALOGUED OBJECTS BY LEVELS

An asterisk indicates that the object meets the criteria for inclusion in the household assemblage. A question mark with an asterisk indicates that the object meets the criteria, but there is some doubt if it should be included. Square brackets indicate objects discarded during the use of the well.

Level 1b			Joins in Level		Level 2			Joins in Level
*1	BF	Amphora	2, 5		37	BF	Skyphos	
13	BF	Lekythos			38	BF	Skyphos	
15	BF	Lekythos	2		*39	BF	Skyphos	5
16	BF	Lekythos	2		44	BF	Skyphos	
22	BF	Closed vessel			51	BF	Skyphos	
24	BF	Phiale			53	BF	Skyphos	1b
25	BF	Stand			54	BF	Skyphos	1b
27	BF	Open shape	2		55	BF	Skyphos	
33	BF	Skyphos			56	BF	Skyphos	
36	BF	Skyphos			57	BF	Skyphos	
43	BF	Skyphos			58	BF	Skyphos	3
53	BF	Skyphos	2		59	BF	Skyphos	1b
54	BF	Skyphos	2		60	BF	Skyphos	
59	BF	Skyphos	2		61	BF	Skyphos	1b
61	BF	Skyphos	2		63	BF	Skyphos	
64	BF	Skyphos	2		64	BF	Skyphos	1b
67	BF	Skyphos			65	BF	Skyphos	
71	BF	Cup-skyphos	2		66	BF	Skyphos	
76	BF	Cup			69	BF	Skyphos	
80	BF	Lid			70	BF	Skyphos	
99	RF	Cup			71	BF	Cup-skyphos	1b
137	BG	Cup			72	BF	Protocorinthian kotyle	
138	BG	Cup			*77	BF	Cup?	5
161	BG	Lekanis lid	2		*79	BF	Lekanis lid	5
180	HH	Lekane			*83	BF	Miniature Corinthian kotyle	
*181	HH	Lekane			85	RF	Closed vessel (pelike?)	
194		Lamp			86	RF	Closed vessel (chous?)	
*? 202	TC	Herm			*87	RF	Cup	
*? 206		Loomweight			*88	RF	Cup	
*? 209		Spindle whorl			94	RF	Cup	
*? 216		Clay stopper			96	RF	Cup	
					97	RF	Cup	
Level 2			Joins in Level		98	RF	Cup	
*1	BF	Amphora	1b, 5		100	RF	Cup	
*2	BF	Amphora	4		101	RF	Cup	
*4	BF	Stamnos			102	RF	Cup	
*6	BF	Kalpis	5		103	RF	Cup	
9	BF	Lekythos			*109	BG	Psykter	
*10	BF	Lekythos			*122	BG	Type B skyphos	
12	BF	Lekythos			126	BG	Skyphos	
15	BF	Lekythos	1b		*127	BG	One-handler	
16	BF	Lekythos	1b		*129	BG	Cup	
17	BF	Lekythos			139	BG	Cup	
18	BF	Lekythos			*143	BG	Stemmed dish	
19	BF	Lekythos			*148	BG	Salt cellar	
20	BF	Lekythos			*149	BG	Salt cellar	
21	BF	Lekythos			*156	BG	Covered bowl	
26	BF	Dinos or louterion?			159	BG	Lekanis lid	
27	BF	Uncertain open shape	1b					
31	BF	Skyphos						
*34	BF	Skyphos	5					
35	BF	Skyphos						

TABLE 2—*Continued*

Level 2			Joins in Level		Level 5			Joins in Level
160	BG	Lekanis lid			*84	RF	Pelike	
161	BG	Lekanis lid	1b		*89	RF	Cup	
*162	BG	Lekanis lid	5		*90	RF	Cup	
*163	BG	Psykter lid			*92	RF	Cup	
*165	BG	Lid or bowl?			*93	RF	Cup	
*166	BG	Askos			*95	RF	Cup	
*168	BG	Disk			[*104]	BG	Amphora	6
189		Lamp			*105	BG	Amphora	
*197		Lamp			*106	BG	Pelike	
*? 199	TC	Female head protome			*107	BG	Pelike	
*? 201	TC	Seated female			*112	BG	Trefoil oinochoe	6
*? 207		Loomweight			*113	BG	Trefoil oinochoe	6
					*114	BG	Jug	
Level 3			*Joins in Level*		*123	BG	Cup-skyphos	6
*41	BF	Skyphos	5		*124	BG	Cup-skyphos	
*48	BF	Skyphos	5		*125	BG	Cup-skyphos	
58	BF	Skyphos	2		*128	BG	Cup	6
111	BG	Psykter			*132	BG	Cup	6
					*133	BG	Cup	
Level 4			*Joins in Level*		*134	BG	Cup	
*2	BF	Amphora	2		*135	BG	Cup	
110	BG	Psykter			*136	BG	Cup	6
*184	HH	Chytra	5		*144	BG	Stemmed dish	
					*145	BG	Stemmed dish	
Level 5			*Joins in Level*		*146	BG	Stemmed dish	
*1	BF	Amphora	1b, 2		*147	BG	Stemmed dish	
*3	BF	Amphoriskos			*150	BG	Salt cellar	
*5	BF	Oinochoe			*151	BG	Salt cellar/small bowl	
*6	BF	Kalpis	2		**152**	BG	Bowl	
*11	BF	Lekythos			*157	BG	Lekanis	6
14	BF	Lekythos			*158	BG	Lekanis lid	
*23	BF	Phiale			*162	BG	Lekanis lid	2
*28	BF	Skyphos			*170	BG	Ring	
29	BF	Skyphos			*172	HH	Kados	
30	BF	Skyphos			[174]	HH	Trefoil jug	
32	BF	Skyphos			*175	HH	Jug	
*34	BF	Skyphos	2		*176	HH	Jug	
*39	BF	Skyphos	2		[177]	HH	Jug	6
*41	BF	Skyphos	3		[178]	HH	Jug	
42	BF	Skyphos			**179**	HH	Water jar	
*45	BF	Skyphos			*182	HH	Lekane	6
*46	BF	Skyphos	6		*183	HH	Bowl	
*47	BF	Skyphos			*184	HH	Chytra	4
49	BF	Skyphos			*185	HH	Chytra	
50	BF	Skyphos			*186	HH	Chytra	
52	BF	Skyphos			*188	HH	Cooking bell	
68	BF	Skyphos	6		*191		Lamp	
*77	BF	Cup?	2		*192		Lamp	
78	BF	Open shape (plate?)			**193**		Lamp	
*79	BF	Lekanis lid	2		*195		Lamp	
					*?200	TC	Seated female	

TABLE 2—*Continued*

Level 5			Joins in Level	Level 6 (Period of Use)			Joins in Level
203	TC	Quadruped		[120]	BG	Mug	
204	TC	Fragment of horse		*121	BG	Skyphos	
*210		Astragalos		*123	BG	Cup-skyphos	5
*211		Astragalos		*128	BG	Cup	5
*212		Modified astragalos		*130	BG	Cup	
*213		Modified astragalos		[131]	BG	Cup	
*214		Modified astragalos		*132	BG	Cup	5
				*136	BG	Cup	5
Level 6 (Period of Use)			**Joins in Level**	*141	BG	Stemmed dish	
[7]	BF	Lekythos		*142	BG	Stemmed dish	
[8]	BF	Lekythos		[153]	BG	Bowl	
[40]	BF	Skyphos		[154]	BG	Bowl	
*46	BF	Skyphos	5	*155	BG	Covered bowl	
[62]	BF	Skyphos		*157	BG	Lekanis	5
68	BF	Skyphos	5	*164	BG	Lid for covered bowl?	
[73]	BF	Cup		*167	BG	Unguent pot	
[74]	BF	Cup		*169	BG	Stand	
[75]	BF	Cup		*171	BG	Argive monochrome juglet	
[81]	BF	Thymiaterion		[173]	HH	Jug	
*82	BF	Miniature hydria		[177]	HH	Jug	5
*91	RF	Cup		*182	HH	Lekane	5
[*104]	BG	Amphora	5	*187	HH	Chytra	
[*108]	BG	Pelike		*190		Lamp	
*112	BG	Trefoil oinochoe	5	*196		Lamp	
*113	BG	Trefoil oinochoe	5	*198	TC	Female plaque figurine	
[*115]	BG	Jug		[205]	TC	Fragment of human figurine?	
*116	BG	Trefoil olpe		*208		Loomweight	
*117	BG	Olpe		*215	Bone	Disk	
*118	BG	Olpe		[217]		Lead sheet	
*119	BG	Olpe					

thrown in immediately on top of the period of use pottery (Level 6), then cleanup continued with additional fragments being dumped into the well later in the process. The disposal of the wellhead parallels that of some of the fragmentary pottery.[13]

The excavators hit the modern water table at 50.30 m above sea level, and provisions were made to pump out water interfering with the excavation. The tight conditions of well excavation combined with the difficulty of distinguishing soil changes in mud under poor lighting conditions justify a less rigid interpretation of the recorded archaeological stratigraphy.[14] Excavation generally proceeded down the well in horizontal sweeps, although in reality, debris tossed into the well probably landed in a conical heap rather than settling into flat layers.[15] The effect is similar to a farmer's

13. There was no attempt to reconstruct the wellhead of well J 2:4. The full circumference of rim or base does not appear to be preserved. The fabric of the clay has degraded to small chips, resulting in the total deterioration of some fragments. Fragments of the rim have an estimated diameter of ca. 56 cm; fragments of the base have a diameter of ca. 88 cm.

14. Graham Webster, in his handbook of archaeological methods, *Practical Archaeology*, warns, "Whether the results achieved from the excavation of wells are always commensurate with the great efforts put into them is often a matter of doubt" (1963, p. 95). He goes on to recommend a "crash helmet" for the excavator.

15. See Vanderpool 1938, p. 366, for a discussion of this filling phenomenon.

silo filled with grain from an opening in the top. The grain forms a peak in the silo. If the farmer were to change grains periodically, the stratigraphy of the silo would not be horizontal but conical, higher at the center than at the edges. The natural stratigraphy of well J 2:4, however, was probably not as pristine as that of the farmer's mechanically filled silo. Use of the well must have centered on the north and west since the eastern edge of the well would have been difficult to access due to the external eastern wall of the house and the east–west wall separating the northeastern courtyard and the southeastern room (see Fig. 9, below). Therefore, pots dropped into the well during use and household debris discarded into the well might have piled up along the northern side of the shaft, forming a slope down into the water table. In the cleanup operation, similarly, debris swept or dumped into the well would also have piled up and intermingled with the period of use deposit.

Given the above conditions, it is not possible to distinguish a clear line between the period of use deposit and the beginning of the dumped fill. A period of use deposit usually contains a combination of water-fetching vessels that have broken during use and rubbish thrown into the well for disposal.[16] I have somewhat arbitrarily defined the upper reaches of the period of use deposit of well J 2:4 as the point where the fine-ware pottery outnumbers the water jars. However, keeping in mind the naturally conical stratigraphy that has been dug horizontally, it is not surprising that there are also numerous water jars in the lower portion of Level 5, the lowest level of the intentional fill. It is necessary to make a distinction between Levels 5 and 6 in order to distinguish Level 5, rich in complete black-figured and red-figured pots, as separate from the period of use deposit.

Beginning from the bottom, Level 6 represents the period of use deposit intermingled with a small amount of fine-ware pottery from the first episode in the cleanup operation. Level 6 includes one nearly complete household fabric jug (**173**) and at least 42 cooking-ware water jars, according to counts of bases.[17] This is not the complete extent of the period of use deposit, though, because Level 5 also includes a large number of complete water jars and fragments. The lower part of Level 5 (46.00–45.90 m) includes six complete or nearly complete household fabric water jars (**172, 174–178**). In the entire range of Level 5 (46.65–45.90 m), there are at least 28 cooking-ware water jars. Water-jar bases give the best estimate for total number of water vessels present, since the mouth or handle of a jar that breaks in the well may remain attached to the rope and be retrieved. In fact, three water jars are missing their vertical handles (**174, 177,** and **178**); in these cases the vessels broke within the well but the handle, to which the rope was tied, was retrieved and disposed of elsewhere.[18] If we count only water-jar bases there are at least 74 water jars (of both household and cooking-ware fabrics) in the lowest portions of the well. Above Level 5 the number of water jars decreases considerably.

Also present in Level 6 were non-water jar odds and ends tossed into the well for disposal or by accident during the period of use.[19] This miscellaneous material includes: the stem and floor of a black-figured Type Sub-A cup with a satyr (**74**); a single fragment of a Type A or B black-figured cup (**73**); an eye cup (**75**); two black-figured skyphoi fragments (**40, 62**); a fragment of a black-glazed Type C cup with concave lip (**131**);

16. *Agora* V, p. 123; *Agora* XII, p. 44.

17. See Table 5 for minimum number of vessels, plus Chapter 3 for quantification methodology. The ring bases of cooking-ware hydriai, jugs, and kadoi are indistinguishable; see Rotroff and Oakley 1992, p. 29. No effort was made to mend the cooking-ware water jars, so there may be many other complete water vessels within Level 6 as well as Level 5, which also contains period of use material.

18. This will be important to remember when we consider the large number of kadoi rims preserved in Level 2 of the deposit.

19. No transport amphora fragments were found in Level 6; see discussion in Appendix I.

a fragmentary black-figured stem of a thymiaterion (**81**); a fragment of a
Phanyllis Group lekythos with a warrior leaving home (**7**); lamps (**190, 196**);
a miniature hydria (**82**); and a terracotta female plaque figurine (**198**). A
circular lead sheet (**217**) probably covered the end of the well rope, and it
either fell off or the entire rope fell irretrievably into the well. The objects
from the period of use deposit date to the last quarter of the 6th century.
In particular, the thymiaterion stem (**81**) dates closer to 525 than to 500,
as does the plaque figurine (**198**). The fragments of black-figured cups also
date between 525 and 500. Faunal remains represent both food portions
and butchering debris.[20] In Table 6, discussed in Chapter 3, I attempt to
distinguish trash generated while the house was in use from debris associated with the post–Persian destruction cleanup.

Complete or nearly complete objects of shapes inappropriate for drawing water indicate that the intentional fill of Persian destruction debris also
reaches into Level 6.[21] The black-glazed olpai **116–119**, nearly all intact;
the large black-glazed jug **115**; and stemmed dishes **141** and **142** all represent table-service objects tossed into the well on top of the period of use
deposit. The red-figured cup **91**, which belongs to the set of red-figured
cups found in Level 5, indicates that this portion of fine-ware material
in Level 6 is not part of the period of use but belongs to the intentional
dumped fill above.[22] Again, the stratigraphy of a well is not likely to be
horizontal, and this mixture of period of use and dumped fill is a result of
the uneven natural stratigraphy of the well forced into horizontal "levels"
for the purpose of study (see Fig. 5).

Almost all the fine-ware fragments excavated from 46.65 m to 45.45 m,
from Levels 5 and 6, could be mended to form complete or nearly complete
pots. These pots must have been tossed into the well intact, and broken in
the shaft.[23] When the conservators had finished mending the vases from
Levels 5 and 6, only a handful of fine-ware sherds remained unjoined in
the storage lots, and some of these joined figured fragments from Level 2.
This indicates that Level 5 included pottery broken aboveground whose
fragments were dispersed around the house and deposited in the well in
different shovelfuls during the filling of the well.

Levels 5 and 6 yielded 68 complete or nearly complete vessels other
than water jars, with some of the sturdier shapes preserved intact. Other
Persian destruction well deposits also contained objects discarded intact.
The phenomenon can best be seen in the vast number of complete vessels, some intact, discarded into the Stoa Gutter Well (SGW) and at least
one other domestic well.[24] The complete shapes in our deposit largely

---

20. L. Snyder, pers. comm. Comments on faunal remains are preliminary observations only; a full study by
Lynn Snyder is forthcoming.

21. With the exception of transport
amphoras, for which many joins could
be found, but no complete pots made
up. See discussion in Appendix I,
where the conclusion is that the amphoras were not thrown into the well

intact, but in large fragments.

22. Faunal remains show a parallel
distribution. Astragaloi are only found
in Levels 5 and 6, and food and butchering debris blends between Level 5
and the top of Level 6 (L. Snyder,
pers. comm.).

23. The pocket of fine wares
discussed here is a type of de facto
deposit, meaning that the objects were

intentionally discarded even when they
could have been reused or recycled.
Thus their deposition cancels their
symbolic and social functions; see
Schiffer 1987, pp. 89–97.

24. Stoa Gutter Well (Q 12:3):
Thompson 1955; Roberts 1986.
Well H 12:15: Thompson 1954,
pp. 51–54, pl. 15.

represent the equipment needed for drinking wine. These include three black-figured cup-skyphoi of hasty, silhouette style (**45–47**), and a large, black-figured Heron Class skyphos by the CHC Group (**28**). Two of the black-figured cup-skyphoi (**45** and **46**) are very close in style, profile, and potting details. There are also three complete black-glazed cup-skyphoi (**123, 124,** and **125**), the latter two of which, again, are nearly identical. Only one Corinthian-type skyphos (**121**), nearly complete, came from Levels 5 and 6. The most common drinking vessel is the Type C cup. There are eight complete or nearly complete black-glazed examples, of which only three have concave lips.[25] This is in contrast to Levels 2 and 3, higher in the well, in which fragments of black-glazed Type C cups with concave lips dominate all other drinking vessels. All of the plain-rimmed black-glazed Type C cups from Level 5 of the deposit are of similar size, ranging from 6.60–7.30 cm in height and 17.50–19.70 cm in diameter, and they have similar capacities (see Appendix II).

Level 5 contained a number of complete or nearly complete red-figured cups. In total, there are six examples of Type C cups with red-figured decoration from these two lowest levels of the well. Four have plain rims (**89–92**), one a concave lip (**93**), and one is a small-scale Type C cup (**95**). In Chapter 3 the identification of these cups as a symposium set based on workshops, shapes, and iconography is discussed. In the deposit as a whole, black-figured fragments outnumber red-figured about four to one; however, in this pocket of complete fine wares, there is more red figure than black figure.

The pocket of fine wares in Level 5 also contained four stemmed dishes of different forms.[26] That the stemmed dishes were found in conjunction with the predominantly "sympotic" equipment suggests that the shape played some role in communal drinking or in the meal that preceded it. They may be the only food-consumption form present in this pocket of fine wares (see discussion in Chapters 4 and 5).

The remaining complete vessels from Levels 5 and 6, with a few interesting exceptions, are wine-serving vessels or tableware. There is a black-figured oinochoe (**5**) and a black-figured amphoriskos (**3**). There are four pelikai: one of red figure (**84**), and three of black glaze (**106, 107,** and **108**), one of which (**107**) is intact. In black glaze there are also two table amphoras (**104, 105**), an intact jug (**114**), and two trefoil-mouth oinochoai (**112, 113**).

Faunal remains from Levels 5 and 6 include both bone artifacts and food and butchering debris. A group of astragaloi (**210–214**) found in Levels 5 and 6 must have been discarded at the same time as the complete fine wares discussed above. Thus, it is likely that they were a set of objects within the house. Other faunal remains include food and non-food (mandibles) bones of pigs, a radius and ulna of a donkey, food and non-food (horn cores) bones of ovid-caprids, fish bones, and three uncut dog bones.[27]

As opposed to the rich levels of fine-ware pottery at the bottom of the well, Level 4 (47.60–46.65 m) was distinguished by loosely packed fist-sized stones, nodules of slag, and large fragments of coarse pottery. Level 4 yielded a small number of black-glazed fragments and two black-figured body sherds. Mortars and pithoi or basin fragments made up the majority of household fragments, with a few lekanai fragments. The bulk of the pottery was transport amphora body sherds, at a weight of 12 kg. Also present were

25. The Type C cup is a stemmed cup shape with a fillet at the bottom of the stem. Stemmed cups are known generally as kylikes; see **128, 130, 131** (concave lip), and **132–136** (plain rim). Cup **129** from Level 2 is nearly identical to **130** in profile and dimensions, further connecting the upper fill with the pocket of fine wares in Level 5. The concave-lip version of the Type C cup is the more common in Archaic black glaze: *Agora* XII, p. 92.

26. These are **144, 145, 147** (chalice-shaped), and **146** (with concave lip).

27. L. Snyder, pers. comm.

about a dozen fragments of roof tiles. Among the few inventoried objects from this level, **184** is an intact chytra with extensive carbon deposits, that is, clear evidence of use. This vessel of fragile cooking-ware fabric must have been tossed into the well and cushioned by the water as it sank to its resting place. A chytra is juglike in form, and it is not impossible that this shape was used to pull up water, but the burning on **184** and its location above the pocket of Persian destruction fill confirm that it was not being used in this manner. In addition, the chytra tells us that the water table must have been higher than 47.60 m during the period of use and the period of Persian destruction cleanup. Tossed into the well, it hit the water and gently sank into its resting spot. Once in the well, fortune and physics protected it from the crushing weight of stones and slag above. The slag is perplexing, for it indicates industrial activity in the neighborhood of the house. The slag nodules represent a "wheelbarrow load" of debris from somewhere outside of the house.[28] Aside from the slag, there is no other evidence for metalworking preserved,[29] although it is possible, of course, that further evidence lies under the disturbed area to the west.

Level 3, 48.60–47.60 m, again, contained very little pottery and few inventoried objects. Level 3 is characterized by a nearly sterile fill of crushed bedrock. The excavators originally thought this bedrock may be the result of the collapse of the upper section of the shaft, but as discussed above, the collapse of the north side of the well occurred during the period of use as shown by the presence of part of the Submycenaean human foot in Level 6. Like the slag, the crushed bedrock must have also come from a source outside the house. The bedrock in the area of the Agora excavations is a soft, easily excavated marl. It is possible that the source of this stratum of bedrock was the excavation of another well near but not within the house or leveling associated with post–Persian destruction construction.

Level 2 (49.75–48.60 m) is characterized by a gravelly fill with fist-sized stones, many fragments of pottery, and small chunks of hardened mud that may either come from mud-brick walls or the mud packing of roofs. The pottery includes both fragments from objects broken in the house and fragments of supplementary material brought in to top off the filling of the well. Small, very worn pottery fragments dating to the early part of the 6th century indicate that a portion of the pottery from Level 2 (as will be the case for Level 1) was introduced from a location where pottery sherds were subjected to abrasion and wear; see, for example, **72** and **189**.[30] These fragments most likely came from the ground surface near the house.[31] Either the cleanup was nearing a conclusion and the well was still not sufficiently filled, or the debris in the well settled and more fill was needed. In either case, several shovelfuls of fill were tossed in from another source, but the mixture of older fragments with contemporary ones

28. See also the layer of stone chips above the well brought in from outside, p. 34.

29. The slag is similar to Mattusch 1977, pp. 357–358, nos. E2 and E3, pl. 87. The iron smithy she describes was located in the courtyard of a struc-

ture, which had "slag, ash, and charcoal mixed with black earth on its packed clay floor" (p. 357). No such stratum was found in the house of well J 2:4; therefore, the house is not likely to have had a metalworking establishment. The slag exhibits slight magnetism,

confirming that it contains iron.

30. For ceramic abrasion, see Schiffer and Skibo 1989.

31. As with the figured fragments, the transport-amphora fragments from Levels 1 and 2 are worn and some date to the early 6th century; see Appendix I.

indicates that the supplementary fill was part of the initial cleanup and not a later addition.[32] It is possible that the homeowners looked no farther than their doorstep or their rubbish heap.[33] In fact, the large number of water-jar fragments in this level—91 rims, handles, and bases, but with a minimum number of vessels of only nine—suggests that the source of the supplementary fill was the location for the disposal of vessels broken in the course of the household's life. The predominance of water-jar rims and handles may be from the vessels that broke inside the well and left their bases at the bottom.

Many of the figural pottery fragments from Level 2 join with other fragments from within this level, fragments from Level 1, or fragments in Levels 5 and 6 (see Table 2). The cross-level joining of fragments represents pottery broken in the Persian destruction but shoveled into the well at different points in the cleanup process. In this way, some of the fragments of a single broken vessel may have been deposited in the first shovelful, while others did not get deposited until the last. Further confirmation of the relationship between the highly fragmentary material in the upper two levels and the lower pocket of fine wares comes in the graffito N found scratched on the underside on two pieces from Level 2, one a salt cellar (**148**), the other a Type C cup base (**139**). The same N appears on the underside of a bowl (**152**) and a water jug (**179**) from Level 5. The graffito is most likely a mark of ownership. It is not uncommon for black-glazed vessels to bear an abbreviation of the owner's name. Excavation of the *Thra* well found beneath the Stoa of Attalos, also a Persian destruction deposit, found numerous vessels with ΘΡΑ scratched onto the vessel after firing.[34]

Fine-ware pottery from Level 2 was highly fragmentary, but plentiful. Fragments represented a minimum number of 70 drinking vessels, including a pair of two intentional red (coral red) cups, one attributed to Euphronios (**87**) and the second (**88**) likely from a related workshop. Some of the objects from Level 2 were preserved in large fragments, including **87** and **88**, an askos (**166**), a covered bowl (**156**), and a black-figured stamnos (**4**); however, they were not as complete as the objects from Level 5. It is likely that these were objects broken in the destruction, as opposed to the objects in Level 5 that were not broken until tossed into the well. Even more abundant than the figured ware in Level 2 were large coarse-ware fragments. It is particularly desirable to understand the relationship of the two intentional red cups (**87** and **88**) to the chronology of the well. With the exception of the significantly earlier sherds, the fragments from Level 2 are contemporary with the pottery from Level 5. According to conventional dating, the intentional red cups are about 10–20 years older than the other red figure from the deposit. The early fragments that were used to top off the well are single, worn fragments; thus, the proportion preserved, multiple fragments, and condition of the intentional red cups again suggests that they were in use in the house and were damaged during the attack. The intentional red cups, then, were among the oldest objects this house owned.

Finally, Level 1 (51.00–49.75 m) can be separated into two sublayers based on the soil of the fill. Level 1b (50.88–49.75 m) was a fill of dark gray clay with densely packed 10.00–15.00 cm stones. The pottery from this level was very similar in character to that of Level 2, with a high proportion

32. Some wells and cisterns in the Agora area do exhibit supplementary fills dating up to a century after the initial fills. See, e.g., well B 13:7, *Agora* XXIX, p. 435, with two Hellenistic fills at the bottom and Roman and Turkish above; and cisterns E 14:1, *Agora* XXIX, p. 446, and F 16:1 (Demeter Cistern), *Agora* XXIX, p. 451.

33. It is not possible to tell if the supplemental pottery represents primary refuse, that is, refuse discarded where it was used, or secondary refuse that was discarded elsewhere, then relocated; see Schiffer 1987, pp. 58–59.

34. R 12:1: Thompson 1951, pp. 50–51; *Agora* XXI, F 32–F 40. At least eight examples of the graffiti were found in the well.

of amphora and lekane fragments, often quite large, and a large number of drinking-vessel fragments. While there were many joins of fragments from Level 1 to Level 2, more fragments from Level 1 showed signs of wear and abrasion. As in Level 2, some of the worn figured fragments can be dated securely to the first quarter of the 6th century: see **22** and **25**, for example, with at least two uncatalogued Late Geometric–Early Iron Age fragments in addition, and **180**, a large fragment of a lekane dating to the middle decades of the 6th century. Level 1a, 51.00–50.88 m, was a stratum of gray, clayish soil at the very top of the fill. This is probably a layer of sediment accumulated as the well fill settled and surface water drained through. Level 1 completes the cleanup of the house, and as with Level 2, the majority of the pottery fragments from Level 1 originated outside the house and formed a supplementary fill to close the well.

In summary, in addition to the period of use deposit, there are three components distinguishable within the stratigraphy of the intentionally dumped fill of the well: the lower, initial cleanup characterized by whole pots (Level 5); the middle, nearly sterile fill of dug bedrock and slag (Levels 4 and 3); and the upper fill consisting of broken pottery from the house and supplementary fill brought in to top off the well (Levels 2 and 1). The joins between the upper fill (Levels 1 and 2) and the lower fill (Levels 5 and 6) confirm that the entire fill, regardless of its individual components, is a single depositional episode resulting from the same event.

Chronology

Excavators of the Athenian Agora have long recognized a destruction debris horizon dating to the Late Archaic period. Closed deposits and numerous strata of broken pottery intermixed with building debris record a massive, area-wide destruction paralleled archaeologically in the Agora excavations only by the Sullan destruction of 86 B.C. and the Herulian sack of A.D. 267.[35] From the early years of excavation, Agora excavators associated the Late Archaic debris horizon with the cleanup and rebuilding of the city after destruction by the Persians during the Second Persian War in 479.[36] According to Herodotos (8.40–41), the Athenians had evacuated the city sometime in 480, leaving it all but deserted when the Persian troops entered.[37] Herodotos also says that when Mardonios, Xerxes's general, left

35. Thompson 1981.

36. Vanderpool 1946, pp. 266, 271–275. Thompson (1981, pp. 344–346) calls the Persian destruction of Athens "the most familiar of all the manmade disasters that were to befall ancient Athens" (p. 344).

37. The timeline is secure if not precise. During the Second Persian War, there were two Persian invasions of Attica and two evacuations separated by ten months (Hdt. 9.3). Herodotos (8.40–41) refers to evacuation efforts during the initial entry of the Persians into Attica under Xerxes in September of 480. A decree to evacuate on the first occasion is preserved in a later inscription found at Troezen, one of the refugee sites; see Jameson 1960, pp. 198–223 and pp. 201–202 for ancient references to the decree. Pausanias saw the decree (2.31.7) and Plutarch mentions one (*Them.* 10.2–3), but the authenticity of the 4th–3rd century Troezen inscription is questionable; see Mattingly 1981. It was during the first evacuation that the Acropolis was taken (Hdt. 8.52–55). After the Battle of Salamis at least some of the Athenians returned to their city for the winter, where they stayed until they realized that the Peloponnesian allies would not send help as the Persians approached again (Hdt. 9.6). However, Plutarch describes another decree passed at Troezen to offer the Athenian refugees public support and to educate their boys (*Them.* 10.3), which implies that some of the families remained in Troezen for the winter. When Mardonios led the Persians into Attica a second time in June of 479 (Hdt. 9.3),

the city on his way to fight the Greek allies at Plataia, "He burnt Athens and utterly overthrew and demolished whatever wall or house or temple was left standing" (9.13.2; trans. A. D. Godley, Cambridge, Mass., 1924). In addition to the debris levels found in the Agora excavations, a significant destruction horizon on the Athenian Acropolis, the *Perserschutt*, was identified as debris resulting from the Persian destruction of an older Parthenon under construction, the *Archaios Neos,* and votive offerings.[38]

That the destruction horizons in the Agora and on the Acropolis represented debris created by the Persian sack was largely accepted until the late 1980s when E. D. Francis and Michael Vickers mounted a challenge to the traditional stylistic dating of monuments of the Late Archaic and Early Classical periods.[39] In response to this challenge T. Leslie Shear Jr. re-studied the evidence for the Persian destruction horizon in the Agora.[40] Shear's 1993 review of the (then) 21 deposits attributed to the Persian destruction convincingly confirmed the original interpretation of the deposits' formation. He documented the homogeneous character of the deposits by carefully recording pottery types and numbers, by carefully re-evaluating the chronological development of key pottery styles and forms, and by showing that the deposits resulted from single filling episodes. The current study accepts that these are deposits formed during the rehabilitation of the city of Athens after the Persian sack, but the author also recognizes that there are still unanswered questions concerning the motivations for their creation. Some of these issues will be addressed below.

The Persian destruction deposits are more properly called Persian destruction cleanup deposits.[41] Thucydides describes what the Athenians found upon their return to the city after the Battle of Plataia: "only short stretches of the circuit wall had been left standing, and most of the houses were in ruins; though a few survived, in which the Persian nobles themselves had quartered" (1.89.3; trans. Shear 1993, p. 416). The first order of business was to rebuild the city walls (Thuc. 1.90.3, 1.93.2), but certainly families returning to the city must have proceeded to clean up their domestic quarters in an informal way in order to create shelter for the surviving members of the *oikos.*[42]

"not even then" did he find the Athenians at home; the Athenians had evacuated again, this time to Salamis (Hdt. 9.3, 6). Herodotos describes the destruction Mardonios caused as he retreated from Athens (Hdt. 9.13), but when Herodotos says, "[Mardonios] utterly overthrew whatever wall or house or temple *was left standing*" (9.13; emphasis mine), he must mean that Xerxes had already done extensive damage in the city. For a more detailed discussion of the relationship of the ancient sources and the archaeological evidence, see Shear 1993, pp. 415–417. For the Persian Wars in general, see Burn [1962] 1984. For debate over the authenticity and chronology of the

Troezen decree and evacuation of Athens, see Burn [1962] 1984, pp. 364–377; and Hammond 1988, pp. 559–563, with bibliography.

38. The identification and chronology of the *Perserschutt* deposits are complicated. See Hurwit 1989, p. 63 and n. 74; 1999, pp. 141–142; Lindenlauf 1997; Stewart 2008.

39. Francis and Vickers 1988, but see also Shear 1993, p. 384, n. 4. Cook (1989, pp. 168–169), in a negative review of the Francis-Vickers proposed chronological down-dating, expresses skepticism about the secure association of deposits on the Acropolis and around the Classical Agora with the Persian destruction of Athens; however,

following Shear 1993, Cook (1997, p. 255) accepts the deposits as a "useful peg" for pottery chronology.

40. Shear 1993. The following comments on the Persian destruction archaeological context in the Agora excavations are based on Shear's thorough presentation and interpretation of data.

41. For the history of the term "Persian destruction deposit," see Lindenlauf 1997, pp. 50–51.

42. Some initial cleanup must have also occurred when the Athenians returned after Xerxes's first destruction of the city, but this would be impossible to recognize archaeologically since the destruction by Mardonios was so thorough.

TABLE 3. CLEANUP DEPOSITS

Immediate, Post–Persian Destruction ca. 479 B.C.	*Delayed, Post–Persian Destruction ca. 475–460 B.C.*
B 19:10	B 18:6
D 15:1	G 3:1
D 17:2	G 11:3
D 17:10	G 11:8
E 14:5	H 13:5
E 15:6	L 5:2
F 19:5	M 17:4
G 6:3	Q 21:3
H 12:15	
J 2:4	
Q 12:3	
Q 20:1	
R 12:1	
R 12:4	

There are two types of Persian destruction deposits encountered by the Agora excavations (Table 3).[43] The difference is a slight, but distinctive chronological one. In the first type of deposit, the material is largely Late Archaic and dates to the late 6th century and first two decades of the 5th century. There are 14 of these deposits from the Agora excavations, most of which seem to have been functioning wells—some domestic—at the time of the Persian destruction.[44] The second type contains transitional shapes of the Early Classical period, and thus is conventionally dated to the third or fourth decade of the 5th century.[45] This second group of "delayed" deposits contains more pits and collapsed wells than functioning wells.[46] Both types of deposits contain similar ceramic forms and a similar range of debris; only the chronologically sensitive fine-ware forms distinguish the two. While a difference of a decade may seem pedantic and overstated, the implication is that some of the deposits represent immediate efforts to clean up the debris, while the others correspond to longer term recovery efforts.[47]

43. Dinsmoor 1934, p. 425; Shear 1993, pp. 414–415, 417; Lindenlauf 1997, pp. 50–51, 75.

44. Discussed by Shear 1993, pp. 413–414.

45. Transitional shapes: Vicup, *Agora* XII, p. 93; stemless cups, *Agora* XII, p. 98; totally glazed one-handlers, *Agora* XII, p. 126. In addition, figured wares also show a later style. Black figure declines in quality and increases in hastiness, see discussion in Shear 1993, pp. 410–411.

46. Only one well in the later group was a functioning household well,

Q 21:3, beneath the Roman period Omega house. Another functioning well filled with delayed debris is G 11:3, the later well of Building F, considered by some to be the predecessor of the Tholos. The function and role of this complex of structures is much debated, but for this study, Building F is considered outside the definition of an ordinary house, and therefore not a purely domestic context. See Thompson 1940, pp. 15–33, for the excavation of Building F; 1962, p. 21, for its earliest identification as the "Peisistratid Palace," and Papadopoulos

2003, p. 296, n. 142, for objections to this identification and an alternative identification as a potter's workshop.

47. European cities spent decades cleaning up after the destruction of World War II. Whether the oath of Plataia is to be believed or not, the damaged religious monuments in Athens remained unreconstructed for many years after the destruction, possibly as a reminder of the impiety of the Persians. For a discussion of the oath of Plataia and its controversies, see Meiggs 1972, pp. 504–507. For delayed deposits on the Acropolis, see Stewart 2008.

The fill of well J 2:4 shares the characteristics of other closed Persian destruction deposits, and the fine-ware forms in the fill indicate that it is the type of Persian destruction deposit formed soon after 479.[48] The closed Persian destruction deposits from the Agora excavations are characterized by a mass of pottery, architectural debris, and other rubble deposited into a well or pit in one operation.[49] Joins from the top of well J 2:4 to the bottom indicate that pottery broken on the surface was deposited into the well at one time as opposed to being a gradual accumulation of debris. The majority of the late Archaic pottery in well J 2:4 and the other Persian destruction deposits bears little sign of wear or abrasion. This indicates that the pottery was not already discarded but was broken sometime shortly before its deposit and that some of the pottery did not have a long use life. Furthermore, many shapes are inappropriate for drawing water from a well, thus they were intentionally deposited in the well. In addition to pottery and household objects, the Persian destruction deposits can contain fragmentary roof tiles,[50] and some deposits preserve evidence of mudbrick.[51] Roof tiles certainly do not belong in a well, and their presence among the fragmentary pottery indicates that they were part of the destruction and underscores the magnitude of the destruction. Over 11 kg of roof tile fragments were recovered from well J 2:4, and a few small pieces of caked mud may also represent part of the roof.[52] There was no trace of mudbrick within well J 2:4, but there was gravel and small pieces of rubble.[53]

The clearest indication that well J 2:4 belongs among the Persian destruction deposits is the pottery itself. The shapes and workshops present in well J 2:4 are in keeping with the other Persian destruction deposits.[54] Figures 6, 7, and 8 illustrate the similarities in graph form. In each of the three graphs red-figured, black-figured, and black-glazed shapes and their relative proportions for well J 2:4 are compared to the relative proportions for the 21 Persian destruction deposits as a group.[55] Figure 6, which presents the proportion of shapes in the red-figured pottery component of well J 2:4 compared to the red-figured component of other Persian destruction deposits combined (thus providing an average), shows that the shapes in well J 2:4 correlate with those in other deposits, especially with the dominance of cups. Figure 7, the proportion of shapes in the black-figured pottery

48. All of the figured pottery stylistically dates before 480. There are no Vicup kylix feet or Acrocup kylix feet. There are no all black one-handlers and no stemless cups.

49. Strata with similar material exist as well, but these lack the defined, closed nature that makes the deposits valuable for contextual studies. For example, there are strata of Persian destruction material within the house of well J 2:4; see Figs. 11, 12, and 13 and discussion below.

50. 13 deposits record roof tiles: B 18:6, D 17:2, F 19:5, G 3:1, G 6:3, G 11:3, H 12:15, H 13:5, L 5:2, M 17:4, Q 12:3, R 12:1, R 12:4. Other deposits may have included tile fragments, but they were not recorded or saved.

51. An entire tin of mudbrick was saved from H 12:15; in other cases, excavators noted clay strata in the wells. Some of these may have been dissolved mudbricks rather than potter's clay; see Shear 1993, p. 454, and fig. 7.

52. This is a small quantity of roof tile and must mean that most of the tiles were salvaged for reuse or deposited elsewhere.

53. Layers of mudbrick were found in the excavation of the house: layer 8 (lots BZ 546, 547), Notebook BZ, pp. 1523, 1527; layer 14c, Notebook BZ, p. 1549; layer 15d (lot BZ 560), Notebook BZ, p. 1653; layer 26d (lot BZ 623), Notebook BZ, p. 1681.

54. Shear 1993, pp. 388, 393–401, tables 1–4. For transport amphoras, see Appendix I.

55. Counts for the Persian destruction deposits are taken from the tables in Shear 1993. The "relative proportion" refers to the percentage of the total number of red-figured, black-figured, or black-glazed fragments. So each score is the number of fragments of a shape divided by the total number of fragments in its technique.

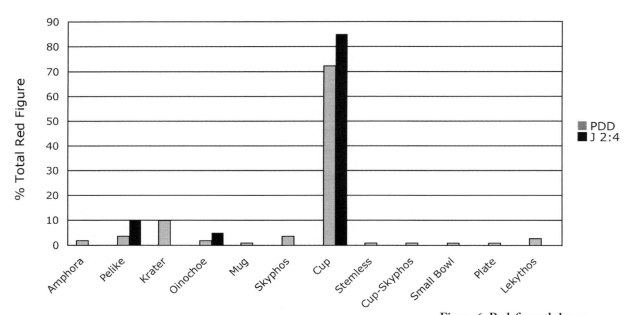

Figure 6. Red-figured shapes
expressed as percentage of total
red-figure component of deposit
J 2:4 compared to percentage of
red-figured shapes in the 21 other
Persian destruction debris deposits
(PDD) combined. Data from Shear 1993

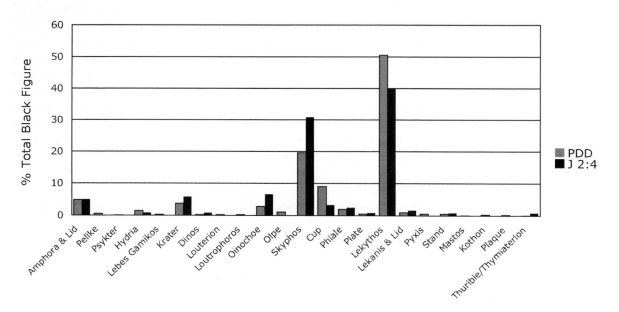

Figure 7. Black-figured shapes
expressed as a percentage of total
black figure component of deposit
J 2:4 compared to percentage of
black-figured shapes in the 21 other
Persian destruction debris deposits
(PDD) combined. Data from Shear 1993

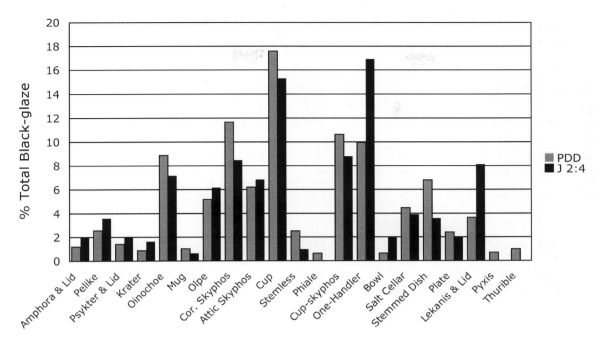

Figure 8. Black-glazed shapes expressed as a percentage of total black-glaze component of deposit J 2:4 compared to percentage of black-glazed shapes in the 21 other Persian destruction debris (PDD) deposits combined. Data from Shear 1993

component of well J 2:4 compared to the black figure in other Persian destruction deposits combined, also demonstrates that J 2:4 contains a similar proportional distribution of black-figured shapes.[56] Only in Figure 8, the proportion of black-glazed shapes in J 2:4 compared to the other Persian destruction deposits combined, does well J 2:4 vary slightly from the established pattern. J 2:4 exceeds the average in one-handlers and lekanides, but falls below it in cups and other drinking shapes. Overall, the general patterns are similar, and the black-glaze may diverge from the expected because of the larger than usual number of red-figured cups and black-figured skyphoi in the deposit or because there was less attention paid in earlier excavation record-keeping to fragments of black-glazed objects including the humble one-handler. The conclusion is that the distribution of shapes in well J 2:4 fits the characteristic pattern of the sealed Persian destruction debris deposits of the Agora excavations.

Well J 2:4's fill, just as the stratigraphy from the lowest house floors, can only date its inauguration to the general period of the late 6th century. There is no material in the bottom of the well, nor are there floor levels, to suggest any use prior to ca. 525.[57] Thus, the well and house were at the most 45 years old when destroyed by the Persians. This approximates a generation and includes the generation that witnessed the fall of the tyrants and the advent of the Kleisthenic democracy.

56. Lekythoi are overrepresented in the Persian destruction deposits because of their presence in the Rectangular Rock Cut Shaft (G 6:3) and the Stoa Gutter Well (Q 12:3), both of which seem to have been retail pottery shops selling skyphoi and lekythoi.

57. In antiquity, wells were sometimes periodically cleared of use debris that gathered at the bottom and inhibited proper functioning of the well. If this were the case for well J 2:4, then we would expect evidence of occupation of the house dating earlier than the period of use material from the well. In addition, there are no provisions for descending in the well, such as the footholds in wells D 15:2, F 19:5, H 12:15, Q 12:3, Q 21:3, R 12:1, and R 12:4.

DISCUSSION OF THE WELL STRATIGRAPHY AND CHRONOLOGY

The stratigraphy of the well provides evidence for post–Persian destruction cleanup activities and provides insight into the cleanup mentality of one group of Athenians. Some of the objects from well J 2:4 and the Persian destruction strata from the house show signs of burning that may be associated with the Persian sack. Some of the vessels are tinged gray at breaks, which may be due to postdepositional conditions, but most are unblemished, and some intact without any signs of damage. As will be argued below, the reuse of the exterior walls of the house in the reconstruction of the Classical period suggests that the house was not completely destroyed by the Persians. What accounts for the complete fine wares in Level 5? There are two possibilities: either the Persians threw the complete pots down the well in addition to the ones they broke around the house, or the homeowners threw the complete pots down the well during the cleanup. It is impossible to know for certain how much damage to attribute to the Persians.[58] At first it might seem illogical for the homeowner to throw functional pottery away, but this problem is related to the bigger issue of why an Athenian homeowner would close a functioning well.

What was the motivation for the widespread closure of 22 wells immediately after the Persian Wars? A secure source of water in Greece, a land prone to lengthy dry periods that prompt mandates of conservation even today, was not a mere luxury but a necessity.[59] Either the motivation for closing the wells was stronger than the need for a private source of water, or a more attractive, alternative source of water was now available nearby. No clear, immediate post-Persian source of water has been found for this house; however, a water pipe dating to the second quarter of the 5th century was found to the south of the polygonal wall, that is, directly outside the house.[60] It is possible that this pipeline fed a public fountain somewhere in the neighborhood. If so, this fountain would be a northwest pendant to the Southeast Fountain house on the southeast corner at the Classical market square.[61]

We must consider the possibility that the wells were sabotaged, since the Persians are known to have used the military technique of cutting off water sources to hamper their enemies. Herodotos tells us that the Persians despoiled the spring of Gargaphia at Plataia (9.49). They had used this tactic before (Hdt. 4.120, 4.140), and it must have been a common aspect

58. The Persians left next to no external material cultural evidence of their presence in Athens other than the damage they did. Arrow points found on the north slope of the Acropolis have been associated with the Persians: Broneer 1933, fig. 13, and p. 342; 1935, pp. 113–117, figs. 4, 5. Broneer also found on the north slope of the Acropolis the skeleton of a fallen Persian(?) warrior: 1935, p. 117, fig. 6.

59. See Camp 1977 for evidence of droughts in the 7th century (pp. 50–51) and the 4th century (pp. 147–149).

60. The "Kimonian pipeline," Camp 1996, p. 242; this is the same pipeline identified behind the Stoa Poikile, Shear 1984, p. 49–50. Both Camp and Shear associate this pipeline with the Athenian statesman Kimon, who Plutarch tells us sponsored a program to bring water to the Academy (*Cim.* 13.8).

61. An unidentified poros ashlar platform to the south of the house of well J 2:4 (southwest of the preserved portion of the house), labeled "Poros Foundation" on Fig. 2, may represent the base of a public fountain, although evidence for its chronology and function remain limited. Three white marble step blocks survive, and they exhibit extensive wear, indicating that the structure received frequent visits from pedestrians, which would be appropriate for a public fountain. See Shear 1997, p. 508.

of warfare (cf. Xen. *Hell.* 3.1.18). It is possible that the Persians poisoned or defiled the wells of the Athenian houses; however, there is no archaeological evidence for the introduction of foreign matter such as dirt or gravel that would "choke" the well or carcasses that would defile it. The gravel and slag in the well occur above the initial cleanup deposit, and joins across these layers indicate that the debris is a unified dumped fill. The joins of fragments from top to bottom present an image of a meticulous cleanup, not a desperate attempt to choke the well. The animal bones, too, occur both in upper levels and within the pocket of the fine wares and so were tossed into the well during the cleanup and not before. If the Persians had introduced dead animals for the purpose of defiling the well, it is unlikely that the bones would have been from butchered animals, and we would expect them to form a solid pocket on top of the period of use deposit.

Perhaps the easiest way for the Persians to defile the wells was to use them as latrines or heap horse feces into them.[62] Neither action would leave macroscopic archaeological traces,[63] but either would render the water impotable for the returning homeowners. In ancient Greece, pollution *(miasma)* played an important role in everyday religion. The sense of violation and miasma would be amplified through the presence of the foreigner's excrement.[64] Even if there is no evidence to prove that the Persians physically defiled the wells, the Athenians may have perceived a sense of pollution of the water from the Persian presence in the city and their destruction of both sacred and domestic structures.[65] The evidence for rebuilding of houses on new lines and the closure of private wells, often to accommodate rebuilding, suggests a post–Persian War mentality of starting over, or renewal. The intact and complete pottery from well J 2:4 supports this view of the cleanup mentality.

The complete vessels appear immediately above the period of use; thus, unbroken pottery was tossed into the well first, before the more labor-intensive cleanup of broken pottery and debris from the collapse of the walls and roof. The disposal of usable material must also mean that the pottery was considered relatively valueless and not worth saving.[66] The question of

62. Poisoning water sources is a common wartime tactic; see Lesho et al. 1998, pp. 512–513. The tactic is particularly useful for retreating forces. During the 1939–1940 Winter War, as the Finns retreated they booby-trapped houses and poisoned village wells with horse manure so that the Russians could not use them: Trotter 1991, p. 68.

63. Palaeobotanical study may have been helpful on this point, but soil flotation produced no useful data.

64. For miasma and pollution, see Parker 1983. Parker does not address the issue of miasma in Athens after the Persian Wars, but he does discuss the sensitivity of the household to pollution, pp. 29–30. See also Connor 1985,

especially pp. 79, 83, on the emotional impact of the destruction of houses.

65. The occupation of some Athenian houses by Persian nobles (Thuc. 1.89.3) may have contributed to feelings of pollution.

66. It is not likely that these functional vessels are the undesired "mates" to broken vessels. Not only are entire sets discarded into the well, but a "set" was a flexible concept, and pots decorated in different techniques could be combined together. In contrast, see Chapter 4 for a discussion of the value of the intentional red cups from Level 2, which were mended extensively in antiquity.

value of Attic pottery has been greatly debated in recent decades.[67] What well J 2:4 shows is that a homeowner—or person doing the cleanup—was willing to incur the loss of these vessels.[68]

Another possibility that must be considered is that the Persians themselves threw the fine wares down into the well as part of the destruction of the house. Several factors argue against this explanation, however. As discussed above, in the pocket of fine wares (Level 5) there are fragments that join other fragments from the upper well fill (Levels 1 and 2). It is unlikely that the Persians, while busy destroying the house, would toss into the well complete pots, smash others on the ground outside the well, then gather up a few stray fragments of the broken vessels and deposit them into the well. Furthermore, the intact pots from Level 5, which hit the water and gently came to a rest, indicate that the fill of Level 5 did not exceed the water table. In other words, the dump of fine wares would not have been enough to render the well unusable, by choking it as was done at Plataia. The intact and complete pots, though, do prove that the Persian destruction was not thorough (as will also be argued for the architectural remains), and some household possessions escaped destruction.[69]

Regardless of the motivation for closing the wells, a question remains as to the funding of the cleanup projects. Thucydides (1.90.3, 1.93.2) states that the first rebuilding efforts were directed at the city walls with all able-bodied residents assisting, including women and children. The wall reconstruction must have required organization, but since building material seems to have been largely salvaged from damaged structures, the project may not have required much funding. The houses, on the other hand, demanded serious reconstruction at, presumably, a significant cost in materials and possibly specialized hired labor. Margaret Miller has argued that the average citizen soldier went away from the battles of Plataia and Salamis a rich man.[70] This is in contrast to scholarly opinions that Athens and Athenians were poor in the years after the victory at Plataia.[71] Perhaps there was an influx of wealth from the spoils taken from the Persians, and it funded the private rebuilding. Unfortunately, we have little good archaeological evidence for Athenian households immediately following the Persian Wars, so it is not possible to compare pre- and postwar quality of life. It is important to remember that the renovations to the house of well J 2:4 (discussed below) and similar other structures of the Agora and surrounding neighborhoods did not occur immediately, but began sometime in the decade of 470–460. It is more likely that the homeowners lacked time than money.

67. Vickers and Gill 1994. One difficulty with the issue is that metal ware rarely survives in the archaeological record. The house of well J 2:4 might have owned numerous pieces of metal ware, but there is no way to know it. This is an unfortunate reality, because it would be very useful to know how a household's ceramic vessels complemented its metal vessels.

68. It is impossible to know if the house was reoccupied by the same family after the return to the city. Even if a different owner took possession of the house after the war, he could have continued to use the existing pottery.

69. The complete pots may have been stored in a different room from the broken pots; see Xen. *Oec.* 9.10 for daily-use objects and special-use objects being stored separately.

70. Miller 1997, pp. 43–45. The same is argued in Vickers 1990, but to support a different thesis.

71. Boardman 1996, p. 135. The prevailing scholarly view is discussed in Vickers 1990, pp. 105–106.

THE HOUSE OF WELL J 2:4

Well J 2:4 and its associated architecture are the first domestic structures of Archaic date found in the area near the northwest corner of the Classical Agora square. Figure 1, a plan of the Athenian Agora area, shows monuments present ca. 480, contemporary with the well and its house. The plan is somewhat misleading, as the areas north and west of the house have not yet been excavated down to Archaic and Classical levels. As more evidence becomes available, it is likely that excavators will find other Archaic domestic structures in the area.

In addition to the evidence from well J 2:4, the structural remains of its house also provide evidence for destruction by the Persians and subsequent rebuilding. Layers of debris, characteristic of the cleanup following the Persian destruction, and alterations to the house plan during post–Persian War renovations attest to the destruction and its aftermath. The picture provided by the closure of the well and rehabilitation of the house provide an image of determined resumption of everyday life in the years following the devastation of the Persian Wars.

SUMMARY OF HOUSE PHASES

The Archaic house as preserved probably had four rooms: the northeastern courtyard with well J 2:4, a northwestern room, a southeastern room, and a southwestern room. The northwestern room may have been a covered space opening onto the courtyard. A doorway connected the two southern rooms.

After the house suffered damage during the Persian sack of Athens, it was renovated over the course of a couple of decades. Post–Persian destruction renovation activities in this house include the following: (1) well J 2:4 was filled shortly after 479 and capped with a stratum of stones and pottery; (2) Persian destruction debris consisting of a dense layer of broken pottery was used as fill throughout the southern half of the house; (3) the east–west crosswall was rebuilt farther to the north, over the southern edge of the mouth of well J 2:4; and (4) a new interior plan was created. The exterior footprint of the house remained the same, but the interior of the house was now divided into at least four new spaces. The Archaic courtyard was turned into a room. A corridor to the northwest indicates the presence of a further room to the west under the western foundation wall of the Roman temple. In the southern half of the house one large room was formed from the two rooms of the Archaic period.

EXTERIOR LIMITS OF THE HOUSE

The archaeology of the area surrounding the well is difficult to unravel because of continuous rebuilding in the area from antiquity to the present. Of immediate concern is the disruption caused to the walls and floors of the eastern portion of well J 2:4's house by the Roman podium temple and a later bothros, and the obliteration of all traces of the western portion of the house by the Roman latrine (Figs. 2 and 3). As a result, it is impossible to know the full extent of the house to the west, and we can only sketch

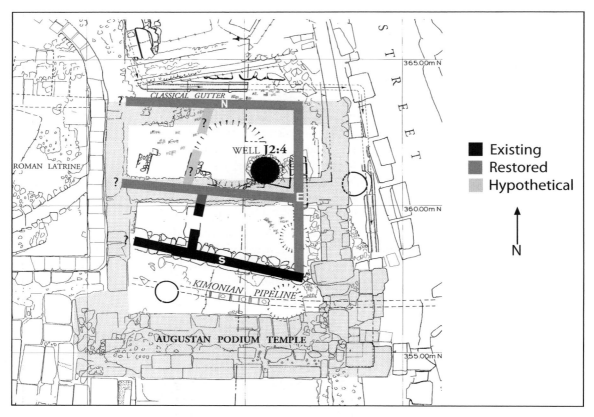

Figure 9. Detail of Figure 3, with plan of the Archaic phase of the house of well J 2:4. Author after Richard Anderson (Camp 1996, fig. 5)

the details of its eastern rooms. The architecture of well J 2:4's house is preserved only in short fragments of walls and small patches of stratified floor levels. The limited evidence available, though, does document two phases to the house: Late Archaic, and Early Classical through Hellenistic.[72] The Late Archaic phase is contemporary with the period of use of the well, and the Classical phase is a post-Persian destruction renovation including the closing of well J 2:4. The eastern portions of the Archaic and Classical houses shared an exterior footprint (Figs. 9, 10). While the obliterated western limits of the house cannot be defined, it is possible to determine its northern, southern, and eastern limits. The southern exterior wall (wall S on Figs. 9 and 10) is an east–west stretch of fine polygonal Acropolis limestone blocks finished on the southern face (Fig. 4). This polygonal wall dates to the Archaic period but continued to be used in the second, Classical, phase of the house.[73] The polygonal wall turns its good face, with diagonally dressed interlocking blocks, toward the altar of Aphrodite (Fig. 4). The construction of the marble altar of Aphrodite dates to ca. 500;[74] therefore, it is likely that the well-built polygonal wall also served as a temenos wall for the sanctuary, if not also for terracing, and the treatment of the southern face is a product of this function.[75]

72. Shear 1997, pp. 512–514. I have been able to refine and revise some of Shear's preliminary statements through study of the context pottery and excavation notebooks.

73. Shear 1984, p. 33; 1997, p. 512.
74. Shear 1984, p. 30, n. 45.
75. Shear 1984, p. 33.

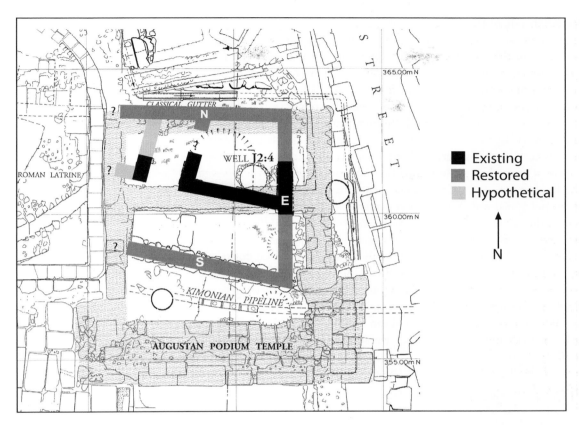

Figure 10. Detail of Figure 3, with plan of the Classical phase of the house of well J 2:4. Author after Richard Anderson (Camp 1996, fig. 5)

The northern exterior wall (wall N on Figs. 9 and 10) is preserved only in its lowest foundations.[76] To the north of the northern wall was an area of road metal dating to the Late Archaic–Early Classical period.[77] This was probably a narrow (1-m-wide) alley along the north of the house, since the lowest course of a parallel polygonal wall from another structure survives about 1 m north of the northern wall of the house.[78] In the Classical period, an open poros water channel flowed eastward through the alley before turning south to follow the line of the north–south street (Figs. 2, 3, 9, and 10).[79] The poros channel cannot be dated more precisely than the mid-5th century on the basis of ceramic evidence, but it rests above the road-metal levels. Another polygonal wall to the north of the house of well J 2:4 at J/2, 2/13–15 runs north–south and may have connected with the east–west polygonal wall (parallel to the house's southern polygonal wall)

76. Notebook BZ, pp. 1731 ff.; Shear 1993a, p. 2; Shear 1997, p. 512.

77. At J/6, 7–2/16, 17; Layers 5b–13b, Notebook BZ, pp. 1581, 1583, 1585, 1589–91, 1595, 1599, 1663, 1667–69, 1731, lots BZ 443, 445, 457.

78. The wall at J/4–7, 2/16 is in an area of Hellenistic disturbance, probably from the robbing out of the northern house wall. As a result, a general date of 5th century is assigned to it,

but it is possible, especially since the path of this wall parallels the south Archaic polygonal wall of the house, that it might date to the Archaic period as well.

79. Houses from both Olynthus and Halieis had alleyways behind them for drainage; see discussion in Ault 1994, p. 40. Near the Athenian Agora, the alley behind Houses C and D, which would become the bed for the Great

Drain, was merely 2 m wide in places: Young 1951, pp. 187–224. Room 6 of House C had two drains that deposited water into the alley before it was converted to the Great Drain: Young 1951, p. 206. There are fragments of a terracotta, U-shaped drain in Levels 5 and 6 of well J 2:4. It is possible that the poros water channel is a post-Persian replacement of an Archaic predecessor.

on the north side of the alley. The polygonal walls north of the house are at a higher elevation than the house's southern polygonal wall. Since the ground level in this area rises toward the north, up from the bed of the Eridanos River, these walls likely served as terracing for the area.[80] It is possible that the polygonal walls north of the house of well J 2:4 represent exterior walls of another house built on a higher terrace.[81]

The eastern exterior wall (wall E on Figs. 9 and 10) was also of polygonal masonry. Its history is complicated, and portions of it may have been rebuilt in the Hellenistic period. A well-constructed north–south stretch of polygonal masonry is preserved within the foundations of the cross-wall for the Roman temple, but it does not feature the diagonal dressing of the southern polygonal wall.[82] This short stretch (ca. 2 m long) represents the middle of the eastern exterior wall. To the north of this middle portion of the eastern wall the area is extremely disturbed, and no traces of the wall were found. To the south of the middle, the wall was removed during the Hellenistic period. A new eastern wall was built, extending the house to the east about 1 m sometime in the Middle to Late Hellenistic period.[83] The object of this renovation is not clear. The house is put out of use by the construction of the Augustan podium temple, which cannibalizes the house's northern and eastern exterior walls and interior, east–west dividing wall.

INTERIOR PLAN: ARCHAIC PHASE

At least three rooms and a courtyard (with well J 2:4) are preserved from the Late Archaic phase (Fig. 9). A date for the construction of the house is given by evidence for the initial leveling of the area. Construction efforts in the southeastern area of the house disturbed and cut off the top of a Submycenaean burial vase set into a shallow pit.[84] Pottery evidence from the lowest floor level in the southeastern room suggests a construction date for the house in the late 6th century (see Fig. 12).[85] Although the disturbed stratigraphy in the northeastern room (the courtyard) did not preserve an Archaic floor level adjacent to well J 2:4 (see Fig. 12), the date of the lowest floor and leveling operation in the southeastern portion of the house agrees with the chronological evidence from the period of use deposit in well J 2:4 (discussed above). The elevations of the lowest floor in the southeastern room and the approximate top of the well are both ca. 51.00 m above sea level, also suggesting contemporary construction.

80. There is a difference of about 0.50 m elevation between the footing stone levels of the two polygonal walls.

81. The Classical period poros water channel turns north at an oblique angle and continues north (traces or remains found in J/2, 3–2/13, 14, 15, 16), which confirms that it post-dates the building utilizing the polygonal walls to the north of the house of well J 2:4 since the water channel respected the plans of both this northern structure and the J 2:4 house.

82. Shear 1997, p. 512.

83. Shear 1993a, p. 3; Shear 1997, p. 512, n. 28.

84. Layer 36a cuts the vase: neck-handled amphora, P 32307. The vessel contained the cremated remains of a young child: Shear 1997, p. 514, n. 35. This is one of several early burials in the vicinity; see also P 32264, a Submycenaean belly amphora found 3 m north of the house, and two Submycenaean inhumations under the northern portion of the house, J 2:10 and J 2:11

(see Appendix III), Camp 1999, pp. 263–265. Builders leveled the area north of the Eridanos before beginning construction, thus obliterating evidence of Iron Age and Early Archaic occupation.

85. Layer 36a, Lot BZ 626 in the southeastern portion of the house (indicated on Fig. 12) dated to the last quarter 6th century on the basis of a cup foot, cf. *Agora* XII, p. 263, no. 401, fig. 4, ca. 525–500.

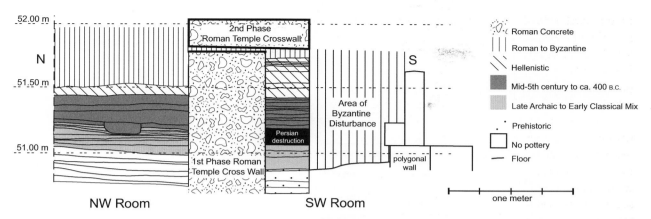

Figure 11. Simplified north–south stratigraphic cross-section at J/3, looking east. Author after excavation Notebook BZ, p. 1496

The preserved portion of the house as originally constructed in the Late Archaic period had two rooms in the southern half, and a courtyard with well J 2:4 and probably a third room in the northern half (Fig. 9). Again, the very disturbed stratigraphy of the area obscures some important details of the house plan; however, in the absence of architecture, the scrappy stratigraphy provides some clues to the plan.

In the Classical period the east–west wall dividing the house was rebuilt and shifted to the north so that it overlapped the edge of well J 2:4. The rubble Roman temple cross-wall engulfs the Classical wall, and no trace of an earlier east–west Archaic wall was found in the excavation. The stratigraphy, though, does provide evidence for a wall between the northern and southern portions of the house in the Archaic period. A simplified north–south stratigraphic cross-section (Fig. 11) at J/3, through the northwestern and southwestern remains of the house, presents a view of stratigraphic levels as excavated.

Before looking at the specific evidence for the Archaic east–west wall, however, it is necessary to comment on the presentation of stratigraphic evidence. Since the area of the house of well J 2:4, like almost every part of ancient Athens, experienced continuous rebuilding throughout antiquity, good sequences of strata are sometimes restricted to narrow strips that are prone to containing intrusive fragments caused by later building. The simplified stratigraphic drawings presented here in some cases combine layers that were excavated separately, but that I assigned to the same stratigraphic unit when I restudied the context pottery and excavation notebooks.[86] The chronology of these strata is indicated by shading, based on the dominant chronological period indicated by the ceramic evidence, allowing for occasional intrusions of later material. Figure 11 presents an area of good stratigraphy to the north of the obtrusive Roman temple cross-wall and the thin strip of preserved stratigraphy along the south face of the Roman temple cross-wall, the second phase of which, here, projects over the southern side of the earlier temple cross-wall.[87] The excavators identify most of the strata as floors, with the exception of the Persian destruction debris used as fill below the first Classical period floor in the southern half of the house. Figure 11 shows that the layer of Persian destruction debris found in the southern half of the house does not extend into the northern half. In order for this separation to occur, a wall must have been in place when the Persian destruction fill was laid down.

86. Individually excavated layers were most often deemed to be a single stratigraphic unit when ceramic joins were found. In other cases, when soil color and character and ceramic characteristics remained constant I combined like layers into one stratum, although the excavator had cautiously changed units to preserve information. The context ceramics remain stored as excavated.

87. Shear 1997, p. 513, and fig. 4.

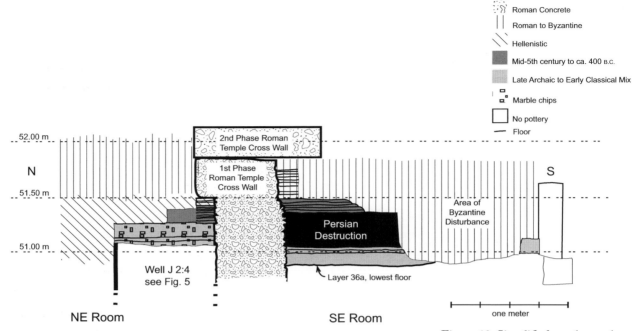

Figure 12. Simplified north–south stratigraphic cross-section at J/6, looking east. Author after excavation Notebook BZ, pp. 1542, 1762

Furthermore, there are no joins between the pottery from strata on either side of the temple cross-wall below the Persian destruction fill, suggesting that floors were not continuous.

A stratigraphic cross-section through the northeastern and southeastern portion of the house (Fig. 12) also indicates the presence of an east–west wall during the Archaic phase of the house. In the southeastern room the stratum of Persian destruction debris is a thick layer of broken pottery. Again, since the Persian destruction debris does not continue seamlessly over the top of the well, this is an indication of the presence of an east–west wall dividing the house. The well is capped with a layer of marble and poros chips that matches the elevation of the debris stratum in the southeastern part of the house, but pottery is scant among the stone chips. Pottery in the Persian destruction debris stratum in the southeastern part of the house dates to about 450, that is, later than the fill in well J 2:4. The well was filled in shortly after the return of the Athenians to their city in 479, but renovations were not made to the house for another couple of decades. The scant pottery among the stone chips also dates to ca. 479, suggesting that the stone layer was an effort to cap the well or limit settling after filling it in. That the well was closed first and house renovations delayed further emphasizes the urgency of filling in the well.

The space in which the well was located was probably a courtyard, since wells were typically situated in courtyards in Athens in the Archaic and Classical period.[88] It is also possible that the more western portion of the northern room was open but covered, either by a shed roof or by a second story.[89] A large portion of the northern half of the house was disturbed by a Byzantine bothros, which interferes with the Archaic and Classical stratigraphy. There is no evidence for Archaic walls in the northern portion of the house, although there are short sections of Classical walls in this area. The excavator does record that the lowest floor surface in the northwestern portion of the house (Fig. 11) contained sand and gravel, which she

88. Camp 1977, pp. 181–182, 245; Shear 1997, pp. 512–513.

89. For a similar relationship of courtyard to roofed, but open area, cf. a partially excavated Archaic house at Sardis: Cahill 2002b, p. 179.

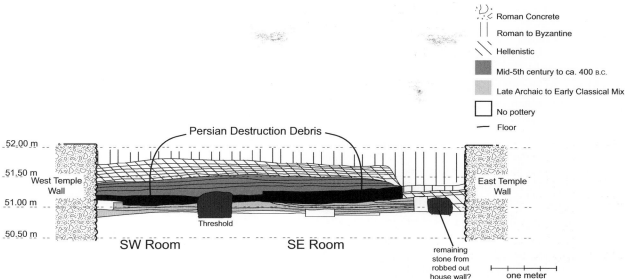

Figure 13. Simplified east–west cross-section along southern edge of Roman temple cross-wall, looking north. Author after excavation Notebook BZ, p. 1562

90. Shear (1997, pp. 512–513) suggests that the entrance was through the courtyard with the well and could have either been from the alley at the north or from the main north–south road.

91. The presence of a vestibule to act as a buffer between street and house is a key element in the discussion of privacy and seclusion of women: see Walker 1983; Jameson 1990a; 1990b, p. 183; Nevett 1995, pp. 92–94.

92. E.g., first phase of Vari Cave house, Jones et al. 1973, fig. 4; house on the north foot of the Areopagos, *Agora* XIV, pp. 177–180, fig. 42; the eastern and western houses on the northeast slope of the Areopagos, Shear 1973a, pp. 146–150, fig. 4 (the excavator states that the eastern house was built in the early 5th century with a courtyard and well, like the house of J 2:4); the "Flügelhofhaus" on the Pnyx, plan in Jones 1975, fig. 8A.

distinguished from other floor surfaces in the house and associated with the surfacing of a courtyard; thus, it is likely that the open courtyard area in which J 2:4 was situated continued over to the west, and possibly beyond the preserved limits of the house. A covered area to the west of the courtyard would have provided work space that was close to the well but sheltered from the elements. A portico might possibly have been backed by unpreserved rooms continuing to the west under the Roman latrine.

The southern portion of the house was divided into two rooms in the Archaic period as indicated by a threshold block (Figs. 9, 13). This threshold probably marks a doorway in a short north–south wall dividing the two southern rooms, although the Roman temple cross-wall obliterated most of the wall to the north of the threshold. Figure 13 presents an east–west stratigraphic cross-section of a narrow strip of preserved strata against the south face of the Roman temple cross wall. Persian destruction debris was placed directly on the latest Archaic floor level, bringing its level even with the threshold block. The southeastern room was ca. 3.50 m by 2.00 m, and the southwestern room an unknown length by 2.00 m wide.

The entrance to the house could have been either from the main north–south street at the east, or from the west in the section no longer preserved. The narrow alleyway at the north of the house with the polygonal terrace wall behind it precludes an entrance from the north,[90] and an entrance from the south through the sanctuary area is also unlikely. If the entrance were on the eastern side of the house, there are arguments for locating the door in either the courtyard room or the southeastern room. Since the southeastern room is separated from the southwestern room by the threshold, the southeastern room would have made an excellent entrance vestibule. However, this would make the vestibule exceptionally large in comparison to the other preserved rooms. Although many Classical-period houses have entrance vestibules,[91] houses with direct entry into a courtyard are known,[92] and this design seems to be favored in houses with irregular floor plans. Therefore, it is also possible that one entered the house through the courtyard. Neither situation seems preferable, which may mean that the original entrance to the house was on its unpreserved western side.

INTERIOR PLAN: CLASSICAL PHASE

Nearly every room of the Archaic house presents evidence for the cleanup
following the Persian destruction. In the two southern rooms there is a
deep stratum of broken pottery (Fig. 13),[93] and in the northeastern room,
in addition to the fill within well J 2:4, there is a stratum of marble and
poros chips,[94] which corresponds to the elevation of the debris stratum in
the southeastern room (Fig. 12). Unfortunately, the disturbed stratigraphy
makes it impossible to know whether the chips continued throughout the
northeastern room or not. No stone chips appear in the northwestern room,
nor do they continue as a layer into the southeastern room.

The Persian destruction debris throughout the house tells us something
about the process of renovation after the owners returned to their damaged
house. The pottery fill in well J 2:4 contains no objects dating significantly
after 480, while the debris stratum found in the southern part of the house
contains objects dating to the second quarter of the 5th century.[95] It appears that the homeowners returned to their house, filled in the well with
unwanted pottery and pottery broken by the Persians, but then waited
some time to carry out the structural renovations to the house. This fits
Thucydides's description of events following the victory at Plataia; he says
that rebuilding the city wall was the first priority of the Athenians (1.89.3),
and that the houses, along with public buildings, were plundered for usable
building materials to repair the walls (1.90.3, 1.93.2).

The exterior footprint of the house appears to have remained largely
intact, at least in the preserved eastern portion, but the interior plan experienced changes. The most significant alteration to the house plan was
the closing of the courtyard well. Classical floors above the well are clay
(Fig. 12), perhaps indicating that the former open courtyard became a
closed room. In addition, a new east–west wall was built, slightly to the
north of where the Archaic wall existed. This new wall passed over the
southern edge of the closed well. The stratum of marble and poros chips
over well J 2:4 may have also provided further footing for the construction
of this wall over the top of the closed well. There is no preserved evidence
of a foundation trench on either side of the Classical east–west wall or its
Archaic predecessor.

The presence of the marble and poros chips demands a brief comment.
The chips consist of fragments of poros, white marble, and blue marble.
White marble predominates, and blue marble (presumably Hymettian) is
the least frequent. Some of the chips preserve tool marks, indicating that
they are all likely to be debitage from stoneworking. In fact, a few small,
well-finished fragments of moldings point to architectural construction

---

93. Shear 1997, p. 513, nn. 31–34.
94. Shear 1997, p. 514.
95. For these two "types" of Persian destruction deposits, see Shear
1993, pp. 414–415, 417. The debris
stratum contained mudbrick, roof
tiles, rubble, and pottery characteristic
of Persian destruction deposits. However, the pottery dates closer to 470–
460 than the pottery of the well, which

is firmly before 480. There are no
joins between the fill of well J 2:4
and the floor stratum. Pottery lots
BZ 618–621: e.g., fragment of flaring rim with red-figured ovolo motif;
black-glazed lekythos cf. *Agora* XII,
p. 314, no. 1119, pl. 38 (ca. 450);
red-figured fragment with head of
an owl, unknown open drinking
shape; several Vicup feet, cf. *Agora*

XII, p. 265, nos. 436, 437, pl. 20,
fig. 5 (ca. 470–460). The pottery
from this fill is of a different nature
from the fill of the well: the floor fill
has little figured pottery and no
black-figured cup-skyphoi, black-
figured lekythoi, or black-glazed
skyphoi, which are numerous in
the well fill.

as the source. In the northeastern room, the chips are densest above the well and do not appear in floor levels in the northern part of the house in the Classical period.[96] A scattering of stone chips also appears in the stratum of Persian destruction pottery in the southern half of the house;[97] in contrast, stone chips are more common among the Classical and even Hellenistic floor levels of the southern half of the house. The excavators suggested that this house may have been a marble worker's establishment,[98] but in comparison to houses in which we can confidently identify marble-working activities, the house of well J 2:4 lacks evidence of pervasive marble dust that would be a product of the working of stone on-site.[99] Instead, it is more likely that the homeowners brought in the stones from a nearby construction site to use as fill, especially to cap the well. One possible existing source of stone chips in the neighborhood may have been debris left over from the construction of the Archaic altar to Aphrodite ca. 500 m immediately to the south.[100] It is tempting to connect the stone chips with the construction of the Classical stoa building to the east of the house of well J 2:4, identified as the Stoa Poikile; however, construction on the stoa was not begun until early in the second quarter of the 5th century.[101] None of the pottery from the stone-chip layer over the well dates later than 480. The stone chips used in the floors of the southern half of the house in the Classical period on the other hand are more likely to be connected with the construction of the stoa. The restriction of stone chips to this portion of the house in the Classical period is perplexing. It is possible that the texture of the stone chips embedded in the clay floors was appropriate for whatever activities occurred in this area.

The east–west wall has a northern return at its western end, and this, in addition to a scrap of another north–south wall at the far west of the preserved area, defines a northwestern "room" in the Classical phase of the house (Fig. 10). The width of this space is a little over 1 m wide, so it was possibly a corridor rather than a room. The northern return of the central, east–west wall indicates that there was direct access from the northern portion of the house to the southern portion of the house after the rebuilding. The north–south wall formed by the return of the east–west central wall must have contained a doorway at its northern end for access to the corridor, although this area of the excavation did not preserve Classical levels. The corridor would then have the dimensions of ca. 1 m by 3 m. It is also impossible to know the full northern and southern extent of the

96. Lots BZ 492–503, above the well and sealed by the lowest Classical floor, contained approximately 1,050 chips (280 poros, 638 white marble, 128 blue marble), 52 of which exhibit clear signs of tool marks or finished surfaces. I thank Agora architect Richard Anderson and David Scahill for discussing the stone chips with me.

97. In the Persian destruction debris in the southeastern room there were only 22 stone chips; in the southwestern room, 7.

98. Shear 1997, p. 514; note, how-

ever, that the excavator was referring to the thick layer of stone chips found above well J 2:4. It is now clear that the stone chips above the well have a terminus post quem of ca. 480 and should be associated with the closure of the well; therefore, they cannot be evidence of an Archaic sculptor's workshop as the excavators first suggested.

99. Cf. the house of Mikion and Menon, Shear 1969, p. 389: "On this point [that marble working occurred in the house] there can be no possible doubt whatever, for the floors of all five

phases were strewn with a heavy layer of marble working chips and marble dust.... Numerous hunks of partially worked marble were also found in every layer."

100. Shear 1984, p. 26. The altar features poros foundations, white island marble orthostates and moldings, and a light blue limestone sill. The blue marble fragments found in association with the house are finer than limestone.

101. Pottery from the foundation trench dates to 470–460: Shear 1984, pp. 13–14, nn. 16, 17.

scrap of wall at the west that forms the western side of the corridor. Since it is not an exterior wall, its presence implies a third northern space farther to the west, obliterated by the western foundation of the Roman podium temple. On Figure 10 I have restored the western wall as hypothetically solid, although it is also possible that there was an opening on the corridor allowing access to a room to the west.

In the southern section of the house, the two rooms of the Archaic period became one in the Classical period (Figs. 10, 13). Formerly the two rooms were divided by a door indicated by the surviving threshold. Persian destruction debris was deposited throughout both Archaic rooms and used to raise the ground level and form one room. Joins between the debris along the Roman temple cross-wall and a stratum of debris found against the north face of the polygonal wall (S on Fig. 10) indicate that the Persian destruction fill probably covered the entire southern half of the house.[102] Floor levels of the Classical period (mid-5th century) pass over the former threshold (Fig. 13). This new room was at least 5 m by 2 m, although its original east–west extent cannot be known.

The house seems to continue in use through the Hellenistic period, although most of the upper levels of the house were destroyed during the construction of the Roman podium temple.[103] The excavators found evidence of Hellenistic floor levels, but they remark that the Early Hellenistic period seems to be absent and that in places the floors jump from mid-5th century to mid-2nd century, although in other areas there are Classical floor levels with artifacts dating down to ca. 400.[104] There is evidence for a Hellenistic rebuilding of the exterior eastern wall.[105] It is possible that the house was unoccupied for a period and then renovated for continued use in the mid-Hellenistic period. Of course, the Hellenistic builders could also have lowered the interior floor level, elevated by years and years of resurfacing, by scraping away a century or two of surfaces. Indeed, the rise in floor level from the earliest Archaic floor to the latest preserved Classical floor is approximately 50 cm. If we presume that the house was continuously occupied and resurfaced at a similar rate, then by the 2nd century, it may have been uncomfortable for a person to stand up inside the house. A lowering of the floor may have been expedient.

DISCUSSION OF HOUSE RENOVATION

The renovation of the house of well J 2:4 after the Persian destruction is in keeping with a pattern observed elsewhere in the Agora excavations. It is difficult to identify the architectural remains of houses associated with wells filled with Persian destruction debris due to continuous occupation and later disruption throughout the site, but in five (of 21) cases, wells filled with Persian destruction debris can be associated with domestic architecture. Their situations are remarkably similar to that of well J 2:4.[106] T. L. Shear Jr., in his review of Persian destruction deposits of the Agora, states categorically,

> In every one of these [five cases], however, the builders of the Classical period took no cognizance whatsoever of the location of Archaic wells in the designs of their houses. . . . [I]n five specific

102. BZ lot 339, against the northern face of the polygonal wall (S on Fig. 10), contained pottery fragments that joined fragments from the strata excavated against the Roman temple cross-wall (BZ lots 618–621).

103. Augustan podium temple: Shear 1997, pp. 498, 507; post-Classical house: Shear 1997, p. 512.

104. Shear 1997, p. 513.

105. Shear 1997, p. 512, and n. 28.

106. These well deposits are B 19:10, B 18:6, D 17:10, H 12:15, and Q 21:3.

cases, it appears that the Classical builders were free to build along totally different lines and made little or no use of preexisting walls, foundations, or building materials, as if they set their new structures upon a tabula rasa from which the Archaic predecessors had been quite literally swept away.[107]

The case of the house of well J 2:4 is not so extreme. Exterior walls were preserved, probably because they had escaped the devastation structurally sound. The amount of roof tile from well J 2:4 is not enough to roof a structure, so it is possible that some undamaged tiles were reused in the Classical renovation. Of the five cases of post-Persian domestic rebuilding, two provide excellent parallels for the history of well J 2:4. Well H 12:15, near the northwestern corner of the Middle Stoa, was filled in, with a new interior wall built over its former mouth, just like well J 2:4.[108] In House G under the Roman period Omega House, the owners filled up their well with Persian destruction debris and created an andron out of part of the space formerly occupied by the courtyard with the well.[109] The change from courtyard to room in the house of well J 2:4 represents a similar shift in the function of the space.

There is no sign of a coherent, imposed plan for the architectural rebuilding of private houses in the vicinity of the Athenian Agora,[110] but a prevailing cleanup mentality suggests socially shaped behavior possibly guided by state orders.[111] That so many private wells were filled in, thus causing residents to shift to reliance on public water sources, may reflect some cleanup oversight by the city. In addition, communal dumping in neighborhood wells and pits may also indicate direction from a central authority—be it a concerned neighbor or the city. The post–Persian War rebuilding of Athens did respect the existing street plan, with minor modifications.[112] In the Piraeus, on the other hand, rebuilding included the institution of a new street grid.[113] Since the Athenian houses were rebuilt following the existing street plan, any renovation of the house of well J 2:4 was seriously restricted by the circumscription of its lot by the north–south street to the east, the east–west alley to the north, and the sanctuary of Aphrodite to the south.

THE HOUSE OF WELL J 2:4 AND ITS NEIGHBORHOOD OVER TIME

The construction of the house and well in the last quarter of the 6th century coincides with other Late Archaic building activity in the area. The house's nearest neighbor, the altar to Aphrodite, was probably under construction at the same time.[114] A portion of a Late Archaic cobbled road was found to the east of the (later) Classical commercial building (see Fig. 2, labeled

---

107. Shear 1993, pp. 405–406.

108. Well H 12:15: Thompson 1954, pp. 51–54.

109. Well Q 21:3: Shear 1973a, pp. 152–153.

110. Boersma 1970, p. 44. He also points out that everyone returned to the city at once, and there was no time to impose either a building or street plan on the returning inhabitants.

111. A prevailing "cleanup mentality" might also motivate the closing of the wells. If the populace perceived the wells to be polluted, through rumor or assumption, hysteria might have provided the incentive to fill in perfectly usable wells.

112. Thompson 1981, p. 345.

113. Boersma 1970, p. 10.

114. Shear 1984, p. 30, n. 45.

"Classical building"), the back wall of which cut through the road bed.[115] There is no evidence yet for other Late Archaic structures between the cobbled road and the house of well J 2:4,[116] although a pit deposit (J/K 2:1) cut through the cobbled road surface contained Persian destruction debris in association with a stratum of similar debris beside it.[117] This pit deposit suggests that there may have been other houses in the area, probably to the north or east of the cobbled road. Terracing to the north of the house of well J 2:4 also seems to date to the Late Archaic period, and it was possibly installed to protect against erosion to the south and to facilitate further development of this area.[118] Traces of an Archaic drain or water channel ran west in the area now behind the Stoa Poikile.[119] Nearby public monuments in place at the time of the construction of the house of well J 2:4 include the Stoa Basileus and the Altar of the Twelve Gods (Figs. 1, 2).[120] The western edge of the Agora had also been developed into a nascent civic center. Well J 2:4 represents one of 31 excavated wells built during the last two quarters of the 6th century. These wells surround the Classical Agora and probably represent houses constructed during a domestic building boom in the wake of the public and commercial development of the area in the late 6th century.[121]

It remains uncertain who sponsored the Late Archaic building boom and to whom to attribute the increased public role of the area that would (at some point) become the Classical Agora.[122] It is generally accepted now that the Archaic Agora lay to the northeast of the Acropolis and that the area of the Classical Agora was officially designated the civic center sometime in the Late Archaic to Early Classical period. The process of relocating the civic center from its Archaic setting to its new one has been associated with the Peisistratids, the new democracy, or post–Persian War reorganization.[123]

The area directly north of the Classical Agora square experienced even greater building activity following the Persian destruction.[124] During the time of the cleanup and renovation of the house of well J 2:4, other major public projects were underway in the neighborhood. The Eridanos was canalized in the second quarter of the 5th century,[125] and the Stoa Poikile constructed shortly thereafter if not simultaneously.[126] A water pipe running behind the Stoa Poikile, between it and the Classical commercial building,

115. Noted on Camp 1999, fig. 24, to the east of the ostraka deposit, but not discussed in text.

116. Excavations in the Classical commercial building reveal that strata beneath it jumped from Classical to Geometric levels. It is possible that Archaic structures were leveled before construction, and no traces survive: Camp 1999, p. 277; Scahill 2001.

117. Camp 1999, p. 274, noted on fig. 24.

118. An Archaic polygonal terrace wall (J/4, 7–2/16) lies north of the house of well J 2:4 (on Fig. 3, north of "Classical gutter") and parallels the Archaic polygonal wall used as the south wall (wall S on Figs. 9 and 10) of the house.

119. Shear 1984, p. 14.

120. Stoa Basileus: Shear 1971, pp. 243–255; *Agora* XIV, pp. 83–90; Shear 1994, pp. 236–239. Altar of the Twelve Gods: Gadberry 1992.

121. Wells: B 19:10, D 15:1, D 17:10, E 14:5, E 15:6, F 19:4, F 19:5, G 11:3, G 11:8, G 15:1, H 12:15, I 17:2, M 17:4, N 18:7, O 19:4, P 17:1, Q 7:1, Q 12:3, Q 17:3, R 12:1, R 12:3, R 12:4, T 19:1, T 24:3, T 24:5, T 25:2, U 23:2, U 24:1, U 25:2, V 23:1, V 24:2. These are in contrast to the 17 wells that went out of use around the mid-6th century (Shear 1978, pp. 4–5; 1994, pp. 229–239); Shear proposes that these represent households expropriated by a central authority.

122. For discussions of the existence of an earlier Archaic Agora northeast of the Acropolis, see most recently Papadopoulos 2003, pp. 280–297; see also Dontas 1983; Shear 1994, pp. 225–228, 245–246; Miller 1995; Schnurr 1995; Robertson 1998; Schmalz 1998; 2006. The idea of an alternative site for the Archaic Agora was first put forth much earlier by Oikonomides 1964.

123. Peisistratids: Camp 1994, p. 11; Kleisthenes: Shear 1994, esp. pp. 239, 245; post–Persian War: Miller 1995; Papadopoulos 1996; 2003, p. 297.

124. Thompson 1981, pp. 345–346.

125. Shear 1997, pp. 517–518.

126. Shear 1984, pp. 13–14, nn. 16, 17.

has been identified as the Kimonian pipeline that brought fresh water to the Academy area. This pipeline was installed in the second quarter of the 5th century, after the completion of construction of the Stoa Poikile.[127] Another possible house in the neighborhood cleaned up a bit more slowly, placing some of their Persian destruction debris in the pit in the cobbled road (J/K 2:1), and in associated strata ca. 475.[128] Around the same time a substantial number of ostraka were dumped on the road nearby.[129] The ostraka pit indicates that the Archaic cobbled road was no longer in service and was being used as a dumping area. Meanwhile the north–south road east of the house was formally surfaced for the first time, with the earliest road metal dating to the first quarter of the 5th century.[130] Traffic was now diverted farther to the west, to accommodate the Stoa Poikile, which blocked the old Archaic cobbled road. In the third quarter of the 5th century the Classical commercial building, which aligns with the Stoa Poikile, was built.[131] It was also around this time that the altar of Aphrodite was rebuilt.[132] It was destroyed sometime shortly after its construction ca. 500, and although the evidence is not certain, it was likely due to the Persians, as the nearby Stoa of Basileus and the Altar of the Twelve Gods also both bear evidence of damage.[133] The delayed renovation of sacred structures seems unusual, but may be explained by the Oath of Plataia,[134] or a more tacit agreement to allow sacred sites damaged by the Persians to remain so as a reminder of the impiety of the barbarians.

The picture is one of prosperity and energy for this neighborhood north of the public square in the Early Classical period. Of especial note is the shift to public and commercial activities. The house of well J 2:4 is currently the only Classical domestic structure known in the area, although excavations continue in the area and will undoubtedly shed light on its domestic neighbors.

THE DOMESTIC CONTEXT

Before examining the contents of well J 2:4 in the following chapters, it is necessary to establish that the pottery originated from a domestic context and represents only one household. A "domestic context" means that the artifacts were used in a house by the household members for household activities. A domestic assemblage can include kitchen equipment, tableware, utilitarian shapes, entertaining equipment, household ritual objects, and objects associated with household industry, such as weaving. That well J 2:4 contains pottery in possession of a single household is shown by the relationship of the well to the architecture of the house, the shapes and quantities of shapes present in the deposit, and the absence of evidence to identify the deposit as votive, public, or purely commercial.

127. Shear 1984, p. 49, n. 101.
128. Camp 1999, p. 274.
129. Camp 1999, pp. 268–274.
130. A portion of the road was excavated in 2002: Scahill 2002. The earliest surface is lot BE 2612, dated to the 480s by an ostrakon of the Alkmaionid Hippokrates, P 34456 *(agathe)*.

131. Camp 1999, p. 277.
132. Shear 1984, p. 32.
133. Stoa Basileus: Shear 1971, pp. 243–255; *Agora* XIV, pp. 83–90; Shear 1994, pp. 236–239; Altar of the Twelve Gods: Gadberry 1992, p. 471.
134. On the Oath of Plataia and its authenticity, see Meiggs 1972, pp. 504–

507. It seems best to acknowledge that many sacred monuments and small shrines were not rebuilt immediately after their damage at the hands of the Persians, whether or not there was a public interdiction against doing so.

As discussed above, well J 2:4 was located in the courtyard in the northeastern portion of the Archaic phase of its house. In the Archaic period, wells in the vicinity of the Classical Athenian Agora could serve cultic, commercial, civic/public, or domestic users. John Camp states that Archaic wells were more likely to be for private use, with one well serving one house.[135] However, there are certainly Archaic wells associated with commercial and cultic activities, and thus a domestic function should not be assumed for all wells in the area.[136] In order to support the identification of well J 2:4 and its architecture as a domestic context, it is necessary to consider alternative identifications.[137]

The architecture associated with well J 2:4, as described above, argues for the identification of the structure as a house, as opposed to a cult center, but the proximity of the structure to the altar of Aphrodite demands that we consider a possible relationship to the cult. Sacred areas around the Classical Agora often featured wells that inevitably became receptacles for discarded votive offerings.[138] Well J 2:4 was not such a receptacle for the shrine to Aphrodite to its south. The fine polygonal wall (Fig. 4; and Wall S on Figs. 9 and 10) acted as a socle for a mudbrick wall, and it preserves no evidence for a door or other opening allowing access from the house to the cult area. Further, distinctive votive offerings left in the cult area are not present in the house. Evidence for votive offerings includes rich layers of faunal remains[139] and small (ca. 4.5 × 4.5 cm), square terracotta votive plaques, some of which retain traces of white and red paint.[140] North of the polygonal wall there is neither abundant bone nor the distinctive plaques. It is not impossible, however, that the resident of the house served the cult in some capacity, but no formal cult activities took place in the house. Items for use in household cult are present in small quantities in well J 2:4, but these are common in most of the Persian destruction deposits. Finally, there are no obvious dedicatory inscriptions among the graffiti on objects from well J 2:4.

The Classical-period houses in Athens in the area of the Agora occasionally acted as both shelter for the family and a location for a commercial enterprise. That enterprise might be the sale of objects made elsewhere or the fabrication and sale of objects on-site. Some of the commercial activities were noisy and dirty industrial pursuits.[141] However, these "home

135. Camp 1977, p. 181.

136. Commercial: pottery sales shop, Roberts 1986; butcher, R 12:1, Shear 1993, p. 469. Cultic: on the north slope of the Acropolis, Wells B and C, Cutting Y–Z (Broneer 1938, pp. 170–172).

137. Similar questions are applied to test the domestic origin of finds from two houses at Lydian Sardis: Cahill 2002b, pp. 182–184. These two houses, of which only a portion of each survives, provide parallels for many aspects of the domestic assemblage of the house of well J 2:4. They were likely destroyed

by fire around 546 by Cyrus the Great during his capture of Sardis (Cahill 2002b, p. 175). The material remains of the Sardis houses are very well preserved, better than the house of well J 2:4. Cahill admits that without comparative evidence, it is difficult to answer questions about the Lydian houses' status and size, just as it is with the house of well J 2:4.

138. For example, the Crossroads well (J 5:1), associated with the Crossroads Enclosure, Shear 1973a, pp. 126–134; 1973b, pp. 360–369; and well H 6:9, a well on the Kolonos Agoraios

filled with miniature vessels.

139. For the faunal remains associated with the altar of Aphrodite, see Foster 1984.

140. The votive plaques are unpublished, but the excavator inventoried two complete examples (T 4243 and T 4244) and fragments of 89 others (T 4245–T 4342) found west of the altar of Aphrodite and south of the polygonal wall during the 1993 excavation season: Shear 1993b, p. 2. All date to the late 6th to early 5th centuries.

141. See Young 1951; Agora XIV, pp. 173–177; Tsakirgis 2005.

businesses," such as that of the marble workers Mikion and Menon and Simon the shoemaker, were located in structures that were, architecturally, houses first, with commercial activity pursued within them.[142] In both of these examples there was ample archaeological evidence of the commercial activity pursued within, and no such evidence is present for the house of well J 2:4.[143] The slag from Level 4 of well J 2:4, as argued above, was probably brought in from outside to help fill the well shaft and does not represent metalworking pursued in the house. Metalworking requires extreme heat sources, and there is no evidence of scorching, crucibles, or other debris related to such an industry.[144] The dense layer of poros and marble chips present above the well in the northeastern room of the Classical house and the scattered chips in the southern half of the house were brought in as fill and do not represent stone-working activity in the house. It is, of course, possible that a light industry utilizing raw materials and products that do not survive in the archaeological record occurred within the house,[145] but the conclusion is that the fill of well J 2:4 does not originate from a primary commercial context.[146]

One final commercial enterprise must be considered: the tavern (καπε-λεῖον). There is not much evidence for public drinking establishments in the Archaic period, but they appear in literature by the end of the 5th century.[147] Both wine shops and public houses existed, and it is not clear how much the two overlapped, that is, how much was "takeout," and how much was drunk on-site. Lucy Talcott interpreted a late-5th-century well deposit as the property of a tavern due to the number of drinking cups, mixing bowls, and transport amphoras present in the deposit.[148] Wine sellers and/or taverns must be represented by a cluster of deposits and traces of architecture in the southeast area of the Classical Agora.[149] Mark Lawall points out that commercial graffiti related to the sale of wine are limited to this one area of the Agora.[150] One deposit must have been associated with a tavern that served both food and wine since it contained a large number of

142. Similarly, an Archaic house at Sardis contains a glass workshop, but otherwise the assemblage of ceramics meets the expectations for a house: Cahill 2002b, pp. 180, 182; 2005, pp. 60–65.

143. Menon and Mikion: Shear 1969, pp. 383–394; Simon the Shoemaker: Thompson 1954, pp. 51–55; Thompson 1960. See also the "industrial district" described in Young 1951.

144. Several slag nodules were found in the stratum of Persian destruction debris found in the southeastern portion of the house (Lot BZ 621), but this debris might have been brought in to help raise the floor level to form one continuous room in the Classical phase of the house.

145. One problem is that many of household pottery shapes—such as the

lekane, mortar, or pithos—might be used in craft settings; see Sparkes 1991, p. 75. One unusual bowl from Level 5 of well J 2:4 preserved traces of a red substance, probably miltos, and was shaped so that the base would sit comfortably in the palm of one's hand (183). This object may have been used to hold paint for a craft pursued within the house.

146. In contrast, compare the Classical commercial building to the northwest of the house, across the north–south street, and the shops and businesses located in the various stoas around the Classical Agora.

147. Davidson 1997, pp. 53–60.

148. R 13:4: Talcott 1935. Drinking vessels: 38; mixing bowls: 5; amphoras: 20, with many more uncatalogued; amides (urinals): 2; cooking pots: 5;

lamps: 5; only one oinochoe catalogued. Commercial graffiti on the transport amphoras adds strength to the tavern identification, Lawall 2000, p. 68. Talcott does not discuss any architecture that may go with the well. The deposit was closed in the third quarter of the 5th century and probably represents more damage from the earthquake in 426; see Rotroff and Oakley 1992, p. 56.

149. Classical walls under the Library of Pantainos may belong to drinking establishments or wine shops that produced the debris found in the deposits nearby; see Shear 1975, pp. 346–361, and fig. 5. For the association of the deposits with a tavern and wine shop, see Talcott 1935; Shear 1975, pp. 357–358; Lawall 2000, pp. 68–69.

150. Lawall 2000, pp. 68–69.

cooking pots and amphoras in its fill.[151] Although these tavern assemblages
share items in common with domestic assemblages, the extraordinary
number of amphoras, in particular, and a large quantity of pouring and
drinking shapes indicate that these deposits are not domestic in origin.
Literary references give the impression that taverns sold premixed wine by
the pitcher accompanied by a cup.[152] We would expect a tavern deposit to
contain a large number of pitchers in balance with cups. While well J 2:4
has a large number of drinking vessels, it does not have an exceptional
number of amphoras, pitchers, or cooking vessels. The conclusion is that
well J 2:4 did not serve a drinking or wine sales establishment.

Wells in the area of the Classical Athenian Agora could also serve public or civic contexts, but well J 2:4 did not. If a well were for public use,
then we would expect it to be easily accessible, but this is not the case with
well J 2:4. The surviving architecture clearly situates the well within the
courtyard of a small structure, which is an unlikely location for a public
water source. Also in the category of "public" functions are wells that served
public dining locations.[153] While the ΔE ligature does appear on cups from
Persian destruction deposits, indicating that some public dining did occur
before the Persian Wars, it was not until the second half of the 5th century
that dining at the state's expense became widespread.[154]

Having ruled out a religious, commercial, or civic context for the use
of well J 2:4, we turn to the contents of the well itself in order to characterize the artifact assemblage. The domestic origin of well J 2:4 will be
established through comparison to other secure domestic assemblages.
Unfortunately, we do not have a completely comparable deposit from the
area of the Classical Agora. Much of the pottery in Persian destruction
deposits "undoubtedly originated in the china cupboards of Athenian
households,"[155] but since many of the deposits cannot be associated with
domestic architecture, we do not know if these deposits represent the
contents of a single household or not.[156] It is entirely possible that several
households—or households and businesses—joined in their use of a deposit as they cleaned up debris. In fact, some of the Persian destruction
deposits contain household pottery and architectural fragments that must
have originated in public settings. Thus those deposits contain material
from both public and private contexts, which makes it likely that more than
one household contributed to the fill material. The deposits containing
architectural fragments are pits and trenches, not wells,[157] but finds such
as ostraka in some wells also call into question the purely domestic origin

151. U 13:1: Shear 1975, pp. 355–
361. Lopadia: over 100; amphoras: 79
complete and 280 fragmentary; bones
of fish, cattle, pigs, sheep, and evidence
of bone working.

152. Euboulos 80 KA, apud Athen.
11.473e: "I told the bartender to mix
me a pitcher [chous] of wine that
cost an obol, and to set the biggest
kantharos he had beside me," trans.
S. D. Olson, Cambridge, Mass., 2009.

153. E.g., H 6:5: Talcott 1936;
G 12:22 (in conjunction with the
Tholos): Thompson 1940, pp. 126–
127.

154. The ΔE ligature appears on at
least two cups in Persian destruction
well fills: *Agora* XXI, Fa 1, p. 51, pl. 29
(well E 15:6); Roberts 1986, no. 41,
p. 25, fig. 13. On the ΔE ligature in
general, see Talcott 1936, pp. 353–354;
Agora XXI, p. 51; Rotroff and Oakley

1992, p. 42, and n. 44. For public
dining, see Rotroff and Oakley 1992,
p. 45.

155. Shear 1993, p. 393.

156. Only five wells can be associated with domestic architecture in addition to J 2:4: B 18:6, B 19:10, D 17:10,
H 12:15, and Q 21:3; see Shear 1993,
pp. 405–406.

157. E.g., trench H 13:5, pit L 5:2,
pit G 3:1.

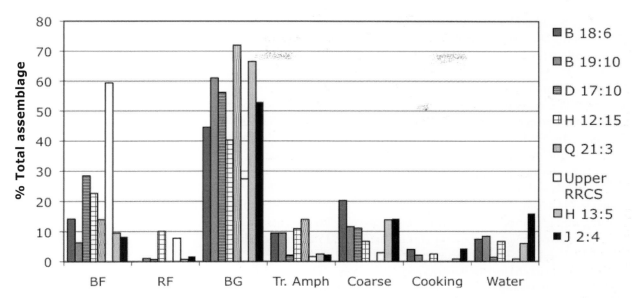

Figure 14. Percentage of different wares in the total assemblage of J 2:4 compared to their percentages in other domestic deposits, a commercial deposit, and a pit with public debris. Data from Shear 1993

158. E.g., ostraka in D 15:1, marble basin fragment in F 19:5, marble head in Q 20:1.

159. Evidence from J 2:4 is limited to complete and diagnostic fragments of vessels. Although the entire deposit was kept for J 2:4, only complete and diagnostic fragments of vessels were kept for the earlier excavated deposits. So as not to skew the statistics, the body sherds from J 2:4, even if a shape can be determined, are not included in the counts used to generate Fig. 14.

of their contents.[158] One further problem that prevents direct comparison of well J 2:4 to other household Persian destruction deposits is that, until recently, excavators did not retain the entire contents of a deposit but culled the coarse wares and body fragments to reduce storage needs. As a result, comparison of quantities or even weights must be limited to the better-preserved objects. We will never know, for example, how many roof tiles were in most of the Persian destruction deposits because only the most diagnostic were kept.

Only five Persian destruction well deposits can be firmly associated with domestic architecture. A comparison of well J 2:4 to these deposits can confirm that it is also likely to be domestic. Since these six deposits vary in total quantity of objects, Figure 14 compares the proportion of the total deposit for seven categories of objects.[159] There is very little difference in the proportions of deposit contents, confirming that all six deposits were formed from similar use contexts. To underscore the consistency of the six household deposits, Figure 14 also includes a deposit formed from a commercial establishment and a pit deposit that received material from public and private contexts. The commercial deposit, the upper portion of the Rectangular Rock-Cut Shaft (RRCS; G 6:3 upper), has an extraordinary number of black-figured objects since the deposit contained debris from a pottery sales shop. This commercial deposit also had fewer coarse-ware vessels since these were not necessary for the shop's activities. Other commercial establishments would have different distributions of pottery forms, but the point is that the contents of deposits with industrial or commercial components usually vary from the pattern visible in domestic deposits. The pit with public debris (H 13:5) had very little figured fine ware but much black glaze, which is a variation from the pattern of domestic deposits. In contrast, the pottery contents of well J 2:4 best approximates the domestic deposits.

A comparison to two later, domestic contexts from Attica further confirms the identification of the contents of well J 2:4 as domestic

(Fig. 15:a, b). The Dema house[160] of the late 5th century and the Vari house[161] of the late 4th century may be more than 100 years later than J 2:4, but they allow for two important comparisons: (1) again, to confirm the contents of a typical domestic assemblage (assuming some diachronic consistency), and (2) to confirm that J 2:4 contains only one household's pottery.[162] The excavators assume that the artifacts recovered from both of the Attic country houses represent only what was in use at the site.[163] Of course, the needs of a country house and an urban house are different, and the chronological difference should also account for variation in the assemblages, but in general, the pottery from the Dema house and the Vari house should provide a profile of a typical Classical household assemblage.[164] Indeed, if we compare the percentage of the total assemblage for categories of wares, we see that J 2:4 agrees well with the character of the two definite domestic deposits in both wares (Fig. 15:a) and functions (Fig. 15:b). Variations include the overall decrease in black figure by the late 5th century and its absence in the 4th century; an increased need for coarse-ware vessels in the country for the processing of agricultural materials; and (Fig. 15:b) a greater number of objects devoted to communal drinking in J 2:4, possibly related to the urban environment in Late Archaic Athens.

The standing condition of the house of well J 2:4 after the Persian sack suggests that this well would not have been a public dumping ground. The exterior walls of the house survived sufficiently for the house to be rebuilt without new exterior construction. This means that well J 2:4, in the courtyard of the house, would not have been accessible or visible to passersby, and thus not a tempting location for neighbors or the state to use for deposition of their own cleanup debris. If neighbors had had access to well J 2:4 for dumping their debris, we would expect a very different pattern of debris within the well. There would be a more consistent distribution of more complete vessels throughout the depths of the well, not concentrated in one pocket, as the neighbors came by to drop off their loads of debris. The jumble of multiple households' broken pottery would also result in a more homogeneous fill, not the discernible levels as discussed here. The

160. Jones et al. 1962.

161. Jones et al. 1973.

162. A similar comparison of the Dema House, the Vari House, and Agora deposit N 7:3 appears in Rotroff 1999, p. 68, table 1; Foxhall 2007.

163. Jones et al. 1962, pp. 88, 100; 1973, pp. 373, 396. Although both sites were abandoned, and it is possible that some objects were scavenged, the excavators assume that the remaining pottery is representative of the entire deposit. Both sites had brief periods of reoccupation, and that pottery is not considered here. Graphs in Figure 15 were created using total number of vessels identified in the original

publications of the Dema and Vari houses. In these publications, the authors frequently catalogue representative examples but mention in the entry that "four more" were represented in the fragments. All were included in the data set used to generate the graphs. In order to account for the difference in assemblage sizes, components are presented as a percentage of the total of all vessels.

164. The number of ceramic vessels in well J 2:4 that meet the criteria described in Chapter 3 for inclusion in the house is approximately 200 (see Table 6). It will be argued that this is a conservative estimate; but interestingly,

it seems to agree well with the number of vessels from a better-preserved house at Sardis: Cahill 2002b, p. 182. Cahill reports there are more than 200 pots in the partially excavated house, implying that the original assemblage was some unknowable factor greater. Cahill also notes that at the 4th-century site of Olynthus, where household assemblages were much more poorly preserved, 106 was the largest number of vessels preserved in any one house (House of the Many Colors, *Olynthus* XII, pp. 183–206; Cahill 2002a, pp. 85–97). Therefore, on this speculative and spotty evidence, the assemblage from well J 2:4 seems to be in line.

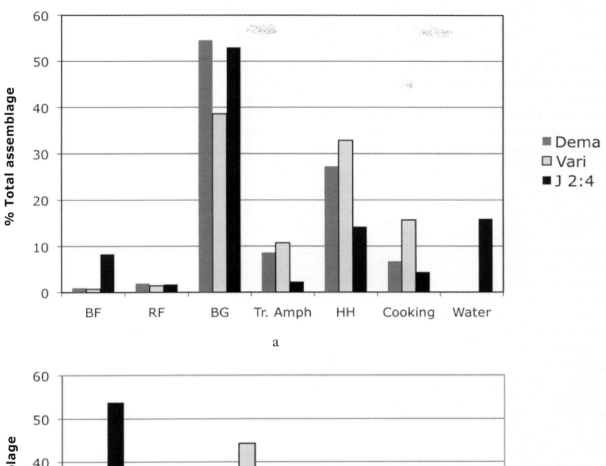

a

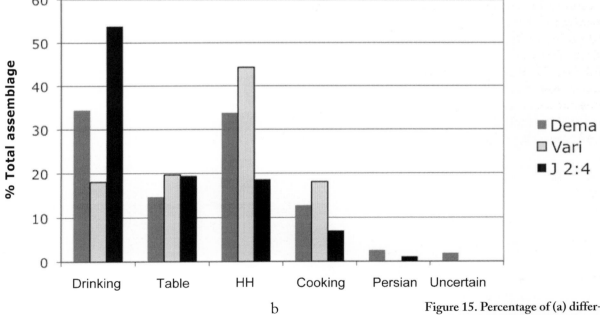

b

Figure 15. Percentage of (a) different wares and (b) pottery by function in the total assemblage of J 2:4 compared to the total assemblages excavated at the Dema and Vari houses. Data for the Dema house from Jones et al. 1962; data for the Vari house from Jones et al. 1973; MinNV used for J 2:4, see Table 5

conclusion is that the material from well J 2:4 originated in a domestic context, that of the house of well J 2:4. The well fill, however, did not all originate from household activity in the house of well J 2:4. The slag present in Level 4, bedrock in Level 3, and the highly worn, much older fragments in Levels 1 and 2 must have been brought in from somewhere outside the house. The highly fragmentary vessels in the fill may represent debris from a household rubbish pit, some of which may have, in fact, originated in the house of well J 2:4. In Chapter 3 I will define a methodology for distinguishing between nearly complete pieces at use in the house when it was sacked and extraneous fragmentary vessels of similar type.

QUANTIFYING THE HOUSEHOLD ASSEMBLAGE

As described in Chapter 2, well J 2:4 was filled at one time, mainly with debris from the destruction of the house of well J 2:4 and with additional material brought in to top off the well. In an effort to characterize a typical household assemblage for a Late Archaic Athenian house, this section will quantify the ceramic contents of well J 2:4, explore the relationship of the dumped fill with the household contents, and use the assessment of the house's pottery to place the household's symposium equipment into the context of the entire household assemblage.

QUANTIFICATION

Excavators retained all artifacts—complete and fragmentary—from the excavation of well J 2:4, in contrast with the policy of earlier excavations to discard nondiagnostic body sherds or to keep only representative objects. Study of the full deposit has the advantage of providing an accurate picture of the proportion of fine wares to household wares present, and, for the purpose of this study, insight into the variety and number of vessels in the household for use in communal drinking activities. Certainly many other questions may be asked of the deposit, and with future inquiries in mind, I have provided the reader a full count of diagnostic fragments in Table 4.

METHODOLOGY

All diagnostic rim, foot, and distinctive body fragments from the deposit were examined and their forms determined when possible.[1] Approximately 10% of diagnostic fragments are too small, unusual, or poorly preserved

---

1. Shape or function was assigned on the basis of original intended use. Of course, many shapes have multiple functions, and some objects could have been used for unintended purposes. Cahill (2002a, p. 71) considers this problem and its effect on ceramic-use statistics. For an example of an extreme unintended use, see the salt cellar in *Agora* XII, p. 300, no. 897 (and others), pl. 34, fig. 9, with a hole through its floor, which the authors propose could have been used as funnel or door knocker. Cahill (2002b, p. 179) discusses evidence for reuse of vessels in an Archaic Lydian house.

for confident assessment of their original form. Categories such as "miscellaneous rims" and "undetermined ring base" allow these fragments to be recorded without assigning them inaccurately to a particular shape. Although the vessel shape can sometimes be determined from body sherds, particularly with fine wares, body sherds were only considered diagnostic when they indicated a form not present as a rim, base, or handle. Table 4 presents all count data for diagnostic sherds, including diagnostic elements (e.g., handles) not used to generate maximum and minimum counts.

Number of vessels was determined in several ways as appropriate to the particular form or ware. In most cases bases were used to determine number of vessels. Bases have a tendency to break into fewer fragments than rims because of their sturdier construction. A single skyphos might shatter into dozens of rim fragments but only three or four base fragments. Serious effort was put into finding joins and joins across levels for fine wares, some of which have been catalogued and discussed in Chapter 2. Table 5 summarizes the maximum and minimum number of vessels for the entire deposit by category. The maximum number of vessels is the total possible if every base fragment represented a different vessel. The minimum number of vessels was determined using a method developed by Susan Rotroff for the study of a similar, but later deposit from the Athenian Agora.[2] She summarizes the calculation in the formula: estimated minimum number of vessels = W + O + (U-O)/2, where W = a whole foot, O = over half of a foot, and U = under half of a foot.[3] To facilitate this formula, in the counts of context pottery reported in Table 4 the proportion of base and rim was recorded as 100%, greater than or equal to 50%, or less than 50%. For chytrai, which have a rounded bottom and thus no foot to count, rims had to be used in the count. It is likely that the numbers for chytrai are too high.

Number of vessels was determined with the entire deposit in mind. As established in Chapter 2, the deposit was formed at one time with discernible levels, but all deposited simultaneously with joins between the levels. Therefore, when determining number of vessels within each level, rim fragments were not usually significant on the assumption that they might belong to a vessel represented by a base fragment in another level. On the other hand, some diagnostic fragments are clearly not complemented by bases,[4] and they would not be represented in the count if only bases were strictly considered. Thus, some of the figured wares and, for example, the mushroom jug, are counted as one, even though no bases were preserved. Tables 4 and 5 present data for the entire deposit and make no distinction between objects in use in the house and objects brought in from the outside to fill the well. Table 6 presents a conservative view of objects that were in use when the house was sacked, according to the methodology described below.

---

2. Rotroff and Oakley 1992, p. 133.

3. Results of the formula are rounded upward if greater than 0.50, downward if less than 0.49.

4. For example, there are fragments of two rims of black-figured kraters in Level 1b but no krater feet are preserved. Therefore, the krater rims are counted in the minimum and maximum number of vessels.

DISCUSSION

The Levels Compared

The fill from the upper portion of the well (Levels 1a, 1b, and 2) contains much more fragmentary pottery than the pocket of fine wares (Level 5). The forms present in the upper levels, however, are similar in date and character to the more complete forms from lower in the well. I proposed in Chapter 2 that Level 5 and the top of Level 6 contained objects from the house thrown into the well intact. Fragmentary pottery with joins between the upper fill and Level 5 (see Table 2) demonstrates that the deposit was formed at one time but also that some of the pottery in this house was broken aboveground and deposited as fragments at different times of the well-filling activity. To be clear: the complete cups **89**, **90**, and **91** from Level 5 and the top of Level 6, for example, were thrown into the well intact. These delicate shapes, particularly their handles, would scatter throughout a room if broken aboveground and would not be so tightly packed in the well fill.

The fragmentary pottery with joins between levels (**1**, **6**, **34**, and **79**, among others) seems, in contrast, likely to represent objects that were broken aboveground and deposited into the well in different "shovel loads." In addition, large fragments of vessels in the upper portion of the fill (**4**, **87**, **88**, **109**, and **166**, among others) are also likely to have belonged to the house and to have been broken aboveground, but preserved in larger portions. It is difficult to know for certain whether the very fragmentary pottery in the upper fill, that is, the pieces that exist as single fragments only, originated in the house, or were brought in with fill collected elsewhere. The presence of early fragments, from the Geometric period through the early 6th century, indicates that portions of the upper fill were acquired outside the house where fragments could accumulate over time. There are four earlier fragments in Levels 1a and 1b, and eighteen in Level 2, including **22** and **72**. Thus, minimum-number-of-vessel (MinNV) counts for Levels 1 and 2 may not refer to pottery used in this household. In contrast, MinNV counts for Levels 5 and 6 do represent pottery used in the house.

Minimum number of vessels may give a good idea of the contents of the house for Levels 5 and 6, but more conservative criteria are needed to determine what objects in Levels 1 through 4 should be considered part of the household's assemblage at the time of destruction as opposed to contemporary fill brought in from outside. To make this distinction, the following criteria were used: the object had to be complete or more than half-preserved, or the object had to have fragments with joins between upper and lower fill. Numbers in italics on Table 6 indicate fragmentary objects with joins above and below the nearly sterile Levels 3 and 4. It is assumed that joins indicate that the object was broken in the destruction, but deposited in the well in two different shovel loads. The objects are tallied under the highest level from which joining pieces come. Table 2 provides more information about joins. That these joining, but incomplete, objects exist suggests that many more of the fragmentary objects from the deposit also originated in the cupboards of the house of well J 2:4.

TABLE 4. DIAGNOSTIC SHERD COUNTS BY LEVEL

"Tins" column reports number of uninventoried diagnostic sherds stored with context pottery. Number of fragments and complete vessels included in the Catalogue of this book are listed in the "Cat." column. bs = body sherd; und = undetermined form; * = likely figured.

	Level 1a Tins	Level 1a Cat.	Level 1b Tins	Level 1b Cat.	Level 2 Tins	Level 2 Cat.	Level 3 Tins	Level 3 Cat.	Level 4 Tins	Level 4 Cat.	Level 5 Tins	Level 5 Cat.	Level 6 Tins	Level 6 Cat.	Levels 5 to 6 Tins	Levels 5 to 6 Cat.	Mixed Levels Tins	Mixed Levels Cat.
FINE WARE																		
BLACK-FIGURE																		
Drinking Vessels																		
Cup bs				1	1	1								3				
Heron Class skyphos, full profile												1						
Heron Class skyphos rim <50%												1						
Cup-skyphos, full profile												3						
Skyphos rims <50%	1		10	4	22	7	2				3	3	2					
Skyphos base, 100%				1		1						1						
Skyphos base >50%																		
Skyphos base <50%			2	1		1						1		1				
Skyphos bs	1		23	5	40	10	4	2			6	3	7	1				
Cup-skyphos handle			1		1													
Skyphos w/canted handles, cf. *Agora* XII, no. 331 rim <50%	1										1							
Service Vessels																		
Krater, column rim			2		1													
Krater bs			2	1	2													
Large bowl w/bf rim					3													
Dinos/louterion rim						1												
Amphora bs				1		1												
Amphora rim <50%			1		1													
Amphoriskos												1						
Stamnos						1												
Kalpis bs						1												
Oinochoe, trefoil, complete												1						
Oinochoe, count as one											2							
Oinochoe bs											1							
Closed bs	2		12	1	23		1				2		2					1
Stand			1	1														

Category	Counts (left to right)
Table Vessels	
Lekythos	3
Lekythos bs	10, 3, 2, 7, 1, 6, 1, 1
Lekanis lid rim	1, 1
Lekanis lid knob	2, 2
Lekanis bs	1, 1, 1
Ritual Vessels	
Plate	1, 1
Thymiaterion	1
Phiale, Six's technique	1, 1, 1, 1
Personal Vessels	
Pyxis bs	1, 1
Earlier	
Earlier, bf	2, 4, 2, 1
Earlier, geo or like	2, 12, 2, 1, 2, 2
RED-FIGURE	
Drinking Vessels	
Cup, full profile	2, 5, 1
Cup bs	1, 1, 8
Service Vessels	
Pelike, full profile	1
Closed bs	1, 2
BLACK-GLAZE	
Drinking Vessels	
Type C, concave rim, full profile	1, 1
Type C, concave rim >50%	1, 13, 1, 1
Type C, concave rim <50%	1, 43, 6, 2, 2, 1
Type C, plain rim, full profile	5
Type C, plain <50%	1, 1, 17, 1
Cup feet 100%	3, 1
Cup feet >50%	3, 4, 1, 1
Cup feet <50%	1, 11, 22, 2, 1
Cup feet, und <50%	2, 4, 1, 1
Handles, cups >50%	1, 7, 1
Handles, cups <50%	7, 43, 5, 4

Continued on next page

TABLE 4—Continued

	Level 1a		Level 1b		Level 2		Level 3		Level 4		Level 5		Level 6		Levels 5 to 6		Mixed Levels	
	Tins	Cat.	Tins	Cat.	Tins	Cat.	Tins	Cat.	Tins	Cat.	Tins	Cat.	Tins	Cat.	Tins	Cat.	Tins	Cat.
Corinthian-type skyphos (Corinthian fabric) rim					2													
Corinthian-type skyphos (Corinthian fabric) base			5		2													
Corinthian-type skyphos (Corinthian fabric) handle			3															
Corinthian-type skyphos (Attic fabric) full profile											1			1				
Corinthian-type skyphos (Attic fabric) rim <50%			2		4						2		1				1	
Corinthian-type skyphos (Attic fabric) base = 100%					2													
Corinthian-type skyphos (Attic fabric) base >50%			1		4						1							
Corinthian-type skyphos (Attic fabric) base <50%			7		13													
Corinthian-type skyphos (Attic fabric) handle			3															
Handles, Corinthian-type >50%					1													
Attic-type skyphos rim <50%			1		12				1		2						1	
Cup-skyphos, full profile												3						
Cup-skyphos, count as one											2							
Cup-skyphos rim <50%	1		23		159	1	2				24		6				4	
Cup-skyphos base >50%			2		7				1		2							
Cup-skyphos base <50%	1		29		51		2				4		1				2	
Handle, cup-skyphos >50%			1		2						1						6	
Handle, cup-skyphos <50%			19		51		2				4						4	
Handles, skyphos >50%	1				1													
Handles, skyphos <50%					1													
One-handler, full profile						1												
One-handler rim >50%					1													
One-handler rim <50%	1		4		22		2		1		3		1					
One-handler base ring >50%					1						3							
One-handler base ring <50%			13		13						2						1	
One-handler base flat <50%			4															
Handles one-handler >50%	1		4		2												2	

	1	2	3	4	5	6	7	8	9	10
Handles one-handler <50%		1								
Subgeometric survival rim	2					1		2		
Subgeometric survival base = 100%	2									
Subgeometric survival base <50%	1									
Type B skyphos			1							
Sessile kantharos handle (spur)		2								
Mug base									1	
Misc. rims		14	1			1				
Open base ring <50%		1				1				
Open base flat <50%		1				1				
Service Vessels										
Krater column handle*		1	1							
Krater column rim <50%										
Pelike, full profile						2	2		1	
Amphora, full profile			1			2	2			
Amphora rim <50%	6	5	1					3		
Amphora ring base <50%		1								
Amphora ring base <50%*	1									
Amphora handle*		2				1		2		
Psykter, full profile		1	1							
Psykter rim >50%		1								
Psykter rim <50%		1	1			1				
Psykter lid, full profile			1			1				
Psykter lid rim										
Psykter foot	1			1	1					
Oinochoe w/trefoil rim, full profile							2			
Oinochoe w/trefoil rim >50%						1				
Oinochoe w/trefoil rim <50%						3		3		
Oinochoe rim, round								1		
Oinochoe handle	5									1
Oinochoe handle, twisted	1									
Oinochoe handle, Corinthian fabric						1				
Banded oinochoe rim <50%	1	11				2				
Banded oinochoe rim+handle 100%						1				

Continued on next page

TABLE 4—Continued

	Level 1a		Level 1b		Level 2		Level 3		Level 4		Level 5		Level 6		Levels 5 to 6		Mixed Levels	
	Tins	Cat.	Tins	Cat.	Tins	Cat.	Tins	Cat.	Tins	Cat.	Tins	Cat.	Tins	Cat.	Tins	Cat.	Tins	Cat.
Banded oinochoe handle			4		2													
Banded oinochoe ring base = 100%					1						1							
Jug, full profile												1						
Unknown closed rim <50%					3						1							
Horizontal handle											1		1					
Misc. vertical handles			1		16						4		5					
Vertical handle, Corinthian fabric					1													
Closed base ring = 100%											1		3					
Closed base ring >50%					2				1		2		1					
Closed base ring <50%			10		12				2		1		2					
Closed base disk <50%					2													
Closed base flat >50%														1				
Closed base flat <50%					3													
Closed base flat, Corinthian fabric					1													
Table Vessels																		
Lekythos base = 100%*			5		4								2					
Lekythos base <50%*					7													
Lekythos rim >50%*			3		1						1		1					
Lekythos rim <50%*					10												1	
Lekythos handle			2		5						1		1					
Globular lekythos, rim			1		2								1					
Olpe full profile														4				
Olpe rim <50%			1		2						1							
Olpe rim, trefoil <50%																	1	
Olpe base, disk = 100%			2								1		1					
Olpe base, disk >50%			1		1													
Olpe base, disk <50%			2															
Olpe base, flat >50%			4		4						2		1					
Olpe base, flat <50%					3								1					
Olpe handle			4		5													
Askos						1												
Bowl rim <50%					1													

Type												
Bowl ring base (810) >50%							2					
Bowl ring base (810) <50%	2				1							
Covered bowl		1			1	1						
Covered bowl lid full profile						1						
Covered bowl lid rim	1				1							
Covered bowl lid knob	1				1							
Lekanis, full profile				1								
Lekanis lid, full profile				1	1							
Lekanis lid rim	3		2				2					
Lekanis lid bs		1	1									
Lekanis lid knob >50%	2					1						
Lekanis lid knob, Corinthian fabric		1										
Open w/ledge rim, Corinthian fabric	1	1						1				
Stemmed dish, full profile	1		1	2		2						
Stemmed dish rim >50%				1	1							
Stemmed dish rim <50%	6	14	1	2	2	1						
Stemmed dish foot = 100%				1	1							
Salt cellar, concave >50%		3										
Salt cellar, concave <50%	1	2		1								
Salt cellar, echinus >50%		1										
Salt cellar, echinus <50%		1										
Salt cellar, convex >50%			2									
Small bowl, full profile				1								

HOUSEHOLD

Service

Type												
Table amphora rim <50%	1			1		1						
Jug w/trefoil rim, full profile				1								
Jug, full profile				4								
Jug rim <50%												
Jug handle	1	1										
Mushroom jug-count as one				1								
HH closed base ring = 100%				2	1							
HH closed base ring >50%		1		2		1						
HH closed base ring <50%		4	1	1			1	1				
HH closed base flat = 100%				1								
HH closed base flat >50%				2								

Continued on next page

TABLE 4—*Continued*

	Level 1a Tins	Level 1a Cat.	Level 1b Tins	Level 1b Cat.	Level 2 Tins	Level 2 Cat.	Level 3 Tins	Level 3 Cat.	Level 4 Tins	Level 4 Cat.	Level 5 Tins	Level 5 Cat.	Level 6 Tins	Level 6 Cat.	Levels 5 to 6 Tins	Levels 5 to 6 Cat.	Mixed Levels Tins	Mixed Levels Cat.
HH closed base, flat <50%					1												1	
Closed base, Corinthian tile fabric																		
Vertical handles											3							
Food Preparation and Utility																		
Lekane, full profile				1								1						
Lekane bases, ring >50%	1		1								1							
Lekane bases, ring <50%	1		10		16		3		2		3						1	
Lekane bases, flat <50%	1		5		5				1		1							
Lekane rim, thickened >50%													1					
Lekane rim, thickened <50%			20	1	22		1				1		1				2	
Lekane rim, rolled <50%			2		3						1							
Lekane rim, ledge >50%									1									
Lekane rim, ledge <50%			9		14								1					
Lekane handles >50%			1		1													
Lekane handles <50%			8		17						1		1				3	
Bowl, full profile												1						
Bowl rim <50%	1								1								1	
Mortar, pale porous rim			2															
Mortar, count as one			1															
Mortar, rim <50%			1		6				2									
Mortar ring base <50%					3						1							
Mortar flat base <50%			3		4				3		1							
Louterion rim			2		3				2									
COOKING WARE																		
Cooking Vessels																		
Chytra w/flange	1		4		5									1				
Chytra w/o flange			3		2					1		2						
Chytra spout													1					
Lid rim			3		2													
Strainer bs					1													
Eschara rim					1													

	C1	C2	C3	C4	C5	C6	C7	C8	C9	C10	C11	C12
Brazier	4		9			1						2
Cooking bell						1				1		
Unknown open			1			1						
Water Jars												
Hydria rim 100%						2						
Hydria rim <50%	2		7			4		3	1		1	
Handles, horizontal	9		17	22			15		1	1		2
Kados, full profile							1		1			
Kados rim = 100%						1					1	
Kados rim >50%						4						1
Kados rim <50%	11		28		1	10		13	1		1	2
Jug w/trefoil rim, full profile								1				
Jug rim 100%						1						
Jugs rim >50%			1			1						
Jugs rim <50%	3		7	1		6		6	1		1	
Narrow-neck jug <50%	1		1									
Jug rim, trefoil 100%						2		1				1
Jug rim, trefoil >50%						1		1				
Jug rim, trefoil <50%	1					5		7	1		1	2
Jug handle			6									
Handles, vertical	16		6			9		8				6
Handles, unknown						8		8				
Base, ring = 100%						12		32				2
Base, ring >50%	3		1			11		3				1
Base, ring <50%	9		17		1	6		16	1		7	4
STORAGE VESSELS												
Basin rim <50%	4		1		1	1			1			1
Pithos bs					1	1						1
Pithos toe												1
Large storage, complete						1						
Large storage, fragment	3		9			8		1				
Stopper		1	1									
RITUAL VESSELS												
Votive miniatures	3		3		1				1			
Votive miniature handle			1									

Continued on next page

TABLE 4—*Continued*

	Level 1a		Level 1b		Level 2		Level 3		Level 4		Level 5		Level 6		Levels 5 to 6		Mixed Levels	
	Tins	Cat.	Tins	Cat.	Tins	Cat.	Tins	Cat.	Tins	Cat.	Tins	Cat.	Tins	Cat.	Tins	Cat.	Tins	Cat.
BF Corinthian kotyle, miniature (Corinthian fabric)						1												
Argive monochrome juglet														1				
Plate broad-rimmed rim <50%	1		1		3													
Miniature open											1							
PERSONAL VESSELS																		
Feeder nozzle					1													
Unguent pot														1				
Pyxis lid rim (large shape)			1															
UNCERTAIN USE																		
BG stand														1				
BG disk						1												
BG ring												1						
Lid/bowl						1												
LAMPS																		
Type 2			1		1	1												
Type 16			9	1	11							3						
Type 17			1		2													
Type 19					1							1		1				
Type 20						1											1	
Type 21			5		2						1							
Type 22			1		1													
Type 23					2						1		2					
Tube					1													
Small/non-Attic					3													
Horizontal handle			1		1													
WEAVING TOOLS																		
Loomweight, complete			7	1	1	1								1				
Loomweight fragment			3															
Spindle whorl				1														

MISCELLANEOUS

Pesos		1								1			
Obsidian blade fr			6	1	1						1		
Terracotta figurine			6		2				3		2		
Astragaloi						17		5		2			
Bone disk										1			
Lead sheet										1			
Quern						1							
Pounder						2							

BUILDING MATERIALS

Tile		41	45	5	17	3		3		1		4
Brick?												1
Tile/large storage uncertain		3	20	15		4						
Wellhead		Yes				Yes		Yes		Yes		
Drain				2						3		
Water pipe			1									
Corinthian fabric bs	1	3	92			1						
Later intrusions bs	1	1	2				1					1

TABLE 5. SUMMARY OF MAXIMUM AND MINIMUM NUMBER OF VESSELS BY LEVEL WITHIN WELL J 2:4 (DATA FROM TABLE 4)

	Level 1a		Level 1b		Level 2		Level 3		Level 4	
	MaxNV	MinNV	MaxNV	MinNV	MaxNV	MinNV	MaxNV	MinNV	MaxNV	MinNV
DRINKING VESSELS										
RF Cup					2	2				
BF Cup (bs only)			1	0	2	0				
BG Cup	1	0	21	13	31	16	1	0	1	1
BF Skyphos			3	1	3	2				
BF Cup-skyphos	1	0	31	16	58	29	2	1	1	1
BG Heron Class										
BG Type B skyphos					1	1				
BG Corinthian-type skyphos (Corinthian fabric)			5	3	2	1				
BG Corinthian-type skyphos (Attic fabric)			8	4	19	11				
BG Skyphos w/canted handles	1	0								
BG One-handler			4	2	15	8				
Subgeometric survival			3	2						
BG Mug										
BG Sessile kantharos					2	1				
Uncertain drinking base					1	0				
DRINKING SERVICE VESSELS										
BF Stamnos					1	1				
BF Amphora			1	0						
BG Amphora			1	0	1	0				
BF Amphoriskos										
BF Oinochoe										
BG Oinochoe										
Banded oinochoe					1	1				
RF Pelike										
BG Pelike										
BG Psykter					3	2	1	1	1	1
BG Psykter lid			1	1						
BF Kalpis					1	0				
BG Closed			10	5	20	10			3	2
BF Krater			2	2	1	0				
BG Krater			1	0						
BF Bowl					3	0				
BF Stand			1	1						
BF Dinos/louterion					1	0				
TABLE VESSELS										
BF Lekythos					1	1				
BG Lekythos*			5	5	11	8				
Askos					1	1				
BG Olpe			5	4	8	6				
BF Lekanis lid					3	2				
BG Lekanis										
BG Lekanis lid			2	2	1	1				
BG Bowl					2	1				
BG Covered bowl + lid					1	1				

	Level 5		Level 6		Mixed Level 5 and 6		Mixed: Redigging Fill		TOTAL	
	MaxNV	MinNV	MaxNV	MinNV	MaxNV	MinNV	MaxNV	MinNV	MaxNV	MinNV
RF Cup	5	5	1	1					8	8
BF Cup (bs only)			3	0					6	0
BG Cup	7	7	4	2			1	0	67	39
BF Skyphos	5	4	1	1					12	8
BG Cup-skyphos	11	8	1	0			2	0	107	55
BF Heron Class	1	1							1	1
BG Type B skyphos									1	1
BG Corinthian-type skyphos (Corinthian fabric)									7	4
BG Corinthian-type skyphos (Attic fabric)	2	1	1	1					30	17
BG Skyphos w/canted handles	1	0							2	0
BG One-handler	5	4					1	0	25	14
Subgeometric survival									3	2
BG Mug			1	1					1	1
BG Sessile kantharos									2	1
Uncertain drinking base	1	0							2	0
BF Stamnos									1	1
BF Amphora									1	0
BG Amphora	2	2							4	2
BF Amphoriskos	1	1							1	1
BF Oinochoe	3	3							3	3
BG Oinochoe	2	2							2	2
Banded oinochoe	1	1							2	2
RF Pelike	1	1							1	1
BG Pelike	2	2	1	1					3	3
BG Psykter	1	0							6	4
BG Psykter lid									1	1
BF Kalpis									1	0
BG Closed	4	3	7	5					44	25
BF Krater									3	2
BG Krater									1	0
BF Bowl									3	0
BF Stand									1	1
BF Dinos/louterion									1	0
BF Lekythos	1	1							2	2
BG Lekythos*			2	2					18	15
Askos									1	1
BG Olpe	3	3	7	6					23	19
BF Lekanis lid									3	2
BG Lekanis	1	1							1	1
BG Lekanis lid	1	1	1	1					5	5
BG Bowl	1	0	2	2					5	3
BG Covered bowl + lid			3	2					4	3

TABLE 5—*Continued*

	Level 1a		Level 1b		Level 2		Level 3		Level 4	
	MaxNV	*MinNV*	*MaxNV*	*MinNV*	*MaxNV*	*MinNV*	*MaxNV*	*MinNV*	*MaxNV*	*MinNV*
TABLE VESSELS										
BG Stemmed dish					1	1				
BG Salt cellar			1	0	9	8				
Small bowl										
BG Jug										
HOUSEHOLD WARE										
Lekane	2	1	17	9	21	11	3	2	3	2
Mortar			4	3	7	4			3	2
Bowl										
Jug										
Mushroom jug										
Closed					6	3	1	1		
Louterion			2	0	3	0			2	0
Basin			4	1	1	0	1	0	1	0
Pithos									1	0
Stopper			1	1	1	1				
Large storage										
COOKING WARE										
Chytra	1	1	7	7	7	7			1	1
Lid			3	1	2	1				
Strainer					1	1				
Cooking bell										
Brazier			4	1	9	1				
Eschara					1	0				
Water jar			12	6	18	9			1	0
RITUAL										
Votive miniatures			3	3	5	5				
BG Broad-rim plate	1	0	1	0	3	1				
BF Phiale			2	2						
BF Thymiaterion										
Argive monocrhome juglet										
PERSONAL										
Unguent pot										
BF Pyxis			1	1						
BG Pyxis lid			1	0						
Feeder					1	1				
UNCERTAIN USE										
BG Stand										
Disk					1	1				
Ring										

	Level 5		Level 6		Mixed Level 5 and 6		Mixed: Redigging Fill		TOTAL	
	MaxNV	MinNV	MaxNV	MinNV	MaxNV	MinNV	MaxNV	MinNV	MaxNV	MinNV
BG Stemmed dish	4	4	3	3					8	8
BG Salt cellar	1	1							11	9
Small bowl	1	1							1	1
BG Jug	1	1							1	1
Lekane	6	4					1	0	53	29
Mortar	2	1							16	10
Bowl	1	1							1	1
Jug	5	5							5	5
Mushroom jug	1	1							1	1
Closed	8	8	1	1	1	0	2	1	19	14
Louterion									7	0
Basin	1	0							8	1
Pithos							2	1	3	1
Stopper									2	2
Large storage	1	1							1	1
Chytra	2	2	2	1					20	19
Lid									5	2
Strainer									1	1
Cooking bell	1	1							1	1
Brazier	1	0					2	0	16	2
Eschara									1	0
Water jar	32	28	51	42	7	4	7	5	128	94
Votive miniatures	1	1	1	1					10	10
BG Broad-rim plate	1	0							5	1
BF Phiale	1	1							3	3
BF Thymiaterion			1	1					1	1
Argive monocrhome juglet			1	1					1	1
Unguent pot			1	1					1	1
BF Pyxis									1	1
BG Pyxis lid									1	0
Feeder									1	1
BG Stand			1	1					1	1
Disk									1	1
Ring	1	1							1	1

TABLE 6. POTTERY AND ARTIFACTS PROBABLY ORIGINATING IN THE HOUSE OF WELL J 2:4

	Level 1b	Level 2	Level 3	Level 4	Level 5	Level 6 [Period of Use]	TOTAL
DRINKING VESSELS							
RF Cup		2			5	1	8
BF Cup		*1*				[3]	1, [3]
BG Cup		1			7	1, [1]	9, [1]
BF Cup-skyphos			*1*		4	[1]	5, [1]
BG Cup-skyphos					8		8
BF Heron Class		*1*			1		2
BF Skyphos		*2*	*1*			[1]	3, [1]
BG Type B skyphos		1					1
BG Corinthian-type skyphos (Attic fabric)					1	1	2
BG One-handler		1			4		5
BG Mug						[1]	[1]
Subtotal							**43**
DRINKING SERVICE VESSELS							
BF Stamnos		1					1
BG Amphora					1 [1]		1, [1]
BF Amphora	*1*	*1*					2
BF Amphoriskos					1		1
BF Oinochoe					3		3
BG Oinochoe					2		2
Banded oinochoe					1		1
BG Jug					1	[1]	1, [1]
RF Pelike					1		1
BG Pelike					2	[1]	2 [1]
BG Psykter		1					1
BG Psykter lid		1					1
BF Kalpis		*1*					1
BG Closed					3	5	8
Subtotal							**26**
TABLE VESSELS							
BF Lekythos		1			1	[2]	2, [2]
Askos		1					1
BG Olpe					3	6	9
BF Lekanis lid		*1*					1
BG Lekanis					1		1
BG Lekanis lid		*1*			1	1	3
BG Bowl		1				[2]	1, [2]
BG Covered bowl and lid		1				2	3
BG Stemmed dish		1			4	3	8
BG Salt cellar		2			1		3
Small bowl					1		1
Subtotal							**33**

TABLE 6—*Continued*

	Level 1b	Level 2	Level 3	Level 4	Level 5	Level 6 [Period of Use]	TOTAL
HOUSEHOLD WARE							
Lekane	1				4		5
Mortar					1		1
Bowl					1		1
Jug					2, [3]		2, [3]
Mushroom jug					1		1
Closed					8	[1]	8, [1]
Large storage vessel					1		1
Stopper	1	1					2
Subtotal							**21**
COOKING WARE							
Chytra				1	2	1	4
Cooking bell					1		1
Subtotal							**5**
Water Jar (MinNV for all Levels)	6	9			28 + 4 Mixed Levels 5 and 6	42	89 (74 in Levels 5 and 6)
RITUAL							
Votive miniatures	3	5			1	1	10
BF Phiale					1		1
Argive monochrome juglet						1	1
BF Thymiaterion						[1]	[1]
PERSONAL							
Unguent pot						1	1
UNCERTAIN USE							
BG Stand						1	1
Disk		1					1
Ring					1		1
OTHER ARTIFACTS							
Lamps		1			3	2	6
Loomweights	8?	2?				1	1, 10?
Spindle whorl	1?						1?
Terracotta figurines	1?	2?			1	1, [1]	2, 3?, [1]
Bone disk						1	1
Pesos	1					1	2
Lead sheet						[1]	[1]
Astragaloi					24		24
Quern					1		1
Pounder					2		2
Tile						1†	
Drain						3†	

Data from Table 4; Levels 1 to 4 subjected to criteria described in Chapter 3; square brackets denote objects discarded during the use of the well. Numbers in italics represent fragments with joins between upper and lower levels, which are counted in the highest level in which a joining fragment occurs. A question mark means the object meets the criteria, but there is some doubt if it should be included.

† Probably Persian destruction debris.

It is surprising, for example, that only two black-figured lekythoi meet the criteria for inclusion in the household assemblage, although there were more than 75 fragments of lekythoi in the deposit. Table 4 also records many fragments of tile and large storage vessels. No tiles and only one storage vessel was preserved complete enough to meet the criteria, but these are, nonetheless, likely to have originated in the house.

On Tables 2 and 6 and in the Catalogue, objects from all levels that are most likely to have been in use in the house at the time of the destruction are denoted with an asterisk. For Levels 1 through 4 the objects had to be over half preserved to earn an asterisk.

Objects from Level 6, the period of use deposit, likely to have been discarded into the well during its use are denoted on Tables 2 and 6 and in the Catalogue with square brackets. I assume that all objects in the period of use of the well (Level 6 and the lower portion of Level 5) originated in the household, although some single fragments might have slipped down from higher levels because Levels 5 and 6 did contain some small earlier fragments (see Table 4). The objects in the period of use portion of the deposit were not in use at the time of the destruction, but they do tell us about the chronology of the house and provide additional evidence for the types of artifacts used by the household. Representative and distinctive examples are catalogued. Period of use deposits are generally characterized by numerous water jars broken in use, which is true of Level 6. However, it is possible that some of the water jars from a little higher in the well, from the upper portion of Level 6 and lower portion of Level 5, might have been functioning at the time of the clean-up but were deposited along with the complete fine wares. It is hard to tell the difference between discard while in use or during the clean up, so some water jars and water fetching closed shapes from Levels 5 and 6 receive an asterisk in Tables 2 and 6 and the Catalogue. Fine-ware closed vessels found broken in the period of use deposit receive both an asterisk and square brackets since they might have been used to fetch water.

It is uncertain if the loomweights, terracotta figurines, and lamps in Levels 1 and 2 originated in the house. Loomweights, a spindle whorl, clay stoppers, and terracotta figurines are listed on Table 6 with a question mark. They meet the criteria for inclusion in the household assemblage because they are more than half preserved; however, all are single fragments of dense forms that might have retained their preservation even in a redeposited fill. Only one lamp is listed for the upper fill (194). Others did not meet the criteria discussed above: all were fragmentary and none had joins with the lower fill. Nevertheless, there were over 50 fragments of lamps in the whole fill, suggesting that the number of six lamps on Table 6 may be too low.

A House's Equipment

My study of the pottery and artifacts that probably originated in the house of well J 2:4 (as summarized in Table 6) can only consider objects disposed of in the well. It is entirely possible that this house used more than one location for disposal of broken household pottery, and that we are therefore seeing only a portion of the actual household assemblage. Absent from

Table 6, for example, is a krater. The abundance of other types of drinking equipment means that this household must have owned a krater; thus, its absence may underscore that our image of this house's equipment is flawed. In addition, moving from the raw data of fragment counts to an assessment of equipment owned by the house is not entirely satisfactory, and the criteria imposed are possibly too rigid, leading to a misrepresentation of the picture. However, Table 6 does provide a starting point for understanding both the variety and quantity of domestic equipment in a household of the Late Archaic period, and even this flawed view helps us to understand the life of the household. As will be explored further in Chapters 4 and 5, a critical observation for this study is that the largest proportion of the house's pottery inventory is devoted to communal drinking activities. Using the figures from Table 6, but discounting the water jars and "other artifacts" category, the household equipment breaks down roughly as follows: 46% drinking cups[5] and service vessels; 22% forms for the table; 21% cooking and household; and 11% miscellaneous (Fig. 16:a).[6] This is an enormous investment in drinking activities for a household.[7] Taking the same data for MinNV in Table 5 instead (Fig. 16:b), with the caveat that some of the fragments used to generate MinNV may have originated in other households, the pattern is nearly identical, confirming that the importance of drinking equipment.

According to Table 6, the most common drinking vessel was the cup (kylix). Approximately half of the house's drinking vessels were of this stemmed variety associated with formal drinking parties (Fig. 17:a). Of these cups, the majority were plain black glaze or red figure, and only one black-figured cup met the criteria for inclusion in Table 6. As will be discussed in Chapter 4, the red-figured cups appear to be a set, and some of the black-glazed cups may have been purchased at the same time. Using the MinNV tallies from Table 5 gives a different view (Fig. 17:b). Cups continue to be important, but more cup-skyphoi enter the picture. Even though we cannot be sure that all objects tallied in Table 5 were in use in the house at the time of the destruction, most of the fragments are contemporary with the destruction debris; therefore, Figure 17:b confirms the importance of cups and cup-skyphoi in houses in Late Archaic Athens. The cup data from Table 4 also confirm the observation of Brian Sparkes and Lucy Talcott that the concave-lipped form of undecorated black-glazed cups was more popular than the plain-rimmed version.[8] Using a modification of Rotroff's MinNV formula to consider only rims provides a way to understand the relative proportion of the two forms of the cup. The ratio

5. Handle counts confirm the plausibility of the drinking-cup figures presented in Table 6. A modified version of Rotroff's formula applied to drinking vessel handles of greater than 50% and less than 50% from Levels 5 and 6 (counts listed in Table 4), $(O + U/2)/2$, gives a result of four additional drinking cups: $(2+ [13/2])/2) = 4.25$. Table 4 attempts, when possible, to attribute a handle to a shape, but fragmentary handles can be difficult to assign to a shape, so the formula groups all fragmentary handles together.

6. Percentages are rounded to the nearest 1% in order to underscore the inherent error in such calculations when the data itself may contain errors. See the similar assessment of pottery from the Dema house, the Vari house, and Agora deposit N 7:3 in Rotroff 1999, p. 68, table 2.

7. Rotroff (1999, p. 68) comes to the same conclusion that "vessels earmarked for use with wine are remarkably common." She goes on to strengthen the picture of how extraordinary the Greek emphasis on wine service vessels was by offering an informal statistical comparison to pottery from 10 non-Western communities in which serving vessels are rare, if present at all.

8. *Agora* XII, p. 91.

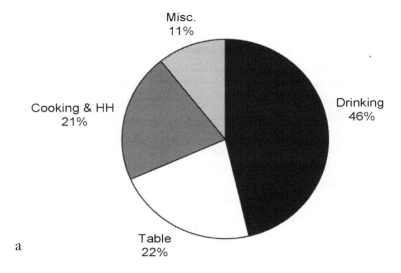

a

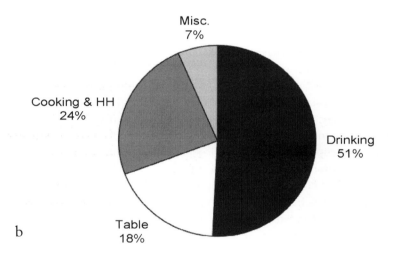

b

Figure 16. Household pottery by function, (a) using data from Table 6; (b) using MinNV from Table 5

of MaxNV concave rims to plain rims is 37 to 14,[9] and although this is not an accurate determination of maximum number of vessels, it does suggest that the deposit contained twice as many concave-rimmed black-glazed cups as plain-rimmed.

The second most common drinking shape was the cup-skyphos, although the criteria used to create Table 6 may lead to an underrepresentation of the form. The raw numbers, as related on Tables 4 and 5, indicate that there are a minimum of 64 black-figured and black-glazed skyphoi present in the deposit.[10] Many of these are single fragments of bases in the upper portion of the well; thus, they were eliminated by the criteria used for Table 6. There are surprisingly few one-handlers and skyphoi of the Attic and Corinthian types.

Chapter 6 examines the objects from this house associated with daily life and chores. An initial look at the household wares using the data from Table 6, not including water jars, shows that closed vessels are the most common (Fig. 18:a). Many of these were pouring vessels. It is no surprise

9. Whole rim + Over 50% rim + (Under 50% rim - Over 50% rim)/2. Numbers from Table 4.

10. When only bases are preserved, it can be difficult to determine whether the complete vessel bore black-figured decoration or not. Thus, 64 is the sum of recognizable black-figured cup-skyphoi and those characterized in the data as "black-glazed."

Figure 17. Proportions of drinking cups, (a) in household, using data from Table 6; (b) in entire deposit, using data from Table 5

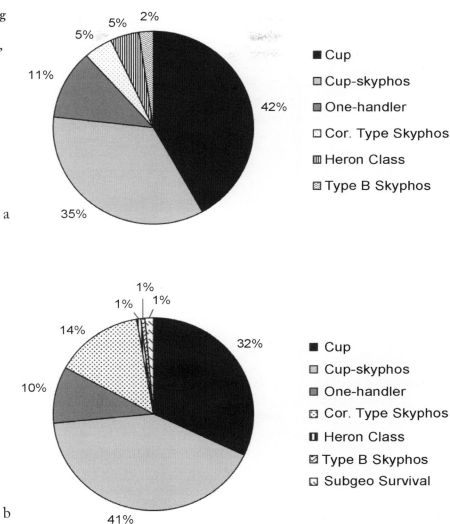

a

b

that lekanai and cooking vessels make up a large component of the household wares. If the MinNV tallies from Table 5 are used instead, the picture is slightly different (Fig. 18:b). Lekanai are more prevalent, closed vessels less so, suggesting that the tally for lekanai in Table 6 is also too low. Also notable on Figure 18:b is the large percentage of mortars. Their number on Table 6 is also likely to be low.

Finally, it is worthwhile in the context of this discussion to consider the large number of cooking-ware water jars in the deposit. For a majority of the water jars, only their bases were preserved, and since potters used the same base on all the cooking-ware water jar forms—hydriai, kadoi, and jugs—it is impossible to determine the form from the base alone. Therefore, using the bases to determine minimum number of vessels gives us an aggregate number for water jars. Using bases only, the minimum number of water jars is 94. In order to refine this picture, the Rotroff MinNV formula was applied to the rim counts from Table 4.[11] The results are presented at the top of Table 7. Analysis of the rims shows that kadoi make up 50% of the

11. Whole rim + Over 50% rim + (Under 50% rim - Over 50% rim)/2. Numbers from Table 4.

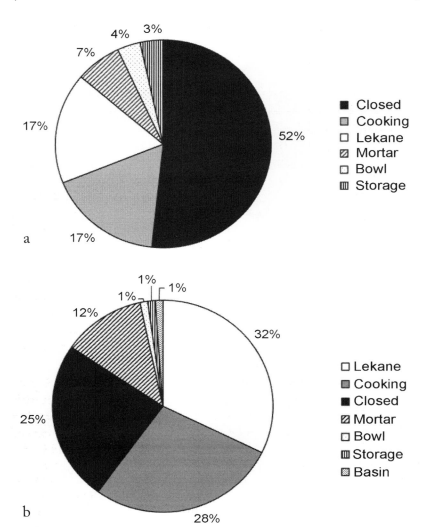

Figure 18. Household wares (not
including water jars): (a) proportions
by form, using data from Table 6; (b)
proportions in entire deposit, using
data from Table 5

water-jar forms, with jugs second and hydriai last. However, handle counts present a different picture. The vertical handles for kadoi, jugs, and even hydriai are similarly made, so that fragments are impossible to associate confidently with a particular form. Thus, the counts in Table 4 break down cooking-ware water-jar handles into "vertical" (kadoi, jugs, hydriai), and "horizontal" (which can only be hydriai). Some number of the vertical handles may properly belong in the hydria column. Table 7 (bottom) presents two possible situations representing maximum and minimum extremes. If all the vertical handles are assigned to kadoi and jugs (no hydriai), and the hydriai handles each represent an individual object, then the hydriai make up 57% of the water jars, with kadoi and jugs combined equaling 43%. Hypothetically, if each hydria took two handles, and this minimum number of hydriai, 34, all took a handle from the vertical handle counts, that would leave 17 kadoi and jugs. In this case, hydriai make up 67% of the water jars, and kadoi and jugs combine to equal 33%. But then there is the problem that kadoi have two handles and jugs have only one. Further refinement of the vertical handle assignments is not possible without

TABLE 7. PROPORTIONS OF COOKING-WARE WATER-JAR TYPES USING RIM AND HANDLE COUNTS

Rims	MaxNV	MinNV	Proportion (Using MinNV)
Kados	75	39	50%
Hydria	20	11	14%
Jug	51 (30 round/21 trefoil)	28 (26 round/12 trefoil)	36%
Handles	MaxNV	MinNV	Proportion (Using MaxNV–MinNV)
Horizontal handles = hydria	67	34	57%–67%
Vertical handles = kados/jug/hydria	51	17 (see discussion, pp. 151–152)	43%–33%

introducing speculative multipliers. Nevertheless, the handles suggest that the proportion of hydriai among the water jars should be between 57% and 67%, which is much higher than what the rims alone tell us. In sum, the hydriai handle counts indicate that hydriai and kadoi were the most popular cooking-ware water-jar forms, with the jug in third place. The exact proportions are difficult to assess.

This chapter has presented the quantification of the deposit's pottery. All aspects of the process of determining numbers are fraught with problems—from the initial determination of form to numerical rounding and philosophy of minimum number of vessel formulae, to, in the case of J 2:4, determining what part of the deposit's contents originated in the household. Therefore, the conclusions sketched out here are tentative at best, but nonetheless provide a plausible picture of the domestic assemblage. The most significant conclusion from this assessment is that this house was committed to communal drinking. They had invested in special-use pottery, and it made up the largest component of their ceramic household equipment.

CHAPTER 4

The Sympotic Context Part I: Drinking Vessels

The previous chapters introduced deposit J 2:4 and established its identification as fill from a house damaged by the Persians during the sack of Athens in 479. Although little remains of the house architecture, the pottery from the fill in well J 2:4 presents an artifactual view of household activities during the Late Archaic phase of the house. Chapter 3 explored the character of the deposit in more depth and identified the material most likely to have been in the cupboards of the Archaic house at the time of the Persian destruction. The contents of this well deposit are particularly important because they include pottery used during communal drinking events—symposia—presumably held in the house. The present and following chapters will examine more closely the individual artifacts from the fill of well J 2:4. Following the detailed presentation of artifacts from the house, Chapter 7 will consider the social importance of the communal drinking associated with this house. In Chapters 4 and 5 the shape and iconography of figured vessels is discussed within the chapter text, and the reader is referred to the Catalogue for further discussion of painter attribution, comparanda, and dating.

THE SYMPOSIUM

Studies of sympotic activity and equipment tend to take a synchronic and nonspatial approach.[1] Communal drinking events were a part of Greek and Roman culture from at least the 8th century B.C. through the 4th century A.D. and underwent significant changes in practice and attendant equipment along the way.[2] Thus a discussion of "sympotic equipment" without reference to chronological period can be misleading.[3] Descriptions of sympotic equipment often conflate shapes used by Athenians with shapes produced by Athenians mainly for export. For example, figured hydriai

1. For example, Vickers 1978; Davidson 1997, pp. 43–49; Smith 2003, pp. 13–46, especially pp. 18–19.

2. Some seek Bronze Age origins for the symposium (Węcowski 2002), and others see its reflection in Christian rites (Smith 2003).

3. For example, the krater, the quintessential vessel for an Archaic or Classical Greek symposium, is absent from the Hellenistic Greek sympotic set; see Rotroff 1996.

are frequently cited as components of sympotic assemblages, when in fact their numbers are disproportionately low in the households of Athens for the figured versions to have been a regular, required member of the typical Athenian sympotic assemblage.[4] The discussion below and the presentation of the sympotic set from well J 2:4 focus on equipment an actual Athenian would use in his house at the turn of the 5th century.[5] An understanding of specifically Athenian symposia will allow us to investigate how a real Athenian, not a hypothetical Athenian, selected equipment for entertainment in his own home.[6]

The archaeological find context and the context of use of figured vessels is increasingly important as we become aware that many pots were decorated with the export market in mind, not the Athenian table. The potters and painters must have known the destination for some of their pots, and a comparison of vases found in Athenian contexts and those exported, especially to Etruria, documents relationships between particular image types and their destinations. By identifying what shapes and scenes Athenians did consider appropriate for their household entertaining, we can better evaluate the meaning of those shapes and scenes *not* used in Athens. As businessmen, the Athenian potters and painters must have worked to please their discerning customers, whether they were Attic or not.[7]

The symposium was a communal drinking party for men held during the evening at the house of an individual.[8] Literary sources place the symposium in a space called the andron.[9] The term andron is frequently associated with archaeological remains of a square room with certain characteristics, including an off-center door, raised platforms along its walls, and floor and/or wall decoration. Recent scholarship has emphasized that not every house had a formal room for the symposium. Rather, the term more likely designates any space defined by the activity taking place at the time. Thus an andron would be the temporary or impermanent place of men's business, including the symposium, no matter whether it was held in a multipurpose room or the courtyard of a house.[10] In other words, you

4. According to Shear 1993, tables 2, 3, and 4, the total number of hydriai from Persian destruction deposits is: 14 black-figured in seven deposits; no red-figured and no black-glazed examples; but 30 household ware in 11 deposits.

5. Until now, discussions of Athenian sympotic assemblages referred to Rotroff and Oakley 1992, which presents a public dining assemblage, not a private one; see, e.g., Fisher 2000, pp. 361–362; Cahill 2002a, pp. 181, 186.

6. Herbert Hoffmann's argument (1994b, p. 71; 1997, pp. 1–17) that ceramic shapes were imitations of metal ware and were intended primarily for deposition in graves is untenable and fails to consider the presence of figured

wares in domestic deposits of pottery from the Athenian Agora excavations.

7. Hannestad 1988 on the home market. On iconography designed for the export market: Blinkenberg Hastrup 1999; La Genière 1999; 2009; Shapiro 2000; Lewis 2002, esp. pp. 116–120; 2009; Osborne 2002; but 2004, esp. pp. 92–93 disagrees; Paléothodoros 2002; Reusser 2002; Lynch 2009a; Schmidt 2009.

8. E.g., Plato's *Symposium* is set at the house of Agathon; Xenophon's *Symposium* at the house of Kallias Hipponikos. Vase-painting images of symposia place the activity in the house by depicting baskets, cups, and other implements hung on invisible walls above the drinkers. Occasionally in images of symposia architectural space is indi-

cated by a column at the side of the scene that demarcates the interior space of the house from the exterior world. The column stands symbolically for the built architecture of the house; see Lynch 2006.

9. See Nevett 1999, pp. 37–39, for a review of the ancient sources.

10. Cahill 2002a, p. 186. In those houses that had architecturally distinct andron rooms, these rooms might have served other purposes during the day, including women's work, when not in use by the men; see Nevett 1999, p. 71. The *gynaikon*, the women's quarters, may also be a space defined by activity at a certain time and not a permanent area of the house; Nevett 1999, p. 155.

do not need to have an andron room to hold a symposium.[11] Groups could gather in any room, or even in the space of the courtyard. Wherever the group gathered, it would arrange itself in a circular manner so that no one person was at a head position.[12] Although depictions of symposia in vase painting frequently show participants reclining on klinai, couches,[13] again, guests could recline on simple mattresses arranged around any appropriately sized space. Reclining, which probably entered Greece from the East,[14] signifies status in that reclining demands the attention of a servant. The relaxed position also emphasizes the participant's disengagement with physical activity for the evening and shifts the focus away from physical to intellectual pursuits.

One important characteristic of the symposium is that it focused on the communal consumption of wine, not food.[15] The host could offer a banquet before the drinking, but this was not necessary. If a meal preceded the drinking, there was a formal break between the activities to mark the beginning of the drinking phase.[16] The term symposion itself emphasizes the communal nature of wine drinking, which the Greeks considered the most appropriate manner in which to consume alcohol.[17] Drinking was not the only pursuit: the symposium was also the site of earnest discussions as preserved in dialogues of Plato and Xenophon and imitated by later authors. Sympotic literature emphasizes communal participation in the conversation as a parallel to communal participation in the drinking.

In order to emphasize the importance of communal drinking, Athenians developed special ceramic equipment exclusive to the functioning of a symposium.[18] Archaeologically, the presence of these special shapes in an assemblage indicates that the owner participated in formal drinking. The most essential item in a sympotic assemblage is the krater, a large "punch bowl."[19] The Athenians mixed their wine with water and prided themselves on the temperate mixture,[20] although the symposiasts could consume up to five kraters full of the temperate mixture.[21] The mixing took place during the symposium in the krater as a part of the drinking ritual. Wine might be brought to the symposium in a table amphora, but this shape is not common in Athenian assemblages, so it is likely that wine was poured directly from a transport amphora into the krater without an intermediary table

11. Lynch 2007.

12. Some vase painters try to represent the squared-circle arrangement of couches disposed around a room, but with moderate success: e.g., red-figured cup by Douris, Florence, Museo Archeologico 3922, *ARV*[2] 432, no. 55, *Add*[2] 237, Buitron-Oliver 1995, p. 79, no. 99, pl. 64, among others pictured there. Lissarrague (1990a, pp. 19–46, esp. 20–23) discusses the meaning of the depiction of space in sympotic scenes.

13. Boardman 1990, p. 122.

14. Dentzer 1971; see Boardman 1990, pp. 129–130, for the Eastern origin of the kline.

15. Murray 1990b, pp. 3–6.

16. See, e.g., Xen. *Symp.* 2.1; also Murray 1990b, p. 6; Schmitt Pantel 1992.

17. In contrast to solitary drinking, see Villard 1992. See also discussion in Davidson 1997, pp. 57–60.

18. All shapes discussed here were originally designed to accommodate a function within the symposium. It is human nature to use objects for practical purposes other than intended; e.g., a secondary use of any closed form might be to fetch water from a well. The present discussion is concerned only with primary intended function.

19. Lissarrague 1990b; Luke 1994, pp. 26–27.

20. Water was measured first, then wine added to it: Xenophanes, *PLG*[4], fr. 4 (= Ath. 11.782a). The proportion of wine and water varied from one to one up to three to four, and was set by the symposiarch in consultation with the drinkers (Pl. *Symp.* 176e, 177d, 213e). For proportions, see (possibly) Hes. *Op.* 593–596; Ath. 10.423–427; Plut. *Quaest. conv.* 3.9.

21. Euboulos, fr. 94 Kock (= Ath. 2.36b); Philochoros, *FGrH* 328 F 5b (= Ath. 2.38c–d).

vessel.[22] The same is true for water: fine-ware table hydriai are not very common in Athenian assemblages, but coarse-ware water jars abound. Water was probably fetched from the well with a suitable vessel, which could be anything from a coarse pitcher to a kados to a black-glazed pelike,[23] and then was poured into the krater.

A servant would then serve the mixed wine from the krater by dunking an oinochoe into the krater and pouring the wine into individual cups.[24] Although metasympotic scenes in vase painting show a male or female servant using a ladle for the task of decanting wine from the krater, few ceramic ladles (kyathoi) have been found in Athens.[25] Not essential to the proceedings, but useful, was the psykter, a wine cooler.[26] A psykter was a smaller, closed vessel that floated inside a krater filled with snow or cold water.[27] In this way, the wine might be chilled and maintained at a steady temperature without becoming diluted.

A symposiast might use any one of a variety of drinking-cup shapes. Stemmed shapes were designed specifically for use while reclining; their stem allows an easy grasp and their shallow bowls eliminate the need to tip the cup back to drink its contents. These cups, also known as kylikes, feature shallow bowls with two horizontal horseshoe-shaped handles on a stemmed foot.[28] A reclining drinker could hold the cup with his right thumb over the rim or handle and with his fingers on the broad bowl. The handle served only as a thumbrest while drinking, but the loop did facilitate the game of kottabos, in which wine lees were flicked from the bowl at a target.[29] When not in use, the cup could also be hung by its handle on a nail on a wall.[30] The tondos of many figured cups are painted so that the scene is not in line with the horizontal axis of the handles but rather is at an irregular angle. In the Catalogue entries for the kylikes from well J 2:4, an approximate orientation off-handle-axis is given for cup scenes. This seeming imperfection is probably another reflection of the use of the cups while reclining. It would be most comfortable to drink from a location approximately at the seven o'clock or eight o'clock area (with the handles at three o'clock and nine o'clock), if one held the cup with a thumb over the three o'clock handle. Drinking from the six o'clock area would put a

22. On the shoulder of a red-figured hydria attributed to Euthymides (Vatican City, Mus. Gregoriano 17752, *ARV*[2] 28, no. 14, *Add*[2] 155, Boardman 1975, fig. 35), a transport amphora is being emptied directly into a krater. This scene appears occasionally in both black figure and red figure.

23. For the use of pelikai as water vessels, see Lynch 2001a.

24. See, e.g., the red-figured cup attributed to the Cage Painter, Paris, Louvre G 133, *ARV*[2] 348, no. 7, Lissarrague 2001, p. 36, pl. 24.

25. See, e.g., the black-figured oinochoe by Kleisophos, Athens 1045, *ABV* 186, Lissarrague 1990a, fig. 77. The kyathoi pictured in vase painting

may be metal. One form of clay kyathos was made by Attic potters for the export market to Etruria: Eisman 1975, pp. 77, 82–83. The few clay kyathoi found in the Agora excavations are a different form, with long handle and hemispherical bowl and are not decorated, *Agora* XII, pp. 143, 306, nos. 996–1001, pl. 35; none of the Agora examples is from a context dating earlier than the mid-5th century. It is possible that metal kyathoi that do not survive were used in clay kraters. Other, small, dipping shapes could also be used to decant wine; see discussion in Catalogue entry for the chytra **186**.

26. *Agora* XII, pp. 52, 238–239, nos. 35–44, fig. 2, pl. 2.

27. Drougou 1975; Lissarrague 1990a, pp. 96–97, figs. 77, 78.

28. *Agora* XII, pp. 88–97, nos. 378–445, pls. 18–20. The genus "cup" includes Type A, Type B, and Type C, distinguished on the basis of formal features.

29. Sparkes 1960; Lissarrague 1990a, pp. 80–86; Csapo and Miller 1991.

30. In vase-painting scenes of the symposium, cups seem to float above the heads of the drinkers: e.g., red-figured cup by Douris, Florence, Museo Archeologico 3922, *ARV*[2] 432, no. 55, *Add*[2] 237, Buitron-Oliver 1995, p. 79, no. 99, pl. 64. The painter is trying to convey that the cups are hung from pegs on the walls.

drinker's right wrist in a cramped, uncomfortable position. In this way, the "off-centered" tondo scene accommodates the viewer's perspective, aligning the scene not perpendicular to the handles, but perpendicular to the drinker's mouth. This effect is clearest on **91**.

Skyphoi are flat-bottomed deep cups that were probably not exclusively used for drinking wine. Some, such as the Corinthian-type skyphos[31] have thin, delicate walls, and might not have been for everyday use. The Attic-type skyphos[32] has a similar form but with sturdier walls, and could survive more demanding use. The cup-skyphos,[33] a stouter version of the skyphos with cup handles, also seems designed for more frequent use. Figured cup-skyphoi (e.g., **46** and **47**) feature Dionysiac and other scenes that relate to the activities of the symposium, associating them securely with sympotic use.[34]

This overview of sympotic equipment has emphasized the relationship of the pottery forms to the unique practices of communal drinking in the Archaic period. Attic potters created a repertoire of forms to complement the activities of the symposium, especially its principles of equality and control. An examination of the sympotic objects in well J 2:4 allows us to move from expectations to an illustration of a single household's sympotic equipment. While the list of equipment is quite short, the reader is reminded that about half of this household's pottery was devoted to drinking wine. The cultural and economic investment in the symposium provides critical insight into the importance of drinking activities in the household. Because of the large scale of the investment it is all the more important to understand the relationship of the images on the sympotic vessels to the cultural goals of both Archaic Athenian society in general and one household in specific.

WINE CUPS IN WELL J 2:4

The contents of well J 2:4 reveal that a household could have more than one set of drinking cups. This house had three or possibly four sets of drinking cups for use in communal drinking. I define a set as more than one cup of a similar form and decoration; as we will see, these sets are further united by similarities of iconographic theme. The various sets of drinking cups do not seem to be accompanied by set-specific serving utensils, so that the same serving vessels must have been used whether they matched the set of cups or not. The interpretation of multiple sets is that each represents a different kind of communal drinking event that took place in the house. A set of red-figured cups best suits the traditional view of sympotic activity, and most likely was purchased to serve a traditional, formal symposium (**89–93, 95**; Color Ill. 1). Two red-figured cups with coral-red glaze (**87, 88**) stand out as a very special set and may relate to a drinking event restricted to just two participants. A set of black-figured cup-skyphoi contains a large number of these sturdy shapes good for frequent use (**45–47**; Color Ill. 2). Finally, a large, black-figured Heron Class skyphos (**28**) may have served a drinking event to which members of a limited community were invited, but perhaps acted as mixing bowl, not drinking cup (Color Ill. 8). In sum, the sympotic sets from this deposit demonstrate that communal drinking

31. *Agora* XII, pp. 81–83, 256–258, nos. 303–329, fig. 4, pls. 14, 15.

32. *Agora* XII, pp. 84–85, 259–260, nos. 334–354, fig. 4, pls. 16, 17.

33. *Agora* XII, pp. 109–112, 275–280, nos. 562–623, fig. 6, pls. 25–27.

34. See more complete black-figured versions: *Agora* XXIII, p. 288, no. 1564, pl. 104 with Dionysos; and p. 290, no. 1588, pl. 105, with Dionysos reclining, maenads, and satyrs. See also *Agora* XXX, p. 300, no. 1256, pl. 118, with a maenad; and p. 303, no. 1278, pl. 120, with a symposiast, later red-figured skyphoi that document the continued association of skyphoi with wine drinking.

was not a monolithic concept, but rather that the household participated in a variety of group drinking activities. It may be best to limit the term "symposium" and the activities it has come to imply to the use of the red-figured cup set and to use the term "communal drinking" for the other sets. The semantic point is to remind us that group drinking could occur in a range of formal types. In fact, one did not even need a matched set of cups to participate in communal drinking. Mixing of wine and water could occur in a utility bowl. The point was that a group drank together and bonded through this shared experience. That a house, such as the one of well J 2:4, did have not one but several sets of drinking cups reflects an increased formalization and specialization of the activity of drinking. Increased formalization further serves to distinguish the event from ordinary activities.[35] More will be said about why this distinction was necessary in Chapter 7.

A SET OF RED-FIGURED CUPS

Five Type C cups[36] with decoration limited to their tondos can be identified as a set through their similar shapes, decorative schemes, iconography, and workshops (89–93; Color Ill. 1). A sixth red-figured cup of smaller scale and different decorative scheme (95; Color Ill. 1), and a red-figured pelike (84; see Chapter 5), complement the set itself, and are linked through workshop and date to the cups. Table 6 records that the household owned a minimum of eight red-figured Type C cups. Level 5 of the deposit contains well-preserved examples, but it is impossible to know if other members of this set were disposed of elsewhere. Because we cannot be certain that all household material was discarded in well J 2:4, this project assumes that the cups are representative of what the household owned. A handful of red-figured cup fragments were found in the upper fill (Levels 1 and 2) of predominantly fragmentary material, and they will also be discussed in relation to this red-figured set, although they do not meet the criteria described in Chapter 3 for certain inclusion in the household's assemblage. Aside from the red-figured pelike and two fragments of other red-figured closed shapes (85 and 86, both from the upper fill of the well), the only red-figured objects in well J 2:4 were cups.

The kylix shape, with its stem and broad bowl, is the most frequently represented drinking vessel in sympotic scenes on vases, and was undoubtedly created for use in a formal sympotic context. It is unlikely—but not impossible—that a kylix would be used for any beverage other than wine. Thus, the red-figured kylikes represent evidence for participation in a more formal type of communal drinking than do black-figured cup-skyphoi, to be discussed below. The presence of the red-figured cups in well J 2:4 tells us that the household was entertaining guests formally. There was a rise in participation in formal symposia beginning late in the last quarter of the 6th century, and this may be tied to a democratization of the symposium or an appropriation of the symposium by participants in the new democracy in Athens. In other words, archaeological evidence for participation in symposia—kylikes—goes up in the last quarter of the 6th century, thus indicating that more people were drinking in this formal manner than ever before.[37] Our household is but one of many that bought a set of red-

35. Not unlike a Victorian dinner party; see Jameson 1987, p. 65.

36. Type C cups: *FAS*, pp. 111–136, pls. 32–36; *Agora* XII, pp. 91–92.

37. Lynch 2007, and below, Chapter 7.

figured kylikes around 500. The implications of the rise in popularity of the symposium and the purchase of sympotic equipment will be discussed further in Chapter 7.

The set of red-figured Type C cups may have included more than five items; however, these five are taken to be representative of the entire set, regardless of number. The evidence will show that these five form a close group selected with some thought, and similarities of form and style demonstrate that at least several were probably purchased at the same time. Each cup will be described individually and cups will be interrelated based on characteristics including workshops, profiles, and iconography. Detailed comparanda and attribution support are given in the individual Catalogue entries.

The first cup, **89** (Color Ills. 1, 3; Fig. 86), has in its tondo a figure of a nude, bearded male moving to the right. He has a himation tossed over his left shoulder and carries a Corinthian-type skyphos in his right hand.[38] He wears a wreath of leaves painted in added red. The figure is a typical adult male komast, and many parallels occur in Late Archaic red figure.[39] He is either on his way to an evening of communal drinking and is bringing along his own skyphos, or he is departing from the event, drink in hand, for a rousing walk about the neighborhood, the *komos*.[40] Either way, the man is associated with communal drinking through the skyphos and the wreath he wears. In the field around the figure is the inscription ΗΟΠΑΙΣ:ΚΑΛΟΣ, "the boy is beautiful" (Fig. 86). The evocation of a beautiful youth also has an appropriate place in the symposium.[41]

The preliminary attribution of this cup was "Close to Skythes,"[42] but it is more likely a product of the Ambrosios Painter, who must have been a student of Skythes. The inscription on **89** is in keeping with a particular stylistic trait of the Ambrosios Painter: the use of punctuation between noun and adjective. The inscription itself is without interest, as the generic formula is overwhelmingly common for the Late Archaic period; however, the painter used the less common punctuation of two vertical dots rather than the regular three-dot divider.[43] The use of the two-dot punctuation mark is seen on at least two other cups by the Ambrosios Painter with the *ho pais kalos* formula, on which it is used by the painter to separate *kalos* from the name of the one deemed beautiful.[44] In general, the use of the

38. The skyphos he holds is depicted with a double line just below the handle zone, thin horizontal handles, and narrowing lower body, which suggests a Corinthian-type skyphos rather than an Attic type. Cf. *Agora* XII, p. 257, no. 311, pl. 14.

39. The composition is a frequent tondo scene in the cups of Makron: Munich 2617, *ARV*[2] 480, no. 1, *Paralipomena* 379, *Add*[2] 247, Kunisch 1997, pl. 1, no. 1; Naples, Stg. 269, *ARV*[2] 466, no. 104, Kunisch 1997, pl. 127, no. 368; et alia.

40. For discussion of the *komos*, see Bron 1988; Gossel-Raeck 1990a,

1990b, 1990c; Kaeser 1990a.

41. On the meaning of *kalos* inscriptions, see Lissarrague 1999; Slater 1999; Brenne 2000.

42. Camp 1996, p. 248, no. 28, fig. 8, pl. 74. The preliminary attributions have provided a welcome starting point for the few refinements I offer here after extensive study of the objects and comparative material.

43. Jeffery 1990, p. 67. Note that Camp (1996, p. 248, no. 28) does not record the punctuation.

44. Boston, MFA Res. 08.31b, *ARV*[2] 174, no. 22, *Add*[2] 184, Vermeule 1969, p. 14, no. 14, pl. 11.2. In the text

Vermeule interprets the punctuation symbol as an iota, but the photograph indicates that this is a misreading. The inscription on London, E 817, *ARV*[2] 175, no. 32, Beazley 1918, fig. 12 bis (drawing) as reproduced has identical letter forms to that of **89**. On Brussels R349, *ARV*[2] 174, no. 24, the inscription is ΤΛΕΣΟΝ:ΚΑΛΟΣ; on Oxford 1911.616, *ARV*[2] 173, no. 1, *Add*[2] 184, the inscription is ΧΣΑΝ[Θ]ΕΣ:ΚΑΛΟΣ. Other cups probably preserve the punctuation mark, but facsimiles of the inscriptions are not always presented in publications.

punctuation mark to separate subject and adjective is not very common in inscriptions on red figure, but it is used by first-rate painters including Douris and the Brygos Painter.[45] In addition, the letters on **89** are spaced evenly and are very legible.[46] Red-figured cup **90** exhibits a nearly identical inscription.

Potting details link this cup to others in well J 2:4. The profile of **89** is nearly identical to that of **90**, indicating that they are the products of the same potter. The formal details of the feet of these Type C cups place them around Hansjorg Bloesch's cup profile subgroup of *Die Fortschrittliche Richtung*.[47] Bloesch includes in this group cups painted by the Epeleios Painter, the Euergides Painter, and the Ambrosios Painter,[48] painters present among the red-figured set from well J 2:4 as well as the two intentional red cups (discussed below).

The second red-figured cup, **90**, (Color Ills. 1, 4; Fig. 87) depicts a youth running to the right holding strips of meat, looking back left. In the field around him is another ΗΟΠΑΙΣ:ΚΑΛΟΣ inscription (Fig. 87) in added red. The youth wears a *zoma*, essentially a loincloth, tied about the waist. This is a garment often associated with slaves, craftspeople, and workers for its freedom of movement.[49] He is probably a slave or delivery boy bringing the evening's snacks to the host's house. The idea of speed is conveyed through the pose, the (modified) swastika disposition of the limbs, a conventional Archaic indication of rapid movement that has a long history in Greek art.[50] The added red on the strips, a somewhat unusual detail for meat on vases, draws the viewer's eye to them and identifies the meat as the real star of the scene.

Cup **90** was also preliminarily attributed to a hand "close to Skythes";[51] however, like **89**, it is more likely associated with the Ambrosios Painter. Not only are there strong similarities between the styles of **89** and **90**, but **90** can independently be attributed to the Ambrosios Painter based on the pose of the figure, the depiction of anatomy, the rendering of the hair and drapery, and the inscription. The inscription on **90** is identical to that of **89**. In particular, the forms of the alphas, pis, and lambdas are exact matches (cf. Figs. 86, 87). The inscriptions also start and stop in approximately the same place in the tondo field, allowing for variation due to the different poses. Finally, the profile of the cup **90** is also nearly identical to that of

45. It was used much more frequently in black figure when inscriptions formed part of the decorative scheme of the vase; see Jeffery 1990, p. 67.

46. This is not always the case with the Ambrosios Painter's inscriptions; see Immerwahr 1984a, p. 11, n. 11.

47. *FAS*, pl. 33, no. 6, Munich 2595, Epeleios Painter, *ARV* ² 148, no. 37.

48. *FAS*, p. 123.

49. Pekridou-Gorecki 1989, pp. 87, 128–130. See also Pritchett 1956, on the inventory of garments on the Attic Stelai. Cf. Berlin, Antikenmuseum 1980.7, Pekridou-Gorecki 1989, fig. 74; Brussels, Musées Royaux A717, *ARV* ²

20, no. 1 [Smikros], Boardman 1975, fig. 32.1; London E 23, *ARV* ² 179, no. 1 [The Carpenter Painter, name vase], Boardman 1975, fig. 124; Providence, RISD 25.109, *CVA* Providence RISD 1 [USA 2], pl. 17 [70]:1a, b; Vienna, University 53c 1, *ARV* ² 560, no. 154 [The Pan Painter], *CVA* Vienna 1 [Germany 5], pl. 10 [204]:18. A garment wrapped around the waist is not always associated with slaves or workers. It appears also on hoplites and komasts. E.g., hoplite: Amsterdam, Allard Pierson Museum 591, *ARV* ² 177, no. 1 [Painter of the Agora Charias Cups], *CVA* Amsterdam Allard Pierson Museum 1 [Netherlands 6],

pl. 23 [278]:2; komasts: Tübingen S/665, *ABV* 375, no. 219 (Leagros Group), *CVA* Tübingen 2 [Germany 44], pl. 39 [2140].

50. On the Ambrosios Painter's Oxford cup with Dionysos in the tondo, the god also moves to the right in the modified swastika running pose, holding objects in his outstretched hands; the position of the feet is nearly identical to **90**, Oxford 1917.55, *ARV* ² 174, no. 21, *CVA* Oxford 1 [Great Britain 3], pl. 1 [93]:3.

51. Camp 1996, p. 248, no. 29, fig. 8, pl. 74. The inscription as recorded in Camp 1996 does not present the punctuation.

89 (cf. Figs. 86, 87), indicating that they are products of the same potting establishment, if not of the same potter. They both belong in Bloesch's *Die Fortschrittliche Richtung* group.

The subject of the tondo decoration relates to entertaining within the house. The meat being hurriedly brought home foreshadows the enjoyment of a future meal. The speed of the youth's pace, implied by the swastika disposition of the limbs, will ensure that the meat is fresh and indicates that it is needed at home for immediate preparation.[52] Similar strips of meat are frequently depicted draped over the low tables in front of drinkers in vase-painting images of symposia.[53] The presence of foodstuffs is usually taken to be a reference to the dining that occurs prior to the drinking, that is, a telescoping of the evening's events into one image, but snack items such as sausages, bread, and small cakes accompanied the drinking itself. Such snacks would help the drinkers pace their alcohol consumption.

The youth wears an added red wreath on his head. If the garment he wears is that of a slave or worker, it is possible that the wreath marks him as an "honorary" member of the drinking festivities who facilitated the activity—like the wine bearers, who also wear wreaths in sympotic scenes.[54] The activity on cup **91** (Color Ills. 1, 5; Fig. 88), with a youth treading grapes, complements this scene of the youth bringing the meat, and they should be taken as a pair representing preparations that culminate in the viewers' simultaneous enjoyment of them. It is also possible that the youth's wreath is a reference to the sacrificial event from which he procured the meat for his master.[55] Some scholars assume that all meat consumed in ancient Greece originated in sacrifice and that the average Greek ate meat rarely, but the abundance of bones in domestic deposits suggests that Greeks ate meat regularly.[56] It seems unlikely that all meat consumed originated from ritual sacrifice.

52. It is possible that these are fresh sausages, as opposed to salted, dried sausages; on the different kinds of sausages, see Dalby 2003, p. 294.

53. E.g., Munich, Antikensammlungen 2301, *ABV* 255, no. 4 [Andokides Painter bilingual], Boardman 1974, fig. 161. However, these too may be sausages.

54. Wreaths were a common sympotic accessory; see Blech 1992, pp. 63–74, and sources: Ath. 15.669c–686c; Archestratus, fr. 60 (62 Brandt), line 1, Olson and Sens 2000, pp. 224, 226–227, p. 227 on references to businesses selling wreaths in 5th-century Athens.

55. Jenifer Neils (pers. comm.) first suggested this connection. Sparkes (1995, pp. 158–159) points out that crowns were a "popular space-filling decoration in late black-figure," and hesitates to connect the wreathed heads with officiants or participants in a sacrifice. Even the carpenter on the Carpenter Painter's name vase, a cup, wears a wreath; thus, the wreathed figures more likely reflect the sympotic environment in which the drinker participates than sacred activity. Sparkes (1995, pp. 158–159) believes that the butchers of meat and fish are images of secular nature. He does not explore the relationship of meat procurement and sacrifice, and he seems to accept that some meat came from a secular butcher. The case may be similar to Kosher butchering, in which a rabbi's blessing on the animal is required before slaughter, but the meat end-products are consumed on the daily table. Household ritual should not be ruled out as accounting for some of the faunal remains found in houses, but it is not the only possible origin.

Fish butchers in two black-figured images wear the same garment and wreaths as the figure in **90**; see Berlin, Antikenmuseum F1915, *ABV* 377, nos. 247 and 382 (Leagros Group), *CVA* Berlin 7 [Germany 61], pl. 36 [3029]. Figures also wear the *zoma* in sacrificial scenes: krater by the Pan Painter, Naples, *ARV*² 551, no. 15, Beazley 1931b, no. 12, pl. 30. Another example of the garment worn by attendants in scenes of sacrifice: Warsaw 142464 (ex Goluchów, Musée Czartoryski 79), *ARV*² 797, no. 142, *CVA* Goluchów, Musée Czartoryski 1 [Poland 1], pl. 34 [34]:3a–c.

56. Durand and Schnapp (1984), Davidson (1997, p. 18), and others see all meat as related to sacrifice and all scenes of butchering as related to the act of sacrifice. Wilkins and Hill (2006, pp. 143–144) present a less dogmatic view and argue that meat from sacrifice could have been preserved for consumption later.

The third red-figured cup, **91**, preliminarily attributed to the Epeleios Group[57] but here to a painter in the Manner of the Euergides Painter, depicts a frontal youth squatting in a large vessel.[58] The youth is probably treading grapes, so the vessel he stands in should be taken as a lug-handled vat akin to a bell krater.[59] His torso and limbs are seen frontally, but his head is profile looking to the left. His left leg is raised up, while his right is below the line of the vat. This is a treading motion and is seen on a cup in Boston (in reverse, with right leg up) with another frontal figure, an adult male this time, in a vat.[60] On **91**, the youth holds short, sticklike objects in each hand, which are probably meant to be attached to supporting ropes to help him keep his balance in the round-bottomed vessel made slippery with grape skins. In comparable scenes of treading grapes, the treader often grips a rope hanging from above even if he stands in a flat-bottomed container such as a basket.[61] In a recently published cup in Taranto associated with the Euergides Painter, a youth treads in a krater, his right hand raised in a fist, but there is no sign of a stick or rope.[62] Both stick and rope are implied, as is the rope on **91**. The exterior scenes of the Taranto cup depict komasts, strengthening the interpretation that its treading youth is preparing grapes to produce the wine needed for *komos* activities.

The youth treading grapes is the conceptual equivalent of the youth bringing the meat on **90**. In both cases the youths are preparing elements of the evening's entertaining. These "genre" scenes come to life as the guest consumes the meat and wine figuratively depicted on the cups. Both youths are wreathed, possibly indicating their status also as honorary "members" of the evening's activities, even though they are not direct participants. These two processes of daily life are idealized and complement the sentiments of *ho pais kalos*. That handsome youths prepared the food and drink may be a bit of fantasy for the drinker.[63]

57. Camp 1996, p. 250, no. 30, fig. 8, pl. 74. Note that the transcription of the inscription published there is incorrect; see Fig. 88:d for a facsimile.

58. The Euergides Painter and those associated with him are related to the Epeleios Group; see *ARV*[2] p. 104: "Cups Mingling Epeleian Elements and Euergidean."

59. There are many examples of youths and satyrs in or beside large bell-krater-shaped vessels, and there has been much discussion about what the figures are doing; see Robertson 1992, pp. 75–76. Beazley describes London, V&A 4807.1901, *ARV*[2] 89, no. 14 as "youth in a bell-krater (treading grapes)." Immerwahr (1992, pp. 124–25, n. 15) reviews some of the hypotheses. A once-popular hypothesis was that figures associated with the lug-handled vessels are bathing, but Ginouvès (1962, pp. 51–54) concludes that processing grapes is more likely

than bathing for most of the scenes in which the youth is depicted *inside* the vessel. Sparkes (1976, p. 53, and n. 59) agrees. See Castle Ashby 56, *ARV*[2] 91, no. 50 [Euergides Painter], *CVA* Castle Ashby [Great Britain 15], pl. 34 [689]:4, for a similar lug-handled krater on a flat base, which must be a separate stand, since it does not recall any known pottery base forms.

60. Boston, MFA 24.453, *ARV*[2] 129, no. 28 [unattributed, Pamphaios potter], Immerwahr 1984b, no. 43, pl. 44. Another cup with a frontal youth in a vat (London, V&A 4807.1901, *ARV*[2] 89, no. 14, Sparkes 1976, fig. 15, attributed to the Euergides Painter himself) also suggests a treading motion, but the youth squats so low in the vat that his legs are not visible. This cup is discussed below.

61. On the cup Boston MFA 24.453, *ARV*[2] 129, no. 28 [unattributed, Pamphaios potter], Immerwahr 1984b,

no. 43, pl. 44, the adult male grabs a single loop descending from the tondo border with his raised right hand. Another frontal, treading youth, once Arlsheim, Schweizer Collection, *ARV*[2] 1593, mentioned in text of no. 37, Sparkes 1976, p. 53, fig. 17, holds on to two similar loops hanging from the tondo border. Treading in a basket: Immerwahr 1992, p. 125. The motif is common in black figure; see Sparkes 1976 for discussion. A red-figured example: Basel, Private Collection (Cahn), *ARV*[2] 1632, added as no. 49 bis [Kleophrades Painter], Sparkes 1976, fig. 19.

62. Taranto, Vinc. 108/2, *CVA* Taranto 4 [Italy 70], pl. 22 [3189]:2. In the text to the plate the subject is described as an athlete bathing.

63. A modern analogy might be the kind of calendar often found in mechanics' garages that features images of buxom women in revealing outfits pretending to repair cars. The mechanic

The cup should be assigned to the Manner of the Euergides Painter rather than to the painter himself. The stylistic details, the composition, and the inscription all point to a group of cups in the Manner of the Euergides Painter that use some of the same subjects.[64] The Euergides Painter himself favored scenes with youths and big round-bottomed vatlike vessels,[65] but the youths in his vats are usually in profile and bending over so that their backs form an arch that balances the abbreviated bottom of the vat.

The inscription around the figure on **91**, ΠΡΟΣΑΓΟΡΕΥΩ (Fig. 88), also relates the cup more to the Manner of the Euergides Painter.[66] Only one cup on which the Euergides Painter himself placed this inscription survives,[67] but it is very common on cups attributed to the Manner of the Euergides Painter.[68] The cups with the *prosagoreuo* inscriptions are all related through the workshops of the potters Paidikos and Pasiades, who may be the same man.[69] The inscription is translated as "I address you!" or "I greet you!"[70] but it is unclear whether the youth addresses the viewer, the inscription is merely a convivial toast, or the greeting is a surrogate for the host's welcome.[71] Convivial inscriptions such as *chaire!* were fashionable on black-figured band cups shortly after the middle of the 6th century.[72] A renewed interest in convivial inscriptions is apparent among the Pioneer red-figure artists, who were very interested in the written word on pots.[73]

Both the tondo scene and the inscription reflect the cup's use in communal drinking. The boy prepares the wine, the essential element of the gathering. Without wine the gathering would not occur. Just as the *ho pais kalos* inscriptions evoke a sympotic setting, the convivial greeting would also evoke a friendly evening where the drinker is welcomed and warmly included in the activities. The first-person address, as opposed to the imperative, further personalizes the greeting.[74]

The profile of **91** is nearly identical to two black-glazed cups from the deposit, **135** (Fig. 112) and **136** (Color Ill. 1; Fig. 112). Not only are the proportions and dimensions similar, but all feature a well-molded fillet between carefully incised lines at the base of the stem. These three cups

---

does not really believe the young women are fixing cars, but the juxtaposition of expected roles for attractive women and the rough and dirty world of car repair is a pleasant fantasy for the viewer.

64. *ARV²*, pp. 97–101.

65. The Euergides Painter is so consistent in his compositional types that Rouillard (1975, pp. 41–43) has classified his compositions into several different schemes. The youth with the vat is Scheme B.

66. Immerwahr (1998, no. 2558) agrees that the inscription places the cup around the Euergides Painter and not around the Epeleios Painter.

67. Bologna 561, *ARV²* 88, no. 10. There is no record of a tondo inscription on London, V&A 4807.1901, *ARV²* 89, no. 14.

68. The *prosagoreuo* inscription also appears on other shapes and in several other hands that must all be related: on alabastra in the Manner of the Euergides Painter and on alabastra of the Group of the Paidikos Alabastra, *ARV²*, pp. 98–101; on a group of cups that Beazley describes as belonging "to the same stylistic group as Louvre CA 487 [*ARV²* 103, no. 13]"; on an alabastron signed by the painter Paidikos, *ARV²*, p. 103; and on a cup "Related to cups in the manner of Euergides Painter" by a hand identified as the Painter of Bologna 433: Bologna 433, *ARV²* 106, no. 2.

69. *ARV²* 102, bottom.

70. LSJ, s.v. προσαγοράζω.

71. Giving voice to the cup is discussed in Lissarrague 1985; 1990a, pp. 60–67; 1992.

72. See Immerwahr 1990, pp. 45–54, in the context of his discussion of Little Master cups; Fellmann 1990; Lissarrague 1990a, pp. 60–65, with examples. See also Slater 1999, pp. 153–154, who uses the addresses as an example of dialogue prompted by the inscriptions on vases.

73. See Immerwahr's discussion (1990, pp. 58–74) of the various types of inscriptions on the Pioneer vases, and the discussion of the meaning of *kalos* inscriptions by Slater (1999, pp. 143–161), who sees them as part of the discourse and performance of the symposium. He does not discuss the *prosagoreuo* inscriptions. See also Neer 2002.

74. Lissarrague 1990a, pp. 59–67, esp. 61–62.

must have been made by the same potter and provide additional evidence for a single potter producing vases for both figured and plain decoration.[75]

The fourth red-figured cup, **92**, (Color Ills. 1, 6; Fig. 89) features an owl in the tondo.[76] The owl has a frontal head and stands profile to the right with wings folded under. His body feathers are indicated with black-glazed dots in rows. A single line defines the wing, and the wing feathers are indicated with a series of parallel lines separated from the body by a wavy line.[77] On both sides of the owl is a reserved curly tendril. Thin fronds or leaves in added white, now fugitive, appear above the tendrils in pairs, and a single frond appears in the field between the right tendril and the owl's foot. There is an inscription in added red, also fugitive, in the field to the left of the owl (discussed below).

The owl on this cup is similar in design to the owls on the popular Type B skyphoi called glaukes, which probably begin contemporary with this cup, ca. 500.[78] Our cup shares the characteristics that Franklin Johnson defines as early for the skyphoi: "large dot for the pupil," "two circles around [the eye]," "the beak is triangular," "the entire face is dotted except for eyes and beak," "wavy lines across the wings indicating the end of feathers."[79] Owls appear less often in vase painting than one would expect, which may have something to do with a belief that owls are afraid of pots;[80] however, they do appear on a variety of shapes made ca. 500.[81]

The owl is a reference to Athena, and by extension a symbol of the Athenian state. The owl began to appear on the coinage of Athens from the last decades of the 6th century, and thus became identified with the state of Athens.[82] The owl also appears on amphoras of official measure with one example, now in Munich, attesting to the use of the type ca. 500,[83] although most examples of official use date much later than **92**.[84] The tondo

75. On potters producing both figured and black-glazed pottery, see *Agora* XII, pp. 13–15, 28–31. Oakley notes (2004, p. 65) that evidence for the relationship of figured and black-glazed production is welcome validation of assumptions and hypotheses.

76. Camp 1996, p. 250, no. 32, pl. 75. Preliminarily attributed to the Sabouroff Painter; however, I have not found evidence to support this attribution. Kreuzer (1999, pp. 224–225) places it in a workshop with an owl oinochoe, Capua 222, *CVA* Capua 2 [Italy 23], pl. 19 [1094]:10. Note that the inscription as reported in Camp 1996, p. 250, no. 32, is incorrect; see Fig. 89:d for a facsimile.

77. Lamberton and Rotroff (1985, pp. 12–13) discuss the species *Athene noctua* and its development as the symbol of the Athenian polis; see also Pollard 1977, p. 39; Kreuzer 1999.

78. On the dating of **92**, see Kreuzer 1999, p. 224. On the dating of the glaukes, see Dinsmoor 1934, pp. 419–420. Glaukes from early-5th-century contexts: Graef and Langlotz II, varia, see Johnson 1955, pp. 119–120, 123, figs. 30–38, pl. 37. The majority of the Agora glaukes belong to the middle decades of the 5th century; see *Agora* XXX, p. 64 and nn. 21, 22.

79. Johnson 1955, p. 119.

80. Ar. *Av.* 358; Pollard (1977, p. 39, n. 158), however, notes that the meaning of this line of Aristophanes is still unclear.

81. Other early solitary or nonsubsidiary owls on pots other than cups and glaukes: a red-figured kalpis, Getty 86.AE.229, *CVA* Getty 7 [USA 32], pl. 352 [1629] (Group of the Floral Nolans); a black-figured amphora, Munich 9406, Schauenburg 1988, figs. 3, 4; a red-figured Type B amphora, Kyoto, inv. no. 8 (Berlin Painter?), *CVA* Japan 1, pl. 1 [1].

82. See Kreuzer 1999 for the symbolic role of the owl as a representation of the order of the polis. She also explores the relationship of the owl vase motif with owls on coins. See *Agora* XXVI, p. 5 and n. 6, for scholarship supporting an association of the Athena head/owl type with the Peisistratid Hippias. The owl also appears on official dry measures as early as the first half of the 5th century; see *Agora* X, p. 49, DM 4, DM 5, pls. 13, 18, 33. Hoffmann (1994a, pp. 37–38) explores the relationship between Athena, the owl, and the olive. Essentially, the owl is a fearsome hunter and shares the "bright eyes" of Athena. See also the discussion in Lamberton and Rotroff 1985, pp. 12–13; Bron 1992, pp. 47–63; Hurwit 1999, p. 8.

83. Munich 9406, unattributed, ca. 500; Kaeser 1987, pp. 228–231, figs. 5, 6, 9.

84. For the Agora evidence: see *Agora* X, pp. 59–60, LM 12–20, black-figured amphoras with the head of Athena, owl, and the inscription *demosion*.

of **92** was painted in this milieu of developing owl imagery; therefore, it is likely that the viewer was expected to make a connection between the cup's iconography and the Athenian state.

Cup **92** includes an inscription in added red starting below the reserved tendril to the left of the owl and continuing to the top of his head: Ε[Λ]ΟΧΟΣΕΝ (Fig. 89). The letters are small, but formed clearly enough not to doubt this reading.[85] It probably expands to: "ἐγὼ χοῦς ἤν"[86] or "ἐγὼ χοῦς ἦν."[87] ΕΓΟ, the first-person pronoun, is rare in vase inscriptions.[88] The tent-form gamma is perfectly acceptable for the early 5th century.[89] We would expect the nominative of chous to be spelled χοῦς but Ο can represent omega in Late Archaic orthography, and omega can in turn stand for the ΟΥ diphthong in Archaic Attic dialect.[90] ΕΝ could either be ἤν ("look!") or ἦν (the first person singular imperfect of εἰμί). The first reading translates, "Look! I am a chous"; the second, "I was being a chous." In the first case the emphasis is on the quantity with the particle drawing the attention of the reader. In the second reading, the drinker would drain his cup to find this humorous but exaggerated reminder of how much he has drunk. This cup has a volume of 633 ml, which is 3/16 of the official measure of a chous, 3,200 ml.[91] The cup certainly does not hold a chous. There is a parallel for the inscription on a two-handled cup of Subgeometric type (early 7th century) found by Carl Blegen at an early shrine in the vicinity of the Argive Heraion.[92] This cup bears the retrograde, local script inscription ΧΟΣ{Η}ΕΜΙ.[93] The ΧΟΣ is taken by all as a reference to the chous measure. Barry Powell sees the inscription on this Subgeometric cup as a joke, "I hold a whole gallon!"[94] If Powell's theory is right, then the inscription on **92** may be a joke backed up with the state's "authority" as portrayed by the owl symbol.

The inscription on **92** may also be a joke about the potency of the cup's contents implying "Drinking me has the effect of drinking a whole chous," or "Keep (re)filling me and you will drink a whole chous." It may also refer to the second day of the Anthesteria festival, the Choes, which involved a speed-drinking contest in which the first to drink down a chous of wine was the winner.[95] The cup's inscription may be a prompt for the drinker to drink the wine in one gulp in imitation of the practice of the Choes drinking contest.

A second, simultaneous joke may be on the sound the small owl makes. An ancient Greek word for owl, κουκούβη, is onomatopoeic, incorporating the "cooo cooo" sound the owl makes.[96] On a Type B red-figured amphora

85. *Epoisen* and *egrapsen* do not fit the letters even with generous allowances for misspellings.

86. Matthias Steinhart suggested this reading (pers. comm.).

87. Rex Wallace suggested this reading (pers. comm.).

88. It appears on a black-figured band cup from the Agora (P 30782, Camp [1986] 1992, p. 136, fig. 110), spoken from the mouth of a man playing a dice game.

89. Immerwahr 1990, p. 135.

90. Immerwahr 1990, p. 81 and n. 3.

91. *Agora* X, p. 47. Richard Anderson, architect for the Athenian Agora Excavations, assisted with the calculations of volume.

92. Blegen 1939, pp. 425–426, no. 414, fig. 13.

93. *SEG* XI 306: χός ἐμί; Jeffery 1990, p. 150, no. 11: χός ηεμι, which she (p. 149) attributes tentatively to a dialect of Kleonai.

94. Powell 1989, p. 329, no. 31. Jeffery (1990, p. 149, n. 1) admits that

the translation of this inscription is difficult. She suggests that a local standard chous might have been much less than an Attic chous and that "chous" need only refer to the cup itself.

95. See Hamilton 1992, pp. 10–33, for literary testimony and description of the contest.

96. LSJ Supplement, s.v. κουκούβη. In Aristophanes's *Birds* (261), the owls make the sound κικκαβαυ.

with an owl now in the Hashimoto collection[97] there is a postproduction graffito under the owl's beak: KYYY. Beazley suggested that a young Greek boy must have wanted this striking owl to speak and animated the figure with the addition of the call "cooo."[98] The similarity of the sound the owl makes to the word "chous" might have created a pun in the ears of the reader/drinker.

The first-person address also reminds us of the greeting on **91**, the cup with the youth treading grapes. Unlike the greeting, the owl's inscription seems more likely to emanate from the owl himself and not the cup or another intangible source. In contrast with a glaux skyphos, the arresting, frontal owl in the cup tondo would have suddenly appeared to the drinker as he drained his wine.

The size and shape of **92** is very similar to **89**, **90**, and **91**, but the profile may indicate a different potter. The upper surface of the foot of **92** is more inclined than the others, and the profile has no direct parallel in Bloesch but comes closest to the same group as those above.

Cup **93** (Color Ills. 1, 7; Fig. 90) differs from the preceding cups in several ways. In its tondo is an eight-spoke wheel. A pleasing geometric design filling the tondo field is unusual for red figure and departs from typical figural images in cup tondos. The eight spokes meet at a round hub, or nave, at the center, where the spokes are lashed together with bindings.[99] The border of the tondo forms the exterior of the wheel rim (felloe), and the interior rim is scalloped with arcs between each spoke.[100] The spokes create eight black-glazed sections, and in the curved, outer edge of each section is a thick crescent of added white, somewhat fugitive. At least one section has a blob of added white at the point near the hub. In each black-glazed section is a single letter in added red. Unfortunately, the color is fugitive and the letters are carelessly written so that the inscription is nearly illegible (see Fig. 90).[101] The letters seem to be oriented with their tops toward the tondo border. A larger, better-drawn letter may indicate the top of the wheel. This letter is a round letter and most resembles an O. Moving counterclockwise, the next letter is probably a K. The following letter is more difficult to interpret, but it may be a T or an A. If it is a T then this may be a word with an οκτ- prefix written retrograde around the wheel. Γ seems certain for the letter five from the first (counterclockwise), but no word fits the spaces and shapes of letters properly.

The chariot is popular in black- and red-figure iconography, and it appears in a variety of scenes such as marriages and the introduction of Herakles. Spoke wheels appear in scenes of Ixion in Hades and as shield devices, but **93** is the only example I have found where a wheel is used alone as a tondo motif. The most common wheels on vehicles and as shield motifs in red figure have four spokes, not eight.[102] The eight-spoke wheel occurs

97. Kyoto, inv. no. 8, with a single owl, *CVA* Japan 1, pl. 1 [1].

98. Beazley 1927, p. 348.

99. See Crouwel 1992, pp. 34–38, for the vocabulary and details of wheel construction.

100. These may be triangular wedges to give the spokes support:

Crouwel 1992, pp. 36–37.

101. See Immerwahr 1990, 47: "the invention of red-figure is bad for Attic calligraphy." Added red inscriptions in red figure use a softer brush than added red inscriptions on black figure.

102. See Crouwel 1992, p. 35: "Since four-spoke wheels appear so

often and in different media, it seems likely that this number is not merely artistic short-hand to indicate *any* spoke wheel but that it reflects actual practice in Greece." He lists some of the six- and eight-spoke representations (pp. 34–35, n. 104).

in vase painting infrequently, and often much later than **93**.[103] In several examples where the chariot appears to have an eight-spoke wheel, I think that the painter is attempting—unsuccessfully—to show both wheels of a chariot simultaneously.[104] In fact, it is difficult to argue that any of the so-called eight-spoke wheels are not simply two four-spoke wheels superimposed, spokes distributed in a balanced, decorative manner.[105] The only incontrovertible examples of eight-spoke wheels are on shield devices used by the Niobid Painter.[106] It is possible his use of this shield device may be a reference to Hera's chariot described in the *Iliad* as having eight spokes, and thus it would lend a heroic touch to his battle and departure scenes.[107] The eight-spoke wheel did exist; it was particularly popular for chariots used in east Greece and the Near East, and one was found at Olympia.[108] One final explanation for the number of spokes should be considered. The arrangement of spokes on **93** might simply be designed to accommodate the eight sections required for the eight-lettered inscription.[109] The explanation

103. Eight-spoke wheels: Ferrara 1499, *ARV*² 554, no. 83, *Paralipomena* 386, *Add*² 258 [Pan Painter], *LIMC* VIII, 1997, p. 62, no. 97, pl. 37, s.v. Triptolemos (G. Schwarz); Louvre C 10833, *ARV*² 558, no. 130, *Add*² 259 [Pan Painter], *LIMC* VIII, 1997, p. 62, no. 98, pl. 37, s.v. Triptolemos (G. Schwarz); Boston, MFA 98.935 (unattributed oinochoe of ca. 400), Vermeule 1970, fig. 4; Berlin Staat-liche Museen F2372 (unattributed loutrophoros of ca. 430, ex Sabouroff Collection), Oakley and Sinos 1993, figs. 72, 73; Oxford 1981.683 (V.315), *ARV*² 229, no. 47 [Eucharides Painter], *CVA* Oxford 1 [Great Britain 3] pl. 33 [125]:1 (but the author suggests "spokes of both wheels given?"); Louvre G 368, *ARV*² 502, no. 10 [Painter of the Yale Oinochoe], *CVA* Louvre 3 [France 4], pl. 8 [169]:2; Berlin F2521, *ARV*² 516, no. 18, *CVA* Berlin 3 [Germany 22] pl. 130 [1059]:6. Greek depictions of the Ixion myth all feature a four- or six-spoke wheel; see *LIMC* V, 1990, s.v. Ixion (C. Lochin).

104. Cf. examples where the painter has carefully drawn both wheels as overlapping, but at first glance there appears to be only one wheel of eight spokes: Acropolis 742, *ARV*² 205, no. 117 [Berlin Painter], Graef and Langlotz II, pl. 59, no. 742; Brussels R235, *CVA* Brussels 2 [Belgium 2] pl. 19 [72]:4b; London, E 183, *ARV*² 1191, no. 1 [Painter of London E 183], *CVA* London British Museum 6 [Great Britain 8], pl. 84 [359]: 2a; Louvre, G 452, *ARV*² 921, no. 33 [Aberdeen

Painter], *LIMC* VIII, 1997, p. 962, no. 101, pl. 645, s.v. Persephone (G. Günter). Vermeule (1970, p. 101) has her doubts about the wheel on the Dexileos vase and attributes the eight spokes to the painter's confusion about how to depict both wheels. The same may be true of Ferrara 1499, the Cleve-land Painter's vase where only seven spokes are shown. The evenly placed spokes on a "six-spoke" wheel illustrate the disposition two four-spoke wheels with the chariot car blocking two of the far wheel's spokes: red-figured krater, Tarquinia, Museo Nazionale, no inv. no., *ARV*² 1073, no. 14, *Add*² 326 [akin to the Group of the Villa Giulia Painter], *LIMC* III, 1986, p. 750, no. 6, pl. 563, s.v. Eos (C. Weiss).

105. Neils (1996), in a discussion of the name vase of the Cleveland Painter, Cleveland, 1930.104, *ARV*² 516, no. 1, on which an eight-spoke wheel appears on a chariot in a processional scene, interprets the scene as an illustration of *Il.* 5.723, in which the wheels of Hera's chariot are described as ὀκτάνημα ("eight-spoke"), a hapax legomenon in ancient Greek; discussion repeated in Neils 2004. However, the chariot wheel on the Cleveland Painter's vase has seven spokes: one is obscured by the car. I take this as evidence that the painter is trying to show two four-spoke wheels, not one eight-spoke wheel.

106. Among others: the name vase, Louvre G 341, *ARV*² 601, no. 22, *CVA* Louvre 2 [France 2]: pl. 1 [95]:1; Bo-logna, Pell. 269, *ARV*² 599, no. 8, *CVA* Bologna, Museo Civico 5 [Italy 33],

pl. 97 [1471]:4; Munich 2324, *ARV*² 604, no. 55, *CVA* Munich 5 [Germany 20], pl. 215 [930]:1. But the Niobid Painter also uses a four-spoke wheel: San Francisco, Legion of Honor 1814a, *ARV*² 610, no. 27 [Manner of the Nio-bid Painter], *CVA* San Francisco 1 [USA 10], pl. 18 [478]:1a, 19 [479]:1b.

107. Beazley (1954, p. 79) laments that shield devices became increasingly dull in the Classical period and cites the Niobid Painter's simple wheel device as a case in point.

108. Crouwel 1992, pp. 35, 71. Ersoy (1998, p. 116) demonstrates that the number of spokes on surviving wheels increases with the diameter of the wheel. Therefore, it is possible that the wheel on **93** is meant to imply a larger-than-expected wheel. Surviving eight-spoke wheels include the hub of a wheel found in a well at Olympia dated to the third quarter of the 5th century: Hayen 1980–1981, pp. 185–189, figs. 26–28; and two chariots from burials at Salamis in Cyprus dated to the end of the 7th century and ca. 600 respectively: Karageorghis 1967, Tomb 2, pp. 22–24, no. 68, pls. 18, 115, 116; Tomb 3, Chariot B, pp. 49–51, pls. 30, 120, 121.

109. A conventional *kalos* inscrip-tion appears on a contemporary red-figured cup with a depiction of Ixion and the wheel: Geneva, HR 28, *LIMC* V, 1990, p. 859, no. 9, pl. 555, s.v. Ixion (C. Lochin). The inscription is within the segments created by the four-spoke wheel.

for this enigma must lie in the inscription, and until a reasonable reading is proposed, it will retain its mystery.

The shape of **93**, too, is different from those we have already discussed, as it is the only red-figured Type C cup with a concave lip. The Type C cup with concave lip is the preferred shape of cups in black glaze.[110] Plain rims, on the other hand, are most often associated with figural cups, and all other red-figured cups from this deposit, excluding one of the intentional red cups, have a plain rim. In fact, there are no potter signatures on red-figured cups of Type C with concave lip.[111] The profile of **93** has parallels with two red-figured cups from the Stoa Gutter Well (SGW), one by the Painter of the Agora Chairias Cups, P 24102,[112] and another attributed to Epiktetos.[113] It also matches the profiles of two black-glazed cups from well J 2:4: **129** and **130**. It seems likely that all of these cups originated in the same potter's workshop.[114]

The final red-figured Type C cup, **95** (Color Ills. 1, 9; Fig. 92), is also different from the previous cups in form and decoration, but relates to the set of red-figured Type C cups through its painting attribution.[115] Cup **95** is smaller with less skilled drawing, but it is the only nearly complete red-figured cup from the deposit decorated on both the interior and the exterior. On both sides of the exterior there is a pair of youthful hoplites in combat between palmettes. On the interior, the tondo decoration is a nude youth running to the right. The exterior has the feel of stock scenes, and the awkward balance of the tondo composition may indicate that the figure was excerpted from a pair of combatants or komasts. The drawing is hasty and clumsy; the eyes and ears of the figures are particularly problematic.

The youth in the tondo moves rapidly to the right and carries a crooked staff in his right hand. A mantle covers his entire left arm from shoulder to hand. Head and legs are profile, and the torso attempts something between frontality and three-quarter view.[116] The eye is a large, open-ended almond with a dot for a pupil placed tangential to the lower lid. The pupil gives the tondo youth's eye a slightly less-than-frontal appearance, but the eyes on the exterior figures do not repeat the off-center placement of the pupil, so we may consider the less-than-frontal eye of the tondo youth a fortuitous mistake. The tondo youth suffers a neck problem that can be explained by the black glaze intrusions on his right shoulder. The outline of the figure was drawn with the intention of his hair resting on his right shoulder, but the painter has hastily incised a hair contour that ignores the original plan. The result is that the neck has a disjointed look.

110. *Agora* XII, p. 91. The concave lip makes it a sturdier vessel than the plain-rimmed variety. Note that it is unusual that there are more complete examples of black-glazed Type C cups with plain rim than concave lip from this deposit. See discussion in Chapter 3.

111. Roberts 1986, p. 7.

112. *ARV*² 176, no. 1; *Paralipomena* 339, 1; *Add*² 185. *Agora* XXX, p. 341, no. 1562, pl. 147. For profile, see Roberts 1986, pp. 10, 13, no. 9, fig. 3.

113. *ARV*² 76, no. 80; *Paralipomena* 328, no. 1; *Add*² 168. *Agora* XXX, p. 339, no. 1554, pl. 146. For profile, see Roberts 1986, p. 10, no. 2, fig. 2; it can be dated to 520–510 based on the *kalos* name: Shapiro 1980.

114. On a single potter producing forms for both plain black and figured decoration, see Papanastasiou 2004.

115. Note that the cup was originally published as a Type B cup (Camp 1996, p. 250, no. 31), but the profile is not continuous from rim to foot.

116. Cf. Louvre C 10473, a red-figured cup attributed to Epiktetos, *ARV*² 76, no. 79, *CVA* Louvre 10 [France 17], pl. 12 [766]:1, with a youth moving left carrying a spear or stick and with a cloak over his arm. The painter of **95** probably had this type of image in mind as he painted this tondo.

Illustration 1. Red-figured and black-glazed cups

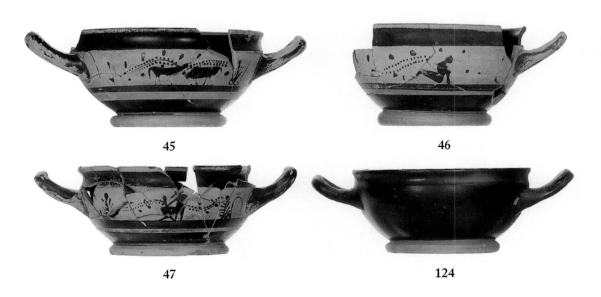

Illustration 2. Black-figured and black-glazed cup-skyphoi

Illustration 3. Type C cup (89), detail

Illustration 4. Type C cup (90), detail

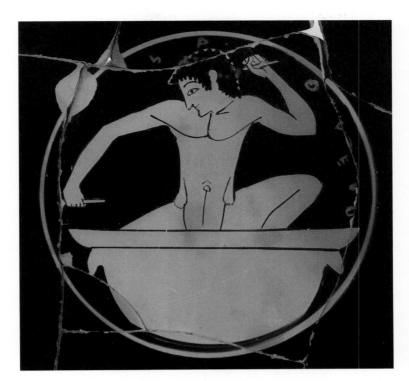

Illustration 5. Type C cup (**91**), detail

Illustration 6. Type C cup (**92**), detail

Illustration 7. Type C cup, concave lip (93), detail

Illustration 8. Skyphos, Heron Class (28)

Illustration 9. Type C cup (95), side view and detail

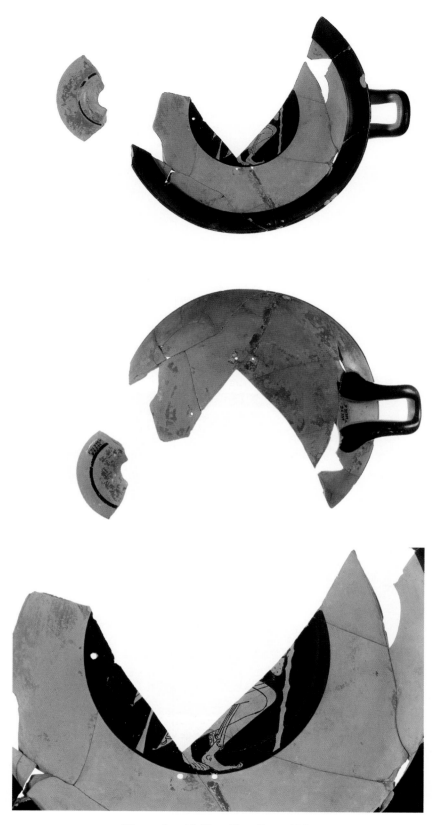

Illustration 10. Type B or C cup (87)

104

121

123

128

133

191

Illustration 11. Misfired objects from well J 2:4

Illustration 12. Skyphos, Ure's Class K2 (45)

Illustration 13. Pelike (84)

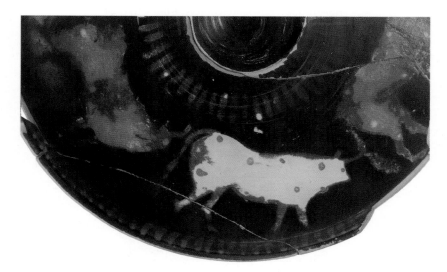

Illustration 14. Omphalos phiale, Six's technique (23), detail

The youth in the tondo is probably meant to be a hunter. He carries a throwing stick—lagobolon—used for flushing out hares.[117] The arrangement of the chlamys, covering the left arm, is also a characteristic of hunters.[118]

The pairs of combatants on the exterior battle each other armed with shields, but no visible weapons. On side A we ought to see the right youth in back view with the weapon in the right hand and shield on the left, on analogy with the skirted right youth on side B; however, the painter has given the right youth on side A frontal features and thus rendered him left-handed. On side B the raised arms suggest the possibility of rock throwing, but the arms of the youths on side A are lowered in a thrusting position, not in a typical throwing position. There is no sign of rocks in the undefined hands, although the fist is roughly round. The presence of shields on **95** seems to demand spears or swords, but neither is present. It is possible that the painter intended to include thin, reserved weapons, but in his haste chose to avoid the detailed brushwork. There is no sign of an abandoned preliminary drawing for spears, nor relief outline, nor is there evidence that weapons were drawn in an added color.

On a mug from Pontecagnano, which has some stylistic similarities with **95**, one warrior with sword drawn approaches a second who crouches with a stone in his hand.[119] The clutched fists on **95** are too poorly rendered to determine if the warriors held stones, but stone throwing may account for the lack of visible weapons.[120] The light-armed troops of gymnetes in the Greek army included stone throwers with shields.[121]

Stone throwing has a heroic quality, as it frequently appears as a backup defense in the *Iliad,* often with devastating accuracy and effect.[122] Athena even throws a stone, or rather a boulder, at Ares (*Il.* 11.265). In only one scene from the epics is it clear that the stone is of human-fist proportions (*Il. 16.734*). The scene on **95** may not be true combat, but a mock battle. Plato (*Leg. 8.834A*) states that young men should train for war by participating in games that include contests of stone throwing (by hand and by sling).

Stone throwing may have been a part of organized warfare; however, the light-armed troop was not the most glamorous of contingents in the Greek army. Herodotos preserves a Delphic oracle that contrasts the king of Sikyon with a common stone thrower, as if these were two social opposites (5.67.10). The use of a sling, which is the brother of stone throwing, is

117. Barringer 2001, pp. 95, 177–179.

118. Barringer 2001, pp. 23, 26, and n. 55.

119. Pontecagnano, Museo Archeologico T1240, Lissarrague 1989, p. 42, fig. 56. A fallen warrior reaching for a weapon at hand, a rock, is commonly depicted; e.g., Athens 661, *ABV* 200, no. 11 [Wraith Painter], Ure 1932, no. 86, pl. 3; London B 249, *CVA* London British Museum 4 [Great Britain 5], pl. 61 [206]:1; London 99.7–21.5,

*ARV*² 1052, no. 29 [the Group of Polygnotos], *CVA* London, British Museum 6 [Great Britain 8], pl. 103 [378].

120. Cf. white-ground alabastron with a youth clearly throwing a stone, London, GR 1910.4–15.3, Williams 2002, p. 345, pl. 88a–c. Youths use stones in hunting, but, to my knowledge, never in conjunction with a shield. For examples of hunting scenes with stone throwing, see Barringer 2001, figs. 9, 10, 12.

121. Xenophon (*An.* 5.2.12–14)

describes how stone throwers helped his troops deal with a rugged mountain band at Drilai. He places the gymnetes alongside the peltasts and archers. Tyrtaeus (fr. 11.35–38 W) provides an early source for the light-armed, stone-throwing troops. For stone throwing, see Pritchett 1991, pp. 1–67, esp. 65–66.

122. *Il.* 4.518–526; 5.302–310; 7.264, 268; 11.265; 12.380; 14.402–420 (Hector is nearly killed by a rock thrown by Telamonian Ajax); 16.411, 587; 20.285–291.

considered appropriate for slaves and an unsuitable vocation.[123] Therefore it is understandable why stone throwing, even with its heroic implications, may not have been a popular image. Other than images of Amazonomachies, Gigantomachies, and Centauromachies, in which stones are used as weapons, vase-painting images of stone throwing appear only in the work of less skillful painters such as the Painter of Munich 2562 and the Painter of Berlin 2268.

The closest parallel for the drawing style of **95** is found on an unattributed cup fragment from Adria.[124] Other comparisons show that this cup has a workshop relationship with painters associated with both the Epeleios Painter and the Euergides Painter. Thus, it may not parallel the decorative schemes or size of the other red-figured cups from this set, but it was produced in the same or related workshop.

The small size of **95** is paralleled by another set of small cups from Agora Persian destruction deposits. Three small Type C cups with tondo decoration only and a fourth black-glazed example, all from the Rectangular Rock-Cut Shaft (RRCS), have a rim diameter of around 13 cm.[125] The profile of **95** is very close to that of the cups from the RRCS, but **95** has a slightly deeper bowl, which may indicate a chronological difference within the production of this workshop. The drawing on the other Agora cups, which are attributed by Beazley to the Group of Acropolis 96, is mediocre but far superior to **95**.[126]

The small size of these cups has prompted several interpretations of their use. It has been suggested that a small cup in the Bryn Mawr collection "may have been for a child or held banquet sweetmeats."[127] This latter suggestion is unlikely, as there were other shapes for holding snacks at the table.[128] The former suggestion, that these diminutive cups were "child-sized," is more plausible.[129] In Xenophon's *Symposium* (1.8) the youth Autolykos, the one for whom Kallias threw the party, sits upright by his father's side. There is no indication that he drinks with the men, nor mention of a special cup for him, but this may have been a context for such a small cup. Alternatively, the smaller volume of the cup may point to a special role it had in the consumption of a "sipping" wine as opposed to a "drinking" wine. There is evidence that 5th-century Athenians appreciated the regional varieties of wine and recognized its varying qualities.[130] So, it is possible that certain wines were reserved for small tastes as opposed to heavier drinking.

123. See Dem. 23.148: not only did Aristokrates, the defendant, serve as a slinger, but he did so against Athens. The slight is double; that he also owned a pirate ship makes it treble: Pritchett 1991, pp. 53–54.

124. Adria B312, *CVA* Adria 1 [Italy 28] pl. 23 [1271]:7.

125. Vanderpool 1946, pp. 279–280, no. 33, pl. 30 (= *Agora* XXX, p. 342, no. 1571, pl. 148); p. 280, no. 34, pl. 30 (= *Agora* XXX, p. 342, no. 1573, pl. 149);

p. 280, no. 35, pl. 30 (= *Agora* XXX, p. 342, no. 1572, pl. 148); *ARV*². pp. 104–105, the Group of Acropolis 96. The fourth, black-glazed cup, is Vanderpool 1946, p. 316, no. 226, pl. 63. See Roberts 1986, p. 8, fig. 5, for profiles.

126. *ARV*², pp. 104–105.

127. Bryn Mawr P-219, *CVA* Bryn Mawr 1 [USA 13], pl. 5 [585]:4, 5; H. 4.5 cm, Diam. 11.7 cm.

128. See discussion of service vessels in Chapter 5.

129. Böhr (2009) proposes that small cups (ca. 20 cm in diameter) were used in the initiation of boys into their phratry, or as "philotesia," loving cups offered by an erastes to his eromenos.

130. Evidence discussed by Dalby 1996, pp. 97–102. Note especially the quotation from Hermippos, who describes a delicate wine appropriate for his friends and a vile one for his enemies.

TWO CORAL RED CUPS

The set of coral red cups probably contained only two members. Cups **87** (Color Ill. 10; Fig. 84) and **88** (Fig. 85) are two Type B or C red-figure cups that use the technique of intentional red glaze on the interior and exterior. The technique is relatively rare and seems to have been practiced by a limited number of craftsmen due to its challenging nature.[131] The two cups from well J 2:4 have similar profiles, with **88** having slightly thicker walls. The lip of **88** is strongly offset on the interior and concave on the exterior, while **87** has a more delicately offset lip on the interior, but only a narrow band of black-glaze on the plain exterior lip. On both **87** and **88**, intentional red glaze covers the surface below the lip on the interior and the exterior except for the tondo, which has the traditional black-glazed background for the red-figured composition. Only one foot is preserved, and it is probably the foot of a Type B cup.[132] Both upper- and underside surfaces of the foot have intentional red glaze, and the stem is also red as far as preserved. There is a black-glazed line on the foot on the chamfer and a corresponding line on the underside of the foot.

There are several aspects of these two cups that unify them as a set. To begin with, they both feature extensive ancient repairs. On **87** the damaging break ran from the rim below the tondo figure's feet, through the tondo, and presumably back out to the now-missing rim at about the ten-o'clock position (see Color Ill. 10). It was repaired with both lead staples and lead strips. Two and a half sets of drilled holes for lead staples are preserved, but none of the staples is preserved. Traces of lead along the crack both on the interior and exterior indicates that thin lead strips covered the break in the area between the rim and the tondo. The repairs were carefully made so as not to interfere with the tondo decoration; the lead strips halt at the edge on the tondo on the interior, but continue on the exterior.[133] Cup **88** suffered a similar mishap and bears one set of drilled holes indicating similar staple repairs in the area of one handle, but there is no evidence preserved for lead strips. Lead rivets or staples are a common repair technique, but lead strips are less so.[134] The attention given to these repairs is atypical for objects from this deposit and for pottery in Late Archaic Athens, where, presumably, you could easily replace a broken pot with a new one. Only one other figured object from this deposit (**4**, a stamnos) had extensive repairs.[135]

131. Vanderpool 1946, pp. 285–287, no. 52, pl. 35, with Talcott's comments on Richter and Hall 1936, p. xliv; Richter 1951; Farnsworth and Wisely 1958; Winter 1968; Cohen 1970–1971; 2006, pp. 48–51; Noble 1988, pp. 137, 140; Maish 2008; Walton et al. 2008.

132. Type B cups have a continuous profile from rim to foot with a chamfer on the upper surface of the foot plate. Type C cups have a similar profile but have a raised fillet, or incised lines imitating a fillet, at the base of the stem

and usually do not have a chamfer on the top of the foot; cf. a Type C cup with chamfer, Vanderpool 1946, pp. 285–287, no. 52, pl. 35 (= *Agora* XXX, p. 341, no. 1566, pl. 148), profile given in Roberts 1986, p. 11, fig. 6 (P 2698). The foot fragment is of Type B, and has been assigned to **87** based on profile analysis. See discussion of profiles below. See *FAS*, pp. 41 and 111–112, with figures, for the forms. There is no indication of a fillet on **87**, but it is possible that there was one.

133. A respect for the figural decoration was reported for several repaired vases in the Getty Collection; see Elston 1990.

134. See Noble 1988, p. 175, who does not mention lead strips as a mending option; Elston 1990, passim, who does not report lead strips on any of the Getty vases.

135. A fragment from the neck of a pithos from Level 5 had a single drill hole. Several black-glazed fragments from Level 2 also had drill holes.

Cup **87** is attributed to the red-figure Pioneer Euphronios;[136] too little remains of the tondo of **88** to permit an attribution. Two of the five cups attributed to Euphronios by Beazley, including one that bears the signature of Euphronios as painter and Kachrylion as potter, use intentional red.[137] All five cups attributed to Euphronios can be linked to the potter Kachrylion, whose workshop produced the largest number of intentional red cups during the Archaic period.[138] The profile of **87** is very close to the profile of a fragmentary cup with intentional red from Thasos attributed to Euphronios and signed by Kachrylion as potter.[139] The profile of **88** is closest to the profile of a Type C cup (P 2698) with concave rim and intentional red that recalls Euphronios.[140] The profile of P 2698 in turn is related to Boston, MFA 00.336, which Bloesch includes in a group of conservative Type C cups under the influence of Kachrylion.[141] Therefore, it seems secure to associate both **87** and **88** with the workshop of the potter Kachrylion, who worked regularly with Euphronios and knew the secrets of the intentional red glaze.

Both red-figured cups with intentional red glaze from well J 2:4 feature scenes of life in the palaestra. The scene on **87** should be restored with a male, probably a youth, wearing a himation sitting on a stool with only one leg preserved (Color Ill. 10).[142] He holds a knobby staff in his left hand, and from his wrist hangs a speckled sponge.[143] A trace of a round object preserved at the break by the sponge is the edge of an aryballos also suspended from the wrist. This detail is enough to set the scene in the palaestra, as sponges were an accompaniment to the strigil and aryballos and are often shown hanging in the background of such scenes. On **88** a youth holding *halteres* is in the process of jumping or practicing for the jump. One *halter* is preserved in his (left?) hand, thrown behind his back. The jumping weight is of the club type, and we can imagine that the jumper is in the final step of his jump when the weights are thrown backward, behind the back.[144] It is possible, however, that he is using the jumping weights as dumbbells, as it seems a figure in the tondo of a cup in Munich by the Antiphon Painter is doing.[145] In the field to the left of the figure is

136. Attribution in Camp 1996, no. 36, by C. Pfaff; supported by D. von Bothmer and J. Camp (pers. comm.)

137. Munich 2620, *ARV²* 16, no. 17: signed by both Euphronios as painter and Kachrylion as potter; St. Petersburg, Ol. 18181, *ARV²* 17, no. 20: attributed to Euphronios, argued by Cohen (1970–1971, p. 5) to be also a work of the potter Kachrylion, based on the use of coral red and the fact that two of the five Euphronios cups with coral red bear the signature of Kachrylion.

138. Cohen 1970–1971, pp. 4–5; 2006, pp. 48–50.

139. Thasos 80.51.21, 80.144.21, 80.144.22. Fragment 80.51.21 bears the signature of Kachrylion as potter on the

exterior. This cup also uses coral red on the interior below the black-glazed offset rim. See Maffre 1988, 1992.

140. P 2698, from the RRCS: Vanderpool 1946, pp. 285–287, no. 52, pl. 35 (= *Agora* XXX, p. 341, no. 1566, pl. 148); profile given in Roberts 1986, p. 11, fig. 6 (P 2698).

141. Roberts 1986, p. 13, no. 10, fig. 6, links the profile of Vanderpool 1946, pp. 285–287, no. 52 (P 2698) to Boston, MFA 00.336. Bloesch groups Boston MFA 00.336 with cups under the influence of Kachrylion: *FAS,* p. 120, no. 8.

142. For a similar scene, cf. the cup Agora P 2575, unattributed, *Agora* XXX, p. 341, no. 1567, pl. 148, on which a draped adult male sits on a

stool to the right, holding a knobby staff, and a sponge and aryballos hang in the field behind him, although the sponge is not identical in shape and texture to that on **87**.

143. *Agora* XXX, p. 340, no. 1556, pls. 146, 147, Manner of Euphronios, *ARV¹* 19, no. 7, preserves a similar sponge along with an aryballos and strigil.

144. Gardiner 1904, p. 189.

145. Munich, Antikensammlungen 2635, *ARV²* 339, no. 57, *Add²* 218, Vanhove 1992, p. 210, no. 69, with figure. Gardiner (1904, p. 193) accepts that some of the vase-painting scenes may depict weight training. Harris (1964, p. 84) emphasizes that since the jump was so difficult, the athlete

a discus in a bag hanging from the wall. The jump and the discus throw were individual events of the pentathlon, and the hanging discus adds both an interesting formal element to balance the scene as well as an emphasis on the athlete's talents. The multidisciplinary event required a variety of athletic skills, a fact that was duly appreciated at least in Aristotle's time.[146] It is noteworthy that cups **87** and **88** are the only vessels from this deposit with images of athletes.

Athletics in ancient Greece, especially Athens, were a showcase for the aspects of beauty associated with being young and victorious.[147] Athletics also implied the world of the aristocracy, for the gymnasium scenes relate to the world of elite youths with free time to train and with the resources to afford personal trainers.[148] More than any other images from this deposit, these two cups convey the idealized world of youthful beauty that forms the hallmark of Greek art and culture in the Archaic and Classical periods. This is significant when taken in conjunction with the special respect these cups received. The athletic imagery alone makes these two cups stand out among the others, and the relatively rare intentional red technique and fine draftsmanship of the painter (at least on **87**) place the two cups on an aesthetic level above the other pottery owned by the house. The extensive ancient restoration of the cups means that they were highly valued. I assume that the home owned only two intentional red cups since there were no other stray fragments with intentional red found in the well or in the stratigraphic levels of the house.[149] Their number demands a very special context for their use within the house. Two drinkers—the homeowner and a special guest—may have used these cups.[150] Regardless of the specific purpose of the meetings, these cups would bring a dignity and distinction to the encounter through their decoration, technique, and imagery. The extraordinary objects would signal to the invited guest the host's respect for the guest and the occasion.[151]

needed to practice extensively the synchronization of arms and legs. Depiction of an athlete practicing or exercising would further emphasize the palaistra setting, as opposed to the more public setting of competition. For a summary of the current view of the jump with earlier references, see Golden 1998, pp. 60–62.

146. Arist. *Eth. Nic.* 3.9.3.1117b.

147. Cohen (2006, p. 49) points out that many of the coral-red-glaze cups found in Athens feature elite male imagery. On athletics and beauty, see Lissarrague 1989, pp. 39, 41; Sansone (1988, pp. 79–81) associates personal exertion in the name of victory with religious sacrifice.

148. See Mark Golden's chapter "Elite Athletics at Athens: Assent and Animosity" (1998, pp. 157–169, esp. 160–164). He draws a contrast between the democratic process in which the

community prevails and the individual pursuits of the gymnasium. Also on the role of elites and athletics, see Morgan 1989, esp. pp. 191–223.

149. Of course, it is possible that other members of this set were disposed of elsewhere, but the rarity of the technique makes it unlikely that there was a significant number of additional cups in this set. The following discussion follows the assumption that the house owned only two intentional red cups.

150. Possible occasions may have included business arrangements, private alliances, celebrations of victories, and even the meeting formalizing the *engye*, the betrothal contract between a future father-in-law and groom prior to a wedding (on which, see Oakley and Sinos 1993, p. 10; see also Pind. *Ol.* 7.1–6, for the use of a special cup for use at a marriage symposium). Cohen (2006, p. 49) proposes that since many

of the Late Archaic coral-red-glaze cups featured elite male images, they may have been "philotesia," loving cups given to an eromenos by his erastes. Agora P 7690 + P 8890 (*Agora* XXX, p. 319, no. 1410, pl. 131; in color: Cohen 2006, p. 49, fig. 7) has a graffito on the black-glazed field of the tondo: ΦΙΛ]ΟΤΕΣΙΟΝ. The tondo preserves only the legs of a male couple, closely face-to-face. Beazley 1947 [1989], no. γ16, p. 24, first proposed the reading for the inscription. See note 129 for a similar interpretation of **95**.

151. This association of particular vessels with special events has parallels today. A Finnish friend's family owns two glasses, inherited from an ancestor, which have been used only twice this generation: on her and her only sibling's wedding days. Restricting the objects to a special use marks the occasion as extraordinary.

RED-FIGURED CUP FRAGMENTS

I discuss red-figured cup fragments from well J 2:4 here, although it is difficult to know their exact relationship with the set of red-figured cups described above. Most of the fragments come from the upper portion of the well deposit (Levels 1 and 2); therefore, they either represent whole cups broken by the Persians and tidied up by the homeowners, or fill brought in from outside in an effort to top off the well. In the latter case, it is possible that the fill came from a place used by the household for waste disposal, so it is still possible that the fragments come from cups that were in use at one time by the household. The following fragments do not meet the criteria for inclusion in the household assemblage as described in Chapter 3 and Table 6. Nevertheless, it is worth noting that the shapes and figural decoration on some of the fragments are similar to the complete red-figured cups discussed above, and those similarities may suggest that some of the fragments belonged to cups that originally filled out the set.

Fragment 94 is the floor and partial stem of a Type C cup, probably decorated in the tondo only. The scene is a Scythian archer kneeling to the left, drawing his bow. The ear flaps of the Scythian cap, the *kidaris,* and the tail of the bow confirm this identification.[152] The style is easily identifiable with the Pithos Painter, or perhaps the Manner of the Pithos Painter. He and his colleagues are exceedingly fond of the Scythian archer motif, and there are two examples from the Agora itself.[153] The popularity of the Scythian images relates to a cultural trend in Late Archaic Athens to adopt images related to the Persian world into the Athenian iconographic repertoire.[154] The reason for the success of the images of Scythian archers and Scythian symposiasts is complex, as Margaret Miller demonstrates in her work on Athens's reception of Persian culture. Using imagery of the foreign enemy neutralizes, through familiarization and domestication, the power the image evokes and represents.[155] A less sophisticated explanation might suggest that these are images of a foreign cultural sphere and are appealing because of their exoticness and because they depict "the other" in contrast to the heroic Greek.[156] The work of Herodotos stands as a testament to Greek fascination with foreign cultures, and if the archers were a somewhat familiar presence due to their role in the Athenian military, then the images might explore an interest in their exotic presence within the cultural world of the painter, the purchaser, and presumably, the

152. Vos 1963, pp. 47–48. *LIMC* I, 1981, p. 513, nos. 72, 73, pl. 391, s.v. Alexandros (R. Hampe), identifies the single Scythian archers in the tondo of two cups as the Trojan prince Paris (Alexandros), but it seems unlikely that the hastily drawn archers of the Pithos Painter and his circle are intended to be heroic figures.

153. The archer motif: *ARV*² 139, nos. 19–22, plus the series of Scythian symposiasts, *ARV*² 139–141, nos. 23–

63. Agora examples of the archer motif: *Agora* XXX, p. 334, no. 1516, pl. 143, *ARV*² 139, no. 18; *Agora* XXX, p. 334, no. 1517, pl. 143, *ARV*¹, p. 1952.

154. Miller 1997, passim. Vos (1963, pp. 61–65) confusedly perceives a decline in the number of images of Scythians in Attic vase painting during the years 500–490, which she goes on to explain by associating the recruitment of Scythians with the Peisistratid tyranny. She sets off on the wrong foot

by misdating some of the material and does not consider the Pithos Painter's Scythian archer scenes. Williams (1991, p. 47 and n. 38) links the Scythian images to the return of Miltiades the Younger to Athens ca. 493 (Hdt. 6.39–40) from eastern campaigns.

155. Miller 1997, pp. 243–258, esp. 248–250.

156. Lissarrague 1990c, pp. 125–149, esp. 141.

drinker.[157] The Scythian symposiast might be humorous as well, for the closed community of the drinking group would be the last place one would expect to find a Scythian.[158]

Cup fragment **96** provides only the second example (along with **95**) of a cup with exterior decoration from this deposit. Fragment **96** comes from an area of the cup to the left of a handle. Three joining fragments preserve a draped figure moving right. The front foot of the figure touches an oddly shaped reserved form that must be intended as a piece of landscape. The landscape element continues under the handle attachment. The placement of the figure and the landscape element so close to the handle indicate that this was a multifigured scene. Landscape details sometimes appear in Judgment of Paris scenes, to locate the shepherd on Mt. Ida.[159] One very hypothetical reconstruction of our small sherd would identify the preserved figure as Paris trying to escape his destiny by fleeing up the mountain, but he often wears a shorter garment and sandals or rustic boots.

Fragment **97** is from the tondo of a cup. It preserves a trace of the reserved border of the tondo, so it should be positioned to the left of the center of the tondo. The trace of the cup stem on the exterior confirms this reconstruction. There is no indication of exterior decoration. Preserved on **97** is a shield with a device of the hindquarters of a feline. A bow projects above and below the shield, presumably gripped in the shield hand of the missing figure. Only the top recurve and a trace of the bottom recurve can be seen. The spacing of the tondo indicates that this was a single-figure scene. The shield motif is not common.[160] It is likely to be a single Amazon or Scythian running to the left. A cup by Douris in Baltimore gives a general idea of the type of scene, but his example is much more elaborate.[161] Fragment **97** was found in Level 5, associated with the complete vessels. It is possible that this fragment belonged to a cup complementing the set of complete cups discussed above but broken above ground and the majority of it disposed of elsewhere.

The two joining fragments of cup **98**, from the left side of a tondo, preserve little of the red-figured decoration. The exterior preserves no trace of decoration. Within a reserved border is a pillow and a trace of the back of the head of a male. The pillow is puffy and covered with exquisitely decorated material (see Catalogue for the use of relief line for details). The pattern on the pillow is a band of black bordered by dots and rows of

157. For Herodotos's treatment of Scythia, see Hartog 1988.

158. DeVries (1977, p. 546) would like to see the Eastern-themed products of the Pithos Painter as "attempts to cater to Eastern interest" and markets; see also DeVries 2000 on Attic iconography with Eastern themes in general. Although many products of the Pithos Painter have been found in the East (see Clairmont 1955, pp. 120, 130), that they are also being used in Athens means that the imagery is not specifically targeted to the foreign consumer. This

may be a case in which we can document the reception of the same image by different viewers. A similar point about overinterpreting distribution and users is made by Lissarrague (1990c, p. 145, and n. 75).

159. The landscape continues under the handle of the cup Louvre G 151, *ARV*[2] 406, no. 8, *Paralipomena* 371, *Add*[2] 232 [Briseis Painter], *LIMC* VII, 1994, p. 179, no. 35, pl. 112, s.v. Paridis Iudicium (A. Kossatz-Deissmann), ca. 480; Paris sits on a lump of landscape next to the handle on Berlin, Staatliche

Museen F2291, *ARV*[2] 459, no. 4, *Paralipomena* 377, *Add*[2] 244 [Makron], *LIMC* VII, 1994, p. 179, no. 36, pl. 112, s.v. Paridis Iudicum (A. Kossatz-Deissmann), ca. 480; Paris flees toward the handle of a stamnos on London E 445, *ARV*[2] 217, no. 1λ [Group of London E 445], *CVA* London 3 [Great Britain 4], pl. 21 [186]:5d.

160. It is not mentioned by Chase [1902] 1979.

161. Baltimore Johns Hopkins B8, *ARV*[2] 442, no. 215, *Add*[2] 240, Buitron-Oliver 1995, no. 6, pl. 4.

dots. The scene is probably a symposiast sitting (not reclining) on a kline, with the pillow propped behind him. He may be sitting upright to play an instrument, as on a cup in Orvieto attributed to the Colmar Painter.[162] Symposiasts facing right are far less common on tondos than those reclining or sitting to the left. Both fragments that join to form **98** came from the upper portion of the well deposit.

Fragment **99** is a single fragment from the upper portion of a cup tondo. It preserves the head of a male facing right. He raises his left arm and braces it palm up against the border of the tondo. A trace of something else can be seen in the field to the right of his head. The tail ends of his fillet hang down, indicating that the proper orientation for the fragment is with his hand in the twelve-o'clock position. It is not uncommon for figures to interact with the tondo border, and a satyr on a cup by the Painter of Agora 2578 from the Agora also braces himself, presumably because he is so excited by the amphora of wine in front of him.[163] The style is in keeping with the hasty work of many cups from other Persian destruction deposits in the Agora, but it defies precise attribution.

Fragment **100** is very similar in style to **99** and is also very poorly preserved. Again, a trace of the tondo indicates that this is probably the top of the field. A man's balding head faces right, and an object hangs in the field above him. The work is hasty and the black-glazed background does not follow the relief outline. It is possible that this is not a balding man, but is a satyr. Satyrs, however, usually have a receding hairline and not a bald patch.[164] A ∪-shaped object, something like a discus bag, hangs in the field, but the painter has painted over the relief lines to reduce the form to a stalactite hanging from the tondo. It somewhat resembles a shoe or a *halter* in this form.

Fragment **101** is a small fragment from the center of a tondo. It preserves the naked buttocks of a figure to the left. There is not much to say about this fragment, but the shape of the buttocks and the three-quarters view do recall a slightly larger fragment from the Agora attributed to the Chaire Painter.[165]

Fragment **102** is three joining fragments of the lower portion of a single figure. A section of a very narrow tondo border is preserved. The figure's back leg pushes off the border, indicating he is in motion toward the right. A tail of drapery hangs down from above, indicating that the garment continued to the shoulders. The drapery is similar to that of the Group of Acropolis 96. This fragment preserves a single letter (O) and the trace of another (possibly a Λ) to the left of the foot. *Ho pais kalos* is likely.

The final fragment, **103**, is also a red-figured tondo, but only the reserved border and the tip of a single finger survive.

At the very most, the cup fragments add evidence for 11 more red-figured vessels. This is probably an exaggerated number, since, as discussed above, it is likely that some of the fragments were broken earlier in the history of the house or even brought in from elsewhere with fill. Nevertheless, this is still a small number for the house—a maximum number of 21 cups if all fragments are taken to represent one cup.[166] This number is truly low in comparison with the large number of black-figured objects and fragments from the deposit.

162. Orvieto 589, *ARV*² 359, no. 19 [Colmar Painter], *CVA* Orvieto, Umbria (varia) 1 [Italy 16], pl. 7 [764]:2. Another in Palermo, V.662, *ARV*² 812, no. 57 ["Followers of Makron II: The Clinic Painter or close to him"], *CVA* Palermo 1, [Italy 14], pl. 13 [670]:2, shows a back view of a symposiast with a pillow at the left.

163. *Agora* XXX, p. 341, nos. 1563, 1564, pl. 147, *ARV*² 142, nos. 2 and 3 [Painter of Agora 2578].

164. Cf. the satyrs of the Pithos Painter and the Painter of Agora 2578 mentioned above. Priam can sometimes have a bald pate, not just a receding hairline: amphora by Euthymides (signed), Munich 2307, *ARV*² 26, no. 1, Boardman 1975, pl. 33.1.

165. *Agora* XXX, p. 348, no. 1613, pl. 152, *ARV*² 144, no. 3.

166. Only two red-figured fragments from the deposit were not catalogued. Camp's statement (1996, p. 245) that the number of largely complete pieces of red figure is about equal to the number of largely complete black figure is true, although misleading; there is a far higher proportion of black figure when one looks at the fragments.

THE RED-FIGURED CUPS: SUMMARY AND COMMENTS

The six red-figured cups described above are united as a set based on several factors: their shapes and decorative technique, the workshops responsible for their potting and painting (and thus date), and their iconography. The cups **89**, **90**, and **91** are particularly close in profile and potting details. Five plain, black-glazed Type C cups with plain rim (**132–136**) are also very close to the profiles of the red-figured cups, and at least two of the black-glazed cups with plain rims have a nearly identical profile to **89** and **90**. Thus, it seems reasonable to place the black-glazed cups alongside the red-figured ones as part of the same set. The undecorated versions may represent extra cups that were used when a larger group assembled than the number of red-figured cups in the house could serve and thus created a flexible set (see Color Ill. 1). Two of the black-glazed cups (**133**, **134**) are identical in profile, and both have the same, misfired, matte greenish-black glaze with orange spots (Color Ill. 11). Clearly these come from the same potter's shop, and their odd firing indicates that homeowners were not averse to using imperfectly produced pottery in their homes.[167] Capacities of the Type C cups with plain rim, both red-figured and black-glazed, are all about the same, which will not be true across the sets (see volume analysis in Appendix II).

As discussed in the Catalogue entries for each cup, a comparison of cup foot profiles to the studies of Bloesch shows that the cups **89** and **90** belong in Bloesch's group that includes potters working for the Ambrosios Painter, the Euergides Painter, Epiktetos, Skythes, and Onesimos around the turn of the 5th century. The two intentional red cups, **87** and **88**, also have profiles that fall into this same group as defined by Bloesch.[168] Furthermore, Beth Cohen has shown that the intentional red technique was largely limited to the workshop of the painter Kachrylion.[169] Thus we have a conjunction of potters, painters, and technique serving the home market.[170] It is possible that the homeowner bought his set of red-figured kylikes as well as the black-glazed versions from a single shop that carried the wares of this production group of potters and painters.

Dating of red figure, although there is so much of it from the period immediately before the Persian Wars, continues to be a very subjective exercise.[171] While we have a terminus ante quem of 480 for all of the material from well J 2:4, the critical question of just how ante 480 the red figure

167. Other examples are illustrated in Color Ill. 11. The Corinthian-type skyphos, **121**, and the lamp, **191**, are misfired a dramatic orange color; the black-glazed table amphora, **104**, is misfired mottled red; and the concave lip cup, **128**, and the cup-skyphos, **123**, both have patches of misfired red slip. It is not possible to know if they cost less than properly fired pots.

168. The Ambrosios Painter also decorated intentional red cups from the workshop of Kachrylion: S.82.AE.24, Bareiss 260, *Greek Vases* 1983, no. 146.

169. Cohen 1970–1971, pp. 6–7; 2006, pp. 48–51.

170. We tend to use the word "workshop" to describe the relationships among painters and/or potters, but we know little about the organization of the potter's quarter. On the problem of the definition of "workshop," see Rudolph 1988.

171. The subjectivity of red-figure chronology was brought to the attention of the field of Classical archaeology by the extreme chronological revisions proposed by Michael Vickers

and David Francis in the 1980s; see, among many similar statements of their thesis: Francis and Vickers 1981, 1988; Francis 1990. Their downdating of red figure, along with many other monuments of the Late Archaic period, has largely been refuted; see most succinctly Amandry 1988 and Cook 1989. The debate over chronology has resulted in greater scholarly attention to one's own assumptions; see Neer 2002, pp. 186–205; Rotroff 2009.

dates involves assessing the style and assigning a subjective date based on assumptions of stylistic development. A conservative stylistic date for the red-figured cups would be ca. 500, with the assumption that the date could move either earlier or later. Cups **89**, **90**, **91**, and **95** comfortably fit this date, and, as argued above, the owl on **92**, as an early, nonconventional version of the owl that becomes very canonical later in the 5th century, should also date to ca. 500 or the early years of the 5th century. The red-figured cup with the wheel (**93**) defies stylistic dating since it has no parallels. The two intentional red cups (**87** and **88**) date about a decade or so earlier than the other red-figured cups.

The profiles of the cups, however, can offer more evidence for dating. The development scheme for Type C cups as put forth by Sparkes and Talcott has the shape progressing from a stout-looking cup with short stem, broad foot, and deep bowl to one with a tall, slim stem, and a smaller foot that angles up to the stem.[172] The shape of the cone on the underside, too, develops from a broad flat cone to a pointy, narrow cone.[173] The type of foot and especially the cone on the underside in use at 482 is seen in the ostraka of Themistokles that accompany those of Aristeides, who is known to have been ostracized in 482.[174] The cups from deposit J 2:4, none of which demonstrate these developed, later traits, must date somewhat before 482. Bloesch dates his *Die Fortschrittliche Richtung* group of Type C cups, to which most of the cups from well J 2:4 belong, to a period of development around 500–490.[175] Therefore, the profiles of **89**, **90**, and **91** comfortably date to the first decade of the 5th century.

The forms of **92** and **93**, on the other hand, show a few traits of the later developments of the Type C cup. Cup **92** has a greater slope of the foot plate up to the stem and a taller stem without a fillet, which has been replaced by grooves at the base of the stem. A clearer signal of a later date is the sharper cone on the underside, which is approaching the form of the cup-foot ostraka of Themistokles, that is, approaching a date of 482.[176] Cup **93**, with a concave lip, is also closer to the form of the Themistokles ostraka. It has a straight stem, fillet, and gently sloping foot plate. Neither **92** nor **93** has the steep slope of the upper face of the foot plate as seen on the Themistokles ostraka; therefore, these should also be dated closer to 490 than to 482.

With the workshop discussion and chronological ranges for the cups in mind, it seems likely that the owner of these vases purchased **89**, **90**, **91**, and **95**, at least, in addition to the black-glazed cups, either at one time, or over a brief period from the same pottery shop. A date ca. 490 for **92** and **93** means that they may have been purchased at the same time or only shortly after the other red-figured cups. We do not see a pattern of one cup early on, three later, and so on, which would indicate the purchase of individual cups over a period of time either to build up a set or to replace broken members of the set. We also do not see a pattern of cups purchased from various workshops. For instance, the painters Skythes, Onesimos, the Brygos Painter, Douris, and the potters Pamphaios and Hermaios are not represented in the Persian destruction pottery from the Agora, but their products are found elsewhere in Athens, particularly on the Acropolis.[177] Instead, the painter and potter attributions for red-figured cups found in the Agora excavations depict a pattern of purchases from a limited number of artisans who are possibly represented by only a few shops.

172. *Agora* XII, pp. 91–92.

173. Roberts 1986, p. 9.

174. For a profile drawing, see Broneer 1938, p. 229, fig. 60:I, and pp. 242–243 for discussion of the dating of the ostraka. See *Agora* XXV, pp. 4–5, for the dating of ostracisms of the 480s and 490s.

175. *FAS*, p. 123.

176. See Broneer 1938, pp. 242–243.

177. See the limited but important presentation of the statistics in Hannestad 1988, pp. 226–227, and fig. 3.

The purchasing pattern seems significant. The cups were purchased ca. 500–490, and used for a decade or two until the Persian War. Black-figured drinking vessels, on the other hand, continued to be purchased until the close of the deposit.[178] The fragments of red figure from this deposit are few, but even considering the fragmentary cups, none of the cups exhibit red figure in its conventionally expected ca. 480 style. It is possible that the homeowner bought the set of red-figured cups for one particular occasion ca. 500 but continued to use them for the next two decades on other occasions. If so, this means the imagery was not so specifically celebratory or commemorative as to preclude use on more generic occasions.[179]

The limited number of red-figured cups, especially the set of two intentional red examples, may relate to the perceived value of the red-figured cups.[180] Value can be either an economic concept or a social concept. One model that explains the relationship of red figure to black figure in this house focuses on the economic value of the cups. Scholars generally agree that metalware vessels had the greatest economic value and that pottery certainly had a lesser value. There may be, however, a range of economic values for pottery. This homeowner's care of the intentional red cups suggests that the rare technique and fine draftsmanship had real value to him.[181] Although it is impossible to know, the homeowner may have had a sentimental attachment to these special cups that motivated him to repair them.[182] It is also important to remember that the other red-figured cups that he owned are modest products with simple, single-figure scenes. These cups might have cost less than ones with elaborate multifigured scenes on the interior and exterior. That the homeowner seems to have bought the red-figured cups at one time but continued to buy modest black-figured objects throughout the early 5th century may mean that red figure was more expensive, and therefore more economically esteemed, than black figure.

A second model focuses on the social value of the red-figured cups. Small numbers of vessels in a specific decorative style may relate to limited or special use. For example, for this house a relationship may be: the more frequently used, the greater the number of vessels in a set, and the poorer the decoration. Thus, the finest cups, the intentional red cups, might have been reserved for select occasions, and the hasty, black-figured cup-skyphoi (see below) for everyday use. The red-figured cups fall in between because they were reserved for entertainment of guests within a specific environment, the symposium. It is possible that red figure was associated with more formal entertaining in this house and that its use was limited to communal

178. This pattern is observable in other Persian destruction deposits. Hannestad (1988, p. 224) presents statistics on the continued popularity of black figure in the home market after the introduction of red figure.

179. T. B. L. Webster (1972, p. 291 and passim) describes a great number of vases as "special commissions" commemorative of many types of events. Although some vase images must have been bespoken, the vases from domestic contexts in Athens tend to be generic.

Most of the vases Webster uses for evidence were found in Etruria. For Webster's theory to work, commissioned vases made for Athenian patrons, used perhaps only once for a special symposium, would have to be sold on a "secondhand market" to Etruscan consumers.

180. Using the quantities for black-figure and red-figure pottery from the Acropolis and the Agora from Hannestad 1988, p. 224, shows that the percentage of red figure to black figure on

the Acropolis from 550–470 is 39%, for the Agora, 16%; therefore, there was a distinction made between the relative value of red figure and black figure. Hannestad (1988, p. 226) even describes red figure as a "luxury" compared to black figure.

181. On the relative value of figured wares, see Bažant 1981, p. 7.

182. Note that whatever sentimental value the cups had, the homeowner did not take them with him when he evacuated the city.

drinking events demanding a level of quality and presentation. Just as the intentional red cups were brought out for the most auspicious drinking events, the red-figured cups may have been used for more typical, but formal entertaining of important business associates or potential political allies. The black-figured cup-skyphoi might have been used for more ordinary gatherings or even for daily use in the household.[183]

Iconographically, the set of red-figured cups presents images reflective of the act of communal drinking. The wine treading on **91** and the meat on **90** anticipate the actual activities of communal drinking. The komast (**89**), if he is approaching the party, is also anticipatory of the evening's events. The owl (**92**), with its humorous, first-person inscription, brings the viewer into the sphere of the image and the act of drinking as well, especially if the joke refers to the potency of his wine. Even **93** with the eight-spoke wheel demands the viewer to interact with its inscription, puzzling out the letters and turning it about. The tondo of **93** may also invoke the spinning motion of a chariot wheel as a metaphor for the spinning sensation caused by excessive drinking. All of these images require the viewer to participate in fulfilling their completion. The youth with the meat is running, the komast is moving, the youth is treading—they all are in the middle of an action that has as its culmination the very room where the drinker sits. The viewer, by consuming the wine and meat in the context of a symposium, completes the images temporally and in action.[184] The images on the pelike, **84** (discussed in Chapter 5), also require the viewer to fulfill the time between the images. The key is that the viewer—the symposium participant—is at the end of each process described by the images. Not only do the images culminate with his presence in the very room where he is viewing the image, he participates by mentally completing the images and seeing his participation in the symposium as their outcome. The viewer is engaged as part of the group through his interaction with the images, but he is also made to feel an essential member of the group that is united through use of cups of the same form and decoration. Of course, the ritualized activities of the symposium—mixing of wine and water, serving from a single krater, sequential singing, and so on—amplify the sense of group unity.

This set of cups with self-reflective images associated with the act of communal drinking does not necessarily present subjects we would expect at a symposium. There are no scenes of heroes and gods (unless the eight-spoke wheel can be associated with Hera), no scenes of the drinkers participating in symposia, no women, no overt courting (although Eros is represented in the thoughts of *ho pais kalos*), and no entertainment, particularly no hetairai. The pelike **84**, which probably complemented this set of red-figured cups, has a man carrying a barbitos, implying musical entertainment, but otherwise we have no hint how the evening will be spent beyond the implied consumption of wine. It is useful to remember that these complete cups may not represent the entire set of red-figured cups owned by this house, and thus any discussion of subjects absent should be cautiously accepted. There is, however, a noticeable absence of scenes of gods and heroes on all the cups from the Persian destruction deposits of the Classical Agora,[185] and drinking cups from domestic contexts favor images of daily life.

183. Cf. Xen. *Oec.* 9.2–10, where the homeowner, Ischomachos, is recounting how the household possessions are stored. He says, "Whatever we use for festivals or entertaining guests or at rare intervals we handed over to the housekeeper" (9.10; trans. S. Pomeroy, Oxford, 1994), as opposed to the daily-use objects that were stored in a different, presumably more accessible, location. Bažant (1981, pp. 4–12), in an analysis of this passage, asserts that the role of all vases used for entertaining, both metal and ceramic, was "to graphically display the prosperity of their owner and thus remind the guests of the respect due to the former." He repeats the argument (1985, pp. 56–57) with even more emphasis on the presentation and definition of status through entertaining. For commentary on the passage from Xenophon, see Pomeroy 1994, pp. 291–301. A red-figured skyphos in the J. Paul Getty Museum depicts a storage area of a house, arranged as neatly as Ischomachos prescribes: 86.AE.265, Neils and Oakley 2003, pp. 258–259, no. 63, fig. 63b and p. 120.

184. On the role of the viewer in "producing" image meaning, see Wolff 1984, pp. 95, 97.

185. The exception is the Gorgos cup (P 24113), *Agora* XXX, pp. 317–318, no. 1407, pl. 130, which stands out as one of the finest products present in the Persian destruction debris. It is possible that it was intended for a nondomestic use but was damaged in the shop.

In addition, products of only certain painters active at the turn of the 5th century appear in the Persian destruction deposits. It appears that these painters painted for the domestic-use market, and it appears that they chose iconography they deemed appropriate to that context. Of the painters present in the Persian destruction debris, some demonstrate an ability to tailor their work to use context. For example, mediocre products of Epiktetos and the Euergides Painter are found in domestic contexts, but outstanding examples of their skills are found on pottery from the Acropolis, presumably serving a votive function.[186]

There are, however, whole quarters of the Kerameikos not represented in the Persian destruction material. The Proto-Panaetian Group, Onesimos, the Kleophrades Painter, and especially Douris, Makron, and the Brygos Painter do not make a showing in the Agora, although their products are present on the Acropolis. These patterns reveal some details of an otherwise poorly understood system of pottery workshops and sales shops. Painters and potters must have worked together and often in close proximity,[187] but they did not all serve the same markets. The evidence from the Persian destruction cleanup deposits also underscores that some painters designed products for multiple markets but with particular consumers and contexts of use in mind.

Athenian consumers favored domestic pottery that avoided scenes of myth and selected scenes that evoked their world or witty plays on their world. A structuralist's analysis might explain the "genre" images as reassuring and reinforcing of the drinker's way of life, especially when images of satyrs and other "others" are included among them.[188] But the images are also part of the whole symposium environment, the purpose of which was to define one's peer group through bonding and sharing. The images reflect the world from which the drinkers hail, and the elevation of the ordinary to the image similarly elevates the drinker's (possibly boring) life. Cup **90**, with the *prosagoreuo* inscription, welcomes the drinker, emphasizing that he is a part of the group. In this way, the images encourage group identity. No one individual is distinguished as superior, but all participate in a shared—and superior—culture.

The images on pottery from Late Archaic Athenian households are frequently humorous. More will be said about humor in the discussion below, but the red-figured scenes on the cups are amusing; the jokes of the pelike (**84**) and the owl (**92**) must have invoked laughter from the viewers. The SGW and RRCS also contained cups with humorous iconography.[189] The subjects of the domestic sympotic pottery reflect the context, which was one of amusement and pleasurable entertainment. The symposium provided an escape from the difficulties of daily life, while at the same time permitting bonds to form that would facilitate success in life. This is important because humor, just like wine, is a key to relaxing the barriers between individuals, thus permitting bonds to form during the symposium or any evening of communal drinking. The particular homeowner who purchased these cups wanted to emphasize humor and fun when he hosted his group of drinking companions. The scenes, like comedy costumes, reminded the viewer/guest that the evening was meant to be pleasurable, not somber or dull.

186. E.g., plate by Epiktetos, Acropolis 2.6, *ARV*[2] 78, no. 102, Graef and Langlotz II, p. 1, no. 6, pl. 2:6a; cup by the Euergides Painter, Acropolis 2.166, *ARV*[2] 92, no. 64, Graef and Langlotz II, pp. 12–13, no. 166, pl. 6:166.

187. There is ample evidence for potters working with different painters, suggesting a kind of fluidity to the "workshop" organization: *FAS*; Rudolph 1988; Osborne 2004.

188. Lissarrague (1988, 1993, 1990a, 1990d, 1990e) explores this role of satyrs. See also recently Cohen 2000a, pp. 4, 6–13; Padgett 2000, pp. 43–48; and Neils 2000, among others in the Cohen 2000b volume.

189. E.g., the hetaira with her dwarf on the interior of a Type B cup, with youths making dogs jump on the exterior, *Agora* XXX, p. 319, no. 1411, pl. 132 (unattributed); or the satyr with a peltast's shield and spear performing a pyrrhic dance, *Agora* XXX, pp. 334–335, no. 1518, pl. 143, *ARV*[2] 142, no. 1 [Painter of Agora P 2578].

A SET OF BLACK-FIGURED CUP-SKYPHOI

Another set of drinking vessels from this deposit consists of black-figured cup-skyphoi (Color Ill. 2). These are squat cups with a torus foot and a narrow figure zone framed by palmettes between two cup handles.[190] P. N. Ure calls this shape skyphoi of Class K2, and their painters are generally members of the Haimon workshop. The floruit of Class K2 skyphoi was 500–480, although they appear earlier and continue later. The deposit contains none of the hastiest examples of this style, usually dated after 480, nor do any other of the Persian destruction cleanup deposits.[191] The draftsmanship is near the nadir of black figure, but the skyphoi themselves are often well-potted. Some of the Class K2 skyphoi from well J 2:4 do have black-figured decoration with incision, and these are related to the Haimon Painter and sometimes even in his manner.[192] Skyphoi of the same shape but with silhouette decoration outnumber those in true black figure in this deposit. The silhouette figures lack incision and occasionally have added color for details. These, too, must be related to the Haimon Painter's workshop, but probably represent other hands at work than those skyphoi with incision.[193] Both the black-figured and silhouette-style skyphoi from well J 2:4 share a careless approach to the decoration, hasty application of the figures, and a preference for stock scenes repeated sketchily. The result is an image that is a vague shadow of the intended design (e.g., Color Ill. 12). As similar as the black-figured skyphoi appear, it is possible to see discernible variations of potting and painting within the examples from well J 2:4, which must relate to different hands.[194]

Catalogued here are representative or distinctive examples of black-figured skyphoi, of which five meet the criteria for inclusion in the probable household assemblage (see Chapter 3). Skyphoi of Ure's Class K2 are represented by 22 entries, mainly from Level 2. Seven fragments that preserved figural scenes or otherwise unrepresented details were inventoried for the Agora pottery database but do not appear in the Catalogue,[195] and 67 smaller or nonfigural fragments of the shape remain in the context pottery tins.[196]

ICONOGRAPHY OF THE BLACK-FIGURED SKYPHOI

The majority of the Class K2 skyphoi from deposit J 2:4 are decorated in a hasty silhouette technique without incision and with little added color. The canonical scheme of decoration is followed in every example; however, there are subtle potting and drawing differences. The K2 skyphos form is characterized by a glazed concave rim, torus ring foot with reserved exterior face, a broad black band and reserved band below the scene, and

190. Ure 1927, pp. 68–69.
191. Hatzidakis 1984, pp. 120–121.
192. Cf. *ABV*, pp. 568–569.
193. *Agora* XXIII, p. 61.
194. Hatzidakis (1984) developed a typological scheme that uses painting and potting stylistic variations to

identify different hands at work in this otherwise unseparated workshop. I will refer to his observations, but will not follow his detailed typology here.
195. See *agathe:* P 32793, P 32796, P 32801, P 32807, P 33181, P 33183, and P 33193.

196. Some of the 67 fragments may belong to catalogued pieces, but there were no joins to guarantee. The fragments returned to the storage tins have parallels in the catalogued material.

a one- or two-figure image, sometimes without incision, between crudely drawn five- to eleven-frond palmettes repeated on both sides. Horizontal cup handles are canted to the level of the rim. The cup-skyphoi most frequently bear themes of Dionysos and his followers, but there is also an interest in Herakles, chariot races, and battles. Deposit J 2:4 provides an overview of the typical images found on Class K2 skyphoi, and features one previously unknown image (45).

Panajotis Hatzidakis attributes all of the skyphoi of this silhouette group (those without incision) to the same hand.[197] It seems reasonable that the skyphoi from well J 2:4 could all be products of one potter and a few very closely aligned painters. This group of silhouette skyphoi follows the work of the Haimon Painter's workshop, whose skyphoi use similar themes, but with incision and more detail; therefore, it is likely that the silhouette K2 skyphoi were produced within the Haimon Painter's workshop, possibly by a single hand.

Three silhouette style cup-skyphoi (45–47, Color Ill. 2) were found nearly complete in the pocket of fine wares (Level 5 and the top of Level 6). The three have very similar profiles, and 45 and 46 are nearly identical, indicating that they are all the products of a single potter. The subject of 45 (Color Ill. 12), two bovines facing each other, one with its head bent down, is rare among the normally repetitive black-figured skyphoi of this type. I have found only one parallel on a silhouette skyphos of a slightly different form.[198] The painter has not made a clear distinction of sex except for an extra "bump" on the right animal's rear which may be a misplaced penis or udders. It is possible that this is meant to be an affectionate scene, a play on the Dionysiac "romantic" scenes of satyrs and maenads. The two-figure composition is unusual for the group, which favors single figures in a field with branches and fruits flanked by rough palmettes.[199] A fragment of a smaller-scale skyphos of this type (51) preserves another quadruped, but not a cow. The animal on 51 is probably a poorly drawn lion or a dog.

The other two nearly complete examples, 46 and 47, are more typical of the subjects of the silhouette-style cup-skyphoi. Cup 46 bears the image of a figure seated on the ground line to the left, looking back around to the right. His arms are cradling an object that loops up and to the left. The curving object is probably a barbitos added onto the stock symposiast figure.[200] The scene may occur on another fragment from this deposit (49), but the figure is too fragmentary to be certain. However, there is no exact parallel for the image outside the deposit.

Cup 47 bears a very common scene of a figure seated on a stool to the left. The figure is most likely seated Dionysos holding a drinking horn.[201] A better-executed example of the scene from the RRCS, by a more patient hand and with incision, gives a better idea of the figural details.[202] The blobs at the head are a beard and possibly a wreath. On 47 the figure's hand seems to grip the vertical drinking vessel by the bottom. A fragment (48) preserves another example of the seated figure, probably Dionysos, for only he and nymphs sit in images on this type of black-figured skyphos. The drawing on 48, though, is of a more controlled hand and does not appear so hasty.

One more fragment preserves the figural scene of a silhouette skyphos of this group. Fragment 50 is very worn, but a female figure with wings

197. Hatzidakis 1984, his Group BIb, pp. 119–120.

198. Art Market, New York, Royal Athena Galleries, HFU59, May 2004.

199. Hatzidakis (1984, pp. 119–121) mentions only three other two-figured examples and one with three figures. In addition, scenes with animals do not occur in any other of Hatzidakis' subgroups of black-figured skyphoi and only occur on eight examples in his list of black-figured skyphoi without incision. On a black-figured cup-skyphos with incision nearer to the Haimon Painter (Hatzidakis Group BIIe) from the RRCS a reclining symposiast type is approached by a bull; Vanderpool 1946, p. 295, no. 86, pl. 46.

200. Cf. the figure in Vanderpool 1946, p. 296, no. 96, pl. 47 (= Hatzidakis 1984, no. 368). The subject is in Hatzidakis's "symposium" category. See Hatzidakis 1984, p. 120, for a list of others.

201. See Hatzidakis 1984, p. 120, for a list of others.

202. Vanderpool 1946, p. 294, no. 81, pl. 45 (= Hatzidakis 1984, no. 338, Group BIa).

can be made out from the ghost of the fugitive black glaze. This is a Nike figure, and a parallel is found in the RRCS that gives an idea of the original composition.[203]

The Class K2 skyphos with reserved exterior face of the torus ring foot can also be decorated with a horizontal band of ivy in the figural zone. There are two similar examples from this deposit, catalogued under **61**. Both have a frieze of reflected ivy leaves connected to a horizontal vine by short stems. Between the leaves are dots, or berries, near the points of the leaves. There is a very similar example from the RRCS.[204] Again, the ivy leaf motif places this cup in the realm of Dionysos.

The remaining fragments of silhouette-style skyphoi are handle palmettes, all hastily drawn with sketchy fronds. Fragment **52**, and others mentioned in its Catalogue entry, all belong to the silhouette-style skyphoi, for no other type takes this form of sketchy palmette. Furthermore, the fragments with palmettes each represent different vessels and do not join with any of the above fragmentary figural scenes. A good effort was made to link nonjoining fragments to one vessel, but this task is greatly hindered by the similarity of the mass-produced skyphoi.

The cup-skyphoi in the next subgroup are also associated with the Haimon Painter's workshop and are true black figure in that details of the figures are incised.[205] The subjects of the skyphoi repeat the subjects of the lekythoi from the Haimon Painter's workshop. The hastiness of the mass-produced black-figured lekythoi is also present in the cup-skyphoi of this workshop. The quality of the cup-skyphoi varies greatly, but in general, the black-figured Haimonian skyphoi with incision are higher-quality products with more careful painting and potting than the silhouette-style skyphoi that also came out of the same workshop. Some of the finer cup-skyphoi from well J 2:4 may be by the Haimon Painter himself, but the subjects are oft-repeated, and the style wilts with repetition. The term "Haimonian" is usually applied to the less skilled products to indicate that they come from the Haimon Painter's workshop and are under his influence, but probably not by the master himself. The black-figured cup-skyphoi of the Haimon Painter's workshop have a torus ring foot often with glazed exterior face, the typical black-glazed lower body with reserved band, figural zone framed by palmettes, and glazed rim. The torus ring foot favored by this workshop is heavier and often has a sharper resting surface than that of the typical silhouette-style skyphos profile. The walls on the Haimon Painter's skyphoi are also straighter, and the ring foot is broader, so that the wall does not curve in so far to meet it at the junction. The rims can be slightly concave, offset, plain, or in two cases, slightly incurving. The overall effect is of a stouter, broader vessel than those of the silhouette-style cup-skyphoi. The implication is that there are at least two potters at work: one producing for the silhouette-style cup-skyphos wing and one producing for the true black-figure wing of the Haimon Painter's workshop.

The true black-figured versions of the cup-skyphoi have palmettes with multiple fronds in a fan-shaped array, sometimes with an added white heart. The figural scenes usually feature two or three figures interacting with each other. Dionysos again dominates the themes, but a few deeds of Herakles appear, and the ubiquitous chariots known from black-figured Haimonian

203. Vanderpool 1946, p. 296, no. 104, pl. 47 (= Hatzidakis 1984, no. 388).

204. Vanderpool 1946, p. 297, no. 114, pl. 47 (= Hatzidakis 1984, no. 356). See also Hatzidakis 1984, no. 360, pl. 45, which is also similar. Fragment **70** is a fragment of a small skyphos with a row of black-glazed verticals on white ground. This is probably a row of lotus buds, similar to the ivy, but I can find no parallel.

205. Hatzidakis 1984, pp. 139–160, Groups BIIe–h.

lekythoi also find a home on the skyphoi. There are examples of all of these subjects from well J 2:4. I have attributed most of the skyphoi broadly to the Haimon Group by designating them "Haimonian." In a few cases, traits suggest a painter closer to the eponymous workshop leader. These I have attributed to "Manner of the Haimon Painter." All the cup-skyphoi from this workshop probably date to the first two decades of the 5th century.[206]

Dionysos and his retinue are popular subjects for the Haimon workshop cup-skyphoi: **55** preserves Dionysos between a satyr and a maenad, while **56** preserves a male carrying a large, apparently soft object in his arms that is probably a wineskin.[207] Fragments **57** and **65** also have satyrs, and **58** has a female probably carrying a lyre.

Another popular subject on the Haimonian skyphoi is the deeds of Herakles. The corpus of scenes is limited to four: the Nemean lion, the Erymanthian boar, the Cretan bull, and the Delphic tripod. Only the first, Herakles wrestling the Nemean lion, is represented in this deposit (**59**), and indeed, this is the most popular of the four on both skyphoi and lekythoi.[208] The stock scene has Herakles down on his knees on the left, wrestling the crouching lion on the right. In the field above him hang his quiver and his mantle and club, usually dangling from one of the decorative branches. The incision varies greatly from very clear, detailed work to hasty, impressionistic scratches. The technique on **59** comes closer to the latter, but it is not the worst. Knowing the scene type, which is very standard, helps to puzzle out the forms on small fragments.

It is interesting that the workshop favored only these few specific Heraklean themes. An obvious motivation for these scenes is their ease of drawing. The Nemean lion, Cretan bull, and Erymanthian boar scenes are nearly identical in composition; only the animal varies. Herakles wrestles all these opponents. This would explain the presence of the boar, which was not one of the more popular of Herakles's deeds in Archaic art. The bull was popular, and we will see it again on the black-figured oinochoe (**5**), to be discussed in Chapter 5. The fight with the lion, though, was the most popular, as the quintessential deed of the hero and a symbol of the mortal turned immortal.[209] The struggle for the Delphic tripod, too, offers an easily recognizable compositional element, the tripod, which allows the painter to express the scene in a very schematic manner while assuring proper identification. The importance here is not the subjects but the suitability of the scenes for a hastily drawn, small-scale, limited-figure composition. The Heraklean combats the skyphos painters chose not to show—the Hydra, Kerberos, and Geryon—raise compositional difficulties that may have been uncomfortable for the middling draftsmen. The really interesting absence is the combat between Herakles and the Amazons. Two-person combat was depicted by the skyphos painters (**66** is one example), but never Herakles and an Amazon, although this was a very popular scene in Archaic black figure.

A final common Haimon Workshop scene found in this deposit features a three- or four-horse chariot.[210] The chariot can either be shown in full gallop or at a starting line. A draped male stands in the chariot holding the reins. The scene has direct parallels with the lekythoi of the Haimon Painter's workshop, but the lekythoi show more variation in the

206. Hatzidakis 1984, p. 140.

207. Cf. *Agora* XXIII, p. 283, no. 1511, pl. 103, for a satyr(?) with wineskin.

208. Hatzidakis 1984, pp. 146–148. Cf. *Agora* XXIII, pp. 222–223, nos. 961–967, for Haimonian lekythoi with Herakles and the Nemean lion. The compositions are identical.

209. There are political interpretations for the popularity of Herakles in the Archaic period, but this hypothesis has little impact on the discussion here; see Boardman 1972.

210. Hatzidakis 1984, pp. 155–160, Group BIIh.

scene type. Subsidiary figures are few on the skyphoi, unlike the lekythoi, on which the chariot can be in a race or a procession, and carry divine or mortal occupants.[211] The upper part of a charioteer is preserved on **60**, and his hunched-over position indicates that he is at full gallop. This is the only chariot scene on the black-figured skyphoi from this deposit, and it probably dates to 490–480, although the type continues down into the mid-5th century on Class K2 skyphoi, pinch-base skyphoi, and lekythoi. Over time, the rhythmic row of horse legs, often of incorrect number, becomes more of a pattern decoration than a representation of a specific subject. This is the key to the chariot's popularity on both small and large shapes: the vertical elements of the horse legs create a striking visual pattern, and the decoration overwhelms the meaning of the image.

Since the multifrond palmettes with strongly curving tendril are so distinctive of the Haimon Painter's workshop, it is possible to identify several fragments to the Haimonian black-figured skyphoi even though none of the figural elements remain.[212]

The next group is also composed of true black-figured cup-skyphoi.[213] The characteristics of this group are a slightly concave glazed rim, glazed exterior face of the torus ring foot, and the canonical figural zone with black-glazed and reserved bands below. The black figure has incision, but it is hasty and the figures are not very innovative, but they do show occasional traces of added color. The figural scenes are more populated than on the Haimonian skyphoi, but the fragments from well J 2:4 unfortunately do not preserve enough of their scenes to demonstrate it. Most fragments are assigned to this group based on the distinctive palmette with "many fresh leaves around black hearts and strongly curved volutes."[214] There are two fragments that probably belong to this group, **53** and **54**. Fragment **53** preserves a seated male and a standing woman, probably Dionysos and a nymph. There is a trace of added color on the garments. The second fragment is just a palmette, but its ten fronds have the same form as those typical of the group.[215] Hatzidakis attributes this group to the Painter of Elaious I by adding to a list assigned to that painter by Beazley.[216] With the small fragments here, even to offer "Manner of the Painter of Elaious I" seems ambitious, thus it will suffice to note that these two fragments appear to be by a different hand than those skyphoi that follow from the Haimon Painter's workshop.[217]

A few fragments of skyphoi related to the Class K2 shape remain to be discussed. Fragment **66**, of unusually lightweight fabric, has a scene of combat between two warriors, one falling down on his knee. This is the only black-figured combat scene preserved in this deposit. The incision is more careful than that of the Haimonian black-figured skyphoi. This must not be a Haimonian product, but it does not readily fit the characteristics of the other workshops producing black-figured skyphoi. Another unusually well-executed fragment, **62**, preserves a nicely potted base with shiny black glaze. The ring-foot profile varies slightly from the others, suggesting an experiment or a different potter. A trace of a small-scale human foot is preserved on the ground line. The foot on the ground line has very delicate added red details, perhaps for sandals. None of the other examples from this deposit matches this subtle detail or fine brushwork. It is difficult to associate this fragment with a workshop, but it is important to note that

211. Cf. *Agora* XXIII, pp. 246–247, nos. 1186–1197, pl. 87, for Haimonian lekythoi with chariot scenes populated by both mortals and gods.

212. These are **64**, **65**, P 32793 *(agathe)*, and P 33183 *(agathe)*. See note 217 below on the relationship between the Painter of Elaious I and the Haimon workshop.

213. Hatzidakis 1984, pp. 134–139, Group BIId.

214. Hatzidakis 1984, p. 135.

215. The palmette on Hatzidakis 1984, no. 430, pl. 13, is very similar.

216. *ABV* 575, nos. 8–13, and 708.

217. *Agora* XXIII, p. 61, associates the Painter of Elaious I with skyphoi under the Haimon Painter's influence. The implication is that the Haimonian workshop was large and fluid, and many identifiable hands had associations with it alongside undistinguishable painters.

there are no skyphoi from the White Heron workshop, the most careful of all the black-figured skyphoi groups, in this deposit.[218]

Finally, there is another class of skyphoi related to the Class K2 skyphoi called "pinch-base" for the contraction of the wall at the junction with the foot. The shape has a rounded bowl and sits on a very broad disk foot. The result is a shape reminiscent of band cups and a distant cousin of the stemmed kylix. There are only two possible examples of this shape from the deposit, **68** and **69**. Fragment **68** is from a thin-walled skyphos. No other black-figured skyphos from this deposit has such a thin wall. The drawing, too, is above average and preserves much added color. A draped figure, probably female, runs right, pursued by a male preserved only as a leg and hand holding a spear or staff. The woman's garments are covered with added color, and the incision is hasty, but detailed. The second possible pinch-base skyphos, **69**, is a fragment with a small-scale symposiast reclining on a dilute ground line. The size of the figure and the curvature of the wall also point to a pinch-base form; however, this fragment is warped, and it is impossible to confirm the shape.

A stray skyphos fragment needs to be mentioned here. The rim fragment **71** is from a skyphos of a shape most frequently decorated in totally black glaze.[219] The rim is straight, but offset, and the interior of the rim is reserved with a frieze of dolphins balancing on their noses. The bodies of the dolphins had both added white and red details, now fugitive, but no incision.[220] Two nonjoining fragments of the skyphos were found, but in the upper fill. The motif is relatively common, especially on drinking vessels.[221] The conceit of dolphins or ships floating on the surface of wine was used often on black-figured cups and mixing bowls and so implies that this skyphos held wine.[222]

BLACK-FIGURED CUP-SKYPHOI: SUMMARY COMMENTS

Five black-figured cup-skyphoi meet the criteria described in Chapter 3 for use in the house (see Table 6); however, the large number of fragments of cup-skyphoi suggest that the set had many more members. At the very least, the abundance of fragments attests to the popularity of this form and decoration in the decades before the sack of Athens. All are poor, late black-figured products with little inspiration and hasty execution, even though some stand out as better than the others. The workshop of the Haimon Painter was responsible for nearly all of the skyphoi present in the deposit. The majority of the examples from this deposit have Dionysiac scenes. The exceptions are the single examples of the usually ubiquitous Herakles and chariot scenes, the Nike, and the rare image of the two bovids (Color Ill. 12). The appearance of Dionysiac imagery on the skyphoi is so common that it assures us that the cup-skyphoi were designed for the consumption of wine. Nonetheless, other liquids or even foods could have been served in the deep, broad bowl. The skyphos with cattle is part of a bovine theme in this deposit, for this house owned other shapes decorated with cattle and related imagery (**23**, **28**). Perhaps this trend is a mere coincidence of archaeological survival, but it may also be revealing an iconographic theme particularly appealing to this homeowner.

218. For the products of the White Heron workshop, see Hatzidakis 1984, Group BIIc, pp. 129–134.

219. Cf. *Agora* XII, p. 276, no. 577, pl. 25, ca. 480.

220. The added colors on the dolphins are visible when the fragment is tilted in raking light.

221. *Agora* XXIII, pp. 263–264, no. 1353, compiles a list of occurrences to which *CVA* Athens 4 [Greece 4], pl. 60 [60]:6, 7, p. 65, adds others.

222. Lissarrague 1990a, pp. 107–122.

Although the absolute number of black-figured skyphoi this house owned is not clear, there are more fragments of this shape and technique than of any other drinking vessel. The house could have owned a set suitable for serving a large gathering of drinkers, but the coarse, generic imagery of the cup-skyphoi suggests that the context would not be one where subtle iconography would be appreciated. It is possible that these sturdy skyphoi represent the quotidian wine drinking vessels of this house. The skyphos is a tabletop shape more easily handled when seated in an upright position, as opposed to the kylix, the stem of which would have been useful to a reclining drinker. The large number may reflect the size of the household or may represent a supply of a shape used regularly and broken frequently, as the fragmentary evidence from the upper portions of the well indicates.

Just as the red-figured cups were complemented by plain black-glazed versions of the shape, so too, the black-figured cup-skyphoi are complemented by plain, black-glazed versions of the shape. The black-glazed cup-skyphos **124** has a very similar profile to **47** (for both, see Color Ill. 2), indicating that they were probably made by the same potter. Again, it is likely that the homeowner bought the plain black-glazed versions of this shape at the same time as he bought the black-figured versions and that the plain were used to fill out the figured set.

A SET OF HERON CLASS SKYPHOI?

The Heron Class skyphos is an overgrown relative of the black-figured cup-skyphoi discussed above. The two share the basic skyphos form of a deep bowl, ring foot, and horizontal handles, but the large size and unusual iconography of the Heron Class skyphos suggest that it might have had a specific cultural use.

P. N. Ure's 1927 volume on the black-figured pottery from the excavations at the cemetery site of Rhitsona in Thebes presented a typology for Attic black-figured skyphoi based on shape, size, and decoration.[223] The Ure typology will be used here to organize the discussion of large black-figured skyphos shapes. The largest of skyphos shapes is called the Heron Class (also known as Ure's Class B and C),[224] named for the white heron that is sometimes found underneath the handle.[225] The shape is characterized by a concave rim, a tall body with a nearly vertical upper wall curving inward to the foot, where a fillet marks the transition, a projecting torus ring foot, and canted horseshoe handles. Its height ranges around 17 cm, with diameters of up to 25 cm. The shape was produced mainly in the years 500–475, but might have appeared in the last years of the 6th century, and was decorated only in the black-figure technique.[226] The decoration of the main frieze area varies, but subsidiary details are generally standard.[227] Skyphoi of this shape bear a number of unparalleled scenes, including the one found on **28** (Color Ill. 8).[228]

Only one nearly complete Heron Class skyphos (**28**) and one small portion of a skyphos made up of joins between Levels 2 and 5 (**34**) meet the criteria for inclusion in the household assemblage; however, fragments of several others attest to their popularity. The most complete example of

223. Ure 1927, pp. 59–62.

224. In Beazley's vocabulary, "'Class' refers to shape, 'Group' to style of drawing" (*ARV*², p. xliii). "Groups" can include identifiable hands, but acknowledges the homogeneity of style, shape, and iconographic preference of multiple painters. E.g., Beazley's discussion of the Leagros Group in *ABV*, p. 354.

225. Ure 1955, p. 90. The bird may, in fact, be a crane; see Borgers 1999, n. 3.

226. Ure 1955, p. 102.

227. *ABV* 617; *Agora* XXIII, p. 60; Ure 1927, pp. 59–62.

228. Borgers 1999, pp. 88–89.

the Heron Class shape from this deposit, **28**, is a skyphos of Ure's Class C, the class defined as having the figural decoration limited to a frieze in the upper half of the vessel and a solid black band below.[229] There are more fragments of Class C skyphoi in the deposit as well as several similar, but smaller skyphoi with coarser decoration assignable to Ure's Class D or E.[230] There are no Class B skyphoi in the deposit. This is a significant point, for finer painters decorated Class B skyphoi, which are similar to Class C, but have images that fill the entire field of the wall with large figures, eschewing the frieze format and its smaller figures.[231] Class B skyphoi of the Theseus Painter and his workshop were found in the SGW and the RRCS and a well recently excavated in the Eleusinion,[232] but there is no sign of his work among the skyphoi in deposit J 2:4. Although these late black-figured products can often suffer from the stagnation of the style, they occasionally introduce very interesting scenes.

The nearly complete Heron Class skyphos, **28** (Color Ill. 8; Fig. 44), was found in the pocket of fine wares, Level 5. The scenes on both sides are the same, with slight but important variations. On both sides of the skyphos are two reclining male drinkers with a female musician seated between them. Each group of three is seated on a single large mattress placed directly on the ground. Numerous birds stand or perch to either side of the central groups.

On side A, the better-preserved side, but not necessarily the dominant side, two bearded drinkers flank a flute player. Both drinkers recline on their left elbows and look to our right. They wear ill-defined himations decorated with hastily incised fold lines. The left drinker extends his right arm outward and grasps a stemmed cup by the stem. The left drinker wears a turban headdress, the layers of which are indicated with stripes of added red. The turban gives his head a conical shape with a "knob" at the back. This is probably meant to be a bun or hair extending from the turban.[233] At the front of the left drinker's head are three hornlike projections. The top and bottom projections are curved inward. The differing lengths of the projections suggest that the painter was attempting to show the projections in perspective, extending from the drinker's profile head.

To the right of the man with the three-pronged headdress is a seated female flute player. She sits up propped on a pillow behind her and faces left. She also wears a wrap head covering, which may be a sakkos since it is looser than the headdress of the left drinker. Both of her hands are raised to a double flute. The flute survives as dilute glaze, and it is possible that it was originally added white. Her face and hands would also have been added white, but only the ghost of the added color survives.

To the right of the flute girl is the second drinker. He, like his left companion, looks right, wears an ill-defined himation, rests his invisible left elbow on a pillow, and raises a stemmed cup in his right hand. His hair is gathered up and tied with a fillet. A small bump at the back of the head represents a bun, or flap of hair.[234] This right drinker also wears a horned headdress. There are four projections extending from the top of the right drinker's profile head. The outer two are hornlike and curve like parentheses. Between the two horns are two lobed projections that resemble ears. Here the painter seems to be giving a frontal view of the headdress on a profile head.

229. Ure 1927, p. 61.

230. Ure 1927, pp. 62–66.

231. Ure's Class B: Ure 1927, p. 59. The Theseus Painter, the Krokotos Painter, and their associates are the leading painters of the large-frieze Class B skyphoi. For the Theseus Painter, see Borgers 2004.

232. From RRCS: *Agora* XXIII, p. 279, no. 1484, pl. 100; *Agora* XXIII, p. 279, no. 1486, pl. 100; *Agora* XXIII, pp. 279–280, no. 1487, pl. 101; *Agora* XXIII, p. 280, no. 1488, pl. 101; *Agora* XXIII, p. 280, no. 1489, pl. 100; *Agora* XXIII, p. 280, no. 1490, pl. 101; *Agora* XXIII, p. 280, no. 1492 (= Vanderpool 1946, pp. 289–290, no. 62, pl. 37); *Agora* XXIII, p. 297, no. 1657, pl. 107. From SGW: Roberts 1986, p. 29, no. 51, fig. 17, pl. 8. See also P 34436, from deposit U 21:1, Camp 2007, pp. 652–653, fig. 26.

233. See, e.g., Kurtz and Boardman 1986, p. 50, fig. 29.4.

234. Boardman (Kurtz and Boardman 1986, pp. 50–51) discusses this "tied head cloth" versus the turban.

There are birds to the left and right of the central group. To the left of the mattress is a crooked stump upon which a bird with incised feathers is perched. This bird faces the drinkers, and a line of four dots of diminishing size flows from his beak toward the left drinker. To the left of the stump is preserved the back half of a bird with incised feathers standing on the ground, facing the group. To the left of these birds, centered under the handle, is another bird, which faces left, but turns its neck and head around to face the group on side A. To the right of the central group is another crooked stump and group of birds. A bird with incised feathers perches on the stump but faces right, away from the drinkers. The right drinker looks in its direction. On the ground, overlapping the stump, a bird faces left and cranes its neck toward the mattress. To the right, centered under the handle, a bird with incised wing feathers faces left but looks right, toward the group on side B.

The figural scene on side B is not as well preserved as that on side A due to surface abrasion and critical missing fragments. It is clear, however, that it repeats the structure of side A. On this side there is a seated female lyre player between two reclining drinkers. The drinker at the left is poorly preserved owing to missing fragments, but the front of the profile face and beard are present to indicate that he reclines on his left elbow and looks back to the right. The angle of the beard and face suggest that his chin is tucked in, so that he looks downward at the lyre player's hands. Although the surface is very worn, a trace of the curving tip of a projection resembling the end of a goat's horn can be seen to the right of the break, which means the left drinker also wore a headdress featuring at least one hornlike projection.

To the right of the left drinker is a female lyre player. She sits upright, facing left with a pillow beneath her. Her head is slightly conical in shape, suggesting that the head wrap is a turban like the one worn by the left drinker on side A. Her hands and face would have been in added white, but the color is no longer preserved. She holds the lyre against her chest and raises her left hand to the invisible strings. Three or four dots arc around and to the right in the field above her head, possibly indicating music emitted by her instrument.

The right drinker reclines in the now-familiar position. This figure is the only drinker on the vase not to wear an odd headdress. His head is bound in a wreath or tainia of added red. He has no projections extending from his head. He raises his right arm above his bent knee and holds an added white drinking horn. The white was applied directly to the surface and is now nearly gone. In the field above the drinking horn is a swallow flying to the right with its wings extended.

Again, to both the left and right of the central group on side B are clusters of birds. Unfortunately, the group to the left of the mattress is largely missing, but the tail of one bird and bottom of a stump indicate that the group was similar to the one to the left of the central group on side A. To the right of the central group on side B, a bird perches on another gnarled stump and looks down at the right drinker, who lifts his head to return the gaze. On the ground in front of the stump, a bird with incised tail feathers faces the drinkers and cranes its neck toward the mattress. To the right and behind this bird is another that faces the central group, but turns its head to the right. The top of its head abuts the bottom of the left-side of the handle. The birds total 11 in all if we restore one to the stump at the left on side B. The sparrow adds another.

The skyphos is a product of the CHC Group.[235] This group of black-figure painters was active in the last decades of the 6th and first decades of the 5th century and is named for its favorite scenes: either Amazons with chariots or courting groups (CH = chariot, C = courting). Repetitive subjects and shapes link the group, but individual hands can be detected within the group, although these have not been fully sorted out.[236]

A successful interpretation of the imagery of 28 (Color Ill. 8) requires a complete understanding of the roles of two peculiar aspects of the scenes: the headdresses and the birds. I have found no clear explanation for either. The preliminary report on well J 2:4 cautiously suggested either a dramatic or cultic interpretation, but neither is satisfying.[237] The overall tone of the skyphos is ordinary, as if nothing were special. That it seems odd to us may mean that we are not equipped with the visual vocabulary possessed by the intended viewers of the skyphos. The formal arrangement of two reclining drinkers flanking a musician is fairly common in "sympotic" scenes and would not be considered unusual were it not for the birds and the headdresses. Both sides of the skyphos depict a drinking party occurring outdoors, as indicated by the single swallow above the right-hand drinker on side B.[238] The mattresses are placed directly on the earth, at the level of the tree stumps. The supernumerary birds and the gnarled stumps place the gathering in an extraurban location, not the civilized world of the urban andron. Here the emphatically rural setting may mean either that this is a group reveling in its excursion to the great outdoors or that the painter is contrasting city drinking with rural entertaining. The birds are most likely vultures, based on their shapes, positions, and markings.[239] Their number and their interaction with the central human group, especially the perching bird on side B who exchanges gazes with the right drinker, impart a humorous element to the scene and reinforce the group's proximity to nature.

The two birds located under the handles may also be a joke at the expense of the more distinguished White Heron painters. The White Heron group of painters, including the Krokotos Painter, placed a single white heron under each handle of their Heron Class skyphoi (thus giving the class its name). On 28 the noble heron is replaced by the ignoble vulture.

235. Originally attributed to the White Heron Group, Camp 1996, p. 246, no. 22, pl. 72. For support of the revised attribution, see Catalogue. For the CHC Group in general, see *ABV* pp. 617–626; *Paralipomena*, pp. 306–308; *Add*², p. 144.

236. For instance, Beazley saw the Amazons with chariot scenes as "all by one hand": *ABV*, p. 617 bottom.

237. Camp 1996, p. 246, no. 22.

238. Outdoor symposia are dis-cussed in Kaeser 1990b; Topper 2009. The presence of a single bird has also been associated with the presence of Athena; see Bron 1992, pp. 64–68.

239. Elke Böhr (pers. comm.). Dr. Böhr remarks that vultures were probably more common in ancient Greece than they are in modern Greece, and that they served an important role as street cleaners both in town and in the countryside. The vulture is dying out in modern Greece because their prime food source, the donkey, is no longer essential to village life. Eleni Hatzivassiliou (2009, pp. 116–117) suggests that birds on skyphoi by the Theseus and Athena Painters are ravens. The study examines scenes of birds perching on altars and tumuli, and some do resemble the body form, but not the feather incisions of 28. It is possible that some of her birds are vultures.

Surely this substitution brought a chuckle to fellow members of the CHC Group at the very least.[240] The Dog Group, another group of painters who painted Heron Class skyphoi, placed dogs under the handles, which might also have been a joke. Perhaps we are seeing interactions between workshops akin to those well documented for the Pioneer red-figure painters, here in a large, late black-figure workshop.

The headdresses remain a puzzle, but it is useful to start with what they are not. In his article on the "Getty Birds" vase, J. R. Green collects vase-painting images depicting scenes of comic choruses.[241] His examples of comic choruses all feature a group of men performing in costume. The earliest vases in Green's study date to the late 6th century and depict groups of costumed men moving in unison.[242] These depictions show that comic performance in the Archaic period already featured the comic choral dances that would be a characteristic of Classical Attic comedy. In contrast, the figures on **28** are not engaged in a dance, so cannot be described as a comic chorus. In vase painting depictions of choruses, the only reference to staging is the occasional inclusion of the theatrical musician, a lyre- or flute-player.[243] The internal, dramatic setting is not depicted in any way through the use of figures or sets. Only the costumes indicate the theme of the chorus. This lack of setting in choral images also contrasts with the obvious outdoor setting of **28**. While the choral figures do wear headdresses, these are clearly part of a costume.[244] A black-figured amphora, Berlin, Staatliche Museen F1697, depicts a chorus that wears crested helmets with a superficial similarity to the headdresses of **28**.[245] In the Berlin scene, three men wearing horse costumes (their faces are clearly depicted beneath a horse-head mask) bear men dressed as "knights" on their backs. Each of the three knights wears a helmet with a distinctive crest. The first wears a helmet with projecting donkey ears. The donkey ears are rendered with convincing perspective to suggest that the ears are perpendicular to the profile head. While the crests do bear similarities to the projecting headgear of **28**'s drinkers, the amphora painter is careful to show that the knights wear helmets and the devices are integral to the helmets. On **28**, however, the turbans and hair wraps preclude the wearing of a helmet, and there is no indication that the figures are wearing masks.

240. A kiln site excavated in Athens may document a workshop relationship between the CHC Group and the Krokotos Painter and followers; see Baziotopoulou-Balabani 1994.

241. Green 1985.

242. This aspect of the vase-painting depictions of pre-comedy is also emphasized by Sifakis (1971, pp. 86–87) and Brijder (1986, pp. 79–81); see also Green and Handley 1995, pp. 14–21.

243. See the discussion of early choruses in Webster 1970, pp. 1–23.

244. Sifakis (1971, pp. 76–77) lists theriomorphic choruses known from

ancient sources (both fragments and references) but bulls are not among them. Fisher (2000, p. 382, n. 29, fig. 10) illustrates a Boiotian Kabirion Class skyphos (once Berlin 3286) decorated on one side with a symposium scene in which the participants appear to be wearing comic theatre masks and have a strange triangle projecting from the tops of their heads. Fisher cites this Boiotian example to suggest, although hesitatingly, that **28** also represents a comic theatrical symposium. I agree with Boardman (cited as pers. comm. in Fisher 2000,

p. 382, n. 29) that the odd triangular projection above the heads of the Boiotian comic symposiasts is meant to represent fancy headbands, and thus it should not be compared to the more elaborate and distinctive headdresses of **28**. The same triangular headband is seen on the figure of Kabiros on a fragmentary Kabirion Class skyphos, Athens 10426, Boardman 1998, fig. 506:2; thus the headband is not exclusively associated with comic contexts.

245. Green 1985, p. 101, no. 3, fig. 6; *ABV* 297, no. 17; *Paralipomena* 128 [Painter of Berlin 1686].

On a Heron Class skyphos in the Guardini Collection each side features a line of armed dancers moving in unison toward an aulos player.[246] The figures, satyrs and humans, wear helmets, and Ingeborg Scheibler has interpreted a projecting shape at the hairline of some of the dancers as horns.[247] On a closer look, the projections are more likely to be the upturned cheek flaps of the helmets. Regardless, even if these are horns, their form is different from those on 28, and the Guardini skyphos scene certainly portrays a dancing group, possibly a comic chorus.

One final depiction of a comic chorus is worth mentioning here. On the shoulder of a black-figured hydria in a private collection, four chorus members dance in unison toward a flute player, their front feet kicking and their hands in their armpits, elbows out "chicken dance"–style.[248] Green describes the chorus members and the flute player as "wearing animal ears in their headbands."[249] A closer look at the headbands, though, reveals that the projections are not animal ears but feathers. The projections, in added white, are the shape of feathers, and at least the piper's has a distinct quill. This may be another bird-related spoof and not a chorus of mules.[250] Regardless of identification, the almond-shaped objects are fitted into a distinct headband and are not of the same form as the headdresses depicted on 28. Therefore, using the evidence put forth by Green as examples of comic representations contemporary with or earlier than 28, the scene depicted on both sides of 28 does not fit into the well-defined characteristics of the representation of early comic choruses.

The headdresses find their closest parallels in elaborate helmets of the Orientalizing and Archaic periods. Vase painters depict helmets with elaborate attachments ranging from horns to zoomorphic crests such as the ones on the Berlin amphora with knights, examples of which are also known from surviving bronze helmets of the Archaic and Orientalizing periods. A helmet in a private collection in Würzburg provides a good example of the type.[251] Two horns and two ears are attached to a Corinthian helmet. The horns sit atop the helmet, and project out in a wide ∨ perpendicular to the profile. The ears appear below the horn and jut out nearly horizontally. Each horn and ear is one hammered piece, and is flat, not fully rounded.[252] Vase painters also depict horned helmets in battle scenes.[253] There is even

246. Guardini 48, Todisco 1984, pp. 45–46, pl. 43.

247. Scheibler 2000, p. 26.

248. Green 1985, p. 100, no. 2, fig. 5; Sweden, Private Collection, *Münzen und Medaillen (Auktion)* 1967, pp. 57–58, lot no. 121, pl. 31.

249. Green 1985, p. 100.

250. See Webster 1970, p. 94, for early choruses that anticipate the plays of Old Comedy including the *Birds* and the *Knights*.

251. Collection of Prof. K. Wyss, published in Lorenz 1980, pp. 135–138, pls. 31, 32.

252. For other examples, see Born 1994, figs. 6, 63, 66, 68–71, among others. For Born 1994, fig. 66 (AG 308), see now Christie's South Kensington, 28 April 2004, lot no. 58.

253. See the useful diagrams in Born 1994, pp. 38–53, for a range of helmet-crest types. Horned helmets on vases: Louvre, Camp. 150, *CVA* Louvre 6 [France 9], pl. 60 [399]:1 [hydria, early 6th century]; NY Met. 25.78.4, *ABV* 119, no. 9 [Related to Lydos], *CVA* Metropolitan Museum 2 [USA 2], pl. 10 [10]:12b [lip cup tondo, mid-6th century]; NY Met.

44.11.1, *CVA* Metropolitan Museum 2 [USA 2], pl. 25 [25]:39c, 39d [eye cup, ca. 525, helmets with horns, ears, and feathers]; Munich 2244, *CVA* Munich 10 [Germany 56], pl. 44 [2765], 45 [2766], [oversized Droop cup, figures A10, B15, B32 (among others?) have horns or ears on their helmets, ca. 525]; Berlin-Charlottenburg, 1970, 9, cup by the Triptolemos Painter, Knauer 1973, figs. 1, 2. See also the East Greek black-figured fragment from Lindos, Rhodes, figured in Born 1994, fig. 65.

a three-pronged feather-holding crest on a vase in Belgium that recalls the three-pronged headdress of the left-hand drinker on side A of **28**.[254] The helmet is a part of the iconography of battle, and as Vance Watrous argued for the Siphnian Treasury, the distinctive helmets distinguished individuals on the battlefield.[255]

The headdresses on **28** do not, however, seem to be elaborate helmets; there is also no reference to military matters in the image. The poor draftsmanship of **28** hinders interpretation of the images, but the striping on the back of the head of the left drinker on side A certainly means that he is wearing a turban and not a helmet, and the bun of the right drinker on side A also precludes a helmet. On the Agora example used to confirm the attribution to the CHC Group,[256] we see that Dionysos there has a single incised line from hair to beard defining his face, which is characteristic of the CHC Group. Therefore, the beard forms on **28** are not cheek pieces of helmets, nor are they masks.[257] However, the painter expresses no obvious relationship between the head and the projections on **28**. We are left wondering how they attach to the head. Did the painter intend for the figures to be wearing helmets and fail to complete the headgear logically?

A second suggestion is that the scene on **28** refers to cultic activity.[258] Our understanding of private, everyday cult (versus public cult) in Athens remains unclear; however, ritual dining, and subsequently drinking, were regular aspects of cult practice. One possible interpretation of **28** would link it with local festivals of Dionysos. The Rural Dionysia were festivals of Dionysos held in villages throughout Attica during the winter, and each community celebrated on a different day of the festival calendar of Athens. Each festival included a procession, performances, sacrifices, and feasting. Plutarch describes the state of the Rural Dionysia in his day. He bemoans the ostentation of the events and longs for the simple days of yore. Amid his rhetoric may be a clue to the scene on **28**. He mentions, among other things, that in his day the processions included people in expensive costumes and masks.[259] Admittedly, Plutarch is a source distant from the period of the vase, but perhaps the exaggerated aspects of the festival in the Roman Imperial period had their roots in the traditions of Archaic Rural Dionysia. As observed above, the extraurban setting of the scenes on **28** is emphasized, and the local festivals of Dionysos were intended to unite rural communities and to contrast from the ritual activities of the city.

The bull's horns themselves may be a reference to Dionysos. Dionysos appeared to humans as a bull (e.g., Eur. *Bacchae*, 617–622, 920–923, 1017–1018, 1159), and "bull-god" was an epithet of the god in the Archaic and Classical periods.[260] Horns became an attribute of images of Dionysos only in the Hellenistic period, so it is unlikely that the horns on **28** are meant to denote the god himself.[261] There is no textual or visual evidence for worshippers of Dionysos wearing horns. Nevertheless, the association of Dionysos with the bull is worth keeping in mind as we consider the spectrum of bovine references in this deposit.

If not the specific activity of the Rural Dionysia, then perhaps the scene is referring to an irregular feast in a rural cult setting. A source more than a century later than the production of this skyphos, Menanader's Middle Comedy *Dyskolos*, includes a plot point that revolves around

254. Brussels R391, figured in Born 1994, fig. 48.

255. Watrous 1982, pp. 162–167.

256. For attribution of **28**, see Catalogue; *Agora* XXIII, p. 290, no. 1588, pl. 105.

257. It is possible that the drinkers are wearing masks that the painter depicts as their actual physiognomy. Later, in red figure, it is sometimes difficult to tell the difference between a satyr and a human wearing a satyr costume for a satyr play. There the costumes are not always so obviously depicted. However, all Late Archaic images of theatrical performances, discussed above, feature figures unambiguously wearing masks and costumes.

258. Also proposed by Scheibler (2000, p. 24) for **28**.

259. Plut. *Mor.* 3.527D.

260. *Homeric Hymn to Dionysos* 1.3 (West 2003).

261. Carpenter 1997, p. 106.

the preparations for a rural feast. In the play, the family has gone to the countryside to make a sacrifice to Pan. Important to note is the distinction between city and country. The family does not travel together, suggesting that the location is not too far outside the city, but the site is selected for its rural setting.[262] Intrinsic to the plot is that the day of feasting is capped by a night of drinking on the spot. A slave and a caterer arrive early to prepare the food and arrange the equipment, including mattresses and στιβάδας, which are probably mats of grass or weeds.[263] Is it possible that **28** depicts such an evening of entertainment following an informal (versus regularly scheduled) rural sacrifice. Costumes were an important part of some cults, for example, the *arktoi* of Artemis of Brauron.[264] It seems unlikely, though, in the Late Archaic period, for a cultic setting to be handled as humorously as the abundant birds demand and to be portrayed with the formal characteristics of a symposium. Known vase-painting scenes of cult activity are sober and emphasize sanctuary settings through the inclusion of altars and occasional columns representing temple architecture.[265]

Until further evidence appears, a good interpretation of **28** may be one somewhere between purely secular and purely cultic. The event depicted is a pleasant, enjoyable one. The men raise their cups festively and find amusement in their feathered company. However, there are distinctions among the participants. The only man without a headdress, the right drinker on side B, is distinguished also by his white drinking horn, the positioning of the swallow above his head, and his direct engagement of the perching bird to the right. Dionysos and satyrs are frequently the bearers of drinking horns in Archaic art,[266] so could this be Dionysos? If so, there are no other attributes to identify him. This drinker's status at the gathering is different from that of the other three men, but what is the nature of his status? Initiated or uninitiated? Leader or follower? The other three men share the similarities of headdress and drinking vessel (although we cannot be sure about the left drinker on side B, as his cup is not preserved). Perhaps the right drinker on side B is enjoying his "initiation" into a group. The nature of this group is likely crucial to the explanation of the headdresses. At the very least, communal drinking in Athens and elsewhere served to form personal bonds between the individual and the group. A common way to reinforce a feeling of membership is a restrictive code of dress or behavior: a group uniform or secret handshake. To wear the outfit or hold the secret knowledge is to belong to the group.[267] Perhaps what we are seeing here is the "uniform" of a group, possibly, but not certainly, with a religious purpose (cf. the Arval Brotherhood, and others). More will be said about the bovine connection below. The rural, outdoor setting also suggests a special, even extraordinary, location. Exclusive location or access is another means of defining group identity. The unadorned right drinker on side B, then, may be celebrating his new membership in this fraternity of friends.

An unusual scene can sometimes indicate that a vase was specifically commissioned. This is a very unusual scene for the CHC Group, which favored repeated stock scenes, and the careless style may make private commission less likely. The assumption is that bespoke pieces should be better painted, but we cannot know this for certain. The scene may also be the

262. Men. *Dys.* 260–265, 393–426, 855–860.

263. Men. *Dys.* 420; for mattresses on the Attic Stelai, see Pritchett 1956, p. 247, no. 5.

264. Kahil 1977; Sourvinou-Inwood 1990, with bibliography.

265. Some examples of ritual processions or libations, the predominant type of religious scenes in vase painting: Tarquinia, RC 1918, *ARV*² 366, no. 88, Bérard and Durand 1989, p. 32, fig. 33; once Basle Market, *Münzen und Medaillen* 22 (1958), Bérard 1989, p. 108, fig. 152; Boston, MFA 13.195, *ARV*² 35, no. 1 [Gales Painter], Boardman 1975, fig. 211; London, British Museum, WT 220, *ABL* 219, no. 65 [Edinburgh Painter], Boardman 1974, fig. 243.

266. Carpenter 1986, pp. 117–118; Davidson 1997, p. 64. The drinking horn is associated with rapid and excessive drinking and so represents a less civilized way of drinking.

267. Fornis and Casillas 1997, p. 37.

result of an unrecoverable whim on the part of the painter or a depiction of a local story or activity in which he himself participated.

In its evocation and humorous treatment of the symposium, the very activity in which the viewer/drinker was taking part, **28** is analogous to the red-figure set of Type C cups owned by this household. Between the number of birds and the unusual headdresses, this skyphos must have been amusing to the viewer sitting in a house in downtown Athens. Skyphos **28** may or may not have been purchased at the same time as the red-figured cups or the red-figured pelike, but it shares their spirit. At the very least, this skyphos contributes visual information on a new form of costumed communal drinking previously unknown in the Archaic period.

OTHER LARGE BLACK-FIGURED SKYPHOI

There are fragments of at least three other large skyphoi of Ure's Class C, that is, the Heron Class, present in well J 2:4, although they do not meet the criteria for inclusion in the household assemblage. These are three nonjoining fragmentary bases and lower walls with alternating red and black tongues, a trait unique to Ure's Class C, inventoried under **30** and **31**. There are also fragments of identifiable figural scenes (**29, 33**), others too fragmentary to identify (**34**), and ca. 10 uncatalogued small fragments of rims generally with the dot-band wreath that may belong to skyphoi of Class C shape. It is possible that the figural and rim fragments belong to skyphoi represented by one of the inventoried bases.

In contrast to **28**, the remainder of the fragmentary Heron Class and related skyphoi from this deposit have, for the most part, images more typical of their class. All the large skyphoi are products of the CHC Group. Preserved on **29** is the only example of Amazons with a chariot wheeling around, which the CHC Group alone painted, and only on the Heron Class skyphoi. The fragments of **29** preserve the head of a single Amazon and parts of the four-horse chariot wheeling around at center and parts of the two sphinxes that framed the scene.[268] The incision on **29** is a bit more detailed and slightly less hasty than on other examples of this type.[269]

In addition to the large black-figured skyphoi of Class C, there are numerous examples of other large skyphoi of Ure's Classes D and E from this deposit. These classes can be difficult to distinguish without the entire vessel. In general, Class D skyphoi are slightly smaller than Class C and more poorly decorated, sometimes without any incision. They always bear a scene between seated sphinxes and all-black tongues at the base of the wall.[270] Class E skyphoi, which are even smaller, are similarly decorated with poorly painted images but may or may not have black tongues at the base of the wall.[271] The four fragmentary bases catalogued under **42** and **43** with all-black tongues belong to either Class D or E skyphoi, and **44**, without tongues, must belong to a Class E, the only class of this shape without tongues.

A fragment of a skyphos with an identifiable scene, **32**, depicts on both sides a ram framed by sphinxes. The tongues at the base of the wall are not preserved, but the smaller size, poor painting and potting, and added color point more to D1 than C1 (the "1" indicating dot-ivy wreath at rim). Each

268. Von Bothmer 1957, pp. 86–87. He suggests that the pairing of the Amazons with chariot and sphinxes may have been inspired by scenes on larger vessels.

269. Cf., among many others, Athens, National Archaeological Museum 13905, *CVA* Athens 4 [Greece 4], pl. 48 [48]:1–3; Athens, National Archaeological Museum 21064, *CVA* Athens 4 [Greece 4], pl. 48 [48]:4–6; Athens, British School, *ABV* 618, no. 15, Boardman 1974, fig. 292.

270. Ure 1927, p. 62.

271. Ure 1927, p. 63.

ram moves to the right, and the sphinxes face the handles. There is abundant added color in lieu of incision. The rams wear added red garlands around their necks, suggesting that they are adorned for sacrifice. Ure describes but does not picture a smaller skyphos of Class D1 with a single ram, no incision, with a purple fillet around its neck.[272] It is likely that **32** should be restored on the lines of the Rhitsona skyphos.

Courting and dancing scenes are the second- and third-favorite skyphos designs by the CHC Group, and both are present in fragmentary examples within this deposit.[273] These scenes appear on either Class D or E vessels, so it is difficult to assign figural wall fragments to a specific shape. Fragment **33** preserves the dot-ivy rim of a deep, large vessel, and a single head to the left. Since the products of the CHC Group are so uniform and repetitious, this small fragment is enough to suggest a courting scene.[274] The diagonal line running through the fragment may be the tail of a cock, the love gift frequently depicted in a variation of the scene.[275]

Preserved on **35** is a fragmentary courting scene on a Class D skyphos. Only the lower portion of the figural zone is preserved, but there is a sphinx to the left, presumably mirrored on the right, and four males at center. The two at the center face each other while a companion walks away on either side of them.[276] The body positions of figures in both the courting and dancing scenes are very similar, and some of the fragments may belong to either subject type. A few more fragments preserve only a portion of a male figure, therefore the scene could be either dancers or courting. Fragments **39** and **40** each preserve only a portion of a single figure and, in the case of **40**, a bit of the framing sphinx.

The dancing scenes are slightly easier to identify because of the presence of women. There are some courting scenes with women, but the fragments of dancing scenes here all feature women in motion and cannot be confused with courting scenes.[277] Fragments **36, 37, 38,** and **39** all depict dancing scenes. Of these, **36** and **37** are the most complete fragments, but again, the stock scene is readily identified from even the smallest scrap of a women's skirt.

Finally, there are a few small fragments of sphinxes that flank the scenes on both Class D and E skyphoi. Preserved portions of seated sphinxes are catalogued under **41**. Class E skyphoi tend to have handle palmettes in addition to sphinxes, and there are no traces of handle palmettes among the fragments. Therefore, it is more likely that the above fragments of courting and dancing belong to skyphoi of Class D than to E. The only implication is that Class D skyphoi are larger than Class E, and a preference for the larger vessels is noted for the house.

The shape of the large skyphos, echoing the form of its modestly sized cousins, usually causes it to be classed as a drinking vessel. It is obvious from this discussion that the shape was popular, but according to the criteria described in Chapter 3, only one (**28**) can be assigned to the household assemblage with certainty. Unlike the red-figured cups and the black-figured cup-skyphoi, the large skyphoi are not preserved as a set or a remnant of a set. This may be a result of the cleanup process, or even of chance.

The size of Heron Class skyphoi results in a capacity of about three liters, which is about five times the amount that a kylix held (see Appendix II).

272. Ure 1927, p. 62, no. R 26.92. There is a somewhat similar scene with two rams on a Heron Class skyphos, but these rams have incision and more active poses: Athens, National Archaeological Museum 20097, *CVA* Athens 4 [Greece 4], pl. 49 [49]:3, 4.

273. For CHC Group courting scenes and their variations, see discussion in *CVA* Athens 4 [Greece 4], pp. 52–56 (entry for pl. 45:1–3). For CHC Group dancing, also see *CVA* Athens 4 [Greece 4], p. 58 (entry for pl. 52:1, 2).

274. Cf. complete examples: Ure 1927, no. R 80.260, pl. 19; Athens, National Archaeological Museum 636, *CVA* Athens 4 [Greece 4], pl. 46 [46]:1–3.

275. Beazley 1947, pp. 22–23.

276. For a complete example of a courting scene, see Ure 1927, no. R 80.260, pl. 19.

277. For a complete example of a dancing scene, see Athens, National Archaeological Museum 1112, *CVA* Athens 4 [Greece 4], pl. 52 [52]:1–2. Sometimes satyrs and maenads dance: cf. Athens, National Archaeological Museum 364, *CVA* Athens 4 [Greece 4], pl. 54 [54]:4, 5.

There are references in sympotic literature to the use of different-sized cups throughout the night of drinking. There are calls for "the big cups," with the implication that the drinker wished to get drunk faster than the current small-cup pace would allow.[278] In Xenophon's *Symposium*, the clown Philip finishes his dance and declares he is thirsty, calling for τὴν μεγάλην φιάλην.[279] Socrates puts a halt to the request and advises the continued use of μικραῖς κύλιξι.[280] Are the Heron Class skyphoi the big cups? Some symposium scenes depict drinkers holding both a kylix and a large skyphos.[281] It is possible that such depictions imply the transition from the regular to big cups. In these scenes, the skyphos most often resembles an Attic skyphos or a Corinthian-type skyphos. The handles are not canted as they are on the Heron Class vessels, and the vase painters often add lines in the handle zones, as we find on both the Attic and Corinthian skyphoi shapes in black glaze. A skyphos of Heron Class type does appear on a black-figured amphora in Munich, interpreted as depicting activities of the Anthesteria festival. It shows a woman drinking from a large skyphos with canted handles and horizontal lines that indicate the wreathed mouth and the bottom of the figural zone of a Heron Class skyphos of Class B.[282] However, the iconography of Heron Class and other large skyphoi, along with their prevalence, argues against their being exclusively associated with women or a festival.[283]

The three liters that **28** holds would have weighed three kilograms. It seems unlikely that the vessel was raised to the lips when a drinker was seated in the reclining position. Certainly the handles would not have withheld the strain, especially since the reclining drinker could have grasped only one. It is true, however, that drinkers depicted in vase paintings often appear to carry or use very large vessels for drinking.[284] On a vase attributed to the Kleophrades Painter, a figure carries a large skyphos and another figure grabs a transport amphora by its handle as if it is light or empty.[285] The amphora in the scene by the Kleophrades Painter is probably not empty, because that would signal an end to the evening. Seemingly weightless objects are examples of the painter's artistic license. Vase painters were only minimally interested in realism and proper scale, and they frequently exaggerated certain elements either for effect or for ease of drawing. The same may apply to the scale of the skyphos the other reveler holds on the Kleophrades Painter's amphora. The largest Attic-type skyphos preserved in the Agora excavations has a height of 15 cm and diameter of 18 cm.[286] This is still less than the 17 cm height and 22 cm diameter of **28**. There is a

278. Davidson (1997, pp. 63–64) discusses the use of different-sized cups and their implications. He uses literary evidence from a wide range of periods, but Xenophon is the author closest in date to this deposit. Scheibler (2000, pp. 38–39) also proposes that the Heron Class skyphoi might have been the "big cups."

279. Xen. *Sym.* 2.23.

280. Xen. *Sym.* 2.26.

281. Cf. komasts on Douris, Berlin 2289, *ARV*² 435, no. 95, *Paralipomena*

375, *Add*² 238, Buitron-Oliver 1995, no. 143.

282. Munich 1538, *ABV* 395, no. 3, *CVA* Munich 9 [Germany 48], pl. 10 [2307]:1. There is a Heron Class skyphos with a subject related to the Anthesteria in Bologna that shows a procession with the boat of Dionysos: Bologna, D.L. 109, *CVA* Bologna 2 [Italy 7], pl. 43 [342].

283. Scheibler (2000) discusses the possibility that some of the Heron Class skyphoi were associated with

festivals, but not all. She even connects some with rural festivals of Dionysos (p. 27).

284. For example, in a cup tondo attributed to the Salting Painter, once London, Mitchell Collection, *ARV*² 178, no. 5, Boardman 1975, fig. 125.

285. Würzburg 507, *ARV*² 181, no. 1, Boardman 1975, fig. 129.

286. P 21377, *Agora* XII, p. 259, no. 343, pl. 16, dated to the middle of the 5th century.

general trend toward larger skyphoi through the Archaic into the Classical period, but there is no archaeological evidence to suggest that the Attic- or Corinthian-type skyphoi ever approached the scale depicted in Attic vase painting. Therefore, I do not believe that the cups depicted on vases reflect real models in every detail.

Alternatively, the large, deep, open skyphoi, particularly of Class B and C, could have been mixing bowls for small gatherings at which a large krater would have held too much wine. Average Type C cups (kylikes) have a volume of between 500 and 700 ml when full, thus the three-liter volume of the Heron Class skyphos could serve about four to six people a single cup of wine (see Appendix II).[287] These skyphoi/mixing bowls, then, may have been reserved for use in small gatherings, perhaps of informal but intimate nature. It is possible that the house owned a few of these small-scale mixing bowls for use in small gatherings or in less formal drinking occasions such as the mixing of wine for consumption with a daily meal. Skyphos **28**, with its very odd images, may have served as a mixing bowl for a few guests "in on the joke." In contrast, the uninspired, repetitious images of the other fragments suggest that these were used when the vase painting held little meaning beyond the decoration of a functional object for drinking.

BLACK-FIGURED CUP FRAGMENTS

There are only six fragments of black-figured cups from the deposit, only one of which, **77**, meets the criteria described in Chapter 3 for inclusion in the household assemblage because it is made up of two fragments that join between the upper and lower fill of the well. It is possible that the other wall and rim fragments are from the same vessels, but even if all fragments represent individual objects, this is a very small number of black-figured cups for the house, especially in contrast with the number of red-figured cups. Three of the black-figured cup fragments were found in the deepest level of the well among the period of use material (Level 6): **73**, **74**, and **75**. This suggests that the fragments resulted from breakage in the course of daily life in the house and not from the Persian destruction. Two fragments, **76** and an uncatalogued fragment from Level 2, were found in the upper fill of the well, and thus may also have been broken earlier than the Persian destruction and brought into the well as supplementary fill. Therefore, there is no firm evidence that black-figured cups were in use in the house at the time of the Persian destruction, but their presence in the period of use deposit indicates that the household had used them in the past.

The black-figured cup fragments belong to Type A or Type Sub-A cups.[288] Type A cups are often eye cups with the figural decoration appearing between eyes on the exterior.[289] The difference between the Type A and Type Sub-A is that the Type Sub-A form does not have a fillet at the junction of the stem and bowl, and the bowl is slightly shallower. There are few eye cups from the Athenian contexts.[290] On **75** a fragmentary eye appears at the left of the sherd, and at the right is a chariot wheeling around. The eye is carefully drawn, with a compass-drawn iris distinguished in added

287. Also proposed by Borgers (2004, p. 26). See sections on vessels for mixing wine and water and vessels for serving mixed wine in Chapter 5, for further discussion on this role for the Heron Class skyphoi.

288. On the development of the black-figured cup, see Villard 1946, particularly pp. 178–180 for the late cups.

289. On the Type A cup, see Beazley [1951] 1986, p. 62. See also Jordan 1988, pp. 14–152, for a development of the Type A and Sub-A eye cups.

290. A few are known from the Athenian Agora excavations: *Agora* XXIII, pp. 66–67, 306–307, nos. 1753–1756, pl. 113.

white, and a contour outline that includes the tear duct.[291] The contour of the eye on **75** has a sketchy quality to it at the corners that may mean that the reserved area the contour encloses was once added white, now fugitive. Truly reserved "corneas" have nicely drawn outlines. The second fragment, a rim **73**, may be a nonjoining fragment from the same cup as **75** since the clay characteristics, glaze, and style are similar; however, the style is common enough that the point cannot be pressed further. Enough of the decorative scheme is preserved on **73** to indicate that the scene is Dionysos reclining with a drinking horn.[292] Branches with leaves and grape clusters fill the field. The cup should probably be placed within the prolific group of cup painters named the Leafless Group by Beazley, active ca. 500 and down into the first quarter of the 5th century.[293] The Leafless Group encompasses a number of hands, but the decorative approach and general style is similar among all. Nearly all the Agora black-figured cups are attributed to the Leafless Group or members within it.[294] It is probable that both **73** and **75** and the stem fragment **74** should also be assigned to the Leafless Group. The cup stem **74** is from a Type A cup, as the flat fillet at the top of the stem indicates, and the tondo bears a single running satyr seen in back view. The satyr is not far from the satyrs of the Caylus Painter, a hand Beazley identified within the Leafless Group.[295] The stem fragment **76**, on the other hand, lacks a fillet and thus is a Type Sub-A cup, and its tondo is too fragmentary to identify, let alone attribute. The hasty drawing style places the black-figure cup fragments between 500 and 480.

The conclusion is that this house did not own a set of black-figured stemmed cups. There are black-figured Type A and Type Sub-A cups from both the SGW and the RRCS, although the number is small in both cases.[296] As popular as this shape was in black figure around the turn of the century, the evidence from the SGW and RRCS confirms that it was not a favorite shape for Athenian consumers.[297] Boardman says of its careless style, "Most [examples] . . . dispense with the eyes and present a weary repetition of Dionysiac scenes, generally of the slightest merit, but on the whole better than the similar but mainly later Haimonian cups."[298] The unpopularity of the black-figured cup at Athens cannot be due to the

291. In her extremely detailed study of the black-figured eye cups, Jordan (1988) organizes the material around the treatment of the eye, whether outline (contour), white, or black. Unfortunately, she does not follow the series of black-figured eye cups to its inauspicious end with the likes of the Leafless Group.

292. Cf. *Agora* XXIII, p. 308, no. 1769, pl. 113, the Leafless Group, compared to the Caylus Painter, *ABV* 637, no. 62 and *Agora* XXIII, p. 307, no. 1761, the Leafless Group, *ABV* 716, no. 66 ter.

293. *ABV* pp. 632–653; *Paralipomena*, pp. 310–313.

294. *Agora* XXIII, p. 96.

295. Cf. Tübingen S/10 1486, *CVA* Tübingen 3 [Germany 47], pl. 32 [2277]:1, *ABV*, pp. 650–651.

296. SGW: *Agora* XXIII, p. 307, nos. 1758, 1761 (not illustrated); Vanderpool 1946, p. 309, no. 187, pl. 56 (= *Agora* XXIII, p. 308, no. 1769, pl. 113); Vanderpool 1946, p. 309, no. 188, pl. 58 (= *Agora* XXIII, p. 308, no. 1768); Vanderpool 1946, p. 309, no. 189, pl. 58 (= *Agora* XXIII, p. 308, no. 1767). One is unattributed (*Agora* XXIII, p. 307, no. 1758), but the other four examples were attributed to the Leafless Group. Note that in Shear 1993, p. 390, table 2 ("Distribution of

Black-Figured Pottery by Shape"), he includes the palmette cups in his total for black-figure cups; thus, his number represents more than figural cups. Shear 1993, p. 389, table 1 ("Figured Pottery of the Same Painter, Class, or Group in more than one deposit"), lists 13 objects attributed to the Leafless Group throughout all of the 21 Persian destruction deposits he considers.

297. Perhaps they shared Beazley's opinion of the eye cup: "I cannot remember any class of bf vases I dislike so much" (quoted in von Bothmer 1985, p. 15).

298. Boardman 1974, pp. 150–151.

"slight merit" of the "weary Dionysiac scenes," because these qualities are amply represented by the black-figured cup-skyphoi. Instead, the combination of shape and technique must not have been appealing to the Athenian consumer. The time for black-figured stemmed cups had passed, usurped by the red-figured version of the shape.

In the case of the house of well J 2:4, red figure was the preferred technique for the decorated stemmed cup, which is intrinsically associated with communal drinking. The question remains why red figure was preferred to black figure for formal, sympotic vessels in Late Archaic Athens. One answer returns to the value of the red figure. The dearth of black-figured cups in the Persian destruction material, then, may be explained by their being "out of fashion," demonstrating that the Athenian consumer did discriminate between black figure and red figure, and consciously chose objects in red figure for more formal occasions in this period when both were being produced. It is also possible that the black-figured cups had specific roles other than domestic communal drinking. From a purely economic viewpoint, the hastily made and painted late-black-figured products required less labor and time than even the simplest of red figure.[299] All this implies that the pottery was examined by the viewers, that is, the guests at a symposium, and that they used the pottery, as certainly the food and the entertainment, to assess the host's socioeconomic and cultural standing. Athenians were competitive by nature, and although the symposium was designed to be an equitable experience, the one person who could stand out at any gathering was the host. It seems clear that Kallias and Kritias strive to impress their guests in Plato's and Xenophon's symposia. Their efforts do not go unnoticed. Therefore, the lack of black-figured stemmed cups in the Persian destruction deposits may be a result of the changing markers of status and economic standing in contemporary Athens.

299. Villard (1946, p. 178) adds that the "prolongation" of the eye cup series was due, in part, to the fact that it is easier to trace eyes than to draw figures, and so this decoration appealed to the less talented artists of the prolific late black-figure workshops.

CHAPTER 5

THE SYMPOTIC CONTEXT
PART II: SERVICE VESSELS
AND ACCESSORIES

The previous chapter introduced the symposium and the table equipment needed to conduct it in a private household, then presented the drinking vessels from well J 2:4. It was shown that the house of well J 2:4 owned three or four different sets of drinking cups, with each set characterized by cups of the same form and decorative style. The different sets probably represent different types of communal drinking hosted in the house, from intimate, special occasions to the everyday.

This chapter will present the serving vessels used to prepare and distribute the wine, along with additional objects not directly used for wine consumption or service, but associated with activities of the symposium. One might assume that the service vessels would complement the style and iconography of the specific cup sets, so that a red-figured oinochoe would serve a red-figured set of cups. In fact, as will be shown below, this is not the case.

VESSELS FOR WINE STORAGE

The deposit contains both figured and plain, black-glazed storage vessels. While the figured vessels can be clearly associated with wine service, the case is not so clear for the black-glazed versions of the same shapes, which could have stored any liquid or even grains. The black-glazed shapes are introduced here, but with the caution that they may have performed multiple functions in the house. Although the figured vessels can be more confidently associated with the symposium, these are fewer in number than the black-glazed versions; thus, some of the black-glazed versions must have fulfilled sympotic functions as needed.

Vessels considered to be part of the household's assemblage at the time of the Persian sack, according to the criteria described in Chapter 3, will be presented first, then fragments from the deposit that may possibly represent objects used in the house. Attributions are discussed in the Catalogue entries for individual pieces.

A small, black-figured neck amphora (3), referred to as an amphoriskos due to its diminutive size, is complete and was found in the pocket of fine wares in Level 5, so is associated with the household assemblage. This vase is fairly well potted, but very hastily decorated. It belongs to a class of small neck amphoras with a band of dots below the figural scene, Beazley's Dot-band Class.[1] A similar scene decorates both sides of 3: Dionysos, draped, sits on a high-backed chair and holds a kantharos. On side A a female sits opposite him, and on side B a female dances opposite him. Under the handles are a satyr and another dancing woman. The decoration encircles the vase, and there are none of the decorative palmettes under the handles that often appear on Dot-band Class amphoras.[2] Beazley describes the Dot-band Class as having three palmettes on either side of the neck. The neck of side A has the three palmettes with the central one upside down, but side B has a double ivy band. Otherwise, the subsidiary decoration is canonical for the class: a row of black-glazed tongues marks the junction of the shoulder with the neck, and a row of rays decorates the bottom of the wall below the dot band.

Stylistic and iconographic traits connect 3 with painters of the Kalinderu Group, best known as painters of Class of Athens 581 lekythoi. This workshop briskly produced cups, lekythoi, and small vases from around 500 through the first quarter of the 5th century. A preliminary report on a Late Archaic kiln excavated in Athens records the presence of fragments of lekythoi of the Class of Athens 581, the Cock Group, skyphoi of the CHC Group, and the Krokotos Group.[3] It makes sense that a workshop would specialize in small shapes, and that the decorative approaches would carry over from one to another. The kiln evidence provides proof that several of the painter groups represented in well J 2:4 at least fired pots together. As will be discussed below, well J 2:4 contains many examples of the lekythoi of the Class of Athens 581.

A substantial fragment of the base of a black-figured closed storage vessel (4) is probably from a stamnos. It is from Level 2, but the large fragment of the lower wall and foot is similar to the red-figured cups with intentional red (87, 88) in that it was mended extensively in antiquity. All three of these objects are considered to be part of the house's assemblage since they are preserved in large fragments consisting of multiple joining fragments. The closed vessel 4 preserves a ground line, with feet of four human figures, a crouching feline, and a curving tendril of a floral. The tendril indicates that the figural zone was not restricted to a panel but extended around the vase, probably with palmettes and tendrils around the handle zones. This combination of frieze, black-glazed zone, and rays below with a torus foot is not common for black-figured amphoras of conventional size.[4] However, there is enough of the wall remaining to indicate that 4 had a profile more like a stamnos than a standard amphora. If 4 is a stamnos, it is the only black-figured example from the Agora excavations. Stamnoi were generally exported to the West, so it is odd to find one at use in Athens.[5]

The ancient mends, four lead clamps holding the foot to the body, are rare for this deposit. The careful and extensive repair suggests that this vase, like the red-figured cups with intentional red, was mended with the intention of prolonging its use.[6] Barbara Philippaki dates the black-figured stamnoi to the last decade of the 6th century, after which all stamnoi are red figure.[7] If 4 is a stamnos, then her scheme places it "early" among the material in well J 2:4, that is, perhaps contemporary with 87 and 88 in the

1. *ABV*, pp. 483–485.

2. See, e.g., New York, Met. 21.88.92, *ABV* 478, no. 7 [Edinburgh Painter], Richter and Milne 1935, fig. 16.

3. Baziotopoulou-Balabani 1994, p. 45.

4. See the Catalogue for discussion of the relationship between decorative treatment and form.

5. La Genière 1987.

6. For similar staple repairs, see *Olynthus* X, pp. 329–334, esp. pls. 98, 99; Isler-Kerényi 1979, p. 11, n. 2, pl. XI:21; Noble 1988, p. 175; Elston 1990, pp. 65–66, figs. 26–28; see also discussion in Papadopoulos 2005, pp. 562–563.

7. Philippaki 1967, p. 9.

last decades of the 6th century. The traces of figures on **4** do not otherwise provide stylistic dating evidence.

The decoration of **4** was a series of figures standing or moving to the right. The central figure of the fragment is a female, the added white paint now gone, accompanied by a feline. Another female runs to the right in front of her, and at least one of the two figures to the left of the central woman is male. The fragmentary state of the figural zone makes identification of the scene impossible. The female with crouching feline may be Athena. She is occasionally accompanied by a panther or a lion,[8] but one first thinks of Artemis with animals[9] or even the retinue of Dionysos.

Whether **4** is a stamnos or amphora is not relevant to the observation that the house of well J 2:4 had very few closed vessels with figural decoration. There are two other black-glazed amphoras of small scale (**104, 105**) that can be associated with the household's assemblage, but none of conventional size. In discussions of the symposium, the assumption is that wine was brought to the symposium space in a figured amphora, but the lack of evidence for conventional-sized amphoras suggests that the shape was an optional element of the wine serving service.[10] Pelikai can serve as wine-storage jars, and their presence in the deposit will be discussed below.

Other figured storage vessels cannot confidently be associated with the household's assemblage but do represent the variety of forms present in Agora households at the time of the Persian Wars. There are two fragmentary amphoras of conventional size from the deposit. Fragment **1**, a body fragment from the wall of a black-figured panel amphora, preserves traces of three armed figures running. It is possible that this is a battle scene or a hoplitodromos, in which case the fragment may come from a Panathenaic or pseudo-Panathenaic amphora.[11] Fragment **2** preserves the neck and shoulder of a pseudo-Panathenaic amphora. The scale is too small to be a real Panathenaic, but the decorative scheme and form follow the model of the full-size ones.[12] Athena's crested helmet protrudes into the band of tongues at the base of the neck.

One complete red-figured pelike (**84**; Color Ill. 13) meets the criteria for inclusion in the household assemblage. This vase is decorated with single figures without panels on both sides. The pelike is a multifunctional shape that could hold water, oil, or wine depending on its context of use.[13] The intended purpose of figured pelikai seems to be reflected in their iconography.[14] The iconography of **84** firmly sets it within the symposium, and therefore it most likely served as a storage container for unmixed wine. It is, of course, possible that it held water or even oil instead, but its association with the symposium is clear.[15]

8. See Catalogue for examples.

9. E.g., on the handle panel of the François Vase: Boardman 1974, fig. 46.2.

10. Johnston (1984) notes that amphoras are both rare in the archaeological record of Athens and rarely depicted in Attic vase paintings of symposia. He concludes that figured amphoras were largely made for an export market.

11. For Panathenaic amphoras, see Bentz 1998; Bentz and Eschbach 2001.

12. For pseudo-Panathenaics, see Neils 1992b, pp. 42–46, with bibliography; also discussion in *Agora* XXIII, p. 141, no. 319, pl. 32.

13. Richter and Milne 1935, pp. 4–5; von Bothmer 1951, p. 44; *Agora* XII, p. 49; Kanowski 1983, pp. 113–114; Shapiro 1997; Lynch 2001a, p. 171.

14. See Shapiro 1997 for pelike iconography that reflects its use as an oil storage vessel. It is true that all vessels can be used in unintended ways as necessity demands; therefore, the discussion here centers on primary, intended use of the vessel.

15. On the association of oil with the symposium, see discussion of lekythoi below, this chapter.

Side A (Color Ill. 13) features an adult male moving to the right with a himation around his shoulders playing the barbitos, from which hangs a wicker basket.[16] He is wreathed and wears low soft boots. His mouth is probably open in song, although this area of the vase is not well preserved. There is a fragmentary added red inscription to the right of his chest: IKI[. The ending of the inscription is unfortunately lost because of a missing fragment. Side B (Color Ill. 13) features a standing beardless youth facing right, inducing himself to vomit.[17] The youth leans on a straight stick propped under his left armpit. His left hand reaches up to the top of his head, and he uses the forefinger of his right hand to gag himself, successfully. A stream of vomit in added red flows from his mouth. There is a vertical added red inscription below his elbow: EIOI.

This pelike was originally attributed to the Nikoxenos Painter, but the drawing style belongs neither to him nor his student, the Eucharides Painter. There are more satisfying similarities with the late Pioneer Pezzino Group,[18] a small group of painters who fall between the Pioneers and their students and are united through similar approaches to drawing and subject.[19] None of the pieces assigned to the Pezzino Group match **84** exactly, but there are stylistic similarities. The profile of **84**, however, does connect it with a potter with whom both the Nikoxenos Painter and the Eucharides Painter worked.[20]

The two sides of the pelike are interrelated and promote a discourse on sympotic activity.[21] There is no indication that the two figures are related in the way that figures on vases of the Kleophrades Painter and the Berlin Painter often "speak" across large expanses of black space. Instead, **84**'s figures are each isolated and juxtaposed conceptually. The contrast of youth and adult male on **84** may bear a reference to the *eromenos* and pederastic *erastes* relationships that flourished in the context of communal drinking. There are no overt clues to such a relationship here, but there may be an implication that the evening of drinking they both attend will promote the interaction of boys and men. The combination of the images alludes to many aspects of Greek cultural definitions but does so implicitly. It is up to the viewer to supply the assumptions, so in this way **84** also bears images that require viewer contemplation for the fulfillment of meaning, as did the tondo designs of the red-figured cups.

16. The instrument is a barbitos, not a lyre as published in Camp 1996, no. 27. See Maas and McIntosh Snyder 1989, chap. 5, "The Barbitos in Classical Athens," esp. pp. 114–117, on the barbitos in *komos* and symposium scenes.

17. On vomiting and vases as receptacles, see Cohen and Shapiro 2002, p. 89. Note that **84** contradicts their claim that "only bearded men employ their fingers to induce themselves to vomit," which they describe as an experienced drinker's technique "in

preparation for the next round." They oppose this to youthful drinkers who "appear to vomit spontaneously." A similar assumption about age and behavior is intimated by Sutton 2000, pp. 193–194. Nevertheless, the contrast between adult and youth on **84** conveys the same message of experience and youthful excess.

18. I thank Elizabeth Langridge-Noti for the suggestion to look at the Pezzino Group.

19. See *ARV*² 32; *Paralipomena* 324; *Add*² 157. See also Robertson 1992,

p. 58; *ARV*², p. 32 middle.

20. See Catalogue for discussion of potter.

21. This is a trait common to the Eucharides Painter and less so to the Nikoxenos Painter; see Langridge 1993, esp. p. 131. Shapiro (1997, pp. 63–70) discusses the iconography of black-figured pelikai, which he discovers focus on only a few themes. He also explores how seemingly unrelated scenes on either side of a vase may actually be related.

The adult male sings as he approaches the evening's venue.[22] His traveling shoes[23] and cloak indicate that he is outdoors and is moving toward a destination. The youth, on the other hand, also moves toward a destination, hopefully home, as he, too, wears traveling shoes and carries a cloak. The youth induces himself to vomit and to lose control of his facilities, while the adult male not only maintains his facilities but masters a song. There is an adult–youth, moderation–excess dialogue between the images, perhaps with the younger's overindulgence as a joke about the vagaries of youth. Adult males vomit just as readily on vases,[24] so the contrast here is specific to the context of the pot and not a general cultural principle. There is also a temporal contrast between the male, who is on his way to the evening's festivities, and the youth, who is on his way home. The unrepresented time between the two moments is being fulfilled by the participants of the symposium, the intended viewers. They see themselves on the journey from sobriety to drunkenness, and perhaps a little beyond.

The contrasting images on the vase were meant to be amusing, although the vase carries with it possible social comments. The vomiting youth is comical. Images of vomiters often evoke a bit of sympathy from the viewer by including a second figure who holds the head of the ill male. In this case the youth has to hold his own head,[25] a pose that exaggerates his suffering,[26] and we feel less sympathy than amusement at his condition. The stream of vomit that flows from his mouth makes an amusing contrast to the stream of song coming from the adult male's mouth. The inscriptions, too, reinforce the humor. The man sings a well-enunciated tune, IKI[, while the youth grunts EIOI.[27] It is probably significant, too, that the gesture for singing in Archaic vase painting is one hand at he back of the head tilted upward, as opposed to the youth on **84** whose head is tilted downward, but with the hand in a similar position.[28] Drinking and music go together, and thus, music often accompanies vomiting.[29] Athenaios (11.783e) mentions

22. It is also possible that he is returning home, since a basket with snacks and crockery tied to the instrument would be too heavy to permit playing the barbitos, and presumably the basket would be lighter on the way home. However, on an amphora once attributed to Euthymides, a satyr carries both a lyre to which a basket is tied and a transport amphora of wine: Munich 2424, *ARV*[1] 129, no. 4, but omitted in *ARV*[2], see p. 193 middle, Robertson 1992, fig. 42. The transport amphora indicates that Euthymides's satyr is on his way to the party to which he is offering a contribution. Thus, I think the weight of the basket was not a concern for painters who exercised license with the forces of gravity.

23. The Nikoxenos Painter likes to paint sandals on his figures, but at least

one of the Eucharides Painter's figures wears low boots: once Basle Market, *Münzen und Medaillen*, December 1977, p. 53, no. 50.

24. Sutton 2000, p. 194; Cohen and Shapiro 2002, p. 89.

25. There are many examples, but a cup by Onesimos gives a good contemporary parallel: Getty 86.AE.285, Williams 1991, fig. 4. A standing youth leans over and holds the head of a seated male who has red vomit streaming from his mouth. His right hand is held with the first two fingers pointed as on **84**, indicating that he has just gagged himself. The youth on the Onesimos cup also wears booties, has a cloak thrown over his shoulder, and has a staff.

26. The downturned head position indicates sadness or humility: McNiven 1982, p. 64.

27. On a red-figured kalathoid vase by the Brygos Painter (Munich 2416, *ARV*[2] 385, no. 228, Boardman 1975, fig. 261), Alcaeus sings while Sappho looks on. The inscription, "OOOOO," emanates from Alcaeus' mouth to represent song. In other cases song inscriptions are actual words recognizable from poetry; see Lissarrague 1990a, pp. 123–139.

28. McNiven 1982, p. 64; Lissarrague 1990a, pp. 123–139.

29. Simon. apud Ath. 2.40a (= fr. 142/647 Page): "Wine and music have the same source." See, e.g., the fragmentary cup from Falerii, attributed to the Panaitios Painter, Villa Giulia 18558, *ARV*[2] 326, no. 92, Beazley 1949, p. 4, no. 6, pl. 2:2, where a flute case also hangs in the field behind a crouching vomiter.

the *amystis,* the practice of downing a whole cup of wine to the sound of frantic flute music. He quotes the scolion, "Pipe me a tune, and you sing to her music; and meanwhile I'll drink up." Vomiting must have been the frequent result of rapid consumption. The representation of different states of drunkenness, of which vomiting is nearly the final stage, is also known in vase painting.[30] The stages of consciousness are preserved in the scolion (Ath. 15.695d), "Drink with me, play music with me, love with me, wear a crown with me, be mad with me when I am mad." The decoration on **84** seems to be a visual parallel for this song.

To summarize, this house owned few fine-ware vessels for wine storage. In fact, as noted in Chapter 4, vessels for table service—storage and serving—of wine are few in the Persian destruction deposits. It is possible that wine was not transferred to a separate vessel for presentation in the symposium room, but instead was poured directly from a transport amphora into a krater.[31]

VESSELS FOR WATER STORAGE

Although water is an essential ingredient for a proper symposium, there is only one figured vessel for water storage that meets the criteria for inclusion in the household assemblages, **6**.[32] Scholars typically associate figured hydriai with water storage and the symposium. Some of the other domestic Persian destruction deposits did contain black-figured hydriai, but not red-figured or black-glazed.[33] It is always possible that this house owned a metal hydria, and it did not survive, but it is also possible that water was brought into the symposium room in vessels other than fine-ware hydriai. For example, the deposit preserved a number of black-glazed oinochoai, black-glazed pelikai, banded jugs, household kadoi, and even household hydriai (see Chapter 6), any of which could have served the function of a hydria in the symposium. There is certainly no evidence preserved for hydriai that match the style of drinking-cups.

VESSELS FOR MIXING WINE AND WATER

The quintessential shape for the proper practice of the symposium is the krater, the mixing bowl in which wine and water are blended.[34] Surprisingly, well J 2:4 does not preserve a krater. Two catalogued fragments, both black-figured mixing vessels, **26**, a rim of a dinos, and **27**, a body fragment of a thick-walled vessel, come from the upper fill of the well and do not meet the criteria for inclusion in the household's assemblage. Levels 1 and 2 also contained an additional 10 krater or large bowl fragments. The absence of a krater is perplexing, but several hypotheses exist. First, the krater may have been disposed of elsewhere and thus is not preserved in well J 2:4. Second, it is always possible that the house owned a metal krater and the owners did not discard it since it had a measurable value. Third, if the krater was metal, the Persians could have taken it as booty as they destroyed the house. It is impossible to prove the existence of a metal krater in this case, but if the house did own one, they may have invested in a single large metal piece, the krater, and used ceramic cups with it.

30. Cf. the symposium scene on the krater from Morgantina attributed to Euthymides: Neils 1995, pp. 436, 440–442.

31. For example, as on a red-figured stamnos by Smikros, Brussels, A717, *ARV*² 20, no. 1, Lissarrague 1990a, p. 23, fig. 10, and discussion in Lissarrague 1990a, p. 23.

32. A fragment consisting of several pieces (**6**) is probably from a black-figured kalpis, a hydria with continuous curve.

33. Shear 1993, tables 2–4.

34. Lissarrague 1990b; Luke 1994.

Finally, it is possible that this house did not own a fine-ware krater because it used black-glazed psykters set in lekanai, household utilitarian mixing bowls. The psykter served as a wine cooler: the wine-and-water mixture was placed inside the psykter, and the psykter was placed inside a bowl, usually a krater, filled with ice or cold water.[35] In this way the wine chilled without becoming diluted. At least three psykters were preserved in the deposit (**109, 110, 111**); the most complete of these, **109**, was found in Level 2 of the deposit, and may be associated with the two intentional red cups (**87** and **88**) and the stamnos (**4**), and thus was probably in use in the house. There is even a distinctive psykter lid (**163**), also from Level 2, but not of the correct size for any of the preserved psykter rims. Vase painting depicts psykters typically placed in kraters, but there is at least one representation of a psykter placed in a lekane.[36] That psykters are typically lidded probably means that they sat in a chilling bath for much of the day prior to an evening symposium. Kraters do not have lids, and presumably their wide expanse of liquid surface would have been even more attractive to pests than the narrow mouth of a psykter. The contents of the krater must have been consumed shortly after their preparation, unlike the psykter's contents. The presence of the psykters confirms that the house of well J 2:4 did entertain in sympotic fashion, but the absence of kraters is both disappointing and a puzzle.[37]

VESSELS FOR SERVICE OF MIXED WINE

The shape most commonly associated with pouring wine is the oinochoe, although any jug or pitcher could perform the same function. In addition to pouring, oinochoai or jugs could be used to remove the wine from a krater. If this house only owned pyskters, and no kraters, then the oinochoe would not have been used in this way since the mouth of a psykter is too narrow to accommodate it. Instead, a ladle or very small vessel would be needed to reach down into the psykter and decant the liquid into an individual cup or into a jug. As mentioned in Chapter 4, ceramic ladles are not common in Athens, so it is likely that these were metal.[38] It is also possible that the contents of the psykter could have been poured directly into an oinochoe, without the use of a ladle, by lifting and tilting it. Along with lids, psykters usually had tubular attachments on their shoulders to accommodate a rope-basket handle.

35. *Agora* XII, p. 52; Richter and Milne 1935, pp. 12–13; Drougou 1975, pp. 7–10, 58–59. The psykter is a short-lived shape invented around 530 and lasting only until the early 5th century. How it cooled the wine is debated: some think ice was packed in the psykter, which was then placed in a krater full of wine; others think the krater held the ice or cold water and the psykter held the wine; see Kanowski 1983, pp. 123–125, for discussion and bibliography. Ashmead (1990, pp. 100–103) proposes that the psykter on a red-figured lekythos attributed to the Pan Painter belonging to Haverford College (no inv. no.), *ARV*² 557, no. 116, *Paralipomena* 387, holds warm soup, not cold wine. I accept that the psykter held wine and the krater held water or ice.

36. Red-figured cup tondo, Compiègne, Mus. Vivenel 1102, *ARV*² 341, no. 1 [Manner of the Antiphon Painter], Sparkes and Talcott 1958, fig. 19, recreated in fig. 20.

37. Black-figured, black-glazed, and red-figured kraters were present in small numbers in other Persian destruction deposits; see Shear 1993, tables 2–4. Cahill (2002a, pp. 181–190) observes the small number of kraters recovered from Olynthus and concludes that households must have owned metal kraters (and drinking cups) that were either plundered when the site was sacked or removed by fleeing citizens (p. 187).

38. Clay ladles do exist, but Attic potters made these for the export market to Etruria: Eisman 1975, pp. 77, 82–83.

A complete black-figured trefoil-mouth oinochoe of shape 1 (5) comes from Level 5, the pocket of complete fine wares. The shape 1 oinochoe has an ovoid body with a flattened shoulder, a small flaring ring foot, a concave, black-glazed neck, a pinched trefoil mouth with flat rim, and a high-swung handle. The decoration on 5 is a frieze, although the figures concentrate on the front of the vase and only branches appear on the back beneath the handle. The scene is Herakles restraining the Cretan bull (Fig. 23).[39] Hermes and Athena flank the scene.

Herakles is shown as a youth; he has a meager beard, not the full beard of an adult male. His club rests against Athena's shield. He tries to restrain the bull by grabbing its horn while his other hand reaches around its neck. The figure of Herakles is bent in a powerful pose of exertion, and his efforts are complemented by the implied forward motion of the bull. The bull struggles against Herakles, pawing at the air and bellowing in protest. The pair is a study in forces in equilibrium: the scene as depicted here has no obvious victor, as the bull is not yet subdued. The anatomy of Herakles is detailed with incision, and he is shown in a convincing profile view. The anatomical details of the bull are both incised and indicated in added red.

Hermes, in a chiton and himation, sits to the left of Herakles and the bull on a block stool facing right (Fig. 23). His face and legs are profile, but his torso is frontal in a pose that is not very successful. In his right hand he holds his kerykeion, although the top of the staff is missing. His left hand with two fingers and the thumb extended gestures toward Herakles. Athena sits at the right of the scene facing Herakles and the bull (Fig. 23). Her flesh was once added white, but the paint is now fugitive. She sits upon the same type of block stool as Hermes. She wears a snaky aegis over the top of a long garment with incised and painted patterns. Her right arm is extended, holding her helmet. In her left hand she holds a spear horizontally with the tip touching the neck of the bull.

This oinochoe was originally attributed to the Athena Painter, but it is better associated with the Acheloos Painter within the Leagros Group, who was singled out by Beazley in his frustrated attempt to sort out the hands of the Leagran painters.[40] Beazley highlighted the balanced battles on the Acheloos Painter's vases in contrast to those by the mass of the Leagros Group to help isolate the personality of the Acheloos Painter. He says of the Acheloos Painter, "This painter has a comic vein, and never shows the deep seriousness that characterises the Leagros Group as a whole."[41] Moignard points out that in the adventures of Herakles as depicted by the Acheloos Painter, "Herakles is not quite the successful hero who appears on the Leagran vases."[42] Thus, the mood and content of the scene as depicted on 5 also suits the Acheloos Painter.

39. See Brommer 1973, pp. 194–204; *LIMC* V, 1990, pp. 59–67, nos. 2315–2317, pl. 75, s.v. Herakles (L. Todisco).

40. Attribution to Athena Painter: Camp 1996. Acheloos Painter: *ABV*, p. 354; painter first identified in Beazley 1928, pp. 28, 46–47. See also Moignard 1982.

41. Beazley [1951] 1986, p. 79.

42. Moignard 1982, p. 202.

Aside from the ubiquitous Dionysiac scenes, **5** is the only vase from well J 2:4 with a mythological subject. The black-figured cup-skyphos **59** and black-figured lekythos **16** both have stock scenes of Herakles and the Nemean lion, but otherwise, **5** is the only indisputable example of a scene with a god or hero. It is possible that some pieces from the household's assemblage may not be preserved in this deposit, but the pottery that survives is assumed to be representative; thus, it appears that this household did not favor vases with mythological narratives. The household of well J 2:4 owned pottery that, instead, favored general scenes of Dionysiac revels for everyday use and scenes related to the symposium for more specific communal drinking occasions. There was evidently no wish to introduce images of gods and heroes into these communal drinking settings in this house.

The volume of the oinochoe when it is filled to the bottom of the neck is about 1,330 ml (see Appendix II). If an average cup held 600 to 700 ml, then this oinochoe could fill only a couple of cups at a time, assuming that cups were not filled to the rim. Two black-glazed oinochoai of about the same size as **5** and also from the pocket of fine wares (**112, 113**) may represent additional pouring vessels used at the same time as **5**. If used alone, **5** would serve only a very small gathering.[43] If taken in conjunction with the amphoriskos (**3**) with a volume of 450 ml, and the Heron Class skyphos (**28**) with a volume of about 3,500 ml, a possible set of wine-serving equipment develops. If the wine from the amphoriskos were to be mixed with water at the proportion of two measures wine to five measures water, as was occasionally prescribed for temperate drinking,[44] then it would require about 1,125 ml water. Mixed, this would total 1,575 ml, or about half the volume of the Heron Class skyphos and slightly more than the capacity of the oinochoe. If the cups hold 600 to 700 ml filled to the rim, then the yield of the amphoriskos represents about two or three cups' worth of mixed wine. It is possible that a combination of amphoriskos, mixing bowl (the Heron Class skyphos), and the oinochoe represent a service for a very small gathering. In fact, the volume of the amphoriskos is so small as to suggest that it might have served an individual drinker.

This attention to volume allows us to visualize the serving process better. Since most figured oinochoai are about the same size as **5**, and most cups are around 600–700 ml, then the volume relationships described here must have been common. If there were seven guests, then the oinochoe would need to be dipped twice to fill all the cups, if eleven, then five or six times. An alternative is that several servants worked simultaneously, dipping

43. Another alternative is that the oinochoe held mixed wine to freshen the cups, but the literary evidence suggests that cups were filled, drained, then refilled. If the cups were only half-filled, then the oinochoe could have served up to four drinkers. Clark (2009) also explores the serving function of oinochoai and their proportional relationship to the capacity of both kraters and cups.

44. Ath. (10.426a–427c, 430a–431f) discusses the different mixing ratios described in literary references. At 10.426e the speaker interprets the proverb "Drink either five or three, but not four" as meaning that one should drink two parts of wine to five of water or one part wine to three of water. For the sake of the argument, I will use 2:5 as a temperate mixture.

individual oinochoai in the krater. Perhaps the two black-glazed oinochoai (112, 113) could have been employed at the same time as 5.[45]

Well J 2:4 contained only one possible fragment of a red-figured oino-choe (86). It is from the shoulder of a closed vessel with continuous profile from neck to body. Its thinness suggests that it might be from a shape 3 oinochoe (chous). It preserves a very finely drawn palmette that resembles some of the palmette chain ornaments used by the Berlin Painter in his early period (495–485). Fragment 86 comes from Level 2 of the well, so it is not certain that it represents a vessel used in the house.

This household owned several different types of wine-serving vessels. Three black-figured oinochoai (only 5 is catalogued) meet the criteria for inclusion in this household's assemblage (see Table 6). Two black-glazed trefoil-mouthed oinochoai (112, 113) and at least one banded oinochoe from Level 5, not catalogued, were also in use in the house. Fragmentary evidence suggests that the picture should be expanded. For example, eight rim fragments of black-glazed oinochoai were found in Levels 5 and 6 of the deposit, and 15 fragments of rims from round-mouthed banded oinochoai come from both upper and lower levels (see Table 4).[46] Although the fragmentary material does not qualify for inclusion in the household assemblage, it does indicate the prevalence of these forms in domestic settings. It is also likely that pouring vessels are represented among the black-glazed closed bases, of which there are a maximum of 44 and a minimum of 25 vessels (see Table 5). It is also possible that the plain, household-fabric jugs—functionally the same as an oinochoe, but unglazed and with a slightly different form—could have been used at the table. The household jugs 173–178 were found in Level 5 and 6, and were thus in use in the house. The black-figured oinochoe (5) was decorated with sympotic use in mind; the plain-ware jugs, on the other hand, could have been used in the symposium, but this was not their primary or exclusive use. They could have also been used in household chores such as cooking and washing. Nevertheless, the assortment of pouring vessels from this deposit encourages a broader, more flexible view of the relationship of service ves-sels to fine-ware drinking vessels in terms of their fabric and decoration.

One final pot may belong in this category of wine-service vessels. In symposium scenes by Douris and the related Painter of London E55, wine boys are shown holding a small, round-bottomed jug instead of an oino-choe.[47] The profile of the juglet is very similar to the small cooking-ware vessel of chytra shape (186). The carbon residue on other chytrai from this deposit indicates that they were used over fire for food preparation (see discussion, Chapter 6), but the exterior of 186 preserves no such evidence.

45. Cf. the sympotic scene on a red-figured kylix by Douris, London, E 49, *ARV*[2] 432, no. 52, *Add*[2] 237, Buitron-Oliver 1995, p. 78, no. 96, pls. 28, 29, on which two servants, each holding an oinochoe, circulate around the andron to fill the drinkers' cups.

46. Of the black-glazed trefoil oinochoai rim fragments, all but one fragment were less than 50% preserved. Of the banded, round-mouthed oino-choai rim fragments, all but one frag-ment were less than 50% preserved.

47. London, E 49, *ARV*[2] 432, no. 52, *Add*[2] 237 [Douris], Buitron-Oliver 1995, p. 78, no. 96, pls. 28, 29; Florence, Museo Archeologico 3922,

ARV[2] 432, no. 55, *Add*[2] 237 [Douris], Buitron-Oliver 1995, p. 79, no. 99, pl. 90; Florence, Museo Archeologico, Vagnonville 48, *ARV*[2] 432, no. 58, *Paralipomena* 374, *Add*[2] 237 [attributed to Douris by Beazley, removed by Guy], Buitron-Oliver 1995, p. 86, no. E1, pl. 177.

Nevertheless the intriguing similarity of the serving juglet to the chytra prompts one to wonder if this is another instance of a multifunctional shape.

Other figured closed storage forms are too fragmentary to determine the original shape. Fragment **85** is probably from a red-figured pelike, as the curvature of the fragment suggests a baggy-shaped vessel.

VESSELS FOR THE SYMPOTIC TABLE

This section presents objects that may have been associated with food consumption during the symposium. As noted in the previous chapter, the symposium, technically, involves only the consumption of wine. Nonetheless, as any good cocktail-party host knows, it is important to offer your guests something to temper the effects of alcohol. The 4th-century poet Archestratus describes drinking without snacks as uncivilized.[48] He recommends both savory foods and *tragemata,* "things to chew," such as bread, cheese, honey, and nuts.[49] The ceramic objects from this deposit associated with sympotic snacks include lekythoi and olpai, a lekanis and other bowls, stemmed dishes, and salt cellars. The lekythoi and the lekanis are included due to their black-figure decoration that relates to sympotic activities. There are certainly other uses for all of the shapes discussed here, but the point is that they do have a place in the symposium room, and thus they should be considered sympotic accessories in this context of use.

LEKYTHOI

There are 36 fragments of black-figured lekythoi from this deposit. Fifteen are catalogued here as representative of shapes or subjects. Some of the uncatalogued fragments may be nonjoining fragments of the same object, especially nonjoining feet and mouths; furthermore, the majority of the fragments (26) come from Levels 1 and 2, which may include material that did not originate in the house. Six black-figured and black-glazed lekythoi come from Level 6, the period of use, confirming that the shape was used in the house earlier in its lifetime (**7** and **8**). Only two of these meet the criteria for inclusion in the household assemblage owing to their state of preservation. None of the lekythoi are white-ground, but there is one example of white-ground shoulder decoration (**21**) from the deposit.

The earliest lekythoi in the deposit are fragments of black-figured lekythoi by the Phanyllis Group and the Cock Group (**7, 8, 9**). These two closely related groups are active from the fourth quarter of the 6th century through the first quarter of the 5th century, but they paint an old-fashioned version of the shape, the shoulder lekythos.[50] Their lekythoi have a squatter, fatter shape than the cylindrical lekythoi also popular at the time. This distinctive shape is called "The Phanyllis Class" lekythos because painters of the Phanyllis Group preferred it. Thus, in addition to style, the bulging wall profile helps to identify these fragments as products of the Phanyllis or Cock Groups. One of the Phanyllis Group lekythos fragments (**7**) was found in the period of use deposit, thus helping to place the period of use at 510 or after. Fragment **7** is from a small-sized lekythos, and the preserved

48. Archestratus, fr. 60 [62 Brandt], apud Ath. 3.101b–e; Wilkins and Hill 1994, pp. 97–98; Olson and Sens 2000, pp. 224–238.

49. Dalby 2003, p. 330; Xenophanes, *PLG*⁴, 1.9–10.

50. *ABL,* p. 63; *Agora* XXIII, pp. 45–46.

scene of a warrior with a shield with an added white tripod device places the fragment in the subgroup E (Group of the Hoplite Leaving Home). The second fragment of a Phanyllis Group lekythos (8) is the mouth and neck of a lekythos that is exceptionally large for this deposit. Painters of Phanyllis Group A (the Phanyllis Painter) and Group B (the Group of the Hoplite Arming) decorate large lekythoi and often use the distinctive dog's-tooth pattern of rays on the neck, occasionally marking the bottom of the neck with an added red line.[51] Fragment 8 comes from Level 6, but it might be associated with the Persian destruction cleanup and not the period of use. There are no other fragments from deposit J 2:4 that may belong to a suitably large lekythos, and no large lekythoi of the Phanyllis Group have been found in the Agora excavations, although they have been found in Athens.[52] In Athens both sizes come from graves, and several smaller Phanyllis Class lekythoi were found in the Stoa Gutter Well.[53] The large neck and mouth of 8 may have had a secondary reuse in the house, perhaps as a funnel.[54]

The third early lekythos fragment belongs to the Cock Group. Fragment 9 comes from the body of a lekythos with a slightly convex wall. The scene is as on 7, a warrior departing, and the composition is similar, although the execution as well as the shape is different from the Phanyllis Class. The fragment preserves a warrior to the left with shield and two spears. Behind him stands a draped figure with a spear or staff. There is ample added color, but the incision is hasty and impressionistic. As stated above, the Cock Group is closely related to the Phanyllis Group by their subjects and the slightly bulging profile of their shapes.[55] The main difference between the two is the shoulder decoration. A single uncatalogued shoulder fragment with a very degenerate cock did not join 9, but represents the eponymous shoulder decoration for the Cock Group. Fragment 9 was found in Level 2, the fill at the top of the well. There are 12 other Cock Group lekythoi from Persian destruction deposits, and at least eight from the excavations of the environs of the Agora come from sepulchral contexts.[56] The evidence for domestic use of the Phanyllis Class and Cock Group lekythoi of the late 6th century is not as secure as it is for the early-5th-century examples.

51. The dog's-tooth pattern goes back, as does the shape itself, to an earlier period in the history of the lekythos form; see *ABL*, p. 63, n. 2, and pp. 42–43. Decorated necks are rare on black-figured lekythoi, but the Phanyllis Group liked them; see Kurtz 1975, p. 85, n. 4. The range of mouth diameters of large lekythoi of Groups A and B is 6.2–8.5 cm. For an example of the complete shape and decoration, see Giudice 1983, no. 54, pl. 15:1, among many others.

52. Giudice 1978, pp. 631–640; 1983, p. 23. *Agora* XXIII, p. 207, nos. 824, 825, pl. 77, are fragmentary examples of lekythoi painted by Group B (The Group of the Warrior Arming)

and are large, but more midsized in the range of Phanyllis Class lekythoi. Fragment 8 is from a larger vessel than any of these.

53. Graves: *Agora* XXIII, pp. 207–208, nos. 829–832, 836, pl. 77; Kerameikos: 35.XX.25 (= Giudice 1983, no. 304), 35.XX.27 (= Giudice 1983, no. 373), Ker 8248 (= Giudice 1983, no. 237), Ker 8668 (= Giudice 1983, no. 321), Ker 8717 (= Giudice 1983, no. 320). SGW: *Agora* XXIII, p. 207–208, nos. 826–828, 835, pl. 77 (= Roberts 1986, p. 36, nos. 94–97, fig. 25). None from the RRCS. More Phanyllis Class lekythoi are known from western Greece, and the Athenian market does not appear to be as important; see

Giudice 1978. For the relationship of the Phanyllis Class lekythoi and the workshop of the Nikosthenes Painter, which had a similar distribution pattern, see Kurtz 1975, p. 118.

54. For secondary use of broken pottery, see Cahill 2002b, p. 179, which describes a hydria neck being used as a stand for an oinochoe.

55. *ABL*, p. 67; *Agora* XXIII, p. 46. Also see Kurtz 1975, pp. 118–119: "Some Cock lekythoi were produced in the 581 Workshop which is connected with the Phanyllis Workshop in both shape and pattern."

56. *Agora* XXIII, pp. 208–210, nos. 836, 837, 841, 842, 851, 854, 856, and 857, pl. 78.

The majority of the black-figured lekythoi from well J 2:4 are poorly drawn, hasty products of the large lekythos workshops active at the beginning of the 5th century. Nearly all examples are Class of Athens 581, a class of small to midsized lekythoi produced by a single workshop and decorated rapidly with black-figured subjects painted by many hands.[57] The Class of Athens 581 is subdivided into "The Class of Athens 581, i," and "The Class of Athens 581, ii" on the basis of the shoulder ornament. The shoulder of subclass i has hanging lotus buds and tongues; subclass ii has rays and tongues. The complexity of the ornament on Class of Athens 581, i, usually, is paralleled by a more patient drawing style on the black-figured scene. Lekythoi of the Class of 581, ii, however, are hastily drawn and incised. There is only one certain example of the Class of Athens 581, i among the lekythos fragments from well J 2:4 (20), but some body fragments without a joining shoulder may belong to that subclass. The remainder are Class of Athens 581, ii, if the class can be assigned at all.

The Class of Athens 581, ii lekythoi from this deposit cluster into two groups based on size. The smaller lekythoi have a diameter around 4.5 cm, and the larger around 7.0 cm. It can be difficult to judge the size from fragments, but it seems that the distribution of larger and smaller lekythoi is about even in this deposit.[58] To begin with the smaller lekythoi, there are three catalogued lekythoi with figural decoration (10–12) and one with palmettes (13). Individual painters of lekythoi of the Class of Athens 581 can be identified in some cases;[59] unfortunately, none of the class from well J 2:4 can be so identified.

Fragment 10 preserves the entire body of a small lekythos intact. The subject is a woman, possibly Athena, mounting a chariot. Apollo with his lyre stands beside the chariot, and Hermes with his kerykeion, petasos, and winged boots leads in front of the horses. The figure may be Athena, if the elongated blob on the woman's head can be taken for a helmet. The chariot is a common motif on lekythoi, as it was on cup-skyphoi. The driver and attendants can vary, and on these second-rate products the figures seem to be assembled without much thought. The painting without incision reminds us of the silhouette-style skyphoi, and it is possible that this is also a product of a painter working for the Haimon workshop.

The body of a small lekythos of the Class of Athens 581, ii (11) depicts a typical Dionysiac scene of a maenad between two satyrs. Dionysos and his companions are very common on the mass-produced lekythoi, again pointing out the relationship between these vessels and the black-figured cup-skyphoi being produced contemporaneously in the same workshops.

The final catalogued smaller lekythos with figural decoration is 12, with the subject of a male attacking a female. The central figure is preserved and three additional females flank the scene. The male grabs the central female around the waist. The scene is probably Peleus and Thetis, but unlike representations of the scene on larger vessels, this depiction shows no attributes of Thetis to help to confirm the identification. This could also be a satyr attacking a maenad, and the poor draftsmanship makes it difficult to know if the blurred projection near the male's thigh is a hasty brushstroke or a satyr's erection. The shoulder of 12 is not preserved. The tall, straight wall suggests a more cylindrical shape than the Class of

57. *Agora* XXIII, p. 95. The shape is also painted by the Gela Painter and the Marathon Painter, but with different subsidiary decoration: *ABL,* pp. 93–94, 82; Kurtz 1975, p. 18. The shape also has red-figure connections; see Kurtz 1975, p. 81; *ARV*², p. 676.

58. A similar ratio holds for the lekythoi of the RRCS and the SGW as published. There are many uncatalogued lekythoi fragments from these deposits as well.

59. *ABV,* pp. 489–506; *Paralipomena,* pp. 222–246; *Add*², pp. 122–126. The sorting out of hands within the Class of Athens 581 is done primarily in *Paralipomena.*

Athens 581, a shape associated with the Haimon Painter's workshop, but not enough of the lekythos is preserved to be certain.[60]

The palmette lekythos (13) represents a type of lekythos well known from Persian destruction deposits.[61] These lekythoi are decorated with a chain of upright palmettes standing on a row of O's with added white for details. There are fragments of several others in deposit J 2:4. They were very popular during the first quarter of the 5th century, and the differences in the execution of the pattern allows some classification.[62] They are certainly grave gifts, but their presence in many of the Persian destruction deposits indicates that they had a use within the house as well.[63]

Fragment 14, from Level 5 of the deposit, is from the lower body of a smaller lekythos. The lower wall has a zone of black glaze with a band of black glaze above. There are two added red lines at the top of the black-glazed zone at the bottom of the body, and a single added red line on the black-glazed band. This combination of black-glazed zones and added red is used by the Sappho Painter and the Diosphos Painter, as well as by the Haimon Painter, who is related to them. The shape, with its rounded lower body, and tall, straight wall, looks more like a slim product of the Haimon Painter than it does the earlier pair's forms.

The larger lekythoi are more fragmentary, and no complete example survives from well J 2:4. The fragments often preserve only part of the wall, the shoulder, the foot, or the heavier but nonfigural lower body. Since the shoulders do not always survive with the figural area, it is difficult to know if the shape was the Class of Athens 581, i, or ii, or neither. Four catalogued larger lekythoi have figural decoration. Fragment 15 is a product of the Haimon Painter's workshop, and is in his manner. The subject is Dionysos reclining, and a maenad with krotala dances in front of him. The relationship between the lekythoi and the cup-skyphoi produced by the Haimon Painter and his associates is clear. The same scenes appear on both, and the drawing is similarly hasty (cf. 59). The Haimon Painter's workshop's penchant for repetition of subjects is also found on 16 with Herakles and the lion, a very popular subject for both the cup-skyphoi and lekythoi of the Haimon Group. Fragment 16 should probably belong to the Haimon Group, but not enough is preserved to be certain.

The fragmentary lekythos 17 preserves a warrior and a single eye that can be restored as a warrior between two eyes. The shoulder and profile indicate that the shape is Class of Athens 581, ii. The disposition of a figure between eyes is not common in this class of lekythoi.

A fragment of a larger lekythos, 18, preserves a tall shape with a slightly convex wall unlike that of the Class of Athens 581.[64] The figure is a draped female, and the incision for the folds is rendered in a very unusual feathery manner. The shape is somewhat like the tall cylinders of the Haimon Painter after ca. 490. A lekythos from the Kerameikos gives an impression of the complete shape, but the style does not match.[65]

Another fragment (19) has a rounded bottom also unlike the form of the Class of Athens 581. Below the figure are two broad black-glazed bands above the black-glazed zone at the bottom of the body. The shape is near the form of another lekythos from the Kerameikos.[66]

60. For shape, see *ABL*, p. 131: it originates in the workshops of the Diosphos Painter and Sappho Painter.

61. Shear 1993, pp. 410–411.

62. See *ABL*, pp. 93–94, 185–186; Kurtz 1975, p. 147; *Paralipomena*, pp. 242–243.

63. See Shear 1993, p. 389, table 1. Palmette lekythoi appear in nine of his 21 deposits.

64. It may be an example of Kurtz's "compromise" shape between the old-fashioned, bloated profile and the new cylinder; see Kurtz 1975, p. 78.

65. *Kerameikos* IX, no. 21 (SW 67), pl. 23:4, 5.

66. *Kerameikos* IX, no. 20 (HW 198), 1, pl. 19:2.

In addition to the black-figured lekythoi, there are two larger cylinder lekythoi with totally black-glazed bodies. The black body normally has added red lines at the top of the wall, and a single one at the lower body.[67] Usually the shoulder patterns can be linked to painters who also painted figured lekythoi,[68] but the reserved shoulder of **20** bears an otherwise unattributed pattern. The second black-bodied lekythos (**21**) is also a shoulder fragment with just the start of the wall. The white-ground shoulder is decorated with the conventional rays and tongues.

There are several uncatalogued fragments that may be from small black-bodied lekythoi of the Little Lion Class,[69] but none could confidently be assigned to this class. This is a significant observation because lekythoi of the Little Lion Class were found in abundance in the Stoa Gutter Well and in the Rectangular Rock-Cut Shaft. However, only two additional examples come from domestic Persian destruction deposits.[70] It would appear that the Little Lion Class did not have a strong role in domestic contexts.

DISCUSSION OF LEKYTHOI IN DOMESTIC CONTEXTS

Black-figured lekythoi were the most common grave offering in Attic graves of the Archaic and Early Classical period,[71] but the evidence from well J 2:4 and other domestic Persian destruction deposits from the Agora shows that the shape had a use in the house as well. The contemporary SGW and the RRCS deposits both included extraordinary numbers of black-figured lekythoi: 246 were catalogued from the Stoa Gutter Well and 104 from the RRCS, with hundreds more in the context tins. The presence of replicas and many products of the same painter, in addition to other factors, allows these deposits to be associated with pottery sales shops.[72] Since so many well-preserved examples of black-figured lekythoi from the Agora excavations come from these two shop deposits, a domestic use for the shape has not been emphasized.[73] Shear, in his review of the Persian destruction pottery, points out that black-figured lekythoi appear in all but one of the 21 Agora deposits that he studied.[74]

The domestic role of the lekythos is probably responsible for its appropriateness as a grave offering. The objects placed in the Archaic burials of the Kerameikos, for example, include offerings that could have been taken from the cupboard of the house of well J 2:4. A typical assemblage

67. It is possible that these black-glazed lekythoi were decorated in Six's technique. No lekythoi in Six's technique are present in the deposit, although they are known from the Agora; cf. *Agora* XXIII, p. 244, no. 1175, pl. 86.

68. Kurtz 1975, pp. 115, 120–122.

69. *ABL,* pp. 98–100, 116–120, 134. For the class, see *Agora* XII, p. 314, nos. 1115, 1116, fig. 11, pl. 38.

70. See Shear 1993, p. 389, table 1. The entry for *Agora* XII, p. 314, no. 1116 notes that there were others

uncatalogued from both the SGW and RRCS, so the number listed in Shear 1993 is a conservative figure for these two deposits.

71. Kurtz and Boardman 1971, p. 209; *Agora* XII, p. 150.

72. *Agora* XII, p. 397; Thompson 1955, pp. 62–66.

73. *Agora* XXIII, p. 43, puts the priority on the funerary use of the black-figured lekythoi: "Most of the Agora black-figured lekythoi are small vessels of the type used to furnish out common

graves." *Agora* XII, p. 150, does the same for the black-bodied variety: "Classical grave furnishings are rare in the Agora and the lekythos, the commonest container for oil and one of the vases most generally associated with burial customs, is in some cases an intruder among the pots for everyday use presented here." *ABL,* pp. 128–130, focuses on the role of lekythoi as grave gifts, but offers some evidence that they had a daily use as well.

74. Shear 1993, p. 393.

of grave offerings includes at least one lekythos, an olpe, a salt cellar, and a covered bowl.[75] There are variations, and no firm rules, but in general, the shapes that appear in the Kerameikos graves of ca. 500 have parallels, some exact, in the pottery of well J 2:4. Furthermore, it should be noted that the iconography of the Kerameikos black-figured lekythoi is comparable to examples found in well J 2:4, and the grave offerings do not appear to be selected on the basis of images suitable for a sepulchral context.[76] Therefore, the black-figured lekythoi should be seen as domestic objects first and grave offerings second.

Their size and decoration indicate that lekythoi had many different roles within the household. Images of lekythoi on vases depict them hanging on walls, helping to establish the setting of the image as a home.[77] Certainly they held oil, but oil had different uses: as a body cleanser, as a perfume, and as a food flavoring. If it held body oil, the shape, unlike the portable aryballos, was not designed to be carried easily, and thus was most likely used for body cleansing within the house, not in the gymnasium.[78] The lekythoi very often have Dionysiac themes (**11**, **15**) or oft-repeated themes of Herakles and the lion (**16**), chariots (**10**), and warriors (**17**)—all scenes also seen on black-figured drinking vessels. The appropriate sphere for these images is communal drinking. In a sympotic context, the oil could have been perfumed for personal adornment or flavored as a condiment. The small black-figured lekythoi probably contained perfumed oils.[79] The very small lekythoi, like **10** and **11**, may have held just enough for one application of scent. If not perfumed oils, then the lekythoi of both sizes might have held savory oil for use at the individual table. For example, oil could have been poured into a stemmed dish (see below), flavored with spices, and sopped up with a piece of bread.

The viewers and users of these mass-produced, poorly painted lekythoi may not have given much attention to the images, but the painters did. The painter chose images that he felt were appropriate to the shape and use of the vessel. The increased popularity of the lekythos at the end of the 6th century paralleled the increased popularity of the kylix for drinking. This is a pattern that may reveal a cultural trend of either increased communal dining or increased formality imposed on a long-standing activity through the use of special-purpose tableware. That lekythoi follow this trend further suggests that they had a role in communal drinking.

75. See, e.g., *Kerameikos* IX, Grave 9 (SW 35), pl. 44:1: for pyxis 9, 4, cf. **155**; salt cellar 9, 3, cf. **150**; banded olpe 9, 2, cf. **118**, **119**; black-figured lekythos 9, 1, cf. **11**.

76. This also holds for the material found in the Marathon mound. Haspels explains that the offerings were required in a hurry, so the Marathon tumulus lekythoi represent what was on hand at the moment in a potter's shop: *ABL*, p. 77 and n. 5, pp. 92–93. It may be possible that these were deemed suitable gifts, even for heroes, because the lekythoi emphasized their importance to the domestic world.

77. See list of examples in *ABL*, p. 129.

78. Parko 2001, p. 57 and n. 27.

79. See the discussion on this topic in *ABL*, pp. 124–126, and the fragmentary lekythos by the Diosphos Painter inscribed with the name of iris perfume on its mouth: Athens, National Archaeological Museum 12271, *ABL* 235, no. 66. For the oils, see Gerhardt, Searles, and Biers 1990; Biers, Gerhardt, and Braniff 1994. Sources: Ath. 15.688c–692f; Archestratos fr. 60 (62 Brandt). Olson and Sens 2000, pp. 227–228, for additional sources and discussion.

Olpai

The olpai, **116, 117, 118, 119,** the first two black-glazed and the other two banded, held a small quantity of liquid, which might have been vinegar or another liquid other than oil. Several of the small banded olpai from Persian destruction contexts have *demosion* inscriptions on them that mark them as official measures of some type.[80] The similar capacities of ca. 270 ml for the *demosion* olpai lends weight to this interpretation, but the officially marked versions are larger than any found in well J 2:4.[81] The 95 banded olpai and very similar black-glazed versions found in Persian destruction deposits argue that these were more than measures within a house. If the lekythos held oil for the table, then perhaps the olpe held vinegar. While there is no evidence absolutely linking olpai to sympotic activities—the table shape rarely receives figured decoration—I include it here as a complement to the lekythoi, but it probably belongs best under food-consumption accessories, as opposed to those for wine consumption.

Bowls and Lekanides

There are a number of fragments of bowls, some covered, and lekanis lids from well J 2:4 that may relate to food storage or presentation, possibly during the symposium. Two of the fragments of black-figured lekanis lids have iconography that links them to the symposium. The lekanis is a broad, shallow bowl with handles and is often covered.[82] The shape is a very practical form for storage of small items such as personal effects, sewing needs, or toys, but, as Sparkes suggests, the form could also be used for storing or serving food.[83] It is this last function that places the shape within the symposium. The covered dish could be used to hold olives or other prepared foods that might attract insects if left uncovered. In black figure the shape has a long history, but black-figure painters cease decorating lekanides around 500.[84] The shape continues down into the 4th century in both black glaze and red figure. Of course, lids are often found without the body of the vessel, and this is the case here.

Several nonjoining fragments of the same lid (**79**) with a distinctive double ivy-leaf pattern on the rim were recovered from Level 5, the pocket of fine wares, and Level 2, the fragmentary upper fill; this continuity between the upper and lower dump episodes makes it likely that the lid comes from an object at use in the house at the time of the Persian destruction. The fragmentary scene on **79** preserves two nude figures flanking a large skyphos-shaped krater or large household lekane. The horizontal incised line below the open vessel's handles recalls the household lekane's black-glazed stripe below the handle attachments more convincingly than it recalls a skyphos krater. Nevertheless the function of the vessel for the mixing of wine and water is conveyed by the youth at right, who holds an oinochoe over the vessel. The position of the oinochoe suggests pouring of liquid into the mixing bowl. He may be using the oinochoe as a water pitcher, or he may be about to dip the entire oinochoe into the mixing bowl to fill it. On the other side of the open vessel an adult male stands, holding a very long, curving object with a trumpet-shaped mouth rendered in added white over top of black glaze. If shorter, the shape would be called a drinking horn, but the length is extraordinary. This may be an ivory drinking horn

80. *Agora* X, pp. 56–58, nos. LM 1–LM 7. There is a concentration of officially marked olpai in the SGW; Lang suggests that this is because the potter's shop was selling replicas of the official state measure to customers for personal home use.

81. See *Agora* X, p. 57; dimensions of the official measure: H. 14.0 cm; max. Diam. 7.0 cm. Volumes of complete olpai (see Appendix II): **117,** 60 ml; **118,** 110 ml; **119,** 95 ml.

82. *Agora* XII, p. 164, lids: pp. 167–168.

83. Sparkes 1962, p. 124; *Agora* XII, p. 164. Both bowls and lids of black-glazed versions of the shape are present in the deposit (**157** and lids **158–162**), and these could have been used during the symposium as well.

84. Lioutas 1987, p. 16.

fashioned from the long curving form of an elephant's tusk. Athenaios, in the section on drinking vessels in the *Deipnosophistai,* describes something called "the elephant."[85] He says it has two spouts and it holds three choes (9.6 liters). It is possible that the two spouts refer to the wide mouth at the broad end, and a smaller, mouth-size hole at the thin end of the tusklike form. The shape might have been filled by plugging the small hole and pouring wine into the funnel-shaped mouth. Drinking from an "elephant" implies consumption of a great quantity of wine in a short period of time. If the man is holding an "elephant," whose use must have had very funny implications, then this, along with the red-figured pelike **84,** is a humorous scene based on the activities of drinking.

The sympotic subject of **79** is rare for lekanis lids. Throughout the history of the shape, black-figured artists prefer to decorate both lids and bodies with animal friezes and ornamental bands. Toward the end of the 6th century the iconographic repertoire of lids expands to include the subjects of combat or chariot scenes.[86] In the last quarter of the 6th century, though, Dionysiac and sympotic scenes occasionally appear. Two such scenes from the excavations at Xanthos provide help with the attribution of **79.**[87]

The fragmentary black-glazed bowls (**152, 153, 154**) are exceptionally well potted and glazed, but only the bases survive. The undersides received incised and molded treatment similar to the undersides of bolsals and stemless cups. Although the upper portions do not survive, a slight nipple on the interior floor may be a sign that they were originally lidded. It is not certain that this shape is connected with the symposium, but is included here as a potential serving vessel.

Two covered bowls (**155, 156**) are smaller in scale than the black-figured lekanides. The shape is a hybrid of the lekanis and the stemmed dish (see below), and as its name conveys, it was fitted with a cover to protect its contents, which may have been food. One possible lid (**164**) survives in the deposit. Again there is no certain connection with the symposium.

STEMMED DISHES AND SALT CELLARS

Stemmed dishes and salt cellars are also present in a large enough number in this deposit to propose an individual table use for them and to posit a function in the symposium. Eight complete or nearly complete stemmed dishes meet the criteria for inclusion in the household's assemblage. An additional six fragments were found in Levels 5 and 6, and thus probably originated within the house (see Tables 4 and 6). Of the complete dishes, **141, 142, 143, 144,** and **145** are standard thickened-rim stemmed dishes, although the shape shows a great variation in details. The stemmed dish **146** has a concave lip but the standard bowl and stem shape, while **147** is a variation of the concave rim taking the form of a chalice. All of these share a small-capacity bowl mounted on a tall stem. In all but **147** the bowl is rounded without any sharp corners. The ancient function of this vessel form remains elusive, and Beazley, among others, has speculated that it might have served as a "nut-dish."[88] Indeed, nuts and fruits were served

85. Ath. 11.468f, 497a, b; discussion in Davidson 1997, pp. 64–65.

86. Lioutas 1987, pp. 64–68.

87. For details, see Catalogue.

88. *Agora* XII, p. 138; Beazley 1931a, p. 21; Sparkes and Talcott 1958, text to figs. 24, 25.

alongside the wine during an evening of drinking.[89] The thickened rims make it unlikely that the vessels were designed for drinking. Like salt cellars, the dishes have a small volume, indicating that only a small amount of their contents was needed.[90] It is more likely that they were a receptacle for the mixing of oils or vinegars and spices for dipping of bread. Honey, too, could be dripped from a larger container into this individual stemmed dish.[91] The wide bowl would permit the dipping of food—bread or meat—into the mixture. The stem allows the vessel to be held in one hand while one reclines on one elbow and dips with the other hand. In fact, the feet of some stemmed dishes are identical to those of kylikes, indicating that the same potters are producing both.

The long life of the salt cellar in Attic pottery indicates that it was an integral part of an unchanging aspect of dining. The shape first appeared in the late 6th century, which means it was still young at the time of the Persian Wars. Salt cellars **148**, **149**, and **150** are typical examples of the late Archaic form, while **151**, with an unattested small bowl form with a palmette drawn in added red on its floor, is an oddity.[92] These four small dishes meet the criteria for inclusion in the household assemblage (see Table 6), and in total there are a maximum of eleven and minimum of nine salt cellars, plus the one complete small bowl (**151**). This quantity may be sufficient for setting the table for sympotic guests, but salt cellars often bear incised ownership marks, frequently letters, alone or in pairs. The graffito OΣ is incised on the bottom of **150**, with two linear designs scratched into its wall. On **148** we find the single letter N scratched on the underside. This letter is repeated on the underside of **152**, one of the well-made bowls discussed above, under the foot of **139**, a Type C cup stem, and on the underside of **180**, a cooking-ware water-jar base. Another Type C cup stem (**138**) has EA scratched on its underside, retrograde. The only reason to mark your property, as both the letters and the designs on **150** do, is to make sure the object is returned to you. This implies that diners took salt cellars with them when they dined out.[93] This same piece, **150**, has a reserved rim and concave wall, and Sparkes and Talcott speculate that the reserved rim of this variation was designed to take a lid to keep the contents in place.[94] The other shapes of salt cellars, though, had no such provision, so they were likely transported empty. It is possible that the diner brought his own salt cellar and that the host provided the oil or spices that each diner mixed individually; therefore, we should not expect a single home to own a "set" of salt cellars.

89. Dalby (1996, pp. 102–104) discusses the types of snacks that accompanied wine.

90. The black-glazed stemmed dish **144** has a volume of 120 ml filled to the rim, and the salt cellar **150** has a volume of ca. 50 ml, both much smaller than the smallest of the drinking-cup volumes. See Appendix II.

91. Xenophanes (*PLG*⁴ 1, = Ath. 11.462c) describes the transition from

dining to drinking: "Golden-brown loaves of bread have been set beside us, along with a table full of honor and heavy with cheese and dense honey," trans. S. D. Olson, Cambridge, Mass., 2009.

92. In the later 5th century small bowls often had stamped palmettes on their floors. This may be a predecessor to that tradition; cf. *Agora* XII, p. 298, no. 864, pl. 59, and others.

93. Somewhat similarly, a cache of

Lydian stemmed dishes with various graffiti was found in a household storage area of a house at Sardis: Cahill 2002b, p. 178. Cahill notes that there are several distinct "hands" doing the incision. As with the salt cellars, it is unclear why these would be individually marked, unless they were being used outside the home.

94. *Agora* XII, pp. 136–137, nos. 922–938, pl. 34.

STAND AND DISK

The stand (**169**) and its formal companion the disk (**168**) both represent forms popular only in the Late Archaic period and of unknown function.[95] The stand is made up of a disk on a stem. Their careful forms and decoration are impressive, but offer little help in identifying their function. The disk has part of a graffito on the upper surface, but not enough to identify it as an owner's mark. Stands can also be decorated in black figure and red figure, and one is shown on a table in a sympotic scene, but its function there is likewise unclear.[96] The disk may have been a lid of some sort, although it has no provisions for keeping itself in place.

VESSELS FOR RITUAL, POSSIBLY SYMPOTIC

The deposit contained two objects associated with the performance of religious ritual in the house: a phiale (**23**) and a thymiaterion (**81**). The phiale is a shape for making libations, and thus has a role in the symposium, as a libation marked the opening of drinking activities, especially following a meal.[97] The thymiaterion, on the other hand, is an incense burner, and it has a less direct relation to the activities of the symposium, although it is not impossible that it was used there.[98] Therefore, the phiale is included in this discussion of forms associated with sympotic activity, and the thymiaterion is discussed in Chapter 6, in the context of household activities.

There are numerous references to libations to the gods, particularly Zeus Soter, at the beginning of the sympotic part of an evening of drinking.[99] The omphalos phiale shape, with a raised central boss, clearly originates in a metal prototype and is not common in clay,[100] but 19 have been found in Persian destruction debris of the Agora,[101] and there are many others from the Acropolis Persian debris.[102] The peak of their production in clay seems to have come around the turn of the 6th to 5th centuries, and the preferred decoration uses Six's technique:[103] the figures are painted onto the black-glazed background in a colored suspension of clay, into which details may be incised. The colors are often white, red, and yellow. There is one nearly complete phiale and another fragmentary one in Six's technique from well J 2:4.

The nearly complete omphalos phiale in Six's technique, **23** (Color Ill. 14), from Level 5 of the deposit, may have served the household in a

95. Stand: *Agora* XII, pp. 179–180, 329, nos. 1327–1329, fig. 11, pl. 43; Richter and Milne (1935, p. 31) suggest it was a stand for sweetmeats, but this seems unlikely because of the small size. Disk: *Agora* XII, pp. 178, 329, nos. 1321–1326, fig. 11, pl. 43.

96. Bilingual amphora, Munich J388 (2301), *ARV*² 4, no. 9, *Paralipomena* 113, 320, *Add*² 71, *CVA* Munich 4 [Germany 12], pls. 155 [533]:1, 156 [534]:1. The stand is located to the left of the kylix on the table. It is not present on

the black-figured side of the amphora.

97. See the discussion of libations in the context of the "ritual" of the symposium in Lissarrague 1990a, pp. 25–28.

98. Xenophanes, *PLG*⁴ 1 = Ath. 11.462c–d.

99. Xen. *Symp.* 2.1; Pl. *Symp.* 176a.

100. *Agora* XII, pp. 105–106; *Agora* XXIII, pp. 56–57; see Cardon 1973–1974, p. 133, n. 12, for a list. Note that the phiale shape was inspired by Eastern forms, but the omphalos phialai in Six's technique are not direct imitations

of an Achaemenid shape. For a discussion of Achaemenid phialai in Athenian pottery, see Kurtz 1975, pp. 116–120, esp. p. 117, n. 6; Miller 1997, pp. 136–140.

101. Shear 1993, p. 390, table 1.

102. Graef and Langlotz I, nos. 1111–1252; Tsingarida 2008, pp. 187–193.

103. First described in Six 1888, but coined by Beazley 1928, p. 8; see Juranek 1978–1979; Grossman 1991; Cohen 2006, p. 77 (on phialai).

variety of rituals. Its imagery, however, complements the scenes on several of the black-figured drinking vessels discussed above, thus connecting it to the sympotic activity in the house.[104] The shape is a wide, shallow bowl with a raised central omphalos that corresponds to a central depression on the underside. The interior is decorated in Six's technique with a procession of cattle to the right. The cattle alternate white bodies with red spots and red bodies with white spots. The painted decoration is very well preserved in a thick layer on the bodies of the cattle. Around the cattle the inscription *kalos* is repeated in various misspellings. The two preserved red cattle have projecting triangular forms on their undersides that may be an effort to distinguish the red ones as males.

The spotted bovines on this phiale are another link in a chain of images dealing with cattle. In the first instance presented here, the end product of the cattle—meat—is the subject of a red-figured cup tondo (**90**). A reference to cattle appears again on the Heron Class skyphos (**28**) with the peculiar horned headdresses worn by the drinkers. The black-figured skyphos of Class K2 featured a pair of cattle (**45**). The Cretan bull and Herakles decorate an oinochoe, **5**, which is the most developed mythological scene from the deposit. Cows and bulls are not common imagery in vase painting, with the exception of the Cretan and Marathonian bulls, and this seems to be an extraordinary collection of them for one household. It may be impossible to recover the meaning of the cattle, but perhaps this homeowner was affiliated with cattle ranching or marketing in Athens.[105]

The fragmentary phiale in Six's technique (**24**) preserves enough of the bowl to see that it did not have figural decoration as **23** does. The interior is decorated with a series of rows of slanted lines and dots. This fragment of a phiale is from Level 1b, and thus it may not have originated in the house; nonetheless, it represents the popularity of Six's technique as a decoration for phialai in the Late Archaic period.

THE NEED TO SEE: LAMPS AND THE SYMPOSIUM

A final accessory for an evening of sympotic activity is a terracotta lamp. These, too, are in the category of objects that had many functions in the house and are not exclusively associated with sympotic activity.[106] Still, communal drinking took place at night, and therefore lighting implements were necessary. The small candle power of an ancient oil lamp meant that the only way to brighten a room was to increase the number of lamps or wicks per lamp. Lamp **191**, for example, had two wicks. The other catalogued lamps (**190, 192–197**) are single-wicked, but most bear a carbonized area around the wick hole, indicating that they were used repeatedly. Lamps

104. Other omphalos phialai in Six's technique bear sympotic scenes, making the connection between the shape and sympotic activity even clearer; see Juranek 1978–1979, p. 109, figs. 1–4.

105. There is evidence in the 4th century of cattle ranching to supply the sacrificial needs of the city. A decree of Lykourgos dating to ca. 335 describes purchasing cattle for the annual Panathenaic festival sacrifice with the assistance of cattle buyers, ὁ βοωνής, *IG* II² 334 = *Syll*³ 271. This decree is discussed in Parke 1977, pp. 46–48. The term

appears again in Dem. *Meid.* 21.171.

106. In a well-preserved Archaic house at Sardis, lamps were found in several rooms but also in the kitchen where they were stored with other domestic pottery and equipment: Cahill 2002b, pp. 177–178.

190, **191**, **192**, **195**, and **196** come from Levels 5 and 6, and are likely to have originated in the house; of these, **190**, **191**, **195**, and **196** are complete or nearly complete. Lamp **197**, from Level 2, is three-quarters complete and also meets the criteria for inclusion in the household assemblage.

SUMMARY

This chapter has broadly considered the objects other than drinking cups that might be used during a communal drinking event. Some objects, such as psykters and oinochoai, are directly related to the preparation and serving of wine, but other objects, such as the lekythoi and small dishes, are included here because they might represent snacks that accompanied the drinking. For this latter category an exclusive sympotic use is not assumed; rather, these objects could be used for food service at any time.

One observation about the entirety of the sympotic assemblage—objects associated with wine drinking and food—is that figured ware was comfortably accompanied by black-glazed and even household-ware vessels. We should not imagine a sympotic set made up completely of figured wares. Instead, we find that this house mixed black figure with red figure, and figured with plain wares.

Those objects that are figured continue the themes developed in Chapter 4's discussion of the drinking vessels. In particular, the black-figured oinochoe (**5**) and the Six's technique phiale (**23**) both feature bovines. These complement the horned headdresses on the black-figured Heron Class skyphos (**28**) and the pair of cattle on the black-figured cup-skyphos (**45**). The iconographic parallels for these scenes are either few or nonexistent. Their presence in this household's sympotic assemblage must have been more than coincidence. As suggested above, this emphasis on cows may perhaps relate to the homeowner's interests or profession. And finally, the figured wares presented in this chapter also include a number of humorous elements that complement the puns and visual jokes discussed in relation to the cups in Chapter 4. Among these, **86**, the red-figured pelike with a striding barbitos player and vomiting youth, may have been the funniest. The contrast of adult self-control and youthful overindulgence, emphasized by the inscriptions of song and grunt, must have made the drinkers laugh and contemplate the potential outcome of their evening. The fragmentary black-figured lekanis lid (**79**) with a pudgy drinker holding a very long, curved drinking horn is another reference to excessive and playful drinking.

In sum, the sympotic assemblage provides a view of a household that avoided complex mythological tales and elaborate scenes of the gods,[107] favoring instead simple, funny images that caused the symposium participants to reflect on their own actions and to laugh.

107. This is in contrast to the prevailing view that pottery images reinforce cultural ideals, especially religious ideology; see Scheffer 2001b.

CHAPTER 6

HOUSEHOLD ACTIVITIES OTHER THAN THE SYMPOSIUM

As for the unhappy pan, you may see that resting
beside the socket of the back door
in a pile of sweepings.
　　　—Ath. 11.487e (trans. C. B. Gulick, Cambridge, Mass., 1933)

The previous two chapters examined the evidence for sympotic activity in the house. More fine-ware pottery in the domestic assemblage of the house of well J 2:4 related to communal drinking than to any other single activity, which attests to its importance in Athenian houses (see discussion in Chapter 3). Even though the household invested in communal drinking equipment, these vessels were used only occasionally. In contrast, the household and nondrinking objects were utilized on a regular or daily basis. In fact, the examination of these ordinary objects can reveal more about daily life in ancient Athens than the specialty drinking ware. This chapter will present artifacts from the deposit that relate to the daily life of the house and consider how these provide insight into everyday dining, chores, play, and ritual.

The previous chapters have emphasized that this household used figured pottery alongside plain black-glazed pottery and even coarse wares. Therefore, we should not assume that all undecorated pottery was relegated to chores; instead, we must imagine a much more practical and fluid use of most shapes, whether decorated or not.

EVERYDAY DINING

As discussed in Chapters 4 and 5, communal dining, while it did occur in private homes, was not as much a focus of elaborate customs—rituals—as drinking. Complex rules govern communal food consumption and sharing in many of the world's cultures, but food consumption was not the most significant act of ingestion in ancient Greece.[1] Instead, communal bonding experiences within the private sphere were focused more on the consumption of wine. Dining, the *deipnon*, in Late Archaic and Classical Greece was

1. Ritualized dining did occur in ancient Greece, mainly in public settings in Athens, or semipublic settings such as *syssitia* in Sparta and also in Athens. On public dining in Athens, see Rotroff and Oakley 1992 and Steiner 2002.

less regulated, with fewer rules and less specialized equipment.[2] Wine seems to have been drunk during the *deipnon,* but a formal break was declared between it and the "symposium" portion of the evening.[3] It follows that the material culture of dining does not parallel sympotic patterns: there are no figured and few black-glazed wares devoted to dining, no shapes specifically designed for food presentation, no emphasis on uniformity to express commensality, and no space devoted to food consumption in the household. Perhaps the clearest indication of the secondary role of dining to drinking is that there are no ceramic shapes specifically designated as an individual food receptacle during the Late Archaic/Early Classical period. Plates are known from the period, but they are used as votive objects to be hung and displayed, as their suspension holes indicate.[4] Bowls, which occur infrequently in this period, are very well potted and well glazed and thus too delicate for everyday tableware, although they may have been used to present food or cover a platter.[5] The contents of well J 2:4 illustrate the importance of food preparation through the abundance of lekanai and chytrai (discussed below), but the dearth of fine-ware forms for food consumption underscores in turn the importance of drinking for our Athenian house. The archaeological evidence amplifies the view we have from texts and clarifies the lower importance of dining relative to drinking.

The one all-purpose shape is the one-handler, a sturdy bowl-like form with a single horizontal handle.[6] The incurving or thickened rim of the one-handler argues against a primary function as a drinking cup, but such a use is not improbable. The shape would accommodate single servings of stews or soups. It occurs in a variety of sizes; **127** is a small catalogued example and the only one of five that meet the criteria for inclusion in the household's assemblage. However, Table 5 shows that there was a maximum of 25 and minimum of 14 one-handlers found throughout the deposit, indicating that it was a popular form in domestic contexts and suggesting that this household owned more than one one-handler. In light of the dearth of ceramic evidence for individual food receptacles, it seems likely that everyday dining equipment was made of wood or other perishable materials such as dried gourds.

The lekanis is also a multifunctional shape that may have been used as a food-serving bowl.[7] The form is usually lidded and comes in a range

2. In contrast, "Homeric" banquets did feature rules governing sharing and consumption of food; see Bruns 1970; Murray 1990b, p. 6; van Wees 1995; Węcowski 2002. In the Hellenistic period dining became more elaborate, with complex menus, and although Hellenistic banquets were, technically, communal affairs, the emphasis was more on the status of the host and less on the *isonomia* of the group as in the Late Archaic and Classical symposium; see Murray 1996.

3. Wilkins and Hill 2006, pp. 77–78.

4. Calliopolitis-Feytmans 1974,

pp. 18–19. One fragment possibly from a black-figured plate, **78**, was found in the deposit.

5. Three such examples from this deposit (**152, 153, 154**) had walls of ca. 1 mm in thickness; see *Agora* XII, p. 294, nos. 810–813, pl. 32, for examples. The undersides are exquisitely molded and incised in a manner similar to later stemless cups, e.g., *Agora* XII, p. 270, nos. 496–500, fig. 5, pls. 23, 50. Bowls such as **152, 153,** and **154** may be the progenitors of that class. If the bowl were turned upside down to function as a lid, the outturned foot profile

would permit a good grip, and this would make the underside detail visible.

6. One-handler: *Agora* XII, pp. 124–126; *Agora* XXIX, p. 155.

7. *Agora* XII, p. 164; Richter and Milne 1935, pp. 23–24; Kanowski 1983, pp. 90–93. Photios (s.v. lekane) says that the "ancients . . . called lekanis vessels with handles for cooked food and the like." Hesychius (s.v. lekanides) describes them as dishes in which gifts were brought to newlyweds. The latter function will be explored below, under the discussion of items for the personal toilet.

of sizes.[8] The lid indicates that contents required protection from pests or were stored over time. As discussed in Chapter 5, some lekanides bear figured decoration, and one black-figured example from this deposit (**79**) features drinking-related iconography. As a result, I proposed that some lekanides had a role in the symposium, probably to hold snack items such as olives that might attract pests if not covered. The same role can be posited for lekanides in everyday meals. Our deposit includes a fragmentary lekanis body (**157**) and fragmentary black-glazed lids (**158, 159, 160, 161,** and **162**). One of the fragmentary lids (**159**) has circular scrapes on its interior surface, suggesting that it was inverted and used as a mixing bowl. The function of lekanides must have been similar if not identical to a class of objects usually classed separately: covered bowls. Covered bowls differ in form from lekanides by being smaller and sometimes having a stem.[9] Examples from this deposit are **155** and **156**; **164** is a lid probably for a covered bowl. One lekanis, three lekanis lids, and three covered bowls meet the criteria for inclusion in the household's assemblage (see Table 6).

Other than the lekanis, which was not exclusively for food service, there are no shapes dedicated to the presentation or service of "main dishes." This means that food was either served out of utilitarian bowls, such as the lekane (discussed below), or directly from cooking vessels. The latter seems quite likely, and in fact, a family may have eaten directly from the cooking pot by scooping food with bread.

Dishes for condiments, on the other hand, served in lekythoi, olpai, stemmed dishes, and salt cellars, are numerous in well J 2:4 and other Persian destruction deposits.[10] The abundance of these shapes was discussed in Chapter 5, where it was proposed that they might appear on the symposium table to accompany snacks. The black-figured lekythoi do bear iconography that link them to sympotic activities, but all these shapes may have been used on an everyday basis as part of typical dining equipment. The numbers of lekythoi, olpai, stemmed dishes, and salt cellars suggest that these were individual table items, that is, that each diner had his own, as opposed to there being a single vessel used in common by all. It is possible that lekythoi, especially the smaller variety, held oils to flavor bread.[11] Olpai, also small containers for liquids, may have held oil or vinegar for a similar purpose.

The liquid condiments may have been poured into small dishes, stemmed dishes, and salt cellars, and seasoned with spices. This household owned at least eight stemmed dishes and three salt cellars, but numerous additional fragments attest to the importance of the form in the house. A plausible role for stemmed dishes and salt cellars on the sympotic table is proposed in Chapter 5, and details of the examples from well J 2:4 are

8. *Agora* XII, p. 168. Lekanis lids take on a life of their own in the late 5th to 4th centuries. They are particularly associated with women and are decorated in red figure with nuptial scenes; see, e.g., *Olynthus* XIII, pp. 119–

121, no. 63, pl. 86.

9. *Agora* XII, pp. 172–173; example, p. 325, no. 1269, pl. 42.

10. See Shear 1993, tables 2, 3.

11. Or oils to perfume the body; see discussion in Chapter 5 and below.

discussed there. As with the liquid containers, these receptacles probably had a daily, nonsympotic function as well. The endurance of the salt cellar from the late 6th century to the 4th century, when its function is taken over by small bowls and saucers, indicates that it played an integral part in an unchanging aspect of dining.[12]

It is uncertain whether or not wine accompanied everyday meals.[13] If it did, the drinking cups from this house most likely used are the black-figured cup-skyphoi (**45** and others) discussed in Chapter 3. They are numerous and sturdy, and they do not have a form specially designed for reclining, as do the kylikes. If decoration is a clue, the hasty and ill-defined black-figured scenes suggest that the viewer/drinker would not spend time examining them closely. The cultural apprehension over women's drinking probably means that women were not given wine with daily meals.[14]

HOUSEHOLD CHORES

When we think of household activities, we most often think of the daily chores and maintenance that keep the household running. In ancient Athens, women, slaves, and servants were responsible for most of these activities. In the idealized version of home life provided in Xenophon's *Oeconomicus*, a wife has ultimate responsibility for a team of slaves, who perform the actual tasks.[15] In reality, we can imagine middle-class and lower-class Athenian homes in which the wife and children work together with slaves. It is impossible to know to what class the family that owned the house of well J 2:4 belonged; the small size of the rooms and the house's location along the north side of the Classical Agora may argue for middle class, with a modest number of servants. Certainly the household could afford to host communal drinking events, so it was not impoverished.

Ischomachos, the homeowner and main voice of Xenophon's dialogue, describes dividing up the household equipment for proper storage. He stresses that the division is based on those things that are used daily and those used only for feasts (*Oec.* 9.7). Of those needed for everyday, he describes vaguely those needed "for baking, cooking, spinning, and so forth" (*Oec.* 9.8–9). His "and so forth" is disappointing, but baking, cooking, spinning, and related tasks must have taken up much of the day in an urban house.

The objects in well J 2:4 attest to the daily activities Xenophon mentions: fetching water from the household well, food preparation, cooking, and weaving. Certainly other activities were necessary, such as cleaning and keeping the house in order and procuring supplies outside the house, but these leave few if any traces in the archaeological record. The artifacts discussed here, as is true throughout this work, provide a window into everyday life but cannot shed light on every detail. In particular, the window the objects provide allows a view into the life of Athenian women. The artifacts described here were used by women, unlike the fine wares discussed in Chapters 4 and 5, which are nearly all associated with the symposium and the world of men.

12. *Agora* XII, pp. 132–138; Sparkes and Talcott (p. 132) speculate that the endurance of the shape is in part due to its being a consistent measure.

13. Dalby 2003, p. 351.

14. See, e.g., Ar. *Thesm.* 735–738.

15. Xen. *Oec.* 7.35–36, 41–42; 9.15–17; Pomeroy 1994.

EVERYDAY CHORES: FETCHING WATER

Having a household well must have made daily chores easier. Public water sources, in the form of fountain houses, did exist in the area, but so far there is no evidence for any within a few minutes' walk of the house of well J 2:4.[16] Many private houses in the Late Archaic period did have their own wells, which must have been considered a useful and necessary expense at the time of construction.[17] This house's foundations were close enough to the water table to need a moderately deep well of about 5 m, but some wells in the area around the Classical Agora reached 10 m or more in depth.[18] Water jars are frequently found in the period of use deposit at the bottom of wells, indicating that breakage was common, which is one reason why the vessels are unpretentious and probably were inexpensive.

In order to fetch water from the well shaft, vessels were tied to a rope, lowered down into the well, filled, and hauled back up. In the Late Archaic/ Early Classical period, water jars were made from the same type of gritty clay fabric used for cooking shapes. This fabric, "cooking ware," refers to the type of clay used and not strictly to function.[19] The great porosity, lightness, and probable low cost of the fabric made it ideal for vessels holding water. Vessels were formed largely by hand with the exception of the rim and base, which were wheelmade. The household shape specifically designed for fetching water from a well is the kados. It has a wide mouth and two earlike handles that permit the well rope to be tied around its neck. This deposit has a nearly complete example of a kados (**172**) from Level 5.[20]

Another water-vessel shape from the deposit is the water jug, a cooking-ware pouring vessel with a wide mouth, single handle, and ring base. Table 7 shows that cooking-ware jugs were the second most prevalent type of water jar, after kadoi. An example, **173**, is not very large and would not bring up a very useful amount of water. The hydria, the quintessential water vessel, is better suited for carrying water from afar since its narrower neck prevents the water from splashing out if jostled.[21] Hydriai are also superior to the kados as pouring vessels. No complete example of a hydria is preserved in this deposit, but the distinctive rim and horizontal handles attest to its presence. It is the least common of the three forms in the household.

In the period of use (Level 6) and the lower part of Level 5 there was a maximum of 90 and a minimum of 74 cooking-ware water-jar bases (see Table 5).[22] Unfortunately, it is nearly impossible to distinguish, from the

16. Camp 1977, pp. 73–100.

17. See discussion in Chapter 2.

18. See well cross sections figured in Shear 1993. Camp (1977, pp. 198–220) gives well depth in catalogue entries for Archaic and Classical wells.

19. *Agora* XII, pp. 34–35; Amyx 1958a, pp. 186–190.

20. The kados could also be fitted with a metal or rope basket handle and carried. See, for example, a depiction by the Brygos Painter in a cup tondo:

Boston, MFA 95.29, *ARV*[2] 220, no. 6, Sparkes and Talcott 1958, fig. 27, *Agora* XII, p. 201 and nn. 2, 3. See Sparkes 1962, pp. 129–130 and n. 74, for discussion of the shape and literary references to it.

21. Sparkes 1962, p. 129 and n. 73; *Agora* XII, p. 200.

22. In addition to the cooking-ware water jars, the six closed household fabric bases from Levels 5 and 6 were likely serving as water fetching vessels,

as were the seven nearly complete black-glazed amphoras, oinochoai, and pelikai. See discussion in Chapter 5 of the multifunctional nature of closed vessels. For pelikai in wells, see Lynch 2001a. The maximum number 91 includes water jars in Level 6 and Level 5, some of which might have been discarded in the cleanup, but bases from the lower portion of Level 6, the period of use deposit proper, represent water jars broken in the lifetime of the house.

base alone, the three common water-jar types: kados (**172**), hydria, or jug (**173**). On the other hand, the statistics for water jar rims from well J 2:4 can give some general idea of proportion of water-jar shapes, although the gross distinction of "greater than 50%" and "less than 50%" rim preserved for fragments introduces great error when the pieces are significantly less than 50% preserved. Thus, even the minimum number of vessels is likely to be too large. Rotroff's formula discussed in Chapter 3 can be applied to rims, as it was for bases. Table 7 shows that kadoi make up the majority of water jars, with jugs second and hydriai third, when only the rims are considered. Handles can provide additional information, but this data is even more difficult because of the potters' use of generic vertical handles on all three shapes. A fragmentary handle from a kados can resemble the midsection of a jug handle, and of course, a hydria also has a vertical handle, indistinguishable in fragments from other vertical handles. Horizontal handles are somewhat easier to distinguish as they lack the thumb depression often used at the base of vertical handles. Adding to the identification difficulty, a fragmentary straight (not upswung) horizontal handle can resemble a vertical kados handle. In sum, the handle data can be misleading. Nevertheless, as a measure, the horizontal handle counts give a different view of hydriai than the rims alone do. Table 7 shows that there are more horizontal handles than vertical. This may mean that hydriai were about as common as kadoi.

Another explanation for the discrepancy between the number of hydriai rims and handles may relate to how the vessels broke. If the well rope was tied to the vessel's vertical handle, or handle and neck, then it is possible that the vertical hydria handle and upper portions of the vessel were yanked up and out of the well while its base and—in the case of hydriai—horizontal handles fell to the bottom. In fact, this breakage scheme accounts for the fact that the minimum number of water-jar bases from the deposit is greater than the minimum number of combined rims.

Two observations are worth emphasizing. If this well were in use for 25 years, then the household broke approximately four water jars a year, which is a modest number. There are an additional minimum of 24 water jars in household fabric (including **174–178**) in the well, and various black-glazed and even black-figured vessels may have been used to fetch water, thus raising the average breakage rate from four to six a year, which still seems like a modest breakage rate. A second related observation is that shapes other than kadoi and jugs could be used to fetch water. The intact and nearly complete pelikai (**107** from Level 5 and **108** from Level 6) must have been employed as water jars. Hydriai are usually thought to have been used for fetching water from public fountain houses, not the household well, since their extra handles facilitated lifting as well as pouring. The evidence presented here argues for a more practical view of water jars: if it holds water, it will do the job.[23]

This deposit preserves an unusual series of water jars: **174**, **175**, **176**, **177**, and **178** are all wheelmade jugs made of coarse-ware fabric, not the typical cooking-ware fabric. The fabric is somewhere between the gritty cooking ware and the coarse ware of unglazed vessels such as banded oinochoai. There are no Agora parallels for these non-cooking-ware water jugs. Three (**174**, **177**, **178**) are of similar dimensions and form, with an

23. In fact, the jars do not even have to hold water. It is not uncommon to find holes in the walls of water jars formed by the explosion of lime inclusions during firing in the kiln. For example, the jug **173** has a 1 cm hole in its body. Such serious flaws did not seem to hinder the use of these vessels, and the holes must have been stopped with wax or another perishable substance.

ovoid body, more or less cylindrical neck, and wide mouth. Jug **174** has a slight trefoil rim to facilitate pouring, but the others are round-mouthed. Jugs **175** and **176** are of the same form, but on a slightly smaller scale than **174**. The handles are preserved on **175** and **176**, and we should probably restore similar high-swung oval handles on the others. That the others lack handles and a portion of the neck and rim indicates that they broke against the wall of the well when used to fetch water. On **175** is a nonalphabetic graffito on the shoulder near the handle. Imported water jugs are common for Athens,[24] and these deviations from the typical cooking-ware fabric may be imports.[25] Not only does the fabric have little relationship with the normal water jars, the shape is also unlike any other. The shapes of **175**, **176**, and **177** are closest, but by a stretch, to the banded oinochoai of the 6th century.[26] The water jugs of this series have no comparanda within Athens, and their fabric is unlike typical Attic clay; this supports their identification as imports.

Finally, the period of use deposit of well J 2:4, Level 6 and the lower reaches of Level 5, contained three black-glazed pelikai: one intact (**107**), one broken but nearly complete (**106**), and a third missing its rim, neck, and upper handles (**108**). As was noted in the discussion of the red-figured pelike **84**, the shape had many functions, which are often reflected in the iconography of the figured versions. In the case of well J 2:4 and other Agora well deposits, it is also clear that the shape was being used to fetch water.[27] The condition of the vessels reflects their use as water jars. We can assume that **106** and **107** slipped from the well rope; one broke against the wall, while the other sank intact to the bottom. The rope must have been tied to the neck of **108**, so that when the pelike broke against the side of the well, the neck and handles remained attached to the rope and were removed, while the body sank to the bottom, in fragments. It is possible that these black-glazed versions of the shape bore water into the symposium room to be mixed with wine, but they also could have served an everyday, utilitarian function.

EVERYDAY CHORES: FOOD PREPARATION

Household food consumption implies a whole series of activities from provision to preparation. Unfortunately, flotation analysis did not yield any floral evidence, so it is not possible to say anything about the consumption of fruits, vegetables, or grains by the household. The presence, however, of ceramic mortars and an andesite quern, not inventoried, indicate that grain was milled within the house (see Table 4).

The faunal material reveals that the house consumed the meat of pigs, sheep, dog, and cattle.[28] It seems unlikely that animal bones were thrown

24. *Agora* XII, p. 204.

25. There is always the possibility of a "short-lived household-ware workshop" responsible for a sudden and unsustained appearance of this household-ware type. The phenomenon occurs at the end of the 5th century, with a single workshop responsible for household shapes not made out of the normal cooking-ware fabric; see *Agora* XII, pp. 187–188, 200.

26. Cf. *Agora* XII, p. 246, no. 139, pl. 8.

27. Lynch 2001a.

28. The faunal material from well J 2:4 will be the subject of a full study by Lynn A. Snyder of the Smithsonian Institution. Comments here are based on discussions with Snyder on her preliminary findings.

into the well while it was still being used for water. Rather, they must have been tossed down during the initial cleanup along with the whole pots. Butchering marks indicate that these are bones of animals consumed as food, thus they were either redeposited as fill or they were thrown into the well after meals that took place during the cleanup process. There are no whole animals present, but instead portions of several different animals. There are a few remains of inedible parts such as mandibles, hooves, and horns, but not on a scale that would indicate commercial activity.[29]

During the Late Archaic period the predominant cooking shape was the chytra, a round-bottomed vessel with one or two handles and round mouth, made of the same thin-walled, gritty fabric as the water jars.[30] The round-bottomed chytra sat on top of a brazier,[31] fragments of which are present in Levels 2 and 5 of the deposit, or on a tripod of stones. Aside from a few early examples of a casserole-type cooking vessel, the lopas, which becomes popular in the years after the Persian Wars, the only ceramic cooking shape in the Persian destruction cleanup deposits was the juglike chytra.[32] The chytra shape favored the preparation of liquid food such as soups, broths, and stews, which explains why there was no cultural need for food plates when a bowl or one-handler would do. The deposit contained a maximum of 20 and minimum of 19 chytrai, and a maximum of five and minimum of two chytra lids (see Table 5). The four catalogued examples of chytrai (184–187) can be confidently associated with the household's assemblage.[33] They range in shape from very small (186)[34] to quite large (187). The remarkable preservation of these brittle, thin-walled shapes—184, 185, and 186 are all intact—means that they were thrown into the well during the cleanup, hit the water, and sank into their positions, where they miraculously escaped being crushed by the other vessels and the layer of gravel and slag above them. They are not in the period of use, but are in Level 5, the material intentionally deposited during the cleanup of the house. Traces of burning, even on the inside of 185 and 187, indicate that these vessels were used. Burning on the interior may have resulted from overcooking, or the chytra may have been used to transport burning coals to a different location in the house.[35]

The form of 187 is otherwise unattested for the period. It is large, has the typical wide-mouthed and lidded chytra body form and also has an

29. The bones from the Persian destruction well R 12:1 included numerous ox skulls, which are interpreted as evidence of a butcher or bone-processing workshop.

30. Nearly all of the Persian destruction cleanup deposits contained cooking pots, and when they are not present, such as in the RRCS, it is likely that they were not kept by the excavator. The wealth of figured pottery may have overwhelmed the humble cooking pots in some cases.

31. Sparkes 1962, p. 130. For a complete example, see *Agora* XII, p. 377, nos. 2016, 2017, pl. 97. See

also Amyx 1958a, pp. 211–212.

32. A few Persian destruction deposits contain examples of the eschara, a type of brazier with supports for spits: D 15:1, G 3:1, two from L 5:2 (all delayed Persian destruction cleanup deposits), and H 13:5 and L 5:2 (both trenches with mixed public and domestic material). We associate skewers with roasted meat, and it is possible that meat consumption increased with post–Persian War prosperity, and that the increase in numbers of household escharai is a reflection of this change of dietary habits; see discussion in Rotroff and Oakley 1992,

pp. 47–48. Level 2 contained one eschara rim fragment (uninventoried).

33. The majority of fragments come from the upper fill, particularly Level 2; the intact chytrai, however, come from Level 5 and were more likely to be in use in the house at the time of the sack.

34. See comments in Chapter 5 on the possibility that 186 was a wine-service vessel, on comparison with similarly shaped wine-service utensils in red-figured depictions of the symposium.

35. For a chytra used to transport coals, see Ar. *Lys.* 297, 308, 315.

upright, open spout.[36] The rim is flanged to take a lid, but it is also pierced at least four times on the projecting horizontal flange with holes ca. 7 mm in size. The purpose of these holes in the flange is unclear. The spout was not for pouring, since the small diameter of the hole in the side of the vessel connecting the spout to the vessel would not have permitted the transfer of the contents of the chytra through the spout. Instead, the spout allowed steam to escape from the lidded, boiling contents.[37] Perhaps the holes in the flange are also a provision to allow steam condensing on the lid to drip back down into the pot. The shape of **187** is at the beginning of a new, less juglike chytra type that becomes popular around the middle of the 5th century.[38] This seems to be an early, experimental form.

Bread was a defining element of Archaic and Classical Greek cuisine, and baking bread was a key activity in the house.[39] One method for baking bread involved the use of a cooking bell, a portable oven chamber. This deposit has a very well-preserved example of the type (**188**). It is made from the same material as braziers, a thicker-walled version of the coarse, gritty cooking-ware fabric. Coals were piled up on a flat surface such as a clay floor, over which the bell would be placed for warming (preheating). Once hot, it would be removed, the coals swept to the side, and the dough placed on the warmed earth. The cooking bell would be replaced, the coals heaped over the sides, and the bread baked within.[40] It could also serve as an extinguisher for a fire or low brazier.

Neither cooking nor baking in this household required a built hearth. It is often assumed on the basis of literary evidence that all ancient Greek houses had built hearths, but in fact, there is little evidence for any built hearths in Archaic and Classical Athens.[41] Instead, portable devices such as braziers and cooking bells underscore that the "kitchen" was not a fixed room in the house. Food-preparation activities could move with the weather—to the courtyard in fair weather, to a portico in foul—or to accommodate other activities in the house.[42]

Aside from the devices used for the act of cooking, there are a few shapes that can be associated with food preparation. Although all examples were fragmentary and none were catalogued, the deposit also contained a maximum of 16 and minimum of 10 mortars (see Table 5), of which one can be associated with the household assemblage (see Table 6). This is another multipurpose shape for food preparation.[43] Its sturdy, broad bowl, often with roughened floor, secure handles, and spout, suggest that it was used for grinding, and the contents were then poured into another receptacle. Sparkes and Talcott associate it with bread making specifically, but

---

36. Cf. *Agora* XII, pp. 225 and 372, no. 1944, pl. 94; Sparkes 1962, p. 131.

37. The shape is known in Roman pottery as a hole-mouthed jar and called a "milk boiler" or "wine cooler." In Roman pottery, it occurs both in coarse, kitchen ware, and fine ware, see Hayes 2000, p. 295, fig. 28:2 and discussion. Cooking vessel **187** finds some formal similarities with Attic

red-figured Falaieff kraters, which also have a projecting ledge with pierced holes on the interior; see McPhee 2000. Functions for both coarse and fine-ware examples remain unclear.

38. *Agora* XII, pp. 226 and 373, nos. 1952–1955, pl. 94.

39. Sparkes 1962, pp. 123–129; 1981, pp. 172–178; Dalby 1996, pp. 90–93.

40. Sparkes 1962, p. 128.

41. Jameson 1990b, p. 192; Swinford 2006; Tsakirgis 2007.

42. See Cahill 2002a, pp. 162–163, for the portability of food preparation at Olynthus, where some of the houses had built-in flues but apparently did not use them for cooking (p. 156).

43. *Agora* XII, pp. 221–223, example: *Agora* XII, p. 370, no. 1900, pl. 90; Cahill 2002a, pp. 166–167.

it could have been used for grinding nuts or even dried fruits for recipes. An andesite saddle quern and two stone pounders from Level 5 were most likely used for grinding grain for household bread.[44]

The lekane is an all-purpose large bowl,[45] which probably filled the roles of modern-day mixing bowl and bucket combined. It could be used for preparing food, kneading dough, and soaking beans, but it could also be used as a basin for washing clothes, cleaning the house and children, and an infinite number of other household tasks. It was also the household chamber pot and could be found in a symposium as a receptacle for vomit or as a krater.[46] Two examples of the shape are catalogued here (**181, 182**), but there are a maximum of 53 and minimum of 29 examples, mainly bases, in a range of sizes from the deposit. Only five lekanai meet the conditions for inclusion in the household's assemblage (see Table 6), but the large number in the deposit indicates that they were a common household form.

EVERYDAY CHORES: WEAVING

Weaving was probably a never-ending household chore. The wife of the house was responsible for overseeing the production of clothes and linens for everyone in the house, including slaves. In Ischomachos's house, described in Xenophon's *Oeconomicus,* some of these garments are considered for "festival" use only and were stored separately from everyday garments, meaning that household members may have had multiple sets of clothes.[47]

In the house, women prepared and spun the wool first, before weaving.[48] The wool may have been purchased "raw" or brought from the family's farm in rural Attica. At the urban house, the women carded the wool and cleaned it, then prepared threads by spinning. Spinning requires a distaff and a weighted spindle, usually a stick with a stone whorl attached to its end. The distaff held the raw wool, and was usually made of wood and thus does not survive. One whorl (**209**) comes from this deposit, but it is in the uppermost portion of the deposit, Layer 1b, so it may not have originated in the house.

After the threads were prepared, they were woven into cloth using a loom. Looms were made of wood, and thus also do not survive in the archaeological record.[49] Threads, as they hung on the loom, were weighted with terracotta loomweights to maintain tension, and these weights survive because of their dense ceramic forms. They take a pyramidal form in the Late Archaic period, with a single hole pierced through the upper portion to accommodate the thread. Well J 2:4 contained 10 complete loomweights and fragments of three more. Representative examples are catalogued as **206, 207,** and **208.** All but one of these were in the upper levels of the deposit, but because of their preservation, they technically met the criteria for inclusion in the household's assemblage. Since their preservation is a result of their density, we may not be right to associate them with the household assemblage, so I have listed them and the spindle whorl on Table 6 with question marks. There is little consistency in their weights, although this does not mean they were not used together.[50] Cahill estimates that a household loom at Olynthus would need between 10 and 40 loomweights, depending on the type of textile.[51]

Weaving was a defining characteristic of women in Classical Greece.[52] The ability to spin and weave was a desired trait in all women, but especially

44. For the role of terracotta mortars in preparation of bread, see Sparkes 1962, p. 125. For the distinction between stone grinders and terracotta mortars, see Amyx 1958a, pp. 236–238; Villing 2009.

45. *Agora* XII, pp. 211–216, example: p. 361, no. 1781, pl. 83; on the form, see Lüdorf 2000.

46. Chamber pot: Cohen and Shapiro 2002, p. 87; vomit receptacle: Cohen and Shapiro 2002, p. 89; as a substitute for a krater, see discussion in Chapter 5.

47. Xen. *Oec.* 9.6, 10.

48. For an overview of the spinning and weaving process, see Barber 1994, pp. 34–41.

49. Vase depictions give us an idea what looms looked like, but as always, the vase-painter's goal was not realistic accuracy, so one should be careful about over-interpreting details. See images in Barber 1994.

50. They range from 42 to 75 g; see discussion on variable weights in Cahill 2002a, p. 179; 2002b, pp. 179, 181.

51. Cahill 2002a, pp. 171–175.

52. Fantham et al. 1994, pp. 103–104; Ischomachos proudly boasts that the only skill his 14-year-old bride brought to the marriage was the ability to weave and direct slaves to assist (Xen. *Oec.* 7.5).

those who were "model" women. Practically, the wife herself would not have been able to fulfill the textile needs of the entire *oikos,* but with the assistance of slaves it would have been possible, although we must imagine the women spinning and weaving during any "idle" moments. Looms, unlike the implements of cooking, were not as portable once set up. They were probably located in rooms near the courtyard that had good lighting and circulation, but were protected from foul weather and dirt.[53] Spinning, though, could be done anywhere and for short periods of time and could be done by young girls as well.

EVERYDAY CHORE OR LIVELIHOOD?

This section on daily activities must include the unusual object **183,** a coarse bowl of a gritty fabric similar to cooking-ware fabric, but denser. It is a form that has no parallels in the period: it has a flat base, angled walls, and a tall straight rim. The interior is covered with a residue of white and red pigments. The base is just the right size to sit securely in the palm of one's hand. Although no obvious use comes to mind, the pigments and the form suggest a palette of sorts. One can imagine **183** as a paint pot for a worker decorating a large object as he moved about (as opposed to a small object that would allow him to use more fixed equipment). In Chapter 2 evidence is presented that challenged the previous identification of marble-working industry in the house of well J 2:4. While there is no certain evidence that manufacturing of any sort took place in the house, it is possible that a paint bowl like **183** was used by a wall or monument painter. There is, of course, no way to prove this hypothesis. The bowl comes from Level 5 of the deposit, indicating that it was in use in the house at the time of the Persian destruction.

HOUSEHOLD STORAGE

Ischomachos explains in great detail his theories about proper household storage in Xenophon's *Oeconomicus* (8.2–9.10). What we can glean from his description and anecdotal information is that there were separate storage rooms for goods not used on a daily basis. A storage room is depicted on a red-figured skyphos in the Getty.[54] Wooden chests, which would have been useful for storing clothing and other items likely to attract pests and dirt and be of temptation to others, do not survive in the archaeological record. Wicker baskets and wooden containers also held goods for storage, but these too have been lost.[55] Therefore, again, we must remember that any view of the domestic household based on the ceramic evidence alone is severely limited. But since it is the only thing we have, it is worth considering how ceramics provided storage in the house.

The largest of all ceramic shapes in existence in ancient Greece was the pithos. It is a human-sized storage container usually sunk into the ground so that it could also function as a refrigerator. Pithoi are usually made of a very coarse fabric with very large inclusions. The deposit preserves fragments of pithos rims, toes, and body sherds, one of which has an ancient mend.[56] There is also a fragmentary storage vessel of pithos size but of cooking-ware fabric with a slipped surface, and a broad, open form with

53. Cahill 2002a, pp. 173–177; Greek has a term for "loom-room" (p. 175), but Cahill's study showed that almost any room could be used for weaving. Just as "andron" is a temporal-spatial term used to describe any space where men are drinking together, so too the "loom-room" is whatever space the women are using for weaving at that time.

54. Malibu, Getty Museum 86. AE.265, Neils and Oakley 2003, pp. 258–259, no. 63, fig. 63:b, p. 120, fig. 63 (right).

55. They are mentioned, however, in the Attic Stelai: Amyx 1958b, pp. 264–275.

56. For mended pithoi on the Attic Stelai, see Amyx 1958a, p. 168.

rounded bottom.[57] Sparkes and Talcott thought that the round bottom of a similar example (P 1218) indicated that it functioned as a cauldron,[58] but there is no evidence of burning on their example or on the vessel from well J 2:4, and the slip would also argue against exposure to direct fire. Its overhanging rim and nonfunctional handles (petite in comparison to the hulking stature of the vessel) suggest that it was a storage vessel with a covering tied on or a very large lid. It probably sat in a hole in the floor or on a stand similar to the one P 1218 occupies today (see *Agora* XII, plate 81). Additional fragments of large shapes of indeterminate form may be either tubs or troughs.[59]

JUGS

One black-glazed jug for storage of liquids (**114**) and one black-glazed possible jug (**115**) were found in the well in Levels 5 and 6, respectively. Jug **114** is intact. Its narrow neck allowed for secure closing with a stopper.[60] The possible jug **115** is missing its upper body, and on the basis of the break, it looks as if the vessel had one handle, but it is impossible to know if it had a pouring rim, or a rim similar to that of **114** that could be stopped for storage. Jug **114** was probably dangled into the cool water of the well to chill its contents or preserve them, and then slipped off its rope, which explains why it is intact. Jug **115** probably broke while in use, as did many of the water-fetching shapes, by hitting the side of the well. The body of the vessel sank to the bottom, but its handle/rim, to which the rope remained tied, was withdrawn. Both **114** and **115** are made of a hard, pink-purple fabric and are dipped in glaze (as opposed to the glaze being applied with a brush). Two other objects share these fabric characteristics: **116**, a trefoil olpe, and **157**, a lekanis. The fabric color is similar to Lakonian, but Sparkes and Talcott note that the technique of dipping was common also in Corinth in the Archaic period.[61]

TRANSPORT AMPHORAS

Among the objects pictured in the storeroom on the Getty skyphos are transport amphoras. Households would need to store staples such as grains and dried fruit and meat, as well as wine. Transport amphoras, once emptied, could be refilled with the same contents or reused for storage of other substances. Appendix I provides a complete study of the more than 50 fragmentary transport amphoras from well J 2:4. Remains from the other Persian destruction deposits confirm the prevalence of transport amphoras in the home.[62] A great number of large, sharp-edged fragments of amphoras come from Level 5, the pocket of fine wares, indicating that these were

57. The form of the rim, neck, and handles matches P 1218, *Agora* XII, p. 359, no. 1743, fig. 19, pl. 81, which is described as a "majestic lebes" and linked to makers of pithoi (p. 212). Fragments of pithoi and the large storage lebes were left in the context

tins due to their size and highly fragmentary condition.

58. *Agora* XII, p. 212.

59. Fragments of about four. One is rectangular and has a drain hole and is similar to an unpublished example from the Agora, P 23466.

60. *Agora* XII, p. 208; cf. *Agora* XII, p. 353, no. 1665, pl. 77, from well R 12:1, another Persian destruction cleanup deposit; see also Thompson 1951, p. 50, pl. 25:a.

61. *Agora* XII, p. 208, n. 26.

62. Cf. Roberts 1986, pp. 62–72.

thrown into the well during the same cleanup event. Unlike the fine wares, no amphora can be completely mended from the fragments. The production sites represented by the amphora fragments include Corinthian, Adriatic/Ionian, northern Aegean, Lesbos/Region, Chian, southeastern Aegean, and south Italian. This geographic range of origins parallels patterns from other Persian destruction deposits.

Two further objects may be related to the use of transport amphoras as storage containers in the house. A clay stopper (**216**) is of the size to fit into a vessel with a neck diameter of about 15 cm.[63] It had a stemmed knob for easy removal. It is possible that **165** was also a stopper of sorts. It is a simple, domed form that could have stopped a vessel with a neck of about 10 cm. Its domed form could also have doubled as a scoop for the removal of a vessel's dry contents.

TOILET ITEMS

This category refers to containers for personal use items and objects for adornment. It includes boxes to hold jewelry and cosmetics and containers for perfume. The multifunctional lekanis has been introduced already, with a discussion of its potential role as a food-presentation vessel. In addition, the lekanis could also hold jewelry or other trinkets or cosmetics.[64] This shape was connected with the world of women and their adornment: by the end of the 5th century the lekanis acquired an association with brides as a suitable marriage gift, and the figured versions are dominated by wedding imagery. The black-glazed versions found in this house (**157** and the fragmentary lids **158, 159, 160, 161,** and **162**) thus unfortunately defy exclusive association with either food presentation or personal storage. The same is true for the covered bowls **155** and **156** and for lids **164** and **165**.

Personal adornment also included perfumed oils. I have already discussed the role of lekythoi as containers for perfumed body oil and their potential connection with the symposium (see Chapter 5). Other shapes are exclusively designed for perfumed oil, including the aryballos. Although well J 2:4 contained no aryballoi, one is depicted in the red-figured gymnasium scene on the cup **87** (see discussion in Chapter 4). Well J 2:4 did contain several distinctive perfume vessels. Included in the household assemblage is the perfume jar ("unguent pot") **167**, probably imported from East Greece.[65] It has a deceptively heavy wall that reduces its capacity to a slender tube. This top-shaped perfume vessel might go with **170**, half of a cone-shaped ring stand that would support a small vessel with a pointy bottom.[66]

63. There is a second uncatalogued example from Level 2.

64. For discussion of multiple functions with references, see Amyx 1958a, pp. 202–205.

65. See *Agora* XII, p. 317, no. 1165, pl. 39; see p. 157 for a discussion of the form and its origins.

66. Cf. the image of a similar amphoriskos-shaped perfume jar placed in a ring stand of a different form but same function (Sparkes and Talcott 1958, fig. 55). For the complete shape, cf. *Agora* XII, p. 330, nos. 1335, 1336, pl. 43.

Another container for liquids is the black-glazed askos (**166**).[67] The form is well known from the generations after the Persian Wars, but **166** may be the earliest example of an Attic ring askos. The shape was imported from the East, and an example in East Greek fabric from the Stoa Gutter Well is the closest parallel for the shape of **166**.[68] The decoration of **166**, though, is different. The East Greek example from the Stoa Gutter Well has black bands on a predominantly buff surface, while the early Attic version is totally glazed.[69] The canonical form of the Attic askos will have a ring base, a stouter body, and a handle that arches from spout to the back edge of the ring.[70] Thus **166** is an early attempt to imitate the imported form directly; Attic potters must have found their own innovations more practical, and so **166** remains unparalleled as an early experiment. The ring shape of the early askoi is meant to increase the surface area of the vessel. Askoi probably held a viscous oil, and the ring would permit the vessel to be submerged in heated water to liquefy the contents for pouring.

TOYS

As important as children were to the prosperity and future of Athens, evidence for their lives is hard to identify and has received little scholarly attention until recently.[71] Children of all times and places learn to negotiate adult worlds through play. A few terracotta and bone objects from well J 2:4 may represent children's toys, but, just as with the pottery, these are frustratingly ambiguous, as they can also have a religious function.

Fragments **203** and **204** come from small hand-formed terracotta figurines. Both were quadrupeds, but **204** preserves only a foreleg. The better-preserved **203** does not bear evidence of a rider and has traces of a whitish-yellow slip with curving black lines. This may be a sheep rather than a horse. It is difficult to assess the function of these small figurines; like the terracotta figurines discussed in the next section, these too could have been votive objects in a household shrine.

Knucklebones, *astragaloi*, are asymmetrical tarsal bones of the hind leg of a quadruped. These bones have four distinct, somewhat flat faces, and were used for both games and divination. In divination each face of the bone

67. One theory is that askoi held wine for the cult of the dead: Hoffmann 1977, p. 1; countered by Boardman 1979; restated by Burkert and Hoffmann 1980; rebutted again by Boardman 1981. Later askoi with strainers may have held vinegar: Monaco 1993.

68. *Agora* XII, p. 358, no. 1725, pl. 80 (= Roberts 1986, no. 394). For the shape and typical East Greek decoration, cf. *Délos* X, nos. 80–102, pls. 16–18; *Délos* XVII, nos. 42–59, pls. 47, 48. All of the askoi from Delos have a round bottom and handle that attaches to the near side of the ring,

traits that are present on **166** but not canonical in the later Attic askoi.

69. "East Greek" may sound vague, but see Cook and Dupont 1998, p. 133: "[the askoi] are probably North Ionian and were widely exported and probably copied in the sixth century"; thus the general geographic attribution.

70. See *Agora* XII, p. 158, on the canonical "deep" black-glazed askoi: "none are earlier than 480 though they are preceded by two red-figured examples which would seem to be the earliest of the shape in Attica." The two red-figured examples can be dated to ca. 490 based on style: Providence

(RISD) 25.074, *ARV*² 480, no. 338; *Add*² 247 [Makron], Kunisch 1997, no. 3 and *CVA* Providence 1 [USA 2], pl. 17 [70]:4a, b for a profile view. See Kunisch 1997, pp. 18–21, for a discussion of the difficulties of assigning dates to the career of Makron; he calls the Providence askos an early work. The second is Boston, MFA 13.169, *ARV*¹ 188, no. 50 [Tyszkiewicz Painter], Vermeule 1965, p. 47, fig. 15.

71. See Cohen and Rutter 2007 and Neils and Oakley 2003; the latter includes a catalogue of the Hood Art Museum exhibition "Coming of Age in Ancient Greece."

was given a meaning, so that the reading of knucklebones was similar to the reading of I Ching sticks. Many games were also played with knucklebones, some similar to modern jacks.[72] Children are often represented at play with knucklebones and sometimes receive them as grave gifts. Well J 2:4 contained 26 knucklebones, all from Levels 5 and 6, the intentional cleanup. There were 24 from sheep or goat (*Ovis* sp. and/or *Caprus* sp.) and two from cattle (*Bos* sp.). On many of these the projecting points were worn or intentionally ground down. Six of the astragaloi, represented in the Catalogue by **212**, **213**, and **214**, were modified by intentional shaving off the projecting points to create a more cubic form (**214**), or by holes drilled through from top to bottom (**212, 213**; **214** also has a diamond-shaped hole punched through it). The purpose of these holes, sometimes one (**212**), sometimes three (**213**), and sometimes off center (**212**), is not clear.[73] Examples from other deposits preserve lead in the holes, but no traces of fillings were found in the holes on the astragaloi from well J 2:4.[74] The modifications to the astragaloi effectively change their weights. It is possible that the shaving and drilling reduced the overall weight, and filling the drilled holes would increase the weight.[75] The two bovid astragaloi (e.g., **214**) weighed 52.5 g and 38.6 g. The ovid/caprid astragaloi varied from 2.85 g to 11.0 g, with an average weight of 6.3 g. Again, the purpose of this practice is unclear, but it may be related to functions other than divination or games.[76]

HOUSEHOLD RITUAL

We know very little about the material culture of household ritual. Although literary references emphasize the importance of the household hearth as a focus of rituals,[77] few houses if any in Archaic and Classical Athens, as mentioned above, had fixed hearths. Instead, we must imagine rituals performed around portable braziers.[78] Although household altars are also mentioned in literary sources, there is no archaeological evidence for either fixed or portable altars in Athenian houses.[79] The house itself was sacred, however, and liable to be polluted by death and birth.[80]

72. See discussion in Amandry 1984, pp. 375–378; Neils 1992a, p. 234, nn. 40, 41; Poplin 1992; Vanhove 1992, p. 176; Neils and Oakley 2003, pp. 276–277 and nos. 85–90. Sources: Ar. *Vesp.* 291–296; Paus. 6.24.7, 7.25.10; Plu. *Alc.* 2.1d.

73. Shaving and drilling is not uncommon. See, among others, Vanhove 1992, p. 176, no. 31.

74. Astragaloi with drilled holes filled with lead are known from the Bronze Age through the Roman period; see Reese 1985, pp. 387–388, for overview. On worked astragaloi, see Amandry 1984, esp. pp. 363–370, for astragaloi with lead fillings. Note that none of the astragaloi from well J 2:4

bear incised inscriptions, as many of the examples offered at the Corycian Cave do.

75. Weights used on pan balances sometimes feature the image of an astragalos; see *Agora* X, p. 25, BW 1, pl. 1 (ca. 500), and p. 27, LW 3–7, pls. 2, 3 (4th century–Hellenistic). It is possible that natural astragaloi functioned as household weights for small quantities.

76. A group of 78 astragaloi was found stored with vessels and objects associated with personal ornament in an Archaic house from Sardis: Cahill 2002b, p. 180. It is possible that some of the knucklebones with holes were also necklaces or at least strung on a

cord. Cahill does not say if any of the 78 from Sardis were pierced or otherwise modified.

77. E.g., Aesch. *Ag.* 1055–1057; Eur. *Alc.* 162; Thuc. 1.136. Jameson 1990b, pp. 192–195 and Tsakirgis 2007, p. 225, on household ritual, the hearth, and Hestia.

78. Dikaiopolis in Aristophanes's *Acharnians* (887–888) calls for the servants to "fetch me forth the brazier and the fan." See discussion of sources in Swinford 2006.

79. Portable altars have been found at Olynthus: *Olynthus* VIII, pp. 322–325; Cahill 2002a, pp. 87–88.

80. Parker 1983, p. 63; Burkert 1985, p. 76.

Of the objects found in well J 2:4, several may be connected with household ritual activity. Already discussed was the omphalos phiale in Six's technique (**23**), which may have been used during the symposium, although it could also have been used for other household libation rituals.[81] The imagery of cattle on the phiale may refer to sacrificial offerings of bulls and cows, and thus the inscriptions, *kalos,* may then refer to the beauty of the gift being made to a deity.

A fragment of a black-figured thymiaterion, an incense burner (**81**), also relates to ritual activity.[82] This fragment was recovered from the bottom of Level 6, the period of use portion of the well, indicating that it was used in the house and broken, probably before the Persian destruction. The style of the drawing places it in the last quarter of the 6th century, but closer to 525 than to 500. Incense burners—the stemmed thymiaterion or the nonstemmed version, the thurible—were found in nine of the 21 Persian destruction deposits studied by Shear, for a total of 19 examples.[83] Only one of the other 19 was in black figure, so **81** adds to our knowledge of black-figured thymiateria from domestic contexts.

Fragment **81** is a piece of the tall stem on which a small bowl would have sat, and there would have been a broad, stable foot for setting the incense burner on a table or the ground.[84] On the figural versions, there are friezes both above and below a horizontal central fillet on the stem. This fragment probably represents the upper element of the stem due to the flare of the stem near the bottom break. The bowl would have sat upon the top of **81**.[85] Unfortunately the bowl was fashioned separately and has left no traces of its shape.

The thymaterion **81** is carefully decorated with three pairs of women. In each pair the draped women face each other, and all but one raise one hand hidden under drapery.[86] The women are all individualized by their garments of different colors and patterns, yet the woman with her hand exposed is not the most elaborately adorned. The miniature style is unlike other figural thymiateria decoration. Examples from Eleusis are more elaborately executed with recognizable myths and fewer but larger figures.[87] A parallel for the scene on **81** may be found on another, less carefully executed example from the Agora, but the subject of both remains unclear at present.[88]

---

81. Phialai occur in 11 of the 21 Persian destruction cleanup deposits: B 18:6 (1), D 15:1 (1), E 14:5 (1), F 19:5 (1), G 6:3 (7), G 11:8 (2), H 12:15 (2), H 13:5 (32), M 17:4 (10), Q 12:3 (5), Q 21:3 (1). Three of these deposits (B 18:6, H 12:15, Q 21:3) are well deposits associated with domestic architecture.

82. Wigand 1912, pp. 40–56; Kanowski 1983, pp. 144–146.

83. Shear 1993, tables 2, 3.

84. For a restored example of the shape, see Kournouniotes 1936, fig. 2.

85. This is a common place for the thymiateria to break; cf. *Agora* XII,

p. 331, nos. 1351 and 1358, pl. 44; *Agora* XXIII, p. 317, no. 1851, pl. 44.

86. The woman whose hand is exposed has a black-glazed hand with added white applied on top.

87. Kournouniotes 1936, figs. 1–4.

88. Cf. *Agora* XXIII, p. 317, no. 1851, pl. 119: on the upper zone there are four women facing right; on the lower, five women facing right. The women on this example do not appear to interact with each other, but vertical rows of dots between the figures in imitation of inscriptions may be an effort to animate the scene.

VOTIVES

Votives are gifts given to the gods as markers of ritual activity within cultic contexts. They can be monumental or ephemeral. Small token gifts were a popular category of affordable offerings that commemorated the ephemeral experience of worship.[89] In addition to the possible plate **78**, which may have been a votive offering, the house contained votive terracotta figures and miniature pottery vessels.[90] Eleven votive miniatures and five terracotta figurines meet the criteria for inclusion in the household assemblage. Three terracotta figures from Levels 1 and 2 meet the criterion for inclusion in the household assemblage owing to their large, dense fragments. These are listed with a question mark on Table 6.

One of the terracotta figures, a small herm (**202**), may provide a solution to a vexing discrepancy between the literary and archaeological evidence for Greek houses. It is assumed from the details of the affair of the Hermokopidai at the end of the 5th century that houses had herms somewhere near their entrances.[91] Herms are sometimes represented on vases as large, freestanding objects set before a house.[92] At this time, no evidence for freestanding herms has been found associated with private houses of Athens.[93] Instead, **202** may be an example of typical household herm. Fragments of several other similar small herms have been found in the excavations of the Athenian Agora.[94] They are small enough to be affixed to a door frame or to sit in a niche on the exterior wall of a house. Because **202** comes from Level 1b, it cannot be absolutely associated with this house, but nonetheless, it probably originated in a domestic setting.

Fragments of a seated slab female figure, a female protome, and two standard seated females round out the terracotta votive figures. The terracottas were probably arranged in a household shrine.[95] The hand-formed seated slab figure (**198**) was once painted: and a trace of white wash can be seen on the front and sides, and on fragment b a trace of a yellow dress with black details is preserved. The head projects forth from the slab of clay and is crowned with a radiate diadem made of diamond-shaped appliqués. Fragment (b) preserves the bottom edge where her feet project out from

89. The classic source on votive offerings is Rouse 1902, but see more recently Burkert 1985, p. 93; 1987; *ThesCRA* I, pp. 269–318, s.v. 2.d. Dedications, Greek (J. Boardman). For minor objects as votive gifts, see, e.g., Gebhard 1998; *Corinth* XVII.4, pp. 323–325. On miniature vases as votive gifts, see Shanks 1999, p. 189; Ekroth 2003, p. 36.

90. On the domestic use of terracotta figurines, see Merker 2003, p. 240; *Corinth* XVII.4, p. 322; Ammerman 1990, p. 43 and n. 69. Domestic terracottas of the Hellenistic period have received more attention than those of the Archaic and Classical periods. See also Cahill 2002a, chap. 3 ("The

Houses Described"), for the presence of terracotta figurines in houses.

91. Thuc. 6.27; 61.1.

92. E.g., a herm outside a house on a red-figured loutrophoros, Karlsruhe, Badisches Landesmuseum 69/78 (Naples Painter), Oakley and Sinos 1993, fig. 19. Scholars have used these depictions as evidence for the existence of household herms; see Rose 1957, p. 103.

93. Monumental, public dedications of herms did exist; see discussion of herms in the northwestern corner of the Classical Agora, Thompson 1976, pp. 93–94. Jameson (1990b, p. 194) suggests that household herms were made of wood, and thus do not survive,

but no bases or cuttings suitable for herms have been found outside houses.

94. See Catalogue entry for **202**.

95. Cf. House of the Tiled Prothyron at Olynthus (Cahill 2002a, p. 146), with an artifact assemblage that led the author to identify a ritual suite in the house. See *Olynthus* XIV, pp. 72–73, for the suggestion that some of the household terracottas, especially the hanging masks similar to **199**, might have had a decorative or talismanic function as opposed to a votive function. *Olynthus* XIV, pp. 64–68, notes that most houses had two to seven figurines, and links them to domestic cult.

the slab. This is a style of votive offering found on the Acropolis,[96] but no other examples are known from the Agora. Although this figure comes from Level 6, its preservation suggests that it was still in use at the time of the destruction. By contrast, **205**, also from Level 6, possibly a fragmentary crouching female, is more poorly preserved, and may be more likely to have been thrown away during the life of the well.

The second terracotta is **199**, a protome of a woman's head. The fragment preserves only the top, curved portion with a suspension hole and the beginning of the woman's coiffure. A complete example would depict the face and shoulders of a woman with a veil and *stephane* over her hair.[97] The form is frontal, with a hollow back. Terracottas of the type of **199** have vertical suspension holes that allow for the terracotta to be hung up. This type of votive, with a widespread distribution throughout the Mediterranean, originated in the mid-6th century and continued in a modified form until the 4th century;[98] however, **199** is also the only example of a protome from Persian destruction cleanup debris in the Agora area. The figure is moldmade from a non-Attic clay. The gray core may point to an East Greek origin, where the type originates.[99]

In addition, the deposit contained two moldmade seated figures, **200** and **201**.[100] Both are women seated on a high-backed chair with their hands on the their knees; neither figure's head is preserved, but the style is again Archaic. Scholars have linked the dedication of votive terracotta figurines with female worshippers.[101] They are gifts given to a range of deities,[102] but female deities of interest to the life cycles of women are the most common recipients of terracotta figurines.[103] The identity of these figures is purposely ambiguous. They may be a goddess or the dedicator herself, or simply a beautiful object suitable to be a gift to a god.[104]

Three nearly complete miniature pottery shapes and eight fragmentary ones were found in the deposit.[105] A miniature hydria (**82**), a miniature Corinthian kotyle (**83**), and a miniature "Argive" monochrome jug of uncertain production site (**171**) are the most complete and best made of the examples. Others from the deposit are generally poorly made, with poor or nonexistent glaze. Miniatures usually had votive purposes, either as grave gifts or as offerings in a sanctuary.[106] Their presence in the house

96. Brooke in Casson 1921, pp. 398–404, figs. p. 400.

97. Cf. Uhlenbrock 1988, fig. 1, for a reconstruction; for complete examples: Higgins 1967, pl. 26:b; *Olynthus* XIV, pp. 69–73, nos. 1, 2, pls. 1–3, with extensive discussion of the type and its origins; Kottaridi 2002, pp. 79–80, pl. 14:d, from sepulchral contexts. Kottaridi states an association of figurines with graves of women, girls, and children, but does not specify during which periods this association applies.

98. Higgins 1967, p. 64; Uhlenbrock 1988, p. 19.

99. Croissant 1983, p. 315. The type

is made on the mainland as well: Szabó 1994, p. 127 and fig. 148; *Olynthus* XIV, pp. 69–71.

100. Ten of the other 21 Persian destruction cleanup deposits contained seated female figures, often in multiples: D 15:1 (3), D 17:10 (1), F 19:5 (10), G 6:3 (9), G 11:3 (3), M 17:4 (2), Q 20:1 (8), Q 21:3 (1), R 12:1 (3), R 12:4 (5).

101. Ammerman 1990, p. 43.

102. Alroth 1989, pp. 106–113.

103. Ammerman 1990, p. 43.

104. See the discussion of terracotta dedications at Sicilian sanctuaries in Zuntz 1971, pp. 89–108; he

presents a variety of interpretations and problems.

105. Miniatures appear in five other Persian destruction cleanup deposits, often in multiples: D 15:1 (3), G 11: 3 (1), H 12:5 (4), M 17:4 (9), Q 12:3 (4).

106. Kourou (1988) proposes that the "Argive Monochrome" miniatures are generally associated with cults of Hera or Demeter, although the presence of the type at Isthmia (Morgan 1999, pp. 288–289), where at least Poseidon and Melikertes-Palaimon were worshipped, make the association less certain.

may mean that they had a role in the domestic cult, or perhaps they were objects on hand in the house for future dedications.[107]

The miniature **82** has the characteristics of a hydria, two horizontal handles and a vertical handle midway between, but the broad neck and large horizontal handles do not resemble the proportions of full-scale versions of the shape. The decorative scheme, too, of horizontal lines on the body and vertical lines on the shoulder does not resemble the full-scale versions. This scheme is similar to, but not identical to, a group of miniatures associated with the Swan Group and dated to the end of the 6th century to the beginning of the 5th century.[108] The decorated miniatures of the Swan Group, though, normally imitate ritual shapes such as louteria and kotha.

The two other well-preserved miniatures were both imported. There may be a connection between imported objects and dedications, in that the unusual was deemed attractive to the deity.[109] The miniature Corinthian kotyle **83** is Corinthian in fabric and decoration. Miniature Corinthian kotylai shapes were imitated by Attic potters, but decorated only in black glaze.[110] The closest parallels for **83** are not in Athens but in the Archaic Linear style of Corinth.[111] The handmade Argive monochrome[112] jug **171** may date to the 2nd or 3rd quarter of the 6th century. It probably predates the house construction and might have been brought to the house as an heirloom.

SUMMARY

Although this study focuses on the symposium, this was but one, very specialized activity in the household. In reality, the material presented in this chapter more accurately represents the daily life of the house. There are all-purpose, utilitarian forms, specialized cooking forms that represent the everyday chore of preparing meals for the *oikos,* and a variety of water jars for fetching water from the household well. Yet, this house had few specialized ceramic forms relating to dining and the consumption of food. This absence underscores the lack of emphasis placed on communal dining in Archaic Athens, but we must keep in mind that everyday food receptacles may have been made of perishable materials such as wood, basketry, or gourds. There are more ceramic forms to accommodate meal condiments, which may strengthen the connection of these shapes with the provision of sympotic snacks, not everyday meals.

While the sympotic wares provide insight into the world of men, the household objects offer glimpses of the world of women. In addition to the

107. On the relationship of their diminutive size and meaning, see Shanks 1999, p. 189; the small size is thought to assure an intimate relationship with the deity through the need for "scrutiny of inspection rather than public view." Jameson (1990b, p. 194) gives parallels from Halieis; he also proposes that the miniatures functioned in household cult. Horsnaes (2001, esp. p. 84) explores the possibility that miniatures from sites in Lucania have been used to classify sites incorrectly as sacred instead of domestic.

108. *Agora* XII, pp. 186, 334–335, nos. 1404–1416, pl. 45.

109. Shanks 1999, pp. 189, 192–193.

110. Cf. *Agora* XII, p. 333, nos. 1377, 1378, pl. 45.

111. *Corinth* XV.3, p. 310, nos. 1684–1686, pl. 67.

112. This is a conventional term, but similar vases were made in various locations; see Kourou 1987; 1988; and Dunbabin 1962, pp. 314–315.

food preparation equipment, weaving implements, personal toilet shapes, and votive offerings represent objects that women would have used on a daily basis. These objects all reflect their aspirations to be a good wife and mother, one who maintained the health and prosperity of the household, spun and wove with skill, adorned herself appropriately to bring honor to the family, and maintained the household cults.[113] Literature leaves us few instances of women's voices, and visual and literary images of women created by men bear a complex relationship to the real lives of women. By exploring the archaeology of the mundane, ordinary house, we get closer to the world of women than ever before.

113. At Olynthus, terracotta figurines were found widely distributed in the houses; there were no conventional locations for them: see Cahill 2002a, chap. 3 ("The Houses Described").

CHAPTER 7

Conclusions and Contexts

This study has placed the deposit, well J 2:4, and its contents back into a number of different contexts in order to inform many dimensions of Late Archaic culture in Athens. The advantage of contextual studies is that they recognize that artifacts and architecture are part of a matrix of culturally determined material culture. To look at one aspect of the cultural puzzle without the others may miss essential characteristics.[1] With an emphasis on "context of use," how the artifacts were used, by whom, and when, the objects are placed back into their setting and we can recognize how material culture defines and reinforces cultural activities. In the current study, the well and its house have been placed into a historical context of post–Persian destruction renovation, and the contents of the deposit have been placed into a social context of household activities (especially communal drinking). Along the way, individual objects have been placed into the context of their type's production and development. This chapter will serve to summarize major arguments and to explore further how the contexts can inform our understanding of late Archaic Athenian culture.

The value of this deposit is that it preserves for us objects a Late Archaic Athenian house might own and use. It is important to remember that only that which survives is available to the archaeologist: metal, wicker, wood, most floral remains, and other perishable materials are not preserved in the Athenian soil, and thus their important role in the material culture of the house cannot be explored. Inevitably, any archaeological analysis that wishes to move beyond description and categorization must face positivism, admit to it, and move on. We will never have a complete picture of the material culture of an ancient Greek house. To admit defeat would be ruinous to the desire to understand culture and would bring the fields of archaeology (and philology) to a halt. We need to use the information we have, but responsibly, and with the goal of using it to sketch out broad details of culture fully knowing that the fine details may never be accessible. With this defense in mind, this chapter offers some broad sketches, better colored through contextual studies.

1. See the theory of systems of cultural activity described by Rapoport 1990.

THE ARCHAEOLOGICAL CONTEXT

In Chapter 2 it was shown that well J 2:4 contains artifacts deposited during the cleanup after the Persian destruction of Athens in 479. Well J 2:4 fits the characteristics of the other 21 known Persian destruction cleanup deposits in the vicinity of the Classical Agora and reinforces the domestic origin of much of the Persian destruction material from this area. The scrappy architectural remains of the house document a private residence very close to the northwest corner of the Classical Agora. The house was constructed in the late 6th century and was renovated with a new interior plan after its partial destruction by the Persians. The cleanup mentality seen in the disposal of complete vessels from the house of well J 2:4 is documentable in other Persian destruction cleanup deposits. This behavior represents an emotional reaction to the disaster and a desire to create a clean slate for a new beginning. Fill from the upper portion of the well contained broken pottery from the house of well J 2:4 and fill brought from outside the house. Overall, the fill in the well provides confirmation that the deposition activity occurred at one time and further characterizes pottery shapes and iconography in domestic use in Athens.

The house continued in use as a domestic residence until the Hellenistic period. Its neighborhood experienced a post–Persian War 5th-century building boom with the construction of the Stoa Poikile and the Classical Commercial Building. As with other neighborhoods in this area of ancient Athens, the juxtaposition of private residences and public, sacred, and commercial enterprises presented no "zoning" problems. Only with the construction of the Early Roman podium temple did the house go out of use.

The status of the household is difficult to assess without comparative evidence. Since so few houses excavated in Athens preserve sufficient evidence to characterize their household artifact assemblage, there is no context in which to place the markers of status (or lack of status) from this house. Many of the later Classical houses near the Athenian Agora featured household-level commercial activity. These houses of marble workers and shoemakers are the houses of the middle-class citizens, or possibly even metics, foreigners living and working in Athens. The house of well J 2:4 did not preserve any identifiable evidence for household industry, but it is possible that production occurred without leaving archaeological traces. The overall size of the house cannot be known because of the destruction of its western portion by later monuments, but the modest size of the preserved rooms in both the Archaic and Classical phases of the house suggests a modest status.[2] Without an "upper-class" elite house to which to compare the evidence from the house of well J 2:4, there is no way to establish the upper limit of the homeowner's status. However, that he could afford to host symposia, and thus could afford the necessary equipment and wine, indicates that he was at least middle-class, and certainly not poor.

The Persian destruction cleanup deposits in wells cluster around the area of the Classical Agora. It seems reasonable that many of these wells were within private houses. We can imagine Late Archaic houses ringing an open central area (although excavation along the east side of this central

2. Estimating the size of an ancient "household," or even defining what is meant by a "household," is a difficult task. Gallant (1991, pp. 11–33) proposes a range of four to six people, but with the caveat that the population of the house may change over time. The occupancy of the house of well J 2:4 seems likely to be somewhere in this range.

area has not been as intensive as on the north, south, and west). When this area formally becomes the civic heart of the city remains debatable, but a public function in the Late Archaic period is implied by respect for the open central area that woud be known as the Agora in Classical and later periods.

THE HOUSEHOLD CONTEXT

Through study of the material in well J 2:4, we can better understand daily household activities. Xenophon's *Oeconomicus* is often cited in discussions of household management. As a work of literature it embodies ideals that reflect reality, but distort it as well. The nonsympotic household pottery in well J 2:4 includes shapes for cooking and a variety of multifunctional forms serving diverse household chores. Whereas the sympotic pottery is shaped and decorated for a specific function within the ritual of communal drinking, the pottery for household activities is generic and plainly decorated. In other words, the lack of formal distinction signals its minor social importance and positions the objects and the activities related to them in the background of communal drinking.

Aside from chores, the household assemblage also preserved evidence for household cult. Terracotta figurines, miniature votive pottery, and a phiale all relate to a domestic cult. The phiale may have had a role in the sympotic ritual of invoking the gods before drinking, as well. Literature provides us with glimpses of the importance of household cult, but much of the activity was ephemeral and not accessible through archaeology. On the other hand, archaeology provides evidence for the everyday cult that was so customary that it did not appear in literature.

THE SOCIAL CONTEXT

Perhaps the most obvious observation about the ceramics from well J 2:4 is that communal drinking activities were important enough to this household that the homeowner assembled an array of specialized shapes to accommodate it. The investment in specialized equipment with figured decoration, in contrast to the plain, multifunctional coarse wares, further signals the importance of this activity. The role of the symposium in Archaic and Classical Greek culture is well documented and explored in current scholarship, but well J 2:4 provides an opportunity to examine the drinking practices of an authentic Athenian house and serves as a check for our assumptions developed from literary and iconographic depictions of the symposium.

The house had not one, but several different sets of drinking cups. The quintessential form of wine cup, the kylix (Type C cup), was represented by a set of six red-figured cups complemented by up to eight plain black-glazed cups of the same form. In addition, the house had a set of two intentional red cups with red-figured tondos, a set of black-figured cup-skyphoi with hasty decoration, and possibly a set of large black-figured Heron Class skyphoi. Each set represents a different kind of communal drinking: the set of two intentional red cups for intimate meetings, the black-figured cup-skyphoi for less formal gatherings or everyday use and probably not used while reclining, and the red-figured kylikes for a typical small group symposium. The Heron Class skyphoi are challenging in that one well-preserved example with unusual iconography stands out from other fragments in the deposit with more typical decoration. These may constitute a drinking set, or they may be individual mixing bowls, since they held up to three liters of liquid. The sets of red-figured kylikes and the black-figured cup-skyphoi are both complemented by plain black-glazed versions of the same shape, some from the same potters that made their figured companions. Not only does this provide evidence for the organization of pottery workshops, but it also indicates that figured wares could be used alongside plain black-glazed versions. It seems that the shape was the most important aspect unifying the set, with decoration a close second. The conclusion is that there are a range of communal drinking activities in the house, but they are all united in their use of specialized drinking cups and the communal nature of the drinking.

On the other hand, the house did not own set-specific serving utensils. For example, the one black-figured oinochoe (5) might have served wine into cups decorated in red figure, since there is no comparable serving shape in red figure. The red-figured pelike (84) could have held wine to be drunk from the black-figured skyphoi. Alternatively, plain black-glazed or even undecorated coarse versions of these vessels may have served wine into figured cups.

The well contents did not include a krater. This is a troubling absence, and again, reckoning with positivism, we should admit that it is possible that it was disposed of elsewhere. However, it is also possible that it does not survive because it was metal and was melted down at some point or taken away as loot by the Persians. If it is permissible to imagine a metal krater in this house, then this household might have mixed ceramic and metal together. Similarly, that there are so few kyathoi—ladles—surviving from Athens means that the form existed mainly in metal and was probably used in conjunction with ceramic kraters. Why is it not possible that metal serving and ceramic drinking vessels (or vice versa) were used together as well? To push the metal krater hypothesis one step farther, I could also suggest that if a homeowner wanted to invest in one piece of metalware for his symposium set, the krater would be a good choice. It is the requisite form for communal drinking, the center of all activity, and it could be used for any of the different drinking activities in the house.

The Persian destruction cleanup deposits provide us with a snapshot of communal drinking at the end of the Archaic period. In an effort to understand how the house of well J 2:4's participation in sympotic activities related to the development of the symposium at Athens, let us compare the sympotic contents of deposits closed in the Late Archaic period to those closed earlier in the 6th century (Table 8). I have chosen to focus on the presence of kylikes, as these are a certain marker of sympotic activity. Kraters may be the more obvious choice of a marker, but since they are large and expensive, and heavy enough not to be moved around and broken very

TABLE 8. KYLIKES IN ARCHAIC DEPOSITS FROM THE ATHENIAN AGORA

Deposit Number	Number of Kylikes
DEPOSITS CLOSED BETWEEN 600 AND 525 B.C.	
U 25:2 (lower)	8
A 17:2	0
A 17:1	0
C 18:8	0
F 12:6	0
G 6:3 (lower)	8
I 16:4	4
J 18:4	10
P 8:5	0
Q 13:5	7
Q 17:8	0
Q 18:1	0
R 11:2	5
R 13:3	3
T 18:1	3
T 18:2	0
T 18:3	2
U 25:2	23
V 24:2	7
DEPOSITS CLOSED BETWEEN 525 AND 480 B.C.	
J 2:4	47 (MinNV; see Table 5)
U 25:2	9
R 12:3	13
R 21:3	18
T 24:3	35
T 24:5	8
T 25:2	8
U 23:2	7
U 24:1	12
V 23:1	8
B 18:6	10
B 19:10	25
D 15:1	4
D 17:2	15
D 17:10	31
E 14:5	9
E 15:6	12
F 19:5	2
G 3:1	32
G 6:3	58
G 11:3	3
G 11:8	11
H 12:15	17
H 13:5	86
L 5:2	7
M 17:4	101
Q 12:3	38
Q 20:1	1
Q 21:3	0
R 12:1	13
R 12:4	18

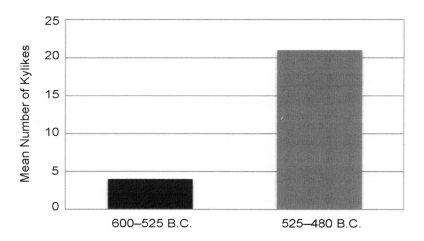

Figure 19. Mean number of kylixes
in early-6th-century and late-6th–
early-5th-century deposits from the
Agora excavations

often, they do not enter the archaeological record as readily as do the more plentiful and delicate kylikes. Furthermore, the stemmed cup is a shape specifically designed to be held while reclining in more formal drinking. In Table 8 the deposits are divided into two chronological groups: before and after 525.[3] This cutoff date is somewhat arbitrary, but it guarantees that deposits before 525 were solidly mid- to early 6th century, and deposits after were more likely to be ca. 500.

The comparison showed that there were significantly more kylikes on average in the Late Archaic deposits, which include the Persian destruction cleanup deposits (see Figure 19). The mean number of kylikes in the earlier 6th-century deposits was four, and in the Late Archaic deposits (closed 525–480) it was 21. Of course, there are many conditions that affect how accurately these numbers reflect actual practice: many deposits are garbage dumps, and not single household deposits like well J 2:4; many were excavated at a time when fragments were discarded and only well-preserved vessels kept. In most cases I restudied the context pottery, so that the numbers given in Table 8 reflect both inventoried and uninventoried objects. The statistical means are overconfidently precise but should be taken as relative numbers. Again, thinking in broad strokes, it appears that there is an increase in the use of kylikes, thus participation in the symposium, at the end of the 6th century. The magnitude of that increase is difficult to assess due to the incomplete nature of the data.

The household of well J 2:4 represents a trend of increased participation in the symposium in the Late Archaic period. The motivating force behind this change may be the new democratic system. The relationship of democratic principles and the social principles of the symposium have been noted previously.[4] The evidence presented here documents that more men were participating in formal symposia—that is, a communal drinking event using specialized equipment and following social rules—around the time that democratic reforms were taking place in the last decade of the 6th century.[5] If it is possible to connect the increase in symposium participation and the democracy, then we have a case for the democratization of the symposium. In the earlier Archaic period, the symposium is the province of the elite and is even associated with Archaic oligarchies as a means of social control

3. This data and analysis also appears in summary form in Lynch 2007 and Lynch 2001b. Quantities represent a minimum number of vessels for each deposit consisting of both inventoried and uninventoried figured and black-glazed kylikes. Fragmentary pottery may have been discarded from some deposits, so minimum counts may be too low.

4. Schmitt Pantel and Schnapp 1982, p. 72.

5. My choice of 525 for a division of the deposit categories reflects the fact that pottery chronologies are not as sensitive as historical chronologies. Some pottery can only be dated to a quarter century, as is true of many of the deposits in toto. It would be impossible to divide the deposits at 507, for example, since the pottery and deposits do not date as nicely. The date 525 was a compromise, and as a result it is possible that the increase in kylikes actually begins before the democratic reforms.

through prestige.[6] The association of the symposium with the elite does not mean that men of other classes were not drinking in groups, rather, they did, but not with the formality and the specialized equipment used by the elite.[7] The increased participation in formal symposia at the end of the 6th century, as denoted by the adoption of formal drinking equipment, then, may be an appropriation of elite social practices by the newly enfranchised. The objectives of communal drinking, including the formation of group bonds, fit the needs of the new democracy well. Men from all over Attica had to interact with each other and share decision making in a way they had not before.[8] The social experience of the symposium allowed them to become acquainted, but it also helped define cultural values that they should all embody.

THE POTTERY IN CONTEXT OF THE SYMPOSIUM

If we consider the context of use, the sympotic pottery from the house of well J 2:4 reveals how material culture can shape the participants' experiences. As noted above, nearly all the figured ware in this house was devoted to use in communal drinking activities. This formal distinction signals to the users and viewers that the objects are beyond the ordinary and underscores that this activity is separate from typical household activities.

The iconography of the figured wares from well J 2:4 permits us to consider what imagery an authentic Athenian household would have on its sympotic pottery. This is a significant question, since Attic figured pottery is typically associated with Athenian symposia without regard to the find context of the pieces. It is my argument here that the iconography of figured pottery used in Athenian homes was a subset of the range of iconographic themes in the artistic repertoire of painters in Attic pottery workshops. Assuming that most of the red-figured kylikes from Persian destruction clean-up deposits originated in the houses of Late Archaic Athens, then the iconography of these cups should provide insight on image preference. The types of images found on red-figured cups from Persian destruction deposits can be characterized as simple single- or double-figure compositions, with decoration usually limited to the tondo with the exterior often left plain.[9] Their subjects include athletes,[10] warriors,[11] satyrs,[12] hetairai,[13] symposium preparations,[14] and symposiasts.[15] The symposiasts featured are single figures in the tondo, and there are no elaborate symposium scenes depicting the entire room, as are so commonly used to illustrate scholarly

6. Schmitt Pantel and Schnapp 1982, pp. 60–61, 64; Murray 1983a, p. 263; 1983b, p. 198; Luke 1994, pp. 26–30.

7. In support of this view, see Wilkins and Hill 2006, p. 178.

8. Murray 1983a, pp. 266–267.

9. One notable exception to this observation is the Gorgos cup: *Agora* XXX, pp. 317–318, no. 1407, pls. 129, 130.

10. E.g., *Agora* XXX, p. 333, nos. 1514, 1515, pl. 143; p. 318, no. 1408, pl. 131 (with battle on exterior); p. 341, nos. 1566, 1567, pl. 148.

11. E.g., *Agora* XXX, pp. 334, 335, nos. 1516, 1517, 1519, pl. 143.

12. E.g., *Agora* XXX, pp. 333–334, nos. 1513, 1518, pl. 143; pp. 340–341, nos. 1558, 1563, 1564, pl. 147.

13. E.g., *Agora* XXX, p. 319, no. 1411, pl. 132; p. 339, no. 1554, pl. 146; p. 341, no. 1562, pl. 147.

14. E.g., *Agora* XXX, p. 340, no. 1555, pl. 146.

15. E.g., *Agora* XXX, p. 342, nos. 1572, 1573, pls. 148, 149; p. 335, no. 1520, pl. 143.

discussions of sympotic gatherings.[16] There are also few images with elaborate myths of gods or heroes. The deeds of Herakles do appear, as on the black-figured oinochoe **5** from well J 2:4, but with some notable exceptions, there are few scenes of mythological narrative in the Persian destruction cleanup deposits. The narratives that do appear relate to everyday life, and some of the compositions are moments in time demanding the viewer to provide the sequence of events before and after. For example, the running boy with two transport amphoras on P 1275, from the Rectangular Rock-Cut Shaft, is a narrative parallel for **90**, a youth running with strips of meat. Both demand that the viewer/drinker see the activity depicted as a step that facilitates his own actions at that very moment. The figured boys bring the food and the wine that the drinker consumes at that very moment. In this way the imagery is self-reflective of the sympotic activity. The narrative of events is generic, not a specific literary one, and brings the viewer/drinker into the narrative as the objective of the image's activity. Other images are more directly reflective of the cup drinker's recent actions but are still a temporal narrative. For example, the symposiast on **89**, an adult walking with a skyphos, reflects the action of either coming to the symposium or leaving the symposium and carousing in the street (the *komos*). It is unclear which is intended, but again the viewer/drinker is meant to see himself and his actions in the activity, again inserting himself into the image's meaning and seeing himself in the narrative of the evening in which he participates.

Examining the pottery from the house of well J 2:4 as a set also allows us to recognize patterns across the entire assemblage that relate to meaning for the individual who owned the house. Presumably, the homeowner is involved in the purchase of sympotic wares. The images on the red-figured cups present a reflective view of the act of drinking, sometimes in a witty way. The first-person addresses of **91** and **92** involve the viewer/drinker in the image in yet another dimension. The owl of **92**, with his comment about his potency, and the spinning wheel of **93**, which might spin ever faster as the viewer/drinker becomes more intoxicated, both focus on the more realistic and humorous side of drinking alcoholic beverages. It is precisely excessive drinking that lowers the inhibitions of the viewers/drinkers and allows them to share experiences and form bonds that would not happen on a typical, sober occasion. The red-figured pelike (**84**) echoes the jokes of the cups. It juxtaposes a man singing with a youth vomiting; the parallel projections, one pleasant, one not, were emphasized with inscriptions.

In addition to the humorous, reflective theme, there is a bovine theme running through this house's set of pottery. The phiale in Six's technique (**23**), the black-figured skyphos (**45**), the black-figured oinochoe (**5**), and the headdresses on the Heron Class skyphos (**28**) involve images of cattle and are almost unparalleled in contemporary vase painting. It appears that our homeowner was a man with a sense of humor who, for some reason, liked cattle. I speculated in Chapter 4 that the homeowner may have been involved in cattle ranching, or perhaps his participation in the association of men with horned headdresses carried over into his aesthetic choices. A fragment of a foot of a cup (**140**)—not from well J 2:4 but from the stratum of Persian destruction debris in the southern part of the house—bears a

16. E.g., the Brygos Painter's cup, London E 68, *ARV²* 371, no. 24, 1649, *CVA* London, British Museum 9 [Great Britain 17], pls. 58, 59 [834, 835].

careful inscription on the resting surface of the foot:]ΥΜΒΡΟΣΕΜΙ, "I am]umbros' [cup]." Unfortunately the beginning of the name is not preserved, and as fill, the debris strata in the house might not have originated within the house. However tempting it may be, it would be incautious to call this the house of]umbros the cattleman.

What the Late Archaic homeowners did not choose for their home sympotic sets is just as important as what they did choose. The material from the Persian destruction deposits does not include any graphic sexual images of the type in contemporary production, which are so frequently used to illustrate Athenian sexual mores. These erotic scenes, elaborate mythological scenes, and scenes of the sympotic room are, instead, made for the export market.[17]

The work of some prominent, innovative red-figure painters is absent from the pottery in the Persian destruction deposits. For example, the Brygos Painter, Makron, Douris, and the Berlin Painter[18] are only tentatively associated with fragments found in the Agora excavations, and not at all in the Persian destruction material. Instead, the painters serving the households of Athens are second-tier craftsmen, working in the wake of their more creative and technically ambitious colleagues. Examining vase painting in conjunction with find context allows this pattern to become visible and provides insight into the pottery industry at Athens. It appears that painters are choosing images based on the destination of their product and that some painters have an exclusive relationship with the export market.[19] Products of the first-tier painters are, indeed, found in Athens, but as dedications on the Acropolis. This indicates that consumers were also associating innovation and quality design with higher value and were making a distinction (possibly economic?) between what was appropriate for use in the home and what was appropriate for the gods.

In conclusion, this study has shown that pottery can be a barometer for more than just chronology. Vase painting studies have focused extensively on painters and iconography in a manner that ignores—or worse, assumes— a viewer without considering the original context of use of the vase. Unfortunately, since so many vases throughout the Mediterranean were excavated before proper archaeological documentation became customary, or were looted without regard for archaeological context, we will never have precise findspots for many of the vases in museums around the world. On the other hand, if a vase is complete, it is most likely to have come from a tomb, which is most likely to have been in Italy. Figured pottery from excavations may have the disadvantage of being highly fragmentary, but it has the advantage of an archaeological context that can inform a context of use. Through establishing a context of use, we can identify the user and the context of viewing for the vases, both of which affect interpretation of the objects' meanings. By studying vases and vase imagery in context, we are able to come closer to understanding an emic view of ancient Greek culture.

17. Some elaborate mythological scenes appear on kylikes dedicated on the Acropolis; see, e.g., the wedding of Peleus and Thetis signed by Euphronios on Acropolis 176, *ARV*[2] 17, no. 18, *Add*[2] 153, Graef and Langlotz II, pp. 13–14, pl. 8, no. 176. This indicates that the Athenians took context of intended use into consideration when choosing an object with appropriate imagery. On erotic scenes, see La Genière 2009; Lynch 2009a.

18. Some scholars attribute the Gorgos cup to the Berlin Painter; see *Agora* XXX, pp. 317–318, no. 1407, pls. 129, 130, with discussion of debate in text of entry.

19. Hannestad 1988; Reusser 2002.

Catalogue

The Catalogue is divided into the following sections: black figure, red figure, black glaze, household ware, cooking ware, lamps, terracotta figurines, weaving implements, worked bone, and miscellaneous objects. Within the pottery sections, the material is divided by shape, with closed forms followed by open forms according to the organization of *Agora* XII. Within each shape, the entries generally proceed by subshape. Objects other than pottery are arranged by type and/or chronological development.

Catalogue entries give the Catalogue number (in boldface), Agora inventory number (in parentheses), shape, and reference to illustrations on the first line, followed by the elevations within well J 2:4 at which fragments of the object were recovered. These elevations are given both in meters above sea level (abbreviated simply as "m") and in stratigraphic "Levels" as described in Table 2 and Figure 5. When multiple fragments were found in contiguous levels, the elevations are given as a continuous range. When joining fragments were found in levels at the top and at the bottom of the well, both elevations are given (e.g., +49.14–48.73 and +47.60–46.60 m).

Next, object measurements are given (in centimeters). Whenever possible, an estimated diameter is given for objects preserving a significant portion of the rim. A list of the abbreviations used appears below. Following the measurements are references to previous publication (if any).

A description follows of the object's condition, shape, decoration, and any inscriptions or graffiti. If an object exhibits the characteristics of a well-known shape, such as Type C cup, the shape is not described in full. Black-figured skyphoi are identified by the classification system devised by Ure (1927, pp. 57–73). For red figure, additional information is provided on the presence of: (1) preliminary drawings, (2) black-glazed contour lines (the 1/8" inch strip), (3) relief lines, and (4) dilute glaze. Since most red-figured vases of the time period covered by this project use contour lines, only their absence will be noted. Otherwise, if a preliminary drawing or dilute glaze are not mentioned in the entry, then they are not used on the object. In the entries for kylikes with figured tondos, an approximate orientation off-handle-axis is given for cup scenes. Fabric color decriptions are given for non-Attic objects and refer to the Munsell Soil Color Chart.

A discussion of comparanda follows, and attribution to a painter is given (where possible). The name of the scholar responsible for the attribution appears in parentheses, and any emendations to the attribution are indicated by the presence of more than one name and the date the attribution was made. If no name is given, the attribution is by the author. Finally, a date for the object is given.

All ceramic objects are Attic unless otherwise noted.

All dates are B.C. unless otherwise noted.

The following abbreviations are used:

RRCS = Rectangular Rock-Cut Shaft (deposit G 6:3)

SGW = Stoa Gutter Well (deposit Q 12:3)

Diam. = diameter (greatest)

est. = estimated

D. = depth

H. = height

L. = length

max. p. dim. = maximum preserved dimension

p. = preserved (i.e., p.H. = preserved height)

Th. = thickness (greatest)

W. = width

Wt. = weight

An asterisk (*) beside the catalogue number indicates an object is considered to be part of the house's assemblage according to the criteria described in Chapter 3. A question mark before an asterisk signals that the object is from the upper fill of the well (Levels 1 and 2) but meets the criteria for inclusion in the household assemblage because it is greater than half preserved; however, its preservation is largely due to the fact that it is a single fragment of a dense form, and thus might preserve well even though re-deposited from elsewhere. Square brackets around a catalogue number indicate single fragments from the period of use deposit (Level 6 and the lowest portion of Level 5) likely broken and discarded as trash during the time of the well's use. Square brackets *and* an asterisk denote fine-ware closed vessels from the period of use possibly used to fetch water and over half preserved.

All photographs courtesy Agora Excavations.

BLACK FIGURE

Amphora

*1   (P 33259) Amphora   Fig. 20

+50.31–49.76; +49.14–48.73; +46.00–45.90 m (Levels 1b, 2, and 5)

Max. p. dim. (a) 8.4, (b) 8.2

Two fragments of body of large amphora, each mended from two fragments (nonjoining fragment left with context pottery in Tin BZ 721). Good black glaze on (a); (b) is abraded, glaze discolored and flaking.

Preserved black-glaze bordering to right of black-figured panel on a. In panel, hoplite running left. Fragment (a) preserves hoplite's shield and back leg down to calf. Two incised compass-drawn circles for border of shield. Part of shield device, a round object, preserved. At top of fragment, half of drilled hole for ancient mend. On (b), a second shield, edge of a third, and trace of a greaved calf. Center of the second shield reserved; trace of a figure in Six's technique, buff clay, as the device,

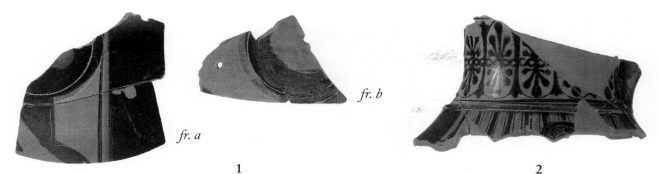

Figure 20. Amphoras 1, 2. Scale 1:2

fr. a *fr. b*

1   2

possibly a Nike. Drilled hole for ancient mend in field to left. Added red: edges of shields, shield device on (a), circle on shield on (b).

Shape is possibly a Panathenaic amphora or a Panathenaic-type amphora; if so, the scene would be the hoplitodromos. The wall is thin, continuously curving, and the scale of the figures is likely appropriate for a full-sized Panathenaic amphora. On Panathenaic amphoras, see Bentz and Eschbach 2001.

Ca. 525–500

*2   (P 33558) Amphora   Fig. 20

+49.14–48.73 and +47.60–46.60 m (Levels 2 and 4)
Max. p. dim. (a) 13.05, (b) 10.4
Two joining fragments of neck and shoulder of a neck amphora. Start of one handle. Sharp raised ridge at bottom of neck, incised line below. On neck, between handles, reflected palmette chain without incision. Alternating red and black tongues at top of shoulder. Crest of a helmet intruding into tongues preserved on a. Added red: line on crest, line on raised ridge, line below tongues. Relief line: curves framing palmettes, outlines of tongues.

Shape is probably a pseudo-Panathenaic amphora with Athena. Cf. *Agora* XXIII, p. 141, no. 319, pl. 32 (but note error there; date should be late 6th century, not late 5th).

Late 6th century

*3   (P 32416) Amphoriskos   Fig. 21

+46.00–45.90 m (Level 5)
H. 17.1; Diam. rim 8.65, body 10.0, foot 5.9
Camp 1996, p. 248, no. 26, pl. 73; Lynch 2009b, p. 75, fig. 73.
Complete except for a few body fragments; mended from several fragments. Thin wash on reserved surfaces.

Disk foot with recessed underside and nipple. Exterior face of foot convex; flat upper face slopes upward slightly. Flaring raised fillet at junction of foot and body. Ovoid body tapering sharply to foot. Slightly raised fillet at junction of body and neck, incised line below. Cylindrical neck, concave, flaring to rim. Echinus profile to exterior of rim, interior with wide concave groove, top flat. Vertical handles flattened, double-round attached from mid-neck to outer shoulder.

Below figural zone: zone of rays on lower body with dot-band between dilute lines above. Above figured zone a row of very debased tongues in black on shoulder. Side A of neck has alternating, interlaced palmettes; side B has reflected ivy-leaf pattern with three uneven horizontal lines. Side A: At left, Dionysos seated facing right on an okladias. Wears himation and holds kantharos, shown in side view, away from his body. At right, female figure seated on an okladias facing left. Wears a himation and extends one hand out, possibly holding a krotalos. Two branches

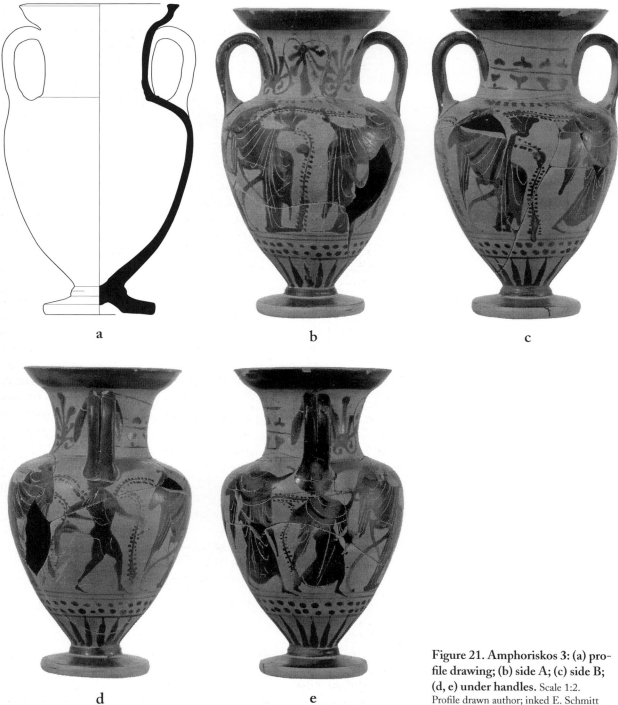

a   b   c

d   e

Figure 21. Amphoriskos 3: (a) profile drawing; (b) side A; (c) side B;
(d, e) under handles. Scale 1:2.
Profile drawn author; inked E. Schmitt

with leaves and one blob-fruit in field around them. Side B: At left, Dionysos seated
facing right on an okladias. Wears a himation and holds a kantharos, shown in
side view, away from his body. At right, draped female figure dancing with krotala
moves right and looks back left. Two branches in field around them with one
blob-fruit. Under one handle, a satyr moving right and looking back at Side A.
Under opposite handle, draped female figure in same pose as dancer on Side B.

Her head overlaps the handle. Reserved: underside and exterior face of foot, top of lip, interior of handles, and interior below neck. Added white: female flesh, part of Dionysos's wreath, neckline of Dionysos's garment, joints of okladiai, possibly hearts of palmettes. Added red: beards of Dionysos and satyr, tail of satyr, garment folds, Dionysos's wreath, satyr's fillet, fillet on females, dots on grape clusters, probably band on fillet above foot. Hasty drawing and incision.

For small-scale amphoras, see *Agora* XXIII, pp. 128–131, nos. 206–225, pls. 24–26. The combination of neck motifs is not common for the class. It is found on a slightly larger Dot-band Class amphoriskos London, BM 63, 7–28, 443, *CVA* London, British Museum 4 [Great Britain 5], pl. 70 [215]:7a, b, and on at least two amphoriskoi of Light-Make Class (*ABV*, pp. 593–600), Tarquinia RC 1629, *ABV* 598, no. 31, *CVA* Tarquinia 2 [Italy 26], pl. 35 [1184]:3, 4; and Bologna 42, *ABV* 598, no. 24, *CVA* Bologna 2 [Italy 7], pl. 22 [321]:1, 2. The style does not match any of the hands Beazley assigned as painters of the Dot-band Class. For amphoriskoi, style is closest to Munich J1218, *CVA* Munich 9 [Germany 48], pl. 35 [2332]:4, and 36 [2333]:1–3, which the author associates with the Krotala Group of painters of lekythoi, and two amphoriskoi by the Michigan Painter, Michigan 2599, *ABV* 344, no. 9, *CVA* Michigan 1 [USA 3], pl. 14 [99]:3a, b; and Copenhagen 8757, *CVA* Copenhagen, National Museum 8 [Denmark 8], pl. 316 [319]:2a, b. The style in general most closely matches that of the Kalinderu Group of lekythos painters, *ABV*, pp. 503–504, *Agora* XXIII, pp. 234–235, nos. 1075–1082, pl. 85 for examples. In particular, the folds of Dionysos's garment emanate from both the arm and the knee, and the head declines slightly. A satyr on a lekythos by the Kalinderu Group from Rhitsona (R135.75, *ABV* 504, no. 13, Ure 1927, pl. 15) matches the satyr under the handle on **3**. The Kalinderu Group is near the style of the Campana Painter of black-figured cups (*ABV*, pp. 653–654, *CVA* Louvre 10 [France 17] pls. 117 [752], 118 [753], 119 [754]:1, 2), whose Dionysoi are near replicas of Dionysos on **3** and the Kalinderu Group lekythoi. Pose, drapery, and wreath are among the consistent details. The wreath is such a typical trait that the small fragment Louvre C 10457, *ABV*, p. 654, no. 10, *CVA* Louvre 10 [France 17], pl. 118 [753]:12, can be attributed to the Campana Painter. Moore hinted at the relationship between the lekythos painters and painters of small amphoras based on the shared subsidiary patterns on both forms (*Agora* XXIII, p. 12). It is well known that better painters, such as the Edinburgh Painter and the Theseus Painter, worked on both lekythoi and small closed shapes, thus it is likely that their less skilled associates did the same.

Dot-band Group (D. von Bothmer in Camp 1996)
Kalinderu Group (Lynch 1999)
Ca. 500

Stamnos

*4 (P 32345) Stamnos   Fig. 22

+49.76–49.14 m (Level 2)
P.H. 18.0; Diam. foot 15.5

Mended from 20 fragments to make up two joining fragments, foot (b) and lower wall (b), about the bottom third of vessel. The joining fragments have not been mended because contact area is so slight. Four lead clamps represent ancient repair, holding foot to body. Peeling black glaze, mottled red in places. Attic clay with several large white inclusions.

Spreading ring foot with thick torus outer face rising on underside to rounded bottom of vessel with slight nipple at center. Flat, vertical fillet at junction of foot and wall bounded at top and bottom by an incised groove. Ovoid body. Lower third and underside of foot reserved.

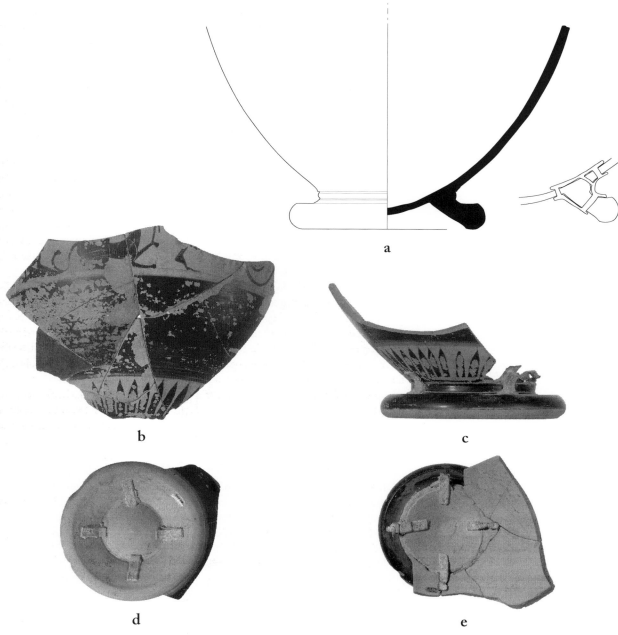

a

b

c

d

e

Band around lower body reserved and decorated with black rays 4 cm high. Above rays, thick, brown line at bottom of 8-cm-wide black band. Above band, reserved area decorated with figures (only feet preserved) walking toward right on a dilute ground line. From left: trace of figure's toes; feet of second figure standing to right, with a tail of drapery beside the back foot. Lower garment and feet of a third, female, figure standing to right. Third figure wears a straight skirt with hem decorated with C pattern between double lines. A crouching feline figure with left paw raised sits on far side of female figure, looking back and up. Feet of a fourth figure running right, front foot fugitive, tail of drapery falls behind. At far right, curving tendril. Added white: foot of female figure, dots on hem of second figure, hem of figure at right. Added red: stripe on skirt of female figure. Somewhat hasty, but detailed incision.

Figure 22. Stamnos 4: (a) profile drawing; (b) mended lower wall fragment; (c–e) mended foot fragment. Scale 1:3 (a, b, c); 1:4 (d, e). Profile drawn author; inked E. Schmitt

In addition to the profile, the decorative treatment of the fragment connects it with the conventional scheme of stamnoi. For shape and decoration, cf. Armonk, Pinney Collection, Philippaki 1967, p. 19, pl. 12:2; Naples, Santangelo 175, Philippaki 1967, p. 19, pl. 13:2; Cabinet des Médailles 251, Philippaki 1967, p. 19, pl. 14:2. For profile, cf. London B 691, Philippaki 1967, fig. 1.

The tendril at the right of the fragment indicates that the figural zone is not in a panel. Amphoras without panels usually have more complex bands below the scene, such as a band of lotus buds. The combination of rays and broad band on **4** is not usually found on amphoras without panels, except those of the Affecter Painter, which have a larger black band. The combination of rays and black band occurs more frequently on amphoriskoi, cf. Verona 18 Ce, *CVA* Verona 1 [Italy 34], pl. 1 [1516]:2a, and pl. 2 [1517]; Geneva 11586, *CVA* Geneva 2 [Switzerland 3], pl. 53 [109]:1, 3; and on conventionally sized neck amphoras, cf. Oxford 1965.125, *CVA* Oxford 3 [Great Britain 14], pl. 16 [631]:3 (profile at back of text volume); Munich NI 9001, *CVA* Munich 9 [Germany 48], pl. 59 [2356] (profile: fig. J), in the text of the entry the scheme of black-glazed body and frieze is called "unusual"; London B 235, *CVA* London 4 [Great Britain 5], pl. 54 [199]:4a, b; Rhodes 11931, *CVA* Rhodes 2 [Italy 10], pl. 21 [497]:3, 4.

This could also be a hydria, but the combination of band and rays is usually accompanied by an exergue panel below the main scene. The only shape that does have the characteristics of a band, an unbounded scene, and torus foot is the stamnos.

The woman may be Athena, who is shown with a feline on a black-figured neck amphora, Oslo, Museum of Applied Art 8673, *CVA* Oslo 1 [Norway 1], pl. 6 [6]; and a black-figured lekythos, Agrigento C846, *ABL* 226, no. 26 [Sappho Painter], *CVA* Agrigento 1 [Italy 61], pl. 71 [2755].

For the ancient repair, cf. the krater, Caltanisssetta, Museo Archeologico, inv. no. 102, from Sabucina, tomb 25, Nadalini 2003, p. 203, figs. 18, 19. For the clamps to have been installed, either the vessel must have been very wide mouthed or the neck was also broken from the body.

Ca. 525–500

Oinochoe

*5 (P 32415) Trefoil oinochoe   Fig. 23

+46.00–45.90 m (Level 5)

H. with handle 25.5; Diam. 14.5

Camp 1996, p. 246, no. 21, pl. 72; Lynch 2009b, p. 75, fig. 73.

Mended from many fragments; complete except for small fragments from body. Good black glaze, lower band worn on one side; smudge of black glaze above Athena's head.

Shape 1 oinochoe with disk foot, concave and recessed on underside, offset neck and trefoil mouth, high-swung strap handle, oval in section, attached from rim to shoulder.

Lowest part of body and top two-thirds of foot black-glazed; neck, rim, handle, and interior of neck black-glazed. Shoulder decorated with debased tongues set off from decorated zone by a line of dilute glaze. At left, draped Hermes seated on a block stool facing right, wearing petasos and winged boots, holds kerykeion in right hand. Figural scene on front of vessel: Herakles and the Cretan bull. Herakles, nude, moves right, escorting the Cretan bull; his left hand grasps one horn, with right hand on the animal's chest. His club leans against Athena's shield. At right, Athena seated facing left on block stool wears aegis, holds her spear horizontally with left hand and holds helmet in extended right hand. Her shield in three-quarter view leans against her knee. Branches with leaves in field around figures, continuing around the back of the vase. Added white: Athena's flesh, Herakles's

Figure 23. Trefoil oinochoe 5:
(a) profile and overhead drawing;
(b) left side, seated Hermes; (c) front,
Herakles and Cretan bull; (d) right
side, seated Athena. Scale 1:3. Profile
drawn A. Hooton; inked E. Schmitt

a

b

c

d

scabbard and sword hilt, triple dots on Hermes's himation, two large white dots on shield. Added red: fillets on Athena and Herakles and on Hermes's hat, dots and stripes on Athena's garment, dots on crest of helmet, muscles of bull on neck and body, dots on Hermes's garment and at neckline, horizontal lines on stools. Fine incision for details of males (hair, eyes, muscles) and bull.

For shape, see *Agora* XII, p. 243, no. 100, pl. 5.

Attribution: Although the style shares similarities with the work of the Athena Painter (see, e.g., Athens, National Archaeological Museum 1138, *ABL* 257, no. 73, pl. 47, 2; Athens, National Archaeological Museum 1132, *ABL* 256, no. 50, pl. 47:3a, b), the Athena Painter's male anatomy is different from that on **5**. The Athena Painter draws male legs with a single long line from thigh to ankle, which ends in a hook; a second line runs down the front of the thigh (*ABL*, pp. 148–149). Herakles on **5** does not have the long line running down the entire leg, but he does have a ∪-shaped calf muscle, which is never seen in the work of the Athena Painter. The Athena Painter's males' beards are much longer and are formed by a single line running from forehead down to lips. He sometimes indicates the cheekbone and the faces become "over-refined," according to Haspels (*ABL*, p. 148).

The details of the painting match the Acheloos Painter's male anatomy, which Moignard summarizes, down to the "pothook shape" of the calf muscles, described here as "∪-shaped" (Moignard 1982, p. 203; cf. Herakles on Toledo 1958, 69A, Moignard 1982, pl. 8:a, b). The heads on **5** also illustrate the typical forms described by Moignard (1982, pp. 203–205; cf. NY Met 26.60.29, *ABV* 384, no. 17, *Paralipomena* 168, Beazley [1951] 1986, pl. 88:5). The nose has a distinct flaring nostril and is long and pointy at its end. The lips are outlined, making them look fleshy. The eye is formed by two concentric circles flanked by two incised triangles. The ear has two concentric circles and a dangling ∪-shaped lobe (cf. *Agora* XXIII, p. 184, no. 640, pl. 61 for the ear and eye. This ear is also seen on figures of the Rycroft Painter, cf. Boston, MFA 03.880, *CVA* Boston 2 [USA 19], pl. 83 [917]:1, 2, but the Rycroft Painter is an earlier and better painter).

A Type B amphora with Herakles wrestling Acheloos attributed to the Leagros Group (Louvre F 211, *ABV* 368, no. 104, *CVA* Louvre 3 [France 4], pl. 25 [160]:3) provides confirmation that **5** belongs closer to the Acheloos Painter than to the Leagros Group in general. There Athena sits on a block stool but is entirely in profile, as is preferred by the Leagros Group as a whole (cf. Louvre F 249, *ABV* 372, no. 166, *CVA* Louvre 4 [France 5], pl. 50 [216]:3–5). Other similarities, however, including the pose of Herakles and the balance of forces, and the three-quarter view of Athena's shield with two added white dots, indicate that the painter of **5** is coming from the same workshop tradition.

The best comparison for style and composition is the name vase of the Acheloos Painter (Berlin 1851, *ABV* 383, no. 3, Beazley [1951] 1986, pl. 88:1), a neck amphora with Herakles and the Erymanthian boar (Rome, Guglielmi Collection, Beazley [1951] 1986, pl. 88:2), and another version of Herakles and the Cretan bull with a clothed Herakles and Iris instead of Hermes (a lekythos, Palermo GE 1896.2, *ABV* 385, no. 50, *ABL*, pl. 15:4a–c). The composition on the Palermo lekythos is similar to **5**, including Athena's aegis and shield and her spear tip hitting the bull in the chest. Differences include that Herakles is fully dressed and positioned on the far side of the bull, and Iris, not Hermes, appears to the left.

The workshop of the Acheloos Painter can be hard to distinguish from the master himself (Moignard 1982, pp. 206–211; Holmberg 1990, pp. 85–103), and Beazley declared that it is "hard to say whether a vase is by the Acheloos Painter himself or only in his manner" (*ABV*, p. 385).

Athena Painter (D. von Bothmer in Camp 1996)

Acheloos Painter or Manner of (Lynch 1999)

Ca. 525–500

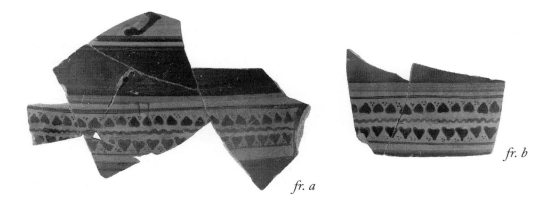

fr. a

fr. b

Figure 24. Kalpis 6. Scale 1:2

KALPIS

*6　(P 33261) Kalpis　　　　　　　　　　　　　　Fig. 24

　　+49.76–48.73 and +46.00–45.90 m (Levels 2 and 5)
　　Max. p. dim. (a) 16.0, (b) 8.6
　　Fragment of shoulder (a), mended from seven joining fragments. Start of horizontal handle at right. Smaller fragment of shoulder (b) mended from two joining fragments. Sloping shoulder curving into rounded belly. Pinkish clay, matt black glaze.
　　Fragment (a) preserves small section of shoulder panel with rear leg of a feline and a hoofed leg of quadruped facing left. Below, reserved line, broad black-glazed band. In handle zone, elaborate horizontal ivy band with squiggly line between reflected heart-shaped leaves. Between each leaf, three or four dots. Black glaze below. Fragment (b) has more of ivy band. Added red: line at top of black-glazed band below shoulder panel; line at top of black-glazed zone on body. Added white (fugitive): leg of quadruped directly on reserved surface.
　　Ca. 500

Figure 24. Kalpis 6. Scale 1:2

LEKYTHOS

[7]　(P 33234) Lekythos　　　　　　　　　　　　Fig. 25

　　+45.45–45.20 m (Level 6)
　　Max. p. dim. 4.42
　　Fragment of wall, broken all around. Large burnt-out inclusion on surface.
　　Convex wall. Preserves upper part of hoplite with shield and draped male, both facing left. Added red: edge of shield, fold of drapery. Added white: tripod shield device, dots on garment.
　　For the shape and scene, cf. *Agora* XXIII, p. 208, no. 831, pl. 77 (Phanyllis Group E, the Group of the Hoplite-leaving-home). For the Phanyllis Group in general, see Giudice 1983; *ABL,* pp. 63–68, 199–205; *ABV,* pp. 463–466. For the Group of the Hoplite-leaving-home, see Giudice 1983, pp. 88–118, nos. 187–263; *ABV,* pp. 464–466, and *ABL,* pp. 66–67, 205.
　　Phanyllis Group E, the Group of the Hoplite-leaving-home
　　Ca. 510–500

Figure 25. Lekythos 7. Scale 1:1

[8]　(P 33237) Lekythos　　　　　　　　　　　　Fig. 26

　　+45.90–45.60 m (Level 6)
　　P.H. 7.31; Diam. mouth 7.0
　　Fragment of mouth and neck. Glaze flaking on handle side, but good elsewhere.

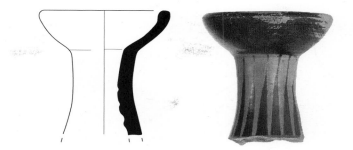

Figure 26. Lekythos 8. Scale 1:2. Profile drawn author; inked E. Schmitt

Wide, flaring mouth with rounded lip. Tall, cylindrical neck flares toward shoulder. Mouth glazed on exterior and interior to top of neck. Vertical rays on neck (dog's teeth). Added red line at bottom of neck.

For a complete example, see Giudice 1983, no. 54, pl. 15:1, among others. See 7, above, for the Phanyllis Group. The painters of both Group A (the Phanyllis Painter) and Group B (Group of the Warrior Arming) decorate large lekythoi with the dog's tooth ray pattern on the neck and occasionally an added red line at the junction of neck and shoulder.

Phanyllis Group
Ca. 500

9   (P 33236) Lekythos   Fig. 27

+49.76–49.14 m (Level 2)
P.H. 5.7
Fragment of wall. Thin black glaze. Powdery Attic clay.

Tall, straight body. Departure of a warrior. Hoplite with shield and two spears at center facing left, draped male with staff at right facing left. Trace of a figure at left with staff facing right. Figures stand on thicker black-glazed ground line. Hasty incision. Added red: dots on edge of shield, crest of helmet, folds of drapery. Added white: snake shield device, dots on garment, lower panel of garment. Compass point at center of shield.

For scene and style, cf. *Agora* XXIII, p. 209, no. 841 et alia, pl. 78 (the Cock Group). For the Cock Group, *ABV*, pp. 466–472, and *ABL*, pp. 67–68.

Cock Group
Late 6th century

Figure 27. Lekythos 9. Scale 1:1

*10   (P 33109) Lekythos (smaller)   Fig. 28

+49.76–49.14 m (Level 2)
P.H. 7.1; Diam. 4.51
Single fragment preserves body intact. Missing neck, mouth, handle, and foot. Glaze mottled red in places.

Tapering cylindrical body. Shoulder slopes away from narrow neck. On shoulder, tongues and rays identify it as a Class of Athens 581, ii lekythos, see *Agora* XXIII, pp. 46–47. Uneven double line at top of front two-thirds of body. At bottom of wall, broad black-glazed band, narrower band above. On body, figure mounting chariot. Apollo facing right with lyre. Hermes in front facing right, looking back left. Hermes carries two spears and wears a petasos and winged boots. No incision.

The figure mounting may be Athena. The flat part on the top of her head may be a helmet. There may have been added color, including a meander at top of wall.

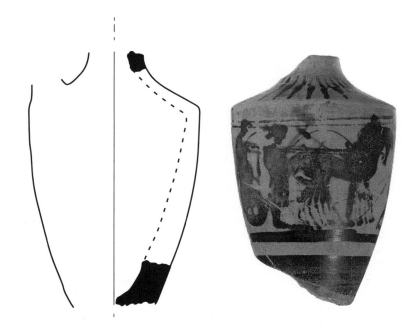

Figure 28. Lekythos 10. Scale 1:1.
Profile drawn author; inked E. Schmitt

Cf. a lekythos by the Diosphos Painter with a much neater version in which the figure is clearly Athena: Athens, National Archaeological Museum 463, *ABL* 233, no. 34, pl. 38:2a, b. There are more careful lekythoi with the subject of a goddess mounting a chariot by the Haimon Painter and in the Manner of the Haimon Painter. There can be a whole range of characters acting in the same scene; see *ABL,* p. 132 for a discussion and for examples, *Agora* XXIII, p. 246, nos. 1186–1188, 1190, pl. 87.

    Class of Athens 581, ii.

    Early 5th century

*11   (P 32426) Lekythos (smaller)   Fig. 29

    +46.00–45.90 m (Level 5)

    P.H. 8.55; Diam. 4.5

    Intact, but missing foot, handle, and mouth. Surface worn in places. Black glaze fired red and flaking on lower black-glazed band.

    Maenad between two satyrs. She moves right, looking back over her shoulder at satyr moving right, grasping her arm. Second satyr approaches from right. Branch with leaves in background. On shoulder, tongues and rays as **10**. Added white for female skin (fugitive). Added red dots on dress.

    For subject, cf. *Agora* XXIII, p. 233, no. 1069 (not figured; Class of Athens 581, ii), of which **11** is possibly a replica.

    Class of Athens 581, ii.

    Early 5th century

12   (P 33230) Lekythos (smaller)   Fig. 30

    +49.76–49.14 m (Level 2)

    P.H. 6.7; Diam. body 4.1

    Two joining fragments of wall. Tall, straight cylinder tapering to foot. Dull, streaky black glaze.

    Lower wall black-glazed with broad and thin black-glazed lines above. Double line above the scene and trace of band at top of wall. Figural scene on front two-thirds of lekythos. Preserves four females moving right. Lower bodies only of three, but central complete. Central female is attacked by a male who grabs her at the waist. Branches with small leaves in field between figures. Hasty incision. Added

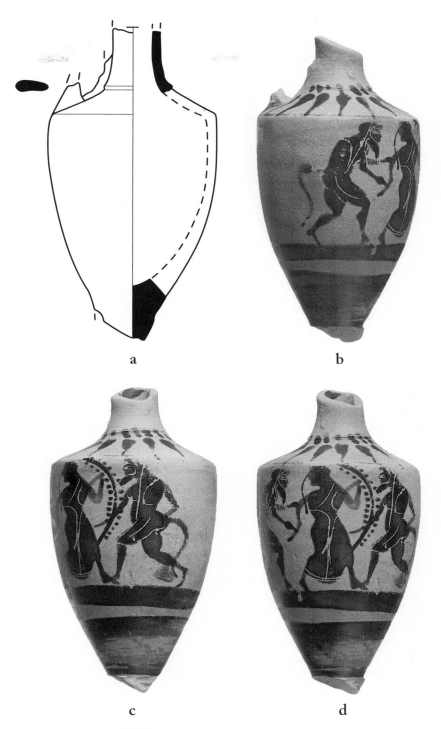

a   b

c   d

Figure 29. Lekythos 11: (a) profile drawing; (b, c) satyrs; (d) maenad.
Scale 1:1. Profile drawn A. Hooton; inked E. Schmitt

white (fugitive): for flesh (limbs directly on reserved ground), dress folds. Added red (fugitive): fillet on man and woman, dots and stripes on garments.

For the scene on contemporary lekythoi, see *Kerameikos* IX, p. 105, no. 68, 7, pl. 38:3, 4; p. 100, no. 45, 2, pl. 48:4; and Vanderpool 1946, p. 304, no. 152, pl. 55. For the scene on a slightly later lekythos, see *Kerameikos* IX, p. 113, no. 98, 2, pl. 28:3 and p. 119, no. 122, 1, pl. 32:7. Probably Peleus and Thetis or satyr and maenad; the above parallels are generally taken to be Peleus and Thetis.

Class of Athens 581, ii

Early 5th century

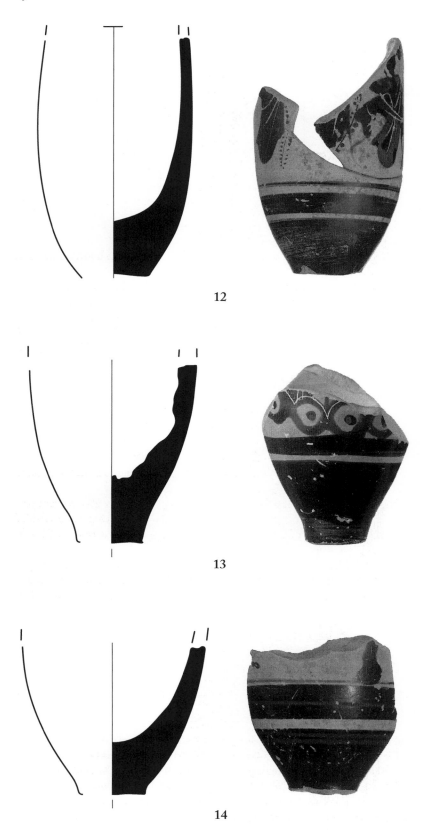

12

13

14

Figure 30. Lekythoi 12–14. Scale 1:1.
Profiles drawn A. Hooton; inked E. Schmitt

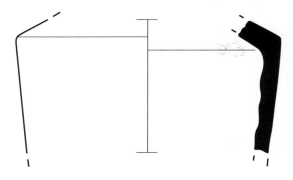

Figure 31. Lekythos 15. Scale 1:1.
Profile drawn A. Hooton; inked E. Schmitt

13 (P 33228) Lekythos (smaller)   Fig. 30

+50.31–49.76 m (Level 1b)

P.H. 5.2; est. Diam. body 4.5

Two joining fragments of straight wall and tapering lower body. Shiny black glaze. Dilute wash uneven on reserved surfaces.

Lower body black-glazed, uneven broad black-glazed band above. Row of uneven, interlaced, upright palmettes on body. Added white: dots in center of circular tendrils, dots in an arc around heart, line arcing around palmette.

Other lekythoi probably from the same workshop: Vanderpool 1946, p. 308, no. 182, pl. 53; and *Kerameikos* IX, p. 103, no. 57, 6, pl. 25:1; p. 106, no. 69, 2–7, pl. 39:1; p. 105, no. 68, 5, pl. 38:3; et alia.

Class of Athens 581, ii (most likely)

Ca. 490–480

14 (P 33231) Lekythos (smaller)   Fig. 30

+46.60–46.30 m (Level 5)

P.H. 4.3; est. Diam. body 4.5

Fragment of lower body with tall, straight wall tapering to base. Good black glaze. Wash on reserved surfaces.

Lower wall black-glazed. Broad band and dilute ground line above. Scene preserves a blob at right (possibly the stem of a vine) and the tip of a foot at left. Added red: double line at top of black-glazed zone and single line at center of black-glazed band.

Added red lines on black-glazed bands below scene are used by the Sappho and Diosphos Painters and also by the Haimon Painter, who is stylistically related to both. All are possible workshops for this lekythos. See *ABL*, pp. 94, 131, and 134.

500–480

15 (P 33229) Lekythos (larger)   Fig. 31

+50.31–49.14 m (Levels 1b and 2)

P.H. 3.5; est. Diam. shoulder 7.25

Four joining fragments of shoulder and upper wall. Sloping shoulder. Tall, straight wall meets shoulder at a sharp angle.

Rays on shoulder. Dot band at top of wall between two horizontal lines. On body, Dionysos sits facing left. Holds a rhyton in his outstretched right hand. Branches in background sprout behind his body. Hands of a maenad with krotala at left. Minimal incision. Added white: stripe on torso of Dionysos, flesh of female; dots on horizontal lines framing black-glazed dots at top of wall.

The scene is probably the same as one on a smaller-scale lekythos from Gela, Museo Archeologico, no inv. no., Panvini and Giudice 2003, p. 449, no. pF31

(Little Lion Class). For style and white over dots at top of wall, see *Kerameikos* IX, no. 21 (SW 67), pl. 23:4, 5, and Vanderpool 1946, p. 305, no. 158, pl. 55. Style resembles the Manner of the Haimon Painter

    Ca. 490

16   (P 33227) Lekythos (larger)   Fig. 32

    +50.31–49.14 m (Levels 1b and 2)

    P.H. 4.0; est. Diam. shoulder 7.5

    Two joining fragments of wall and start of shoulder. Wall tall and cylindrical. Rays on shoulder. Neat dot band at top of wall. On body, Herakles and the Nemean lion. Quiver hangs in field above. Lion's haunches preserved below. Branches at right and left. Hasty incision. Added white: baldric of quiver, lion's underbelly.

    The scene is very common on lekythoi, but there is no precise parallel for the style and details of this particular composition. See Vanderpool 1946, p. 303, no. 147, pl. 55 for an example. Style resembles the Haimon Group.

    500–480

Figure 32. Lekythos 16.
Scale 1:1

17   (P 33226) Lekythos (larger)   Fig. 33

    +49.76–49.14 m (Level 2)

    P.H. 4.75; est. Diam. shoulder 7.25

    Four joining fragments of shoulder and upper wall. Surface chipped at central figure. Sloping shoulder. Straight, tall, and cylindrical wall.

    On shoulder, black-glazed rays with tongues above as on **10**. At top of wall, dot band. Dots stop at edge of scene, but horizontal framing lines continue. Warrior facing left with one arm raised, spear in hand. At right, large eye with thin eyebrow. Incision for helmet and eye. Added white: outline of eye, iris of eye. Added red: warrior's eye, patch on his leg.

    For scene, cf. *ABV*, p. 502, no. 114–118, except for those of the Kalinderu Group; the eyes of the Kalinderu Group are not as tall as on **17**.

    Class of Athens 581, ii.

    500–480

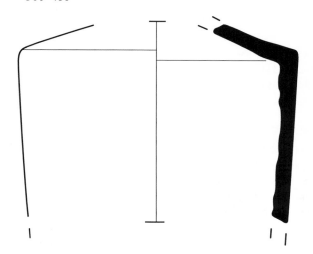

Figure 33. Lekythos 17. Scale 1:1.
Profile drawn A. Hooton; inked E. Schmitt

18   (P 33235) Lekythos (larger)   Fig. 34

    +49.76–49.14 m (Level 2)

    Max. p. dim. 5.0; est. Diam. body 7.0

    Fragment of wall, broken all around. Wall tall and very slightly convex. Dilute wash on reserved surface.

Figure 34. Lekythos 18. Scale 1:1

Preserves draped female figure from neck down. Below, black-glazed band, reserved line, black-glazed zone at bottom of body. Hasty incision. Added white: flesh (directly on reserved surface), drapery folds.

Shape is probably like *Kerameikos* IX, no. 21 (SW 67), pl. 23:4, 5.

500–480

19 (P 33464) Lekythos (larger)   Fig. 35

+49.76–49.14 m (Level 2)

P.H. 7.9; Diam. body 7.4

Five joining fragments of lower wall. Wall convex and tapering to foot. Streaky black glaze.

Bottom of scene preserves trace of figure to right on an uneven ground line. Two broad black-glazed bands below, and black-glazed zone at bottom of wall onto foot.

For shape and subsidiary pattern, see *Kerameikos* IX, no. 20 (HW 198), 1, pl. 19:2.

Ca. 490

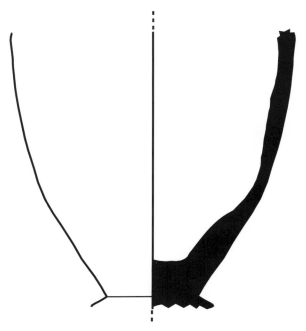

Figure 35. Lekythos 19. Scale 1:1.
Profile drawn author; inked E. Schmitt

20 (P 33233) Lekythos (larger)   Fig. 36

+49.76–49.14 m (Level 2)

Max. p. dim. 6.81; Diam. shoulder ca. 7.5

Fragment of shoulder and start of wall. (Two nonjoining fragments of body left in Tin BZ 684.) Good black glaze.

Slight offset at junction of neck and shoulder. Sharp angle at junction of shoulder and wall. On shoulder, row of tongues and hanging lotus buds. Tendrils connecting buds skip two in between. Black-glazed body. Added red: lines in between the buds, double line at top of wall.

The pattern of lotus buds follows that of the Class of Athens 581, i (*Agora* XXIII, p. 46) but is unconventional in that tendrils only connect the lotus buds on the upper side, i.e., they are pendant. Normal shoulder decorations of linked lotus buds have the tendrils connecting the buds from upper and lower points. The stems skip two buds, a scheme favored by the Sappho Painter (Kurtz 1975, pp. 8, 120, n. 6). The

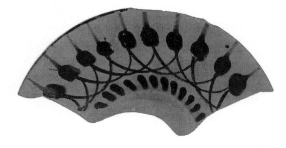

Figure 36. Lekythos 20. Scale 1:1

addition of a white line between buds, but without connecting tendrils, is seen on the Little Lion Class (a product of the Diosphos and Sappho Painters' workshop, *ABL,* p. 98) of small black-bodied lekythoi, but **20** is definitely larger than this class. Kurtz (1975, p. 120) describes the addition of the added white line as a petal between the buds and points out that it appears also on the shoulder of lekythoi by the Dolphin Group.

    Class of Athens 581, i
    Ca. 500–480

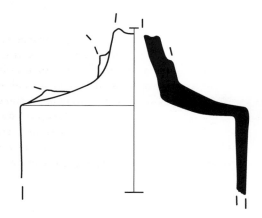

Figure 37. Lekythos 21. Scale 1:1.
Profile drawn A. Hooton; inked E. Schmitt

21   (P 33232) Lekythos (larger)   Fig. 37
    +49.76–49.14 and +48.88–48.70 m (Level 2)
    P.H. 4.3; Diam. shoulder 6.05
    Three joining fragments of neck, shoulder, and top of wall. White-ground worn off at edge of shoulder. Narrow neck with narrow opening. Light offset at junction with shoulder. Sloping shoulder meets wall at sharp angle. Wall and handle black-glazed. White-ground neck and shoulder. Rays and tongues on shoulder as **10**. Added red: narrow, close-set double line at top of wall.

    At the handle break, the white-ground continues under the handle attachment, indicating that this surface was put on before the handle was applied.

    The Diosphos Painter's workshop utilized the combination of white-ground shoulder with rays and tongues but on a more cylindrical body than that of the Class of Athens 581, ii; cf. Kurtz 1975, p. 120. Without the profile, it is difficult to assign the piece to a more specific hand within the Class.

    Class of Athens 581, ii
    Ca. 500–480

Figure 38. Closed vessel 22. Scale 1:3

CLOSED: SHAPE UNCERTAIN

22 (P 33238) Closed vessel   Fig. 38

+50.88–50.31 m (Level 1b)

Max. p. dim. 5.3

Convex wall fragment, broken all around.

Large but indistinguishable animal figure. Locks of hair indicated with incision and added red.

For style and date, cf. *Agora* XXIII, p. 102, no. 14, pl. 3 (early 6th century). The scale of the figure suggests an amphora. The figure is likely to be a feline or horse head.

Early 6th century

PHIALE

*23 (P 32414) Omphalos phiale, Six's technique   Color Ill. 14; Fig. 39

+46.00–45.90 m (Level 5)

H. 5.4–5.9; Diam. 18.8

Camp 1996, pp. 250–251, no. 34, fig. 9, pl. 75; Neer 2002, p. 202, n. 77.

Mended, about two-thirds complete. Four small fragments of rim not mended. Glaze flaking on the exterior rim, staining on exterior. Added clay of Six's technique largely missing everywhere except bodies of cattle.

Low shallow bowl, raised omphalos within with corresponding depression on the underside. Rim concave and slightly offset. Exterior reserved with buff slip except for black-glazed rim. Interior black-glazed. Raised omphalos decorated with five concentric circles in white, now fugitive. Zone around the omphalos and the lip decorated with thick white radiating lines. Thin added red lines at bottom of rim rays and at outside of omphalos rays, fugitive. On bowl six spotted cattle walk to right, parts of five preserved. Cattle alternate white body with red spots, and red body with white spots. Added clays fairly well preserved on bodies, fainter at legs and tails. Inscriptions in added red in field around cattle, largely fugitive: *kalos*

Figure 39. Omphalos phiale 23: (a) profile drawing; (b) interior; (c) transcription of inscription.
Scale 1:3. Profile drawn A. Hooton; inked author; transcription drawn and inked author

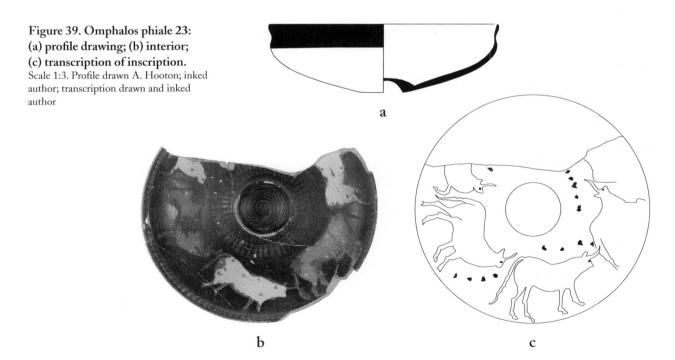

a

b   c

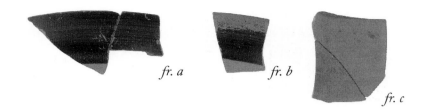

fr. a   *fr. b*

fr. c

**Figure 40. Phiale 24: fragments of
rim (a, b) and bowl (c).** Scale 1:2

near each figure although two inscriptions missing a single letter; the fourth with
only one letter preserved.

For shape and technique, see *Agora* XXIII, pp. 273–274, nos. 1430–1439,
pl. 98 (late 6th to early 5th centuries). The red cattle may be bulls as they have
somewhat triangular protuberances under their bellies that may be penises. The light
cattle do not have this feature, but nor do they have udders.

See *Agora* XXIII, p. 244, no. 1175, and p. 56, n. 1, for bibliography on Six's
technique.

Ca. 500

24   (P 33243) Phiale, Six's technique   Fig. 40

+50.31–49.76 m (Level 1b)
Est. Diam. 21.0; max. p. dim. (a) 4.84, (b) 3.1, (c) 5.93
Fragments of rim (a, b) and bowl (c).

Continuous curve from rim into bowl. Exterior reserved with broad black-
glazed band at rim. Interior (not shown) black-glazed with decoration in Six's technique (fugitive). Added white: on rim (a, b) row of dots below diagonal lines. On
bowl (c): two rows of dots. Added red: on rim (a, b) right-slanting diagonal lines
with horizontal line below. On bowl (c): smaller, right-slanting diagonal lines around
center.

For shape and technique, cf. *Agora* XXIII, p. 273, no. 1433, pl. 98; also **23**.

Ca. 500

STAND

25   (P 33239) Stand   Fig. 41

+50.88–50.31 m (Level 1b)
Th. wall 1.1; max. p. dim. 9.9
Fragment of thick wall, broken all around. Worn. Buff clay with occasional
medium to small white inclusions and some mica. Edge of drill hole from ancient
mend at lower break.

Preserves portions of two registers divided by a dilute line. Above: body and
two feet of quadruped, probably a deer, facing right. Two rosettes each with carefully
incised petals and two concentric circles within. Below, body of a bull moving to
right. In field above and to left, rosettes, one without incision. Added red: details
of bull's musculature, details of quadruped, interior of rosettes, some petals.

For shape, style, and date, cf. *Agora* XXIII, p. 171, no. 550, pl. 52 (first quarter
of the 6th century).

Early 6th century

Figure 41. Stand 25. Scale 1:2

OPEN: SHAPE UNCERTAIN

26   (P 33220) Dinos or louterion(?)   Fig. 42

+49.76–49.14 m (Level 2)
Est. Diam. 32.5; max. p. dim. 9.8
Fragment of thick rim. Good black glaze.

Figure 42. Dinos or louterion(?) 26.
Scale 3:4. Profile and drawing author; inked
E. Schmitt

Figure 43. Open shape 27. Scale 1:1

Rectangular rim with slightly inward sloping exterior face. Wall of vessel springs outward nearly horizontally from bottom of rim. At right break, traces of an attachment on upper surface and exterior surface. On upper surface, bull facing left. Added red (fugitive): neck and patch on body of bull.

For similar rim profile, cf. Copenhagen 4219, *CVA* Copenhagen 3 [Denmark 3], pl. 124 [126]:3 (photo, no drawing). The attachment on **26** may be an upright horizontal handle or the start of a spout.

525?

27   (P 32799) Open shape   Fig. 43

+50.31–49.14 m (Levels 1b and 2)
Max. p. dim. 3.4

Three joining fragments of wall. Good black glaze on exterior. Streaky, mottled black glaze on interior. Dilute wash on reserved surface. Tall, straight wall. Preserves arm and torso of figure, probably on horseback. Careful incision.

For the pose, cf. *Agora* XXIII, p. 165, no. 500, pl. 47; p. 295, nos. 1630, 1631, pl. 107. The fragment is thick, and the scale of the figure large; therefore, it is unlikely to have come from a drinking vessel. It is more likely from a krater.

Context: 525–480

Skyphos

*28   (P 32413) Skyphos, Heron Class; Ure's Class C1   Color Ill. 8; Fig. 44

+46.00–45.90 m (Level 5)
H. 16.2–16.9; Diam. 22.35; W. with handles 29.9

Camp 1996, p. 246, no. 22, fig. 7, pl. 72; Fisher 2000, p. 381, n. 29, fig. 9; Scheibler 2000, p. 24; Lynch 2009b, p. 75, fig. 73.

Nearly complete. Missing fragments of rim and body. Mended from 32 fragments. Surface abraded on side B. Fragments tinged gray at breaks.

Ring foot with torus outer face; underside rises to convex bottom of vessel. Fillet at junction of foot and body. Deep body. Concave rim, slightly outturned at lip. Canted horseshoe handles attached to wall. Reserved: line on interior rim; center of interior floor with a circle at center; underside with broad circle, second thinner inner circle and dot at center; resting surface; interior of handles; fillet, with miltos.

Figure 44. Skyphos 28, Heron Class:
(a) profile drawing; (b) side A;
(c) side B; (d, e) handle zones;
(f) detail, side A; (g) detail, side B.
Scale 1:4 (a–e); not to scale (f, g).
Profile drawn A. Hooton; inked author

Lower body reserved and decorated with row of debased tongues in alternating purple and black. Below tongues, two thin lines of dilute slip. Above tongues, three dilute lines. Wide black-glazed band at bottom of wall. Above the band, two thin dilute lines, one thicker black-glazed line, two dilute lines, the topmost of which serves as the ground line for the figural frieze. Upper half of body filled with black-figured frieze. Thin dilute line at top of frieze. Thick line above. Reflected, debased ivy leaves with dilute line between on rim.

Side A: two bearded drinkers with a flute player between them recline on a single large mattress with pillows, framed by groups of birds. Left drinker turns to right. He wears a draped himation covering all but neck and extended right arm. Holds a long-stemmed kylix by the stem in right hand. Wears a turban, fillet, and headdress with three curving projections (horns?) at front. At center, female double flute player sits up, facing left. Wears a sakkos and a draped garment. Right drinker looks to right. Wears a draped himation covering all but his raised right arm. Holds a stemmed kylix by base. Wears a fillet and headdress with two curving horns and two lobed projections between. To the left of the group, two plump, short-necked birds look right. Near bird perches on a knobby stump. To right of figural group, two similar birds: one perched on knobby stump looks right, one on ground looks left.

Side B: similar scene. Two bearded drinkers with a lyre player between them recline on a large mattress with pillows, framed by groups of birds. Left drinker looks right. Wears a himation and a poorly preserved headdress with at least one projecting, curving horn. At center, female lyre player sits up, facing left. Wears sakkos and himation. Right drinker holds a drinking horn in raised hand (unclear which hand). Wears a himation and fillet, but no headdress. In the field above is swallow flying to right with outstretched wings. To the left of the figural group, fragmentary group of birds. Preserves bottom of knobby stump and bird on ground facing right. To the right of the figural group, three birds: one bird perched on a knobby stump looking at right drinker, two others stand on the ground facing drinkers, the second looks back to right. Under each handle, one bird. (Total: 11 plump, long-necked birds restoring one on missing stump on side B.)

Dots appear in field above figures. On side A, dots emitted from left perching bird; on side B possibly from the lyre. Added white (fugitive): female flesh, plumage and feet of some birds, rocks at base of stump on side A, rhyton of right drinker on side B directly on reserved surface, wave pattern on mattress, stripes on pillow on side A, dots on pillow on side B. Added red (fugitive): fillets, folds and decorative dots of garments, sakkos of flute player, wave pattern on mattress, stripes on pillows, beards. Hasty incision.

See Chapter 4 for possible interpretations of the scene. The headdresses are unusual but seem to be combinations of horns and ears. The birds have been identified by Elke Böhr as vultures (pers. comm.). On the fragmentary section of side B, one can restore two birds similar to those on side A. Only the head of the bird on the ground is missing; the bottom of a knobby stump suggests that a second bird was perched there. The preservation of added red and white is very poor, and in places is only discernible as a faint ghost. The foreground arm and hand and the hairline of the flute player on side A are visible when the pot is angled. It is possible that the headdress horns on side A were also white.

Attribution: The CHC Group paint various shapes of skyphoi, but their Heron Class skyphoi affiliate them with potters working in the workshops of the Krokotos Painter and the Theseus Painter (Ure 1955, p. 90; *ABL*, p. 144). The products of the Theseus Painter are of higher-quality draftsmanship and feature the larger decorative zone of Class B skyphoi at the expense of the black-glazed band on the lower body. The Heron Class skyphoi of the CHC Group outnumber those of the Theseus Painter, but their mass-produced quality lacks the sophistication of

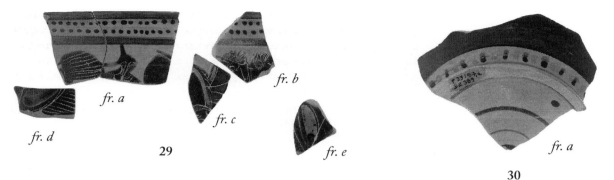

fr. a
fr. b
fr. c
fr. d
fr. e
29

fr. a
30

Figure 45. Skyphoi 29, 30, Heron Class. Scale 1:2

the Theseus Painter's subject matter, and the narrower Class C decorative scheme favors repetitive iconography.

The subsidiary decoration of tongues, bands, and dilute lines on **28** is identical to another Heron Class skyphos from the Agora, P 1140 + P 1160 (*ABV* 620, no. 86; *Agora* XXIII, p. 290, no. 1588, pl. 105), attributed by Beazley to the CHC Group. Agora P 1140 + P 1160 also provides parallels for odd figural details on **28**. On P 1140 + P 1160, the reclining figure, Dionysos, wears a turban or head wrap with a bun of hair at the back of the head, resulting in a silhouette like the left drinker on side A. The upper limit of the beard of Dionysos on P 1140 + P 1160 is formed by a line that arcs down from the forehead, where it also forms the hairline. This same beard motif can be seen on all of the drinkers preserved on **28**. The mattress on which Dionysos reclines also featured a wave pattern, now fugitive.

White Heron Group (Camp 1996)
CHC Group (Lynch 1999)
Ca. 500

29 (P 32777) Skyphos, Heron Class; Ure's Class C1   Fig. 45
+46.60–46.30 m (Level 5)
Max. p. dim. (a) 7.2, (b) 3.9, (c) 3.2, (d) 3.25, (e) 2.4
Two joining (a) and four nonjoining (b, c, d, e) fragments of rim and wall. Good black glaze on interior, exterior dull in spots.

Tall, straight wall. Lightly concave rim with dot-ivy between black-glazed bands. Wall preserves Amazon with chariot wheeling around between sphinxes. On (a), rim and wing of sphinx, upper part of Amazon with shield. Amazon wears a pointy cap with a tail and earflaps. On (b), rim and three horse heads; (c), horses's necks, foreleg; (d), body and wing of sphinx; (e), body of sphinx. Reserved line on interior of lip. Added white: Amazon's skin, bodies of sphinxes, one horse. Added red: details on shield, horses' manes. Hasty but detailed incision.

For shape, group, and decorative scheme, see *Agora* XXIII, p. 289, nos. 1578–1581, pl. 105. For a complete example of the scene, see Athens, National Archaeological Museum 21064, *CVA* Athens 4 [Greece 4] pl. 48 [48]:4–6, and Athens, British School, *ABV* 618, 15, Boardman 1974, fig. 292, which is even closer in style.

CHC Group
Ca. 500

30 (P 33197) Skyphos, Heron Class; Ure's Class C   Fig. 45
+46.60–46.30 and +46.00–45.90 m (Level 5)
Est. Diam. at fillet 10.0; max. p. dim. (a) 9.6, (b) 7.75, (c) 4.0
Three nonjoining fragments of lower wall, fillet, and part of floor (a). Foot missing. Glaze cloudy and streaky. Dilute wash on reserved surfaces.

Beveled fillet at junction with foot, scraped grooves above and below fillet. At base of wall, reserved band with alternating black and red debased tongues. Unintentional rough groove at center of band. Underside reserved with three circles. On interior, reserved circle at center of floor.

On underside, stray oval black-glazed dot between foot and first circle. Below dot, incised graffito: A[.

For shape and decorative scheme, see *Agora* XXIII, p. 290, no. 1588, pl. 105.
Probably CHC Group
Ca. 500

31   (P 33190) Skyphos, Heron Class; Ure's Class C   Fig. 46

+49.76–49.14 m (Level 2)
Est. Diam. at fillet 11.5; p.H. 2.7; max. p. dim. 11.0
Fragment broken all around. Interior floor, lower wall, and fillet above foot. Pinkish-gray clay (5YR 6/4), tinged gray at breaks. Beveled fillet at junction of wall and foot. Underside reserved with broad central circle. Reserved circle on interior floor with thin black-glazed circle at center.

At base of wall, reserved band with alternating black and red debased tongues. Two thin, dilute lines below, three above. Dilute glaze or miltos on fillet.

Also from Level 2: P 33191 *(agathe)*, fragment of lower wall and fillet above foot with band of alternating black and red debased tongues. For shape, decorative scheme, and date, see *Agora* XXIII, p. 190, no. 1588, pl. 105.
Probably CHC Group
Ca. 500

32   (P 32780) Skyphos, Ure's Class C1 or D1   Fig. 47

+46.60–45.90 m (Level 5)
P.H. (a) 9.0; est. Diam. 17.0; max. p. dim. (b) 10.4, (c) 4.4, (d) 6.6
About one-third preserved. Mended into two large nonjoining fragments (a, b) and two small floating fragments (c, d). Roughly potted and finished. Bulge in wall where handle was pressed on. Hasty drawing. Added color largely fugitive, but shiny black glaze.

Tall, convex body with nearly straight upper wall. Slightly outturned rim, lightly concave beneath on exterior. Canted horizontal handle attached to upper wall. At bottom of wall, black-glazed zone with two black-glazed lines above. Degenerate dot-ivy on exterior of rim; top of rim glazed; broad, dilute line below. Same scene on both sides: Ram facing right between sphinxes facing out to handles. Reserved: inside of handles, line on interior of rim, but irregular and partially covered. No incision. Added white: faces of sphinxes, band on sphinxes, horns of rams. Added red: fillet on sphinxes, bands on sphinxes' bodies and wings, spots and band on rams.

Figure 46. Skyphos 31, Heron Class. Scale 1:2. Profile drawn author; inked E. Schmitt

Figure 47. Skyphos 32, Ure's Class C1 or D1. Scale 1:3

fr. a

fr. b

fr. c

fr. d

Three additional inventoried fragments of similar vessels, probably by the CHC Group, from J 2:4: P 32800 *(agathe),* fragment of a sphinx's body, from Level 2; P 33186 *(agathe),* fragment of wall with trace of figure, from Level 1b; P 32776 *(agathe),* fragment of wall at handle with lightly incised ✕ on exterior, from Level 1b.

For a similar scene and style, see Vanderpool 1946, p. 293, no. 76, pl. 44. For complete example of a similar scene, see Athens, National Archaeological Museum 20097, *CVA* Athens 4 [Greece 4], pl. 49 [49]:3, 4. For a single ram between sphinxes, see Ure 1927, p. 62, no. R26.92.

Without the reserved band of tongues, it is difficult to know whether this is a Class C1 or Class D1 skyphos. The diameter is smaller than the average C1, so it is more likely to be D1.
  CHC Group
  Ca. 500

33   (P 32794) Skyphos, Heron Class; Ure's Class C1 or D1   Fig. 48

+50.31–49.76 m (Level 1b)
  Max. p. dim. 8.0; est. Diam. 21.0
  Two joining fragments of rim and wall. Roughly potted. Worn. Scrape on rim and dent at top of figural zone. Tall, straight wall. Concave rim. Rim with degenerate dot band. Figural zone preserves two human heads: one facing left with incision for eye and hairline; at right, back of second head facing right. One dilute glaze line at top of zone. Reserved line on interior of rim. No added color preserved.

This is probably a courting group. The diagonal line extending behind the first figure's head is probably the tail of a cock. For a similar scene, see Athens, National Archaeological Museum 636, *CVA* Athens 4 [Greece 4], pl. 46 [46]:1–3. Without the tongues at the base of the wall, it is impossible to tell whether this is a Class C1 or D1. The scale of the figure is too small for Class B.
  CHC Group
  Ca. 500

Figure 48. Skyphos 33, Heron Class.
Scale 1:2

*34   (P 32802) Skyphos, Heron Class?   Fig. 49

+49.76–49.14 and 46.00–45.90 m (Levels 2 and 5)
  Max. p. dim. 3.0
  Two joining fragments of wall to left of handle. Thin-walled. Good black glaze on the interior.

Preserves trace of handle attachment with black glaze at right. Body and tail of bird facing right. No incision. Added white: horizontal stripe on tail. Added red (fugitive): spot on body.

Possibly a bird between handle attachments. The thickness of the wall matches that of the Heron Class skyphos **28**, but this fragment does not belong to that skyphos, which has both handle birds preserved.
  Ca. 500

Figure 49. Skyphos 34, Heron Class?
Scale 1:1

35   (P 33210) Skyphos, Ure's Class D or E   Fig. 50

+49.76–49.14 m (Level 2)
  P.H. 5.5; max. p. dim. 8.2
  Seven joining fragments of wall.
  Tall, convex wall. Preserves lower portion of figural zone with two black-glazed lines and black-glazed zone below. Tip of wing and tail of sphinx to left. Lower half of four males: two at center facing each other, framed by two walking away. Added red at waist of second male from left.

A courting scene. For a complete example, see Ure 1927, no. R80.260, pl. 19.
  CHC Group
  Ca. 500

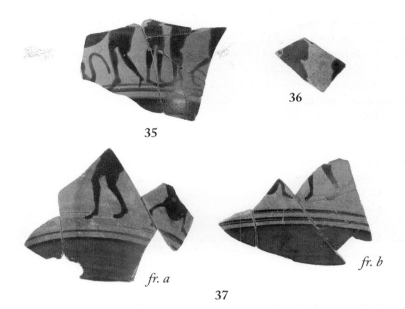

Figure 50. Skyphoi 35–37, Ure's Class D or E. Scale 1:2

36 (P 32804) Skyphos, Ure's Class D or E Fig. 50
+50.31–49.76 m (Level 1b)
Max. p. dim. 3.5
Two joining fragments of wall. Surface flaws in black glaze on interior.
Preserves part of two figures. Female figure facing right, holding right arm in front of body. Rear of male facing right. Added white (fugitive): female flesh directly on reserved surface. Added red: dots on garment. No incision.
This is probably a dancing scene. Dancers between sphinxes are the third most common theme for the CHC Group. See *CVA* Athens 4 [Greece 4], p. 58, discussion of pl. 52 [52]:1, 2, for a list of others and their variations. Additional inventoried examples from J 2:4: P 33202 *(agathe)*, fragment of wall with back foot of male and skirt of female in nearly identical pose to those on **37**, from Level 2; P 33203 *(agathe)* and P 33204 *(agathe)*, both fragments of walls with legs of dancers, both from Level 2.
CHC Group
Ca. 500–480

37 (P 33199) Skyphos, Ure's Class D or E Fig. 50
+49.76–48.70 m (Level 2)
P.H. (a) 7.3, (b) 6.5; max. p. dim. (a) 10.2, (b) 8.6
Fragments of wall, three joining (a) and six joining (b). Black glaze cloudy. Surface irregularly finished.
Black-glazed lower wall, two black-glazed lines above, the upper fades out. Figural zone on (a) preserves bottom half of male facing left, female running to right. Figural zone on (b) preserves one foot and skirt of female running right, male facing left. No incision. Added white: at waist of man on (a). Added red dots on women's skirts.
Probably a dancing scene; see **36** for references.
CHC Group
Ca. 500

38 (P 33200) Skyphos, Ure's Class D or E Fig. 51
+49.76–49.14 m (Level 2)
P.H. 5.4; max. p. dim. 11.5

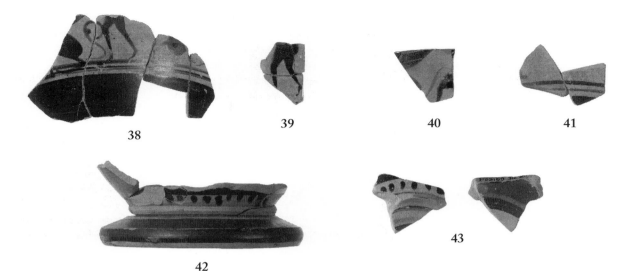

Figure 51. Skyphoi 38–43, Ure's Class D or E. Scale 1:2

Five joining fragments of wall. Black glaze dull on interior, shiny on exterior. Dilute wash on reserved surfaces.

Black-glazed lower wall, two dilute black-glazed lines above. Figural zone preserves lower half of sphinx to left, male to left, female running right, and foot of another figure running to left. No incision. Added white: wing of sphinx. Added red: dots on dress.

Scene similar to **37**, but smaller-scale figures here and thinner wall. Probably a dancing scene; see **36** for references.

CHC Group

Ca. 500

*39   (P 33201) Skyphos, Ure's Class D or E   Fig. 51

+49.76–49.14 and +46.30–46.00 m (Levels 2 and 5)

Max. p. dim. 3.5

Three joining fragments of wall.

Preserves lower half of male figure facing left. No incision. Trace of black-glazed line below. Added red at waist.

Probably from **38** or a replica. The scale of the figure matches. Probably a dancing scene; see **36** for references.

It is possible that **39** and **41**, which both have joining fragments from top and bottom of well, are from the same object. Both have a reddish wash on the surface, walls of similar thickness, and similar wheelmarks on the interior. In contrast, **34**, also a large black-figured skyphos, has a much thinner wall.

CHC Group

Ca. 500

[40]   (P 32792) Skyphos, Ure's Class D or E   Fig. 51

+45.45–45.20 m (Level 6)

Max. p. dim. 3.2

Fragment of wall, broken all around. Good black glaze on interior; more diluted for figures. Dilute wash on reserved surface.

Tall, slightly convex wall. Preserves wing and backside of left-facing sphinx at left. On right, one leg of a male moving to left. Added red: spot on sphinx's wing. Added white: stripe on sphinx's wing.

Probably a dancing scene; see **36** for references.
CHC Group
Ca. 500–480

*41 (P 32782) Skyphos, Ure's Class D or E   Fig. 51

+48.50 and 46.00–45.90 m (Levels 3 and 5)
Max. p. dim. 4.6

Two joining fragments of wall. Good black glaze. Red wash on reserved surface. Preserves tip of foot to right. Two black-glazed lines below, lower dilute. Black-glazed zone at bottom of wall.

The figure is probably a sphinx. It is possible that **41** and **39**, which both have joining fragments from top and bottom of well, are from the same object. Both have a reddish wash on the surface, walls of similar thickness, and similar wheelmarks on the interior. In contrast, **34**, also a large black-figured skyphos, has a much thinner wall. Attribution uncertain because of small fragment without diagnostic characteristics.
CHC Group?
Ca. 500

42 (P 33205 + P 33196) Skyphos, Ure's Class D or E   Fig. 51

+46.60–46.30 m (Level 5)
P.H. 4.6; Diam. foot 12.3

Fragment of foot and lower wall. Mended from many fragments. Somewhat roughly potted.

Projecting torus foot. Beveled fillet at junction of wall and foot with scraped groove below. Tall, deep wall. Reserved: tondo on interior, underside, resting surface, bottom quarter of torus face, fillet, narrow strip on top of foot below fillet, lower wall. On underside: broad, streaky central circle and dot. Band of debased black-glazed tongues on reserved band at base of wall.

For shape and decorative scheme, cf. *Agora* XXIII, p. 291, no. 1597, pl. 105. Shape could either be a Ure's Class D or E, but probably E since the size is smaller.

Another fragment of a base from a similar form from J 2:4: P 33185 *(agathe)*, fragment of projecting torus foot with band of black-glazed debased tongues at bottom of wall, from Level 1b.
Ca. 500

43 (P 33189) Skyphos, Ure's Class D or E   Fig. 51

+50.31–49.76 m (Level 1b)
Max. p. dim. 3.9

Single fragment of lower wall and fillet above foot, broken all around. Flat fillet at junction of wall and foot. Black-glazed lower wall. At base of wall, reserved band with narrow debased black-glazed tongues, dilute glaze line below. Added red: line on interior floor encircling reserved tondo; drip mark slightly above line. Reserved: underside with at least one wide, broad, black-glazed circle; circle on interior floor.

The shape is similar to *Agora* XXIII, p. 291, no. 1597, pl. 105, but the added red line on interior floor is peculiar. Could either be Ure's Class D or E but seems big enough to be a D.
Ca. 500

44 (P 33192) Skyphos, Ure's Class E?   Fig. 52

+49.76–49.14 m (Level 2)
P.H. 3.5; Diam. foot 13.0

Two joining fragments of lower wall and foot (floor not preserved). Interior and upper part of underside fired red. Projecting torus ring foot; upper surface flat, but irregular. Lightly beveled fillet between two scraped grooves at junction of wall and foot. Reserved: exterior face of foot, resting surface, and underside of foot.

For shape and decorative scheme, see *Agora* XXIII, p. 293, nos. 1609, 1610, pls. 105, 106. Although this fragmentary skyphos carries no sign of figured decoration, it is more likely to belong to a black-figured skyphos than a plain black-glazed because a black-glazed version is not known from the Agora (cf. *Agora* XII). Ure's Class E3 does not have tongues, which would explain why there is no reserved band at the bottom of the wall. The red glaze on the interior is even enough to suggest that it is intentional, but the streaking and variations on the exterior and underside indicate that the color is a result of misfiring.

Ca. 500–480

Figure 52. Skyphos 44, Ure's Class E?
Scale 1:3

*45 (P 32423) Cup-skyphos, Ure's Class K2   Color Ills. 2, 12; Fig. 53
+46.60–45.60 m (Level 5)
H. 7.4–7.6; Diam. 14.3; W. 21.3
Camp 1996, p. 246, no. 23, fig. 7, pls. 71:b, 73.

Nearly complete. Mended, one-third of rim missing. Black glaze peeling, especially in figured area and on handles. Torus ring foot. Low convex walls. Concave rim. Canted handles attached to top of wall. Two bands of black glaze at bottom of wall, lower thicker. Rim and exterior of handles glazed. Same scene on both sides, better preserved on side A: pair of bovines facing each other. Branches and blob-fruits in field. Five frond palmettes with tendrils by handles. Poor painting

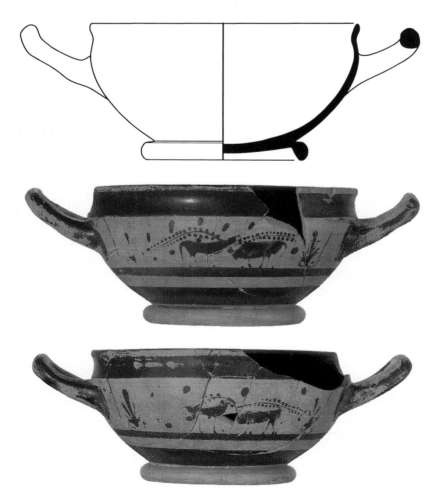

Figure 53. Cup-skyphos 45, Ure's Class K2. Scale 1:2. Profile drawn author; inked E. Schmitt

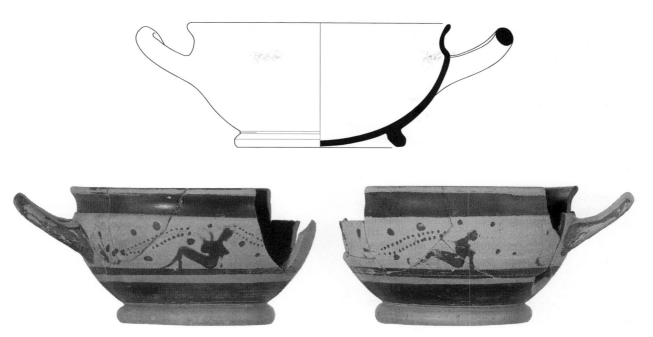

Figure 54. Cup-skyphos 46, Ure's Class K2. Scale 1:2. Profile drawn A. Hooton; inked E. Schmitt

with no incision, but well potted. Reserved: exterior face and underside of foot with black-glazed central dot and circle, interior of handles, line on interior of lip.

For shape and decorative scheme, cf. *Agora* XXIII, pp. 287–288, nos. 1555–1565, pls. 104, 105; Hatzidakis 1984, pp. 119–128. For scene, cf. Hermogenean skyphos, Art Market, New York, Royal Athena Galleries, HFU59, May 2004; Hermogenean skyphos, Reading, Ure Museum no. 29.11.5, *CVA* Reading 1 [Great Britain 12], pl. 11 [538]:2, on side B of which both bovines are clearly bulls. Style, decorative scheme, and shape resemble the large number of skyphoi produced by the workshop of the Haimon Painter and called generally, Haimonian (*Agora* XXIII, p. 96).

Ca. 500–480

*46 (P 32424) Cup-skyphos, Ure's Class K2 Color Ill. 2; Fig. 54

+46.60–45.45 m (Levels 5 and 6)
H. 7.5–7.8; Diam. 13.8; p.W. 16.3
Camp 1996, pp. 246, 248, no. 24, pl. 73.

Full profile. About two-thirds preserved. Mended from 13 joining fragments. Missing one handle and parts of rim and wall. Good black glaze, but misfired a dull brown-red in places and flaking in figural zone, worn off exterior of rim. Dilute wash on reserved surfaces. Some prefiring dents on lower exterior wall.

Torus ring foot. Low convex wall. Concave rim. Canted handles attached to top of wall. Two bands of black glaze at bottom of wall, lower thicker. Rim and exterior of handle glazed.

Similar scene on both sides: a figure reclines on the ground, facing left, supported on the left arm, with head turned back to the right. Schematic curved object held in the right hand. Branches and blob-fruits in background. Five frond palmettes with tendrils by handles. Poor painting with no incision, but fairly well potted. Reserved: underside except for central dot and circle, exterior face of foot and resting surface, line on interior of lip, interior of handle.

For shape and decorative scheme, cf. *Agora* XXIII, pp. 287–288, nos. 1555–1565, pls. 104, 105. A figure in the same position, without the curved object, appears on the fragmentary skyphos P1290, Vanderpool 1946, p. 296, no. 96, pl. 47. The object is probably a lyre. Hatzidakis (1984, p. 120) lists examples of "symposium" scenes, in which he would place this example. Style as **45**. Haimonian.

Ca. 500–480

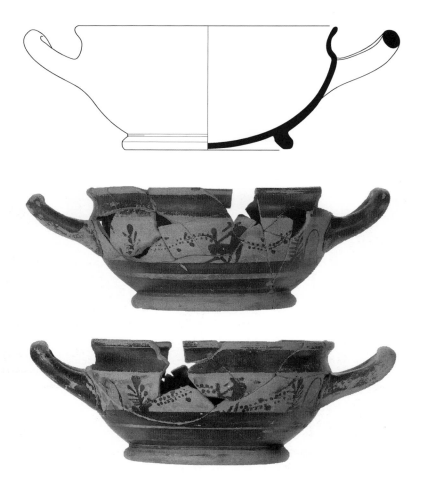

*47 (P 32474) Cup-skyphos, Ure's Class K2   Color Ill. 2; Fig. 55
+46.60–45.90 m (Level 5)
H. 6.8; Diam. 13.7
Camp 1996, p. 248, no. 25, pl. 73.

Almost complete except for sections of rim and body. Mended from many fragments. Good black glaze, brownish and thin in places. Dilute wash on reserved surfaces.

Torus ring foot. Low convex walls. Concave rim. Canted handles attached to top of wall. Two bands of black glaze at bottom of wall, lower one thicker. Rim and exterior of handles glazed.

Similar scene coarsely painted on each side: Dionysos seated facing left on a low stool, one arm in front and bent, holding an abstract rhyton. Projecting blob from the area of the head toward the raised hand; back of head irregularly formed. Branches with leaves and blob-fruits in background, hasty palmettes with tendrils by handles. Poor silhouette painting, no incision. Reserved: underside with two concentric circles (inner one thicker), exterior face of foot, resting surface, line on the interior of rim and interior of handles.

For shape and decorative style, see *Agora* XXIII, pp. 287–288, nos. 1555–1565, pls. 104, 105. Very similar profile to **124** and **125**. Hatzidakis (1984, p. 120) lists other seated Dionysos scenes (cf. especially no. 338 for a better-drawn example of the scene); and cf. Corinth, CP-799, Brownlee 1995, pl. 96 (objects stolen from Corinth Museum, see p. 337, n. 1). The protrusion from the front of the face is probably Dionysos's beard. The irregularity on the back of the head is probably hair in a bun or turban. Style as **45**. Haimonian.

Ca. 500–480

48

49

Figure 56. Cup-skyphoi 48, 49, Ure's Class K2. Scale 1:1

*48 (P 32808) Cup-skyphos, Ure's Class K2 Fig. 56

+48.70–48.60 and +46.00–45.90 m (Levels 3 and 5)
Max. p. dim. 6.5

Two joining fragments of wall, broken all around. Fragment from Level 3 worn, and clay gray. Shiny black glaze. Reddish wash on reserved surfaces on fragment from Level 5.

Convex wall tapering toward foot. Black-glazed zone at bottom with black-glazed band above. On wall: figure seated on stool facing right. Trace of branch in field to left. No incision.

For shape, style, and motif, cf. *Agora* XXIII, p. 288, no. 1564, pl. 104. Probably Dionysos seated as on **47**. The drawing is more careful than on other silhouette skyphoi in this deposit. Shape and decorative scheme as **45**. Haimonian.

Ca. 490–480

49 (P 33198) Cup-skyphos, Ure's Class K2 Fig. 56

+46.60–46.30 m (Level 5)
P.H. 3.5; est. Diam. 9.5

Three joining fragments of rim and wall. Glaze flaking, chips on surface. Very fine mica in clay.

Slightly convex wall. Concave rim. Indeterminate figural scene. Possibly figure seated facing left, holding lyre, looking back to right. No incision. Branch in field at right. Blob-fruits above and below. Broad ground line, reserved band below. Reserved line on interior of lip.

For shape and decorative style, see *Agora* XXIII, pp. 287–288, nos. 1555–1565, pls. 104, 105. Cf. **45, 46, 47**. This is probably another symposiast with lyre as on **46**. Hatzidakis (1984, p. 120) lists other examples of symposiasts. Style and decorative scheme as **45**. Haimonian.

Ca. 500–480

50 (P 33206) Cup-skyphos, Ure's Class K2 Fig. 57

+46.60–46.00 m (Level 5)
Max. p. dim. 7.7

Four joining fragments of wall. Good black glaze on interior, but fired brown flaking on the exterior. Dilute wash on reserved surface.

Preserves center of one side with single female figure with wings (Nike?) between branches with blob-fruits. No incision. Black-glazed band below.

Cf. Vanderpool 1946, no. 104, pl. 47. Style and decorative scheme as **45**. Haimonian.

Ca. 490–480

51 (P 32784) Cup-skyphos, Ure's Class K2 (small) Fig. 58

+49.76–49.14 m (Level 2)
P.H. 2.5; est. Diam. 10.0

Figure 57. Cup-skyphos 50, Ure's Class K2. Scale 1:2

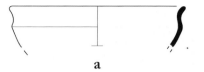
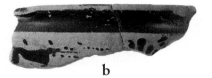

a   b

Figure 58. Cup-skyphos 51, Ure's Class K2. Scale 1:2 (a); 3:4 (b). Profile drawn A. Hooton; inked E. Schmitt

Two joining fragments of rim and wall. Roughly potted. Black glaze flaking in places. Worn. Rim pinched and distorted in places before firing.

Low, slightly convex wall. Concave, black-glazed rim. Quadruped, possibly a lion or a dog (no incision) between palmettes (one preserved). Branches in field. Reserved line on interior of lip.

This is a small version of the shallow Class K2 skyphos. See Hatzidakis 1984, p. 120, for a list of skyphoi of this form with animals. Style and decorative scheme as **45**. Haimonian.

Ca. 490–480

52 (P 32806) Cup-skyphos, Ure's Class K2   Fig. 59

+46.60–46.30 m (Level 5)

Est. Diam. 12.5; max. p. dim. 7.1

Two joining fragments of rim and wall, to left of handle (missing). Streaky black glaze.

Low, slightly convex wall. Concave, black-glazed rim. Reserved line on interior of rim. On wall: hasty palmette, tendril to right, branch with leaves to left, dots, grape cluster, and blob-fruit in field. Trace of figure at the left edge of fragment. No incision. Below, black-glazed band with trace of reserved band below.

For shape and decorative scheme, see *Agora* XXIII, pp. 287–288, nos. 1555–1565, pls. 104, 105. Palmette is nearly identical to **47**, and very similar in style to **45** and **46** as well as other inventoried fragments associated with the Haimon Group from J 2:4: P 32807 *(agathe)*, with a portion of an eight-frond palmette from Level 5, and P 33181 *(agathe)*, also with a hasty palmette from Level 1b. Style and decorative scheme as **45**. Haimonian.

Ca. 490–480

Figure 59. Cup-skyphos 52, Ure's Class K2. Scale 1:2. Profile drawn author; inked E. Schmitt

53 (P 32774) Cup-skyphos, Ure's Class K2   Fig. 60

+50.31–49.14 m (Levels 1b and 2)

H. 6.1

Three joining fragments of wall. Good black glaze on interior, mottled orange and dull gray on exterior. Dilute wash on reserved surface. Tall, slightly convex wall. Plain black-glazed rim. Preserves standing figure facing right and seated male facing left, looking right. A clublike projection extends from man's hand. Probably nymph and Dionysos or possibly Herakles. In the field, branches. Hasty but detailed incision. Traces of added white and red (fugitive) on garments, fillets.

For shape and style, see *Agora* XXIII, pp. 282–283, nos. 1504–1516, pls. 102, 103. The rim fragment **64** may be from the same object. It has the same orange

54

55

53

Figure 60. Cup-skyphoi 53–55, Ure's Class K2. Scale 3:4 (53), 1:2 (54, 55)

discoloration and similar clay. The palmette on **64** is also of similar scale to figures here. The added color and incision, although hasty, elevate this skyphos above many of the other examples here. Hatzidakis (1984, p. 135) creates a group around several cup-skyphoi attributed to the Painter of Elaious I by Beazley; **53** may belong to this group.

Ca. 490–480

54 (P 33182) Cup-skyphos, Ure's Class K2 Fig. 60

+50.31–49.14 m (Levels 1b and 2)
Max. p. dim. 5.2

Three joining fragments of wall, broken all around, to right of handle (missing). Black glaze mottled red-brown on upper part of palmette, good on interior.

Slightly convex wall. On wall: ten-frond palmette. Trace of a branch to right. Wide black-glazed band below.

Cf. palmette on *Agora* XXIII, p. 286, no. 1550, pl. 104. Possibly Manner of the Painter of Elaious I; cf. Hatzidakis 1984, no. 430, pl. 13.

Ca. 490–480

55 (P 32773) Cup-skyphos, Ure's Class K2 Fig. 60

+49.76–49.14 m (Level 2)
P.H. 5.7; p.W. 17.9; est. Diam. body 20.0

Ten joining fragments of wall mended into two joining fragments (largest fragment illustrated). Surface worn. Glaze fired red-orange on interior, orange-gray on exterior. Dilute wash on reserved surface.

Preserves one side with Dionysos seated on stool, facing right, between satyr at left and maenad at right. Figures framed by two palmettes with many fronds. Branches with leaves and blob-fruits in field. Below, black-glazed band, black-glazed zone at bottom of wall. Limited, hasty incision.

For style and shape, see *Agora* XXIII, p. 283, nos. 1513, 1519, pl. 103. The spirals of the curling tendrils of the palmettes are similar to *Agora* XXIII, p. 283, nos. 1513, 1519, pl. 103, and place this fragment near the Haimon Painter.

See also another fragment from J 2:4 with a similar style: P 32801 *(agathe)*, which preserves the top of a figure facing left and the bottom of the concave rim, from Level 2.

Manner of the Haimon Painter
Ca. 490–480

56 P 32791 Cup-skyphos, Ure's Class K2 Fig. 61

+49.76–49.14 m (Level 2)
Max. p. dim. (a) 5.2, (b) 3.7

Six fragments of wall, five joining (a), one nonjoining (b).

Tall, slightly convex wall. On a, figure of nude male moving right. Has a pointy beard and is stooped slightly as he carries something (wineskin?) in front of him. Front foot rests on a black-glazed ground line. Branch in field to right and trace

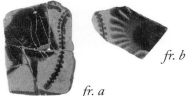

fr. b

fr. a

Figure 61. Cup-skyphos 56, Ure's Class K2. Scale 1:2

of one above. To right, heel of another figure. On b, palmette with many fronds, branch in field to left. Added white (fugitive): center of palmette(?). Otherwise no added color preserved.

Cf. *Agora* XXIII, p. 283, no. 1511, pl. 103, for a satyr carrying a similar formless object, which Moore suggests may be a footless krater, attributed to the Manner of the Haimon Painter; *Agora* XXIII, p. 283, no. 1511, 1513, et al., pl. 103, for the palmette. The palmette places this fragment near the hand of the Haimon Painter himself.

Manner of the Haimon Painter
Ca. 490–480

57   (P 32783) Cup-skyphos, Ure's Class K2   Fig. 62

+49.76–49.14 m (Level 2)
Est. Diam. 18.0; max. p. dim. 4.4
Three joining fragments of rim and wall to left of handle. Good black glaze. Well potted.

Tall, straight wall. Plain black-glazed rim with thickened lip. Preserves head of a bearded male facing right. Two branches in field. Edge of a palmette. Reserved line on interior of lip.

For the shape and style, see *Agora* XXIII, pp. 282–283, nos. 1508–1513, pl. 103. The figure is probably a satyr. Another inventoried fragment from J 2:4, P 32788 *(agathe)*, preserves a similar section of branches with leaves and blob fruits, from Level 1b. Palmette and attribution as **55**.

Manner of the Haimon Painter
Ca. 490–480

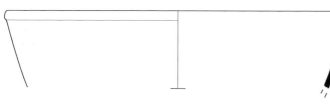

Figure 62. Cup-skyphos 57, Ure's Class K2. Scale 1:2. Profile drawn A. Hooton; inked E. Schmitt

58   (P 32790) Cup-skyphos, Ure's Class K2   Fig. 63

+49.76–49.14 and 48.50 m (Levels 2 and 3)
Max. p. dim. 4.5
Two joining fragments of wall. Dull black glaze on exterior, shinier on interior. Uneven dilute wash on reserved surface.

Slightly convex wall. Plain, black-glazed rim. On wall: draped figure facing left. Figure has elongated head and a black-glazed loop extending from left shoulder. Several branches in field to right. One with blob-fruits. Hasty incision. No added color preserved.

For the shape, cf. Vanderpool 1946, p. 297, no. 107, pl. 47. The loop object may be a lyre, and the elongated head, a turban. Probably a scene of satyrs and maenads; see Hatzidakis 1984, p. 139, for a list of others. Style and decorative scheme as **45**. Haimonian.
Ca. 490–480

Figure 63. Cup-skyphos 58, Ure's Class K2. Scale 1:1

59   (P 32775) Cup-skyphos, Ure's Class K2   Fig. 64

+50.31–49.14 m (Levels 1b and 2)
P.H. 7.5; max. p. dim. (a) 7.5, (b) 2.7, (c) 2.0, (d) 1.5
Fragments of wall and rim, three joining (a) and three nonjoining (b, c, d). Good black glaze. Orange wash on reserved surface. Tall, slightly convex wall. Plain black-glazed rim.

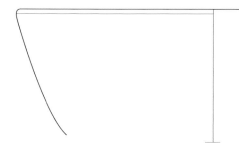

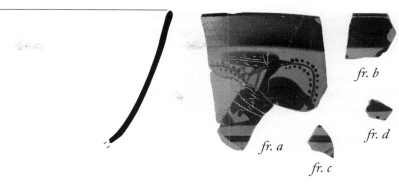

Figure 64. Cup-skyphos 59, Ure's Class K2. Scale 1:2. Profile drawn A. Hooton; inked E. Schmitt

On (a), crouching lion, forepart of kneeling Herakles, quiver above, and branches in field. Below, black-glazed bands. On (b), a rim fragment, traces of two objects. On (c), ground line and reserved band. Above, trace of figure, probably tail of lion. On (d), black glaze below rim and two leaf dots. Hasty incision for Herakles and the quiver, but none on the lion. Reserved band on interior.

Cf. *Agora* XXIII, p. 284, no. 1519, pl. 103. Hatzidakis (1984, pp. 146–153) places the scenes of Herakles in a single category; see p. 146 for a list of others with the Nemean lion, all in the same pose. Shape and style as **57**, linked to **55** through palmette.

Manner of the Haimon Painter
Ca. 490–480

60 (P 32787) Cup-skyphos, Ure's Class K2   Fig. 65
+49.76–49.14 m (Level 2)
Max. p. dim. 4.4
Two joining fragments of wall and rim. Rim roughly finished and gouged before firing. Dull black glaze on interior. Dilute wash on reserved surface. Tall, straight wall. Outturned black-glazed rim, thickened lip.

Preserves upper part of charioteer in chariot. Branch in field. A diagonal line crosses in front of the figure. No incision. Reserved line on interior of rim.

For shape, style, and motif, see *Agora* XXIII, p. 282, no. 1504, pl. 102 (Manner of the Haimon Painter); Hatzidakis 1984, no. 512. The hunched position of the charioteer's body suggests a chariot in rapid motion, as opposed to a processional scene. The diagonal line may be a goad or an accidental mark.

Manner of the Haimon Painter
Ca. 490–480

Figure 65. Cup-skyphos 60, Ure's Class K2. Scale 1:1

61 (P 32778) Cup-skyphos, Ure's Class K2   Fig. 66
+50.31–49.14 m (Levels 1b and 2)
P.H. (a) 3.3, (b) 2.2; est. Diam. 9.0
Two joining fragments of base and lower wall (a) and three joining fragments of rim (b). Good black glaze, flaking on rim. Fragment (a): torus ring foot, groove at junction of foot and wall; flaring convex wall. Fragment (b):

Figure 66. Cup-skyphos 61, Ure's Class K2. Scale 1:2. Profile drawn A. Hooton; inked E. Schmitt

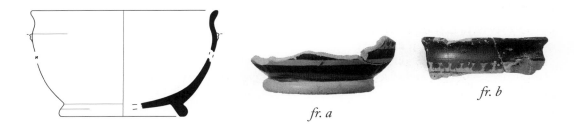

black-glazed concave rim with one handle scar. Reflected horizontal ivy on wall. Dots between leaves of lower register. Black-glazed band, zone below. Reserved: line on interior of rim, exterior face of foot, resting surface and underside of foot.

Cf. Vanderpool 1946, p. 297, no. 114, pl. 47. Hatzidakis (1984, p. 120) lists other examples with floral motifs: no. 360, pl. 45 is very similar. See also another similar inventoried fragmentary skyphos from J 2:4: P 32796 *(agathe)*, also with reflected ivy leaves, from Level 2. Style and decorative scheme as **45**. Haimonian. 500–480

[62]   (P 33207) Cup-skyphos, Ure's Class K2   Fig. 67

+45.90–45.60 m (Level 6)
P.H. 3.8; est. Diam. foot 9.5
Single fragment of almost half of foot. Good black glaze on exterior, dull on the interior.

Torus ring foot. Tall, convex wall. Bottom of wall black glaze with reserved band. Bottom edge of figural zone preserved. Preserves trace of a foot(?) with added red details. Reserved: resting surface, underside with a broad central circle. Traces of miltos on reserved surface of underside.

Cf. *Agora* XXIII, p. 282, nos. 1504, 1501, pl. 102, for the wider black-glazed band below the figural zone and the black-glazed torus foot.

This is a better-quality product than most Class K2 skyphoi from this deposit with a different foot profile, suggesting that it is by a different potter from the other Class K2 skyphoi in this deposit. Another inventoried example from J 2:4 with a similar profile is P 33193 *(agathe)*, fragment of foot and lower wall, from Level 2. P 33193 preserves the bottom of a figural zone with very small figures.

Ca. 500–480

Figure 67. Cup-skyphos 62, Ure's Class K2. Scale 1:2. Profile drawn author; inked E. Schmitt

63   (P 32803) Cup-skyphos, Ure's Class K2   Fig. 68

+49.76–49.14 m (Level 2)
Max. p. dim. 3.4
Fragment of rim and wall. Black glaze fired brown on exterior of rim. Concave black-glazed rim. Reserved line on interior of lip. Added red: line at bottom of rim and on interior. Graffito on wall:]ΔΙ.

The potting marks indicate that the handle attachment begins immediately after the second letter, so there are no further letters to the right.
Ca. 500–480

Figure 68. Cup-skyphos 63, Ure's Class K2. Scale 1:1

64   (P 33180) Cup-skyphos, Ure's Class K2 with incurving rim   Fig. 69

+50.31–49.14 m (Levels 1b and 2)
Est. Diam. 18.0; max. p. dim. 6.1
Three joining fragments of wall and rim, to right of handle (missing). Black glaze fired red-brown on exterior, mottled red on palmette fronds; good on interior. Dilute wash on reserved surfaces. Vertical wall. Straight, black-glazed slightly

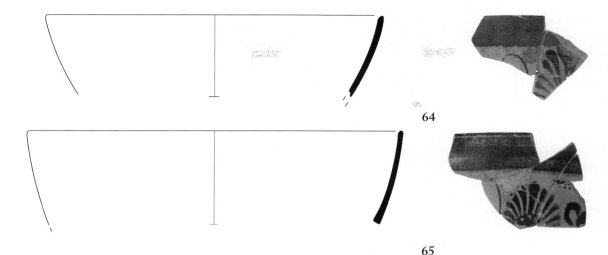

64

65

Figure 69. Cup-skyphoi 64, 65, Ure's Class K2. Scale 1:2. Profiles drawn A. Hooton; inked E. Schmitt

incurving rim. Reserved line at top of rim on interior. On wall: palmette with many fronds, of which the central is oversized; single tendril at left.

For shape and decorative scheme, see rim of *Agora* XXIII, p. 285, no. 1532, pl. 103. The rim is unusual for the skyphoi of this deposit and is not discussed by Hatzidakis 1984. This may be from the same object as **53**, a fragment of a skyphos wall that does not preserve the rim. Both have the same orange misfiring and similar clays. If it is the same, then the attribution should also be possibly the Manner of the Painter of Elaious I.

Ca. 490–480

65 (P 32789) Cup-skyphos, Ure's Class K2 with straight rim   Fig. 69

+49.76–49.14 m (Level 2)

Est. Diam. 26.0; max. p. dim. 7.3

Seven joining fragments of rim and wall, to right of handle (missing). Dull black glaze, worn on rim. Tall, straight wall. Straight black-glazed rim. Micaceous clay with one large milky quartz inclusion on surface.

On wall: multifrond palmette, single tendril curving up and left. To right, tail and rear end of a satyr facing right. Branch in field above. No incision. Reserved line on interior of lip. Added white (fugitive): dot in center of palmette.

Cf. *Agora* XXIII, p. 285, no. 1532, pl. 103 (Manner of the Haimon Painter), for palmette and profile. The palmette brings this fragment closer to the Haimon Painter himself. Two other inventoried fragments of skyphoi with straight rims from J 2:4 preserve similar palmettes, also in the Manner of the Haimon Painter: P 32793 *(agathe)*, from Levels 1b and 2; P 33183 *(agathe)*, from Level 2.

Manner of the Haimon Painter

Ca. 490–480

66 (P 32797) Cup-skyphos, Ure's Class K2 miscellaneous   Fig. 70

+49.76–49.14 m (Level 2)

P.H. (a) 4.9; est. Diam. 14.0; max. p. dim. (a) 5.4, (b) 4.3

Two nonjoining fragments of rim and wall. Dull, cloudy black glaze on exterior. Interior dull and fired mottled red. Dilute wash on reserved surface. Very light clay. Fragment (a): slightly convex wall; concave, black-glazed rim. Fragment (b): gently tapering lower wall.

Figural scene preserved on (a): warrior with helmet and shield, down on one knee, facing right, looking left. Holds one arm up, closed-fisted, but without a visible

fr. a

fr. b

Figure 70. Cup-skyphos 66, Ure's Class K2. Scale 1:2. Profile drawn A. Hooton; inked E. Schmitt

weapon. At left, shield and knee of second warrior. On (b), lower leg of another figure, facing left with foot resting on ground line of black-glazed band. Black-glazed zone at bottom of wall. Reserved line on interior of lip. Added white (fugitive): garment of warrior, helmet, shields. Added red (fugitive): dots on shields, dots on garments, cheek panel, and crest of helmet.

This skyphos is made from a different type of clay than the other Class K2 skyphoi from this deposit. It is a lighter-weight, thinner-walled version of the shape. The scene, too, is more ambitious and the incision better done, while still hasty. The details of the face under the helmet are neater than any other incision on the skyphoi in this deposit, so an attribution to the Haimon Group seems unlikely. The scene has parallels in P 1359 (Vanderpool 1946, p. 294, no. 83, pl. 46), on which a draped female figure (a goddess) takes on a fallen warrior, and *Agora* XXIII, p. 282, no. 1501, pl. 102, where a mounted rider meets a running warrior.

Ca. 500–480

67   (P 33184) Skyphos, uncertain form(?)   Fig. 71

+50.31–49.76 m (Level 1b)

Max. p. dim. 5.5

Two joining fragments of lower wall, broken all around. Surface chipped, fragments worn. Good black glaze. Thick wall, tapering and thickening toward bottom (above foot). Figural zone preserves feet of two(?) figures. No incision. Two wide black-glazed bands below. Added white on figure at left.

For shape, cf. P 20781 (*Agora* XXIII, p. 196, no. 1649, not pictured). The shape must have a narrower junction between body and foot than Class K2 skyphoi, but has the same decorative scheme.

Ca. 500–480

68   (P 33241) Skyphos, pinch-base?   Fig. 71

+46.00–45.90 and +45.60–45.45 m (Levels 5 and 6)

P.H. 4.8; max. p. dim. 5.01

Eight joining fragments of thin, convex wall. Very good black glaze and fine potting.

Preserves lower part of draped figure moving right. Leg and hand of second figure following at left. Trace of third figure to right. Black-glazed band below. Added red: folds of himation. Added white: large patch and dots on himation. Good drawing, but somewhat hasty incision.

Probably a pinch-base skyphos. The wall is convex in both directions, indicating a bulging vessel. For shape, see *Agora* XXIII, p. 61. Note that *Agora* XXIII, p. 61, n. 21, refers to Ure 1927, "Group R," but the pinch-base skyphoi from Rhitsona are later than 480 and not contemporary with the material from well J 2:4. The style of the Rhitsona pinch-base skyphoi is the typical late black-figured degenerate style. The type begins in the last quarter of the 6th century as a development of the black-figured band cup. See Hatzidakis 1984, p. 31, his "Class A." Hatzidakis (1984, p. 33) states that pinch-base skyphoi were mainly for export, which would explain the small number of them in Persian destruction deposits.

Ca. 500–480

67

68

69

fr. a   *fr. b*   *fr. c*

70

Figure 71. Skyphos 67, uncertain form(?); skyphoi 68, 69, pinch base?; skyphos 70. Scale 1:2.

69 (P 32798) Skyphos, pinch-base? Fig. 71

+49.76–49.14 m (Level 2)

Max. p. dim. 4.7

Fragment of wall, broken all around. Good black glaze, but prefiring dent in wall.

Slightly convex wall. Preserves draped male reclining on elbow on mattress with pillow. Branch with blob-fruit in field. Trace of dilute ground line below mattress. Added red (fugitive): stripes on garment, semicircles on mattress and pillow.

The ground line indicates that this is not a Class K2 skyphos, but the figure is too small to occupy a frieze on a Class C, D, or E skyphos. The wall has a strong vertical curve, which suggests a pinch-base skyphos, which can have ground lines. Cf. *Agora* XXIII, p. 282, no. 1502, pl. 102. The semicircles on the mattress are typical of the CHC Group; compare similar ones, but fugitive, on **28**. For pinch-base skyphoi, see discussion under **68**.

CHC Group

Ca. 500–480

SKYPHOS: OTHER

70 (P 32805) Skyphos Fig. 71

+49.76–49.14 m (Level 2)

Max. p. dim. (a) 2.8, (b) 2.2, (c) 2.4; est. Diam. 9.0

Three nonjoining fragments of rim and wall. Surfaces very worn, white-ground nearly gone on (b) and (c). Interior black glaze mottled red. Concave black-glazed rim. Reserved line on interior of rim. On bowl, white-ground with black-glazed verticals, probably lotus buds.

The Lindos Group decorates miniature skyphoi with white-ground, but fragments of **70** have a larger diameter than the Lindos Group skyphoi.

490–480

71 (P 32779) Cup-skyphos Fig. 72

+50.31–49.14 m (Levels 1b and 2)

P.H. 5.2; est. Diam. 19.0; max. p. dim. (a) 5.2, (b) 1.7

Two nonjoining fragments of rim and upper wall. Brown-black glaze, worn on the exterior of rim. Tall, straight wall. Thickened lip, inset below, offset on interior. Interior of rim reserved with frieze of dolphins balancing on noses. No incision.

Figure 72. Cup-skyphos 71. Scale 1:2. Profile drawn A. Hooton; inked E. Schmitt

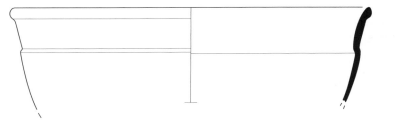

fr. b

fr. a

Added red (fugitive): nose, dorsal fin, and underbelly of dolphins; double line on inset on exterior of rim. Added white (fugitive): bodies or portions of bodies of dolphins.

Agora XXIII, pp. 263–264, no. 1353, compiles a list of examples of dolphins on rims, to which *CVA* Athens 4 [Greece 4], pl. 60 [60]:6, 7 (p. 65) adds more.

525–500

72   (P 33195) Protocorinthian kotyle   Fig. 73

+49.76–49.14 m (Level 2)

Max. p. dim. 1.4

Small fragment of rim. Light buff clay (Corinthian import). Surface abraded.

Rim slightly incurving at lip, with straight, sharp lip. Preserves three S-shaped vertical squiggles between two black-glazed horizontal lines. Interior black-glazed. Reserved: interior and exterior of lip, line below rim on interior.

For design and date, cf. *Agora* VIII, p. 50, no. 155, pl. 9.

8th–6th century

Figure 73. Protocorinthian kotyle 72.
Scale 2:1

Cup

[73]   (P 32785) Cup, Type A or Sub-A   Fig. 74

+45.45–45.20 m (Level 6)

Est. Diam. 25.0; max. p. dim. 3.3

Fragment of rim and wall. Good black glaze. Well potted.

Plain rim and convex wall. Top of lip glazed with dilute line below. Preserves head and arm of seated bearded male facing left, holding trumpet-shaped drinking horn. Branches with leaves and grape bunches in field. Reserved line on the interior of the rim. Added white (fugitive): mouth of drinking horn. Added red: beard, dot on garment.

For shape and decorative parallel, see *Agora* XXIII, p. 308, no. 1769, pl. 113 (side A), the Leafless Group, compared to the Caylus Painter, *ABV* 637, no. 62, and *Agora* XXIII, p. 307, no. 1761, the Leafless Group, *ABV* 716, no. 66 ter.

The incision on this fragment is better than average for the black-figure from this deposit. The figure is possibly a satyr or Dionysos reclining, as on *Agora* XXIII, no. 1769. If the latter, then the bump below the drinking horn would be his raised knee. It may be an eye-cup as *Agora* XXIII, p. 307, no. 1756, pl. 113. The specific cup shape cannot be determined without the joining stem and foot.

Probably associated with the Leafless Group

Early 5th century

Figure 74. Cup 73, Type A or Sub-A. Scale 1:2. Profile drawn A. Hooton; inked E. Schmitt

[74]   (P 32427) Cup, Type A or Sub-A   Fig. 75

+45.45–45.25 m (Level 6)

P.H. 3.0

Single fragment, broken all around. Good black glaze.

Part of interior floor and stem of a kylix. Conical stem with reserved fillet at junction with bowl on exterior. In tondo: a satyr moves right, preserved from shoulders to thighs with base of tail. Added red on tail.

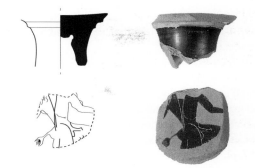

Figure 75. Cup 74, Type A or Sub-A. Scale 1:2. Profile and drawing author; inked E. Schmitt

Cf. *Agora* XXIII, p. 309, no. 1777, pl. 113. It is possible that this satyr tondo goes with one of the cup wall fragments, **73** or **75**. The satyr is similar to satyrs by the Caylus Painter, an identified hand within the Leafless Group, cf. Tübingen S/10 1486, *CVA* Tübingen 3 [Germany 47], pl. 32 [2277]:1; *ABV*, pp. 650–651.

Probably the Leafless Group
Early 5th century

[**75**]   (P 32786) Cup, Type A? Fig. 76

+45.45–45.20 m (Level 6)
Max. p. dim. 7.2

Fragment of wall, broken all around. Good black glaze. Well potted. Broad, shallow bowl of a cup.

Preserves half of circular black-glazed eye formed by three concentric, compass-drawn, incised lines within thick black-glazed eye-shaped outline with tear duct at lower right. To right, rear portion of chariot wheeling around and back legs of horses. Branch with leaves over top of chariot. Hasty incision for horse legs. Below, thin and thick dilute lines, black-glazed zone toward stem. Added white: iris of eye, patch on chariot or horse.

Probably the Leafless Group
Early 5th century

76   (P 33188) Cup, Type Sub-A? Fig. 76

+50.31–49.76 m (Level 1b)
P.H. 3.6; Diam. stem 3.0

Fragment of stem and interior floor of cup, broken all around. Roughly potted on stem. Dull black glaze, flaked and worn, fired red-brown in tondo. Concave stem rising to flat cone on underside. Underside reserved with trace of glaze indicating lower part of cone was glazed.

Indeterminate tondo figure, but incised lines preserved indicating a black-figured tondo; hasty incision.

Possibly a satyr in tondo. Lack of fillet on stem suggests a cup of Type Sub-A. Cf. *Agora* XXIII, p. 309, no. 1777, pl. 113.

Early 5th century

Figure 76. Cup 75, Type A?; cup 76, Type Sub-A? Scale 1:2

75   76

*77   (P 32781) Cup?   Fig. 77

   +49.76–49.14 and +46.00–45.90 m (Levels 2 and 5)
   Max. p. dim. 4.0
   Two joining fragments of wall. Good black glaze and good incision. Red wash
on reserved surface. Slightly convex wall. Preserves one leg and backside of nude
male. Hand (his?) at left holding spear angled downward.
      The wheel marks indicate that this is a fragment from a broad, open shape and
not a skyphos. Better-quality drawing and incision than on most of the other black-
figured skyphoi and cups. For the horizontal abdominal incisions, cf. *Agora* XXIII,
p. 297, no. 1657, pl. 107, a shallow cup-skyphos of special shape from the RRCS,
attributed to the Theseus Painter.
      525–500

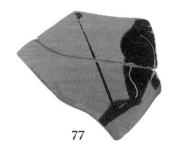

77

Plate?

78   (P 33208) Unidentified open shape   Fig. 77

   +46.00–45.90 m (Level 5)
   Max. p. dim. 2.4
   Fragment of floor, broken all around. Powdery Attic clay.
      Underside: reserved with a black-glazed circle and central dot. Black-glazed cir-
cle or band beyond. Interior: slightly convex and reserved with black-glazed radiating leaves and tongues.
      Cf. *Agora* XII, p. 311, no. 1081, pl. 37, a plate from the middle of the 5th cen-
tury. The catalogue entry to no. 1081 notes that the star motif is common as far back
as the 6th century, and a version of it can be seen on Kerameikos 74, Callipolitis-
Feytmans 1974, pp. 26–29, no. AI:1, pl. 1.
      Context: 525–480

78

**Figure 77. Cup? 77; unidentified
open shape (plate?) 78.** Scale 1:1

Lid

*79   (P 32425) Lekanis lid   Fig. 78

   Ca. +46.60 m; +49.14–48.73 (Levels 2 and 5)
   Est. Diam. 31.0; max. p. dim. (a) 15.5, (b) 6.57, (c) 3.97
   Three nonjoining fragments. Glaze fired mottled red on the underside. Large
white (lime) inclusion on underside of (a). Flat top rising to convex center. Downturned, projecting flat rim.
      On exterior of rim, band of reflected ivy leaves with dilute line between. Two
black-glazed lines form ground line for figural zone on top. On (a), two figures on
either side of a large skyphoid krater resting on ground. At left, a bearded, wreathed
nude male facing right, holding in left hand a long curving object flaring at the end
near his hand. Right hand extends behind body, missing. At right, a nude, beardless
youth facing left, holding an oinochoe over krater. Behind youth, a knobby pole. Above
decorated zone: rays extending from handle, and two black-glazed lines. On (b),
hand and heel of figure facing left, in same pose as youth on (a), foot of second figure facing right. On (c), trace of a figure to left (probably heel). Underside: resting
surface and center reserved, one dilute black-glazed circle at center preserved.
Added white: curving object held by left man. Added red: wreaths with berries
on figures, beard of man on left; on underside: broad line near rim, thin line at
junction of rim and top, broad line at center of black-glazed zone, line at edge of
reserved center.
      For the shape, cf. *Agora* XII, p. 323, no. 1234, pl. 41, fig. 11 (ca. 480). The style
is very similar to *Agora* XXIII, p. 267, no. 1386, pl. 95 (unattributed, last quarter

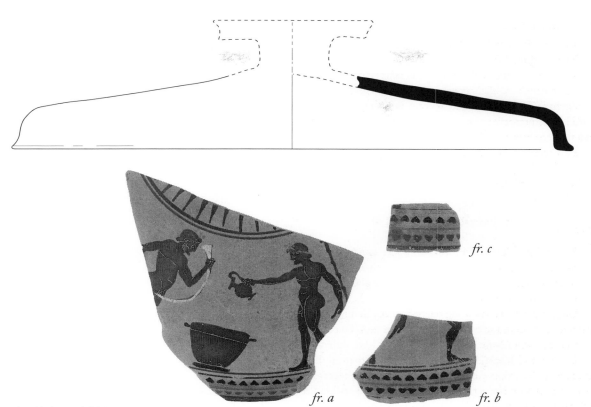

Figure 78. Lekanis lid 79. Scale 1:2.
Profile drawn author; inked E. Schmitt

6th century). *Agora* XXIII, p. 264, no. 1354, p. 93 (unattributed, last quarter of the 6th century) also has the double ivy motif on the rim.

The white object held by the man may be an "elephant," a drinking horn described in Athenaios (11.468f, 497a–b; discussed in Davidson 1997, pp. 64–65).

Attribution: The fat bellies and horizontal incisions on the abdomens of **79** resemble the human komasts on fragment D of a lid from Xanthos, attributed to the Leagros Group (Metzger 1972, pp. 122–124, no. 242 [A15–1113 + A15–1177], pl. 55 = Lioutas 1987, p. 66, no. D85, *ABV* 695, no. 242 bis, *Paralipomena* 163, no. 242 ter). The reflected ivy rim pattern occurs on another lid fragment from Xanthos attributed to the Leagros Group, as well as on an unattributed Agora fragment (both with chariot scenes): Xanthos: Metzger 1972, p. 124, no. 243 (A15–1223), pl. 58 = Lioutas 1987, p. 66, no. D84, *ABV* 695, no. 81 bis, *Paralipomena* 162, no. 294 bis. Agora: *Agora* XXIII, p. 264, no. 1354, pl. 93 (unattributed), from deposit E 15:6, well deposit of Persian destruction fill. These four lid fragments with double ivy rim pattern also share the details of a single horizontal line dividing the ivy, black glaze on the lip, the double line above and below the scene, and rays between the stem and the frieze. These four lids and **79** must come from the same workshop. Two other Xanthos lid fragments have lotus buds and a meander on the rims, but share all other subsidiary details with double ivy lids: Metzger 1972, pp. 124–125, no. 244 (A15–1118), pl. 58 (Edinburgh Painter) = Lioutas 1987, p. 67, no. D86; Metzger 1972, p. 125, no. 245 (A34–2627), pl. 59 (unattributed) = Lioutas 1987, p. 65, no. D68). See discussion in Lioutas 1987 for development of form and workshops.

Probably the Leagros Group
Ca. 525–500

80   (P 33212) Lid   Fig. 79

+50.31–49.76 m (Level 1b)

Max. p. dim. 3.82

Fragment, broken all around, from near center of convex lid. Black glaze fired red and mottled.

At base of handle, band of rays between two black-glazed lines. Below, figured zone preserves branch with leaves and uncertain portions of two figures. Underside reserved.

Last quarter 6th century

Miscellaneous Forms

[81]   (P 32428) Thymiaterion   Fig. 80

+45.23 m (last object removed) (Level 6)

P.H. 4.6; Diam. shaft 3.3

Single fragment of stem. Broken above and below; nearly solid with narrow central void. Trace of flaring bowl or decorative element at top of fragment with groove at junction. Upper portion of exterior glazed down to top of stem. Drips of glaze on interior of stem.

Six draped women wearing fillets standing in three pairs facing each other, each with one hand raised in front. In all but one case the raised hand is covered by the garment, the other bent at the side. Women have individualized garments, some with chiton and himation, others with just himation. Decorative patterns vary but include red stripes, incised crosses, and white rosettes. Added white: skin of women, dots and decorative details on garments. Added red: folds of garments, fillets, pupils of eyes where preserved. Tidy, miniature work.

For thymiateria from Athens, see *Agora* XII, pp. 182, 331, nos. 1344–1355, pl. 44; *Agora* XXIII, pp. 69–70, 317, nos. 1851–1853, pl. 119; from Eleusis, Kournouniotes 1936.

For decorative scheme, cf. *Agora* XXIII, p. 317, nos. 1851, 1852, 1853, pl. 119; no. 1851 comes closest to the decorative scheme of **81**. None of these is as well painted or incised as **81**.

Ca. 525

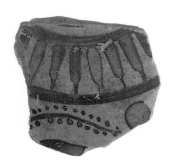

Figure 79. Lid 80. Scale 1:1

Figure 80. Thymiaterion 81. Scale 1:1.
Profile drawn A. Hooton; inked E. Schmitt

Miscellaneous Decorated

*82   (P 33225) Miniature hydria   Fig. 81

+45.90–45.60 m (Level 6)

P.H. 4.35; Diam. 4.01

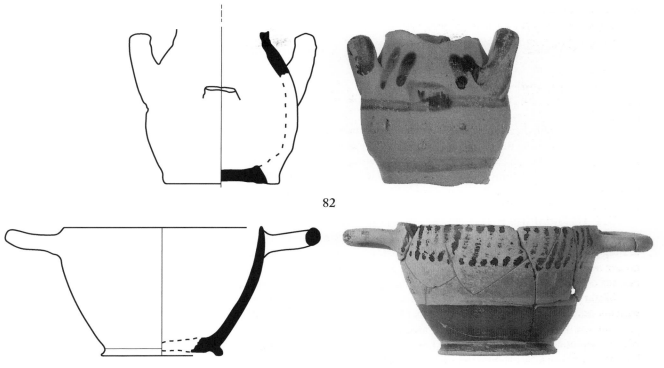

82

Figure 81. Miniature hydria 82; miniature Corinthian kotyle 83. Scale 1:1. Profiles drawn author; inked E. Schmitt

83

Missing neck, rim, and vertical handle. Thin black glaze fired brown. Buff clay with large white (lime) inclusions, many burnt out or puckering. Wheelmade, but finger prints on surface.

Disk foot with string marks, spherical body. Two high loop handles at shoulder. Vertical handle attaches at midpoint of body. Broad neck. Vertical lines on shoulder. Horizontal line below handles and at bottom of wall. Exterior of handles glazed.

Votive. Similar to examples from Pyre B at Eleusis, Kokkou-Vyride 1999, p. 228, nos. B88–B91. Decorative scheme similar to miniatures by the Swan Group, see *Agora* XII, pp. 186, 334–335, nos. 1404–1416, pl. 45.

525–500

*83   (P 32343) Miniature Corinthian kotyle   Fig. 81

+49.76–49.14 m (Level 2)

H. 3.5; Diam. 5.4

Nearly complete; mended from several pieces. Floor of vessel missing. Glaze flaking. Fine, light buff clay. Nicely wheelmade. Corinthian clay, very pale brown (10YR 8/3).

False ring foot imitating flaring ring foot of full-scale Corinthian shape. Tall body with straight rim. Two horizontal handles attached slightly below rim. Brownish-black glaze on interior. Exterior reserved, divided into three bands: lower third with brownish black; central third with a reddish band between thin red lines; top third with vertical black lines, slightly off axis. False ring portion of foot with brownish-black glaze and line of same on exterior face. Outer half of handles glazed.

For shape and a similar decorative pattern, cf. *Corinth* XV.3, p. 310, nos. 1684–1686. Dates are not firmly asserted by Stillwell. Similar from Eleusis, Kokkou-Vyride 1999, p. 229, B99. Miniature version of the Linear Style. Votive.

Late 6th to early 5th century

RED FIGURE

Pelike

*84   (P 32418) Pelike   Color Ill. 13; Fig. 82

> +46.60–45.90 m (Level 5)
>
> H. 27.4–27.7; Diam. rim 11.6, foot 12.8, body 19.4
>
> Camp 1996, p. 248, no. 27, pl. 73; Neer 2002, p. 203, n. 101; Lynch 2009b, p. 75, fig. 73.

Complete profile. Several fragments missing from rim, body, handles, and foot; mended. Short prefiring scrape and gouge on surface of side B to right of figure. Black glaze cracked in places and worn especially on rim, cloudy spot on side B. Spreading ring foot with torus vertical face. Ovoid body. Continuous curve to neck. Torus rim. Vertical strap handles, oval in section attached from neck to shoulder. Reserved: underside and exterior face of foot; interior below neck.

Side A: Bearded male facing right on a reserved ground stripe. Holds a seven-stringed barbitos beneath his left arm and strums strings with left hand, holds pick in right hand. Basket hangs from lower arm of instrument. Figure is nude except for a mantle draped across upper arms and back, and low soft boots. Large frontal eye. Incised hairline. Added red: pick string, tuning knobs, string tying basket to instrument, wreath with four sets of paired leaves at front. Sketchy preliminary drawing throughout figure and drapery. Relief line throughout, including outline of beard and barbitos strings. Black glaze used only for beard and eyeball.

Inscription in added red (fugitive): (horizontally in field above barbitos) IKI[.

Side B: Youth facing right standing on reserved ground stripe. Leans on a staff under his left armpit and induces vomiting with his right forefinger. Left hand holds his head. Nude except for a mantle draped over shoulder and arm and low soft boots. Frontal eye. Incised hairline. Added red: stream of vomit from mouth to slightly above ground line, fugitive in places; wreath with four sets of paired leaves at front. Sketchy preliminary drawing throughout. Relief line throughout. Black glaze used for eyeball and curls at hairline. Inscription in added red (fugitive): (vertically below elbow) EIOI. Widely spaced double line in added red below ground stripes.

For shape, cf. *Agora* XII, p. 237, nos. 16–19, pl. 1.

Similar scene of walking barbitos player: pelike attributed to Myson, *ARV*² 238, no. 6, Panvini and Giudice 2003, p. 307, fig. G28, although the musician is a youth. For vomiting figures, see Cohen and Shapiro 2002, with references. A kantharos by Douris depicts very similar contrasting sides, Athens, National Archaeological Museum (ex Serpieri), *ARV*² 445, no. 255, Buitron-Oliver 1995, p. 72, no. 7, pl. 4. On side A of the kantharos, an adult male plays the barbitos on his way to the symposium, and on side B, a youth stands in a very similar pose to **84**, but instead of leaning on his stick and vomiting, he leans on his stick and looks deep into the cup he holds. Note also that the adult male wears the same low booties as the figures in **84**. Also, on Boston, MFA, 26.61, *ARV*² 383, no. 199, *Paralipomena* 366, *Add*² 228 [Brygos Painter], an amphora, both sides feature youths, on side A playing the kithara, on side B holding his head as if to vomit (it is unclear from available images if added red vomit is present). Images of MFA 26.61 available online, Beazley Archive Database, vase no. 204098.

Attribution: attributed to the Nikoxenos Painter in Camp 1996, whom Beazley (1912–1913, pp. 243–245) characterizes as easy to distinguish. The Nikoxenos Painter's figures are generally fussy–looking, with pinched faces and very orderly drapery, the folds of which are drawn between two lines. The ears of the Nikoxenos Painter's figures are schematic and circular. The eyes are large, but almond shaped, unlike the large rounded eyes of **84**. The prominent nostril and often turned-down mouth are very distinguishing characteristics of the Nikoxenos Painter, and neither is present on **84**. Finally, there are only two pelikai attributed by Beazley to the

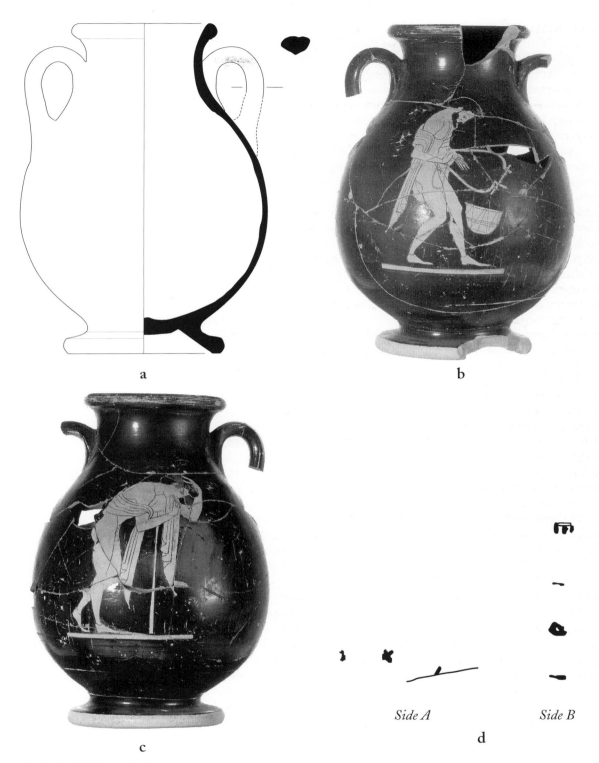

a

b

c

Side A   Side B

d

**Figure 82. Pelike 84: (a) profile draw-
ing; (b) side A, bearded male with
barbitos; (c) side B, youth inducing
vomiting; (d) facsimile of inscriptions.** Scale 1:3 (a–c); 1:1 (d). Profile,
facsimile drawn author; inked E. Schmitt

Nikoxenos Painter (Louvre C 10782, *ARV²* 221, no. 11, Beazley Archive Vase Number 202058, with image; Amsterdam Allard Pierson Museum 1313, *ARV²* 221, no. 12, *CVA* The Hague 1 [Netherlands 1] pl. 3 [33]:3, 4), and these use a framed figural scene, not the silhouetted figure on a ground line as on **84**.

The style does not fit the style of the Nikoxenos Painter's student, the Eucharides Painter, either (Beazley 1911–1912; Langridge 1993, pp. 65–81). The Eucharides Painter did paint numerous vases with single figures on a ground line against a black background, including a pelike of very similar shape in Münster (Münster University 66, Stähler 1967, passim, pls. 1–3, 4:a, and 10:a; Langridge 1993, pl. 46). On another pelike by the Eucharides Painter the ground line does not encircle the vase, but is abbreviated as a floating reserved strip as on **84** (Richmond 62.1.13, *ARV²* 220, no. 10 bis and p. 1637, *Paralipomena* 347, *Add²* 199, Reed and Near 1973, p. 91, no. 107, pl. 107:a, b; Langridge 1993, pl. 47). The Münster pelike features a double-figure composition on each side, but the figures stand on a plain, reserved ground line that seems to go around the entire vase, which Langridge (1993, pp. 85, 292–293) tentatively links to the influence of the Berlin Painter. The pose of the youth on side B of **84** with his far, left leg relaxed and balanced on the ball of the foot behind the weight-bearing foot, is repeated several times in the work of the Eucharides Painter (cf. youth on side A of the Münster pelike; lekythos by the Eucharides Painter in the collection of Christos Bastis, Buitron-Oliver 1987, p. 283, no. 165, pl. 165). However, the Eucharides Painter has a completely different approach to drapery hems, which Langridge describes as ending in a shape like "the bottom of a golf club" (Langridge 1993, p. 25), in a far more fluid line than on **84**. Finally, the Eucharides Painter always uses a relief hair contour as opposed to an incised contour as is found on **84** (Langridge 1993, p. 22).

The late Pioneer Pezzino Group seems a more likely attribution. Some of their ears come close to the weak crescent with central line of the youth's on **84** (see, e.g., the komasts on the calyx krater from Agrigento, *ARV²* 32, no. 2, Arias 1969, passim, pl. 60; wrestlers on a psykter in a Swiss private collection, *Add²* 157, no. 32 bis, von Bothmer 1986, p. 11, fig. 6:a–e). Eyes are large with a round pupil, but in some instances the pupil lolls forward, or the eye narrows. Drapery has a bumpy profile where it is silhouetted against the black background along the figures' backs (e.g., Munich 2420, *ARV²* 32, no. 3, *Add²* 157, Arias 1969, p. 204, pl. 64:2). The feet and hands on the Pezzino Group's figures are long like those of **84** and the Pezzino Group customarily incises its hairlines as on **84**. The vases in the Pezzino Group all have inscriptions, and at least two (Getty 75.AE.83, unpublished, and calyx krater in Agrigento, *ARV²* 32, no. 2, Arias 1969, pp. 205–207, e.g., pl. 60) have inscriptions that repeat combinations of the letters ΕΙΟΠΚ and Γ.

More can be said about the potter of this vessel in relation to the painter attribution. The study of pelikai by Regina-Maria Becker described a distinct group of pelike forms associated with the Nikoxenos Painter and the Eucharides Painter (1977, pp. 11–14). The characteristics of the shape include a wide disk foot, sometimes offset from the bulging body by a fillet or groove, and a flaring, torus lip. The shape is very full-bodied. Bloesch (1951, p. 38), whose techniques Becker utilizes, associated the Nikoxenos Painter with the Club-Foot Potter. Becker and Langridge focus on a second, un-named potter used by the same painters. Becker attributes a group of mainly black-figured pelikai associated with the workshop of the Nikoxenos Painter to the second potter, but includes the unattributed red-figured pelike, Louvre Cp 10785, which has a profile very similar to that of **84** (1977, p. 12, fig. 4b). Langridge adds several red-figured pelikai by the Eucharides Painter to Becker's list, confirming that both painters used the same potter (Langridge 1993, pp. 132–135). **84** is significantly smaller than its closest parallels

Figure 83. Closed vessel (pelike?) 85; closed shape (chous?) 86. Scale 1:2

85   86

in Becker's and Langridge's groups. For example, the measurements of Louvre Cp 10785 are: H. 32.0, Diam. rim 15.3, Diam. foot 18.8, max. Diam. 25.4. Becker does include several smaller pelikai with a H. ca. 27.0 or less in her Nikoxenos-type group (1977, nos. 38, 39, 40, 41, 42). Of these, Becker 1977, p. 15, no. 42, Athens, National Archaeological Museum 1425, *ARV*² 223, no. 6, *Paralipomena* 346 [Nikoxenos Painter], illustrated as Langridge 1993, fig. 28, has a foot similar to that of **84**, but the body of **84** is not baggy, and the rim of **84** is thicker and more of a torus. Thus, **84** is closest to the larger versions of the form by a potter serving both the Eucharides Painter and the Nikoxenos Painter and producing pelikai for decoration in both black figure and red figure.

Nikoxenos Painter (D. von Bothmer in Camp 1996)
Pezzino Group (Lynch 1999)
510–500

85   (P 32772) Closed vessel (pelike?)   Fig. 83
+49.76–49.14 m (Level 2)
Max. p. dim. 6.0
Fragment of wall, broken all around. Thick wall. Good black glaze. Interior reserved with light buff wash. Dilute red wash on exterior reserved surfaces.

Preserves reserved ground line and feet of two figures. Large foot of one figure facing right. Two feet facing left: one foot behind foot of figure to right, and toes of another foot stepping with heel off the ground. Black-glazed zone below ground line. Preliminary drawing on feet at left of sherd. Relief line: outline, toes. Added red: thin double line at top of black-glazed zone at bottom of wall.

Probably a pelike like **84**.
Ca. 500

CLOSED: SHAPE UNCERTAIN

86   (P 32771) Closed shape (chous?)   Fig. 83
+49.14–48.73 m (Level 2)
Max. p. dim. 3.8
Fragment from shoulder, broken all around. Good black glaze and careful drawing. Interior reserved.

Preserves single palmette from shoulder frieze. Right facing, sideways palmette with seven fronds (six preserved), each divided by a single line. Two symmetrical volutes and encircling tendril with side curls sprouting from center. Two arcs and central dot for heart. Above, two reserved lines, upper with added red line overlaid. Relief line: outline of palmette except interior of curls; details of palmette except central dot; lower edge of each reserved line.

Similar to palmettes by the Berlin Painter, Cardon 1977, pp. 57–58 and passim. In particular, the neck ornament on the fragmentary volute krater Leipzig T762, *ARV*² 206, no. 128, drawn as Cardon 1977, fig. 7a. The form is probably a Shape 3 oinochoe (chous).
500–480

Figure 84. Cup 87, Type B or C.
Scale 1:3. Profile drawn author; inked
E. Schmitt

CUP

*87   (P 32344) Type B or C cup   Color Ill. 10; Fig. 84

+49.76–49.14 m (Level 2)

P.H. 3.0; est. Diam. rim 19.15, foot 8.0

Camp 1996, p. 251, no. 36, pl. 76; Neer 2002, p. 202, n. 79; Cohen 2006, pp. 49, 62–63, no. 10, fig. 10:1–3; Böhr 2009, p. 121, n. 97.

Mended from 19 fragments. About half of bowl, one handle, and half of foot (as one nonjoining fragment) preserved. Fine black glaze on interior of lip and narrow band at top of lip on exterior, exterior of handle, tondo, and single line on upper surface of chamfer on foot and single line on underside of foot. Intentional red glaze on exterior below lip, interior between lip and tondo, and both upper- and underside of foot. Intentional red flaking throughout. Shallow bowl. Straight rim, carefully offset on interior. Horizontal horseshoe handle.

Tondo: Lower part of tondo preserved with draped male figure seated right on a diphros, of which only one leg is shown. Rests left hand (missing) on a knobby staff. Sponge and aryballos (edge just visible at break) hang suspended from the (missing) wrist. Feet face right; right foot is balanced on the ball of the foot. Drapery tail with dress weight appears to left of stool; another hangs down to right of stool leg. Preliminary drawing on knee and drapery. Relief line of various weights throughout including major drapery folds, ankle, and toes of right foot. Black glaze for dots on sponge. Dilute glaze for big toe of left foot. Very dilute glaze for minor drapery folds and left shin. Ancient repairs: two pairs and one single drilled holes for clamps, traces of which survive; lead strips cover mended breaks between offset rim and tondo on interior and between clamps on the exterior (the lead strip on the interior does not intrude on the red-figured tondo). No inscription preserved.

The shape is more likely Type B, favored for figured wares; this cup would presumably be among the earliest examples of the shape: see Shear 1993, p. 414 and n. 86.

Probably the potter Kachrylion, with whom Euphronios collaborated extensively. Profile close to Thasos 80.51.21, et al., Maffre 1988, signed by Kachrylion and attributed to Euphronios. The five known cups attributed to Euphronios can be associated with Kachrylion, two of which have intentional red: Munich 2620, *ARV*² 16, no. 17: signed by both Euphronios as painter and Kachrylion as potter; St. Petersburg, Ol. 18181, *ARV*² 17, no. 20: attributed to Euphronios, and attributed to the potter Kachrylion by Cohen 1970–1971, p. 5. Many of the Late Archaic intentional red pieces were produced in association with Kachrylion; see Cohen 1970–1971, pp. 4–5; 2006, pp. 48–50. For further discussion of potting links

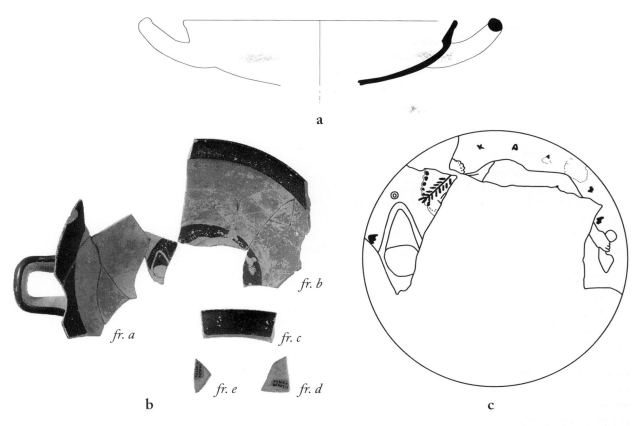

a

b

c

**Figure 85. Cup 88, Type B or C:
(a) profile drawing; (b) fragments,
including tondo with long jumper;
(c) facsimile of inscription.**
Scale 1:3 (a, b); 3:4 (c). Tondo, facsimile
drawn author; inked E. Schmitt

between **87, 88,** and Kachrylion, see discussion in Chapter 4. For the technique of
coral-red, see Maish et al. 2006, pp. 8–11; Maish 2008; Walton et al. 2008.

Attribution: compare the legs and stool of youths seated on side B of the red-
figured krater signed by Euphronios in the Louvre, G 103, *CVA* Paris, Louvre 1
[France 1], pl. 4 [42]:3, 4.

Euphronios (C. Pfaff in Camp 1996; confirmed by D. von Bothmer)
Hegesiboulos Painter (Neer 2002, p. 202, n. 79)
Ca. 515

*88   (P 33221) Type B or C cup   Fig. 85
+49.76–49.14 m (Level 2)
P.H. (a + b) 5.8; est. Diam. (a + b) 21.9; max. p. dim. (c) 5.5, (d) 3.0, (e) 2.8
Cohen 2006, pp. 46, 62.

Mended into two large fragments with three nonjoining fragments. About
one-third of bowl preserved, but only outer edge of tondo. One handle preserved.
Glaze cracked, dull on exterior, flaking in tondo. Intentional red flaking and
scratched. Powdery Attic clay.

Somewhat shallow bowl. Rim concave on exterior, offset on interior. Canted
horseshoe handle. Interior and exterior of rim, exterior of handles, tondo black-
glazed. Intentional red on interior between rim and tondo and on exterior below
rim. Reserved: interior of handle and handle panel, possibly with miltos on surface.
Tondo: Exterior edge of tondo preserved showing long jumper bending forward
to left. Back and top of head, shoulder, and raised arm holding a single halter. A
trace of black glaze can be seen at the crook of the elbow. A discus in a bag hangs
in field to left of head. Incised hairline. Added red (fugitive): wreath with close set
paired leaves, inscription. Relief line throughout. Dilute glaze on shoulder, neck,

and arm. Black-glazed dots for curls at hairline. Ancient repairs: one drilled hole near missing handle and edge of a nonpaired second hole approximately underneath unpreserved handle. Inscription to left of head:]AO[; to right of head: ΚΑΛΟΣ.

For shape and decorative scheme, cf. P 2698, Vanderpool 1946, pp. 285–287, no. 52, pl. 35. For discussion of depictions of long jumping, see Chapter 4.

510–500

Cup: Type C

*89   (P 32420) Type C cup   Color Ills. 1, 3; Fig. 86

+46.00–45.60 m (Level 5)

H. 7.1; Diam. 19.2; W. with handles 25.6

Camp 1996, p. 248, no. 28, fig. 8, pls. 71:b, 74; Immerwahr 1998, p. 165, no. 673; Lynch 2009b, p. 75, fig. 74.

Complete except for chips, fragments missing from rim and bowl. Mended from many fragments. Fragments tinged gray at edges. Good black glaze. Miltos on interior of handles. Very well potted.

Torus disk foot, with concave groove at upper edge, rising to flat-topped cone on underside. Thick stem with rounded fillet at juncture of foot and stem, between two scraped grooves. Somewhat shallow bowl, straight rim. Canted horseshoe handles.

Tondo: Long-haired, bearded male figure moves right, holding Corinthian-type skyphos in outstretched right hand. Crouches slightly, with legs in profile and shoulders in three-quarters view. Nude except for a mantle draped over left shoulder. Almond-shaped, frontal eye with iris drawn around a dot for the pupil. Reserved hairline. Added red: wreath with parallel dot-leaves, inscription. Preliminary drawing visible on mantle, very precisely drawn. Relief line throughout except under soles of feet, but including major anatomy, mantle, skyphos, beard strands, hair curls, and eyeball. Black glaze for hair and left ankle bone. Dilute glaze for ribs and musculature. No preliminary drawing is visible for the figure, but it is possible that the relief line outline follows a steady preliminary drawing very closely and thus obscures it. Inscription clockwise from front of head: ΗΟΠΑΙΣ:ΚΑΛΟΣ. Punctuation not noted in Camp 1996, p. 248, no. 28.

Tondo off perpendicular to handles by about 25°.

For shape, cf. *Agora* XII, p. 264, no. 420, pl. 20, fig. 4; *FAS*, p. 123, no. 36, pl. 33:6a, b. Very close to **90**, from same workshop.

Attribution: Skythes's attempts at anatomy never approach the confidence of the drawing on **89**. The abdominal muscles on Louvre F 129 (*ARV*² 52, 84, no. 20; *CVA* Louvre 10 [France 17], pls. 14 [768]:6, 8, and 15 [769]:2, 5–7) and Louvre G 12 (*ARV*² 84, no. 17; *CVA* Louvre 10 [France 17], pls. 14 [768]:4, 5, 7 and 15 [769]:1, 3, 4), both attributed to Skythes, are stylized, resembling a tortoiseshell with irregular quadrate segments. The epigastric arch and the lateral abdominal muscles are reduced to a single arching line from hip to shoulder blade. On other cups he indicates ribs with a varying number of short parallel lines, e.g., Louvre G 10, *ARV*² 83, no. 3; *CVA* Louvre 10 [France 17], pl. 13 [767]:2, where the painter depicts Hermes in a profile pose with four strokes along the rib cage, the top two shorter strokes may be muscles or more ribs; Louvre S 1335, *ARV*² 83, no. 4; *CVA* Louvre 10 [France 17], pl. 13 [767]:3, where a komast with lyre and drinking cup in an attempted contrapposto profile view has four rib lines but at a very curious angle. The painter of **89** must have learned from Skythes, because some stylistic traits are shared by both. The tondo figure of Louvre F 129, attributed to Skythes, wears a garment draped over his leg with the same whorl pattern as that of the himation over **89**'s left shoulder, but **89**'s angular folds are slightly less natural. Details such as the paired parens on the upper thigh of **89** occur on Skythes's figures,

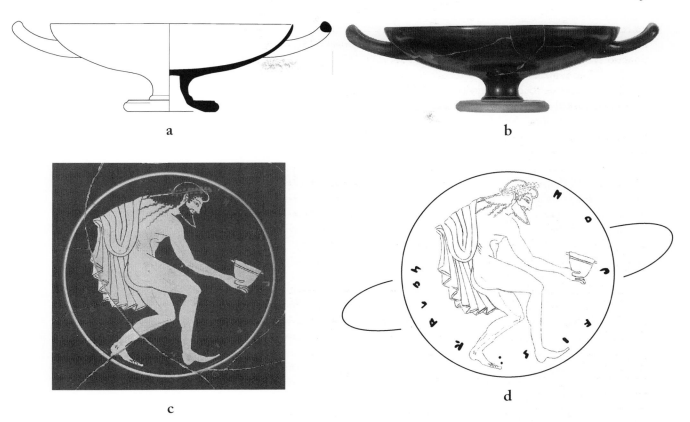

a b

c d

Figure 86. Cup 89, Type C: (a) profile drawing; (b) mended cup; (c) tondo, komast with skyphos; (d) facsimile of inscription. Scale 1:3 (a, b); 3:4 (c, d). Profile drawn A. Hooton; inked author; facsimile drawn author and B. Peruzzi; inked E. Schmitt and B. Peruzzi

e.g., Louvre G 12; Louvre G 10; Louvre S 1335; Louvre CA 2997, *ARV*² 83, no. 9. The pair of komasts from the exterior of Louvre G 12 have the same double shin line as **89** ending in an ankle formed by two short parallel strokes resembling quotation marks. Skythes also prefers more specific *kalos* inscriptions than the general inscription on **89**.

The closest parallel for **89** is found on a cup attributed to the Ambrosios Painter in the Archaeological Museum in Florence (Arch. Mus. 73127, *ARV*² 173, no. 4, *CVA* Florence 3 [Italy 30], pl. 75 [1339]). An archer strings a bow in the tondo, and his body twists in a similar manner to that of the komast on **89**. The profiles of both heads bear a straight hairline-to-nose forehead profile line ending in a rounded tip of the nose, and individual coils of curls fall over the shoulders and back, cf. Berlin, Staatliche Museen 1757 [number given as 2273 in *ARV*²], *ARV*² 174, no. 31, *Add*² 184, Gantz 1971, p. 17, pl. 11:b; on a woman: Munich, Private Collection, Immerwahr 1984a, p. 10, pl. 3:2. There is a small rounded concavity for a nostril, and the mouths are short strokes. The necks are not long, but are silhouetted against the black glaze. The archer also has the Ambrosios Painter's distinctive pupil-within-an-eyeball frontal eye and arched brow. Not all of the Ambrosios Painter's figures have a distinct eyeball, but many do: Getty Museum, no inv. no. (anonymous loan), Frel 1979, n.p., no. 14; Getty S.82.AE.19, *Paralipomena* 338, no. 33 bis, *Add*² 184, *Greek Vases*, p. 42, no. 28; Rome, Villa Giulia, 50458, *ARV*² 173, no. 5, *Add*² 184, Mingazzini 1971, pp. 18–21, no. 640, pls. 107–109; Rome, Villa Giulia, 50535, *ARV*² 174, no. 15, *Add*² 184, Mingazzini 1971, pp. 23–25, no. 642, pls. 110, 111. In sum, the musculature of Skythes strikes one as exaggerated or cartoonish, and the Ambrosios Painter achieves a more sensitive handling of anatomy on this cup with the use of three different dilutions of glaze to indicate anatomical detail; cf. Villa Giulia, 50535, *ARV*² 174, no. 15, *Add*² 184, Mingazzini 1971, pp. 23–25, no. 642, pls. 110, 111, but also Rome, Villa Giulia, 50458, *ARV*² 173, no. 5, *Add²* 184, Mingazzini 1971, pp. 18–21, no. 640, pls. 107–109, which is a tour de force of torsion; Munich 2614, *ARV²* 173, no. 2, *Paralipomena* 338, *Add²* 184, Shapiro 1982, p. 69, pl. 25:a; Athens, Acropolis 56, *ARV²* 174, no. 27, Graef and Langlotz II, p. 5, pl. 3, no. 56.

The drapery on **89** defies gravity and the physics of motion. An accordion, zigzag hem (usually with a double line) and a whorl pattern for the folded garment form the hallmark of the Ambrosios Painter's drapery on the gods on the exterior of the Ambrosios Painter's Florence cup, and other examples: Würzburg L 474, *ARV²* 173, no. 10, Shapiro 1982, p. 69, pl. 25:d; Oxford 1917.55, *ARV²* 174, no. 21, *Add²* 184, *CVA* Oxford 1 [Great Britain 3], pl. 1 [93]:3; Orvieto, Faina 62, *ARV²* 174, no. 17, Philippart 1932, pp. 104–105, pl. 11:1; Berlin, Staatliche Museen 1757 [number given as 2273 in *ARV²*], *ARV²* 174, no. 31, *Add²* 184, Gantz 1971, pl. 11:b; Villa Giulia, 50535, *ARV²* 174, no. 15, *Add²* 184, Mingazzini 1971, pp. 23–25, no. 642, pls. 110, 111, but can also be seen on: Rome, Villa Giulia, 50458, *ARV²* 173, no. 5, *Add²* 184, Mingazzini 1971, pp. 18–21, no. 640, pls. 107–109; Adria B 99, *ARV²* 174, no. 26, *CVA,* Adria 1 [Italy 28] pl. 2 [1250]:1; London E 42, *ARV²* 174, no. 20, Beazley 1918, p. 20, no. 18, fig. 12. The peculiar fall of the garment over a single shoulder is also found in the tondo of a cup with a youth putting on his sandals, Munich, Private Collection, Immerwahr 1984a, p. 10, pl. 2:2. The system is repeated on at least two komasts on a cup by the Ambrosios Painter in Oxford (Oxford, 1911.616, *ARV²* 173, no. 1, *Add²* 184, Shapiro 1982, p. 70, pl. 26:a, b). In contrast, the folds on a cup by Skythes in Athens respond to the effects of gravity, and there is a greater sense of three-dimensionality to the folds, cf. Athens, National Archaeological Museum 16269, *ARV²* 83, no. 13, von Bothmer 1986, p. 15, fig. 14.

Beazley said of the Ambrosios Painter that "nobody could complain if the word bad were applied to [him]" (1918, p. 19), and Henry Immerwahr concurred, saying, "[he] leaves something to be desired as an artist" (1984a, p. 12), but these may be unfair judgments of an ambitious painter of middling talent. His subject matter varies quite a bit, and his interest in the human form enlivens the scenes. In fact, Beazley did concede that "[i]f bad, he is never dull, for he fancies curious subjects, he is prodigal of inscriptions, and he puts his little people into funny poses," which, he continues, "show a real desire to figure fresh aspects of life and movement" (1918, pp. 20, 21).

Close to Skythes (D. von Bothmer in Camp 1996)
Ambrosios Painter (Lynch 1999)
500–480

*90   (P 32417) Type C cup   Color Ills. 1, 4; Fig. 87
+46.00–45.90 m (Level 5)
H. 7.0; Diam. 19.2; W. with handles 25.5
Camp 1996, p. 248, no. 29, fig. 8, pls. 71:b, 74; Lynch 2009b, p. 75, fig. 73.

Complete except for small chips, fragments missing from rim and bowl, right leg of figure missing. Mended from several fragments. Clay tinged gray along breaks. Good black glaze. Miltos on interior of handles. Two vertical black-glazed dots in left handle panel. Well potted.

Torus disk foot with groove at upper edge of exterior face, rising to flat-topped cone on underside. Thick stem with rounded fillet at juncture with foot between two scraped grooves. Somewhat shallow bowl. Straight rim. Canted horseshoe handles.

Tondo: Youth moves rapidly to right, holding in each outstretched hand a long strip of meat. Wears a *zoma* knotted around waist. Legs seen in profile, abdomen in three-quarters view, and chest frontal. Head profile, facing left. Added red: wreath with a few sets of paired, heart-shaped leaves at the front of the head,

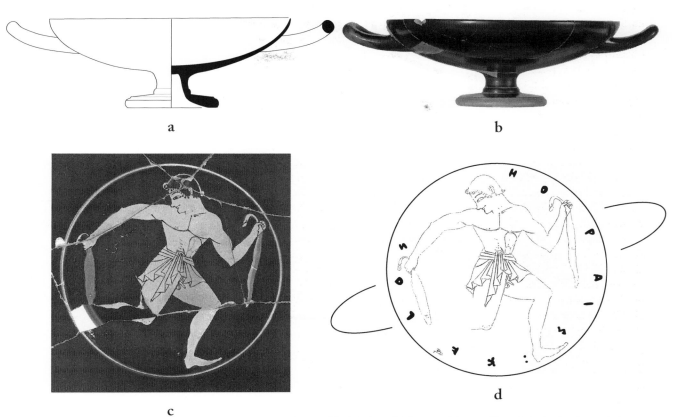

a

b

c

d

Figure 87. Cup 90, Type C: (a) profile drawing; (b) mended cup; (c) tondo, youth with strips of meat; (d) facsimile of inscription. Scale 1:3 (a, b); 3:4 (c, d). Profile drawn A. Hooton; inked author; facsimile drawn author and B. Peruzzi; inked E. Schmitt and B. Peruzzi

meat, inscription (fugitive) in field around figure. Very faint preliminary drawing visible on torso and legs. Relief line throughout, including row of curls at hairline, eyeball, and epigastric arch but not balls of feet. Black glaze for strands of hair along face. Dilute glaze for inner ear, nipples, ribs, abdominal muscles, neck muscles, and muscles of left calf. Inscription: ΗΟΠΑΙΣ:ΚΑΛΟΣ. Punctuation not noted in Camp 1996, p. 248, no. 29.

Tondo off perpendicular to handles by about 25°.

For shape, cf. *Agora* XII, p. 264, no. 420, pl. 20, fig. 4; *FAS,* p. 123, no. 36, pl. 33:6a, b. Profile close to **89**, from same workshop.

Attribution: By the same hand as **89**. The youth's abdominal and neck muscles and ribs are indicated in dilute glaze, which was also present on the arms and legs, but the surface is worn. The youth is shown with a frontal upper chest and profile legs, but the abdominal muscles on **90** do not convey torsion as successfully as on **89** (see above for comparanda). The collarbones end in a characteristic squared-off hook, cf. Getty Museum, no inv. no. (anonymous loan), Frel 1979, n.p., no. 14. The Ambrosios Painter draws his legs with several relief strokes, not one continuous line, producing a sharp ankle bump as can be seen on **89** and **90** and nearly every figure by the painter where the calf is bare; cf. London E 817, *ARV*² 175, no. 32, Beazley 1918, p. 20, no. 18, fig. 12 bis; Oxford 1917.55, *ARV*² 174, no. 21, *CVA* Oxford 1 [Great Britain 3], pl. 1 [93]:3. The hair on **90**, with fringe ending in a light relief dot around the face with large relief dots at the hairline, is used by the Ambrosios Painter for both humans and satyrs: cf. London E 817, *ARV*² 175, no. 32, Beazley 1918, p. 20, no. 18, fig. 12 bis; Boston, MFA 01.8024, *ARV*² 173, no. 9, Boardman 1975, fig. 119; London E 42, *ARV*² 174, no. 20, Beazley 1918, p. 20, no. 13, fig. 12. The drapery on **90**, like that on **89**, fails to respond to gravity.

Close to Skythes (D. von Bothmer in Camp 1996)

Ambrosios Painter (Lynch 1999)

Ca. 500–480

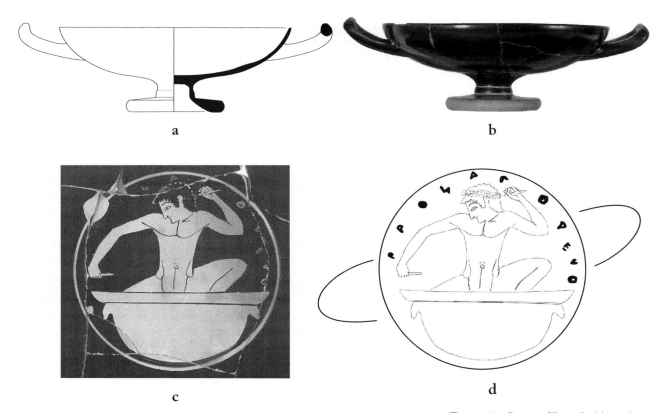

a   b

c   d

**Figure 88. Cup 91, Type C: (a) profile
drawing; (b) mended cup; (c) tondo,
youth treading grapes; (d) facsimile
of inscription.** Scale 1:3 (a, b); 3:4 (c, d).
Profile drawn A. Hooton; inked author;
facsimile drawn author and B. Peruzzi; inked
E. Schmitt and B. Peruzzi

*91   (P 32419) Type C cup   Color Ills. 1, 5; Fig. 88

+45.90–45.60 m (Level 6)

H. 7.0; Diam. 18.2; W. with handles 24.4

Camp 1996, p. 250, no. 30, fig. 8, pl. 74 (inscription incorrect); Immerwahr
1998, p. 165, no. 672; Neer 2002, p. 202, n. 94; Lynch 2009b, p. 75, fig. 74.

Nearly complete. Missing fragments from rim. Mended from 15 fragments.
Good black glaze. Well potted.

Torus foot, rising to flat-topped cone on underside. Thick stem with lightly
beveled fillet at juncture of foot between two heavy scraped grooves. Somewhat
shallow bowl. Straight rim. Canted horseshoe handles.

Tondo: youth squats inside a large vessel. Upper legs widespread and bent, with
the figure's left knee rising above rim of the basin. Torso and legs frontal with
head profile to left. In each hand he grasps a short stick with the left arm raised to
the head. Almond-shaped eye with a small solid dot for the pupil. Added red: wreath
with parallel dot-leaves, inscription clockwise in field around figure. Sketchy preliminary drawing visible throughout. Relief line throughout including anatomical
details, except for lower edges of vessel. Black glaze for hair, eyeball, and profile of
the mouth. Inscription in added red: ΠΡΟΣΑΛΟΡΕΥΟ

Tondo off perpendicular to handles by about 15°.

For shape, cf. *Agora* XII, p. 264, no. 420, fig. 4, pl. 20. Very similar to black-
glazed cups **135** and **136**, possibly by the same potter. The vessel in which the
youth squats has a flaring offset rim above two lug handles, close in appearance to
Agora XII, p. 366, no. 1847, fig. 19, pl. 88, a tub from a pre-Persian context. The
youth is treading grapes (see discussion in Chap. 4).

Attribution: The inscription is not known on any products of the Epeleios
Group (Immerwahr 1998, p. 2329), but is common on products of the Euergides
Painter and in his manner. Stylistic analysis favors the "Manner of the Euergides
Painter." The Euergides Painter depicts youths in vats, but prefers profile treaders

(Rouillard 1975, pp. 41–43). The only frontal youth in a vat attributed to the Euergides Painter, a cup in the Victoria and Albert Museum, shares formal qualities with **91**, but is by a different hand (London, V&A 4807.1901, *ARV*² 89, no. 14, Sparkes 1976, p. 53, fig. 15 = Gerhard 1847, vol. 3, pp. 70–71, pls. 180, 181, but details of Gerhard's drawing do not resemble the photograph as published in Sparkes). The anatomy on the Euergides Painter's version is less clear than the V&A depiction: Is the curving line meant to be a spine? Yet the hands grip the side of the vat frontally. A cup in Taranto (Vinc. 108/92, *CVA* Taranto 4 [Italy 70], pl. 22 [3189]:2) is closer to **91** in composition, but not style. The Euergides Painter uses characteristic collarbones formed of squared-off hooks, whereas the Taranto figure has rounded collarbone lines. The Euergides Painter himself never draws a hand at a right angle to the arm as on the Taranto cup. However, the exterior figures on the Taranto cup are confidently attributable to the Euergides Painter. Cf. the komasts on a cup by the painter Tours, 863–2-67, Rouillard 1975, p. 33, fig. 3. The Taranto cup is an example of the Euergides Painter sharing a job with another craftsman probably within his workshop. The inscription on the Taranto cup says *ho pais kalos* and uses letter forms unlike those of **91**. Thus, **91** should be by someone associated with the Euergides Painter, but not by the master himself. Indeed, **91** is closest to the anatomy of figures attributed to the "Manner of the Euergides Painter," see, e.g., Brussels R 260, *ARV*² 97, no. 10, Kilmer 1993, pp. 60–61, no. R173, pl. at p. 146; Louvre G 98, *ARV*² 98, no. 17 (with a column krater not a vat), *CVA* Louvre 19 [France], pl. 78 [1283]:3.

Epeleios Group (D. von Bothmer in Camp 1996)

Manner of the Euergides Painter (Immerwahr 1998, p. 165, no. 673; Lynch 1999)

Ca. 500–480

*92   (P 32422) Type C cup   Color Ills. 1, 6; Fig. 89
+46.00–45.90 m (Level 5)
H. 7.5; Diam. 18.0; p.W. 19.0
Camp 1996, p. 250, no. 32, pl. 75; Kreuzer 1999, pp. 224–225, pl. 21:a; Neer 2002, p. 203, n. 106.

Complete profile. About three-quarters preserved, missing one handle. Mended from several fragments. Fragments tinged gray at the breaks. Good black glaze. Thin red-brown glaze on reserved outer face of foot and resting surface. Well potted.

Torus disk foot, rising to cone on underside. Two incised grooves at juncture of foot and stem. Somewhat shallow bowl. Straight rim. Canted horseshoe handle.

Tondo: Owl between two reserved, curling tendrils. Owl, decorated with spots except for wing feathers, stands to right and faces front. Added white (fugitive): two leaves in field above left reserved tendril, one curving toward the owl; in field to right of owl's feet, single leaf; in field above right reserved tendril, two leaves, one curving toward the owl. Added red (fugitive): inscription in field to left of owl's head. No relief line outline, used only for outer eye circles, line of wing and straight wing feathers. Black glaze for all other details except dilute glaze wavy lines on wings.

Inscription: ΕΛΟΧΟΣΕΝ in field to left of owl. Published as ΕΛΟΧΟΔΕΝ in Camp 1996, p. 250, no. 32.

Tondo off perpendicular to handles by about 20°.

Shape close to *Agora* XII, p. 264, no. 420, fig. 4, pl. 20. Decoration, cf. fig. 89:e, *Agora* XXX, p. 346, no. 1600, P 31009, pictured upside down on pl. 151, from the SGW, a fragment from a cup with similar tondo scheme. P 31009 preserves the left tendril, an added white or red leaf above the tendril, and a single letter, E, in precisely the same position as on **92**. The exterior of P 31009 preserves

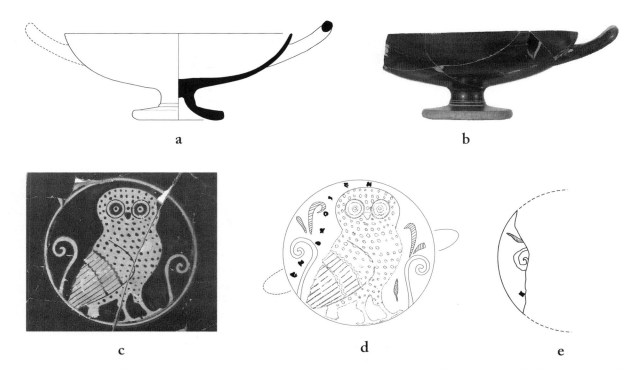

a   b

c   d   e

Figure 89. Cup 92, Type C: (a) profile drawing; (b) mended cup; (c) tondo, owl; (d) facsimile of inscription; (e) drawing of P 31009 from SGW. Scale 1:3 (a, b); 1:2 (c, d, e). Profile and (e) drawn author; inked E. Schmitt; (d) drawn author and B. Peruzzi; inked B. Peruzzi

the beginning of a handle, which also agrees with the handle placement and tondo orientation of **92**; and the diameter of the reserved border of P 31009's tondo is approximately the same size as **92**, 8.2 cm, but the wall of P 31009 is thicker, 0.56 cm, than that of **92**, 0.50 cm, at the tondo border.

There are several cups from the Persian destruction fill on the Acropolis with owl tondos, but none match **92** precisely in style or detail; e.g., Acropolis 75, *ARV*[2] 80, no. 1 [Epiktetos?], Graef and Langlotz II, p. 7, no. 75, pl. 5; Acropolis 1078 [Six's technique], Graef and Langlotz II, p. 99, no. 1078, pl. 84; Acropolis 415–419, Graef and Langlotz II, p. 37, nos. 415, 416, 417, 418, 419, pl. 31 (all ca. 500, except the latter two may be ca. 450).

Attribution: An owl on a mug probably by the same hand, Capua 222, *CVA* Capua 2 [Italy 23], pl. 19 [1094]:10, see discussion in Kreuzer 1999, pp. 224–225. For the chronological problems with attributing this cup to the Sabouroff Painter, see Neer 2002, pp. 203–204, n. 106.

For related examples, cf. Castellani 50478, Mingazzini 1971, p. 635, pl. 51:3; Populonia 208101 (PD 340); Getty 77.AE.96, cup with owl and an olive wreath in the tondo, and on the exterior the handles are flanked by an owl and olive branch; *Agora* XXX, p. 350, no. 1632, "uncertain cup type," from ca. 450–425. An owl from the same tradition appears on a white-ground plaque from the Acropolis, 2499, *ABV* 506, top [Group of Athens 581], Graef and Langlotz I, p. 243, no. 2499, pl. 102. Owls appear as the exterior black-figured decoration of a bilingual cup, Basel 458, *CVA* Basel 2 [Switzerland 6], pl. 3 [259], [Skythes]. Beazley attributed one owl cup from the Acropolis to the Manner of Epiktetos (Acropolis 75, *ARV*[2] 80, no. 1, "bear[s] some resemblance to Epiktetos," Graef and Langlotz II, p. 7, no. 75, pl. 5), but it does not match the style of **92**. Dinsmoor speculated that the olive branches on the glaux skyphoi may relate to the addition of an olive wreath encircling Athena's head on coins, which is further interpreted as a reference to the victory at Marathon (Dinsmoor 1934, pp. 420–421), but the tendrils on **92** are not olive leaves. For interpretation of inscription, see Chapter 3.

Sabouroff Painter (D. von Bothmer in Camp 1996)
Unattributed (Lynch 1999)
Ca. 500

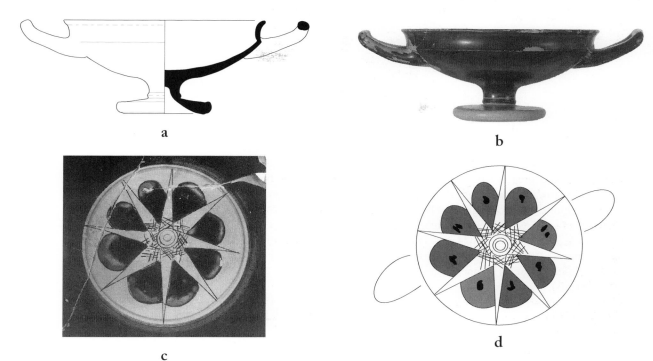

a

b

c

d

Figure 90. Cup 93, Type C, concave lip: (a) profile drawing; (b) mended cup; (c) tondo, eight-spoke wheel; (d) facsimile of inscription. Scale 1:3 (a, b); 1:2 (c, d). Profile and facsimile drawn author; inked E. Schmitt

*93   (P 32421) Type C cup, concave lip   Color Ills. 1, 7; Fig. 90

+46.00–45.90 m (Level 5)

H. 7.5; Diam. 16.1; W. with handles 23.1

Camp 1996, p. 250, no. 33, pls. 71:b, 75; Neils 1996, n. 51; Lynch 2009b, p. 75, fig. 74.

Complete except for chips missing from body. Mended from 15 pieces. Back glaze peeling in places, especially on one side of rim.

Torus disk foot, rising to cone underneath. Beveled fillet at juncture of foot and stem, offset with incised grooves above and below. Somewhat shallow bowl. Concave rim, sharply angled on exterior, slightly offset on interior. Canted horseshoe handles.

Tondo: eight-spoke wheel. Spokes come to a point at rim, which is also the border of the tondo. Inner rim scalloped between spokes. Cross-hatched lines near bases of spokes; three concentric circles for hub. Spokes in two overlapping planes of four spokes each. Added white: crescents at outer edge of each black-glazed section, stroke at point of at least one black-glazed section. Added red (fugitive): inscription, one letter in each black-glazed section. Relief line used for all lines except border of tondo.

Tondo off perpendicular to handles by about 20°.

Inscription uncertain. No parallel for decoration. The cross-hatching represents the binding of the spokes to the hub or to each other; see discussion in Crouwel 1992, pp. 35–36. An eight-spoke wheel, *oktanemos,* is mentioned once in Greek literature (Hom. *Il.* 5.723, in reference to Hera's chariot; discussed in Neils 1996, pp. 24–26; 2004, pp. 78–81). See Chapter 4, pp. 88–90, for list of other eight-spoke wheels. For shape, cf. *Agora* XII, p. 264, no. 409–413, fig. 4, pl. 19. Similar to shape of black-glazed cup **130**, also concave and with a similarly narrow stem and squared handles; possibly the same potter.

Unattributed

Ca. 500–480

94   (P 32763) Type C cup   Fig. 91

+49.76–49.14 m (Level 2)

P.H. 2.8; max. p. dim. 4.4

Figure 91. Cup 94, Type C: fragment of stem; crouching archer in tondo.
Scale 1:2

Fragment, broken all around. Preserves stem and floor of cup.

Narrow stem with low beveled fillet at junction with foot. Single uneven groove at top of fillet. Rises to narrow, flat cone on underside. Underside reserved. Tondo: Archer crouching to left. Back view of torso, one arm extended holding bow. Bottom tail of bow preserved. Ear flap of Scythian-style cap hangs down over back. Preliminary sketch: leg. Relief line: outline, ear flap, spine. Black glaze: details at top of spine, two dots may be hair curls.

For image, cf. *Agora* XXX, p. 334, nos. 1516, 1517, pl. 143, see fig. 54 for restoration (n.b.: figure on **94** holds bow in armed position, unlike *Agora* XXX, no. 1517.)

Pithos Painter or in his manner

Ca. 510–500

*95   (P 32411) Type C cup   Color Ills. 1, 9; Fig. 92

+46.30–46.00 m (Level 5)

H. 4.9; Diam. 12.8

Camp 1996, p. 250, no. 31, fig. 8, pl. 71:b, 74, 75 (published as a Type B cup); Lynch 2009b, p. 75, fig. 74.

Nearly complete except for chips on bowl and sections of lip. Mended from several fragments. Good black glaze. Well potted.

Torus foot, rising to flat cone on underside. Slight, beveled fillet at juncture of foot and stem. Somewhat shallow bowl. Straight rim. Canted horseshoe handles. Reserved: top of cone on underside, resting surface and outer face of foot, handle panels and interior of handles, line below scene, line on exterior of rim, line on interior of rim, line of tondo.

Tondo: youth, nude except for a cloak draped over outstretched left arm and shoulder, moves right, holding a handled stick in his right hand. Hairline incised, but does not follow the preliminary drawing or line of black-glaze dot-curls, causing the head to look displaced on the body. Side A: between one five-frond and one six-frond palmette with tendrils coiled beneath handles, two nude youths in combat. Both youths move right, raise one arm, and carry a shield on the other. The shield of the right youth bears a horse device. Side B: same as Side A, except both youths hold their right arms down. The right youth wears a skirt-garment from waist to knees; shield with a feline device. Left youth's shield with dot-cluster device. The combatants on the exterior have no visible weapons. All eyes almond-shaped and frontal with a black pupil. All hairlines incised. Preliminary drawings throughout. All lines relief, except inner portions of palmette tendril curls. Black-glazed dots indicate curls associated with each figure's hair, however, the incised hairline does not always follow the line of curls. Black glaze used for shield devices and hearts of palmettes. No dilute glaze or added color used.

Tondo off perpendicular to handles by about 15°.

Very small size; see discussion of similar small cups from the RRCS, Roberts 1986, p. 9, fig. 5. The RRCS examples are associated with the potter Kachrylion and the red-figured examples are attributed to the Group of Acropolis 96 (see *ARV*² 105, nos. 2–4, and bottom of page). One of the small cups from the RRCS is black-glazed with a profile that indicates the same potter as the red-figured cups.

Attribution: The closest stylistic parallels for **95** are unattributed cups: Adria B312, *CVA* Adria 1 [Italy 28] pl. 23 [1271]:7; and Bryn Mawr P-219, *CVA* Bryn

Figure 92. Cup 95, Type C: (a) profile drawing; (b) side B, nude youths in combat; (c) tondo, nude youth.
Scale 1:2 (a, b); not to scale (c). Profile drawn A. Hooton; inked author

Mawr 1 [USA 13], pl. 5 [585]:4, 5, but a cup in the Louvre comes close, Louvre G 22, *ARV*² 770, no. 5, *Add*² 287 [the Manner of the Epeleios Painter], Barringer 2001, pp. 22–23, figs. 11, 12. The painter of **95** probably does not belong to the Group of Acropolis 96, which decorated small-scale Type C cups of a similar profile, which Beazley considered near to the Euergides Painter, although there are some similarities between **95** and Tübingen S/10 819, *ARV*² 105, no. 6 [number given as Tübingen E 34], *CVA* Tübingen 5 [Germany 54], pl. 3 [2620], a red-figured cup with a komast on his way to a symposium carrying an oinochoe and holding a handled stick upon which his mantle hangs. Note especially the odd ear. The style of **95** is close to the Painter of Munich 2562, whom Beazley says recalls the Epeleios Painter. On the name vase of the Painter of Munich 2562, a mug, the painter depicts two crouching warriors wearing helmets and armed with shields but no weapons (Munich 2562, *ARV*² 158, no. 2, *CVA* Munich 2 [Germany 6], pl. 96 [292]:1–3. The scene is repeated on Warsaw 142459, *ARV*² 158, no. 1, *CVA* Goluchów, Musée Czartoryski 1 [Poland 1], pl. 23 [23]:2, 3). His figures are clumsy and cartoonish, and he renders shields in perspective similarly to **95**. The warriors on this mug seem to be clutching something round in their ill-defined hands, which may be rocks. Another unattributed small cup in the Bryn Mawr collection has a style that is near to both Euergides and the Epeleios Painter (Bryn Mawr P-219, *CVA* Bryn Mawr 1 [USA 13], pl. 5 [585]:4, 5). Another small cup, Vienna 1848 attributed to Onesimos, *CVA* Vienna 1 [Austria 1], pl. 5 [5]:1 is not similar to the style of **95**. There is a small group of cups that Beazley saw as mingling Epeleian elements and Euergidean, but the members of this group use more ambitious poses and more attentive drawing than the painter of **95** (*ARV*² 104).

Close to the Painter of Munich 2562
Ca. 500–480

CUP: SHAPE UNCERTAIN

96 (P 32768) Cup   Fig. 93

+49.76–49.14 m (Level 2)

Max. p. dim. 9.7

Three joining fragments of wall including stump of left handle attachment. Glaze mottled red near handle. Good black glaze on interior. Broad, flat bowl.

Exterior: to left of handle, draped figure steps to right with left foot extended, toes pointed, touching an inclined reserved area, probably landscape. Handle panel reserved. No sign of preliminary drawing. Relief line: outline, all details, line at bottom of reserved handle panel.

No trace of tondo on interior.

Figure 93. Cups 96–100. Scale 1:2

Attribution: The drapery style suggests Douris or an associate, and allows for a rough, but unsecured, date. Cf. Douris: Vienna 3695, *ARV*² 429, no. 26, *Paralipomena* 374, *Add*² 236, Buitron-Oliver 1995, p. 75, no. 42, pl. 26; Getty 86.AE.290, *Paralipomena* 375, *Add*² 237, Buitron-Oliver 1995, p. 78, no. 93, pl. 61; Munich 2646, *ARV*² 437, no. 128, *Paralipomena* 375, *Add*² 239, Buitron-Oliver 1995, p. 83, no. 173, pl. 96; Bryn Mawr P236, *ARV*² 439, no. 146, *Add*² 239, Buitron-Oliver 1995, p. 83, no. 190, pl. 105, et alia. On these comparanda there is a characteristic high, rounded fold flanked by descending folds placed two or three folds from the edge of the figure. The area of garment which falls behind the figure, that is, the inside of the garment, does not have any folds and the hem is not distinguished.

Ca. 480

97 (P 32764) Cup   Fig. 93

+49.76–49.14 m (Level 2)

Max. p. dim. 5.9

Fragment of floor near stem, broken all around. Good black glaze. Tondo: preserves shield and bow of a figure to left. Round shield with device of the hindquarters of a feline on a ground line in silhouette. Upper re-curve of bow projects above shield, trace of lower below. Compass point and two lightly incised circles on shield, outer forms shield edge. Small section of reserved tondo border above bow. No preliminary drawing. No contour line. Relief line: outline, bow string. Black glaze for shield device. Added red: letter to right of bow string: **K**.

The drawing is very careful. Probably a single figure, possibly a Scythian or an Amazon archer; cf. **94**. The shield device is not common; abbreviations of animals do occur, but more often the front part is represented. The hindquarters of a feline in added white on a black shield occurs as a device in the Leagros Group Florence 94320 [fragmentary hydria], *ABV* 361, no. 16, *CVA* Florence 5 [Italy 42], pl. 33 [1897]:1, and the hindquarters of a feline without a ground line is used by Polygnotos Syracuse 23507 [pelike, signed], *ARV*² 1032, no. 53, *CVA* Syracuse 1 [Italy 17], pl. 4 [809]:1 and again on Syracuse 9317, *ARV*² 1059, no. 132 [Group of Polygnotos], *CVA* Syracuse 1 [Italy 17], pl. 5 [810]:1. The hindquarters of a horse appear as a shield device on Brussels R322, a red-figured cup, *ARV*² 402, no. 12 [Foundry Painter], *CVA* Brussels 1 [Belgium 1], pl. 3 [30]:1d, and what looks like the hindquarters of a pig on Brussels R303, *CVA* Brussels 1 [Belgium 1], pl. 8 [35]:d.

Ca. 500–475

98 (P 32769) Cup   Fig. 93

+49.14–48.73; +48.70–48.60 m (Level 2)

Max. p. dim. 6.0

Two joining fragments of wall, near stem. Black glaze streaky on exterior, slightly dull near figure.

Tondo: Preserves edge of back of profile head of male facing right. Narrow reserved contour around hair. Small black-glazed circles for curls overlapping reserved zone. Below at left, patterned pillow propped against tondo border. No preliminary drawing. Relief line: outline and linear details of pillow. Black glaze for hair, pillow stripe, and dots.

Fine drawing on the pillow. The pattern on the pillow is one seen in the work of the Pioneers. A pillow in a symposium scene on a kalpis in Bonn attributed to Euthymides repeats the pattern of broad black strip with dot border and a row of dots in between, but it is not an exact match (Bonn 70, *ARV*² 28, no. 12, *CVA* Bonn 1 [Germany 1], pl. 16 [16]:1). Euthymides's is a sacklike pillow with a continuous horizontal pattern. The pillow on **98** has two separate panels sewn together at a seam, which is distinguished by a vertical decorative band of dots. On the fragment **98**, the front of the pillow seems less ornate than the back, but it is possible that the patterns are staggered and a thick black stripe begins just below the break. An even closer parallel for the pattern is found in the costume of Amazons on two neck amphoras in the Manner of Euphronios (cf. Louvre G 107, *ARV*² 18, no. 1, *CVA* Paris, Louvre 6 [France 9], pl. 33 [412]:1–4; Louvre G 106, *ARV*² 18, no. 3, *CVA* Paris, Louvre 6 [France 9], pl. 33 [412]:5–7). On both of these related amphoras Amazons wear jumpsuits made of a woven fabric with the same broad stripe with dot border and row of dots in between. The small fragment of the tondo preserved in **98** does not allow an attribution to any painter, but the similarities with work of the Pioneers may suggest a date slightly earlier than the set of cups presented above.

Last quarter of the 6th century

99   (P 32762) Cup   Fig. 93

+50.31–49.76 m (Level 1b)

Max. p. dim. 5.0

Fragment of wall near stem, broken all around.

Tondo: profile head of a male facing right, left arm raised above head with hand touching reserved border of tondo. Reserved hair contour. Trace of second indeterminate object below arm. Added red (fugitive): fillet around head, tied in back with two dangling ends, one over face, the other behind the arm. Sketchy preliminary drawing preserved on face; no details, just blocking. Relief line: outline, facial details. Black glaze for hair and pupil. Added red inscription (fugitive): [ΗΟΠΑΙΣ]ΚΑΛ[ΟΣ].

The orientation of the tondo is given by the dangling ends of the fillet. He is bending forward, and the hand is in the twelve-o'clock position.

Attribution: The style of **99** is close to that of *Agora* XXX, p. 342, nos. 1571, 1572, 1573, pls. 148, 149, cups from the RRCS (Vanderpool 1946, pp. 279–280, nos. 33, 35, 34, pl. 30) by the Painter of the Group of Acropolis 96, and an unattributed fragment, *Agora* XXX, p. 343, no. 1577, pl. 149. Compare the squinty eye and the ill-defined, lumpy ear.

Ca. 500–475

100   (P 32770) Cup   Fig. 93

+49.14–48.73 m (Level 2)

Max. p. dim. 4.9

Fragment of floor near stem.

Tondo: Preserves top of balding head of man facing right. Above right, object hanging from reserved tondo border. Another object below at break, but indeterminate. No contour line. No preliminary drawing. Relief line: outline, details of face and bald spot, ∪ shape at upper right, diagonal line for object at bottom right. Black glaze for hair and eyeball.

101

102

103

Figure 94. Cups 101–103. Scale 1:2

The object in the field to the right of the man's head was drawn with a broad ∪ outline (possibly a discus bag?), but was reduced to a narrow reserved shape using black glaze. Black glaze also spills over the slanting relief line below the ∪ shape. Possibly a satyr.

Ca. 500

101   (P 32766) Cup   Fig. 94

+49.76–49.14 m (Level 2)

Max. p. dim. 3.1

Fragment of floor near stem. Clay tinged slightly gray at breaks.

Tondo: preserves buttocks and top of one thigh of nude figure facing left. Seen from back. Preliminary drawing: center buttock line. Relief line: outline, buttock definition.

Has some aspects in common with the Chaire Painter, cf. buttocks on *Agora* XXX, p. 348, no. 1613, pl. 152, *ARV²* 144, no. 3.

Ca. 500–475

102   (P 32765) Cup   Fig. 94

+49.76–49.14 m (Level 2)

Max. p. dim. 7.2

Three joining fragments of wall, with handle scar. Very good black glaze. Smudge of dark red substance to left of figure's foot on interior. Drilled hole for ancient mend at handle attachment. Handle panel reserved.

Tondo: thin reserved outline. Preserves back foot, draped lower leg, trace of thigh, and triangular fold of drapery of figure moving to right. No preliminary drawing. Relief line: outline, drapery details, toe. Added red inscription to left of foot:]O[.

The red substance may be spilled added red.

Ca. 500–475

103   (P 32767) Cup   Fig. 94

+49.76–49.14 m (Level 2)

Max. p. dim. 41.5

Fragment of wall, broken all around.

Tondo: preserves thumb of one hand. Slanting relief line in field below hand.

The hand may be held behind the body, carrying an object indicated by the relief line.

Ca. 525–480

Figure 95. One-piece amphora 104, Type B. Scale 1:3. Profile drawn and inked author

BLACK GLAZE

AMPHORA

[*104] (P 32757) One-piece amphora (Type B)   Color Ill. 11; Fig. 95

+45.60–45.23 m (Levels 5 and 6)

H. 22.3; Diam. 16.4

Complete profile. About one-third complete, mended from numerous fragments. Missing one handle and most of neck and rim. Glaze fired red (2.5YR 5/6) on exterior and interior of neck, and mottled black on shoulder.

Flaring ring foot, convex underside. Ovoid body. Cylindrical neck. Thickened, rounded rim. Vertical handles, round in section, attached from bottom of neck to shoulder. Reserved: underside and interior below level of upper handle attachment. Pink-red clay with frequent large white inclusions on surface and within fabric, some burned out.

No exact parallel in *Agora* XII, but p. 236, nos. 7 and 8, pl. 1, would place **104** around 500. The one-piece amphora form is not very common in the Agora excavations. Red color of slip means that the kiln did not enter the reduction stage correctly.

Ca. 500

*105 (P 32408) One-piece amphora (Type B)   Fig. 96

+46.60 m (Level 5)

H. 21.1; Diam. body 17.5, rim 11.0

Almost complete. Body, foot, handles, and part of rim preserved as a single fragment, two joining rim fragments. Chips missing from foot from use. Very worn. Peeling, dull black glaze fired unevenly red. Heavy, pink Attic clay with frequent medium to small white inclusions and frequent fine mica.

Flaring ring foot with broad resting surface. Ovoid body rounds to short, concave neck. Thickened, rounded, flaring rim. Vertical strap handles, oval in section, attached at lower neck and shoulder. Added red: double line around shoulder at base of handle, single at upper attachment of handle. Reserved: underside, interior below neck, but significant amount of glaze on interior body, dripped from neck along wall to form puddle at bottom. Dilute wash on underside.

**Figure 96. One-piece amphora 105,
Type B.** Scale 1:3. Profile drawn author;
inked E. Schmitt

Similar in form to *Agora* XII, p. 236, no. 7, pl. 1, which is dated to "late 6th century," but **105** is slightly larger.

Late 6th century

Pelike

*106   (P 32467) Pelike   Fig. 97

+46.63–46.30 m (Level 5)
H. 24.0; Diam. body 17.7; rim 12.6
Complete profile. Largely complete, several body fragments missing. Mended from many fragments. Black glaze mottled red and gray in places.

Flaring disk foot. Globular body with largest diameter slightly below midpoint. Continuous curve to cylindrical neck. Outturned rim, rounded on top. Vertical strap handles with central ridge, attached from midneck to shoulder. Reserved: vertical face of foot, underside, interior below neck, but glaze dripped slightly down one side on interior. Added red: double line below lower handle attachments, single line below rim on neck, corresponding line on interior of neck, single line on rim at interior edge.

No exact parallel in *Agora* XII. It has the most in common with *Agora* XII, p. 237, no. 14, pl. 1, with a flaring ring foot reserved on the exterior face and underside, tall neck, and tight profile, but the rims and handles do not match. This is a hybrid of the one-piece amphora and the pelike.

Ca. 520–500

*107   (P 32405) Pelike   Fig. 97

+46.50 m (Level 5)
H. 27.3; Diam. 19.7
Camp 1996, pl. 71:a; Lynch 2001a, fig. 6.
Intact except for mended chip on foot. Glaze cloudy and red above shoulder.

Spreading ring foot with torus outer face. Concave fillet at junction of foot and body with incised lines above and below. Ovoid body with largest diameter below midpoint of body. Continuous curve to cylindrical neck. Thickened, torus rim. Vertical strap handles nearly rectangular in section, attached from lower neck to top of body. Reserved: underside and lower three-quarters of exterior face of foot.

Figure 97. Pelikai 106–108. Scale 1:4.
Profiles drawn author; inked E. Schmitt

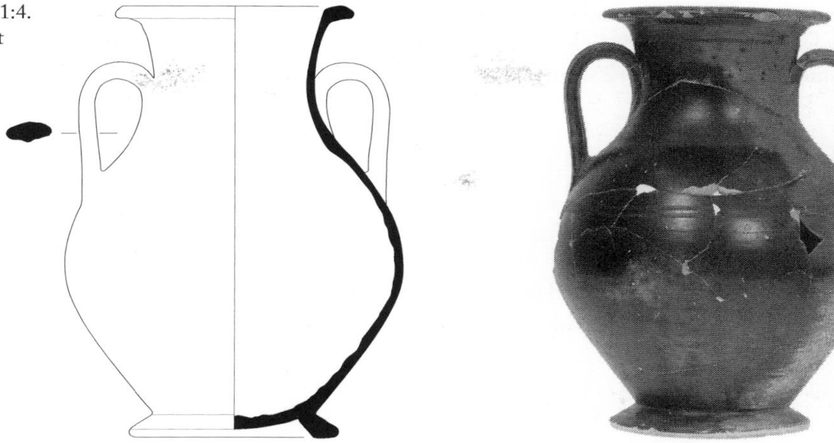

106

107

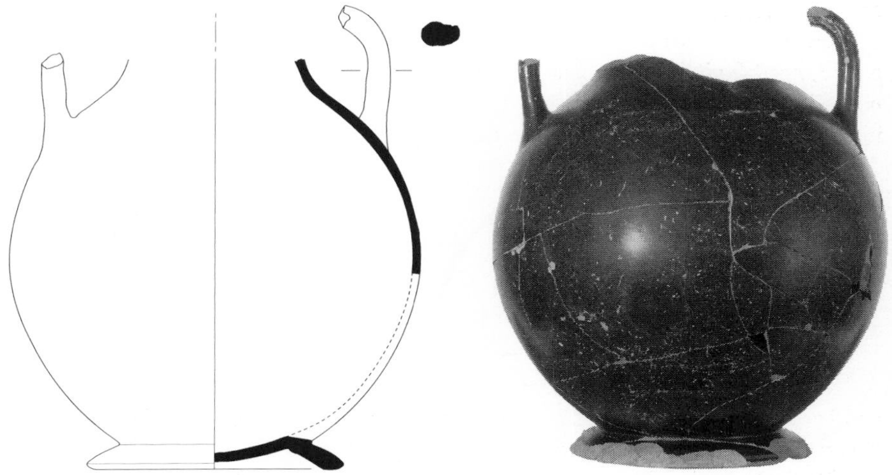

108

Totally glazed within, but streaky and cloudy. Added red (fugitive): wide double line at base of handles, single line on neck below rim.

Similar to *Agora* XII, p. 237, no. 21, pl. 1, but with a different rim.
Ca. 500–480

[*108]   (P 32754) Pelike   Fig. 97

+45.60–45.23 m (Level 6)
P.H. 25.4; Diam. 21.6
Lynch 2001a, fig. 6.

Two-thirds complete. Mended from many fragments. Missing neck and rim, upper part of handles, and a few body pieces. Chips missing at edge of foot from use. Very good black glaze.

Flaring ring foot, slightly convex underside. Spherical body, continuous curve to neck. Vertical handles oval in section, attached at shoulder. Reserved: underside, interior below neck. Added red: line near edge of foot.

Similar in form to *Agora* XII, p. 237, no. 22, pl. 1, but **108** is larger.
Ca. 500–480

Psykter

*109   (P 33215) Psykter   Fig. 98

+49.76–49.14 m (Level 2)
P.H. (a) 12.8, (b) 7.6; Diam. rim 7.67

Two large fragments made up of many small fragments (more small nonjoining fragments remain in Tin BZ 684). Mouth, neck, and body preserved. Missing foot. Good black glaze and fine, thin fabric. Some fragments tinged gray at edges.

Rim and body (a): projecting rim with vertical, upright flange at interior to receive lid. Slightly concave neck offset at junction with shoulder. Flat shoulder curves into squat, bulbous body. One double tube handle preserved on upper wall below shoulder; pierced vertically for string.

Lower body (b); not pictured: diameter widest at bottom of body, then contracts to stem. Reserved: outer face of flange, upper surface of rim, handle, and interior below neck.

Cf. *Agora* XII, p. 238, no. 37, pl. 2; p. 239, no. 38, fig. 2, pl. 2. The concave neck and size resembles no. 37, but the squat bulbous shape is more like no. 38. Lid **163** does not fit.
Ca. 500–480

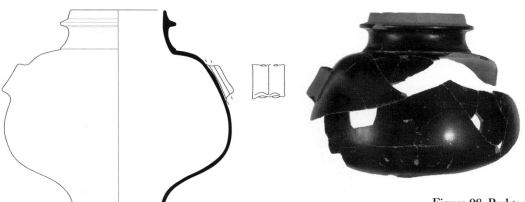

Figure 98. Psykter 109. Scale 1:3.
Profile drawn author; inked E. Schmitt

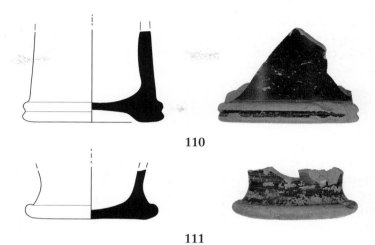

Figure 99. Psykters 110, 111. Scale 1:2.
Profiles drawn and inked author

110 (P 33251) Psykter   Fig. 99

+47.60–46.60 m (Level 4)
P.H. 5.1; Diam. foot 7.6
Single fragment preserving foot. Chipped on edges. Good black glaze on exterior. Dilute black glaze on interior.

Disk foot with recessed underside. Double molding at edge of foot. Lower stem flares slightly to foot. Reserved: upper molding, lower half of lower molding, underside.

Cf. *Agora* XII, p. 239, no. 39, pl. 2, for a similar small double molding and slightly flaring stem. The recessed underside is similar to *Agora* XII, p. 238, no. 35, pl. 2, which is a slightly earlier date (see drawing in Roberts 1986, p. 31, no. 66, fig. 21).

Ca. 500

111 (P 33250) Psykter   Fig. 99

+48.70–48.60 m (Level 3)
P.H. 2.8; Diam. foot 6.8
Single fragment of foot. Glaze streaky and flaking. Dilute glaze on interior.

Flat bottom, torus vertical face. Cylindrical lower body. Base of wall flares outward to foot. Reserved: underside and torus face of foot.

No Agora parallel.
Context: 525–480

OINOCHOE

*112 (P 32466) Trefoil oinochoe (Shape 1 oinochoe)   Fig. 100

+46.00–45.25 m (Levels 5 and 6)
H. to rim 19.7, with handle 25.0; Diam. body 18.1
Full profile. Mended from many pieces. Body fragments missing and foot chipped. Thin fabric. Glaze misfired red in a few isolated places.

Flaring ring foot, underside convex. Squat, rounded body. Cylindrical neck offset lightly from shoulder. Trefoil mouth, slightly concave on interior. Highswung handle, round to oval in section, attached from rim to shoulder. Reserved: underside of foot, interior below neck.

Cf. *Agora* XII, p. 243, no. 96, fig. 2, pl. 5. Shape 1 oinochoai do not continue past the first decades of the 5th century.

Ca. 525–500

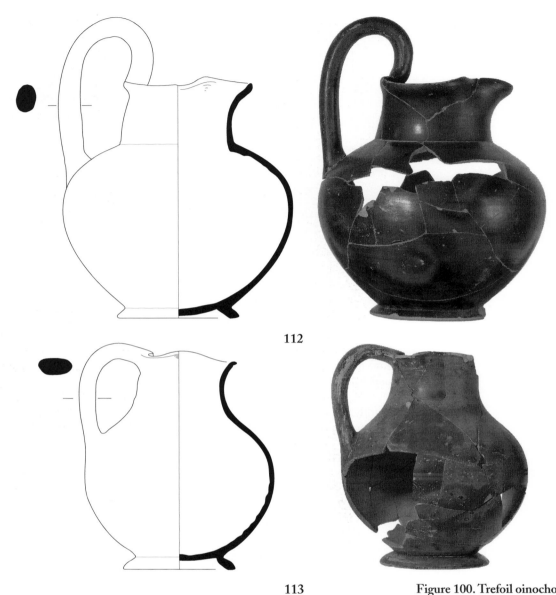

112

113

Figure 100. Trefoil oinochoai 112, 113. Scale 1:3. Profile drawn A. Hooton; inked E. Schmitt (**112**); profile drawn author; inked E. Schmitt (**113**)

*113   (P 32473) Trefoil oinochoe (Shape 3 oinochoe, chous)   Fig. 100

+46.00–45.25 m (Levels 5 and 6)

H. with handle 19.7; Diam. 15.0

Complete profile. Mended from many pieces. Almost complete except for a large fragment from the body and half of the mouth. Uneven black glaze, mottled red and brown.

Flaring ring foot with convex upper face. Globular body, continuous curve to concave neck. Trefoil mouth, flat lip. Low vertical handle, oval in section, rising to just above the rim, thumbrest projects into mouth. Reserved: underside of foot, interior below neck. Added red: double line around greatest diameter.

For shape and date, cf. *Agora* XII, p. 244, no. 108, pl. 6, but larger. Similar in size and shape to Roberts 1986, p. 34, no. 80 (not figured), ca. 500.

Ca. 500

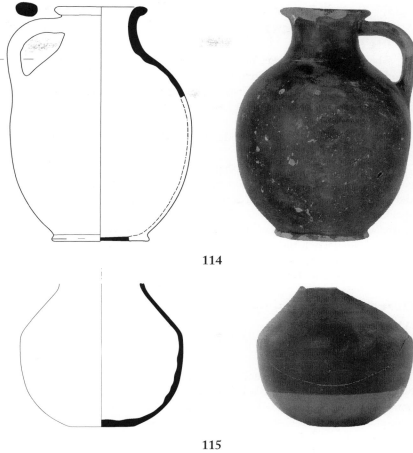

Figure 101. Jugs 114, 115. Scale 1:4. Profile drawn and inked author (**114**); profile drawn author; inked E. Schmitt (**115**)

JUG

*114 (P 32406) Jug Fig. 101

+46.30–46.00 m (Level 5)

H. 25.0; Diam. 19.0

Camp 1996, pl. 71:a.

Intact except for chips on foot and rim and two small holes in body. Matt black glaze worn on upper handle. Dipped. Hard pink-purple fabric (between 2.5YR 6/4 and 10R 6/4) with occasional large white inclusions including small bivalve shells, no mica visible. Imported?

Disk foot. Ovoid body. Narrow neck, slightly concave. Thickened outturned rim. Vertical handle, oval in section, attached from below rim to shoulder. Reserved: underside, interior below rim, but drips run down interior wall and swirl horizontally.

No parallel available for date.

The small holes in the body were caused by the explosion of inclusions during firing; therefore, the vessel had these holes while in use. The holes were probably plugged with wax or the like to render the vessel functional. Similar in fabric to the following: **115**, **116**, and possibly **157**. For fabric, cf. *Agora* XII, p. 243, nos. 97 and 98, pl. 5, which are also dipped and probably Lakonian, or *Agora* XII, p. 353, nos. 1665 and 1666, pl. 77. Note that *Agora* XII, p. 353, no. 1666, pl. 77, has the same small holes in the body.

Ca. 500

[*115]   (P 33223) Jug   Fig. 101

+45.90–45.60 m (Level 6)

P.H. 15.8; est. Diam. 22.0

About one-third of vessel. Mended from three fragments. Missing neck and mouth, handle, half of body. Prefiring scrape on body. Streaky, matt black glaze over upper three-quarters of pot. Trace of glaze on inside at bottom of neck. Hard, pink-purple fabric (2.5YR 7/4) with rare medium to large white inclusions and some fine mica. Imported?

Flat bottom, rounded lower body, cylindrical at middle, beveled to sloping shoulder.

Similar in glaze and general shape, but not fabric, to *Agora* XII, p. 354, no. 1687, pl. 78 (probably Corinthian), from a later context, which is a smaller vessel and does not have the pink fabric. Similar in fabric to the following: **114, 116,** and possibly **157.** For fabric, cf. *Agora* XII, p. 243, nos. 97 and 98, pl. 5, which are also dipped and probably Lakonian, or *Agora* XII, p. 353, nos. 1665 and 1666, pl. 77.

Even though only one-third preserved, the jug's large joining fragments and conspicuously missing rim and handle point to its use and breakage fetching water.

Context: 525–480

Olpe

*116   (P 33219) Trefoil olpe   Fig. 102

+45.90–45.60 m (Level 6)

H. 16.3; Diam. 8.35

Missing handle, parts of rim; one rim fragment mended to intact body. Matt black glaze worn and flaking. Black glaze extends inside neck on interior, and drips onto foot on exterior, but does not cover lowest wall. Probably dipped. Medium pink-orange clay (5YR 6/4) with frequent fine mica.

Flat bottom, slightly concave on underside. Ovoid body with slight bevel at junction with tall, slightly concave shoulder. Flaring trefoil mouth more delicate than heavy body. Strap handle attached from rim to top of body. Underside reserved.

Very similar to *Agora* XII, p. 255, no. 285, pl. 13, a "variant" of the olpe shape, but no. 285 does not preserve its mouth. See also *Kerameikos* IX, p. 95, no. 31.10, pl. 47:1, but with a plain mouth. Similar in fabric to the following: **114, 115,** and possibly **157.** For fabric, cf. *Agora* XII, p. 243, nos. 97 and 98,

Figure 102. Trefoil olpe 116. Scale 1:3.
Profile drawn A. Hooton; inked E. Schmitt

117

118

Figure 103. Olpe 117; banded olpe 118. Scale 1:2. Profiles drawn author; inked E. Schmitt

pl. 5, which are also dipped and probably Lakonian, or *Agora* XII, p. 353, nos. 1665 and 1666, pl. 77.

Although **116** comes from Level 6, it is not considered a water-fetching vessel because of its small capacity. Such a use cannot be ruled out, however.

Ca. 500

*117 (P 32399) Olpe   Fig. 103

+45.50–45.45 m (Level 6)
H. 7.9; Diam. 4.9
Camp 1996, pl. 71:a.

Intact, except for chips from rim. Fine clay with large white stone inclusions and frequent fine mica. Matt black glaze, worn.

Flat bottom. Ovoid body with slight bevel at junction with narrow neck. Slightly flaring outturned rim. Strap handle, irregularly formed and slightly concave, attached from rim to lower shoulder. Added red: line below handle attachment. Reserved: underside and interior below rim. Two intentionally incised circles on underside.

Somewhat like *Agora* XII, p. 254, nos. 266–269, pl. 13, but the articulation at the shoulder is not found in any of these examples. Note the similar form of **114** on a larger scale. On presence in Level 6, see comments under **116**.

Ca. 500–480

*118 (P 32402) Banded olpe   Fig. 103

+45.23 m (Level 6)
H. 8.7; Diam. 6.3
Camp 1996, pl. 71:a.

Intact. Glaze worn on front of rim, but otherwise in good condition.

Flat bottom, plump body, narrow neck. Flaring, rounded rim. Strap handle, oval in section, attached from rim to lower shoulder, rising slightly higher than rim. Black glaze on outside of handle, rim, interior of neck, line on body at handle attachment. The rest reserved with a dilute wash.

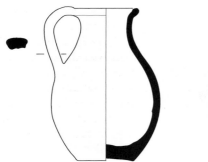

Figure 104. Banded olpe 119. Scale 1:2.
Profile drawn author; inked E. Schmitt

For the type and date, cf. *Agora* XII, p. 254, nos. 255–261, fig. 3, pl. 12, but no exact parallels for plump shape and narrow neck.

On presence in Level 6, see comments under **116**.

Ca. 500

*119   (P 32403) Banded olpe   Fig. 104

+45.23 m (Level 6)

H. 8.5; Diam. 5.8

Intact except for small piece of rim. Glaze flaking and worn. Light dent on one side.

Flat base, underside very slightly concave. Ovoid body, narrow neck. Flaring, rounded rim. Strap handle, oval in section, attached from rim to lower shoulder, rising very slightly above rim. Black glaze on outside of handle, rim, interior of neck, line on body at handle attachment. The rest reserved with a streaky dilute wash with drips at lower body.

For the type and date, cf. *Agora* XII, p. 254, nos. 255–261, fig. 3, pl. 12. The drips of dilute glaze suggest that the object was dipped or the slip was applied in a very watery dilution.

Ca. 500

Mug

[120]   (P 33253) Mug (Shape 8 oinochoe)   Fig. 105

+45.60–45.45 m (Level 6)

Max. p. dim. 7.1

Fragment, bottom of open vessel. Wall broken away. No obvious wear. Excellent black glaze. Well potted.

Underside molded with rounded cushion at edge and sharp aris closer to center. Trace of groove on underside at junction with foot. Reserved circle with

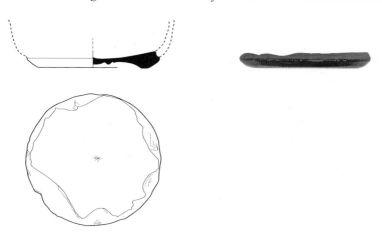

Figure 105. Mug 120. Scale 1:2. Profile drawn author; inked E. Schmitt

black-glazed circle and dot at center of underside. Scraped groove outside aris molding. Interior black-glazed with a slight nipple at center.

For shape, cf. *Agora* XII, p. 249, nos. 190 and 191, fig. 3, pl. 11; *Agora* XXX, p. 252, no. 794, fig. 37. There is enough trace of the wall to see that it flared slightly out and up. The nipple on the inside is paralleled on *Agora* XXX, no. 794, and its presence along with the fine black glaze on the interior indicates a somewhat closed shape. The treatment of the underside is in keeping with *Agora* XII, nos. 190 and 191. The red-figured example, *Agora* XXX, no. 794, has a reserved cushion. The lack of wear on the underside may mean this object did not have a long life. Fine glaze, careful potting, and painting of circles may associate this piece with the delicate bowls **152**, **153**, and **154**.

Late 6th century

SKYPHOS

*121   (P 32477) Skyphos, Corinthian type   Color Ill. 11; Fig. 106

+45.90–45.45 m (Level 6)

H. 7.4; Diam. 11.4

Complete except for pieces of body and rim. Mended from many fragments. Glaze completely misfired bright orange (2.5YR 6/6). Attic clay with rare medium to large white (lime) inclusions. Thin walled, but roughly potted.

Slightly flaring ring foot. Tall, slightly convex wall. Slightly incurving rim. Two horizontal handles attached at rim. Broad, rough groove at junction of wall and foot. Reserved: underside of foot, outer face of foot, and uneven area at bottom of wall. On underside, two incomplete glazed circles and central dot. Added red: two lines below handles, bottom line sags out of parallel; broad band at bottom of wall.

The use of added red in the lower reserved zone disappears by the end of the 6th century; see *Agora* XII, p. 82.

Ca. 525–500

*122   (P 32395) Skyphos, Attic Type B   Fig. 106

+49.76–49.14 m (Level 2)

H. 9.3; Diam. 13.2

Mended from many pieces. About half complete, preserving full profile. Poor matt and streaky black glaze misfired red in places. Many of the fragments gray in color, from burning?

Figure 106. Skyphos 121, Corinthian type; skyphos 122, Attic Type B.
Scale 1:3. Profiles drawn author; inked E. Schmitt

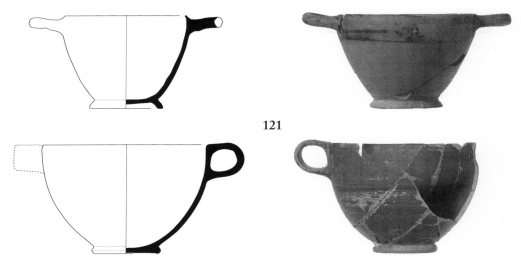

121

122

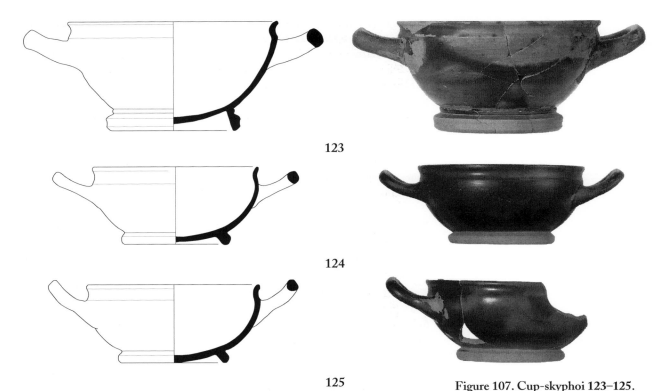

123

124

125

Figure 107. Cup-skyphoi 123–125.
Scale 1:3. Profiles drawn author; inked
E. Schmitt

Plain disk foot, high convex walls, thin vertical strap handle attached to rim at top. Traces of a second, horizontal handle implied by crescent break at rim opposite. Reserved: entire disk foot, interior of handle. Added red: double line below handle attachment, double line on interior of rim. Traces of miltos on reserved surfaces.

No real parallel in *Agora* XII, but similar, except for foot, to p. 260, no. 360, pl. 17. This is the "glaux" shape of skyphos with one vertical and one horizontal handle. The missing handle must be horizontal, not vertical due to the shape of the break and the horizontal pattern of glaze application below.

Ca. 500–480

*123   (P 32472) Cup-skyphos   Color Ill. 11; Fig. 107

+46.60–45.45 m (Levels 5 and 6)

H. 9.2; Diam. 16.5

Nearly complete. Mended from many fragments. Poor black glaze, cloudy in places, mottled red over much of surface, and peeling.

Spreading ring foot with concave vertical face. Fillet at junction of foot and body between two scraped grooves. Rim inset on interior, narrow lip, sharply concave below on exterior. Thick handles canted slightly, attached to top of wall. Reserved: vertical face of foot and resting surface, underside except for five thin glazed circles and central dot, interior of handles and handle panels.

For shape and date, cf. *Agora* XII, p. 276, nos. 573 and 576, pl. 25. This example is larger than **124** or **125**.

Ca. 490–480

*124   (P 32482) Cup-skyphos   Color Ill. 2; Fig. 107

+46.60–46.30 m (Level 5)

H. 6.4; Diam. 13.4

Single fragment preserving two-thirds of cup including entire foot and both handles. Good, thick black glaze.

Spreading ring foot with convex face, short convex wall, concave rim. Canted horizontal handles attached to top of body. Reserved: underside of foot, except for central circle and dot, outer face of foot and resting surface, interior of handles and handle panels.

Same shape as the black-figured Class K2 cup-skyphoi, cf. Roberts 1986, p. 26, no. 48, fig. 16. Very similar to **125**, same potter; probably same workshop as **47**.

Ca. 500–480

*125 (P 32481) Cup-skyphos   Fig. 107

+46.60–46.30 m (Level 5)

H. 6.3; est. Diam. 14.0

Complete profile. Almost half preserved, missing one handle and most of rim. Black glaze fired red on interior floor and on exterior.

Spreading ring foot with convex face, short convex wall, concave rim. Canted horizontal handles attached below rim. Reserved: underside of foot except for irregular, thick central circle and dot, outer face of foot, interior of handle and handle panel.

Same shape as the black-figured Class K2 cup-skyphoi, cf. Roberts 1986, p. 26, no. 48, fig. 16. Very similar to **124**, same potter; probably same workshop as **47**.

Ca. 500–480

126 (P 33194) Skyphos (small)   Fig. 108

+49.76–49.14 m (Level 2)

P.H. 3.7; est. Diam. ca. 8.0

Five joining and two nonjoining fragments of rim, wall, and one handle. Poor black glaze ranging from black to red to brown, and flaking. Somewhat roughly potted.

Deep, convex bowl. Flaring rim with light groove at bottom, offset from bowl. Canted, horizontal handle. Handle panel reserved.

No exact parallel in *Agora* XII, but similar to p. 276, no. 571, pl. 25, but smaller. Probably a cup-skyphos.

Ca. 500–480

Figure 108. Skyphos 126. Scale 1:2.
Profile drawn A. Hooton; inked E. Schmitt

One-Handler

*127 (P 33216) One-handler   Fig. 109

+49.76–49.14 m (Level 2)

H. 3.1; Diam. 9.2; max. p. dim. 2.2

Complete profile. Mended from many fragments with one nonjoining body fragment (not pictured). Missing part of rim and wall. Some restoration.

Torus ring foot. Broad shallow bowl. Rounded, incurving, glazed rim. Bevel at junction of rim with wall. One slightly canted horizontal handle. Interior: glazed with a reserved central disk with two circles and central dot. Exterior: rim glazed.

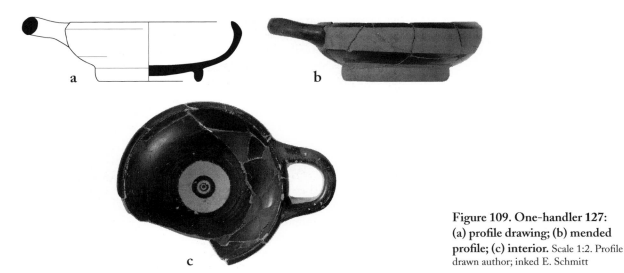

Figure 109. One-handler 127: (a) profile drawing; (b) mended profile; (c) interior. Scale 1:2. Profile drawn author; inked E. Schmitt

Broad black-glazed band below handle attachment otherwise reserved. Exterior of handle glazed. Underside: reserved with five circles, inner two thin. Outer face of foot reserved. Traces of miltos on reserved exterior surface.

For inturned rim, general shape, and decoration, cf. *Agora* XII, p. 288, no. 735, pl. 30. This is the only inventoried example of many fragmentary one-handlers from J 2:4. All have the banded exterior decoration. There are no totally black-glazed one-handlers from this deposit.

Ca. 500

CUP: TYPE C

*128   (P 32479) Type C cup, concave lip   Color Ill. 11; Fig. 110

+46.00–45.45 m (Levels 5 and 6)

H. 8.1; Diam. 15.9

Complete except for fragments of wall and chips of rim. Mended from twelve fragments. Black glaze dull and fired reddish brown in places. Thin, streaky glaze on resting surface and outer face of foot.

Disk foot, rising to flat-topped cone underneath. Thick stem with bulge at juncture with foot. Deep bowl. Concave lip, offset on interior. Reserved: top of cone on underside, resting surface, vertical face of foot, interior of handles, and handle panels.

For shape, cf. *Agora* XII, pp. 263–264, nos. 404–409, pl. 19. The bump on the stem may have been intended as a fillet, but no incised grooves were added to offset it. The flatness of the upper surface of the foot, the gentle concave lip, deep bowl, and broad stem suggest a date of 500 or even earlier.

Ca. 500

*129   (P 32396) Type C cup, concave lip   Fig. 110

+49.76–49.14 m (Level 2)

H. 16.3; Diam. rim 6.6, stem 2.25

Mended from many fragments. Missing lower stem and foot, parts of rim. Thick black glaze, milky inside with an off-centered firing ring, lustrous outside. Well potted.

Body sits on narrow stem with top of flat cone preserved. Somewhat shallow bowl. Rim sharply angled and deeply concave. Canted horseshoe handles. Reserved: inside of handles and handle panels, top of cone on underside. Traces of miltos on reserved surfaces.

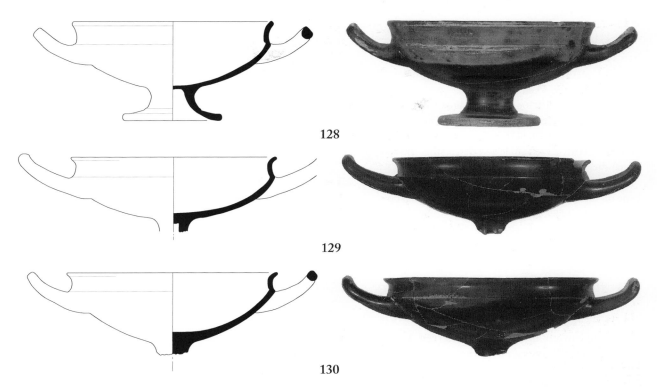

128

129

130

Figure 110. Type C cups 128–130, concave lip. Scale 1:3. Profiles drawn author; inked E. Schmitt

The slender stem and sharply concave rim indicate a date later than 500. Cf. *Agora* XII, p. 264, no. 410, pl. 19, and Roberts 1986, p. 10, no. 8, fig. 3, for the shape and date. Nearly identical to black-glazed cup **130**, from the same potter. Somewhat similar to red-figured cup **93**, possibly the same potter.

Ca. 500–480

*130 (P 32755) Type C cup, concave lip   Fig. 110

+46.60–45.45 m (Level 6)

P.H. 5.7; Diam. bowl 16.9, stem 2.45

Mended from many fragments. Foot, most of stem, a few body and rim pieces missing. Red stacking ring on interior where glaze misfired, otherwise good black glaze and well potted.

Body sits on narrow stem with very tip of cone preserved. Somewhat shallow bowl. Rim sharply angled and deeply concave, offset on interior. Canted horseshoe handles. Reserved: interior of handles and handle panels. Faint traces of miltos on reserved surfaces.

The slender stem and sharply concave rim indicate a date later than 500. Cf. *Agora* XII, p. 264, no. 410, pl. 19, and Roberts 1986, p. 10, no. 8, fig. 3, for the shape and date. Nearly identical to black-glazed cup **129**, from the same potter. Similar to red-figured cup **93**, possibly the same potter.

Ca. 500–480

Figure 111. Type C cup 131, concave lip. Scale 1:3. Profile drawn author; inked E. Schmitt

[131] (P 33222) Type C cup, concave lip   Fig. 111

+45.45–45.20 m (Level 6)

P.H. 5.8; est. Diam. 21.0

Single fragment of rim and wall. Black glaze worn on top of rim. Good black glaze, fired red at rim and near stem on exterior.

Tall concave lip, offset on interior. Rim joins bowl at sharp angle on exterior. For shape and date, cf. Roberts 1986, p. 10 no. 2, fig. 2.

Ca. 520–510

*132   (P 32471) Type C cup, plain rim   Fig. 112
       +46.00–45.45 m (Levels 5 and 6)
       H. 7.3; Diam. 19.7
       Complete profile. Mended from 24 fragments. Missing pieces of rim and bowl.
Good black glaze. Well potted.
       Broad torus disk foot, rising to broad, flat cone on underside with light nipple.
Rounded fillet at juncture of foot and stem between with two incised grooves. Somewhat shallow bowl. Plain rim. Canted horseshoe handles. Reserved: top of cone on
underside, with glazed circle and dot, resting surface and outer face of foot, interior
of handles, and handle panels.
       For shape and date, cf. *Agora* XII, p. 264, no. 416, pl. 20. The short stem, broad
cone on underside with circle and dot, and deep bowl place **132** around 500, if not
earlier, in the development scheme set out by *Agora* XII, pp. 91–92. It is the earliest
in the series of Type C cups with plain rim present in this deposit and probably
dates to the late 6th century rather than early 5th.
       Ca. 500

*133   (P 32478) Type C cup, plain rim   Color Ill. 11; Fig. 112
       +46.00–45.90 m (Level 5)
       H. 6.7; Diam. 18.3
       Complete profile. About half preserved. Mended from six pieces. Black glaze
misfired a cloudy gray-green with some red-orange. Edges of fragments tinged
gray. Dilute glaze on resting surface and outer face of foot. Well potted.
       Torus disk foot, rising to flat cone on underside. Short, straight stem with two
incised grooves at junction of foot and stem, but no fillet. Somewhat shallow, flat
bowl, plain rim. Canted horseshoe handle. Reserved: top of cone on underside,
resting surface, outer face of foot, interior of handle, and handle panel.
       For shape, cf. *Agora* XII, p. 264, no. 417, pl. 20. Identical to **134** in form and
finish; same potter, same firing mishap.
       Ca. 500

*134   (P 32476) Type C cup, plain rim   Fig. 112
       +46.00–45.90 m (Level 5)
       H. 6.6; Diam. 18.3
       Complete except for rim fragments. Mended from eight pieces. Poor black
glaze, very cloudy and greenish over most of the surface. Edges of fragments tinged
gray. Dilute glaze on resting surface and outer face of foot. Well potted.
       Torus disk foot, rising to flat cone with slight nipple on underside, two incised
grooves at juncture of foot and stem, but no fillet. Somewhat shallow, flat bowl,
plain rim. Canted horseshoe handles. Reserved: top of cone on underside, resting
surface, outer face of foot, interior of handles, and handle panels.
       For shape, cf. *Agora* XII, p. 264, no. 417, pl. 20. Identical to **133** in form and
finish; same potter, same firing mishap.
       Ca. 500

*135   (P 32475) Type C cup, plain rim   Fig. 112
       +46.00–45.90 m (Level 5)
       H. 7.0; Diam. 17.5
       Complete except for two small rim fragments. Mended from seven pieces.
Black glaze cloudy in places, especially on interior floor.
       Torus disk foot, rising to flat cone on underside. Careful rounded fillet at
juncture of foot and stem, between incised grooves. Somewhat shallow bowl with
plain rim. Canted horseshoe handles. Reserved: top of cone on underside, resting

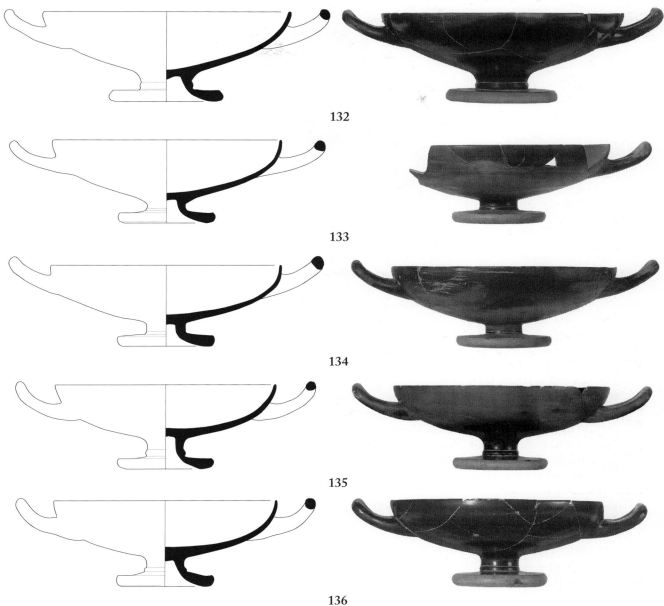

132

133

134

135

136

Figure 112. Type C cups 132–136, plain rim. Scale 1:3. Profiles drawn author; inked E. Schmitt

surface, outer face of foot, handle panels, and interior of handles. Traces of miltos on reserved surfaces.

Slightly lower stem, otherwise similar to *Agora* XII, p. 264, no. 420, fig. 4, pl. 20. Very close to **136**, probably same potter. Profile close to red-figured cup, **91**, possibly the same potter.

Ca. 500–480

*136   (P 32470) Type C cup, plain rim   Color Ill. 1; Fig. 112
+46.00–45.60 m (Levels 5 and 6)
H. 6.9; Diam. 17.7
Lynch 2009b, p. 75, fig. 74.
Complete profile, missing about one-third of rim. Mended from 17 fragments. Good black glaze, slightly cloudy within. Edges of fragments tinged gray. Well potted.

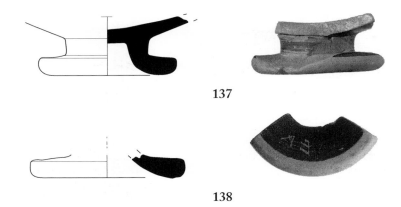

137

138

Figure 113. Type C cups 137, 138.
Scale 1:2. Profile drawn A. Hooton; inked
E. Schmitt (**137**); profile drawn author;
inked E. Schmitt (**138**)

Torus disk foot, rising to flat cone on underside. Medium height stem with rounded fillet at bottom between two incised grooves. Somewhat shallow bowl, plain rim. Canted horseshoe handles. Reserved: top of cone on underside, resting surface and outer face of foot, interior of handles, and handle panels.

Slightly lower stem, otherwise similar to *Agora* XII, p. 264, no. 420, pl. 10, fig. 4. Very close to **135**, probably same potter. Profile close to red-figured cup **91**, possibly the same potter.

Ca. 500–480

137   (P 33187) Type C cup   Fig. 113

+50.88–50.31 m (Level 1b)

P.H. 3.2; Diam. foot 7.4

Four joining fragments of foot, stem, and floor of cup. Worn, with chips missing from edge of foot. Black glaze fired red on interior. Glaze flaking throughout.

Torus disk foot, rising to broad, flat cone on underside. Horizontal surface of foot flat and slightly lipped. Very short, broad stem with two closely spaced scraped grooves at junction of foot and stem. Reserved: outer face of foot, resting surface, center of stem on underside.

For shape and date, cf. *Agora* XII, p. 263, no. 402, pl. 19.

Ca. 525–500

138   (P 33242) Type C cup   Fig. 113

+50.31–49.76 m (Level 1b)

Max. p. dim. 6.75; est. Diam. foot 7.8

Single fragment of foot.

Torus disk foot. Very slightly rising, uneven upper surface. Rising to cone on underside. Reserved: outer face of foot, resting surface. Graffito incised on underside: EA (retrograde).

The foot of *Agora* XII, p. 263, no. 404, pl. 19, incised with ΘPA, is similar in shape.

Ca. 500

139   (P 33245) Type C cup   Fig. 114

+49.76–49.14 m (Level 2)

P.H. 4.0; Diam. foot 7.1

Two joining fragments of foot and bowl. Streaky black glaze, fired brown-red and flaking. Prefiring scrape on upper surface of foot.

Torus disk foot, rising to cone on underside with central nipple. Broad stem with two roughly incised grooves at bottom. Somewhat shallow bowl. Reserved:

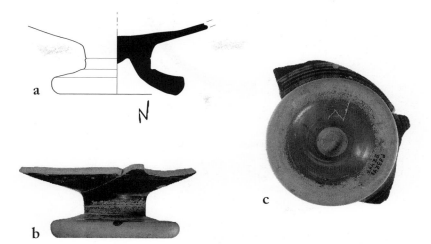

Figure 114. Type C cup 139: (a) profile drawing; (b) fragments of foot and bowl; (c) underside with inscription. Scale 1:2. Profile drawn author; inked E. Schmitt

outer face of foot, resting surface, top of cone on underside. Graffito incised on the underside: N.

The rough grooves on a tall stem suggest a date after 500. Cf. *Agora* XII, p. 264, nos. 409 and 410, pl. 19, for similar shapes.

Ca. 500–480

VICUP

140 (P 33262) Vicup   Fig. 115

+51.40–51.10 m (Layer 24a, Persian destruction debris in SW room of house)
P.H. 3.9; Diam. foot 6.25

Three joining fragments of foot, stem, and floor. Shiny black glaze. Top of foot roughly potted. Trace of miltos on reserved surfaces. Disk foot with concave vertical face. Rising to pointy cone on underside. Reserved: vertical face and resting surface, top of cone on underside. Graffito incised carefully on resting surface:]ΥΜΒΡΟΣΕΜ[Ι].

For shape, see *Agora* XII, p. 265, no. 437, pl. 20, fig. 5.

Inscription is an owner's name: "I am]umbros's [cup]." The name as preserved is not attested in Athens.

Ca. 475

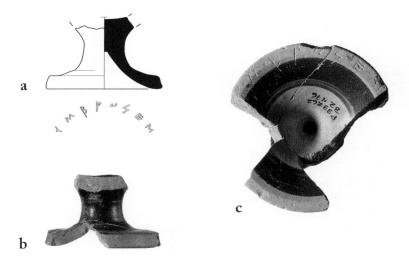

Figure 115. Vicup 140: (a) profile drawing; (b) joining fragments of foot, stem, and floor; (c) inscription on resting surface. Scale 1:2 (a, b); 3:4 (c). Profile drawn A. Hooton; inked E. Schmitt

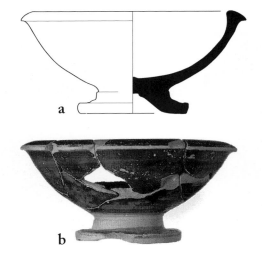

Figure 116. Stemmed dish 141: (a) profile drawing; (b) mended pot; (c) interior floor. Scale 1:2. Profile drawn author; inked E. Schmitt

STEMMED DISH

*141   (P 32480) Stemmed dish   Fig. 116

+45.90–45.45 m (Level 6)

H. 5.7; Diam. 11.9

Mended from 12 fragments. Almost complete. Peeling, cloudy black glaze.

Flat disk foot with pared cone on underside, straight vertical face. Short straight stem with irregular groove at junction with bowl. Rounded bowl with light nipple on interior floor. Rim projects slightly on interior and overhangs exterior wall; slightly convex upper face slopes downward toward exterior. Reserved: underside of foot except for band of glaze at bottom of cone, vertical face of foot, stem, interior and exterior of rim, center of interior floor with black-glazed circle and dot.

Shape similar to *Agora* XII, p. 304, no. 965, pl. 35, fig. 9, though smaller.

Ca. 500–480

*142   (P 32410) Stemmed dish   Fig. 117

+45.90–45.60 m (Level 6)

H. 9.8; Diam. 5.1

Mended from three fragments. Complete except for large chips on rim and foot. Good glaze but fired dull brown on one side, worn on rim.

Torus foot, rising to cone underneath with smooth nipple. Short, straight stem. Thickened rim, convex body, but shallow bowl. Deep groove under glaze below rim on exterior. Reserved: top of cone, resting surface, and outer face of foot.

For shape and date, cf. *Agora* XII, p. 304, no. 969, pl. 35.

Ca. 500

*143   (P 32342) Stemmed dish   Fig. 117

+49.76–49.14 m (Level 2)

H. 5.3; Diam. 10.3

Mended from 11 fragments; greater than half preserved. Excellent, glossy black glaze. Fragments tinged gray at edges.

Disk foot, exterior face with lower torus molding and concave upper. Rises to a narrow cone on underside. Thin stem with two thin, incised lines at base. Rounded bowl. Rounded, thickened lip projects very slightly. Groove under glaze

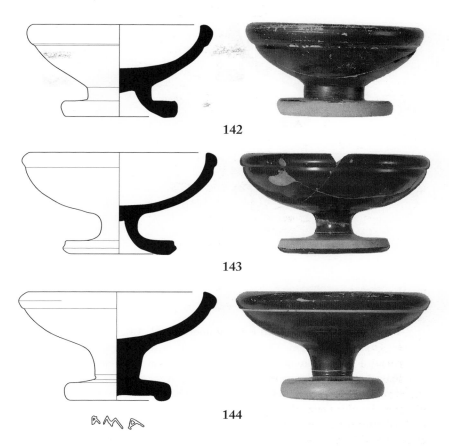

142

143

Figure 117. Stemmed dishes 142–144.
Scale 1:2. Profiles drawn author; inked
E. Schmitt

144

below rim. Reserved: resting surface, top of cone on underside, and upper concave part of vertical face of foot.

Similar to *Agora* XII, p. 304, no. 973, pl. 35, but with a different foot.

Ca. 500–480

*144   (P 32397) Stemmed dish   Fig. 117

+46.60–46.30 m (Level 5)

H. 6.0; Diam. 10.5

Camp 1996, pl. 71:a.

Intact. Thick black glaze. Lightly abraded at places on rim, scratched in two places on exterior bowl.

Torus disk foot, recessed on underside. Tall stem with two fine incised lines at base. Shallow bowl with thickened, rounded rim, sharp scraped groove below. Reserved: underside, resting surface, and outer face of foot, groove at top of wall below rim. Graffito neatly incised on underside: AMA.

Somewhat similar to *Agora* XII, p. 305, no. 983, pl. 35, figs. 1, 9, but different vertical face of foot.

Ca. 500

*145   (P 32465) Stemmed dish   Fig. 118

+46.00–45.90 m (Level 5)

H. 6.2; Diam. 10.6

Almost complete. Mended from 10 pieces, body and rim fragments missing. Glaze good, but dull and lightly mottled red in places.

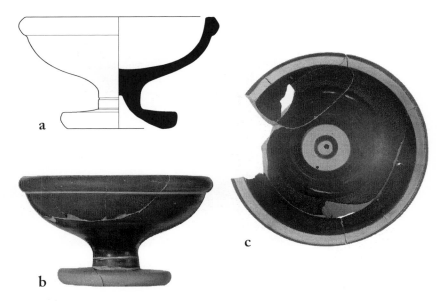

Figure 118. Stemmed dish 145:
(a) profile drawing; (b) mended pot;
(c) interior floor. Scale 1:2. Profile drawn
author; inked E. Schmitt

Torus foot rising to pointed cone on underside. Tall stem with two uneven scraped grooves at bottom. Thickened rim, flat on top, scraped groove below. Reserved: top of cone on underside, resting surface and outer face of foot, top of rim, center of interior floor with glazed circle and dot.

Close to *Agora* XII, p. 304, no. 973, pl. 35. The treatment of the rim suggests that it was made to take a lid.

Ca. 500–480

*146   (P 33218) Stemmed dish, concave lip   Fig. 119

+46.00–45.90 m (Level 5)
P.H. 5.0; Diam. 6.48
Single fragment preserves bowl and rim. Missing foot. Good black glaze; flaking and brown in one spot. Clay tinged gray where flaking. Well potted.

Narrow stem. Deep bowl. Concave rim with sharp junction with bowl; beveled lip.

Similar to the shape of *Agora* XII, p. 305, no. 987, pl. 35, but with a taller bowl and shorter lip.

Ca. 500–470

*147   (P 32483) Stemmed dish, chalice shape   Fig. 120

+46.00–45.90 m (Level 5)
P.H. 6.5; Diam. foot 6.6
Single fragment; missing upper wall and rim. Good black glaze. Clay tinged gray at breaks.

Disk foot rising to pared cone on underside; upper three-quarters of outer face concave, lower quarter rounded. Continuous curve from upper face of foot to stem

Figure 119. Stemmed dish 146, con-
cave lip. Scale 1:2. Profile drawn author;
inked E. Schmitt

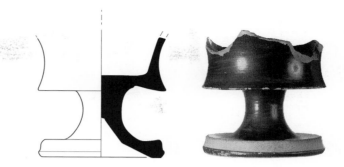

Figure 120. Stemmed dish 147, chalice shape. Scale 1:2. Profile drawn author; inked E. Schmitt

to bottom of bowl. Sharp angle at junction with concave bowl. Reserved: top of cone on underside, resting surface, concave part of vertical face, and edge of top face of foot. Traces of miltos on reserved surfaces.

For shape and date, cf. *Agora* XII, p. 306, no. 993, pl. 35.

Ca. 500

SALT CELLAR

*148   (P 33244) Salt cellar, convex wall   Fig. 121

+49.76–49.14 m (Level 2)

H. 3.25; Diam. 6.45

Complete profile. One-half preserved. Chipped at rim. Exterior, rim, and resting surface worn, but good black glaze. Well potted.

Thick, convex wall. Recessed underside. Black glaze all over with scraped groove at junction of underside and foot. Graffito incised on underside: N.

For the shape, cf. *Agora* XII, p. 299, no. 890, pl. 34, but **148** has a sharper foot.

Ca. 500

Figure 121. Salt cellar 148, convex wall: (a) profile drawing; (b) complete profile; (c, d) inscription on underside. Scale 1:2. Profile drawn author; inked E. Schmitt; facsimile of inscription drawn author

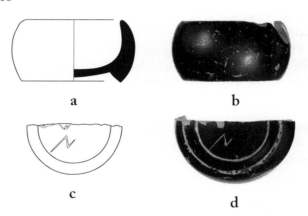

a   b

c   d

*149   (P 32392) Salt cellar, convex wall   Fig. 122

+49.76–49.14 m (Level 2)

H. 3.0; Diam. 5.4

Camp 1996, pl. 71:a.

Mended from two fragments. Complete except for chips at rim. Dull, streaky black glaze peeling inside and out.

Flat, slightly concave underside, bevels up toward wall. Vertical walls curve up and in to plain rim. Reserved: underside, bevel, and bottom of wall.

No exact parallel in *Agora* XII; none have the bevel at the edge of the base. The form with the convex wall and flat underside is usually later than 480, but the bevel suggests that this is an earlier, experimental piece.

Ca. 500

Figure 122. Salt cellar 149, convex wall. Scale 1:2. Profile drawn author; inked E. Schmitt

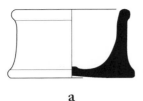
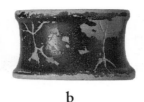

a   b   c

*150   (P 32401) Salt cellar, concave wall   Fig. 123

+46.30–46.00 m (Level 5)
H. 3.9; Diam. foot 6.6
Camp 1996, pl. 71:a.

Intact. Black glaze peeling and worn. Fine clay, very pale brown (10 YR 7/3) with some very fine mica; tinged gray under peeling glaze in places.

Flat underside, torus at base of wall. Concave wall, thickened, rounded lip. Reserved: underside, lower part of base torus, and top of lip. Graffito incised on underside: ΟΣ.

Scratched on wall, two similar designs: vertical, double-ended tridents, placed next to each other. Fingerprint inside on floor.

For shape and date, cf. *Agora* XII, p. 301, no. 923, pl. 34, fig. 9. The double-ended tridents may be thunderbolts, cf. the red-figured cup, Berlin F2293, *CVA* Berlin 2 [Germany 21], pl. 67, 1 [996], pl. 68 [997]:1, where Zeus in Gigantomachy throws a lightning bolt of similar shape.

Ca. 500

*151   (P 32398) Salt cellar/small bowl   Fig. 124

+46.30–46.00 m (Level 5)
H. 3.3; Diam. 7.5–8.0
Camp 1996, pl. 71:a.

Intact. Hasty and careless glazing, misfired red on part of exterior. Poor, irregular potting with accidental scrapes on exterior, finger smudges on interior. Very fine clay, very pale brown (10YR 8/4) with occasional very fine mica.

Narrow ring foot, with nipple on underside. Shallow bowl with convex walls, thickened lip with irregular groove under glaze beneath. Reserved: most of lip, exterior and resting surface of foot, underside. Added red: palmette on interior floor.

No parallels in *Agora* XII, but palmette may prefigure stamped bowls of the late 5th century.

Context: 525–480

Figure 123. Salt cellar 150, concave wall: (a) profile drawing; (b) intact pot; (c) graffito. Scale 1:2. Profile drawn author; inked E. Schmitt

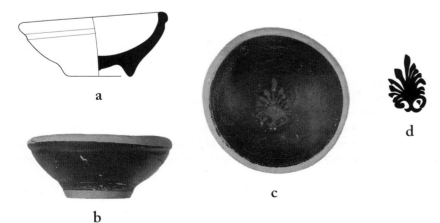

a

b

c

d

Figure 124. Salt cellar/small bowl 151: (a) profile drawing; (b) intact pot; (c, d) palmette on interior floor. Scale 1:2. Profile drawn author; inked E. Schmitt; palmette facsimile drawn author

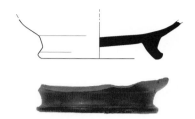

Figure 125. Bowl 152. Scale 1:2. Profile drawn author; inked E. Schmitt

153

154

Figure 126. Bowls 153, 154. Scale 1:2

BOWL AND LEKANIS

152   (P 33254) Bowl   Fig. 125

+46.00–45.90 m (Level 5)

P.H. 2.0; Diam. foot 6.63

Foot and joining fragment of lower wall. Wear on resting surface. Clay tinged gray at breaks. Good black glaze. Well potted.

Ring foot with projecting lower edge, tall concave outer face, convex inner face. Bowl convex and flaring. Thin, delicate wall. Reserved: band at junction of foot and underside. Graffito incised on underside: N.

For the shape and date, cf. *Agora* XII, p. 294, nos. 809–813, pl. 32, fig. 8. Same potter as **153** and **154**.

First quarter 5th century

[153]   (P 33255) Bowl   Fig. 126

+45.60–45.45 m (Level 6)

P.H. 2.0; est. Diam. foot 9.0

Fragment of foot and start of lower wall. Resting surface chipped. Clay tinged gray at breaks. Good black glaze. Well potted.

Ring foot with projecting edge, tall concave outer face, convex inner face. Reserved band at junction of foot and underside. On underside: pattern of broad and thin concentric circles.

For the shape and date, cf. *Agora* XII, p. 294, nos. 809–813, pl. 32, fig. 8. Same potter as **154** and **152**.

First quarter 5th century

[154]   (P 33256) Bowl   Fig. 126

+45.60–45.45 m (Level 6)

P.H. 2.1; Diam. foot 9.4

Foot, intact. Resting surface worn. Clay tinged gray at breaks. Good black glaze. Well potted.

Ring foot with projecting rounded edge, tall concave outer face, convex inner face. Reserved: band at junction of foot and underside. On underside two reserved bands with sets of three concentric circles between three broad bands of black glaze, two circles at center.

For the shape and date, cf. *Agora* XII, p. 294, nos. 809–813, pl. 32, fig. 8. Same potter as **153** and **152**.

First quarter 5th century

*155   (P 32412) Covered bowl   Fig. 127

+45.90–45.60 m (Level 6)

H. 6.2–6.7; Diam. 11.7

Camp 1996, pl. 71:a.

Complete. Foot mended from five fragments, bowl intact; lid missing. Good black glaze but fired red in patch on interior. Roughly potted on upper face of foot.

Torus disk foot, rising to pared cone on underside. Short, broad stem with groove at top and bottom. Convex wall. Rim projects slightly over wall on exterior, flat on top, with vertical, upright flange, angled slightly inward, to receive lid at inner edge of rim. Rim offset on exterior by deep scraped groove. Reserved: top of cone on underside, resting surface and outer face of foot, stem, line at groove below rim, vertical face and top of flange. Miltos on stem, vertical face of flange, possibly on groove.

Cf. *Agora* XII, p. 325, no. 1269, pl. 42, but with reserved stem. The shape is a cross between the stemmed dish with thickened rim and groove beneath (cf. **142–147**) and the covered bowl. Shape similar to **156**, but smaller.

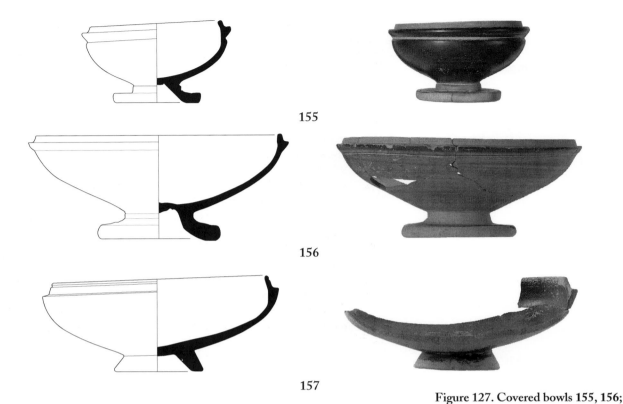

155

156

157

Figure 127. Covered bowls 155, 156; lekanis 157. Scale 1:3. Profiles drawn author; inked E. Schmitt

Although this comes from the lowest level of the well, its excellent condition suggests that it belongs with the clean-up debris and not period of use.

Ca. 500–480

*156 (P 32393) Covered bowl   Fig. 127

+49.76–49.14 and +48.83–48.70 m (Level 2)

H. 8.0–8.6; Diam. 21.0

Mended from numerous fragments. About two-thirds preserved. Missing about one-third of rim. Poorly fired, greenish-red black glaze, pitted and peeling.

Flaring disk foot with torus profile, rough upper surface, rising to broad cone with rough central nipple on underside. Short, wide stem. Broad flaring bowl, projecting lip, flat on top, incised groove below. Inset, vertical, upright flange on rim to receive lid. Reserved: underside of foot, vertical face of foot, stem, top of lip, vertical face and top of flange.

For shape and date, cf. *Kerameikos* IX, pp. 87–88, no. 13 (HW 100), pl. 46:5. Shape is similar to **155** but larger and broader. The lid **158** does not fit.

Ca. 500

*157 (P 33252) Lekanis   Fig. 127

+46.00–45.60 m (Levels 5 and 6)

H. 7.85; est. Diam. 18.25, at flange 17.75

Complete profile, missing most of rim and upper wall. Five joining fragments. Glaze flaking and very worn on exterior, chipped and flaking on the interior. Pink micaceous clay (5YR 7/4), with one pebble inclusion on interior, some small voids. Imported?

Flaring ring foot with broad, flat resting surface. Broad shallow bowl. Rim projects slightly from wall, flat top with vertical flange at interior edge, leans slightly inward. Deep groove beneath rim on exterior. Reserved: resting surface, underside, top and vertical face of flange, top of rim. On underside two dots.

No exact parallel in *Agora* XII, but the wide bowl would place it after 500 in the Agora Attic lekanis chronology. Similar in fabric to the following: **114**, **115**, and **116**. For fabric, cf. *Agora* XII, p. 243, nos. 97 and 98, pl. 5, which are also dipped and probably Lakonian, or *Agora* XII, p. 353, nos. 1665 and 1666, pl. 77.

Ca. 500–480?

Lid

*158 (P 32409) Lekanis lid   Fig. 128

+46.00–45.90 m (Level 5)
H. 6.2; Diam. 20.0
Complete except for chips. Mended from nine fragments. Black glaze fired reddish in places, particularly within.

Convex dome curving to flat lip. Broad, flat handle with pared cone at center, slightly concave and inward sloping vertical face. Reserved: resting surface; a zone near the stem decorated with thin, dilute glazed rays slightly off diameter; top and vertical face of the knob, the former with a glazed circle. Dilute wash on reserved areas of knob. Incised line at top of zone of rays. Added red: on top of lid, double line below reserved zone, two lines at midpoint, single line at rim.

Virtually the same as *Agora* XII, p. 322, no. 1229, pl. 41; from same workshop. A lid for a ribbon-handled lekanis such as *Agora* XII, p. 321, no. 1217, pl. 40.

Ca. 520–500

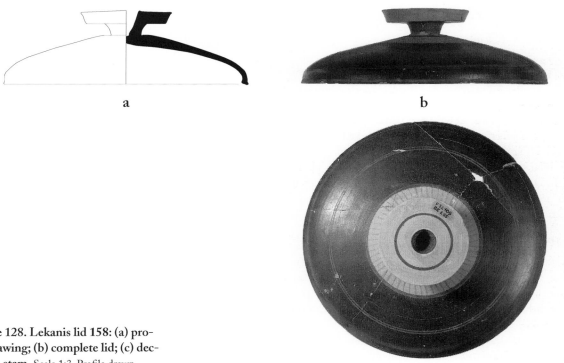

a   b

c

Figure 128. Lekanis lid 158: (a) profile drawing; (b) complete lid; (c) decorated stem. Scale 1:3. Profile drawn author; inked E. Schmitt

159 (P 33209) Lekanis lid   Fig. 129

+49.76–49.14 m (Level 2)
Max. p. dim. 8.2
Fragment of convex top. Glaze dull and flaking. Underside glazed but flaking and scratched. Surface of underside irregular.

Reserved zone at top with rays. Added red line at bottom edge of reserved area.

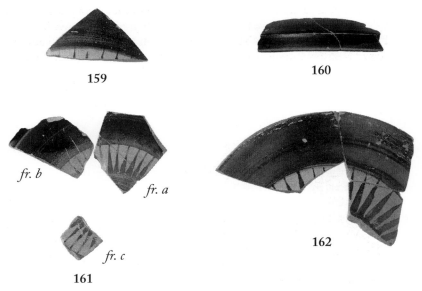

159

160

fr. b

fr. a

fr. c

161

162

Figure 129. Lekanis lids 159–162.
Scale 1:3

For shape and decoration, cf. *Agora* XII, p. 323, no. 1234, pl. 41, fig. 11. The scratches cover the underside of the lid as if it was used for mixing, but they follow the irregular and deep wheelmarks. The steepness of the lid suggests a date closer to 500 than to 480.

    Ca. 500–480

160 (P 33214) Lekanis lid   Fig. 129

    +49.14–48.73 m (Level 2)

    P.H. 3.0; est. Diam. 23.0

    Two joining fragments of rim. Black glaze cloudy on top. Drill hole for ancient mend at break.

    Steeply convex lid, straight rim with slightly thickened, flat resting surface. Sharp edge at junction of rim and top. Reserved: resting surface and underside. Added red (fugitive): double line on top near edge.

    Similar to *Agora* XII, p. 323, no. 1232 or 1234, pl. 41, fig. 11, but no exact parallels. Date is close to 500, but more likely before than after on the basis of the convex profile of the top.

    Ca. 500

161 (P 33211) Lekanis lid   Fig. 129

    +50.31–49.76 and +48.83–48.70 m (Levels 1b and 2)

    Est. Diam. to edge of fragments 10.5; max. p. dim. (a) 6.8, (b) 6.4, (c) 2.85

    Two joining (a) and two nonjoining (b, c) fragments of top of low-domed lid. Glaze mottled brown and black on top, red and black on underside. Flaking on the underside.

    Black-glazed band at base of stem. Narrow reserved zone with rays. Black-glazed zone to edge of top. Added red: on rays, double line at base of stem; in black-glazed zone: single line at top, double line at midpoint and single line toward rim. Two scratches on (b) may be a graffito.

    For shape and decoration, cf. *Agora* XII, p. 323, no. 1234, pl. 41, fig. 11. The flatness of the top indicates a date closer to 480 than to 500.

    Ca. 480

***162** (P 33213) Lekanis lid   Fig. 129

    +49.14–48.73 and +46.60–46.30 m (Levels 2 and 5)

    P.H. 4.5; est. Diam. 23.0

Three joining fragments of high convex lid and rim, missing knob. Glaze streaky and flaking. Roughly potted on interior. Resting surface reserved.

Reserved band with rays at base of stem. Black glaze beyond, down onto rim, where glaze becomes thin and uneven. Underside: black glaze with reserved central circle. Resting surface reserved. Added red (fugitive): single line at top of rays, double line below; double line at middle of black-glazed band on exterior.

For shape and decoration, cf. *Agora* XII, p. 323, no. 1234, pl. 41, fig. 11.

Ca. 480

*163 (P 32468) Psykter lid   Fig. 130

+49.76–49.14 m (Level 2)

H. 1.1 (without handle); Diam. 8.1

Six joining fragments preserving three-quarters of lid. Crack in top ancient, probably prefiring.

Flat top; short, vertical rim, slightly concave. Small pierced loop handle at center. Reserved: underside, resting surface, handle.

For shape, date, and function, cf. *Agora* XII, p. 239, no. 44, pl. 2.

Ca. 500–480

*164 (P 32486) Lid for covered bowl?   Fig. 130

+45.90–45.60 m (Level 6)

H. 3.3; Diam. 10.2

Two joining fragments preserving almost complete lid. Pink clay with frequent fine surface mica. Streaky black glaze, abraded at rim in one area.

Straight low rim, low dome, spherical knob handle. Reserved: underside, resting surface, and handle.

The profile is similar to the lids for small covered bowls both in the Agora and Kerameikos (cf. *Agora* XII, p. 325, no. 1269, pl. 42); however, these lids usually have a glazed acorn knob.

Ca. 500?

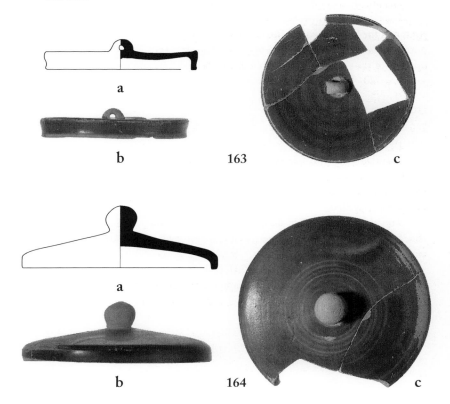

Figure 130. Psykter lid **163**: (a) profile drawing; (b) lid; (c) loop handle; lid **164**, for covered bowl?: (a) profile drawing; (b) lid: (c) knob handle.
Scale 1:2. Profiles drawn author; inked E. Schmitt

Figure 131. Lid or bowl? 165.
Scale 1:2. Profile drawn author; inked
E. Schmitt

*165 (P 33249) Lid or bowl? Fig. 131

+49.76–49.14 m (Level 2)
H. 2.1; Diam. 10.3

Complete. Mended from five fragments. Worn on exterior. Traces of black glaze adhere to exterior surface. Interior surface has traces of light gray slip. Soft, powdery orange fabric with occasional medium white inclusions and frequent mica; one large inclusion on exterior burnt out. Clay tinged slightly gray in places.

Rounded, domed exterior, beveled rim with roughly finished vertical face.

The rough treatment of the vertical face of the rim allows a grip with the fingertips. The object fits in the hand best when used for a scooping motion. May be a temporary lid for a closed vessel, or a multipurpose lid-scooper.

Context: 525–480

Miscellaneous Forms

*166 (P 32394) Askos Fig. 132

+49.76–49.14 m (Level 2)
H. 9.0; Diam. 9.0
Camp 1996, p. 252, no. 37, fig. 10.

About two-thirds preserved. Mended from numerous fragments. Dull black glaze, misfired red at bottom and sides, abraded and worn. Exterior totally glazed. Interior reserved below rim with a few drips.

Deep askos with hollow tube. Rounded base, very high cylindrical body. Flat shoulder. Spout with broad, concave rim around hole. Short strap handle, slightly concave, attached from below rim to near side of tube.

For the shape, cf. *Agora* XII, p. 358, no. 1725, pl. 80, an East Greek import (found in the SGW). Askos **166** is not an import, and probably represents an Attic potter's attempt to imitate the imported form. It stands at the start of the development of the Attic askos, which will have a ring foot and a stouter body.

Ca. 520–490

*167 (P 33217) Unguent pot Fig. 132

+45.90–45.60 m (Level 6)
P.H. 8.7; Diam. 6.43

Mended from two fragments. Missing foot, chip off lower wall, part of rim. Gritty pink-buff clay (7.5YR 7/4) with some medium mica and some medium white-gray inclusions. Imported. Black glaze fugitive on most of surface. Very heavy, thick-walled.

Top-shaped body. Tall, slightly concave neck. Downward sloping, projecting rim. Small central chamber. Interior of rim and neck black-glazed. Black-glazed bands on body, but largely fugitive.

For shape and fabric, cf. *Agora* XII, p. 317, no. 1165, pl. 39. No specific date given for *Agora* XII, no. 1165. The shape is a relative of the Lydion perfume jar.

Ca. last quarter of 6th century?

*168 (P 33246) Disk Fig. 132

+49.76–49.14 m (Level 2)
H. 1.2; Diam. 7.3

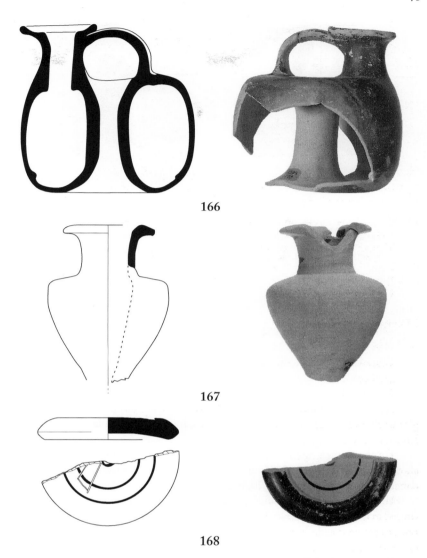

166

167

168

Figure 132. Askos 166; unguent pot 167; disk 168. Scale 1:2. Profiles drawn A. Hooton (**166**), author (**167, 168**); inked E. Schmitt

One half preserved. Black glaze abraded. Large white (lime) inclusions in otherwise fine clay.

Round rim. Recessed center on upper surface. Underside concave. Recessed center reserved with two black-glazed circles. Underside reserved with very dilute wash. Grafitto incised on top: II.

For shape, cf. *Agora* XII, p. 329, no. 1323, pl. 43, fig. 11 (but decorated with different scheme); p. 329, no. 1325, pl. 43. No. 1325 also has an inscription, Δ, which the authors speculate might be a tally mark. Very similar fabric and profile to upper, disk element of **169**. Function uncertain.

Ca. 525–500

***169**   (P 33257) Stand   Fig. 133

+45.90–45.45 m (Level 6)

P.H. 3.05; Diam. 7.6; max. p. dim. (nonjoining fragment) 2.61

Four joining fragments and one nonjoining fragment (not figured) of upper part of stand, missing base. Good black glaze fired red-brown in places. Miltos on reserved surfaces.

Thick, downturned, overhanging rim. Recessed center on top. Concave stem with raised ridge at middle. Underside rises to cone. Reserved: central circle with

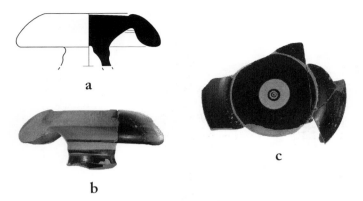

a

b

c

Figure 133. Stand 169: (a) profile drawing; (b) upper part of stand; (c) top of stand. Scale 1:2. Profile drawn author; inked E. Schmitt

two black-glazed circles and dot on top, line at recess; upper part of stem with two black-glazed lines; top of cone on underside.

For shape and date, cf. *Agora* XII, p. 329, no. 1329, pl. 43, fig. 11. Function uncertain.

Ca. 500

*170   (P 33248) Ring   Fig. 134

+46.00–45.90 m (Level 5)

H. 5.45; est. Diam. 8.25

Complete profile. About half preserved. Fine, micaceous buff-gray clay (10YR 7/2); probably Attic clay discolored gray from fire, not imported. Good black glaze but slightly dull.

Inverted cone with convex wall. Curves inward at bottom for resting surface. Rim slopes inward. Reserved: resting surface, interior. Dilute black glaze on rim. Vertical stain of added color or drip on wall.

For the type, cf. *Agora* XII, p. 330, nos. 1330–1336, p. 43; for the specific shape, cf. *Agora* XII, p. 330, nos. 1335 and 1336, pl. 43. The two closest comparanda are dated later than the context of **170**, but are a "definable class," *Agora* XII, p. 180, n. 2, to which add P 34458, unpublished. A slightly heavier version, also from later in the 5th century, *Agora* XXI, p. 13, no. C15, p. 94, no. M9, pl. 61, bears an erotic cartoon of a man having intercourse with a shaggy dog, inscribed prefiring. The ring functions as a stand for pointy-bottomed perfume jars like **167**.

Context: 525–480

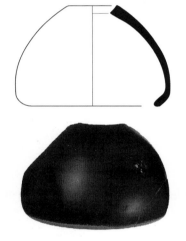

Figure 134. Ring 170. Scale 1:2. Profile drawn author; inked E. Schmitt

*171   (P 33557) "Argive" monochrome juglet   Fig. 135

+45.60–45.20 m (Level 6)

H. 5.6; Diam. 5.9

Complete profile. Mended from 11 fragments. Missing part of rim, pieces of body; handle present but unattached (not pictured in Fig. 135). Powdery white clay (10YR 8/3) with rare medium white inclusions, no mica. Flat bottom, squat spherical body, straight neck with slightly outturned rim. Vertical strap handle attached from rim to body. Handmade.

For identification of ware, cf. *Agora* XII, p. 353, no. 1669–1673, pl. 77; Caskey and Amandry 1952, pp. 202–203. Kourou (1987, pp. 46–47) describes Attic workshops of monochrome, handmade vessels, but **171** does not fit the description of either Attic workshop fabric. **171** seems to fit the description of Kourou's Corinthian workshop, pp. 48–49. For shapes, see Caskey and Amandry 1952, pp. 204–207; Dunbabin 1962, pp. 314–318; Kourou 1988; Morgan 1999, pp. 148–149, nos. 475–480, fig. I.57, pls. 62, 63, but no exact parallel.

Second half of 6th century

Figure 135. "Argive" monochrome juglet 171. Scale 1:2

Figure 136. Kados 172. Scale 1:4.
Profile drawn and inked author

HOUSEHOLD WARE

KADOS

*172   (P 32753) Kados   Fig. 136

+46.00–45.90 m (Level 5)
H. 28.5; Diam. 15.5

Complete profile. Two-thirds complete. Body fragments missing. Mended from six fragments. Foot and rim chipped from use. Thin cooking-ware fabric, reddish brown clay (2.5YR 5/4) with large white and quartz inclusions and mica. Buff surface on interior and exterior.

Ring foot. Ovoid body. Cylindrical neck, thickened, flaring rim. Handles round in section with finger depression at base, attached from shoulder to lower neck.

Cf. *Agora* XII, p. 349, no. 1601, pl. 72. The position of the handles places it closer to 500 than to 480.

Ca. 500

JUG

[173]   (P 32485) Jug   Fig. 137

+45.90–45.60 m (Level 6)
H. 15.5; Diam. 14.4

Complete profile. Two-thirds preserved. Mended from five pieces. Some large body fragments missing. Original, unintentional hole (1 cm) on body. Thin cooking-ware fabric with many medium white and gray inclusions and frequent fine mica. Red clay (10R 5/8) with a buff surface.

Small form. Ring foot, slightly flaring. Squat spherical body. Broad, short neck with a slight trefoil mouth. Vertical handle oval in section, attached from rim to shoulder.

For shape and date, cf. *Agora* XII, p. 352, no. 1655, pl. 76, but **173** is slightly smaller. Jug **173**, from the period of use deposit, obviously had been used to fetch water, therefore the hole in the body must have been plugged with something perishable such as beeswax.

Ca. 500–480

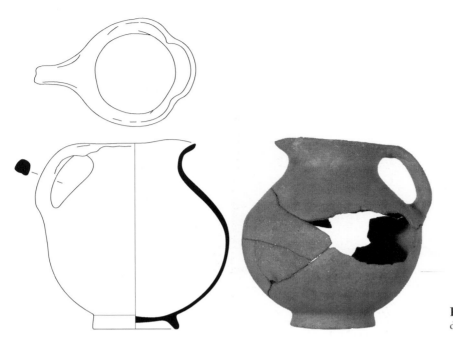

Figure 137. Jug 173. Scale 1:3. Profile drawn A. Hooton; inked E. Schmitt

[174]   (P 32752) Trefoil jug   Fig. 138

+46.30–45.90 m (Level 5)

H. 27.4; Diam. 25.1

Complete profile, except for handle. Seven large joining fragments preserve about half. Wheelmade. Coarse red clay (10R 5/6) with medium white, gray, and mica inclusions; creamy pink surface.

Disk foot, slightly flaring, slightly concave on underside. Ovoid body, wide cylindrical neck with light articulation at bottom. Everted rim with light trefoil.

No exact parallel in *Agora* XII. The wheelmade, coarse, not cooking-ware fabric is unusual for the shape. Shape is very similar to the round-mouth jugs **175**, **176**, **177**, and **178** in form, but the fabric is not as gritty. The wide mouth facilitates fetching water; the handle broke during use in the well and was retrieved.

Context: 525–480

*175   (P 32469) Jug   Fig. 138

+46.00–45.90 m (Level 5)

H. 22.5, with handle 24.9; Diam. 20.4

Largely complete; several body fragments missing. Mended from many pieces. Foot chipped, probably from use. Wheelmade. Gritty, red clay (2.5YR 5/6) with occasional white inclusions and mica.

Disk foot, flaring. Ovoid body. Wide, cylindrical neck with large round mouth pushed in at handle. Slightly everted, rounded rim. High-swung handle, oval in section. Graffito on shoulder to left of handle, X within circle, same as **177**.

No exact parallel in *Agora* XII. The wheelmade, coarse, not cooking ware, fabric is unusual for the shape. Nearly identical to **176**. Shape is very similar to the round-mouth jugs, **177**, **178** and the trefoil jug **174**, but slightly smaller. This is a coarser fabric than **174**. The wide mouth facilitates fetching water.

Context: 525–480

*176   (P 32484) Jug   Not Illustrated

+46.00–45.90 m (Level 5)

H. 21.1; Diam. 18.0

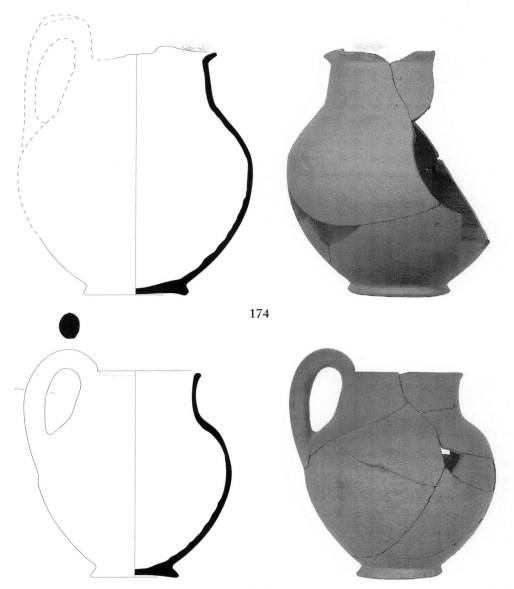

174

175

Figure 138. Trefoil jug 174; jug 175.
Scale 1:4. Profiles drawn author; inked
E. Schmitt

Mended from 11 pieces. Fragments missing from body and chips from rim.
Wheelmade. Gritty orange–dark buff clay, with mica and inclusions.

Disk foot, ovoid body. Wide, cylindrical neck with large round mouth pushed
in at handle. High-swung handle, oval in section.

No exact parallel in *Agora* XII. The wheelmade, coarse, not cooking ware,
fabric is unusual for the shape. The wide mouth suggests it was used for fetching
water. Nearly identical to **175**. Shape is very similar to the round-mouth jugs, **177**,
178, and the trefoil jug **174**. This is a coarser fabric than **174**.

Context: 525–480

[**177**]   (P 32756) Jug   Fig. 139

+46.00–45.60 m (Levels 5 and 6)

H. 27.4; Diam. mouth 15.2 (but not round), body 23.2

Largely complete but missing handle and one-third of rim. Mended from
many pieces. Foot chipped, probably from use. Wheelmade. Gritty light reddish

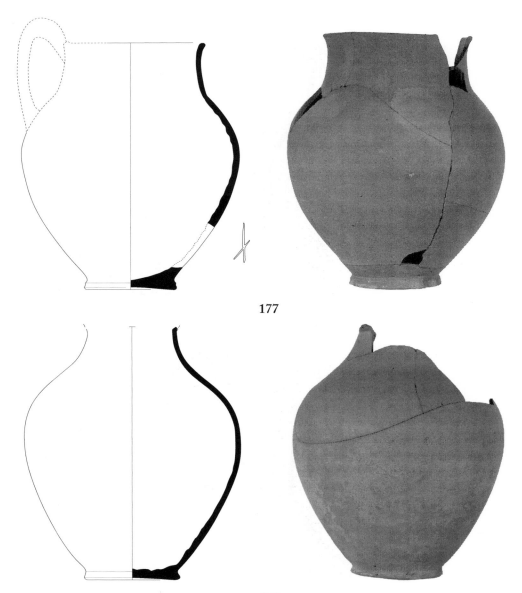

177

178

Figure 139. Jugs 177, 178. Scale 1:4.
Profile drawn author (**177**), A. Hooton
(**178**); inked E. Schmitt

brown clay (5YR 6/4) with small to medium white and black inclusions. Very rare mica. Creamy, uneven buff-pink slip on surface.

Slightly flaring disk foot, slightly concave on underside, light ridge on vertical face. Ovoid body, wide cylindrical neck with slightly everted lip. Mouth not round, possibly very slightly trefoil. Scratch or graffito on front of body, same as **175**: X.

No exact parallel in *Agora* XII. The wheelmade, coarse, not cooking-ware fabric is unusual for the shape. Shape is very similar to the round-mouth jugs **175**, **176**, **178**, and the trefoil jug **174**. This is a coarser fabric than **174**. The wide mouth facilitates fetching water. The handle broke during use in the well and was retrieved.

Context: 525–480

[**178**]   (P 32758) Jug   Fig. 139

+46.30–45.90 m (Level 5)

P.H. 28.0; Diam. body 23.1

About two-thirds preserved. Rim, handle, much of neck, and shoulder missing. Mended from seven large fragments. Wheelmade. Coarse, light red clay (2.5YR 6/8)

Figure 140. Water jar 179. Scale 1:4

with small white and red inclusions and mica. Thin white slip on exterior and thicker greenish-white deposit on interior.

Slightly flaring disk foot, slightly concave on underside. Ovoid body, sloping shoulder to neck. Slight depression on neck suggests a light trefoil.

No exact parallel in *Agora* XII. The wheelmade, coarse, not cooking-ware fabric is unusual for the shape. Shape is very similar to the round-mouth jugs **175**, **176**, **177**, and the trefoil jug **174**, but with a narrower neck. This is a coarser fabric than **174**. The handle broke during use and was retrieved.

Context: 525–480

179 (P 33258) Water jar Fig. 140

+46.60–46.30 m (Level 5)
P.H. 8.0; Diam. foot 11.0
Single fragment of foot and lower wall.

Raised ring foot, flattened resting surface angles upward toward underside. Inner face of foot concave. Pink-buff cooking fabric (gray core: 2.5YR 7/1) with buff slip on exterior (10YR 7/3) and pink interior (5YR 7/4); frequent small to fine white and gray inclusions and mica, occasional red inclusions. On underside, marked with chalklike substance: N.

Ring foot could be from a kados, hydria, or jug; all feature identical ring feet.

The dates for the water jars are difficult to assign. The medium height of the ring foot might place this fragment closer to 500 than to 480, when the feet seem to have a greater height. For a kados inscribed with an ownership mark, cf. *Agora* XII, p. 349, no. 1601, pl. 72.

Ca. 510–480

LEKANE

180 (P 33240) Lekane Fig. 141

+50.31–49.76 m (Level 1b)
P.H. 14.0; est. Diam. 39.0
Fragment of rim, wall and one handle root. Black glaze fired red; streaky on exterior bands; fugitive on band at top of wall. Break at top right may preserve one half of mend hole.

Convex body. Thickened, rounded rim. Thick, round, upturned horizontal handle. Glazed on interior, top of rim, two bands on exterior above and below handle, exterior of handle.

Shape is similar to *Agora* XII, p. 360, nos. 1748, 1750, 1751, pl. 82 (600–525). Date is most likely to be around 550.

Comparanda: 600–525

Figure 141. Lekane 180. Scale 1:3.
Profile drawn author; inked E. Schmitt

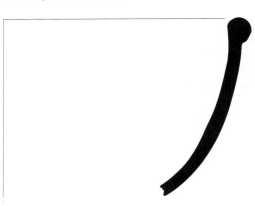

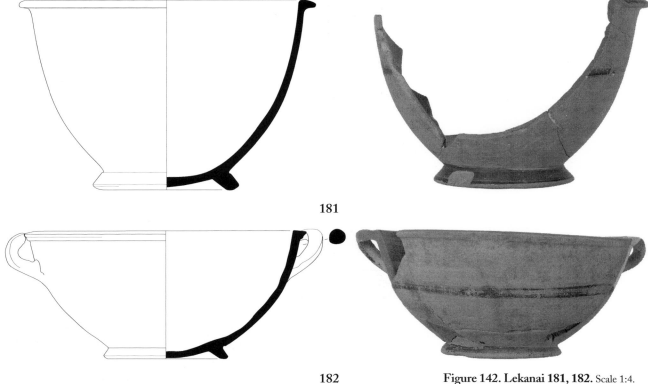

181

182

Figure 142. Lekanai 181, 182. Scale 1:4.
Profiles drawn A. Hooton; inked E. Schmitt

*181   (P 32489) Lekane   Fig. 142

+50.87–50.31 m (Level 1b)

H. 20.9; est. Diam. 34.0

Complete profile; about one-third preserved. Handles not preserved. Mended from 11 large fragments. Pink clay (7.5YR 7/4) with small and large white inclusions.

Flaring ring foot; high wall. Projecting outturned rim, rounded on top.

Streaky brown glaze on exterior of foot, band around body, top of lip. Red and brown glaze (caused by differential firing) on interior, worn on floor.

For shape and date, cf. *Agora* XII, p. 361, no. 1787, pl. 83, fig. 15. Sparkes and Talcott call the rim profile of no. 1787 "the latest of the pre-Persian types."

Ca. 510–480

*182   (P 32488) Lekane   Fig. 142

+46.60–45.60 m (Level 5 and 6)

H. 14.2; Diam. 31.0

Complete profile. Three-quarters preserved. Portions of rim and body missing and half of each handle. Sections restored. Mended from 14 fragments. Light reddish-brown clay (5YR 6/4) with small white inclusions. Thin brown glaze on exterior of foot, around body in band at base of handles, and on exterior of handles; streaky red-brown glaze on interior. Glaze peeling, worn on interior.

Ring foot, slightly flaring. Broad bowl. Thickened rim flat on top. Horizontal handles, round in section, upturned and tangent to rim.

For shape and date, cf. *Agora* XII, p. 364, no. 1825, pl. 86, fig. 15. See text of no. 1825 for further parallels.

Ca. 520–490

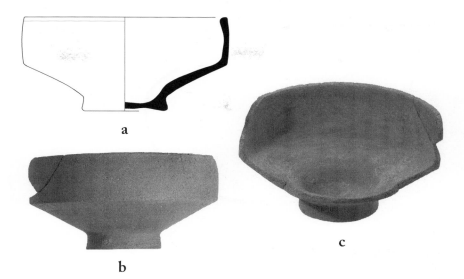

Figure 143. Bowl 183: (a) profile drawing; (b) profile; (c) interior. Scale 1:3. Profile drawn author; inked E. Schmitt

*183 (P 33224) Bowl Fig. 143

+46.00–45.90 m (Level 5)

H. 7.6; est. Diam. 16.2

Complete profile. Missing two-thirds of rim. Aigenetan cooking fabric (J. Hayes and W. Gauss, pers. comm.), light reddish-brown core (2.5YR 6/3) with occasional small andesite inclusions, frequent fine white and gray inclusions.

Tall disk foot, slightly concave on underside. Straight, flaring lower wall to sharp junction with vertical but slightly convex upper wall. On interior, depression at center corresponding to foot. Vertical burnishing on lower wall. Exterior surface finished smoother than interior. On interior, residue of red (ocher?) and white pigments.

The shape of the foot would permit the bowl to sit in the palm of one's hand. It would work well as a paint pot.

Context: 525–480

COOKING WARE

Chytra

*184 (P 32407) Chytra Fig. 144

+46.63 m (Level 4/top of Level 5)

H. 15.0; Diam. 18.5

Camp 1996, pl. 71:a.

Complete. Handle and fragment of rim mended, otherwise intact. Coarse, gritty reddish-yellow clay (5YR 6/6) with occasional large white, frequent small white and gray inclusions, and frequent small to fine black mica. Extensive traces of burning on bottom and side away from handle, and on interior floor and interior side away from handle. Paring marks on lower body. Prefiring dent to right of handle.

Low rounded body, angled to straight shoulder. Short neck. Outturned rim. Vertical strap handle attached from rim to shoulder.

For shape, cf. *Agora* XII, p. 371, no. 1923, pl. 93. The date suggested by the comparandum (575–535) may be too high for this deposit.

Context: 525–480

*185 (P 32404) Chytra Fig. 144

Ca. +45.50 m (Level 5)

H. 12.1; Diam. body 13.4, rim 9.8

Camp 1996, pl. 71:a.

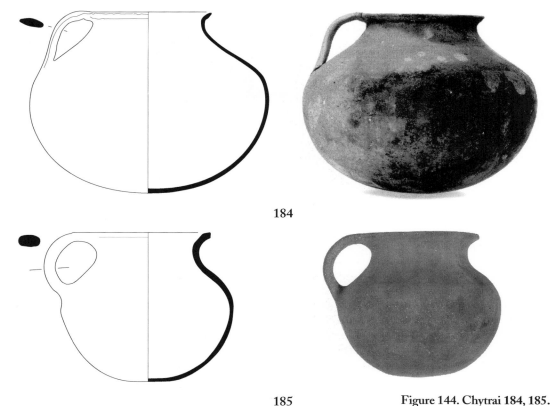

184

185

Figure 144. Chytrai 184, 185. Scale 1:3.
Profiles drawn A. Hooton (**184**), author
(**185**); inked E. Schmitt

Intact. Traces of burning on exterior and on one side of interior. Coarse orange clay (2.5YR 5/6) with frequent fine mica and frequent medium to fine white, frequent fine red and gray, and occasional medium quartz inclusions. Buff wash (7.5YR 6/3) on the surface.

Slightly flattened but rounded base, spherical body. Short, straight neck. Thickened, outturned rim with flat lip. Strap handle, oval in section, with finger depression at base.

For shape and date, cf. *Agora* XII, p. 372, no. 1934, pl. 93. Jug type of chytra. Ca. 525–500

*186   (P 32400) Chytra   Fig. 145

Ca. +46.00 m (Level 5)
H. 7.1; Diam. 8.2
Camp 1996, pl. 71:a.
Intact.

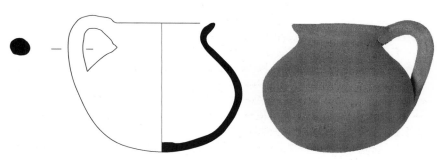

Figure 145. Chytra 186. Scale 1:2.
Profile drawn author; inked E. Schmitt

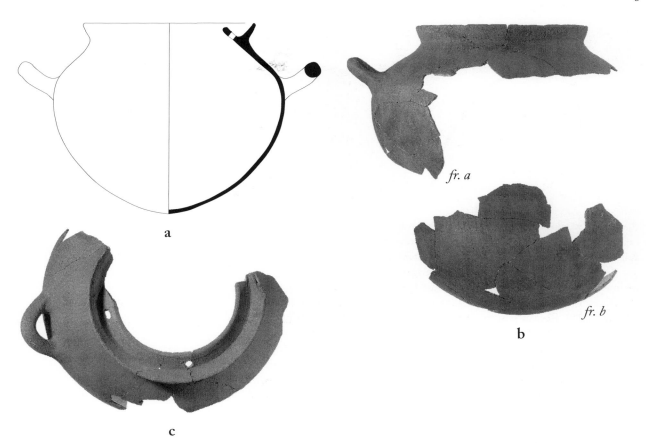

Figure 146. Chytra 187: (a) profile drawing; (b) rim and shoulder, lower body and bottom; (c) top view.
Scale 1:4. Profile drawn and inked author

Rounded bottom, steep shoulder, flaring rim. Vertical handle, round in section, slightly rising above rim, attached from rim to widest part of body.

Medium light reddish-brown clay (5YR 6/4) with frequent black mica and medium white inclusions, burnished vertically on lower half.

No traces of burning. Horizontal wheelmarks on shoulder and above. Probably coil made and finished on the wheel.

For shape and date, cf. *Agora* XII, p. 372, no. 1937, pl. 93. The miniature shape is associated with graves, but it is also found in habitation areas. Some of the domestic examples have carbon deposits on their surfaces, indicating that small-sized chytrai were used for cooking; see Corbett 1949, p. 335, no. 97, pl. 97. However, see also the use of a similarly shaped vessel as a serving jug in sympotic scenes, e.g., Florence, Museo Archeologico, Vagnonville 48, *ARV²* 432, no. 58, *Paralipomena* 374, *Add²* 237 [Douris], Buitron-Oliver 1995, p. 86, no. E1, pl. 117.

Early 5th century

*187   (P 34766) Chytra   Fig. 146

+45.60–45.45 m (Level 6)

P.H. (a) 16.6, (b) 14.0; max. p. dim. (a) 29.0; Diam. rim (b) 18.7; est. max. dim. (b) 28.0–29.0

Many fragments mended into two main pieces: (a) over half of rim and shoulder to belly with one horizontal handle attached below shoulder; (b) one side of lower body and bottom; additional nonjoining belly sherds and second handle not mended. Broad rounded body, hemispherical below, more flattened at shoulder. Straight, nearly upright collar rim with broad, upward sloping, projecting interior flange for lid. The flange is pierced by holes at intervals, four preserved, ca. 7 mm

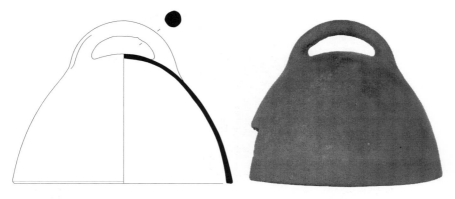

Figure 147. Cooking bell 188.
Scale 1:5. Profile drawn A. Hooton; inked
E. Schmitt

diameter. Two upturned horizontal handles, round in section. Vertical burnishing on exterior of vessel. Traces of burning on exterior and interior. Thin, gritty reddish-yellow clay (5YR 6/6) with gold mica (biotite?) and white and black inclusions.

John Hayes (pers. comm.) thinks it is Aigenetan fabric. The form with strainer on internal flange is also known in fine ware from both Greek and Roman periods; see Hayes 1985, pp. 92–93, C52; 2000, p. 295, fig. 28:1, with further references; McPhee 2000. Roman pottery scholars call the form a "hole-mouthed jar," and they also refer to it as a "milk boiler" or "wine cooler," see Hayes 2000, p. 295. The fine-ware versions are more likely to function as kraters or special serving vessels. **187** is certainly a cooking vessel, and the perforated flange may have permitted condensing steam to drip back into the bowl.

Context: 525–480

*188   (P 32490) Cooking bell   Fig. 147

+46.00–45.90 m (Level 5)
H. 22.5; Diam. 28.8
Two-thirds preserved intact. Large part of rim missing. Dome cracked. Thick yellowish-red cooking fabric (5YR 5/6) with numerous fine white and gray inclusions and silver and black mica. Traces of burning inside and out.

Bell-shaped body with loop handle, round in section across top. Straight rim, flat resting surface.

For shape and date, cf. *Agora* XII, p. 377, no. 2021, pl. 97, fig. 19.
Ca. 520–490

LAMPS

189   (L 6015) Lamp Type 2 B   Fig. 148

+49.76–49.14 m (Level 2)
P.H. 3.3; est. Diam. 9.8
Fragment of rim, wall, underside.

Handmade. Flat underside. Rounded wall. Shoulder slightly concave and rising up to upturned rim. Rim rises (to handle?). Coarse gray-brown clay (10YR 5/3) with large white lime and quartz inclusions, frequent medium mica. Worn, particularly at breaks.

For shape and date, cf. *Agora* IV, p. 11, no. 19, pls. 1, 29.
Late 7th to late 6th century

Figure 148. Lamp 189, Type 2 B.
Scale 1:2. Profile drawn author; inked
E. Schmitt

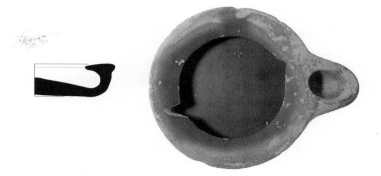

Figure 149. Lamp 190, Type 16 B.
Scale 1:2. Profile drawn author; inked
E. Schmitt

*190 (L 5972) Lamp Type 16 B Fig. 149

+45.90–45.60 m (Level 6)

H. 1.8; Diam. 8.9; L. 11.0

Intact, except for chips from rim. Black glaze on interior floor, rim, and nozzle; misfired red on rim. Dilute wash on remainder. Burning on nozzle.

Flat bottom, low curved wall, broad rim overhangs wall slightly, declines slightly toward well.

Cf. *Agora* IV, p. 34, no. 111, pls. 4, 32.

525–500

*191 (L 5982) Lamp Type 16 B Color Ill. 11; Fig. 150

+46.00–45.90 m (Level 5)

H. 2.3; Diam. 9.7; L. 12.0

Mended from three fragments, chips missing. Black glaze fired orange-red. Glazed everywhere except interior wall and underside of rim. Burning at nozzle.

Concave bottom, rounded body, flat rim overhangs wall slightly.

For shape and date, cf. *Agora* IV, p. 32, no. 96, pl. 4.

500–480

*192 (L 6013) Lamp Type 16 B Fig. 151

+46.00–45.90 m (Level 5)

P.H. 2.15; Diam. 8.9

About half preserved. Missing most of nozzle. Black glaze on rim and interior floor. Dilute wash on other surfaces. Fired red on floor. Surface chipped. Traces of burning at edge of wick hole.

Concave bottom. Continuous curve from rim to bottom. Flat rim overhangs wall slightly with groove below.

For shape and date, cf. *Agora* IV, p. 32, no. 96, pls. 4, 32.

500–480

Figure 150. Lamp 191, Type 16 B.
Scale 1:2

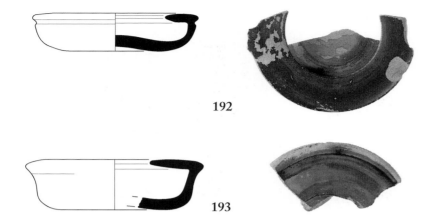

192

193

Figure 151. Lamps 192, 193,
Type 16 B. Scale 1:2. Profiles drawn
author; inked E. Schmitt

193   (L 6012) Lamp Type 16 B   Fig. 151

+46.30–46.00 m (Level 5)

P.H. 2.95; est. Diam. 9.0

Fragment of rim, wall, floor. Streaky brown and black glaze on top of rim continuing onto underside of rim and interior floor. Remainder reserved.

Slightly concave bottom. Rounded junction to straight wall. Wall flares to flat, overhanging rim with large central filling hole.

For shape and date, cf. *Agora* IV, p. 32, no. 97, pls. 4, 32.

500–480

194   (L 6014) Lamp Type 16 B or 21A   Fig. 152

+50.31–49.76 m (Level 1b)

Max. p. dim. 7.56

About two-thirds of concave bottom with rounded wall. Trace of nozzle.

Nozzle and interior of floor glazed. Fired red-brown on interior; dilute wash on underside. Graffito incised on bottom: EM or ΣE.

Difficult to assign type to the fragment, but comes from a lamp with a continuous curve from base to wall and no central tube.

525–480

Figure 152. Lamp 194, Type 16 B
or 21 A. Scale 1:2

*195   (L 5971) Lamp Type 19?   Fig. 153

+46.30–46.00 m (Level 5)

H. 2.1; Diam. 7.3; L. 9.4

Intact. Thin glaze, fired red on interior floor, rim, and nozzle. Remainder reserved. Fine reddish buff clay with flecks of mica; more mica in glaze.

Low, raised base, slightly concave underneath. Continuous curve from wall to rim, with concave offset. Nozzle rises slightly above rim, with traces of burning.

No exact parallel in *Agora* IV, but similar to Type 19 variants, cf. *Agora* IV, p. 43, no. 147, pls. 5, 33.

500–480

*196   (L 5983) Lamp Type 19 A   Fig. 153

+45.45–45.25 m (Level 6)

H. 2.1; Diam. 10.2

Mended from four fragments. Tips of nozzles, parts of rim missing. Dull black glaze on interior floor and tube, top of rim and top of wall. Glaze flaked on rim. Fine, brittle, pink clay (7.5YR 7/4) with frequent fine mica on surface. Imported?

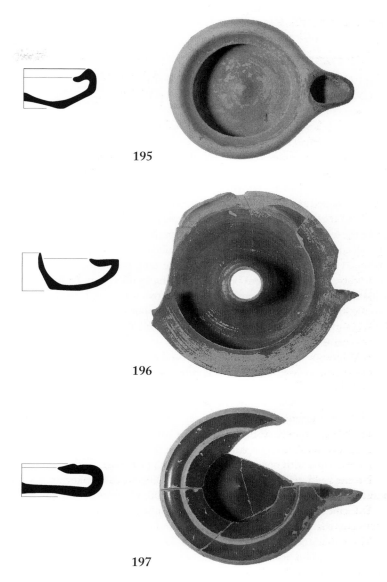

195

196

197

**Figure 153. Lamps 195, Type 19?;
196, Type 19 A; 197, Type 20.** Scale 1:2.
Profiles drawn author; inked E. Schmitt

Convex bottom with central conical tube, flat projecting narrow rim, sloping down toward center, sharp angle at juncture of rim and wall. Two opposing nozzles (only partially preserved) rising above rim. Traces of burning on better preserved. Wick hole intrudes on rim.

For shape, cf. *Agora* IV, p. 40, nos. 131, 132, pls. 5, 33.
500–480

*197   (L 5970) Lamp Type 20   Fig. 153
+49.76–49.14 m (Level 2)
H. 1.8; Diam. 8.6
About three-quarters preserved, mended. Good black glaze. Reserved surfaces with a thin brown wash. Well potted.

Flat bottom, slightly concave underside. Continuous curve to low rounded body. Rim offset from shoulder. Single nozzle. Interior, nozzle, and top of lamp glazed. Reserved line on shoulder below rim offset.

For shape and date, cf. *Agora* IV, p. 44, no. 149, pls. 5, 34.
500–480

TERRACOTTA FIGURINES

PLAQUE

*198 (T 4362) Female plaque figurine   Fig. 154

fr. a

fr. b

Figure 154. Female plaque figurine 198: (a) head; (b) fragment. Scale 1:3

(a) +45.90–45.60 m; (b) +45.45–45.25 m (Level 6)
(a) P.H. ca. 15.0; p.W. 15.5; (b) p.H. 5.7; p.W. 7.8
Camp 1996, p. 251, no. 35, pl. 75.

Broken below shoulders. Painted surface largely missing on (a); better preserved but scratched on (b). Attic clay.

Handmade; finger smoothing visible throughout. Head and upper part of torso of a female figure (a), in relief. Head nearly in the round, lower part no thicker than the plaque. Wears radiate crown, three of the original 10 rays preserved. Three diamond-shaped appliqués at center of crown above forehead, tips broken off. On top of head at center fragment of a thin appliqué perpendicular to plaque plane. This may be the terminus of one of the diamond tips. No clear transition from head gear to forehead. Face lightly modeled, Archaic smile for mouth, but eyes less defined. Appliquéd earrings: a round loop with three long pendants, round in section, which thicken toward bottom before decreasing again at end. At both shoulders are appliquéd round disks from which depend two wavy pendants. Fragment (b): from the lower left corner of plaque; nonjoining, but matches thickness, clay, use of color, and deposit elevation of (a). Foot projects from bottom of plaque from beneath painted drapery, now broken.

a: White surface on front and sides; back reserved. Traces of paint noted in cleaning: black, yellow, red, and white. One pendant of earring preserves yellow with black, slanted design. Trace of red on right disk, central diamond, at neck for necklace or neckline of garment; black on white on right disk pendant cord.

b: White surface on front and sides; back reserved. Broad yellow band at bottom of dress, framed at top and bottom with a horizontal black line, divided vertically with black lines in panels ca. 3.5 cm long × ca. 1.2 cm wide. Above this band, white zone with one horizontal black line preserved.

For the head, cf. Winter 1903, vol. 3.1, pl. 238, no. 2; Brooke in Casson 1921, pp. 398–404, esp. nos. 627 and 688, figs. p. 400; Croissant 1983, pp. 243–244, type L 3, nos. 155–156. Although these fragmentary examples provide convincing parallels for the physiognomy and the diamond crown of **198**, they are protomes (see Mollard-Besques 1954, p. 16, B 92, pl. 12, for a complete version), and some preserve suspension holes at either side of the head. Since **198** has feet, it is not a protome. It is a seated slab figure and would have had a projecting strut to support it; cf. Paul 1958–1959, pp. 199–200, fig. 39; Higgins 1967, p. 43, type 6. The closest parallel is *Kerameikos* XV, pp. 8–9, no. 20 (T 832), pl. 4:1, 2 (with comparanda and bibliography), which preserves the full body and struts for support. The Kerameikos example is less refined in execution, but features the same added clay details.

Camp (1996, p. 251, and n. 22) describes the earrings as rare for the Archaic period. Similar earrings on a fragmentary example (unclear whether protome or slab figure) from Brauron, Themelis 1974, p. 75, b; and the Kerameikos, see above. Similar radiate crown with three diamonds: Croissant 1983, p. 243, no. 155, pl. 99 (from Acropolis); Kokkou-Vyride 1999, p. 237, no. B181, pl. 52 (from Eleusis), but both protomes. Seated slab figures from Eleusis, Kokkou-Vyride 1999, pp. 234–235, 241, 255, nos. B157, B158, B159, B210, Γ35, Γ36, all pl. 49.

The type, whether protome or slab, appears to be limited to Attica and environs. A date of 540–530 is given for the type by the example from the Kerameikos, see above, but R. V. Nicholls (pers. comm.) suggests the third quarter of the 6th century.

Third quarter 6th century

Figure 155. Female head protome 199.
Scale 1:3

PROTOME

*?199 (T 4482) Female head protome   Fig. 155

+49.76–49.14 m (Level 2)
P.H. 7.0; W. 9.5
Five joining fragments of top of upper part of face. Moldmade.

Rounded top with single hole for suspension. Front preserves simple veil head-dress, curve of hair with three rows of wavy curls, and edge of forehead. Powdery clay with greenish gray core (Gley 6/1) with frequent, fine mica, very pale brown surface (10YR 7/4).

Cf. Winter 1903, pl. 236, no. 6; Croissant 1983, pp. 320–321, type N5, nos. 203, 204, pls. 124, 125, (both from Delphi) although an exact parallel is not possible to find since no part of the face of **199** survives. The clay is not Attic, and the gray core may point to a "Northern Ionian" origin; see Croissant 1983, p. 315. The type possibly has its origins on Rhodes (Higgins 1967, p. 64), but is known to be made on the mainland, possibly by immigrant artisans from Ionia (Croissant 1983, p. 315). Examples from domestic contexts in Olynthus: *Olynthus* XIV, pp. 69–73, nos. 1, 2, pls. 1–3, with extensive discussion of the type and its origins. According to Higgins (1967, p. 64) the three waves of hair are a characteristic that should place **199** shortly after 500.

First quarter 5th century

SEATED FEMALE

*200 (T 4480) Seated female   Fig. 156

Figure 156. Seated female 200. Scale 1:2

+47.50 m (Level 5)
P.H. 9.55; W. 5.8; p.Th. 5.75
Missing head, feet, lower part of chair. Edges chipped. Paint largely missing.

Draped female seated on chair, hands on knees. Back flat. Upper part solid, hollow beneath chair. White pigment remains over much of the surface. On front of chair and seat traces of orange and black hatching. Pink-buff clay.

For complete examples, see Winter 1903, pl. 51.

Fourth quarter 6th century

*?201 (T 4479) Seated female   Fig. 157

+49.76–49.14 m (Level 2)
P.H. 7.6; W. 4.2; Th. 4.85
Missing head, chipped at edges.

Draped female figure seated on a chair, hands on knees. Back of chair slightly concave. Solid, but a hole is pierced through from top to bottom. Traces of a buff-gray slip and white pigment in crevices. Light reddish-brown clay (5YR 6/4) with some fine mica and occasional small white, black, and red inclusions.

For complete examples, see Winter 1903, pl. 51.

Fourth quarter 6th century

Figure 157. Seated female 201. Scale 1:2

HERM

*?202   (T 4483) Herm   Fig. 158

+50.31–49.76 m (Level 1b)
P.H. 13.58; W. 4.28; Th. 3.4
Head, arm projections, tip of phallos, and bottom missing.
Solid, rectangular in section. Two small rectangular projections at shoulder level. Erect phallos attached to front. Coarse, pink-buff clay (5YR 7/4) with occasional large white inclusions, occasional small flat voids, little mica, with traces of white slip.
Terracotta herms are not uncommon in the Agora Excavations, although few have been published. Those that have been published demonstrate that the form continues down into the Hellenistic and even to the Roman period, see *Agora* VI, p. 70, no. 861, pl. 22 (3rd century A.D.); discussion of development in Thompson 1952, p. 162, no. 49a, pl. 39 (4th century); 1966, pp. 9–11, 18, no. 18 and Agora comparanda, pl. 4.
Context: 525–480

Figure 158. Herm 202. Scale 1:2

QUADRUPED

203   (T 4477) Quadruped   Fig. 159

+46.33–46.00 m (Level 5)
P.H. 3.25; p.L. 5.56
Missing part of front left leg, head, tail.
Handmade, cylindrical body with short, round legs. Top of broad tail. White-yellow slip with black curving lines on torso.
Context: 525–480

204   (T 4478) Fragment of a horse?   Fig. 159

+46.30–46.00 m (Level 5)
P.H. 4.06
Single foreleg(?) of a horse. Missing foot.
Terracotta core covered with a thick coat of clay with a smooth gray surface. Only a small area of clay still adhered. Some flakes in a small bag with find.
Context: 525–480

UNCERTAIN FORM

[205]   (T 4481) Fragment of human figurine?   Fig. 159

+45.60–45.45 m (Level 6)
p.H 5.25; p.Th. 2.9
Missing head, arms, lower legs. Worn. Probably handmade.
Possibly a crouching figure. Knees bent, back hunched, torso twisted. Red-buff clay. From period of use. Poor condition suggests that it was discarded into the well.
Context: 525–480

Figure 159. Quadruped 203; fragment of a horse? 204; fragment of human figurine? 205. Scale 1:1

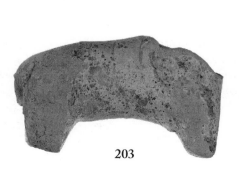

203   204   205

Figure 160. Loomweights 206–208.
Scale 1:2

206   207   208

WEAVING IMPLEMENTS

*?206 (MC 1507) Loomweight   Fig. 160

+50.31–49.76 m (Level 1b)
H. 4.7; W. 2.45; L. 2.5; Wt. 25.65 g
Intact. Edges chipped.
Pyramidal loomweight. Suspension hole pierced off center ca. 0.01 m from top. Black glaze on upper 1.65 cm. Fine purple-buff fabric (5YR 7/3) with very fine mica. No evidence of thread wear.
  Seven additional uninventoried loomweights from Level 1b stored in Tin BZ 683, all at least twice as heavy.
  Context: 525–480

*?207 (MC 1506) Loomweight   Fig. 160

+49.76–49.14 m (Level 2)
H. 6.15; W. 3.88; L. 4.15; Wt. 74.78 g
Intact. Chips at bottom edges.
Pyramidal loomweight with three edges pared down before firing. Suspension hole pierced 1.5 cm below top. Traces of brown to orange glaze over all surfaces, but unclear if pared edges were glazed. Fine buff-orange clay. No evidence of thread wear.
  One additional uninventoried loomweight from Level 2 stored in Tin BZ 684, but smaller.
  Context: 525–480

*208 (MC 1508) Loomweight   Fig. 160

+45.23 m (Level 6)
H. 5.9; W. 2.99; L. 3.4; Wt. 42.3 g
Intact. Small chips at top and bottom.
Pyramidal loomweight. Suspension hole pierced 1.5 cm from top. Traces of creamy white slip (5Y 8/2) over all surfaces, well preserved on bottom. Fine buff clay (2.5Y 8/3) with small red inclusions and fine mica. No evidence of thread wear.
  Context: 525–480

Figure 161. Spindle whorl 209.
Scale 1:2

*?209 (MC 1509) Spindle whorl   Fig. 161

+50.31–49.76 m (Level 1b)
H. 2.8; Diam. 5.35; Wt. 58 g
Intact. Chips on edges, clay cracked in places.
Biconical spindle whorl with central vertical hole ca. 4.8 mm in diameter. Coarse, light olive-gray clay (5Y 6/2), darker in places, with frequent fine white inclusions and occasional large white and gray inclusions.
  Context: 525–480

210

211

212

213

214

Figure 162. Astragaloi 210–214.
Scale 1:2

WORKED BONE

*210 (BI 1088) Astragalos   Fig. 162

+46.60–46.30 m (Level 5)
H. 1.6; W. 1.85; L. 2.93
Intact. Ovid/caprid right astragalos. Worn flat in places.
Four other right ovid/caprid astragaloi from Levels 5 and 6 with similar wear (stored in Tin BZ 735).
Context: 525–480

*211 (BI 1087) Astragalos   Fig. 162

+46.60–46.30 m (Level 5)
H. 2.75; W. 2.15; L. 2.93
Intact. Ovid/caprid left astragalos.
Thirteen other left ovid/caprid astragaloi from Levels 5 and 6. Some with projecting points worn smooth or ground down (stored in Tin BZ 735).
Context: 525–480

*212 (BI 1089) Modified astragalos   Fig. 162

+46.60–46.30 m (Level 5)
H. 1.43; W. 2.05; L. 2.99
Intact. Ovid/caprid right astragalos. Projecting points shaved flat on both top and bottom. Circular hole through center.
One other left ovid/caprid astragalos also flattened but not drilled, from Level 5. One other left ovid/caprid astragalos with drilled hole, off center and not all the way through from Level 5 (both stored in Tin BZ 735).
Context: 525–480

*213 (BI 1090) Modified astragalos   Fig. 162

+46.30–46.00 m (Level 5)
H. 2.2; W. 2.34; L. 3.51
Intact. Ovid/caprid left astragalos. Three circular holes drilled through from top to bottom, roughly in line.
Reese (2002, p. 473) notes that worked astragaloi with three holes are rare, and lists known comparanda.
Context: 525–480

*214 (BI 1091) Modified astragalos   Fig. 162

+46.60–46.30 m (Level 5)
H. 2.05; W. 3.5; L. 5.68
Intact. *Bos,* left astragalos. Shaved flat on all but one surface. Diamond-shaped hole punched through center.
One other unmodified left *bos* astragalos from Level 5, and one similarly modified left ovid/caprid astragalos also from Level 5 (both stored in Tin BZ 735).
Context: 525–480

*215 (BI 1092) Bone disk   Fig. 163

+45.60–45.45 m (Level 6)
Diam. 1.45–1.6; Th. 0.0435

Figure 163. Bone disk 215. Scale 1:1

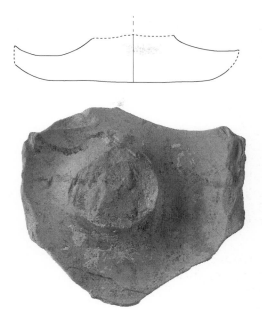

Figure 164. Clay stopper 216. Scale 1:2.
Profile drawn author; inked E. Schmitt

Intact. Pare marks on edge.

Rounded, flat piece of bone. Two holes of different sizes drilled through, one at center, the other to the side.

Context: 525–480

MISCELLANEOUS OBJECTS

*?**216**   (P 33247) Clay stopper   Fig. 164

+50.88–50.31 m (Level 1b)

P.H. 2.95

Chipped on all edges and missing handle. Unglazed, but very good clay and well finished. Worn on underside.

Heavy, convex bottom curving upward and thinning at edge. Upper face concave with large perpendicular stem for handle.

Probably used to stop the neck of an amphora. Handle allowed easy removal for frequent access. Fits vessel with neck diameter of 15–16 cm. Although from Level 1b, preservation meets criteria for inclusion in household assemblage.

Context: 525–480

[**217**]   (IL 1929) Lead sheet   Fig. 165

+45.45–45.20 m (Level 6)

Max. p. dim. 3.9

Rolled round sheet, crumbling at the edges, torn in several places. Two small holes; one at the center of sheet may be intentional.

Probably covered the end of a rope.

Context: 525–480

Figure 165. Lead sheet 217. Scale 1:1

Transport Amphoras from Well J 2:4

by Mark L. Lawall

The transport amphora fragments from well deposit J 2:4 are in many ways similar to amphora finds in other contexts datable to the late 6th and early 5th century B.C. and to the finds in other deposits associated with the cleanup following the Persian sack of Athens. What sets J 2:4 apart is both the evidence for the different phases of deposition even over a very short span of time (Chapter 2) and the total retention of the recovered sherds. Most contemporary deposits do distinguish between a period of use fill and the overlying dumped fill. Once the unitary nature of the fill was established on the basis of cross-mends throughout the well, however, the fill was stored as a single deposit.[1] For this reason, it is now rarely possible to study the various levels of other well fills in detailed stratigraphic order. For J 2:4, however, the definition of four major episodes of filling allows the amphora finds, too, to be considered in a more detailed framework. In this well deposit it is possible to compare the amphora assemblage most likely in use in the immediate vicinity at the time of the Persian sack (the finds in Level 5) with the more general debris of the late 6th and early 5th centuries (the material in upper levels of the fill).

The first part of this report provides a summary of the amphora types found in J 2:4, their major identifying features, the evidence for their places of production, and commentary on finds in other datable contexts. Descriptions of the amphora fabrics are deliberately general in these summary discussions; more detailed description of fabric is included in each catalogue entry. A catalogue of diagnostic fragments follows the description of each type. All drawings are by the author; photographs are courtesy of the Agora Excavations. The catalogued pieces were chosen to illustrate the range of forms and fabrics pertaining to each type. The subsequent quantitative

1. This is particularly true for the amphora material from such deposits. Even if the fine ware and coarse ware were stored in order, the amphora fragments were often separated into their own tins or boxes without preserving the stratigraphic order of the material. I am grateful to Kathleen Lynch for the invitation to contribute this discussion of the amphora material found in well J 2:4; the ideas presented here owe much to discussions with her and with John Papadopoulos. John Camp has been most generous in facilitating my broader study of Late Archaic through Late Hellenistic amphora finds at the Agora excavations. Research on J 2:4 was carried out with the support of grants from the M. Aylwin Cotton foundation, the Social Sciences and Humanities Research Council (SSHRC) of Canada, and the National Endowment for the Humanities (through the American School of Classical Studies at Athens). For the abbreviations used in the catalogue, see p. 178.

discussion provides the numbers of diagnostic fragments found belonging
to each type.

Along with the diagnostic rims, handles (to a lesser extent), and toes,
the fill of J 2:4 also included plenty of body sherds. Such sherds from amphoras are not often closely diagnostic, so it is best to leave them aside from
counts lest the more readily diagnostic fabrics become overrepresented in
any quantification. One point of interest, however, for a well of the Late
Archaic period in Athens is the relative scarcity of local Athenian amphora
fragments compared with imports. Since Athenian amphora body sherds
of this period are readily identifiable by their surface treatment, this comparison is relatively straightforward. The closing quantitative discussion of
the levels of fill in the well considers the relative presence of the Athenian
amphoras and the changing concentrations of amphora fragments through
the fill overall.

AMPHORA TYPES

ATTIC SOS

Only one diagnostic fragment of the Early Archaic Attic SOS amphora
type appears in J 2:4.[2] The type is named for the painted decoration on
the neck, which is composed of zigzag lines (the Σ or sigma) in a vertical
arrangement flanking a circle (the O or omicron), triangle, or other central
motif. The J 2:4 fragment preserves part of a neck wall with traces of the
diagnostic decorative scheme. In complete examples, a high cup-shaped
mouth sits over a short neck with heavy, rounded, stirrup-profile handles.
The often quite large and heavy egg-shaped body is painted with either a
streaky slip or stripes. The jar rests on a heavy, tall, flaring ring toe.

Evidence for Attic production comes from R. E. Jones's optical emission
spectroscopy project published in 1978.[3] He found that the majority of the
96 samples of SOS jars fits an Attic profile while a small minority seemed
to be of Eretrian manufacture.

The type was in use in the 8th and 7th centuries B.C., with some of
the best-preserved and most securely dated examples coming from Archaic
Etruscan tombs and from the necropolis at Pithekoussai.[4] The latest date
for SOS production seems to fall near 590 B.C.,[5] but as in J 2:4, residual
fragments continue to appear in Athenian contexts closed quite late in
the 6th century.

2. Important discussions of this type
are found in Lambrino 1938, pp. 132–
141, who includes discussion of both
the SOS and the *à la brosse* types; and
more recently (and yet to be sup-
planted) Johnston and Jones 1978.

3. Johnston and Jones 1978, pp. 122–
128; Jones et al. 1986, pp. 706–712.

4. Rizzo 1990, figs. 359–366; *Pithe-

koussai I, from tomb nos. 398, 429,
442, 642, and 719, and for further fragments from Pithekoussai, see Di Sandro
1986, pp. 15–22, pls. 1, 2; Johnston and
Jones (1978, pp. 103–121) list numerous further published and unpublished
examples.

5. Gras 1987, pp. 46–49; Docter
1991, p. 46; Dupont 1995–1996, p. 87.

Figure I.1. Attic SOS amphora neck A1. Scale 1:3

A1 (P 35209) Attic SOS amphora neck Fig. I.1
+47.60–46.65 m (Level 4)
P.H. 7.6; est. Diam. interior of neck 13.0
Preserves just under one-sixth of circumference of neck, without any part of rim or handles. Ghost image of decoration shows two concentric circles, of which the inner circle has a much thicker line than the outer; compass dot in the center. Fabric is pale pinkish tan (7.5YR 7/4), almost chalky with very sparse visible inclusions, but those that are visible tend to be large, pale grayish stony and grog.[6]

ATTIC À LA BROSSE

This Attic amphora type is a development from the SOS type appearing in the early 6th century B.C. and continuing into the early part of the 5th century.[7] The primary difference between the SOS amphora and the *à la brosse* type is the loss of the neck decoration and a simplification of the rim from a tall flaring echinoid profile to a narrower rounded rim. The handles, especially by the late 6th and early 5th centuries, are much flatter in section, though they still show a distinctive stirrup-shaped profile. The label for the type comes from the often streakily applied slip brushed over the surface of the body. The toe of the late-6th-century *à la brosse* type is much smaller than the earlier SOS type toe.

Jones's analysis of the Attic SOS type mentioned above included seven samples from *à la brosse* jars, and all matched the Athenian composition.[8] A much darker, more micaceous fabric, similar to other ceramics from Eretria, does appear in *à la brosse* amphoras.[9] For this reason, and given earlier Eretrian production of the preceding form, non-Attic production of some *à la brosse* amphoras seems possible. The light-colored, less micaceous examples, however, are still considered to be Attic products. Further sampling is still needed to confirm non-Attic production.

Mid- to late-6th-century B.C. contexts with *à la brosse* amphoras include tombs at Vulci and Cerveteri,[10] well deposits at Athens, Corinth, and Olympia,[11] and the construction fill for the Aphrodite temple at Histria.[12] Few examples from contexts likely closed within the earliest decades of the 5th century B.C. are known from outside the Agora. A few fragments appear in the latest Archaic levels at Klazomenai (hence predating the

6. In all catalogue entries, the criteria for density of the distribution of inclusions is based on the following ranges illustrated in the introduction to the Munsell Soil Color charts: sparse = 1%–5%; sparse–moderate = ca. 5% (or somewhat higher in places, lower in others); moderate = 5%–15%; moderate–dense = ca. 15%; dense = 20%–25%; very dense = 30% and higher. These figures are approximations meant only to give a general impression of the appearance of the fabric.

7. On this type, see Lambrino 1938, esp. pp. 134–136; Johnston and Jones 1978, pp. 121–122; Boss 1993, pp. 322–324 (though note that his Cat. No. L20 is not Attic but Klazomenian and L21 could be Attic, but if so it is later than ca. 480); *Agora* XII, nos. 1501, 1502.

8. Johnston and Jones 1978, pp. 122–128; Dupont (1995–1996, p. 86) reports similar results from XRF analyses of two *à la brosse* rim sherds.

9. An example of this much darker, more micaceous variant is published by

Campbell 1938, no. 207.

10. Vulci: Rizzo 1990, p. 18, fig. 13, and p. 100, figs. 181, 368.

11. Athens: Roberts 1986, p. 67, no. 418, fig. 42, pl. 18. Corinth: Campbell 1938, nos. 207, 209. Olympia: Gauer 1975, p. 128, pl. 20, no. 3, from well 23 StN.

12. Histria: Dupont 1995–1996, p. 87. The construction fill for the temple is placed in the second and third quarters of the 6th century.

abandonment of the site by 494 B.C.), one example from the Kerameikos
was accompanied by fine wares dated 480–470 B.C.,[13] and another from
Eretria was found in a grave dated perhaps as late as 460 B.C.[14] In other
Persian sack deposits in Athens, the *à la brosse* type is present, but rarely
very common (see Table I.5).

A2   (P 34768) Attic *à la brosse*   Fig. I.2
   +49.75–48.60 m. (Level 2)
   P.H. 3.3; est. Diam. of rim[15] 13.0
   Preserves nearly one-quarter of rim with small bit of neck. Simple heavy
rounded rim with sharp turn down at neck. Blackish brown paint around outer
face of rim. Smooth light brown surface, micaceous, with fine-grained brown
core, sparse visible inclusions, gray glassy, very rare whitish (7.5YR 6/6 and 5/6).

Figure I.2. Attic *à la brosse* A2.
Scale 1:3

Corinthian

The Corinthian Late Archaic amphora types are characterized by a heavy,
flattened, outward-projecting rim over thick outswung handles.[16] The rotund body terminates in a plain cylindrical toe, hollow on the inside. The
fabric is very fine, often quite hard, and commonly features large, sharp-
edged mudstone inclusions. Broadly speaking, the Corinthian amphora
fabric of this period includes two variants: one extremely hard and darkly
fired, the other pale tan and almost chalky in surface feel but still hard
fired and with mudstone inclusions. The latter is much more common in
Athens and is the Corinthian fabric present in J 2:4.

   Attribution of these amphora types to Corinth is based on a wide
range of petrological and chemical studies of samples from the amphoras
in comparison with extensively studied Corinthian clay sources.[17] Hence,
although no kiln sites are known for these amphoras, there is a general
consensus as to their Corinthian manufacture.[18]

   The Corinthian fragments in J 2:4 illustrate chronologically significant
features of the type's form. The rim slopes down slightly; before the late

13. Athens, Kerameikos: *Kerameikos*
IX, HW 173. Klazomenai, from the
necropolis: Doğer 1986, fig. 12. A few
other fragments were excavated on the
acropolis of Klazomenai; I am currently
preparing their publication.

14. Eretria: Andreiomenou 1976,
p. 203, figs. 6, 7.

15. The estimates of rim diameter
throughout this appendix are based on
the topmost edge or surface of the rim,
not the inner or outer face.

16. The most thorough discussion
of this type remains Koehler 1978a,
pp. 9–32; and her articles 1978b,
pp. 231–236; 1981; and 1992, pp. 266–
271. See too Morter and Leonard 1998,
pp. 731–735, for material from Metaponto; Di Sandro 1986, pp. 22–34, for
Pithekoussai; Stocker 2009, pp. 329–
334 and 338–341, for finds from the
Mallakastra Regional Archaeological
Project Survey (Albania).

17. For early studies of Corinthian

fabrics, see Farnsworth 1964, 1970; and
Farnsworth, Pearlman, and Asaro 1977.
For more recent studies, see Whitbread
1986; 1995, chap. 5; 2003; Desy and
De Paepe 1990, pp. 210, 214, 215; and
Stocker 2009, pp. 352–356.

18. Whitbread 1995, esp. pp. 344–
346; 2003, pp. 8–9; cf. Newton et al.
1988, finding correlation between Corinthian Type A amphoras and clay
samples from Megalopolis.

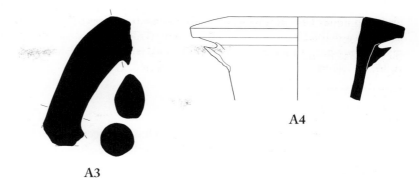

Figure I.3. Corinthian A3 and A4.
Scale 1:4 (A3), 1:3 (A4)

6th century B.C. this rim is more level.[19] The handles are taller in section near the rim and show a slight peak.[20] The broad curve from the body to the sides of the toe is paralleled at Histria in the middle decades of the 6th century and somewhat before 500 B.C. at the Pointe Lequin IA shipwreck.[21] These traits occur in other Persian sack deposits, too, even though Corinthian amphoras are never especially common in Athenian deposits.

A3   (P 34773) Corinthian   Fig. I.3

+47.60–46.65 m (Level 4)
P.H. 13.8
Handle only. Slight peak at upper profile near upper neck attachment, elongated oval in section here; round in section nearer lower attachment. Very pale gray/tan chalky fabric (10YR 7/3), very compact with moderate–dense scatter of large red brown, dark gray, and white opaque; the red brown and dark gray bits are sharply angular mudstone; no mica.

A4   (P 34787) Corinthian   Fig. I.3

Unstratified
P.H. 6.8; est. Diam. rim 11.0
Preserves three-eighths of rim with part of neck wall, upper attachment of one handle. Upright interior profile of mouth with sharp turn out to wide, flat, slightly downsloping top of heavy ledge rim; vertical outer face, downsloping lower surface to sharp turn down to neck wall. Oblong ovoid section handle attaches just below but clear of rim (so far as preserved). Smooth light tan surfaces, smooth except where mudstone is at or near surface (10YR 6/6); very fine compact core; light brown moderate scatter mudstone, scatter of small white and black bits, rare gray glassy and rare mica.

A5   (P 34769) Corinthian   Fig. I.4

+49.75–48.60 m (Level 2)
P.H. 6.1; Diam. toe 5.3
Preserves complete toe with small part of turn out to body. Wall of rotund lower body turns smoothly down to slightly tapering sides of hollow-interior peg

Figure I.4. Corinthian A5. Scale 1:3

19. For the increased slope of the top surface of the Corinthian rims, see Campbell 1938, no. 201; Koehler 1981, fig. 1d; and further discussion in Lawall 1995, p. 59–60, with reference to other examples from Persian sack contexts in Athens.

20. Noted by Koehler 1992, p. 268.

21. Histria (Aphrodite temple fill): Dupont 1995–1996, pp. 87–88, fig. 10. Pointe Lequin IA: Long, Miro, and Volpe 1992, p. 227, fig. 46:2, 3.

toe; sharp turn at bottom of toe to unevenly concave base. Fabric smooth in parts, pale buff, widely scattered mica (10YR 6/4 and 7.5YR 6/6); very compact fabric, sparse large, sharp, dark red brown mudstone bits; rare gray glassy bits; no other visible inclusions.

CORCYREAN-REGION

The amphora class labeled here as Corcyrean has also been labeled Corinthian Type B (as opposed to Type A and A' for the preceding class).[22] The rim in the Late Archaic period may be either a heavy rounded profile or a heavy wedge form. The handles are oval in section, with an upright stance off the shoulder. The rotund body terminates in either a wide cylindrical toe, hollowed inside, or a truncated conical peg. The fabric is very soft, pale and chalky, often with few visible inclusions.

The similarity between this pale amphora fabric and Corinthian coarse-ware fabrics, together with the common presence of the type at Corinth, encouraged the attribution of the type to Corinthian manufacture. Two stamp types, however, point in the direction of Corcyra. The first shows the seven- or eight-pointed star known from Corcyrean coinage,[23] and the second shows the forepart of a bull with the letters KEP, also recalling the coinage of Corcyra.[24] The Corinthian attribution was supported by petrographic and chemical analyses;[25] however, many of these studies also found similarities with Corcyrean clays.[26] Kiln sites for this type are now known on Corcyra, and there have been extensive finds along the western coast of Greece and Albania.[27] In addition, the form was used extensively along eastern and western coasts of southern Italy across the Ionian and Adriatic seas from Greece (albeit often in noticeably coarser fabric). All of these factors encourage shifting attribution of this type away from Corinth and to the general region of Corcyra and the west coast of Greece.

22. The major works on this type remain Koehler 1978a, pp. 33–49; 1978b, pp. 236–237; 1981; and 1992, pp. 272–277. See too Gauer 1975, pp. 121–124, and for later types, pp. 130–131; Di Sandro 1986, pp. 22–24, 34–38; Johnston 1990, pp. 44–46; and Stocker 2009, pp. 334–338.

23. For an early discussion of the Corinthian or Corcyrean provenance of this class, see Grace 1953, pp. 108–109, with references.

24. Both KOP (*SNG Copenhagen* 178–179) and KEP (*SNG Tübingen* 1531) appear on Corcyrean coins with the bull; the same motif also appears on the coins of Dyrrhachium and Apollonia.

25. Farnsworth 1970, pp. 12–13; Farnsworth, Pearlman, and Asaro 1977; Desy and De Paepe 1990.

26. Farnsworth, Pearlman, and Asaro 1977, pp. 457 and 462; Jones et al. 1986, pp. 712–720; Whitbread 1995, pp. 278–285; Stocker 2009, pp. 354–355.

27. On the wide range of production of this type, see Gassner 2003, pp. 183–186. For kiln sites on Corcyra, see Kourkoumelis 1990 and Preka-Alexandri 1992; for finds in Albania, see Desy 1985, p. 414; Ceka 1986, esp. pp. 83 and 89, with pls. 7–9; Bereti 1992, esp. pls. 2, 3 (all proposing that these amphoras are made locally); from Leukas, see Andreou 1990; and from the Kerameikos, Jöhrens 1999, no. 22. Jöhrens follows Andreou in attributing these amphoras to Leukas on the basis of a stamp reading ΛΟΣ (the same stamp type was read as ΓΟΣ by Koehler 1978a, nos. 509–512), interpreted as an abbreviation for ΛευκάδΟΣ; such an abbreviation of the ethnic, using only the first letter and the genitive singular ending, seems unlikely in ancient Greece, cf. Avi-Yonah 1939; McNamee 1981; and perhaps most relevant to the problem of deciphering amphora stamp abbreviations, Florance 1966; all of which clearly show the Greek practice of abbreviating from the end of the word forward and not removing the middle section of the word to leave the ending. Even so, production of amphoras on Leukas seems quite likely; and it is difficult to suggest an alternative to Andreou's suggested reading. No names, whether personal or topographical, seem to start with Λοσ, Γοσ, or even Λοι, taking the Σ as a Corinthian/Corcyrean iota. Jöhrens 1999, no. 23, also publishes a stamp with the abbreviation ZAKY, suggesting production on Zakynthos.

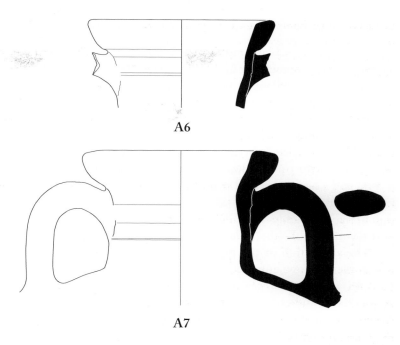

Figure I.5. Corcyrean A6 and A7.
Scale 1:3

The coeval presence of the heavy rounded-rim form with the wedge-shaped rim form in J 2:4 is an important feature distinguishing Late Archaic contexts closed ca. 480 from those closed significantly earlier. A jar top showing the wedge-shaped rim already appears at the Gela shipwreck of ca. 490 B.C.,[28] and both rim forms appear together in early-5th-century B.C. fills from the Aphaia sanctuary on Aigina.[29] The shift to a heavy wedge-shaped rim seems to occur slightly earlier than ca. 480.[30] The fact that both the rounded- and the wedge-rim forms appear here in J 2:4 further links this deposit with others associated with the Persian sack.

A6 (P 34767) Corcyrean   Fig. I.5

+50.88–49.75 m (Level 1b)
P.H. 7.3; est. Diam. rim 14.0
Preserves nearly one-third of rim with bit of neck and one upper handle segment. Flaring mouth, with upsloping flat top of wedgelike rim with rounded-exterior profile; smooth concave transition from rim to neck, deep groove encircles neck at level of handle attachment. Very narrow oval section handle angles up slightly but does not follow line of rim; also does not push in on neck at all. Daintiness of handle suggests fractional amphora. Pale tan, finely gritty surface (2.5Y 7/4), some mica, sparse-moderate scatter large white stony and gray glassy bits, rare very small red-orange bits.

A7 (P 34789) Corcyrean   Fig. I.5

+46.65–45.90 m (Level 5)
P.H. 12.8; rim 12.2 × 13.0
Complete rim, one complete handle, one upper attachment, complete neck, part of shoulder. Mouth flares slightly to tight rounded interior edge of rim; flat top surface, heavy rounded rim with smooth turn down to neck wall; tall relief band at top of neck; wide shallow incised band under this relief band. Nearly white fabric (5Y 7/3), fairly smooth pale greenish white core, grainy, sparse scatter fairly large gray and white glassy bits, rare large opaque red-brown bits, heavily resinated, little or no mica.

28. Panvini 2001, no. 148; note that no. 141 is a neck fragment with a heavy rounded rim with a ridge around the top of the neck, just below the rim, but this piece is identified by Panvini as West Greek.

29. Johnston 1990, nos. 82 and 83.

30. Cf. Koehler 1978a, p. 34.

CHIAN: BULGING NECK WITH PAINTED DECORATION

The Late Archaic Chian amphora type in J 2:4 stands within a lengthy sequence of development for Chian amphoras stretching from the 7th century through the Hellenistic period.[31] The stage present in J 2:4 shows a characteristic narrow outward-rounded rim, bulging neck, and piriform body. The round-section handles arch up from an attachment just under the rim to an upright stance. The type's toe essentially continues the profile of the body but is deeply hollowed underneath. A quite diagnostic feature for this type is the painted decoration. The rim is often painted dark red to brown, and a narrow vertical stripe descends along the outer face of each handle continuing down the side of the body, intersected periodically by thin horizontal bands encircling the body. A circle or cross often appears near the middle of either side of the neck between the handles.[32]

The attribution of the type to Chios depends upon its placement within the developmental sequence noted above. Various amphora forms from this sequence have been tied to Chian production by chemical and petrographic studies,[33] by misfired fragments from workshop sites,[34] by representation of similar jars on Chian coins, and by stamps on amphoras using the images of Chian coins.[35]

The late-6th- through early-5th-century B.C. date for this Chian type, with painted decoration and a clear bulge to the neck, is well established by its common presence in contexts closed no later than 480. These contexts include the terraces for the Aphaia temple at Aigina,[36] a very late Archaic destruction level at Histria,[37] under or in contexts at Miletos and Klazomenai associated with the Ionian Revolt,[38] prior to the destruction of Megara Hyblaea by Syracuse in 483,[39] and a well at Tell el-Maskhuta likely filled in ca. 486.[40] Numerous graves at the Kerameikos excavations strengthen the association between this type and other pottery types dated near 480.[41] The Persian sack contexts in the Athenian Agora provide a rich collection of this stage of Chian amphora.

A8   (P 34776) Chian   Fig. I.6
    +49.75–48.60 m (Level 2)
    P.H. 10.5; est. Diam. rim 10.0
    Preserves three-eighths of rim, bit more of neck circumference, and complete profile neck to turn out at top of shoulder, one upper handle segment. Narrow,

---

31. For overviews of Chian production, see Grace 1979, figs. 44, 45; Lazarov 1982; Dupont 1998, pp. 146–151; Lawall 1998; De Marinis 1999; Abramov 2002; Monachov 2003b.

32. See Dupont 1999b on markings on Chian amphoras of this period; also Lambrino 1938, pp. 211–229 Lawall 1995, pp. 104–115; 1998.

33. Dupont 1982, p. 198; 1983, pp. 30–31; Whitbread 1995, p. 135–153; Seifert 1996; 2004, pp. 36–37 and

figs. 17, 20–23; Johnston and de Domingo 1997, pp. 63–64.

34. Dupont 1982, p. 198; Tsaravopoulos 1986.

35. Baldwin 1914; Mavrogordato 1915a; 1915b; Zeest 1960, p. 77, fig. 3; Grace 1979, figs. 48, 49; for important modifications to the Chian coin chronology, see Hardwick 1993.

36. Johnston 1990, pp. 38–40, nos. 1–36.

37. Dimitriu 1966, fig. 52.

38. Miletos: Voigtländer 1982, p. 44, nos. 31–33, fig. 6; Kerschner 1999, pp. 34–37, fig. 18; Niemeier 1999, pp. 384–392. Klazomenai: Ersoy 1993; 2004, figs. 15, 23; Koparal and İplikçi 2004, fig. 8, illustrates a Chian rim and neck of this type from the destruction of the Archaic phase of an oil-press installation at Klazomenai.

39. Vallet and Villard 1964, pl. 70:1.

40. Holladay 1982, pls. 25:6, 26:5.

41. *Kerameikos* IX, pp. 23–24.

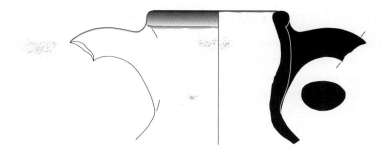

Figure I.6. Chian A8. Scale 1:3

simple out-rounded rim with very narrow undercut join with neck wall; bulging neck, pulled in more at lower part than around rim. Oval section handle; clay covers lower edge of rim. Reddish brown paint over top and outer face of rim down on to upper neck. Thin stripe poorly preserved on outer face of handle. Gritty yellow-brown surfaces, micaceous (7.5YR 6/6); moderate–dense packing light tan small lime bits, small grayish/tan glassy bits.

A9 (P 34770) Chian   Fig. I.7

+49.75–48.60 m (Level 2)
P.H. 4.6; Diam. toe 5.5
Preserves 90% complete toe, very small bit of lower body. Concave-sided pedestal toe with rounded lower resting surface, deep, wide hollow underneath. Gritty yellowish brown surface (7.5YR 6/6), micaceous, fine-grained grayish core (10YR 5/2); moderate scatter gray glassy, can get fairly large; some dusky blackish bits, white opaque, small reddish brown.

A10 (P 33260) Chian(?)   Fig. I.8

+50.88–49–75 m (Level 1b)
Max. p. dim. 12.7
Preserves only shoulder fragment, possibly from Chian amphora. With one preserved line of postfiring inscription: ΣΠΕΜΔΟΙ̣ or perhaps ΣΠΕΝΔΟΜ̣ to be restored as σπένδομαι (I am poured?). There appears to be a further line of text higher on the same shoulder, but not enough of this is preserved to determine the letters. Pale pinkish tan surface with scattered, quite visible mica; grainy break with moderate scatter gray glassy bits, large with chunks especially visible on interior surface, with much smaller and often difficult-to-pick-out bits of greenish or yellowish lime, grainy dark gray patches (burnt lime?) and some red-brown bits (7.5YR 6/6 core).

Figure I.7. Chian A9. Scale 1:3

a

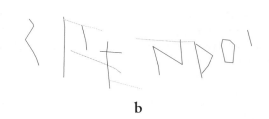

b

Figure I.8. Chian(?) A10: (a) fragment with graffito; (b) facsimile. Scale 1:2

Southeast Aegean with Offset Cuff at Neck

The characteristic feature of Late Archaic southeastern Aegean amphoras is a ridge of clay often rising from the shoulder partway up the neck and forming an offset cuff that encircles the lower part of the neck.[42] The rim is often thickly rounded and the handles attach in the area between the rim and this cuff. The oval section handles have a fairly upright profile. The body either may be broad-shouldered and egg-shaped, terminating in a small flaring ring toe, or may be more bobbin-shaped with a tall, thick knob toe.

The attribution of this type to the southeastern Aegean depends both on images of similar jars on the coins of Samos and on petrographic and chemical analyses associating the production with Samos and Miletos.[43] In general terms, the jars most often associated with Samos show a heavy, fully rounded rim, while those from Miletos carry a rim with a concave interior surface and an echinoid profile. And yet, as more analyses are carried out on amphoras of this general class, the more difficult it becomes to make secure, general statements as to the point or region of manufacture of any one specific form.[44] The examples from J 2:4 (and other contemporary deposits in Athens) tend to belong to the former, heavier group. Stamps, finds from kiln sites, and finds from surveys of possible kiln sites broaden the region of this production north as far as modern Izmir and south at least to the area of Knidos.[45] In light of such finds, the determination of provenance for jars in this class will have to consider a wide range of possibilities.

Few sites outside Athens provide independent chronological evidence for the dates of this class of amphora. The terrace fills from the Aphaia sanctuary, a well deposit associated with the Persian sack of Miletos, and contexts associated with the abandonment of Klazomenai ca. 494 provide the nearest contemporary contexts.[46]

A11   (P 34777) Southeastern Aegean   Fig. I.9

  +49.75–48.60 m (Level 2)
  P.H. 5.0; Diam. neck 10.5
  Preserves just over one-quarter of circumference of neck wall; transition from neck to shoulder. Offset ridge rides fairly high on neck, though position of handles and rim unclear. Smooth light brown micaceous fabric (7.5YR 5/6 and 5YR 5/8), fairly fine, compact break darker red-brown, sparse inclusions, bright white, glassy grayish, rare smudgy black.

42. For general discussions of this type, see Grace 1971; Ruban 1991; Zavojkin 1992; Schattner 1996; Dupont 1998, pp. 164–177 (including his Samian and Milesian types); 1999a; 2000; 2007.

43. For coins, see Brašinskij 1968; Grace 1971. For analyses, see Whitbread 1995; Dupont 1982, pp. 203–208; 1983, pp. 33–34, for Samian pottery without amphoras, and p. 34 for Milesian amphoras; 1986; 2007 (in which very few of the analyzed samples

seem to be of the cuffed neck type); Seifert 1996; 2004, pp. 32–41, and p. 49, noting the difficulty of distinguishing Samian and Milesian samples; and Johnston and de Domingo 1997, pp. 64–65, also noting a similar problem from a petrographic point of view.

44. Dupont 1998, pp. 170–177; 1999a; cf. Dupont 2000 and 2007, noting the possibility that other centers produced a similar form.

45. Later stamped examples in simi-

lar form are known for Erythrai; see Carlson 2003. For information on the results of surveys for kiln sites near and south of Knidos, I am indebted to A. Kaan Şenol. For chemical analyses linking this general form to Ephesos as well, see Kerschner and Mommsen 2005.

46. Aigina: Johnston 1990, pp. 47–49, nos. 99, 100, 102, 105, figs. 7, 9, 10. Miletos: Niemeier 1999. Klazomenai: Ersoy 1993; 2004, fig. 23d.

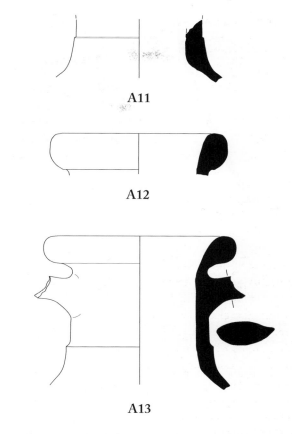

Figure I.9. Southeastern Aegean A11, A12, and A13. Scale 1:3

A12 (P 34778) Southeastern Aegean   Fig. I.9

+49.75–48.60 m (Level 2)

P.H. 3.5; est. Diam. rim 12.0

Preserves just over one-quarter of rim with very small bit of neck wall. Plainly heavy rounded rim, concave curve at bottom edge to join neck; no neck articulation below rim is preserved. Very pale greenish white fabric with little or no mica (close to 5Y 7/3 or greener), coarsely gritty, coarse breaks, dense packing gray glassy bits, very rare red-brown and black bits.

A13 (P 34782) Southeastern Aegean   Fig. I.9

+46.65–45.90 m (Level 5)

P.H. 12.3; Diam. rim 13.5

Preserves seven-eighths of rim with complete profile and much of the rest of the neck; one upper handle segment. Everted, heavy, rounded rim with smooth concave turn down neck wall. High-relief offset collar coming up from shoulder; from collar neck flares out to shoulder. Smooth, finely gritty pale orange surface with much mica (5YR 5/6 and 5YR 5/8), fine-grained breaks, sparse small white bits, rare small black; very rare gray glassy.

A14 (P 34791) Southeastern Aegean?   Fig. I.10

+46.65–45.90 m (Level 5)

P.H. 22.3; Diam. toe 4.4

Nearly complete toe missing small chips, large piece of lower body. Thin-walled, relatively narrow, convex tapering lower body to tall, flaring-sided ring toe with flat base and deep hollow underneath; very slight downward-projecting nub at

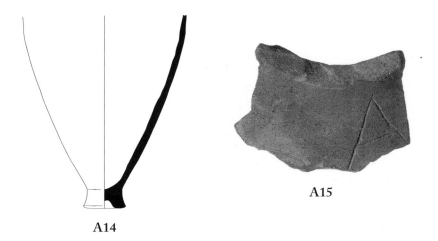

A15

A14

**Figure I.10. Southeastern Aegean?
A14 and Southeastern Aegean A15.**
Scale 1:4 (A14), 1:2 (A15)

top of hollow. Very smooth, pale buff hard-fired fabric, little or no visible mica (5YR 6/6 outer core layer; 7.5YR 5/4 inner core); very compact fabric, sparse–moderate scatter bright white opaque and black bits, rare gray glassy.

A15   (P 35208) Southeastern Aegean   Fig. I.10
   +50.88–49.75 m (Level 1b)
   Max. p. dim. 9.4
   Preserves only the upper part of the shoulder and the lower part of the neck, including a short cuff of clay coming up from the shoulder around the base of the neck. Graffito A on the upper part of the shoulder. Grayish and reddish brown streaky surface with outer third of core gray (10YR 4/2) and inner two-thirds red-brown (7.5YR 5/4) with some grayer areas. Micaceous fabric, with moderate scatter of small gray glassy and yellowish lime bits, darker gray glassy bits especially commonly visible on the surface.

WIDE LOWER SURFACE, ROUNDED RIM

While heavy, rounded rims are often attributable to the southern Aegean (as above), one Late Archaic type with a wide lower surface to the rounded rim, sometimes quite undercut or simply broad and flat as here, has been attributed to the north Aegean and Thrace.[47] These jars lack the cuff of clay coming up around the neck; the body may be either more conical in form or, as is more likely here, more broadly spherical; and the toe, instead of being a ring base, is more of a hollowed, flaring pedestal with a carefully modeled fascia around the outer edge.

The attribution of this type to Thrace was initially proposed with reference to images of similar amphoras on coin types from the city of Abdera.[48] The amphoras bearing similar coin-type stamps, however, do not carry this same form of rim (so far as I have seen). Instead they show a

47. Dupont 1998; 1999a, raising the likelihood of northern Ionian production; cf. Dupont 2007 and 2010; Monachov (2003a and 2003b, pp. 38–42) accepts Dupont's earlier identification. A number of facts remain to

be considered: (1) the often-cited stamped amphoras of Abdera do not show a rounded rim (though such amphoras are found at the site); (2) there are known "profiled" knob toes from Erythrai; and (3) amphoras of this

form are no more common in the north Aegean than they are in the south (the only region where they are extremely common is in the Black Sea).

48. Peristeri-Otatzi 1986; Dupont 1998, p. 182.

wedge-shaped rim typical of the northern Aegean (see below). The broad lower surface or undercut rim type, especially in examples with a more conical body, is far more common in the Black Sea than it seems to be in the southern Aegean.[49]

Recent clay analyses supported the possibility of Thracian production, but northern Ionian reference groups were also considered to be sufficiently similar to represent a possible region of production for the type.[50] Indeed, similar forms also matched both Chian and Milesian reference groups. The hooked, rounded rim form is often found at Klazomenai, the only site in northern Ionia with extensive pottery publication, even if there the lower neck and body often present are not the same narrowly conical forms so common in the Pontic region. The evidence, then, encourages seeing these hooked, rounded rims as the northern Ionian representatives of a southeastern Aegean rounded-rim koine.

The Late Archaic examples of this type are dated primarily by their association with other Late Archaic amphora types, primarily at sites along the north coast of the Black Sea.[51] Similar forms of the rim and toe appear at Klazomenai before the end of the Ionian revolt.[52]

A16   (P 35206) Wide lower surface, rounded rim   Fig. I.11

+49.75–48.60 m (Level 2)

P.H. 4.1; est. Diam. 10.0

Preserves less than one-eighth of rim with part of neck wall, nothing of handle. Small shallow groove around the upper part of the neck below the rim. Light pinkish brown, micaceous fabric (7.5YR 7/6); finely gritty surface, readily visible small to moderate-size gray stony and white opaque bits, dense packing in places.

NORTHERN GREEK: WEDGE RIM, RING OR DISK TOE

Just as amphoras with heavy rounded rims tend to be associated with the southern Aegean, so too amphoras with narrow wedge-shaped rims and ring- or disk-shaped toe tend to be attributable to the northern Aegean.[53] Late Archaic examples of this type, appearing in a wide range of micaceous fabrics, often have a short neck with the handles attaching in the middle or upper half of the neck and swinging outward to a greater or lesser extent (later northern handles are much more upright). The attachment to the shoulder is marked by a thumbprint of varying depth. The egg-shaped body terminates in a ring- or disk-shaped toe. The ring toes are very similar to the southern Aegean toes of the same period, but the body of the northern jars tends to sit above the toe, while the body in the southern examples tends to sit deeper in the toe itself.

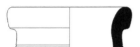

Figure I.11. Wide lower surface, rounded rim A16. Scale 1:3

49. Ruban 1991; Monachov 1999a; 2003a; 2003b; Sorokina and Sudarev 2003; Dupont 1998, pp. 178–186.

50. See Dupont 2007 and 2010.

51. References in note 49 provide the chronological evidence.

52. Ersoy 1993, pp. 416–420; 2004, figs. 15:e, f and 23:h, i.

53. For an overview of the types lumped into this northern group, see Lawall 1995; 1997; Dupont 1998, pp. 186–190; Monachov 1999b. See also Johnston 1990, with examples interspersed throughout pp. 47–57 (some are classified as East Greek, some as northern Greek, others are unidentified).

The rim form in particular ties these amphora types into a general northern Aegean koine traceable from the Late Archaic period through the Early Hellenistic. In addition, the toe forms within this koine seem to go through similar changes of form regardless of fabric and specific forms of rim. The connection of this group in general to northern Greece depends on kiln sites,[54] later stamps with ethnic identifiers,[55] and petrographic and chemical studies tying amphora fabrics to northern clay sources.[56]

Finds outside the Athenian Agora, from contexts datable to the end of the 6th century and earliest decades of the 5th century B.C., support the Late Archaic date for this material. The most securely datable, contemporary examples come from the terrace fills at Aigina and from a series of rubbish pits at Phagris thought to date no later than ca. 490/480.[57] Grave groups at the Kerameikos also associate amphoras in this class with other pottery of the early 5th century.[58] The class also appears among the generally Late Archaic material from Pontic Torikos and at Corinth from a late-6th-century well deposit.[59] The Poros island shipwreck may also provide a further sealed association between this class and Chian amphoras of the sort found in J 2:4.[60]

A17   (P 32759) Northern Aegean   Fig. I.12
+46.65–45.90 m (Level 5)
P.H. 39.2; Diam. rim 9.2; Diam. body 36.8
Complete rim, handles, neck, nearly complete shoulder and much of upper part of body. Squared interior profile, flat-top rim with vaguely inset join to neck wall; lower outer surface of rim variously slightly concave and slightly convex. Oval-section handles attach over upper half of neck and smear join between rim and neck; arched outswung stance. Cylindrical neck, short with tight turn out to broad rounded shoulder. Thumbprints at base of handle. Micaceous very pale orange or buff fabric (5YR 5/8); smooth to very finely gritty; resinated interior, fine-grained core with sparse small stony gray bits and rare off-white lime bits.

A18   (P 34779) Northern Aegean   Fig. I.12
+49.75–48.60 m (Level 2)
P.H. 9.5
Preserves much of one handle from fragment of shoulder to turn of handle toward neck (not preserved). Thick oval-section handle with vertical rib of clay along outer face, thumbprint at base. Fairly smooth, somewhat lumpy dark greenish-brown surface (5YR 4/6); much mica, very dark brown core with moderate–dense distribution of black bits, grayish glassy, dark yellowish green lime.

54. Akanthos: Garlan 2004 and 2006; Trakosopoulou-Salakidou 2004; for further images of the jars in question, see Nicolaïdou-Patera 1986. Samothrace: Karadima-Matsas 1994; Karadima et al. 2002. Thasos: Garlan 1986; 1988.

55. Mende: Corbett 1949; Zeest 1960. Ouranopolis: Garlan 1996. Thasos: Garlan 1999. Oisyme: Giouri and Koukoule 1987. Abdera: stamps published by Peristeri-Otatzi 1986; the jars with the stamps are unpublished but on display in the Abdera Museum. Ainos: Karadima 2004.

56. Mende: Whitbread 1995, pp. 198–209. Thasos: Whitbread 1995, pp. 165–197. Samothrace: Karadima et al. 2002.

57. Aegina: Johnston 1990, nos. 113, 115–119, 130, 135, 138, 147. Phagris: Nicolaïdou-Patera 1987, 1989.

58. *Kerameikos* IX, p. 85, no. 2, HW 169, pl. 44:7, and p. 88, no. 16, HW 167, pl. 44:6; Kübler and Gebauer 1940, p. 330, fig. 11; Schmid 1999.

59. Torikos: Onajko 1980, pp. 124–125, nos. 64, 65, 75, 76. Corinth: Campbell 1938, no. 220.

60. Stavrolakes and McKernan 1975; the Chian amphora was not raised, but the accuracy of the identification of this distinctive form is fairly likely.

A17   **A18**

Figure I.12. Northern Aegean A17 and A18. Scale 1:10 (A17), 1:3 (A18)

A19   (P 34788) Northern Aegean   Fig. I.13

+46.65–45.90 m (Level 5)
P.H. 14.9; Diam. rim 10.4

Nearly complete rim (chipped), one complete handle, one upper segment, complete neck and part of shoulder. Squared-interior, flat-top, wedge rim inset from neck wall. Oval-section handles attach at roughly midway height of neck or slightly higher; outswung, almost stirruplike profile; squat cylindrical neck turns out smoothly at base to shoulder. Graffiti, possible MA ligature followed by O, on neck between handles. Very pale tan smooth slip over pale orange micaceous fabric with darker orange-brown core (5YR 5/8); very rare inclusions, white opaque, small very rare grayish glassy. Resinated.

A20   (P 34772) Northern Aegean   Fig. I.14

+48.60–47.60 and +47.60–46.65 m (Levels 3 and 4)
P.H. 9.3; est. Diam. rim 9.5

Figure I.13. Northern Aegean A19.
Scale 1:3

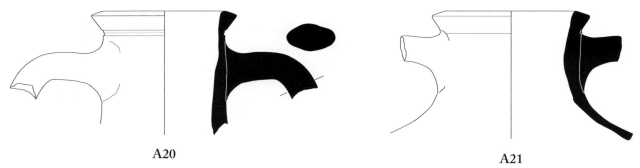

A20   A21

Figure I.14. Northern Aegean A20 and A21. Scale 1:3

Preserves complete rim, part of neck, upper segments of both handles. Slightly everted, sharply squared-interior wedge rim with marked grooves around base of rim, inset sharply from neck wall. One handle attaches below and fully clear of rim; other handle has clay partly covering rim-neck join. Handle projects out fairly far before turning down (stance uncertain). Pale slip poorly preserved over smooth, bright orange micaceous fabric (5YR 5/8 slightly more orangey), moderate scatter smudgy black bits, very light gray glassy and rare lime bits.

A21   (P 34783) Northern Aegean   Fig. I.14

+46.65–45.90 m (Level 5)
P.H. 10.3; est. Diam. rim 9.5

Preserves three-eighths of rim with complete neck profile out onto shoulder, one upper handle segment. Squared interior profile of flat-top rim; sharp outer edge; sharply inset from neck wall; short, wide cylindrical neck turns out quickly at base to quite level shoulder. Oval-section handle with clay just hitting lower edge of rim; arches up slightly. Somewhat lumpy pale pinkish gray surface with lighter slip preserved in places; greenish resin on interior; fine-grained dusky orange-brown core (5YR 6/6); moderate scatter brownish stony bits; some whitish opaque, small gray and blackish bits; micaceous.

A22   (P 34774) Northern Aegean   Fig. I.15

+46.65–45.90 m (Level 5)
P.H. 14; Diam. rim 10.2

Complete rim and neck and both handles (one broken) and part of shoulder. Squared-interior profile wedge rim with flat, slightly downsloping top surface; tight rounded outer edge, concave outer face; slightly and unevenly inset from neck wall; wide, squat cylindrical neck widens somewhat in lower half, then turns out to shoulder. Outswung oval-section handles attach over upper half of neck; only slight rise/arch from neck attachment. Thumbprints at bases of handles. Pale smooth pinkish slip, micaceous, over orangey core (5YR 5/8); resinated; dark brown interior surface; fine-grained orange-brown break, sparse very small white bits and rare gray glassy bits.

A23   (P 34775) Northern Aegean   Fig. I.15

+50.88–49–75 m (Level 1b)
P.H. 12.9; est. Diam. rim 10.0

Preserves three-eighths of rim with one complete handle, small bit of shoulder, part of neck wall. Everted, squared-interior profile wedge rim with flat top, concave outer face, smooth transition to neck wall. Handle attaches just under rim, arches up and out to moderately stirruplike profile; small shallow thumbprint at base of handles. Pale orange surface (5YR 6/6), very smooth and chalky (could be salt damage); very fine red-gray break, very sparse visible inclusions, small grayish stony bits, finely micaceous.

A22

A23

Figure I.15. Northern Aegean A22 and A23. Scale 1:4

A24 (P 34790) Northern Aegean Fig. I.16

+46.65–45.90 m (Level 5)
P.H. 11.1; Diam. rim 10

Complete rim, complete neck, parts of shoulder, both upper handle segments (neither complete). Upright interior profile, squared rim, convex outer face at wedge rim inset from neck wall. Squat cylindrical neck turns out rapidly at base to shoulder. Heavily resinated. Handles attach over upper half of neck under and nearly entirely clear of rim. Very pale buff smooth fabric (7.5YR 5/6), micaceous with much darker brown-orange finely grainy core, moderate scatter small gray and red-brown bits, nothing very commonly visible; dark red-brown interior surface too.

A25 (P 34792) Northern Aegean Fig. I.17

+46.65–45.90 m (Level 5)
P.H. 20.7; max. Diam. toe 5.1

Complete toe and large part of lower body. Wide convex sided lower body, probably fairly egg-shaped; sharp join to flaring-sided disk toe with wide flat base and small hollow in center with small downpointing nub at top of hollow. Resinated. Fairly smooth, pale orange micaceous fabric (5YR 5/8) with dark red-brown interior and bright red-orange-brown finely grainy core, moderate scatter bright white small bits, small grayish bits, and occasional darker red-brown bits.

A26 (P 35210) Northern Aegean Fig. I.17

+46.65–45.90 m (Level 5)
P.H. 39.0; max. Diam. toe 5.5

Nearly complete toe and large part of body. Overall form is very much like **A25**, except that cone does not project as much down into the hollow area under the toe. Resinated. Very smooth, brown micaceous exterior surface with somewhat darker and very finely gritty interior (5YR 6/8); fine-grained core, sparse–moderate mix of red-brown bits, some gray glassy, and some whitish opaque.

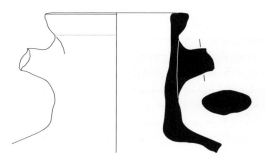

Figure I.16. Northern Aegean A24.
Scale 1:3

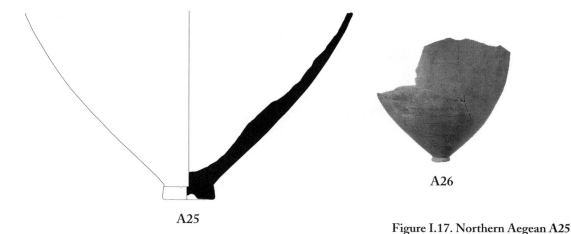

A25

Figure I.17. Northern Aegean A25 and A26. Scale 1:4 (A25), 1:10 (A26)

A27   (P 34784) Northern Aegean   Fig. I.18

+46.65–45.90 m (Level 5)
P.H. 8.7; max. Diam. toe 7.15

Nearly complete toe, part of lower body. Wide body tapers fairly straight to sharply turned join with flaring-sided ring toe; rounded outer edge, sharp interior edge of ring around hollow underneath with downward-projecting nub; prefiring strokes across lower surface of toe. Resinated interior sits down inside toe slightly. Finely gritty micaceous orange-brown surface (5YR 6/8); very sparse, very small light-colored bits.

A28   (P 34786) Northern Aegean   Fig. I.18

+49.75–48.60 m (Level 2)
P.H. 5.1; max. Diam. toe 5.6

Preserves ca. 90% toe with small bit of body wall. Fairly wide lower body turns smoothly out to flaring sides of tall disk/proto-stem toe with beveled outer edge and conical hollow underneath with small downward-projecting nub at top of hollow. Smooth, micaceous bright orange fabric (5YR 5/8), sparse, very small pale inclusions in fine-grained orange-brown core.

A27   A28

Figure I.18. Northern Aegean A27 and A28. Scale 1:4

LESBOS-REGION: RED-BROWN FABRIC

The red-brown-fabric Lesbos-region amphoras are one of a series of different fabric types that show very close similarities of form and are attributable to the region of Lesbos and the adjacent mainland of northwestern Turkey.[61] The Late Archaic red-brown type has a rounded rim, often with a band in relief just below the rim around the top of the neck; tall, slightly bulging neck; round-section handles joining the shoulder with an elongated vertical relief line (a "rat tail"); turnip-shaped body terminating in a tall, plain, narrow toe with a slight depression on the underside. One of the fragments from J 2:4 preserves a fairly tall band below the rim. The fabric

61. For overviews of these types, see Clinkenbeard 1982; 1986; Ruban 1990; Dupont 1998, pp. 156–163; Birzescu 2005.

A29

Figure I.19. Lesbos-Region A29, A30, and A31. Scale 1:3

ranges from brick-red throughout to red-brown with a grayer core and is often quite coarse and micaceous.

Petrographic and chemical analyses made some progress in linking this type to the island of Lesbos, but the results have never been as conclusive for all fabric types as would be hoped.[62] Other evidence in favor of production centers on the island or nearby includes the fact that the form is very common—in a wide range of fabrics—at sites with Archaic strata in the Troad.[63] Amphoras in many of these fabrics, especially the very pale and darker tan fabrics, are rarely found outside the Troad, suggesting production in that region.

The Late Archaic date for the forms present in J 2:4 is supported by finds at many Archaic Black Sea sites with scattered examples in the Levant.[64] The taller band below the rim, as seen in J 2:4, is more commonly encountered in deposits closed within the 6th century than in the early 5th century B.C.[65] These fragments, then, were already quite old when they were swept into the well.

A29   (P 34780) Lesbos-Region   Fig. I.19

+46.65–45.90 m (Level 5)
P.H. 8.2; Diam. of toe 3.2

Chipped but largely complete toe with part of lower body. Concave sides of lower body taper smoothly to simple peg toe; very little or no solid stem part; hollow of body goes nearly to bottom of the toe on the inside. Narrow rounded base with small circular hollow underneath. Finely gritty surface, grayish green with mica (n.b.: form is entirely of the Lesbian Red series); dark brown outer layer of break (under the gray skin) with greenish gray inner core (10YR 5/4); moderate scatter gray glassy and black bits, rare white opaque; traces of resin.

A30   (P 34771) Lesbos-Region   Fig. I.19

+49.75–48.60 m (Level 2)
P.H. 4.6; est Diam. rim 12.0

Preserves ca. one-eighth of rim with part of neck wall. Rounded interior profile up to flattish upsloping upper surface of rim; rounded outer face, sharp turn back in toward neck wall. Tall but very low relief band around top of neck. Somewhat gritty orange surfaces; micaceous, finely gritty core, dusky reddish, darker than exterior (2.5YR 5/6); moderate-dense packing whitish lime infills; red-brown bits, very rare black small bits.

A31   (P 34781) Lesbos-Region   Fig. I.19

+46.65–45.90 m (Level 5)
P.H. 2.2; est. Diam. rim 10.0.

Preserves ca. one-sixth of rim with very small bit of neck. Simple outrounded rim with tight concave curve at lower edge probably to relief band at top of neck (not preserved); smearing from handle at lower half of rim. Gritty coarse orange-brown fabric (5YR 6/6), micaceous, similar core; moderate-dense packing in grainy break; small lime infills off-white, difficult to make out small glassy bits, some grayish/black.

62. Clinkenbeard 1982, p. 264; Dupont 1983, p. 30; Johnston and de Domingo 1997, pp. 65–66.

63. Lawall 2002.

64. See references in Dupont 1998, p. 160; Birzescu 2005.

65. This wider band form is Ruban 1990, type I; for other examples from datable contexts, see Dimitriu 1966, pl. 56, nos. 548, 550 from Archaic level II, dated to mid-6th century; Lawall 2002, nos. 1, 8.

Magna Graeca

The South Italian amphora type present in J 2:4 closely resembles the Corcyrean type and is clearly part of a broad Greek amphora koine for the western Mediterranean.[66] The rim is quite heavy and rounded, usually with a groove and ridge around the lower part of the rim as opposed to a raised band around the top of the neck just under the rim, as is more common among the Archaic Corcyrean jars. The turnip-shaped body ends in a simple, flat base or sometimes an angular knob. The fabric of examples of this class found in Athens tends to be quite pale, ranging from chalky and fairly fine-grained to rough, coarse, and micaceous. The extremely coarse and pinkish Massaliote fabric is not seen in Athens.[67]

The evidence provided by kiln sites, debris likely from kiln sites, and fabric analyses using various techniques indicates many different producers of this class of amphora. And yet, the relatively limited variation in rim forms and overall shape suggest a broad southern Italian koine of amphora production in the Late Archaic and Classical periods. While the best evidence for this production comes from Massalia and Epizephyrian Locris, petrographic and chemical analyses suggest production in the areas of Sybaris and Kroton, Kaulonia, Rhegio, Velia, Poseidonia, the Bay of Naples, and across to Sicily with possible production in the areas of Camarina, Panormus (Palermo), Himera, and the Lipari islands.[68]

The occurrence of folded-over, heavy, rounded rims of the sort found in J 2:4 alongside other late-6th- or early-5th-century Aegean types is quite common in the western Mediterranean. The shipwreck at Braccetto included heavy, rounded South Italian rims alongside Late Archaic Klazomenian, Corinthian, and Lesbian types.[69] On land, the sites of Gravisce, Pyrgi, and Regisvilla repeat this association between the heavy, folded-over, rounded Italian rim and the Corinthian, Klazomenian, Chian, and southern Aegean forms as seen in J 2:4.[70] Indeed, very close parallels for the rim type seen in J 2:4 appear in a destruction level dated near 470 at Velia.[71]

A32   (P 34785) South Italian   Fig. I.20
    +50.88–49.75 and 49.75–48.60 m (Levels 1b, 2)
    P.H. 5.0; est. Diam. rim 12.0
    Preserves ca. three-eighths of rim with small bit of neck wall. Heavy, outrounded rim; upright interior profile; rim folded over outward; thick, offset ridge around lower part of rim above actual thick, rounded, lower undercut edge of rim. Somewhat smooth chalky micaceous pale buff fabric with darker gray fine-grained core, sparse scatter red-brown bits; moderate size, rare gray glassy and whitish bits (10YR 5/3, surface between 10YR 7/4 and 6/4).

Figure I.20. South Italian A32.
Scale 1:3

66. Gassner (2003, pp. 179–219) provides an overview of the various rim forms and fabrics and evidence for locations of production; the more frequently discussed Massaliote amphoras are part of this broad koine (see Bertucchi 1992).

67. The corresponding Massaliote type is Bertucchi's type I (1992, pp. 37–51).

68. The evidence for these production sites is usefully summarized by Gassner 2000 and 2003, pp. 186–206; for similarly wide-ranging results for slightly later western Mediterranean forms, see Desy and De Paepe 1990.

69. Braccetto wreck: Di Stefano 1993–1994.

70. Gravisce: Slaska 1978, figs. 11–

19, likely to go with toes, figs. 24, 25. Regisvilla: Morselli and Tortorici 1985, especially fig. 9. Pyrgi: Colonna 1985, p. 11, nos. 14, 15.

71. Gassner 1999, p. 112, and fig. 4:22 and 24. Similar forms on the Pointe Lequin IB wreck date to the 2nd quarter of the 5th century (Long, Miro, and Volpe 1992, pp. 226–227).

A33

Figure I.21. Unattributed body sherds with graffiti A33, A34, and A35. Scale 1:2

A34

A35

UNATTRIBUTED BODY SHERDS WITH GRAFFITI

A33 (P 34793) Unattributed body sherd: Graffito   Fig. I.21
+49.75–48.60 m (Level 2)
Max. p. dim. 8.4
Preserves only upper part of shoulder and lower edge of neck. The fabric and form are insufficiently diagnostic to identify the type. Graffito possibly Δ or A but there are other small traces of lines seeming to project from what is preserved, perhaps to create some sort of monogram. Light red-brown extremely micaceous fabric (5YR 6/6); fine-grained break; readily visible, moderate scatter small to medium white and yellowish lime bits, few larger gray glassy bits visible. Rarity of gray glassy bits suggests possible southern Aegean fabric, but quite micaceous, so perhaps closer to Samos.

A34 (P 35207) Unattributed body sherd: Graffito   Fig. I.21
+49.75–48.60 m (Level 2)
Max. p. dim. 11.7
Shoulder fragment with the smear of clay from one handle. Graffito E with room for more letters afterward on the same sherd, but there are no further letters. Fairly hard, finely micaceous, red-brown fabric (between 5YR 6/8 and 5YR 5/8); moderate mix of small- to medium-sized gray glassy bits, rare very small lime bits: the fabric could be northern Aegean from this appearance, but this is not certain.

A35 (P 35205) Unattributed body sherd: Graffito   Fig. I.21
+49.75–48.60 m (Level 2)
Max. p. dim. 9.8
Shoulder fragment with graffito K; no traces of handles or neck preserved. Extremely micaceous brownish fabric (5YR 5/6), somewhat redder on the interior; few visible inclusions in grainy break other than mica; could be a coarsely micaceous, dark brown Thasian fabric.

AMPHORA FINDS IN EACH LEVEL

As noted above, differentiation among the filling episodes in well J 2:4 was established on the basis of the fine-ware and plain-ware studies. Using the results of that study as a guiding framework, important distinctions also appear in the amphora finds, particularly as regards likely time of use or importation of the amphoras and their current state of preservation.

No amphora fragments were recovered from the deepest level of the well, Level 6, where the many water jars permit an identification of the fill as resulting from the well's period of use.

TABLE I.1. WELL J 2:4, LEVEL 5: DISTRIBUTION OF AMPHORA TYPES

Type	Number of Diagnostic Fragments*
Attic *à la brosse*	1
Corcyrean	1
Chian: bulging neck with painted decoration	2
Southeast Aegean with offset cuff at neck	1
Northern Greek: Wedge Rim, Ring Toe	11
Lesbos-region (Red-brown fabric)	2
Amphora body fragments	46**

* In this and subsequent tables, "diagnostic fragments" includes both catalogued and non-catalogued rims and toes. Body sherds are listed by counts only at the bottom of this table, comparing simply Attic as opposed to non-Attic sherds.

** 6 Attic sherds; 40 non-Attic sherds and a complete tin (lot BZ 717).

The first major filling episode, Level 5 (see Fig. 5 above, p. 10), which included many complete and some intact symposium vessels, also included many fragmentary transport amphoras (Table I.1). Nearly all amphora types from Level 5 are paralleled in other Persian sack deposits in Athens and in other Late Archaic, closely datable contexts at other sites (see discussion of types, above, and Table I.5, below). As with the fine wares in this level, the amphoras are preserved in large pieces, often with sharp-edged breaks showing little wear before or after deposition in the well. Level 5 provided the largest number of cross-mends in the entire contents of the well. Ten different sets of joining sherds were found in this level, in some cases making up large vessel fragments. The leftover sherds, however, were insufficient for completing any single jar, despite the fact that no sherds were discarded following excavation. The jars were not intact when they were thrown into the well. They must have broken sometime earlier, perhaps during the sack, perhaps even in everyday use.

The next level up, Level 4, was differentiated from Level 5 by the appearance of iron-processing waste and the renewed presence of larger bits of stone in the fill along with roof-tile fragments. At this level and further up in the well, Kathleen Lynch proposes that the debris is no longer largely restricted to the household's contents but is a combination of the remainder of that material with more general debris from the neighborhood. The amphora fragments in Level 4 are more broken up: the only diagnostic elements are handle fragments. While some common Late Archaic types continue to appear in this level, there is also one clearly earlier, residual fragment, that of a late-8th- or 7th-century B.C. Attic SOS amphora (Table I.2). Far fewer and smaller body fragments appeared in this level, with only three Attic and 65 non-Attic fragments. A small group of Chian body sherds in Level 4 produced five joins, but the result was nothing close to an entire vessel. In addition, one sherd from higher up in Level 2 did join a fragment in Level 4, and other sherds in both levels seem to belong to this same vessel (but no further joins could be made). This join across the nearly sterile, crushed bedrock fill of Level 3 makes it clear that broken-up debris on the surface was partly discarded in the stage of Level 4's filling and then the deposition of that same accumulation of

TABLE I.2. WELL J 2:4, LEVEL 4: DISTRIBUTION OF AMPHORA TYPES

Type	Number of Diagnostic Fragments
Attic SOS	1
Chian: bulging neck with painted decoration	3
Northern Greek: Wedge Rim, Ring Toe	3
Corinthian	1
Nondiagnostic handles	3
Amphora body fragments	68*

* 3 Attic, 65 non-Attic.

debris continued after the dumping of Level 3. The fine wares, plain wares, and the amphoras support the proposal that the debris in Level 4 derived from different sources from that in Level 5. Between Levels 5 and 4 there was a shift from depositing the primary (or nearly primary) debris from the immediate household to gathering and depositing secondary debris from the broader surrounding neighborhood.

Level 3, the layer of dug bedrock, contained only one diagnostic amphora fragment: a wedge-profile rim, which joined a set of rims in Level 4. The level also included one poorly diagnostic handle and 10 non-Attic body fragments, all of which were quite small.

With Level 2 the well again began to be filled with debris from within the house, but the fill at this level also began to include a greater proportion of very worn, fragmentary, much earlier 6th-century fine wares and plain wares. Lynch explained this combination of earlier and up-to-date material as resulting from further clearance both of the house itself and of debris, often much worn and older, from the vicinity. The same explanation likely holds true for the amphoras. Many of the fragments are quite worn and are of types that are more commonly found in earlier 6th-century B.C. contexts (Table I.3). The plentiful body fragments, too, were small to moderate in size and quite diverse in appearance. In one set of 14 Corinthian dark fabric wall sherds, no joins could be found even though it was clear from the

TABLE I.3. WELL J 2:4, LEVEL 2: DISTRIBUTION OF AMPHORA TYPES

Type	Number of Diagnostic Fragments
Attic *à la brosse*	2
Corinthian	1
Corcyrean	1
Chian: bulging neck with painted decoration	5
Southeast Aegean with offset cuff at neck	2
Hooked rounded rim (possible Northern Ionian)	1
Northern Greek: Wedge Rim, Ring Toe	4
Lesbos-region (Red-brown fabric)	1
South Italian	1
Other handles	13
Amphora body fragments	450*

* 33 Attic, 417 non-Attic.

TABLE I.4. WELL J 2:4, LEVEL 1: DISTRIBUTION OF AMPHORA TYPES

Type	Number of Diagnostic Fragments
Attic *à la brosse*	3
Corinthian	2
Corcyrean	1
Chian: bulging neck with painted decoration	2
Hooked rounded rim (possible Northern Ionian)	1
Northern Greek: Wedge Rim, Ring Toe	9
South Italian	(1, counted as part of Level 2)
Other handles	5
Amphora body fragments	73*

* 5 Attic, 68 non-Attic.

fabric that all sherds came from one vessel. In two cases very small sherds did join to make a somewhat larger wall fragment. Furthermore, there are many poorly diagnostic handle fragments that do not join better diagnostic rim fragments.[72] Such poorly identifiable bits, making up a substantial portion of the overall assemblage in Level 2, seem more characteristic of fill that remained on the surface for some time before being added to the well fill. Even so, as in the fine wares and plain wares, there are some typical "Persian sack" types still present.

Among the fine wares and plain wares, an even greater percentage were worn and residual in Level 1, the uppermost fill of the well, and there were also many worn animal bones in this fill. Among the amphoras, too, there were again many worn handle fragments, moderate-sized body fragments, and small bits of other parts of rims and toes (Table I.4). There are also a very few joins between amphora fragments in Levels 1 and 2, including the Magna Graeca type rim; such cross-mends were also noted for the fine wares and plain wares.

AMPHORAS IN J 2:4 COMPARED WITH OTHER LATE ARCHAIC AND EARLY CLASSICAL CONTEXTS

The importance of the fill of J 2:4 for understanding Athenian archaeology and history becomes clear when this deposit is set in the context of other Late Archaic and Early Classical deposits around the Agora. An unfortunate reality of any such consideration of the remains from Agora deposits is the fact that, with the exception of J 2:4, we rarely possess the complete contents of these deposits. As a result, any quantitative or statistical consideration of these deposits now has to take account of dramatic differences in sample size (i.e., in the numbers of diagnostic fragments now surviving from the excavation). Similarly, any comparisons must be kept at such a level or with such a focus that these problems of sherd retention are mitigated (e.g., one cannot compare the numbers of body sherds now present across the deposits since these were the first to be discarded when editing the tins).

72. By contrast, in Level 5, where more of the jars seem to have entered the well in large fragments, there are fewer miscellaneous handle fragments.

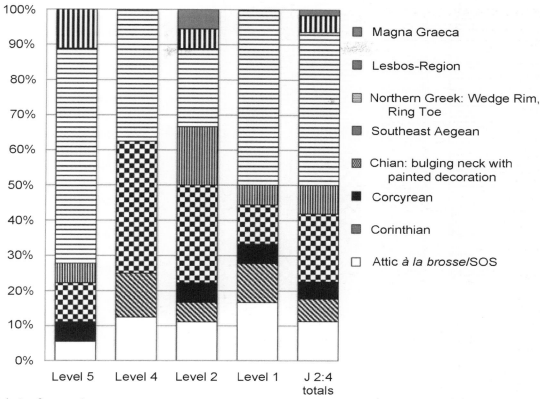

Figure I.22. Relative frequencies of identified amphora types in J 2:4, by level and in total. For the numerical counts in each level, see Tables I.1–I.4.

73. Roberts 1986.

74. The contents of these deposits are discussed by Shear (1993) with lists of the inventoried amphoras; for more details on the amphora contents of each one, see Lawall 1995.

75. Such deposits include wells E 14:5, F 19:5, and (shaft) G 6:3 (upper fill); similarly, wells R 12:4 and G 15:1, closed just before 480, include no more than one restorable vessel.

76. See Lawall 2000.

With these caveats in mind, however, there are still useful observations to be made by comparing J 2:4 with other contemporary deposits.

In many respects, particularly in terms of the amphora types present, J 2:4 closely resembles other deposits thought to have been filled after the Persian sack (Figs. I.22–I.27). J 2:4 differs from some other Persian sack deposits, however, in that, despite full retention of all amphora fragments, no complete vessels could be restored. By contrast, the best known Persian sack deposit, at least the best known in terms of the amphoras, the Stoa Gutter Well (Q 12:3), included many complete or nearly complete amphoras.[73] Likewise, R 12:1, just south of the Stoa Gutter Well, also included complete vessels (though not as many). Two other Persian sack deposits, H 12:15 and G 11:3, also included a few complete vessels, though even fewer than R 12:1; D 15:1 produced one restorable jar.[74] Far more commonly, in fact, Persian sack deposits have not produced complete or nearly complete, readily restorable, amphoras.[75] The more prolific of those that have produced restorable amphoras, Q 12:3 and R 12:1, are found in the southeastern corner of the Agora excavations where later well fillings continue to include numerous complete amphoras and frequent commercial graffiti.[76] This contrast between the J 2:4 filling and these other contemporary fills farther to the south and east may be attributable to the contrast between a largely domestic assemblage of amphoras and a more specifically commercial one.

J 2:4 does share with the other Persian sack deposits the feature of large numbers of amphora sherds, regardless of whether they mend up to

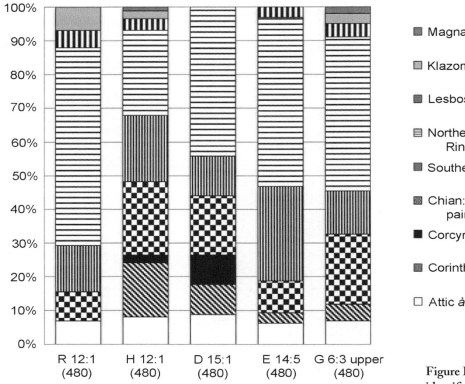

Figure I.23. Relative frequencies of identified amphora types in other Persian sack deposits. For the numerical counts in each level, see Table I.5.

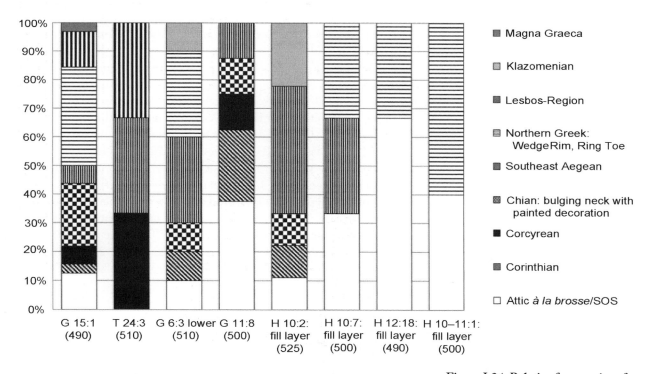

Figure I.24. Relative frequencies of identified amphora types in deposits closed ca. 490 or earlier. For the numerical counts in each level, see Table I.5.

TABLE I.5. DIAGNOSTIC AMPHORA FRAGMENTS FROM SELECTED AGORA DEPOSITS, WITH CLOSING DATES LATE IN THE 6TH CENTURY AND CA. 480 B.C.

Type	Level 5	Level 4	Level 2	Level 1	J2:4 Totals	R12:1 (480)	H12:15 (480)	D15:1 (480)	E14:5 (480)	G6:3, Upper (480)	G15:1 (490)	T24:3 (510)	G6:3, Lower (510)	G11:8 (500)	Fill: H10:2 (525)	Fill: H10:7 (500)	Fill: H12:18 (490)	Fill: H10–11:1 (500)
Attic à la brosse/SOS	1	1	2	3	7	4	7	3	2	7	4		1	3	1	1	2	2
Corinthian		1	1	2	4	0	14	3	1	5	1		1	2	1			
Corcyrean	1		1	1	3	0	2	3			2	1		1				
Chian: bulging neck wiwth painted decoration	2	3	5	2	12	5	19	6	3	21	7		1	1	1			
Southeast Aegean	1		3	1	5	8	17	4	9	13	2	1	3	1	4	1		
Northern Greek: Wedge Rim, Ring Toe	11	3	4	9	27	34	22	15	16	46	11		3			1	1	3
Lesbos-region	2		1		3	3	3		1	4	4	1						
Klazomenian					0	4	2			3			1		2			
Magna Graeca	1		1		1	0	1			2	1							
Total Known	18	8	18	18	62	58	87	34	32	101	32	3	10	8	9	3	3	5
Unknown		3	13	5	21	4	2	2		3	2						1	
Total Fragments	18	11	31	23	83	62	89	36	32	104	34	3	10	8	9	3	4	5

TABLE I.6. AMPHORA TYPES GROUPED INTO BROADER REGIONS, COMPARING WELL J 2:4 (LEVELS 1, 2, 4, AND 5) WITH OTHER DEPOSITS

Type	Level 5	Level 4	Level 2	Level 1	J2:4 totals	R12:1 (480)	H12:15 (480)	D15:1 (480)	E14:5 (480)	G6:3, Upper (480)	G15:1 (490)	T24:3 (510)	G6:3, Lower (510)	G11:8 (500)	Fill: H10:2 (525)	Fill: H10:7 (500)	Fill: H12:18 (490)	Fill: H10–11:1 (500)
Attic à la brosse/SOS	1	1	2	3	7	4	7	3	2	7	4		1	3	1	1	2	2
Corinthia–Corcyra	1	1	2	3	7		16	6	1	5	3	1	1	3	1	1	2	
Lesbos–Chios–Klazomenai	4	3	6	2	15	12	24	6	4	28	11	1	2	1	2			
Southern Aegean	1		3	1	5	8	17	4	9	13	2	1	3	1	5	1		
Northern Greek	11	3	4	9	27	34	22	15	16	46	11		3			1	1	3
Magna Graeca		1	1		1	0	1			2	1							
Total Known	18	8	18	18	62	58	87	34	32	101	32	3	10	8	9	3	3	5

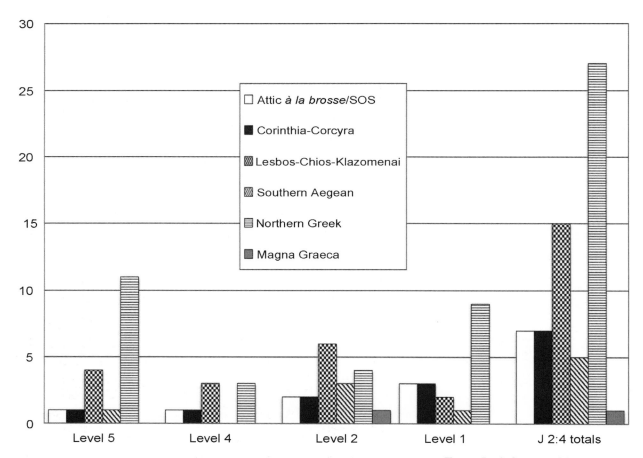

complete amphoras. Deposits closed earlier tend to show some differences in the types present and tend to have far fewer amphora fragments (Table I.5; Figs. I.22–I.24). In terms of specific types: Attic jars are consistently found in both pre-480 and ca. 480 B.C. deposits; Corinthian jars appear slightly more consistently in the later deposits; Corcyraean jars, however, are more often found in the later contexts (indeed, only four fragments are listed in the selected earlier deposits considered here). Chian jars seem more common in the later deposits, too, but southern Aegean jars and northern Aegean types appear with similar frequencies (relative to the total size of each deposit) in both Late Archaic and Persian sack contexts. While the raw figures for Klazomenian jars are similar between earlier and later deposits, the relative presence of Klazomenian jars is greater in the smaller earlier deposits.[77] Two classes—Lesbos-Region and Magna Graeca—appear primarily in the ca. 480 B.C. deposits. This is not to say that all fragments from this class are datable to this later period (cf. Lesbian Red fabric rim A30), but it seems these types are more plentiful in the later period, with the result that the fragments could more consistently enter the archaeological record.

If the groups of imports are combined into somewhat broader regional groupings, the bar graphs of the contributions of each region to Athenian imports over the late 6th century to ca. 480 show the differences in size between earlier and later deposits even more clearly (Table I.6; Figs. I.25 –I.27).

While the numbers, especially in the earlier deposits, are difficult to interpret on account of their sparseness, there is a further indicator of

Figure I.25. Counts of diagnostic fragments grouped according to broader regions in the levels of J 2:4 and in the deposit as a whole (see Table I.6)

Figure I.26 *(opposite, top).* **Counts of diagnostic fragments grouped according to broader regions in the J 2:4 and other Persian sack deposits (see Table I.6)**

Figure I.27 *(opposite, bottom).* **Counts of diagnostic fragments grouped according to broader regions in deposits closed ca. 490 or earlier (see Table I.6)**

77. Amphoras from Klazomenai do not appear in J 2:4; for typological discussion of these amphoras, see Doğer 1986; Ersoy 1993, pp. 396–403; Lawall 1995, pp. 48–54; Dupont 1998, pp. 151–156; Monachov 2003b, pp. 50–55; Sezgin 2004.

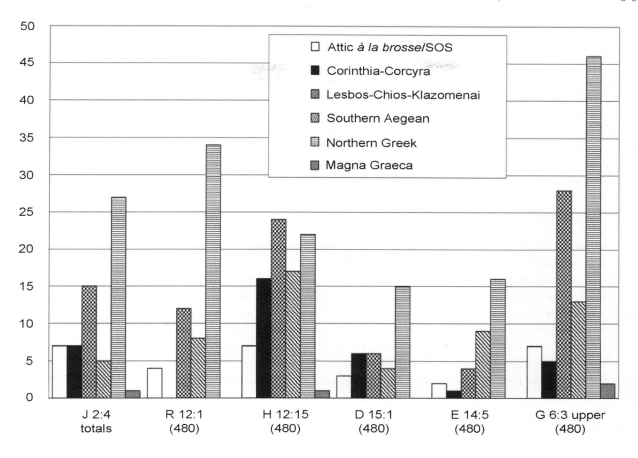

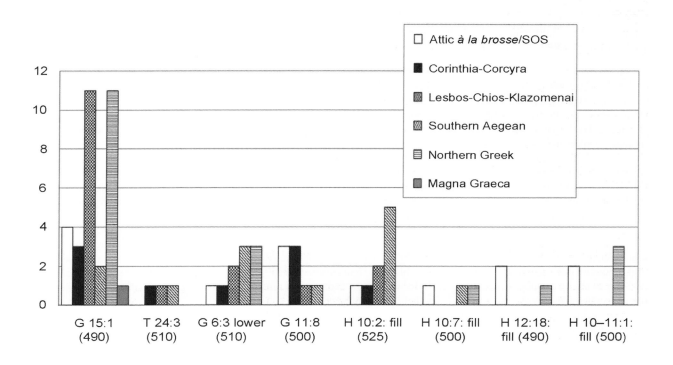

difference between earlier and later deposits: evenness or diversity of each assemblage.[78] An assemblage is considered to have high evenness if all types are equally represented (score closer to 1.00); in a situation of low evenness (score closer to 0.00), a few types will be much more common than others. Keith Kintigh's formula for evenness incorporates the variables of assemblage size, number of different types present, and the number of amphoras in each type: f_i = number of amphoras in type i; k = number of types present; n = sample size; H/H_{max} = evenness as follows:[79]

$$\overset{k}{\underset{i=1}{H}} = [\, n \log(n) - \sum f_i \log(f_i) \,]/\, n \qquad\qquad H_{max} = \log(k)$$

If all regions of production are equally represented, the evenness score is 1.00; if one or a few types are dominant, the score approaches 0.00. This measure can be affected by the extent to which one "lumps" related types into regional classes for purposes of comparing assemblages. If the practices of combining types are constant between the assemblages being compared, however, this difficulty is minimized. The results of this formula for the earlier deposits, those closed within the late 6th century B.C., show significantly higher values between 0.9 and 1.0 compared with the later deposits, with values closer to 0.8 even down to 0.7 (Table I.7). A Student's T-test comparing the earlier and later evenness figures indicates that the two sets of figures are very unlikely to have come from the same pool of samples.[80]

Two underlying factors seem especially relevant to interpreting these differences in evenness. First, evenness might be affected by immediacy of the deposition as compared with the time of use of the assemblage in question. Material deposited shortly after use should show any patterning originally present in the assemblage more clearly than material that is discarded, mixed with further material from other periods, and eventually comes to rest. By this line of argument, "residual" portions of deposits should show more evenness (perhaps many different types but all present with the same frequency) than the up-to-date material. J. Theodore Peña's data from the Palatine East excavations are suggestive of this tendency.[81]

78. Leonard and Jones 1989.

79. Kintigh 1989, p. 29.

80. Comparing the evenness scores of all selected pre-Persian contexts with all selected Persian contexts gives a Student's T score of 0.00027 (0.03% chance that both samples came from the same original population, and that the differences are simply due to random changes over time); comparing the two groups but splitting J 2:4 into the "more residual" and "less residual" levels (Levels 2 and 4 vs. 5 and 1) gives a T score of 0.000023 (0.002% chance of purely random differences); and comparing only the well deposits, excluding the smaller fills, gives a T score of

0.0029 (0.3% chance of purely random differences). Note that G 15:1 is included here in the earlier pre-Persian group, but there is some possibility that this deposit too was closed very near 480. It has been traditionally grouped with pre-Persian contexts since the well went out of use due to bedrock collapse and not human agency.

81. Peña 1998, esp. p. 18, table 2. The main difficulty, Peña rightly notes, is that much of the material in a given assemblage may be somewhat "old" or may be up to date. These pieces fall into his large "indeterminate" category. If one widens the definition of residual to being vaguely "very unlikely to have

been in use near the time of deposition," then some of the "indeterminate" pieces might be reclassified. As it stands for the amphoras presented by Peña, the 13 securely residual amphora types are only present in two or fewer estimated vessels, while the 17 "in phase" or "indeterminate" types are represented by 1 to 12 estimated vessels. Sourisseau's data (1998, pp. 48–50) from Marseille might also be suggestive of the tendency of residual pottery to obscure patterning of the relative presence of different types in assemblages. Sourisseau's data are problematic, however, due to the large numbers in the class "Grecques indéterminées."

TABLE I.7. EVENNESS SCORES COMPARING PRE-PERSIAN WITH PERSIAN SACK CONTEXTS

	Closing Date	*Evenness Score*
PRE-PERSIAN CONTEXTS		
G 6:3, lower	530	0.92
H 10:2	525	0.88
T 24:3	510	1.00
G 11:8	500	0.93
H 10:7	500	1.00
H 10–11:1	500	0.97
G 15:1	490	0.86
H 12:18	490	0.92
J 2:4, Level 2	480 + residual	0.9
J 2:4, Level 4	480 + residual	0.91
PERSIAN SACK CONTEXTS		
J 2:4	480	0.80
D 15:1	480	0.87
E 14:5	480	0.73
G 6:3, upper	480	0.77
R 12:1	480	0.74
H 12:15	480	0.84
J 2:4, Level 5	480	0.71
J 2:4, Level 1	480	0.81

Analysis of the evenness of the different episodes of filling in J 2:4 also suggest greater evenness associated with levels containing more residual pottery. Thus, Level 5, whose large fragments, frequent joins, and sharp breaks indicated use and deposition very near the time of the Persian sack, has a low evenness score (0.7) The middle Levels 4 and 2, argued above to have mixed-in debris from the general neighborhood, show greater evenness (0.90 and 0.91) despite the fact that Levels 5, 2, and 1 are all nearly equal in size. The uppermost Level 1 also has a relatively lower score, perhaps as a result of a greater portion of up-to-date debris in this final stage of the filling.

A second factor potentially influencing evenness scores, also related to depositional history of the amphora assemblage, concerns the broader nature of the area where the material is found. Amphora assemblages from a port site or market building might better reflect the patterns of imports to a city than do individual household assemblages (no matter how close to market buildings). The decisions of individuals within a household might well either flatten out patterns originally existing in imports to a city, or exaggerate patterning through their personal preferences. The greater the distance from the port or market, the greater the chances of the import patterns being diluted by the admixture of other amphora types present in the general population. Such difficulties are somewhat controlled for by considering multiple, roughly contemporary deposits. In the case of the Agora deposits under consideration here, the fact that the evenness scores

Evans and Millett (1992) considered the proportion and approximate age of residual material in given contexts, but they do not discuss the range of residual types present. They do usefully emphasize the importance of depositional history in considering residual pottery. For further discussion of interpretive difficulties posed by residual pottery, see Fontana and Bagolan 1992.

differ with respect to the deposits' closing dates and not in terms of the locations of the deposits points in one of three directions: (1) the Agora assemblages are reflective of general import trends in the Late Archaic/Early Classical period, (2) the Agora in general was more closely linked to marketing and to goods entering the Peiraeus ca. 480 and less so before 500,[82] or (3) some other factor is creating the apparent chronological differences in imports to the city.

This "other factor," and the final one to be considered here, concerns the underlying processes and patterns in contemporary shipping. High evenness might indicate that within the given geographical and/or economic zone there is little selectivity in terms of sources of imports with goods from all suppliers circulating at a similar level. In other words, if Aegean trade operated, for whatever reason, with little patterning or direction but simply with merchants moving from port to port, unloading parts of cargoes and picking up others, then the end result on land might be a basically even distribution of various amphora types. On the other hand, if there is closely directed trade, strong preferences to draw imports from specific sources, perhaps even formal sociopolitical links between cities all shaping the patterns of amphora distributions, then we would expect to see significantly greater unevenness in amphora assemblages reflecting these preferred sources. J 2:4, especially Level 5, and the other Persian sack deposits show greater unevenness in their amphora assemblages than is the case for earlier deposits (and the residual parts of J 2:4). This distinction for the Persian sack contexts might drive the formulation of a hypothesis that shipping within the Aegean did become more formalized in the early 5th century than it had been in the 6th century B.C.

The preceding thoughts should be treated as working hypotheses generated by less-than-ideal data. Given the dramatic differences in deposit size between earlier and later assemblages, the differences in evenness scores might not indicate a truly significant difference in evenness per se. The differences could simply reflect the overall sparseness of the assemblage. Both evenness scores and the range of error likely present in the scores tend to increase in smaller samples.[83] The unique qualities of J 2:4 as a well-excavated, carefully documented, and closely analyzed deposit, however, have permitted us to raise questions and develop such hypotheses related to residuality, patterning in an assemblage, and how this part of the Agora, the broader Agora, and Athens fit into developments in Late Archaic and Early Classical amphora shipping. Further pursuit of these questions depends on continued excavation and analyses of deposits that follow the same high standards as were applied in the case of J 2:4.

82. Papadopoulos 1996; 2003, pp. 280–297.

83. McCartney and Glass 1990, pp. 523–525; on lingering problems correlating sample size and measures of diversity or evenness, see Meltzer, Leonard, and Stratton 1992.

VOLUME STUDIES

Volumes of complete and nearly complete vessels were determined by filling the shape with dry lentil beans or fine-grain sand. In some cases nearly complete vessels were missing critical body fragments, so a dam was formed on the outside of the vase wall to prevent the fill from spilling out. These vessels will have a less accurate estimated volume because the exterior dam produces an extra volume for the thickness of the wall. These are marked with an asterisk (*). Richard Anderson helped calculate the volume of 92, the red-figured cup with owl in the tondo, using a program he wrote for the HP programmable calculator. See now Engels, Bavay, and Tsingarida 2009 for an internet-based program for calculating capacity from a profile drawing.

Catalogue Number	Shape	Estimated Volume (ml)
3	BF Amphoriskos	450*
5	BF Oinochoe	1330*
28	BF Heron Class skyphos	3500
45	BF Skyphos	800
89	RF Type C cup	750
90	RF Type C cup	700–710
91	RF Type C cup	650
92	RF Type C cup	633
93	RF Type C cup, concave lip	550
95	RF Type C cup	250
105	BG Amphora	1,000
107	BG Pelike	3,800
114	BG Jug	3,675
117	BG Olpe	60
118	BG Banded olpe	110
119	BG Banded olpe	95
121	BG Skyphos, Corinthian type	400
123	BG Cup-skyphos	1100
128	BG Type C cup, concave lip	650
129	BG Type C cup, concave lip	600
130	BG Type C cup, concave lip	650–660
133	BG Type C cup, plain rim	550
135	BG Type C cup, plain rim	750
136	BG Type C cup, plain rim	600
144	BG Stemmed dish	120
150	BG Salt cellar, concave wall	50

The Foot in the Well with Osteological Identification

by Lisa M. Little

In Chapter 2 it was argued that the wall of well J 2:4 collapsed early in the period of its use, but without putting the well out of use. This chronology was supported by evidence of bones from a human foot found in the period-of-use deposit. In summary, the Archaic period construction of well J 2:4 narrowly missed a Submycenaean grave nearly tangent with the western edge of the shaft. The burial was excavated in 1997 as grave J 2:11 (skeletal specimen AA 343: female, 17–18 years at death) and dated to the 11th century B.C. on the basis of grave goods. The bottom of grave J 2:11 was reached at a level of 49.90 masl, that is, on level with the upper portion of the shaft of well J 2:4, which had its mouth at approximately 50.00 masl. The proximity of the grave weakened the western wall of well J 2:4, and a section of the fieldstone lining and bedrock fell into the shaft. A portion of the left foot of the skeleton in grave J 2:11 also slipped into the well and was recovered in the period-of-use deposit of well J 2:4. However, the bones of the foot were scattered over a depth of 46.60 to 45.23 masl (Levels 5 and 6),[1] indicating that they did not fall in all at once. The distribution of the bones throughout nearly a meter and a half of period-of-use deposit indicates that the well continued to be used after the initial collapse of the fieldstone lining.

The human bone from grave J 2:11 and well J 2:4 was studied in 1998. The following report confirms that the bones found in the well belonged to the female skeleton of grave J 2:11. Figure III.1 depicts the human left pedal remains recovered from well J 2:4 during the 1995 excavation season (light gray shaded elements) and elements recovered from grave J 2:11 in the 1997 season (dark gray shading). The association of these remains (i.e., the fact that they represent a single individual) is indicated by matching articular surface morphology between elements discovered in the well and the grave, specifically, metatarsal 1 (A = J 2:4)/medial cuneiform (A′ = J 2:11) and the cuboid (B = J 2:4)/calcaneus (B′ = J 2:11).[2]

1. See Fig. 5 and discussion in Chapter 2 on well stratigraphy. The first dumped fill mixed with existing period-of-use material, therefore the cutoff between Level 6 (period of use) and Level 5 (first dumped fill) is not exact, and some period of use is found, technically, in Level 5.

2. I thank Dr. Katherine Whitcome, University of Cincinnati Department of Anthropology, who consulted on the identification, illustration, and text.

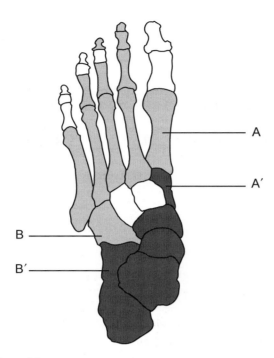

A = metatarsal I
A′ = medial cuneiform
B = cuboid
B′ = calcaneus

■ Elements found within Well J 2:4
■ Elements found within Grave J 2:11

Figure III.1. Human skeletal
remains visual inventory

INVENTORY OF HUMAN SKELETAL REMAINS FROM WELL J 2:4

I. Remains associated with Skeletal Specimen AA 343 from
   Grave J 2:11

Level 5,[3] 46.60 masl

1. Left cuboid—superior surface damaged
2. Left metatarsal I—complete
3. Left metatarsal III—complete, bearing pathological lesion:
   lytic destruction of inferior half of proximal articular surface
4. Left metatarsal IV—complete

Level 5, 46.30 masl

1. Left metatarsal II—complete, but in two fragments
2. One left proximal pedal phalange—complete, identified as
   fourth digit based on relative size
3. One left proximal pedal phalange—proximal articular surface
   missing, identified as third digit based on relative size
4. One left middle pedal phalange—complete, identified as
   second digit based on relative size

Level 6, 45.50 masl

1. Left metatarsal V—superior and lateral surfaces as well as
   distal head are damaged
2. One left distal pedal phalange—distal end damaged, identified as third digit based on relative size

3. Another fragment of phalange
and piece of cranium from Level 5 have
been found since the initial inventory
of human remains was made.

Level 6, 45.23 masl

1. One left proximal pedal phalange—identified as second digit based on relative size
2. One left distal pedal phalange—identified as second digit based on relative size

II. Miscellaneous Human Bone Fragments

Level 2,[4] 49.76 masl

1. Two cranial bone fragments with unfused sutures and root etching of both the ecto- and endocranial surface

4. Two more fragments of possible human cranium from Level 2 have been found since the initial inventory of human remains was made.

REFERENCES

ABL = C. H. E. Haspels, *Attic Black-Figured Lekythoi*, Paris 1936.

Abramov, A. P. 2002. "Tipologija i khronologija amfor o. Chios," *Drevnosti Bospora* 5, pp. 7–26.

agathe = www.agathe.gr. This citation indicates that additional images and information are available for the object in the online catalogue of the Athenian Agora Excavations.

Agora = *The Athenian Agora: Results of Excavations Conducted by the American School of Classical Studies at Athens*, Princeton

  IV = R. H. Howland, *Greek Lamps and Their Survivals*, 1958.

  V = H. S. Robinson, *Pottery of the Roman Period: Chronology*, 1959.

  VI = C. Grandjouan, *Terracottas and Plastic Lamps of the Roman Period*, 1961.

  VIII = E. T. H. Brann, *Late Geometric and Protoattic Pottery, Mid 8th to Late 7th Century B.C.*, 1962.

  X = M. Lang and M. Crosby, *Weights, Measures, and Tokens*, 1964.

  XII = B. A. Sparkes and L. Talcott, *Black and Plain Pottery of the 6th, 5th, and 4th Centuries B.C.*, 1970.

  XIII = S. A. Immerwahr, *The Neolithic and Bronze Ages*, 1971.

  XIV = H. A. Thompson and R. E. Wycherley, *The Agora of Athens: The History, Shape, and Uses of an Ancient City Center*, 1972.

  XXI = M. Lang, *Graffiti and Dipinti*, 1976.

  XXIII = M. B. Moore and M. Z. Pease Philippides, *Attic Black-Figured Pottery*, 1986.

  XXV = M. Lang, *Ostraka*, 1990.

  XXVI = J. H. Kroll, *The Greek Coins*, 1993.

  XXIX = S. I. Rotroff, *Hellenistic Pottery: Athenian and Imported Wheelmade Table Ware and Related Material*, 1997.

  XXX = M. B. Moore, *Attic Red-Figured and White-Ground Pottery*, 1997.

Alroth, B. 1989. *Greek Gods and Figurines: Aspects of Anthropomorphic Dedications* (*Boreas* 18), Uppsala.

Amandry, P. 1984. "Os et coquilles," in *L'Antre corycien* II (*BCH* Suppl. 9), pp. 347–380.

———. 1988. "À propos de monuments de Delphes: Questions de chronologie I," *BCH* 112, pp. 591–610.

Ammerman, R. 1990. "The Religious Context of Hellenistic Terracotta Figurines," in *The Coroplast's Art: Greek Terracottas of the Hellenistic World*, ed. J. Uhlenbrock, New Rochelle, N.Y., pp. 37–46.

Amyx, D. A. 1958a. "The Attic Stelai: Part III. Vases and Other Containers," *Hesperia* 27:3, pp. 163–254.

———. 1958b. "The Attic Stelai: Part III. Vases and Other Containers," *Hesperia* 27:4, pp. 255–310.

Andreiomenou, A. 1976. "Ἐκ τῆς δυτικῆς νεκροταφέως τῆς Ἐρέτριας 2," *AAA* 9, pp. 197–211.

Andreou, I. 1990. "Ἑλληνιστικὴ κεραμικὴ Λευκάδος," in *Β΄ Ἐπιστημονικὴ Συνάντηση γιὰ τὴν Ἑλληνιστικὴ Κεραμική, Ρόδος 1989*, Athens, pp. 54–57.

Arias, P. E. 1969. "Morte di un Eroe," *ArchCl* 21, pp. 190–209.

Ashmead, A. 1990. "A Lekythos by the Pan Painter at Haverford College: Bread and Soup for Dinner?" in *EUMOUSIA: Ceramic and Iconographic Studies in Honour of Alexander Cambitoglou,* ed. J.-P. Descoeudres, Sydney, pp. 95–103.

Ault, B. 1994. "Classical Houses and Households: An Architectural and Artifactual Case Study from Halieis, Greece" (diss. Indiana Univ.).

Avi-Yonah, M. 1939. *Abbreviations in Greek Inscriptions (the Near East, 200 B.C.–A.D. 1100),* suppl. to *QDAP* 9.

Baldwin, A. 1914. "The Electrum and Silver Coins Issued during the Sixth, Fifth, and Fourth Centuries B.C.," *AJN* 48, pp. 1–60.

Barber, E. J. W. 1994. *Women's Work: The First 20,000 Years. Women, Cloth, and Society in Early Times,* New York.

Barringer, J. 2001. *The Hunt in Ancient Greece,* Baltimore.

Bažant, J. 1981. *Studies on the Use and Decoration of Athenian Vases,* Prague.

———. 1985. *Les citoyens sur les vases athéniens du 6ᵉ au 4ᵉ siècle av. J.-C.,* Prague.

Baziotopoulou-Balabani, E. 1994. "Ἀνασκαφές σε αθεναϊκά κεραμικά εργαστήρια των αρχαϊκών και κλασικών χρόνων," in Coulson et al. 1994, pp. 45–54.

Beazley, J. D. 1911–1912. "The Master of the Eucharides-Stamnos in Copenhagen," *BSA* 18, pp. 217–233.

———. 1912–1913. "The Master of the Stroganoff Nikoxenos Vase," *BSA* 19, pp. 229–247.

———. 1918. *Attic Red-Figured Vases in American Museums,* Cambridge.

———. 1927. "Some Inscriptions on Vases," *AJA* 31, pp. 345–353.

———. 1928. *Attic Black-Figure, a Sketch,* London.

———. 1931a. "Groups of Mid-Sixth-Century Black-Figure," *BSA* 32, pp. 1–22.

———. 1931b. *Der Pan-Maler,* Berlin.

———. 1947. *Some Attic Vases in the Cyprus Museum,* London.

———. 1949. "Some Panaitian Fragments," in *Commemorative Studies in Honor of Theodore Leslie Shear* (*Hesperia* Suppl. 8), Princeton, pp. 3–5.

———. 1954. *Attic Vase Paintings in the Museum of Fine Arts, Boston,* in Caskey, Caskey, and Beazley 1937–1963, vol. 2, London.

———. [1951] 1986. *The Development of Attic Black-Figure,* rev. D. von Bothmer and M. Moore, repr. Berkeley.

———. [1948] 1989. *Some Attic Vases in the Cyprus Museum* (The University Committee for Archaeology 27), Oxford.

Becker, R.-M. 1977. "Formen attischer Peliken von der Pionier-Gruppe bis zum Beginn der Frühklassik" (diss. Univ. of Tübingen).

Bentz, M. 1998. *Panathenäische Preisamphoren: Eine athenische Vasengattung und ihre Funktion vom 6.–4. Jahrhundert v. Chr.* (Beiheft zur Halbjahresschrift *Antike Kunst* 18), Basel.

Bentz, M., and N. Eschbach, eds. 2001. *Panathenaïka: Symposion zu den Panathenaïschen Preisamphoren,* Mainz.

Bentz, M., and G. Reusser, eds. 2004. *Attische Vasen in etruskischen Kontext: Funde aus Häusern und Heiligtümern* (Beihefte zum Corpus Vasorum Antiquorum Deutschland 2), Munich.

Bérard, C. 1989. "Festivals and Mysteries," in Bérard et al. 1989, pp. 108–120.

Bérard, C., C. Bron, J.-L. Durand, F. Frontisi-Ducroux, F. Lissarrague, A. Schnapp, and J.-P. Vernant. 1989. *A City of Images: Iconography and Society in Ancient Greece,* trans. D. Lyons, Princeton.

Bérard, C., and J.-L. Durand. 1989. "Entering the Imagery," in Bérard et al. 1989, pp. 23–37.

Bereti, V. 1992. "Amfora transporti te zbuluara ne vendbanimin e Treportit," *Iliria* 22, pp. 129–147.

Bertucchi, G. 1992. *Les amphores et le vin de Marseille, VIᵉ s. av. J.-C.–IIᵉ s. après J.-C.* (*RANarb* Suppl. 25), Paris.

Biers, W., K. Gerhardt, and R. Braniff, eds. 1994. *Lost Scents: Investigations of Corinthian "Plastic" Vases by Gas Chromatography–Mass Spectrometry* (*MASCAP* 11), Philadelphia.

Birzescu, J. 2005. "Die Handelsampho-
ren der 'Lesbos rot'-Serie in Istros,"
AM 120, pp. 45–69.

Blech, M. 1992. *Studien zum Kranz bei
den Griechen* (Religionsgeschicht-
liche Versuche und Vorarbeiten 38),
Berlin.

Blegen, C. 1939. "Prosymna: Remains
of Post-Mycenaean Date," *AJA* 43,
pp. 410–444.

Blinkenberg Hastrup, H. 1999. "La
clientele étrusque de vases attiques
a-t-elle acheté des vases ou des
images?" in Villanueva Puig et al.
1999, pp. 439–444.

Bloesch, H. 1951. "Stout and Slender
in the Late Archaic Period," *JHS* 71,
pp. 29–39.

Boardman, J. 1972. "Herakles, Peisis-
tratos, and Sons," *RA* 1972, pp. 57–
72.

———. 1974. *Athenian Black Figure
Vases,* London.

———. 1975. *Athenian Red Figure
Vases: The Archaic Period,* London.

———. 1979. "Betwixt and Between,"
ClRev 29, pp. 118–120.

———. 1981. "Askoi," *Hephaistos* 3,
pp. 23–25.

———. 1990. "Symposion Furniture,"
in Murray 1990a, pp. 122–131.

———. 1996. *Greek Art,* 3rd ed., rev.,
London.

———. 1998. *Early Greek Vase Painting,* London.

Boersma, J. 1970. *Athenian Building
Policy from 561/0–405/4 B.C.,* Groningen.

Böhr, E. 2009. "Kleine Trinkschalen für
Mellepheben?" in Tsingarida 2009,
pp. 111–127.

Borgers, O. 1999. "Some Subjects and
Shapes by the Theseus Painter,"
in Docter and Moormann 1999,
pp. 87–89.

———. 2004. *The Theseus Painter: Style,
Shapes, and Iconography* (Allard
Pierson Series 16), Amsterdam.

Born, H. 1994. *Frühgriechische Bronze-
helme* (Sammlung Axel Guttmann
3), Berlin.

Boss, M. 1993. "Die Transportamphoren," in *Caere 3.2: Lo scarico arcaico
della vigna parrochilae, parte II,* ed.
M. Cristofani, Rome, pp. 319–349.

Bowden, R. 2004. "A Critique of Alfred
Gell on *Art and Agency*," *Oceania* 74,
pp. 309–324.

Brašinskij, I. B. 1968. "Novye materialy k isučeniju ekonomičeskich
svjazej Ol'vii b VI–IV vv. do n.e.,"
ArcheologiaWar 19, pp. 45–60.

Brenne, S. 2000. "Indices zu Kalos-
namen," *Tyche* 15, pp. 31–53.

Brijder, H. A. G., ed. 1984. *Ancient
Greek and Related Pottery: Proceedings of the International Vase Symposium in Amsterdam, 12–15 April
1984,* Amsterdam.

———. 1986. "A Pre-Dramatic Per-
formance of a Satyr Chorus by the
Heidelberg Painter," in *Enthousias-
mos: Essays on Greek and Related
Pottery Presented to J. M. Hemelrijk,*
Amsterdam, pp. 69–82.

Brommer, F. 1973. *Vasenlisten zur
griechischen Heldensage,* Marburg.

Bron, C. 1988. "Le lieu du comos," in
Christiansen and Melander 1988,
pp. 71–79.

———. 1992. "La gent ailée d'Athéna
Poliade," in *L'image en jeu: De l'antiquité à Paul Klee,* ed. C. Bron and
E. Kassapoglou, Yens-sur-Morges,
pp. 47–84.

Broneer, O. 1933. "Excavations on the
North Slope of the Acropolis in
Athens, 1931–1932," *Hesperia* 2,
pp. 329–417.

———. 1935. "Excavations on the
North Slope of the Acropolis in
Athens, 1933–1934," *Hesperia* 4,
pp. 109–188.

———. 1938. "Excavations on the
North Slope of the Acropolis,
1937," *Hesperia* 7, pp. 161–263.

Brownlee, A. B. 1995. "Attic Black
Figure from Corinth: III," *Hesperia*
64, pp. 337–382.

Bruns, G. 1970. *Archaeologia Homerica:
Die Denkmäler und das frühgriechische
Epos. Küchenwesen und Mahlzeiten,*
Gottingen.

Buitron-Oliver, D. 1987. "Part VI:
Vases," in *Antiquities from the
Collection of Christos G. Bastis,*
ed. E. Swan Hall, Mainz, pp. 241–
295.

———. 1995. *Douris* (Kerameus 9),
Mainz.

Burkert, W. 1985. *Greek Religion,* trans.
J. Raffan, Cambridge, Mass.

———. 1987. "Offerings in Perspective:
Surrender, Distribution, Exchange,"
in *Gifts to the Gods: Proceedings of the
Uppsala Symposium 1985* (Boreas 15),
ed. T. Linders and G. Nordquist,
Uppsala, pp. 43–50.

Burkert, W., and H. Hoffmann. 1980.
"La cuisine des morts," *Hephaistos* 2,
pp. 107–111.

Burn, A. R. [1962] 1984. *Persia and the
Greeks,* repr. London.

Cahill, N. 2002a. *Household and City
Organization at Olynthus,* New
Haven.

———. 2002b. "Lydian Houses, Domestic Assemblages, and Household
Size," in *Across the Anatolian Plateau,*
ed. D. C. Hopkins, Boston, pp. 173–
185.

———. 2005. "Household Industry in
Greece and Anatolia," in *Ancient
Greek Houses and Households,* ed.
B. Ault and L. Nevett, Philadelphia,
pp. 54–66.

Callipolitis-Feytmans, D. 1974.
Les plats attiques à figures noires,
Paris.

Camp, J. McK. II. 1977. "The Water
Supply of Ancient Athens from
3000–86 B.C." (diss. Princeton
Univ.).

———. [1986] 1992. *The Athenian
Agora,* London.

———. 1994. "Before Democracy:
Alkmaionidai and Peisistratidai,"
in Coulson et al. 1994, pp. 7–12.

———. 1996. "Excavations in the
Athenian Agora: 1994 and 1995,"
Hesperia 65, pp. 231–261.

———. 1999. "Excavations in the
Athenian Agora: 1996 and 1997,"
Hesperia 68, pp. 255–283.

———. 2007. "Excavations in the
Athenian Agora, 2002–2007,"
Hesperia 76, pp. 627–663.

Campbell, M. T. 1938. "A Well of the
Black-Figured Period at Corinth,"
Hesperia 7, pp. 557–611.

Cardon, C. 1973–1974. "Two Omphalos Phialai," *GettyMusJ* 6–7, pp. 131–
138.

———. 1977. "The Berlin Painter and
His School" (diss. New York Univ.).

Carlson, D. N. 2003. "The Classical
Greek Shipwreck at Tektaş Burnu,
Turkey," *AJA* 107, pp. 581–600.

Carpenter, T. H. 1986. *Dionysian Imagery in Archaic Greek Art,* Oxford.

———. 1997. *Dionysian Imagery in
Fifth-Century Athens,* Oxford.

Caskey, C., L. D. Caskey, and
J. D. Beazley. 1937–1963. *Attic

Vase-Paintings in the Museum of Fine Arts, Boston, 3 vols., London.

Caskey, J., and P. Amandry. 1952. "Investigations at the Heraion of Argos, 1949," *Hesperia* 21, pp. 165–221.

Casson, S. 1921. *Catalogue of the Acropolis Museum 2: Sculpture and Architectural Fragments with a Section upon the Terracottas by Dorothy Brooke,* Cambridge.

Ceka, N. 1986. "Amfora antike nga Margëlliçi," *Iliria* 16, pp. 71–98.

Chase, G. H. [1902] 1979. *The Shield Devices of the Greeks in Art and Literature,* repr. Chicago.

Christiansen, J., and T. Melander, eds. 1988. *Proceedings of the 3rd Symposium on Ancient Greek and Related Pottery, Copenhagen, August 31–September 4, 1987,* Copenhagen.

Christie's South Kensington. 2004. *The Axel Guttmann Collection of Ancient Arms and Armour, Part 2,* April 28, London.

Clairmont, C. 1955. "Greek Pottery from the Near East," *Berytus* 11, pp. 85–139.

Clark, A. J. 2009. "Some Practical Aspects of Attic Black-Figured Olpai and Oinochoai," in Tsingarida 2009, pp. 89–109.

Clinkenbeard, B. G. 1982. "Lesbian Wine and Storage Amphoras: A Progress Report on Identification," *Hesperia* 51, pp. 248–267.

———. 1986. "Lesbian Wine and Storage Amphoras: Questions Concerning Collaboration," in Empereur and Garlan 1986, pp. 353–362.

Cohen, A., and J. Rutter, eds. 2007. *Constructions of Childhood in Ancient Greece and Italy* (*Hesperia* Suppl. 41), Princeton.

Cohen, B. 1970–1971. "Observations on Coral-Red," *Marsyas* 15, pp. 1–12.

———. 2000a. "Introduction," in Cohen 2000b, pp. 3–20.

———, ed. 2000b. *Not the Classical Ideal: Athens and the Construction of the Other in Greek Art,* Leiden.

———. 2006. *The Colors of Clay: Special Techniques in Athenian Vases,* Los Angeles.

Cohen, B., and H. A. Shapiro. 2002. "The Use and Abuse of Athenian Vases," in *Essays in Honor of Dietrich von Bothmer,* ed. A. Clark and J. Gaunt, Amsterdam, pp. 83–90.

Colonna, G. 1985. "Anfore da trasporto archaiche: Il contributo di Pyrgi," in *Il commercio etrusco arcaico. Atti dell'incontro di studio, 5–7 dicembre 1983,* ed. M. Cristofani, P. Moscati, G. Nardi, and M. Pandolfini, Rome, pp. 5–18.

Connor, W. R. 1985. "The Razing of the House in Greek Society," *TAPA* 115, pp. 79–102.

Cook, R. M. 1989. "The Francis-Vickers Chronology," *JHS* 109, pp. 164–170.

———. 1997. *Greek Painted Pottery,* 3rd ed., rev., London.

Cook, R. M., and P. Dupont. 1998. *East Greek Pottery,* London.

Corbett, P. 1949. "Attic Pottery of the Later Fifth Century from the Athenian Agora," *Hesperia* 18, pp. 298–351.

Corinth = *Corinth: The Results of Excavations Conducted by the American School of Classical Studies in Athens,* Princeton

    XV.3 = A. N. Stillwell and J. L. Benson, *The Potters' Quarter: The Pottery,* 1984.

    XVII.4 = G. S. Merker, *The Sanctuary of Demeter and Kore: Terracotta Figurines of the Classical, Hellenistic, and Roman Periods,* 2000.

    XX = C. K. Williams II and N. Bookidis, eds. *Corinth, The Centenary: 1896–1996,* 2003.

Coulson, W. D. E., O. Palagia, T. L. Shear Jr., H. A. Shapiro, and F. J. Frost, eds. 1994. *The Archaeology of Athens and Attica under the Democracy. Proceedings of an International Conference Celebrating 2500 Years since the Birth of Democracy Held in Greece at the American School of Classical Studies at Athens, 4–6 December 1992* (Oxbow Monograph 37), Oxford.

Croissant, F. 1983. *Les protomés féminines archaïques: Recherches sur les représentations du visage dans la plastique grecque de 550 à 480 av. J.-C.* (*BÉFAR* 250), Paris.

Crouwel, J. 1992. *Chariots and Other Wheeled Vehicles in Iron Age Greece,* Amsterdam.

Csapo, E., and M. C. Miller. 1991. "The 'Kottabos-Toast' and an Inscribed Red-Figured Cup," *Hesperia* 60, pp. 367–382.

Dalby, A. 1996. *Siren Feasts: A History of Food and Gastronomy in Greece*, London.

———. 2003. *Food in the Ancient World from A to Z*, London.

Davidson, J. 1997. *Courtesans and Fishcakes: The Consuming Passions of Classical Athens*, New York.

Délos = Exploration archéologique de Délos faite par l'École française d'Athènes, Paris

X = C. Dugas, *Les vases de l'Héraion*, 1928.

XVII = C. Dugas, *Les vases orientalisants de style non mélien*, 1935.

De Marinis, R. C. 1999. "Anfore chiote dal Forcello di Bagnolo S. Vito (Mantova)," in *KOINA: Miscellanea di studi archeologici in onore di Piero Orlandini*, ed. M. Castoldi, Milan, pp. 255–278.

Dentzer, J.-M. 1971. "Aux origines de l'iconographie du banquet couché," *RA* 1971, pp. 215–258.

Desy, P. 1985. "Il dibattito," in *Magna Grecia, Epiro, e Macedonia. Atti del ventiquattresimo Convegno di studi sulla Magna Grecia, Taranto, 5–10 ottobre 1984* (*AttiTaranto* 24), pp. 413–416.

Desy, P., and P. De Paepe. 1990. "Torre san Giovani (Ugento): Les amphores commerciales hellénistiques et républicaines," *Studi di Antichità* 6, pp. 187–234.

DeVries, K. 1977. "Attic Pottery in the Achaemenid Empire," *AJA* 81, pp. 544–548.

———. 2000. "The Nearly Other: The Attic Vision of Phrygians and Lydians," in Cohen 2000b, pp. 338–363.

Dimitriu, S. 1966. "Cartierul de locuinte din sona de vest a cetatii, în epoca arhaica: Sapaturi 1955–1960," in *Histria* 2, ed. E. M. Condurachi, Bucharest, pp. 19–132.

Dinsmoor, W. B. 1934. "The Date of the Older Parthenon," *AJA* 38, pp. 408–448.

Di Sandro, N. 1986. *Le anfore arcaiche dallo scarico Gosetti, Pithecusa* (Cahiers des amphores archaiques et classiques 2), Naples.

Di Stefano, G. 1993–1994. "Il relitto di Punta Braccetto (Camarina), gli emporia e I relitti di età arcaica lungo la costa meridionale della Sicilia," in *"Nostoi" ed "Emporia": La Sicilia punto di riferimento fino al VI sec. a. C.* I.1 (*Kokalos* 39–40), pp. 111–133.

Docter, R. F. 1991. "Athena vs. Dionysos: Reconsidering the Contents of SOS Amphorae," *BABesch* 66, pp. 45–49.

Docter, R. F., and E. Moormann, eds. 1999. *Proceedings of the XVth International Congress of Classical Archaeology, Amsterdam, July 12–17, 1998*, Amsterdam.

Doğer, E. 1986. "Premières remarques sur les amphores de Clazomènes," in Empereur and Garlan 1986, pp. 461–471.

Dontas, G. S. 1983. "The True Aglaurion," *Hesperia* 52, pp. 48–63.

Drougou, S. 1975. *Der attische Psykter*, Würzburg.

Dunbabin, T. J. 1962. "Monochrome Vases and Coarse Pottery," in H. G. G. Payne and T. J. Dunbabin, *Perachora: The Sanctuaries of Hera Akraia and Limenia. Excavations of the British School of Archaeology at Athens, 1930–1933* II: *Pottery, Ivories, Scarabs, and Other Objects from the Votive Deposit of Hera Limenia*, Oxford, pp. 314–333.

Dupont, P. 1982. "Amphores commerciales archaïques de la Grèce de l'Est," *PP* 37, pp. 193–208.

———. 1983. "Classification et détermination des provenances des céramiques archaiques grecques orientales archaïques d'Istros; Rapport préliminaire," *Dacia* 27, pp. 19–43.

———. 1986. "Naturwissenschaftliche Bestimmung der archaische Keramik Milets," in *Milet 1899–1980: Ergebnisse, Probleme, und Perspektiven einer Ausgrabung. Kolloquium Frankfurt am Main 1980* (*IstMitt-BH* 31), ed. W. Müller-Wiener, Tübingen, pp. 57–71.

———. 1995–1996. "Amphores archaïques de Grèce propre en Mer Noire: État de la question," *Il Mar Nero* 2, pp. 85–98.

———. 1998. "Archaic East Greek Trade Amphoras," in *East Greek Pottery*, ed. R. M. Cook and P. Dupont, London, pp. 142–92.

———. 1999a. "La circulation amphorique en Mer Noire à l'époque archaïque," in *Production et commerce des amphores anciennes en Mer Noire*, ed. Y. Garlan, Aix-en-Provence, pp. 143–161.

———. 1999b. "Marques signalétiques avant-cuisson sur les amphores ioniennes archaïques: Cercles et croix," *Pontica* 32, pp. 9–18.

———. 2000. "Amphores 'samiennes' archaïques: Sources de confusion et questionnements," in *Ceràmiques jònies d'època arcaica: Centres de producció i comercialització al Mediterrani occidental* (Monografies emporitanes 11), ed. P. Cabera Bonet and M. S. Retolaza, Barcelona, pp. 57–62.

———. 2007. "Amphores 'samiennes' archaiques de Mer Noire (approche archéometrique)," in *Greeks and Natives in the Cimmerian Bosporus (7th–1st Centuries B.C.). Proceedings of an International Conference, October 2000, Taman, Russia*, ed. S. L. Solovyov, Oxford, pp. 41–50.

———. 2010. "Les amphores 'samiennes' et 'protothasiennes' de Zeest: La piste nord-ionienne?" in *PATABS 1. Production and Trade of Amphoras in the Black Sea. Actes de la Table Ronde internationale de Batoumi et Trabzon, 27–29 Avril 2006* (*Varia Anatolica* 21), ed. D. Kassab-Tezgör and N. Inaishvili, Istanbul, pp. 39–43.

Durand, J.-L., and A. Schnapp. 1984. "Boucherie sacrificielle et chasses initiatiques," in Bérard et al. 1989, pp. 49–66.

Eisman, M. 1975. "Attic Kyathos Production," *Archaeology* 28, pp. 76–83.

Ekroth, G. 2003. "Small Pots, Poor People?" in Schmaltz and Söldner 2003, pp. 35–37.

Elston, M. 1990. "Ancient Repairs of Greek Vases in the J. Paul Getty Museum," *GettyMusJ* 18, pp. 53–68.

Empereur, J.-Y., and Y. Garlan, eds. 1986. *Recherches sur les amphores grecques* (*BCH* Suppl. 13), Paris.

Engels, L., L. Bavay, and A. Tsingarida. 2009. "Calculating Vessel Capacities: A New Web-based Solution," in Tsingarida 2009, pp. 129–133.

Ersoy, H. K. 1998. "Two Wheeled Vehicles from Lydia and Mysia," *IstMitt* 48, pp. 107–133.

Ersoy, Y. E. 1993. "Clazomenae: The Archaic Settlement" (diss. Bryn Mawr College).

———. 2004. "Klazomenai: 900–500 B.C.: History and Settlement Evidence," in Moustaka et al. 2004, pp. 43–76.

Evans, J., and M. Millett. 1992. "Residuality Revisited," *OJA* 11, pp. 225–240.

Fantham, E., H. Foley, N. B. Kampen, S. Pomeroy, and H. A. Shapiro. 1994. *Women in the Classical World*, Oxford.

Farnsworth, M. 1964. "Greek Pottery: A Mineralogical Study," *AJA* 68, pp. 221–228.

———. 1970. "Corinthian Pottery: Technical Studies," *AJA* 74, pp. 9–20.

Farnsworth, M., I. Perlman, and F. Asaro. 1977. "Corinth and Corfu: A Neutron Activation Study of Their Pottery," *AJA* 81, pp. 455–468.

Farnsworth, M., and H. Wisely. 1958. "Fifth Century Intentional Red Glaze," *AJA* 62, pp. 165–173.

FAS = H. Bloesch, *Formen attischer Schalen von Exekias bis zum Ende des strengen Stils,* Bern 1940.

Fellmann, B. 1990. "Schriftzeite und Beischriften," in Vierneisel and Kaeser 1990, pp. 90–95.

Ferrari, G. 2002. *Figures of Speech: Men and Maidens in Ancient Greece,* Chicago.

Fisher, N. 2000. "Symposiasts, Fish-Eaters, and Flatterers: Social Mobility and Moral Concerns in Old Comedy," in *The Rivals of Aristophanes,* ed. D. Harvey and J. Wilkins, London, pp. 355–396.

Florance, A. 1966. *A Geographic Lexicon of Greek Coin Inscriptions,* Chicago.

Fontana, V., and M. Bagolan. 1992. "Frammenti ceramici e stratigrafia abitativa: Due studi di caso," in *Formation Processes and Excavation Methods in Archaeology: Perspectives,* ed. G. Leonardi, Padua, pp. 323–347.

Fornis, C., and J.-M. Casillas. 1997. "An Appreciation of the Social Function of the Spartan *Syssitia*," *AHB* 11, pp. 37–46.

Foster, G. V. 1984. "The Bones from the Altar West of the Painted Stoa," *Hesperia* 53, pp. 73–82.

Foxhall, L. 2007. "House Clearance: Unpacking the 'Kitchen' in Classical Greece," in *Building Communities: House, Settlement, and Society in the Aegean and Beyond* (British School at Athens Studies 15), ed. R. Westgate, N. Fisher, and J. Whitley, London, pp. 233–242.

Francis, E. D. 1990. *Image and Idea in Fifth Century Greece,* London.

Francis, E. D., and M. Vickers. 1981. "'Leagros Kalos,'" *PCPS* 207, pp. 97–136.

———. 1988. "The Agora Revisited: Athenian Chronology c. 500–450 B.C.," *BSA* 83, pp. 143–167.

Frel, J. 1979. *Painting on Vases in Ancient Greece,* Loyola Marymount University, exhibition catalogue, Los Angeles.

Gadberry, L. M. 1992. "The Sanctuary of the Twelve Gods in the Athenian Agora: A Revised View," *Hesperia* 61, pp. 447–489.

Gallant, T. W. 1991. *Risk and Survival in Ancient Greece,* Stanford.

Gantz, T. 1971. "Divine Triads on an Archaic Etruscan Frieze Plaque from Poggio Civitate (Murlo)," *StEtr* 39, pp. 3–24.

Gardiner, E. N. 1904. "Further Notes on the Greek Jump," *JHS* 24, pp. 179–194.

Garlan, Y. 1986. "Quelques nouveaux ateliers amphoriques à Thasos," in Empereur and Garlan 1986, pp. 201–276.

———. 1988. *Vin et amphores de Thasos* (École française d'Athènes, Sites et Monuments 5), Athens.

———. 1996. "Un nouveau centre de timbrage amphorique: Ouranopolis," *AEMΘ* 10, pp. 347–353.

———. 1999. *Les timbres amphoriques de Thasos* 1: *Timbres protothasiens et thasiens anciens* (Études thasiennes 18), Athens.

———. 2004. "Η ανάγνωση των σφραγισμάτων αμφορέων 'με τροχό' από την Άκανθο," *AEMΘ* 18, pp. 181–190.

———. 2006. "Interprétation des timbres amphoriques 'à la roue' d'Akanthos," *BCH* 130, pp. 263–291.

Gassner, V. 1999. "Zur Chronologie der Lehmziegelhäuser in der Unterstadt von Velia," in *Neue Forschungen in Velia. Akten des Kongresses "La ricerca archeologica a Velia," Rom. 1–2 Juli 1993*, ed. F. Krinzinger and G. Tocco, Vienna, pp. 109–115.

———. 2000. "Produktionsstätten westmediterraner Amphoren im 6. und 5. Jh. v. Chr.," *Laverna* 11, pp. 106–137.

———. 2003. *Materielle Kultur und kulturelle Identität in Elea in spät-archaisch-frühklassischer Zeit: Untersuchungen zur Gefäß- und Baukeramik aus der Unterstadt (Grabungen 1987–1994) (AF* 8, Velia-Studien 2), Vienna.

Gauer, W. 1975. *Die Tongefasse aus den Brunnen unterm Stadion-Nordwall und im Südost-Gebiet (OlForsch* 8), Berlin.

Gebhard, E. 1998. "Small Dedications in the Archaic Temple of Poseidon at Isthmia," in *Ancient Greek Cult Practice from the Archaeological Evidence (SkrAth* 8°, 15), ed. R. Hägg, Stockholm, pp. 91–115.

Gell, A. 1998. *Art and Agency: An Anthropological Theory*, Oxford.

Gerhard, E. 1847. *Auserlesene griechische Vasenbilder*, Berlin.

Gerhardt, K., S. Searles, and W. Biers. 1990. "Corinthian Figure Vases: Non-Destructive Extraction and Gas Chromatography-Mass Spectrometry," in *Organic Contents of Ancient Vessels: Materials Analysis and Archaeological Investigation (MASCAP* 7), ed. W. Biers and P. E. McGovern, Philadelphia, pp. 7–9.

Ginouvès, R. 1962. *Balaneutikè: Recherches sur le bain dans l'antiquité grecque (BÉFAR* 200), Paris.

Giouri, E., and C. Koukoule. 1987. "Ανασκαφή στην αρχαία Οισύμη," *ΑΕΜΘ* 1, pp. 363–375.

Giudice, F. 1978. "La Classe di Phanyllis ed il problema delle importazioni di ceramica attica in Sicilia all fine del VI e agli inizi del V se. a.C.," *Quaderni de "La ricerca scientifica"* 100, pp. 631–640.

———. 1983. *I Pittori della Classe di Phanyllis: Organizzazione produzione distribuzione dei vasi di un'officina di età pisistratideo-clistenica*, vol. 1.1,

Studi e Materiali di Archeologia Greca, Catania.

Golden, M. 1998. *Sport and Society in Ancient Greece*, Cambridge.

Gossel-Raeck, B. 1990a. "Komos–Bürger ziehen durch die Nacht," in Vierneisel and Kaeser 1990, pp. 293–298.

———. 1990b. "Komos–Tanz der Zecher," in Vierneisel and Kaeser 1990, pp. 289–292.

———. 1990c. "Komos–Tanz um den Krater," in Vierneisel and Kaeser 1990, pp. 299–302.

Grace, V. R. 1953. "Wine Jars," in C. Boulter, "Pottery of the Mid-Fifth Century from a Well in the Athenian Agora," *Hesperia* 22, pp. 101–110.

———. 1971. "Samian Amphoras," *Hesperia* 40, pp. 52–95.

———. 1979. *Amphoras and the Ancient Wine Trade (AgoraPicBk* 6, rev. ed.), Athens.

Graef and Langlotz = B. Graef and E. Langlotz, *Die antiken Vasen von der Akropolis zu Athen*, Berlin 1909–1933.

Gras, M. 1987. "Amphores commerciales et histoire archaïque," *DialArch* 5, pp. 41–50.

Greek Vases = Greek Vases: Molly and Walter Bareiss Collection, Malibu 1983.

Green, J. R. 1985. "A Representation of the *Birds* of Aristophanes," *Greek Vases in the J. Paul Getty Museum* 2, pp. 95–118.

Green, R., and E. Handley. 1995. *Images of the Greek Theatre*, London.

Grossman, J. 1991. "Six's Technique at the Getty," *Greek Vases in the J. Paul Getty Museum* 5, pp. 13–26.

Hamilton, R. 1992. *Choes and Anthesteria*, Ann Arbor.

Hammond, N. G. L. 1988. "The Expedition of Xerxes," *CAH* 4, pp. 518–591.

Hannestad, L. 1988. "The Athenian Painter and the Home Market," in Christiansen and Melander 1988, pp. 222–230.

Hardwick, N. 1993. "The Coinage of Chios from the VIth to the IVth Century B.C.," in *Proceedings of the XIth International Numismatic Congress* 1, ed. T. Hackens and G. Moucharte, Louvain-la-Neuve, pp. 211–221.

Harris, H. 1964. *Greek Athletes and Athletics*, London.

Hartog, F. 1988. *The Mirror of Herodotus: An Essay on the Representation of "the Other,"* Berkeley.

Hatzidakis, P. 1984. "Athenian Red-Figure and Black-Figure Cup-Skyphoi of the Sixth and Fifth Centuries B.C., with Particular Reference to Material from Phthiotis" (diss. Univ. of London).

Hatzivassiliou, E. 2009. "Warriors at a Mound: A Puzzle Scene by the Theseus and Athena Painters," in Nørskov et al. 2009, pp. 115–132.

Hayen, H. 1980–1981. "Zwei in Holz erhalten gebliebenen Reste von Wagenräder aus Olympia," *Die Funde* (Neue Folge) 31–32, pp. 135–191.

Hayes, J. W. 1985. *Etruscan and Italic Pottery in the Royal Ontario Museum*, Toronto.

———. 2000. "From Rome to Beirut and Beyond: Asia Minor and Eastern Mediterranean Trade Connections," *RCRFActa* 36, pp. 285–297.

Higgins, R. A. 1967. *Greek Terracottas*, London.

Hodder, I. 1991. *Reading the Past*, 2nd ed., Cambridge.

Hoffmann, H. 1977. *Sexual and Asexual Pursuit: A Structuralist Approach to Greek Vase Painting*, London.

———. 1994a. "*Dulce et decorum est pro patria mori:* The Imagery of Heroic Immortality on Athenian Painted Vases," in *Art and Text in Ancient Greece*, ed. S. Goldhill and R. Osborne, Cambridge, pp. 28–51.

———. 1994b. "The Riddle of the Sphinx: A Case Study in Athenian Immortality Symbolism," in *Classical Greece: Ancient Histories and Modern Archaeologies*, ed. I. Morris, Cambridge, pp. 71–80.

———. 1997. *Sotades: Symbols of Immortality on Greek Vases*, Oxford.

Holladay, J. S. 1982. *Tell el-Maskhuta: Preliminary Report on the Wadi Tumilat Project 1978–1979* (Cities of the Delta 3), Malibu.

Holmberg, E. 1990. *The Red-Line Painter and the Workshop of the Acheloos Painter (SIMA-PB* 87), Jonsered.

Horsnaes, H. 2001. "Miniature Pottery and the Question of Domestic Cult in Lucania," in Scheffer 2001a, pp. 77–88.

Hurwit, J. 1989. "The Kritios Boy: Discovery, Reconstruction, and Date," *AJA* 93, pp. 41–80.

———. 1999. *The Athenian Acropolis,* Cambridge.

Immerwahr, H. 1984a. "An Inscribed Cup by the Ambrosios Painter," *AK* 27, pp. 10–13.

———. 1984b. "The Signatures of Pamphaios," *AJA* 88, pp. 341–352.

———. 1990. *Attic Script: A Survey,* Oxford.

———. 1992. "New Wine in Ancient Wineskins: The Evidence from Attic Vases," *Hesperia* 61, pp. 121–132.

———. 1998. *A Corpus of Attic Vase Inscriptions,* preliminary ed., n.p.

Isler-Kerényi, C. 1979. "Un nuovo stamnos del Pittore di Achille in collezione ticinese," *NumAntCl* 8, pp. 11–35.

Jameson, M. 1960. "A Decree of Themistokles from Troizen," *Hesperia* 29, pp. 198–223.

———. 1990a. "Domestic Space in the Greek City-State," in *Domestic Architecture and the Use of Space,* ed. S. Kent, Cambridge, pp. 92–113.

———. 1990b. "Private Space and the Greek City," in *The Greek City: From Homer to Alexander,* ed. O. Murray and S. Price, Oxford, pp. 171–195.

Jameson, R. 1987. "Purity and Power at the Victorian Dinner Party," in *The Archaeology of Contextual Meanings,* ed. I. Hodder, Cambridge, pp. 55–65.

Jeffery, L. 1990. *The Local Scripts of Archaic Greece,* rev. A. Johnston, Oxford.

Johnson, F. P. 1955. "A Note on Owl Skyphoi," *AJA* 59, pp. 119–124.

Johnston, A. W. 1984. "The Development of Amphora Shapes, Symposium, and Shipping," in Brijder 1984, pp. 208–211.

———. 1990. "Aegina, Aphaia-Tempel 3: The Storage Amphoras," *AA* 1990, pp. 37–64.

Johnston, A. W., and C. A. de Domingo. 1997. "Trade between Kommos, Crete and East Greece: A Petrographic Study of Archaic Transport Amphorae," in *Archaeological Sciences 1995 (Proceedings of a Conference on the Application of Scientific Techniques to the Study of Archaeology, Liverpool, July 1995),* ed. A. Sinclair, E. Slater, and J. Gowlett, Oxford, pp. 62–68.

Johnston, A. W., and R. E. Jones. 1978. "The 'SOS' Amphora," *BSA* 73, pp. 103–141.

Jöhrens, G. 1999. "Kerameikos: Griechische Amphorenstempel spätklassischer und hellenistischer Zeit," *AthMitt* 114, pp. 157–170.

Jones, J. E. 1975. "Town and Country Houses of Attica in Classical Times," in *Thorikos and Laurion in Archaic and Classical Times,* ed. H. Mussche, Ghent, pp. 63–140.

Jones, J. E., A. J. Graham, and L. H. Sackett. 1973. "An Attic Country House below the Cave of Pan at Vari," *BSA* 68, pp. 355–452.

Jones, J. E., L. H. Sackett, and A. J. Graham. 1962. "The Dema House in Attica," *BSA* 57, pp. 75–114.

Jones, R. E., J. Boardman, H. W. Catling, C. B. Mee, W. W. Phelps, and A. M. Pollard. 1986. *Greek and Cypriot Pottery: A Review of Scientific Studies* (Fitch Laboratory Occasional Papers 1), Athens.

Jordan, J. 1988. "Attic Black-Figured Eye-Cups" (diss. New York Univ.).

Juranek, H. 1978–1979. "Beobachtungen eines Doppelbrandes an einer Omphalosschale in Six Technik–Ein seltenes Brennverfahren in der Antike?" *Acta Praehistorica et Archaeologica* 9–10, pp. 107–111.

Kaeser, B. 1987. "Glyptothek und Antikensammlungen," *MüJb* 38, pp. 225–234.

———. 1990a. "Komos–Tanz der Dickbäuche," in Vierneisel and Kaeser 1990, pp. 283–288.

———. 1990b. "Symposion im Freien," in Vierneisel and Kaeser 1990, pp. 306–309.

Kahil, L. 1977. "L'Artèmis de Brauron: Rites et Mystère," *AntK* 20, pp. 86–98.

Kanowski, M. 1983. *Containers of Classical Greece: A Handbook of Shapes,* St. Lucia, Queensland.

Karadima, C. 2004. "Ainos: An Unknown Amphora Production Centre in the Evros Delta," in *Transport Amphorae and Trade in the Eastern Mediterranean. Acts of* the *International Colloquium at the Danish Institute at Athens, 26–29 September, 2002,* ed. J. Eiring and J. Lund, pp. 155–161.

Karadima-Matsas, C. 1994. "Ἐργαστήριο παραγωγής αμφορέων στη Σαμοθράκη," in *Γ´ Επιστημονική Συνάντηση για την Ελληνιστική Κεραμική 1991,* Athens, pp. 355–362.

Karadima, C., D. Matsas, F. Blondé, and M. Picon. 2002. "Workshop References and Clay Surveying in Samothrace: An Application to the Study of the Origin of Some Ceramic Groups," in *Modern Trends in Scientific Studies on Ancient Ceramics. Papers Presented at the 5th European Meeting on Ancient Ceramics, Athens 1999 (BAR-IS 1011),* ed. V. Kilikoglou, A. Hein, and Y. Maniatis, Oxford, pp. 157–162.

Karageorghis, V. 1967. *Excavations in the Necropolis of Salamis* I (*Salamis* 3), Nicosia.

Kerameikos = Kerameikos: Ergebnisse der Ausgrabungen, Berlin
    IX = U. Knigge, *Der Südhügel,* 1976.
    XV = B. Vierneisel-Schlörb, *Die figürlichen Terrakotten* I: *Spätmykenisch bis Späthellenistisch,* 1997.

Kerschner, M. 1999. "Das Artemisheiligtum auf der Ostterrasse des Kalabaktepe in Milet: Stratigraphie und Keramikfunde der Sondagen des Jahres 1995," *AA,* pp. 7–51.

Kerschner, M., and H. Mommsen. 2005. "Transportamphoren milesischen Typs in Ephesos: Archäometrische und archäologische Untersuchungen zum Handel im archaischen Ionien," in *Synergia: Festschrift für Friedrich Krinzinger* 1, ed. B. Brandt, V. Gassner, and S. Ladstätter, Vienna, pp. 119–130.

Kilmer, M. 1993. *Greek Erotica on Attic Red-Figure Vases,* London.

Kintigh, K. W. 1989. "Sample Size, Significance, and Measures of Diversity," in Leonard and Jones 1989, pp. 25–36.

Knauer, E. R. 1973. "Ein Skyphos des Triptolemosmalers," *BWPr* 125, pp. 5–33.

Koehler, C. G. 1978a. *Corinthian A and B Transport Amphoras* (diss. Princeton Univ.).

———. 1978b. "Evidence around the Mediterranean for Corinthian Export of Wine and Oil," in *Beneath the Waters of Time,* ed. J. Arnold, Austin, pp. 231–237.

———. 1981. "Corinthian Developments in the Study of Trade in the Fifth Century," *Hesperia* 50, pp. 449–458.

———. 1992. "A Brief Typology and Chronology of Corinthian Transport Amphoras," in *Grečeskie amfory: Problemy razvitija remesla i torgovli v antičnom mire.,* ed. V. Kac and S. Monachov, Saratov, pp. 265–279 (in Russian).

Kokkou-Vyride, K. 1999. *Ελευσίς: πρώιμες πυρές θυσιών στο τελεστήριο της Ελευσίνος,* Athens.

Koparal, E., and E. İplikçi. 2004. "Archaic Olive Oil Extraction Plant in Klazomenai," in Moustaka et al. 2004, pp. 221–234.

Kottaridi, A. 2002. "Discovering Aegae, the Old Macedonian Capital," in *Excavating Classical Culture: Recent Archaeological Discoveries in Greece (BAR-IS 1031),* ed. M. Stamatopoulou and M. Yeroulanou, Oxford, pp. 75–81.

Kourkoumelis, D. 1990. "Οι Κερκυραίκοι αμφορείς," *Enalia* 2, pp. 14–19.

Kournouniotes, K. 1936. "Θυμιατήρια εν Ἐλευσῖνι," in *Classical Studies Presented to Edward Capps on His Seventieth Birthday,* Princeton, pp. 204–216.

Kourou, N. 1987. "À propos de quelques ateliers de céramique fine, non-tournée du type 'argien monochrome,'" *BCH* 111, pp. 31–53.

———. 1988. "Handmade Pottery and Trade: The Case of the 'Argive Monochrome' Ware," in Christiansen and Melander 1988, pp. 314–324.

Kreuzer, B. 1999. "Athenische Eulen fürs Symposion," in Docter and Moormann 1999, pp. 224–226.

Kübler, K., and K. Gebauer. 1940. "Ausgrabungen im Kerameikos," *AA,* pp. 308–362.

Kunisch, N. 1997. *Makron* (Kerameus 10), Mainz.

Kurtz, D. 1975. *Athenian White Lekythoi: Patterns and Painters,* Oxford.

Kurtz, D., and J. Boardman. 1971. *Greek Burial Customs,* London.

———. 1986. "Booners," *Greek Vases in the J. Paul Getty Museum* 3, pp. 35–70.

La Genière, J. de. 1987. "Vases des Lénéennes?" *MÉFRA* 99, pp. 44–61.

———. 1999. "Quelques réflexions sur les clients de la céramique attique," in Villanueva Puig et al. 1999, pp. 411–421.

———, ed. 2006. *Les clients de la céramique grecque* (*Cahiers du Corpus Vasorum Antiquorum, France* 1), Paris.

———. 2009. "Les amateurs des scenes érotiques de l'archaïsme recent," in Tsingarida 2009, pp. 337–346.

Lamberton, R., and S. Rotroff. 1985. *Birds of the Athenian Agora* (*AgoraPicBk* 22), Princeton.

Lambrino, M. 1938. *Les vases archaïques d'Histria,* Bucharest.

Lang, M. L. 1949. "ΙΣΘΜΙΑ ΦΡΕΑΤΩΝ: Terracotta Well-Heads from the Athenian Agora," *Hesperia* 18, pp. 114–127.

Langridge, E. 1993. "The Eucharides Painter and His Place in the Athenian Potters' Quarter" (diss. Princeton Univ.).

Lawall, M. L. 1995. "Transport Amphoras and Trademarks: Imports to Athens and Economic Diversity in the 5th c. B.C." (diss. Univ. of Michigan).

———. 1997. "Shape and Symbol: Regionalism in 5th Century Transport Amphora Production in Northeastern Greece," in *Trade and Production in Premonetary Greece: Production and Craftsmen. Proceedings of the 4th and 5th International Workshops, Athens 1994 and 1995 (SIMA-PB 143),* ed. C. Gillis, C. Risberg, and B. Sjöberg, Jonsered, pp. 113–130.

———. 1998. "Ceramics and Positivism Revisited: Greek Transport Amphoras and History," in *Trade, Traders, and the Greek City,* ed. H. Parkins and C. Smith, London, pp. 75–101.

———. 2000. "Graffiti, Wine Selling, and the Reuse of Amphoras in the Athenian Agora, ca. 430 to 400 B.C.," *Hesperia* 69, pp. 3–90.

———. 2002. "Ilion before Alexander: Amphoras and Economic Archaeology," *Studia Troica* 12, pp. 197–244.

Layton, R. 2003. "Art and Agency: A
    Reassessment," *JRAI* 9, pp. 447–
    464.

Lazarov, M. 1982. "T'rgoviyata na
    Khios s's zapadnopontiyskite
    gradove," *Isvestiya na narodniya
    museĭ Varna* 18 (33), pp. 5–15.

Leonard, R. D., and G. T. Jones, eds.
    1989. *Quantifying Diversity in
    Archaeology* (New Directions in
    Archaeology), Cambridge.

Lesho, E., D. Dorsey, and D. Bunner.
    1998. "Feces, Dead Horses, and
    Fleas: Evolution of the Hostile Use
    of Biological Agents," *Western
    Journal of Medicine* 168, pp. 512–
    516.

Lewis, S. 2002. *The Athenian Woman:
    An Iconographic Handbook,* London.

———. 2009. "Athletics on Attic
    Pottery: Export and Imagery," in
    Nørskov et al. 2009, pp. 133–148.

Lindenlauf, A. 1997. "Der Perserschutt
    der Athener Akropolis," in *Kult
    und Kultbauten auf der Akropolis,*
    ed. W. Hoepfner, Berlin, pp. 46–
    115.

Lioutas, A. 1987. *Attische schwarzfigu-
    rige Lekanai und Lekanides,* Würz-
    burg.

Lissarrague, F. 1985. "Paroles d'images:
    Remarques sur le fonctionnement
    de l'écriture dans l'imagerie attique,"
    in *Écritures* 2, ed. A.-M. Christin,
    Paris, pp. 71–95.

———. 1988. "Les satyres et le monde
    animal," in Christiansen and Me-
    lander 1988, pp. 335–351.

———. 1989. "The World of the War-
    rior," in Bérard et al. 1989, pp. 39–
    52.

———. 1990a. *Aesthetics of the Greek
    Banquet,* trans. A. Szegedy-Maszak,
    Princeton.

———. 1990b. "Around the Krater:
    An Aspect of Banquet Imagery,"
    in Murray 1990a, pp. 196–209.

———. 1990c. *L'autre guerrier: Archers,
    peltastes, cavaliers dans l'imagerie
    attique,* Paris.

———. 1990d. "The Sexual Life of
    Satyrs," in *Before Sexuality: The
    Construction of Erotic Experience
    in the Ancient Greek World,* ed.
    D. Halperin, J. Winkler, and F. Zeit-
    lin, Princeton, pp. 53–81.

———. 1990e. "Why Satyrs Are Good
    to Represent," in *Nothing to Do with

Dionysos? Athenian Drama in Its
    Social Context,* ed. J. Winkler and
    F. Zeitlin, Princeton, pp. 228–236.

———. 1992. "Graphein: Écrire et
    dessiner," in *L'image en jeu: De l'an-
    tiquité à Paul Klee,* ed. C. Bron and
    E. Kassapoglou, Yens-sur-Morges,
    pp. 189–203.

———. 1993. "On the Wildness of
    Satyrs," in *The Masks of Dionysus,*
    ed. T. H. Carpenter and C. Faraone,
    Ithaca, pp. 207–220.

———. 1999. "Publicity and Perfor-
    mance: *Kalos* Inscriptions in Attic
    Vase-Painting," in *Performance
    Culture and Athenian Democracy,*
    ed. S. Goldhill and R. Osborne,
    Cambridge, pp. 359–373.

———. 2001. *Greek Vases: The Athe-
    nians and Their Images,* trans.
    K. Allen, New York.

Long, L., J. Miro, and G. Volpe. 1992.
    "Les épaves archaïques de la Pointe
    Lequin," in *Marseille grecque et la
    Gaule* (Études Massaliètes 3), ed.
    M. Bats, G. Bertucchi, C. Conges,
    and H. Treziny, Aix-en-Provence,
    pp. 199–234.

Lorenz, T. 1980. "Orientalische und
    griechische Bronzen im Martin-
    von-Wagner-Museum der Univer-
    sität Würzburg," in *Tainia,* ed.
    H. Cahn and E. Simon, Mainz,
    pp. 133–138.

Lüdorf, G. 2000. *Die Lekane: Typologie
    und Chronologie einer Leitform der
    attischen Gebrauchskeramik des 6.–
    1. Jahrhunderts v. Chr* (International
    Archäologie 61), Rahden.

Luke, J. 1994. "The Krater, Kratos, and
    the Polis," *GaR* 41, pp. 23–32.

Lynch, K. M. 1999. "Pottery from a
    Late Archaic Athenian House in
    Context" (diss. Univ. of Virginia).

———. 2001a. "Pelikai in Use De-
    posits," in M. L. Lawall, J. K.
    Papadopoulos, K. M. Lynch,
    B. Tsakirgis, S. I. Rotroff, and
    C. MacKay, "Notes from the Tins:
    Research in the Stoa of Attalos,
    Summer 1999," *Hesperia* 70,
    pp. 171–173.

———. 2001b. "Pottery as Social
    Marker: Evidence for Increased
    Participation in Communal Drink-
    ing at the End of the Archaic Period
    from the Athenian Agora," *AJA* 105,
    pp. 268–269 (abstract).

———. 2006. "When Is a Column Not a Column? Columns in Attic Vase-Painting," in *Common Ground: Archaeology, Art, Science, and Humanities. Proceedings of the XVI International Congress of Classical Archaeology*, ed. C. Mattusch and A. Donohue, Oxford, pp. 372–376.

———. 2007. "More Thoughts on the Space of the Symposium," in *Building Communities: House, Settlement, and Society in the Aegean and Beyond* (*BSA* Studies 15), ed. R. Westgate, N. Fisher, and J. Whitley, London, pp. 243–249.

———. 2009a. "Erotic Images on Attic Pottery: Markets and Meanings," in *Athenian Painters and Potters*, vol. 2, ed. J. Oakley and O. Palagia, Oxford, pp. 159–165.

———. 2009b. "The Persian Destruction Deposits and the Development of Pottery Research at the Excavations of the Athenian Agora," in *The Athenian Agora at 75: New Perspectives on an Ancient Site*, ed. J. Camp II and C. Mauzy, Mainz am Rhein, pp. 69–76.

Maas, M., and J. McIntosh Snyder. 1989. *Stringed Instruments of Ancient Greece*, New Haven.

Maffre, J.-J. 1988. "Kachrylion, Euphronios, et quelques-uns de leurs contemporains à Thasos," in Christiansen and Melander 1988, pp. 379–389.

———. 1992. "Euphronios peintre de coupes," in *Euphronios Peintre*, ed. M. Denoyelle, Paris, pp. 61–78.

Maish, J. P. 2008. "Observations and Theories on the Technical Development of Coral-Red Gloss," in *Papers on Special Techniques in Athenian Vases*, ed. K. Lapatin, Los Angeles, pp. 85–94.

Maish, J. P., M. Svoboda, and S. Lansing-Maish. 2006. "Technical Studies of Some Attic Vases in the J. Paul Getty Museum," in Cohen 2006, pp. 8–16.

Marconi, C., ed. 2004. *Greek Vases: Images, Contexts, and Controversies*, Leiden.

Mattingly, H. B. 1981. "The Themistocles Decree from Troizen: Transmission and Status," in *Classical Contributions*, ed. G. Shrimpton and D. McCargar, Locust Valley, N.Y., pp. 79–87.

Mattusch, C. C. 1977. "Bronze- and Ironworking in the Area of the Athenian Agora," *Hesperia* 46, pp. 340–379.

Mavrogordato, J. 1915a. "A Chronological Arrangement of the Coins of Chios, pt. 1," *NC* 60, pp. 1–52.

———. 1915b. "A Chronological Arrangement of the Coins of Chios, pt. 2," *NC* 60, pp. 373–375.

McCartney, P. H., and M. F. Glass. 1990. "Simulation Models and the Interpretation of Archaeological Diversity," *AmerAnt* 55, pp. 521–536.

McNamee, K. 1981. *Abbreviations in Greek Literary Papyri and Ostraca*, Chico, Calif.

McNiven, T. 1982. "Gestures in Attic Vase Painting: Use and Meaning, 550–450 B.C." (diss. Univ. of Michigan).

McPhee, I. 2000. "Falaieff Bell-Kraters from Ancient Corinth," *Hesperia* 69, pp. 453–486.

Meiggs, R. 1972. *The Athenian Empire*, Oxford.

Meltzer, D. J., R. D. Leonard, and S. K. Stratton. 1992. "The Relationship between Sample Size and Diversity in Archaeological Assemblages," *JAS* 19, pp. 375–387.

Merker, G. 2003. "Corinthian Terracotta Figurines: The Development of an Industry," in *Corinth* XX, pp. 233–245.

Metzger, H. 1972. *Fouilles de Xanthos* 4: *Les céramiques archaïques et classiques de l'acropole Lycienne*, Paris.

Miller, M. 1997. *Athens and Persia in the Fifth Century B.C.: A Study in Cultural Receptivity*, Cambridge.

Miller, S. 1995. "Architecture as Evidence for the Identity of the Early Polis," in *Sources for the Ancient Greek City-State* (Acts of the Copenhagen Polis Centre 2), ed. M. Hansen, Copenhagen, pp. 201–244.

Mingazzini, P. 1971. *Catalogo dei vasi della collezione Castellani* 2, Rome.

Moignard, E. 1982. "The Acheloos Painter and Relations," *BSA* 77, pp. 201–211.

Mollard-Besques, S. 1954. *Catalogue raisonné des figurines et reliefs en terre-cuite grecs, étrusques, et romains* 1: *Époques préhellénique, géométrique, archaïque, et classique*, Paris.

Monachov, S. J. 1999a. *Grečeskie amfory v Pričernomor'e.: Kompleksy keramičeskoj tary VII–II vekov do n. e.*, Saratov.

———. 1999b. "Zametki po lokalizatcii keramičheskoy tary 2: Amphory i amphornye kleyma polisov Severnoj Egeidy," *Antichnyi mir i arkheologiya* 10, pp. 129–147.

———. 2003a. "Amphorae from Unidentified Centres in the Northern Aegean (the So-Called 'Proto-Thasian' Series According to I. B. Zeest)," in *The Cauldron of Ariantas: Studies Presented to A.N. Ščeglov on the Occasion of His 70th Birthday* (Black Sea Studies 1), ed. P. Guldager Bilde, J. Munk Højte, and V. F. Stolba, Aarhus, pp. 247–259.

———. 2003b. *Grečeskie amfory v Pričernomor'e. Tipologija amfor veduščich centrov–eksporterov tovarov v keramičeskoj tare. Katalog-opredelitel*, Moscow.

Monaco, M. C. 1993. "Un cratere già nella collezione 1: Falchi ed il problema delle oxides," *RendLinc* 4, n.s. 9, pp. 67–85.

Morgan, C. 1989. *Athletes and Oracles*, Cambridge.

———. 1999. *The Late Bronze Age Settlement and Early Iron Age Sanctuary* (*Isthmia* VIII), Princeton.

Morselli, C., and E. Tortorici. 1985. "La situazione di Regisvilla," in *Il commercio etrusco arcaico. Atti dell'incontro di studio 5–7, dicembre 1983*, ed. M. Cristofani, P. Moscati, G. Nardi, and M. Pandolfini, Rome, pp. 27–40.

Morter, J., and J. R. Leonard. 1998. "Storage Amphorae," in *The Chora of Metaponto: The Necropoleis* 2, ed. J. C. Carter, Austin, pp. 731–755.

Moustaka, A., E. Skalartidou, M. C. Tzannes, and Y. Ersoy, eds. 2004. *Klazomenai, Teos, and Abdera: Metropoleis and Colony. Proceedings of the International Symposium Held at the Archaeological Museum of Abdera, Abdera, 20–21 October 2001*, Thessaloniki.

Murray, O. 1983a. "The Greek Symposium in History," in *Tria Corda: Scritti in onore di Arnaldo*

Momigliano, ed. E. Gabba, Como, pp. 257–272.

———. 1983b. "The Symposium as Social Organisation," in *The Greek Renaissance of the Eighth Century B.C.: Tradition and Innovation,* ed. R. Hägg, Stockholm, pp. 195–200.

———, ed. 1990a. *Sympotica: A Symposium on the Symposium,* Oxford.

———. 1990b. "Sympotic History," in Murray 1990a, pp. 3–13.

———. 1996. "Hellenistic Royal Symposia," in *Aspects of Hellenistic Kingship,* ed. P. Bilde et al., Aarhus, pp. 15–27.

Nadalini, G. 2003. "Considerazioni e confronti sui restauri antichi presenti sulle ceramiche scoperte a Gela," in R. Panvini and F. Giudice, *Ta Attika: Veder greco a Gela. Ceramiche attiche figurate dall'antica colonia,* Rome, pp. 197–205.

Neer, R. 2002. *Style and Politics in Athenian Vase-Painting,* Cambridge.

Neils, J. 1992a. "The Morgantina Phormiskos," *AJA* 96, pp. 225–235.

———. 1992b. "Panathenaic Amphoras: Their Meanings, Makers, and Markets," in *Goddess and Polis,* ed. J. Neils, Princeton, pp. 29–51.

———. 1995. "The Euthymides Krater from Morgantina," *AJA* 99, pp. 427–444.

———. 1996. "The Cleveland Painter," *Cleveland Studies* 1, pp. 12–29.

———. 2000. "Others within the Other: An Intimate Look at Hetairai and Maenads," in Cohen 2000b, pp. 203–226.

———. 2004. "Hera, Paestum, and the Cleveland Painter," in *Greek Vases: Images, Contexts, and Controversies,* ed. C. Marconi, Leiden, pp. 75–83.

Neils, J., and J. Oakley. 2003. *Coming of Age in Ancient Greece: Images of Childhood from the Classical Past,* New Haven.

Nevett, L. 1995. "The Organisation of Space in Classical and Hellenistic Houses from Mainland Greece and the Western Colonies," in *Time, Tradition, and Society in Greek Archaeology: Bridging the "Great Divide,"* ed. N. Spencer, London, pp. 89–108.

———. 1999. *House and Society in the Ancient Greek World,* Cambridge.

Newton, G. W. A., V. J. Robinson, M. Olapido, M. R. Chandratillake,

and I. K. Whitbread. 1988. "Clay Sources and Corinthian Amphorae," in *Science and Archaeology* (*BAR-BS* 196), ed. E. A. Slate and J. O. Tate, Oxford, pp. 59–82.

Nicolaïdou-Patera, M. 1986. "Un nouveau centre de production d'amphores timbreés en Macédonie," in Empereur and Garlan 1986, pp. 485–490.

———. 1987. "Πρώτα μνήματα απο μια πόλη της πιερίδας κοιλάδας," *ΑΕΜΘ* 1, pp. 343–352.

———. 1989. "Ανασκαφικές έρευνες στις αρχαίες πόλεις Τράγιλο και Φάγρητα," *ΑΕΜΘ* 3, pp. 483–491.

Niemeier, W.-D. 1999. "'Die Zierde Ioniens.' Ein archaischer Brunnen, der jüngere Athenatempel und Milet vor der Perserzerstörung," *AA,* pp. 373–413.

Noble, J. 1988. *Techniques of Painted Attic Pottery,* 2nd ed., rev., London.

Nørskov, V. 2002. *Greek Vases in New Contexts: The Collecting and Trading of Greek Vases,* Aarhus.

Nørskov, V., L. Hannestad, C. Isler-Kerényi, and S. Lewis, eds. 2009. *The World of Greek Vases,* Rome.

Oakley, J. 2004. "New Vases by the Achilles Painter and Some Further Thoughts on the Role of Attribution," in *Greek Art in View,* ed. S. Keay and S. Moser, Oxford, pp. 63–77.

Oakley, J., W. D. E. Coulson, and O. Palagia, eds. 1997. *Athenian Potters and Painters: The Conference Proceedings,* Oxford.

Oakley, J., and O. Palagia, eds. 2009. *Athenian Potters and Painters,* vol. 2, Oxford.

Oakley, J., and R. Sinos. 1993. *The Wedding in Ancient Athens,* Madison.

Oikonomides, A. N. 1964. *The Two Agoras in Ancient Athens: A New Commentary on Their History and Development, Topography, and Monuments,* Chicago.

Olson, S. D., and A. Sens. 2000. *Archestratos of Gela: Greek Culture and Cuisine in the Fourth Century B.C.E.,* Oxford.

Olynthus = *Excavations at Olynthus,* Baltimore
    VIII = D. M. Robinson and J. Graham, *The Hellenic House* (Johns Hopkins Studies in Archaeology 25), 1938.

X = D. M. Robinson, *Metal and Minor Miscellaneous Finds* (Johns Hopkins Studies in Archaeology 31), 1941.

XII = D. M. Robinson, *Domestic and Public Architecture* (Johns Hopkins Studies in Archaeology 36), 1946.

XIII = D. M. Robinson, *Vases Found in 1934 and 1938* (Johns Hopkins Studies in Archaeology 38), 1950.

XIV = D. M. Robinson, *Terracottas, Lamps, and Coins Found in 1934 and 1938* (Johns Hopkins Studies in Archaeology 39), 1952.

Onajko, N. A. 1980. *Archaičeskij Torik antičnyj gorod na severo-vostoke Ponta,* Moscow.

Osborne, R. 2002. "Why Did Athenian Pots Appeal to Etruscans?" *WorldArch* 33, pp. 277–295.

———. 2004. "Workshops and the Iconography and Distribution of Athenian Red-Figure Pottery: A Case Study," in *Greek Art in View: Essays in Honor of Brian Sparkes,* ed. S. Keay and S. Moser, Oxford, pp. 78–94.

Padgett, J. M. 2000. "The Stable Hands of Dionysos: Satyrs and Donkeys as Symbols of Social Marginalization in Attic Vase Painting," in Cohen 2000b, pp. 43–70.

Paléothodoros, D. 2002. "Pourquoi les Étrusques achetaient-ils des vases attiques?" *ÉtCl* 70, pp. 139–160.

Panvini, R. 2001. *La nave greca arcaica di Gela,* Palermo.

Papadopoulos, J. 1996. "The Original Kerameikos of Athens and the Siting of the Classical Agora," *GRBS* 37, pp. 107–128.

———. 2003. *Ceramicus Redivivus: The Early Iron Age Potters' Field in the Area of the Classical Athenian Agora* (*Hesperia* Suppl. 31), Princeton.

———. 2005. *The Early Iron Age Cemetery at Torone* (Monumenta Archaeologica 24), Los Angeles.

Papanastasiou, A. 2004. *Relations between Red-Figured and Black-Glazed Vases in Athens of the 4th Century B.C.* (*BAR-IS* 1247), Oxford.

Parke, H. W. 1977. *Festivals of the Athenians,* Ithaca.

Parker, R. 1983. *Miasma: Pollution and Purification in Early Greek Religion,* Oxford.

Parko, H. 2001. "Small Corinthian Oil-Containers: Evidence of the Archaic Perfume Trade?" in Scheffer 2001a, pp. 55–60.

Paul, E. 1958–1959. "Die böotischen Brettidole," *Wissenschaftliche Zeitschrift der Karl-Marx-Universität, Leipzig* 8, pp. 165–206.

Pekridou-Gorecki, A. 1989. *Mode im antiken Griechenland: Textile Fertigung und Kleidung,* Munich.

Peña, J. T. 1998. "Aspects of Residuality in the Palatine East Pottery Assemblage," in *I materiali residui nello scavo archeologico: Testi preliminari e Atti della Tavola rotonda organizzata dall'École française de Rome e dalla Sezione romana "Nino Lamboglia" dell'Instituto internazionale di studi liguri, in collaborazione con la Soprintendenza archeologica di Roma e la Escuela española de historia y arqueología (Roma, 16 marzo 1996),* ed. F. Guidobaldi, C. Pavolini, and P. Pergola, Rome, pp. 5–19.

Peristeri-Otatzi, C. 1986. "Amphores et timbres amphoriques d'Abdère," in Empereur and Garlan 1986, pp. 491–496.

Pfaff, C. 1994. "Report of Excavations in 1994 within Area BZ," unpublished report, Athenian Agora Excavations.

Philippaki, B. 1967. *The Attic Stamnos,* Oxford.

Philippart, H. 1932. *Collections de céramique grecque en Italie,* Brussels.

Pithekoussai I = G. Buchner and D. Ridgway, *Pithekoussai* I: *La necropole: Tombe 1–723 scavate dal 1952 al 1961,* Rome 1993.

Pollard, J. 1977. *Birds in Greek Life and Myth,* London.

Pomeroy, S. 1994. *Xenophon Oeconomicus: A Social and Historical Commentary,* Oxford.

Poplin, F. 1992. "Les jeux d'osselets antiques," *Dossiers d'Archéologie* 168, pp. 46–47.

Powell, B. 1989. "Why Was the Greek Alphabet Invented? The Epigraphical Evidence," *ClAnt* 8, pp. 321–350.

Preka-Alexandri, K. 1992. "A Ceramic Workshop in Figareto, Corfu," in *Les ateliers de potiers dans le monde grec aux époques géometrique, archaïque, et classique* (*BCH* Suppl. 23), ed. F. Blondé and J.-Y. Perrault, Paris, pp. 41–52.

Pritchett, W. K. 1956. "The Attic Stelai, Part II," *Hesperia* 25, pp. 178–328.

———. 1991. *The Greek State at War,* vol. 5, Berkeley.

Rapoport, A. 1990. "Systems of Activities and Systems of Settings," in *Domestic Architecture and the Use of Space,* ed. S. Kent, Cambridge, pp. 9–20.

Reed, H. S. T., and P. L. Near. 1973. *Ancient Art in the Virginia Museum,* Richmond.

Reese, D. 1985. "Appendix VIII.C," in *Excavations at Kition* V, Part 2, ed. V. Karageorghis, Nicosia, pp. 382–391.

———. 2002. "The Worked Astragalus," in *Busayra, Excavations by Crystal-M. Bennett 1971–1980* (British Academy Monographs in Archaeology 13), ed. P. Bienkowski, Oxford, pp. 472–474.

Reusser, C. 2002. *Vasen für Etrurien: Verbreitung und Funktionen attischer Keramik im Etrurien des 6. und 5. Jahrhunderts vor Christus,* Zurich.

Richter, G. 1951. "Accidental and Intentional Red Glaze," *BSA* 46, pp. 143–150.

Richter, G., and L. F. Hall. 1936. *Red-Figured Athenian Vases in the Metropolitan Museum of Art,* New Haven.

Richter, G., and M. Milne. 1935. *Shapes and Names of Athenian Vases,* New York.

Rizzo, M. A., ed. 1990. *Le anfore da trasporto e il commercio etrusco arcaico* 1: *Complessi tombali dall'Etruria meridionale,* Rome.

Roberts, S. 1986. "The Stoa Gutter Well: A Late Archaic Deposit in the Athenian Agora," *Hesperia* 55, pp. 1–74.

Robertson, M. 1992. *The Art of Vase-Painting in Classical Athens,* Cambridge.

Robertson, N. 1998. "The City Center of Archaic Athens," *Hesperia* 67, pp. 283–302.

Rose, H. 1957. "The Religion of a Greek Household," *Euphrosyne* 1, pp. 95–116.

Rotroff, S. I. 1996. *The Missing Krater and the Hellenistic Symposium: Drinking in the Age of Alexander the Great* (Broadhead Classical Lecture 7), Christchurch.

————. 1999. "How Did Pots Function within the Landscape of Daily
Living?" in Villanueva Puig et al.
1999, pp. 63–74.

————. 2009. "Early Red-figure in
Context," in Oakley and Palagia
2009, pp. 250–260.

Rotroff, S. I., and J. H. Oakley. 1992.
*Debris from a Public Dining Place in
the Athenian Agora* (*Hesperia* Suppl.
25), Princeton.

Rouillard, P. 1975. "Le Peintre d'Euer-
gidès," *RA* 1945, pp. 31–60.

Rouillard, P., and A. Verbanck-Piérard,
eds. 2003. *Le vase grec et ses destins,*
Munich.

Rouse, W. H. D. 1902. *Greek Votive
Offerings: An Essay in the History of
Greek Religion,* Cambridge.

Ruban, V. V. 1990. "O chronologii
krasnoglinjanych amfor s koničes-
kimi nožkami, VII-V vv. do n. e.,"
*Kratike Soobshcheniya Instituta
Arkheologii* 197, pp. 12–19.

————. 1991. "Opyt klassifikacii tak
nazyvaemych miletskich amfor iz
Nižnego Pobuž'ja," *SovArch* 2,
pp. 182–190.

Rudolph, W. 1988. "Workshops: Some
Reflections and Some Pots," in
Christiansen and Melander 1988,
pp. 524–535.

Sansone, D. 1988. *Greek Athletics and
the Genesis of Sport,* Berkeley.

Scahill, D. 2001. "Section BE Final
Report (2001)," unpublished report,
Athenian Agora Excavations.

————. 2002. "(Section BE) North–
South Road (2002)," unpublished
report, Athenian Agora Excavations.

Schattner, T. G. 1996. "Die Fundkera-
mik," in *Ein Kultbezirk an der Heili-
gen Straße von Milet nach Didyma:
Ergebnisse der Ausgrabungen und
Untersuchungen seit dem Jahre 1962*
(*Didyma* III.1), ed. K. Tuchelt,
Mainz, pp. 163–216.

Schauenburg, K. 1988. "Eulen aus
Athen und Unteritalien," *JdI* 103,
pp. 67–85.

Scheffer, C., ed. 2001a. *Ceramics in
Context,* Stockholm.

————. 2001b. "Gods on Athenian
Vases: Their Function in the
Archaic and Classical Periods,"
in Scheffer 2001a, pp. 127–137.

Scheibler, I. 2000. "Attische Skyphoi
für attisches Feste," *AntK* 43,
pp. 17–43.

Schiffer, M. B. 1987. *Formation Processes and the Archaeological Record,*
Albuquerque.

Schiffer, M. B., and J. M. Skibo. 1989.
"A Provisional Theory of Ceramic
Abrasion," *American Anthropologist*
91, pp. 101–115.

Schmaltz, B., and M. Söldner, eds.
2003. *Griechische Keramik im
kulturellen Kontext,* Munster.

Schmalz, G. 1998. "A New Prytaneion
for Augustan Athens?" *AJA* 102,
p. 408 (abstract).

————. 2006. "The Athenian Prytaneion Discovered?" *Hesperia* 75,
pp. 33–81.

Schmid, S. G. 1999. "Eine Gruppe
nordägäischer Transportamphoren,"
AthMitt 114, pp. 143–156.

Schmidt, S. 2009. "Images of Statues
on Attic Vases: The Case of the
Tyrannicides," in Nørskov et al.
2009, pp. 219–237.

Schmitt Pantel, P. 1992. *La cité au
banquet: Histoire des repas publics
dans les cités grecques,* Rome.

Schmitt Pantel, P., and A. Schnapp.
1982. "Image et société en Grèce
ancienne: Les représentations de la
chasse et du banquet," *RA* 1982,
pp. 57–74.

Schnurr, C. 1995. "Die alte Agora
Athens," *ZPE* 105, pp. 131–138.

Seifert, M. 1996. "Überlegungen zur
Anwendung naturwissenschaftlicher
Methoden bei der Herkunftbestim-
mung von Keramik," *Hephaistos* 14,
pp. 29–43.

————. 2004. *Herkunftsbestimmung
archaischer Keramik am Beispiel von
Amphoren aus Milet* (*BAR-IS* 1233),
Oxford.

Sezgin, Y. 2004. "Clazomenian Transport Amphorae of the Seventh and
Sixth Centuries," in Moustaka et al.
2004, pp. 221–234.

Shanks, M. 1999. *Art and the Early
Greek City State: An Interpretive
Archaeology,* Cambridge.

Shapiro, H. A. 1980. "Hippokrates Son
of Anaxileos," *Hesperia* 49, pp. 289–
293.

————. 1982. "Kallias Kratiou Alo-
pekethen," *Hesperia* 51, pp. 69–73.

———. 1997. "Correlating Shape and Subject: The Case of the Archaic Pelike," in Oakley et al. 1997, pp. 63–70.

———. 2000. "Modest Athletes and Liberated Women: Etruscans on Attic Black-figure Vases," in Cohen 2000b, pp. 315–337.

Shear, J. L. 1993a. "Agora Excavations Section BE West 1993," unpublished report, Athenian Agora Excavations.

———. 1993b. "Agora Excavations–Section BZ 1993," unpublished report, Athenian Agora Excavations.

Shear, T. L. 1939. "The Campaign of 1938," *Hesperia* 8, pp. 201–246.

Shear, T. L., Jr. 1969. "The Athenian Agora: Excavations of 1968," *Hesperia* 38, pp. 382–417.

———. 1971. "The Athenian Agora: Excavations of 1970," *Hesperia* 40, pp. 241–279.

———. 1973a. "The Athenian Agora: Excavations of 1971," *Hesperia* 42, pp. 121–179.

———. 1973b. "The Athenian Agora: Excavations of 1972," *Hesperia* 42, pp. 359–407.

———. 1975. "The Athenian Agora: Excavations of 1973–1974," *Hesperia* 44, pp. 331–374.

———. 1978. "Tyrants and Buildings in Archaic Athens," in *Athens Comes of Age: From Solon to Salamis,* ed. W. Childs, Princeton, pp. 1–19.

———. 1984. "The Athenian Agora: Excavations of 1980–1982," *Hesperia* 53, pp. 1–57.

———. 1993. "The Persian Destruction of Athens: Evidence from Agora Deposits," *Hesperia* 62, pp. 383–482.

———. 1994. "Ἰσονόμους τ᾽Ἀθήνας ἐποιησάτην: The Agora and Democracy," in Coulson et al. 1994, pp. 225–248.

———. 1997. "The Athenian Agora: Excavations of 1989–1993," *Hesperia* 66, pp. 495–548.

Sifakis, G. 1971. *Parabasis and Animal Choruses,* London.

Six, J. 1888. "Vases polychromes sur fond noir de la période archaïque," *GazArch* 13, pp. 193–210, 281–294.

Slaska, M. 1978. "Gravisca: Le ceramiche comuni di produzione greco-orientale," in *Les céramiques de la Grèce de l'Est et leur diffusion en Occident,* Paris, pp. 223–230.

Slater, N. 1999. "The Vase as Ventriloquist," in *Signs of Orality: The Oral Tradition and Its Influence in the Greek and Roman World,* ed. E. A. MacKay (*Mnemosyne* Suppl. 188), pp. 143–161.

Smith, D. 2003. *From Symposium to Eucharist,* Minneapolis.

Sorokina, I. P., and I. N. Sudarev. 2003. "Amfory v pogrebenijach gruntovogo nekropolja Kep i gruntovych nekropoley bosporskich gorodov VI–III vv. do n.e.," *Drevnosti Bospora* 6, pp. 297–306.

Sourisseau, J. C. 1998. "Une experience de quantification sur les amphores archaïques et classiques de Provence: Limites et difficultés," in *La quantification des céramiques: Conditions et protocole,* ed. P. Arcelin and M. Tuffreau-Libre, Glux-en-Glenne, pp. 47–52.

Sourvinou-Inwood, C. 1990. "Ancient Rites and Modern Constructs: On the Brauronian Bears Again," *BICS* 37, pp. 1–14.

Sparkes, B. A. 1960. "Kottabos: An Athenian After-Dinner Game," *Archaeology* 13, pp. 202–207.

———. 1962. "The Greek Kitchen," *JHS* 82, pp. 121–137.

———. 1976. "Treading the Grapes," *BABesch* 51, pp. 47–64.

———. 1981. "Not Cooking, but Baking," *GaR* 28, pp. 172–178.

———. 1991. *Greek Pottery: An Introduction,* Manchester.

———. 1995. "A Pretty Kettle of Fish," in *Food in Antiquity,* ed. J. Wilkins, D. Harvey, and M. Dobson, Exeter, pp. 150–161.

Sparkes, B., and L. Talcott. 1958. *Pots and Pans of Classical Athens* (*AgoraPicBk* 1), Princeton.

Stähler, K. 1967. *Eine unbekannte Pelike des Eucharidesmalers im Archäologischen Museum der Universität Münster,* Cologne.

Stavrolakes, N., and J. G. McKernan. 1975. "Survey of a Possible Shipwreck off the Coast of Poros Island, Greece," *JFA* 2, pp. 275–280.

Steiner, A. 1998. Rev. of M. Moore, *Agora* XXX, in *BMCR* 98.1.24.

———. 2002. "Private and Public: Links between *Symposion* and *Syssition* in Fifth-Century Athens," *ClAnt* 21, pp. 347–379.

Stewart, A. 2008. "The Persian and Carthaginian Invasions of 480 B.C.E. and the Beginning of the Classical Style 1: The Stratigraphy, Chronology, and Significance of the Acropolis Deposits," *AJA* 112, pp. 377–412.

Stocker, S. R. 2009. *Illyrian Apollonia: Towards a New Ktisis and Developmental History of the Colony* (diss. Univ. of Cincinnati).

Sutton, R. 2000. "The Good, the Base, and the Ugly: The Drunken Orgy in Attic Vase Painting and the Athenian Self," in Cohen 2000b, pp. 180–202.

Swinford, K. 2006. "The Semi-fixed Nature of Greek Domestic Religion" (M.A. thesis, Univ. of Cincinnati).

Szabó, M. 1994. *Archaic Terracottas of Boeotia* (*StArch* 67), Rome.

Talcott, L. 1935. "Attic, Black-Glazed Stamped Ware and Other Pottery from a Fifth Century Well," *Hesperia* 4, pp. 476–523.

———. 1936. "Vases and Kalos-Names from an Agora Well," *Hesperia* 5, pp. 333–354.

Themelis, P. 1974. *Brauron: Führer durch das Heiligtum und das Museum,* Athens.

Thompson, D. B. 1952. "Three Centuries of Hellenistic Terracottas, IA," *Hesperia* 21, pp. 116–164.

———. 1960. "The House of Simon the Shoemaker," *Archaeology* 13, pp. 234–240.

———. 1966. "Three Centuries of Hellenistic Terracottas 7: The Early First Century B.C." *Hesperia* 35, pp. 1–19.

Thompson, H. A. 1940. *The Tholos of Athens and Its Predecessors* (*Hesperia* Suppl. 4), Princeton.

———. 1951. "Excavations in the Athenian Agora: 1950," *Hesperia* 20, pp. 45–60.

———. 1954. "Excavations in the Athenian Agora: 1953," *Hesperia* 23, pp. 31–67.

———. 1955. "Activities in the Athenian Agora: 1954," *Hesperia* 24, pp. 50–71.

———. 1962. *The Athenian Agora: A Guide to the Excavation and Museum,* 2nd ed., rev., Athens.

———. 1976. *The Athenian Agora: A Guide to the Excavation and Museum,* 3rd ed., rev., Athens.

———. 1981. "Athens Faces Adversity," *Hesperia* 50, pp. 343–355.

Todisco, L. 1984. "Ceramica attica a figure nere," in *Antichità della Collezione Guarini,* ed. B. Fedele, L. Todisco, C. Santoro, C. Laganara, and S. Pansini, Galatina, pp. 38–46.

Topper, K. 2009. "Primitive Life and the Construction of the Sympotic Past in Athenian Vase Painting," *AJA* 113, pp. 3–26.

Trakosopoulou-Salakidou, E. 2004. "Κεραμικοί κλίβανοι Ακάνθου," *AEMΘ* 18, pp. 167-179.

Trotter, W. 1991. *A Frozen Hell: The Russo-Finnish Winter War of 1939–40,* Chapel Hill.

Tsakirgis, B. 2005. "Living and Work-"ing around the Athenian Agora: A Preliminary Case Study of Three Houses," in *Ancient Greek Houses and Households: Chronological, Regional, and Social Diversity,* ed. B. A. Ault and L. C. Nevett, Philadelphia, pp. 67–83.

———. 2007. "Fire and Smoke, Hearths, Braziers and Chimneys in the Greek House," in *Building Communities: House, Settlement and Society* (*BSA Studies* 15), ed. R. Westgate, N. Fisher, and J. Whitley, London, pp. 225–231.

Tsaravopoulos, A. 1986. "Η αρχαία πόλη της Χίου," *Horos* 4, pp. 124–144.

Tsingarida, A. 2008. "Color for a Market? Special Techniques and Distribution Patterns in Late Archaic and Early Classical Greece," in *Papers on Special Techniques in Athenian Vases,* ed. K. Lapatin, Los Angeles, pp. 187–206

———, ed. 2009. *Shapes and Uses of Greek Vases, 7th–4th centuries B.C.* (*Études d'archéologie* 3), Brussels.

Uhlenbrock, J. 1988. *The Terracotta Protomai from Gela: A Discussion of Local Style in Archaic Sicily* (Studia Archaeologica 50), Rome.

Ure, A. 1955. "Krokotos and White Heron," *JHS* 75, pp. 90–103.

Ure, P. 1927. *Sixth and Fifth Century Pottery from Rhitsona,* Oxford.

———. 1932. "Droop Cups," *JHS* 52, pp. 55–71.

Vallet, G., and F. Villard. 1964. *Megara Hyblaea 2: La céramique archaïque,* Paris.

Vanderpool, E. 1938. "The Rectangular Rock-Cut Shaft: The Shaft and Its Lower Fill," *Hesperia* 7, pp. 363–411.

———. 1946. "The Rectangular Rock-Cut Shaft: The Upper Fill," *Hesperia* 15, pp. 265–336.

Vanhove, D., ed. 1992. *Le sport dans la Grèce antique: Du jeu à la compétition,* Brussels.

van Wees, H. 1995. "Princes at Dinner: Social Event and Social Structure in Homer," in *Homeric Questions,* ed. J. P. Crielaard, Amsterdam, pp. 147–182.

Vermeule, E. 1965. "The Vengeance of Achilles: The Dragging of Hektor at Troy," *BMFA* 63, pp. 35–52.

———. 1969. "Some Erotica in Boston," *AntK* 12, pp. 9–15.

———. 1970. "Five Vases from the Grave Precinct of Dexileos," *JdI* 85, pp. 94–111.

Vickers, M. 1978. *Greek Symposia,* London.

———. 1990. "Attic Symposia after the Persian Wars," in Murray 1990a, pp. 105–121.

Vickers, M., and D. Gill. 1994. *Artful Crafts,* Oxford.

Vierneisel, K., and B. Kaeser, eds. 1990. *Kunst der Schale, Kultur des Trinkens,* Munich.

Villanueva Puig, M.-C., F. Lissarrague, P. Rouillard, and A. Rouveret, eds. 1999. *Céramique et peinture grecques: Modes d'emploi,* Paris.

Villard, F. 1946. "L'évolution des coupes attiques á figures noires," *REA* 48, pp. 153–181.

Villard, P. 1992. "Boire seul dans l'antiquité grecque," in *Sociabilité à table: Commensalité et convivialité à travers les âges,* ed. M. Aurelle, O. Dumoulin, and F. Thelamon, Mont-Saint-Aignan, pp. 77–81.

Villing, A. 2009. "The Daily Grind of Ancient Greece: Mortars and Mortaria between Symbol and Reality," in Tsingarida 2009, pp. 319–333.

Voigtländer, W. 1982. "Funde aus der Insula westlich des Buleuterion in Milet," *IstMitt* 32, pp. 30–173.

von Bothmer, D. 1951. "Attic Black-Figured Pelikai," *JHS* 71, pp. 40–47.

———. 1957. *Amazons in Greek Art,* Oxford.

———. 1985. "Beazley the Teacher," in *Beazley and Oxford,* ed. D. Kurtz, Oxford, pp. 5–17.

———. 1986. "An Archaic Red-Figured Kylix," *GettyMusJ* 14, pp. 5–20.

Vos, M. 1963. *Scythian Archers in Archaic Attic Vase-Painting,* Groningen.

Walker, S. 1983. "Women and Housing in Classical Greece: The Archaeological Evidence," in *Images of Women in Antiquity,* ed. A. Cameron and A. Kuhrt, Detroit, pp. 81–91.

Walton, M. S., E. Doehne, E. K. Trentelman, and G. Chiari. 2008. "A Preliminary Investigation of Coral-red Glosses Found on Attic Greek Pottery," in *Papers on Special Techniques in Athenian Vases,* ed. K. Lapatin, Los Angeles, pp. 95–104.

Watrous, L. V. 1982. "The Sculptural Program of the Siphnian Treasury at Delphi," *AJA* 86, pp. 159–172.

Webster, G. 1963. *Practical Archaeology,* London.

Webster, T. B. L. 1970. *The Greek Chorus,* London.

———. 1972. *Potter and Patron in Classical Athens,* London.

Węcowski, M. 2002. "Homer and the Origins of the Symposion," in *Omero: Tremila anni dopo. Atti del Congresso di Genova, 6–8 Iuglio 2000,* ed. F. Montanari and P. Ascheri, Rome, pp. 627–637.

West, M. L. 2003. *Homeric Hymns, Homeric Apocrypha, Lives of Homer,* Cambridge.

Whitbread, I. K. 1986. "The Application of Ceramic Petrology to the Study of Ancient Greek Amphorae," in Empereur and Garlan 1986, pp. 95–101.

———. 1995. *Greek Transport Amphorae: A Petrological and Archaeological Study* (Fitch Laboratory Occasional Papers 4), Athens.

———. 2003. "Clays of Corinth: The Study of a Basic Resource for Ceramic Production," in *Corinth* XX, pp. 1–13.

Whitley, J. 1994. "Protoattic Pottery: A Contextual Approach," in *Classical Greece,* ed. I. Morris, Cambridge, pp. 51–70.

Wigand, K. 1912. "Thymiateria," *BJb* 122, pp. 1–97.

Wilkins, J., and S. Hill. 1994. *The Life of Luxury: Archestratus,* Devon.

———. 2006. *Food in the Ancient World,* Malden, Mass.

Williams, D. 1991. "Onesimos and the Getty Iliupersis," *Greek Vases in the J. Paul Getty Museum* 5, pp. 41–64.

———. 2002. "Perfume Pots, Painters, and a Puzzling Pursuit," in *Essays in Honor of Dietrich von Bothmer,* ed. A. Clark and J. Gaunt, Amsterdam, pp. 341–348.

Winter, A. 1968. "Beabsichtigtes Rot," *AM* 83, pp. 315–322.

Winter, F. 1903. *Die antiken Terrakotten,* Berlin.

Wolff, J. 1984. *The Social Production of Art,* New York.

Young, R. L. 1951. "An Industrial District of Ancient Athens," *Hesperia* 20, pp. 135–288.

Zavojkin, A. A. 1992. "Klassifikatsija fragmentov samosskich amfor iz Fanagorii," *Rossiiskaya Arkheologiya* 1, pp. 40–56.

Zeest, I. B. 1960. *Keramicheskaja tara Bospora* (Materialy i issledovaniya po arkheologii SSSR 83), Moscow.

Zuntz, G. 1971. *Persephone: Three Essays on Religion and Thought in Magna Graecia,* Oxford.

GENERAL INDEX

Bold figures represent catalogue numbers

INDEX OF CATALOGUED OBJECTS

INDEX OF DEPOSITS

INDEX OF BZ CONTEXT LOTS